Praise for The World Remade

"A massive and ambitious effort that strives to cover and explain a very broad range of aspects, including our entry and participation in [World War I], the failure of the 'peace,' and the changes the war brought to our political and social fabric. . . . [G. J.] Meyer offers wonderful insights into many of the key players in this arresting saga. . . . This is a provocative and sometimes harshly judgmental history, but one that should be read to understand our emergence as a global power." —*Booklist* (starred review)

"[Meyer] debunks many myths about America's valiant intentions in joining the war, especially regarding President Woodrow Wilson's sense of destiny on the world stage, and he closely examines why Wilson acquiesced to joining the fight. . . . Meyer gives a good sense of America's future at that negotiating table and Wilson's celebrated role at Versailles as the leader of the free world. . . . A refreshing look at this still-much-debated world debacle."
—*Kirkus Reviews*

"Here, with great skill and fidelity to fact, Meyer . . . relate[s] the complex tale of a nation venturing back into world affairs after a century of comparative isolation. . . . Meyer tells the story with brio. Characters come alive and the past seems near. . . . Meyer succeeds brilliantly with his basic narrative approach, and any reader who wants to learn about American participation in the war will benefit from this book." —*Publishers Weekly*

"G. J. Meyer has written a keen observation about a historic and troubling period. This opus spans the war years, reflecting the [United States'] emergence as a global power while the other countries fought a war of attrition. Wilson is painted first as a complicated man who could be a sharp politician, then as a sick, indecisive man looking for validation. This book is well written, sharp, and has bearing on our present and future involvement in wars. A+" —*Seattle Book Review*

"This lengthy revisionist history will fit well with American history and governmental studies departments in both public and academic libraries."
—*Library Journal*

Praise for A World Undone

"Meyer sets out to integrate the war's discrete elements into a single work of popular history and delivers a worthy counterpoint to Hew Strachan's magisterial three-volume scholarly project, *The First World War*. . . . Accomplished with brio, [he] blends 'foreground, background, and sidelights' to highlight the complex interactions of apparently unconnected events behind the four-year catastrophic war that destroyed a world and defined a century." —*Publishers Weekly* (starred review)

"*A World Undone* is an original and very readable account of one of the most significant and often misunderstood events of the last century. With a historian's eye for clearheaded analysis and a storyteller's talent for detail and narrative, G. J. Meyer presents a compelling account of the blunders that produced the world's first 'great war' and set the stage for many of the tragic events that followed."

—STEVE GILLON, resident historian, The History Channel

"It may seem impossible to write an 'intimate' account of such a global catastrophe, but Meyer has succeeded in doing just that: a masterful narrative history that eloquently conveys the sense of a civilization engaged in massive self-destruction while its leaders, blinded by hubris, nationalism, or outright ignorance, led the charge. Although Meyer pays ample attention to the broad themes of causation and military strategies, he consistently reminds us that the war was a compilation of millions of individual tragedies. He captures the horror and futility of trench warfare, the slaughter at Gallipoli, and the genocide of Armenians as experienced by those who were there. Meyer also offers interesting and controversial insights into the motivations of many of the key participants. This is an outstanding survey of a cataclysm that still casts a shadow over world affairs." —*Booklist*

"This is one of those books where you read every page. . . . Meyer organizes his book chronologically, and accompanies each chapter with a short background essay. . . . [*A World Undone*] has the very best qualities for this kind of comprehensive approach: a gift for compression and an eye for the telling detail." —*Milwaukee Journal Sentinel*

"A comprehensive history aimed at the general reader ... You finish this book feeling you've learned everything anyone reasonably needs to know about The Great War." —*Pittsburgh Tribune-Review*

"Meyer breathes life into the human story within the Great War. He provides in-depth profiles of many of the political and military leaders of that era, and explains why they were so important. . . . This is a literary vision of WWI that few of us have ever encountered. Simply put, this is historical reporting at its best." —*Smoky Mountain Sentinel*

"Thundering, magnificent ... *A World Undone* is a book of true greatness that prompts moments of sheer joy and pleasure. Researched to the last possible dot . . . It will earn generations of admirers." —*The Washington Times*

By G. J. Meyer

The World Remade: America in World War I
The Borgias: The Hidden History
The Tudors: The Complete Story of England's Most Notorious Dynasty
A World Undone: The Story of the Great War, 1914–1918
Executive Blues: Down and Out in Corporate America
The Memphis Murders

The World Remade

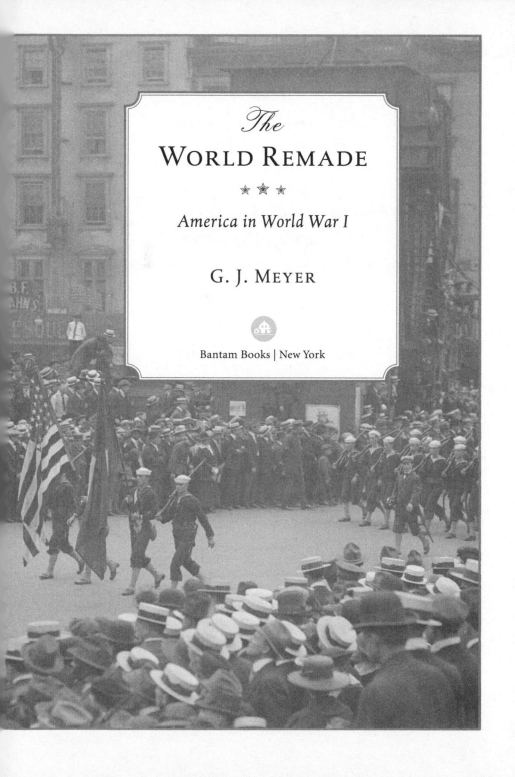

The
WORLD REMADE

★ ★ ★

America in World War I

G. J. MEYER

Bantam Books | New York

LIBRARY OF CONGRESS CATALOGING-IN-PUBLICATION DATA
Names: Meyer, G. J., author.
Title: The world remade : America in World War I / G.J. Meyer.
Description: New York : Bantam, an imprint of Random House, a division of
Penguin Random House, 2017. | Includes bibliographical references and index.
Identifiers: LCCN 2016036502 | ISBN 9780553393347 (pbk.) |
ISBN 9780553393330 (ebook)
Subjects: LCSH: World War, 1914–1918—United States. | BISAC: HISTORY /
Military / World War I. | HISTORY / United States / 20th Century. |
BIOGRAPHY & AUTOBIOGRAPHY / Historical.
Classification: LCC D619 .M465 2017 | DDC 940.3/73—dc23
LC record available at https://lccn.loc.gov/2016036502

For Emily, Damien, and Matias
Gifts who arrived in that order

Contents

Introduction   xiii

PART ONE

The Crooked Road to War

PART TWO

The Price

PART THREE

Sowing Dragons' Teeth

Introduction

THIS BOOK INTERTWINES FOUR STORIES THAT ARE ALMOST ALWAYS told separately:

The story of how the United States came to enter the First World War two and a half long years after it began, when it had already proved ruinous to almost every nation involved.

And the story of how American intervention decided the outcome of the war, with consequences that still reverberate after a hundred years.

Of how the war changed the United States politically and economically and in its very nature, challenging Americans' understanding of themselves as a nation and their nation's place in the world.

And how the hope that the postwar settlement would justify America's sacrifices was dashed first at the Paris peace conference, then again in Washington, D.C.

The combining of these stories sheds light on questions that were controversial a century ago and remain so today.

Why did the United States go to war in 1917, really?

Should she have gone to war? Was the decision necessary? Was it justified by the outcome?

Is it a good thing that American intervention caused the war to end the way it did?

And how much responsibility does the United States bear for the disasters that followed?

World War I, like so many of history's great events, is heavily encrusted with myth. But gradually, over the generations, the truth has been breaking through. Today anyone wanting to defend the old stories about how Germany started the war, and did so because she wanted to conquer the world, takes on a heavy burden of proof. As for who *did* start the war, an uncertain finger of blame points first at Serbia—or is it Austria-Hungary?—before moving on to Russia. After which it hardly knows where to go next.

Which is to say that answers that in 1920 seemed obvious have long since crumbled into dust.

Which in turn is *not* to say that Germany was some kind of innocent victim. There were no innocent victims, though every one of the nations that went to war claimed to be exactly that. Each of them had a story that explained why. Those stories, too, are now threadbare.

So are other stories that once seemed almost too obviously true to require defense. Stories about what the two sides were fighting *for*. And why they refused to discuss peace even as the death toll rose into the millions and kept climbing. About how they came to see submarine attacks on passenger liners and the systematic starvation of millions of civilians as not only justified but necessary.

But even as new and more convincing stories have emerged, the one about American intervention in the war has remained unknown to a surprising extent within the United States itself. There are of course reasons for this—and they, too, are largely unknown.

The first and perhaps the most important is the power of propaganda. Americans have pretty thoroughly forgotten—it is more accurate to say that they never actually knew—that even before the shooting started in August 1914, the United States became the prime target of a British propaganda campaign of unprecedented extent, sophistication, and intensity. Communications from Germany and Austria-Hungary were at the same time essentially shut down. America's newspapers were so accepting of this, and Washington so acquiescent, that the public had scarcely a clue that it was being told almost nothing about the war except what was approved (and often embellished, and not infrequently invented) by platoons of censors in London.

Important truths remained untold, while untruths were spread widely. Small wonder, then, that as months and then years passed, more and more once-skeptical Americans were brought to see the war as a morally simple matter: a conflict between the innocent and the good on one side, the unfathomably evil on the other.

Nor is it remembered that, almost from the day of America's declaration of war in April 1917, the Wilson administration put in place a propaganda machine of its own, one even bigger and more potent than Britain's and aimed at the same target. For the president no less than for the British and French, the war had become a crusade against a Berlin regime (and ultimately a German population) so vicious, so morally degenerate, as to be unworthy of membership in the community of nations. It was made a crime for American citizens to challenge this view, with penalties so severe as to ensure that few would dare to do so. It is Woodrow Wilson's supreme achievement, proof of his success in bending public opinion to his purposes, that he enshrined himself as an international icon, one of history's great champions of liberty, while mounting the most savage attack on individual rights in American history before or since.

He accomplished this by hammering into the national psyche a manufactured but majestically eloquent account of the war's causes, the reasons for his decision to intervene, and the blessings victory would bring. This account was cemented in place by the speed with which Germany's Western Front defenses began to give way soon after (though not simply because) the American Expeditionary Force entered the fight. And by the years in prison—the decades—to which scores and hundreds of Americans could be and were sentenced not only for dissenting from what the White House proclaimed to be true, but merely for failing to display enthusiasm for the cause.

Also important is the fact that what Europe rightly called the Great War never became, for the United States, the nightmare it was for the other belligerent nations. All the others were impoverished; the United States grew fabulously rich. Her "doughboys" were in combat for only half a year and operated as a distinct American army for only the last couple of months. Her casualties, while heartbreaking enough, were a mere fraction of what even the smallest of her allies and enemies suffered. When it was over, Americans simply had less to lament and therefore less reason for anger, bitterness, or defiance.

This goes a long way toward explaining why the war changed the United States in the ways that it did—and why the changes were by no means entirely positive. Understandably but foolishly, Americans saw a direct causal connection between their army's entry into combat and the disintegration of Germany's Western Front defenses that began at exactly that time. The connection was tenuous at best, a case of *post hoc, ergo propter hoc,* but it reinforced a deep-rooted national inclination to see the United States as unique not just in size and wealth but morally and spiritually. It seemed obvious: what else could explain how a war that had been deadlocked for nearly four years became fluid as soon as the Yanks were in the field? It was taken to be as true of the American soldier as of Galahad that

> *His strength was as the strength of ten*
> *Because his heart was pure.*

Finally there is the crucial fact that another war, one even bigger and more global, followed after barely more than twenty years. This time the United States played an incomparably more central part, for reasons incomparably less ambiguous. What was for Americans the smaller, briefer, less painful first conflict disappeared in a sense behind the second. Or disappeared *within* it, by a curious process of historical absorption. It became easy to suppose that Kaiser Wilhelm II, a pathetically ineffectual man turned into a monster by the propagandists, must have been in fact a kind of earlier Hitler, a prototype of the real thing. That Wilhelmine Germany must have been barely distinguishable from Hitler's Germany, so that U.S. intervention was no less necessary and constructive in the first case than in the second.

Thus the purpose of this book: to bring light to old questions by melding into a single narrative what is now known, a hundred years on, about the four stories that make up its subject. To make that narrative as factual as the state of our knowledge permits, and as complete as a single volume can be. And, scarcely less important, to make all of it accessible to and interesting for today's general reader.

I have been at pains to minimize overlap with my earlier *A World Undone: The Story of the Great War, 1914–1918*. That book, being an account of the whole conflict from beginning to end, could give only limited attention to America's place in it, leaving much of that story untouched. My aim has been to make the two works complementary, each providing a dimension beyond the scope of the other.

It hardly need be said that any deficiencies in the pages that follow are my responsibility entirely. They would be more numerous were it not for my good fortune in having Tracy Devine as my editor. She is a superb coach: calling my attention to things that could be done better, gently giving a nudge when I am in danger of becoming careless, making me raise my game. I am indebted also to designer Virginia Norey and production editor Loren Noveck for making this book the handsome object that it is.

I am grateful to the Library of Congress and the libraries of the University of Minnesota and the University of St. Thomas in St. Paul for putting so much essential material within easy reach.

I am grateful to my daughters, Ellen and Sarah, and their families for providing me with two bases from which to do my research.

Above all I am grateful to my wife, Rosie, for allowing this project to devour so much of our lives.

G. J. Meyer
Mere, Wiltshire, England

PART ONE

The Crooked Road
to War

Have you ever heard what started the present war? If you have, I wish you would publish it, because nobody else has, so far as I can gather. Nothing in particular started it, but everything in general.

—WOODROW WILSON, OCTOBER 26, 1916

←

President Woodrow Wilson and the members of his cabinet as they took office in 1913.

Chapter 1

December 1918: Apotheosis

IT WAS DELIVERANCE.

It was like being born again—albeit after an unspeakably difficult birth—free to start over and get it right this time.

It was the end of a nightmare that had threatened never to end, and the beginning, everyone desperately wanted to believe, of a new and permanently better world.

It was peace.

It was victory.

And it was Paris—*Paris!*—with the year's climactic holiday less than two weeks in the future. After four dark, grim, clenched-teeth Christmases spent under the shadow of the apocalypse, the City of Light was free again to be itself, ablaze with the celebration of life.

There was much to grieve, yes—a terrible burden of grief, the incomprehensible sum of something like nine million fighting men dead along with a like number of civilians, plus survivors beyond numbering too broken ever to be put together again. France had suffered as much as any country and more than most, the war having taken nearly 3.5 percent of her population, one of every four men between the ages of eighteen and thirty. But a dozen other nations were similarly bereaved. From Portugal to the Russian steppe, men were learning to live without a limb or all their limbs. And learning to live with the compulsive twitching and trembling that were among the mysterious symptoms of shell shock, a new kind of affliction the name of which reflected ignorance of its causes. Men without eyes were being taught to weave baskets.

But the worst was over. In western Europe at least, the bloodletting had stopped. There were no more enemy armies just beyond the horizon, pressing to break through. There was no need to fear that those enemies might soon be marching in triumph down the Champs-Élysées. Such nightmare visions belonged to the past.

And upon this reborn Paris there now descended the man who had saved it, Thomas Woodrow Wilson, president of the United States. He arrived like a god, the first serving president ever to cross the Atlantic, borne on a great liner that, as it approached the port of Brest, passed through an honor guard of nine of his navy's battleships, twenty of its destroyers, and like numbers of French and British warships.

(That liner, by the way, was herself a symbol of conquest and of new beginnings. Christened the *George Washington* when launched by her German builders, she was the third largest passenger ship in the world and at the start of the war ranked as Germany's finest. She had happened to be in New York harbor when war broke out in August 1914, was unable to return home because Britain's Royal Navy controlled the North Atlantic, and was impounded when the United States declared war on Germany in 1917. She was in every way perfect for this glorious mission.)

The harbor at Brest overflowed with rapturous crowds as Wilson's ship approached her berth. Bands played, cannons boomed. And then that night, all along the route of the special train that carried the president and his wife and their entourage through cities and towns and country crossroads to Paris, people of every age and description came down to the tracks to see their deliverer go rumbling by. Some of them knelt, in attitudes of prayer.

It is said that two million people thronged the streets of the capital the morning of the president's arrival. Even those old enough to remember the pomp of Napoleon III's reign said it paled in comparison with this. The Gare de Luxembourg was turned into the world's biggest flower basket, strains of "The Star-Spangled Banner" filled the air, and crowds cheered and laughed and wept. The Tiger was there, of course: Prime Minister Georges Clemenceau, an old man so combative, so rich in enemies, that he would never have been given the premiership if the only alternative had not appeared to be peace on Germany's terms. The man who, upon taking office, had declared that his only foreign policy was to make war and his only domestic policy was the same. His short, plump body, round bald pate, and fat white mustache were unmistakable to all who caught a glimpse of him. He was joined by a less striking figure, President Raymond Poincaré, taller and almost slender by comparison, elegantly goateed. The two despised each other and made no secret of it. They had come together not just to welcome the American but to bask in the glow of his glory.

The beaming Wilson, slim and dapper and handsome in a way both boyish and austere, rested and at ease after nine days on calm seas, was led to a horse-drawn open carriage and joined there by Poincaré. The pert and pretty Edith Galt Wilson followed in a second carriage with Madame Poincaré. The two chiefs of state and their ladies formed the centerpiece of a grand procession. Led by a regiment of cavalry in full regalia, it made its slow way through the Place de la Concorde, past the statue representing the provinces of Alsace and Lorraine from which a black shroud had recently been removed to mark their recovery from Germany, up a Champs-Élysées lined with captured German guns to the Arc de Triomphe. The carriages soon filled with thrown flowers. The multitudes roared as again and again Wilson raised his silk top hat.

Huge banners were everywhere. *Vive Wilson,* they declared. *Vive l'Amérique. Wilson le Juste.*

The Wilsons were delivered at last to the Murat Palace, which was to serve as their residence during the short time they expected to be in France. They were given a quick tour by its owner, Prince Joachim Napoleon Murat, descendant of one of Napoleon I's great marshals and the emperor's sister Caroline. In size the palace rivaled the White House, with more privacy thanks to the high walls surrounding its wide gardens and an infinitely more exquisite interior. Meanwhile the president's retinue, including the teams of scholars and experts who had been brought along to help him put the world right, was moving into the magnificent Hôtel de Crillon, adjacent to the American embassy. Everything possible was being done to make them happy to be in Paris, to show them that they were among friends.

By early afternoon Wilson was settled in the splendid study adjacent to his equally splendid bedroom on the palace's upper floor. No one was with him except the only man he wanted with him, wily little Edward House, not only his closest confidant but nearly his alter ego. "My second personality," Wilson called him, "my independent self: his thoughts and mine are one." House had been in Europe since October, known to all as the president's personal representative, explaining his objectives and gathering information on his behalf. He called himself "Colonel" and expected to be addressed as such, although he had never served in any army. He said it was a geographic rather than a military title, having been conferred on him by a governor of his native Texas.

House and the president had much to discuss. First were the preparations for the peace conference that was soon to begin, and that had brought Wilson to Europe. House would have been eager to share the latest news about the leading participants—about who thought what, and what kinds of difficulties they were likely to create. Beyond that were all the grand plans that the two of them had spent months and even years perfecting for Europe and the world.

So there sat Wilson in regal splendor, once the obscure son of a southern preacher, now the idol of what was coming to be called the Free World, preparing to rescue the world's unfree portions. Still not sixty-two years old, he was at the midpoint of his second term in office and entirely justified if he regarded himself as the most famous, most admired, most *important* human being on the planet.

And why not? There was nothing in such a claim to make Wilson wince. If he had always been ferociously ambitious, declaring as an undergraduate that youngsters like himself should "acquire knowledge that we might have power," he had wanted power only in order to do good. So he told himself, at least. From his Parisian palace, he could look back on a career in which he had done much good, and not only after reaching the White House: as an educator, too, and as an author, governor of a major state, one of the master orators of his time, and leading figure in that irruption of American reformist zeal known as the Progressive Movement.

His whole life, but especially the past ten years, could be seen in retrospect as an arrow shot straight at this climactic moment. In the three astonishing years that ended with the election of 1912, he had vaulted from the presidency of Princeton University to the presidency of the United States. The war had then made him the man who, as Winston Churchill would write, "played a part in the fate of nations incomparably more direct and personal than any other." Finally he had been brought here, to a Europe that (he saw ample reason to believe) needed him terribly. Could there be a more certain confirmation that he had been destined from eternity to do "high-minded things"? That God had singled him out?

Again: why not? Not even his adversaries—which, being a supremely successful politician, he had in abundance—could have denied that he was brilliantly gifted, impeccably upright, and guided by high ideals. But of course he was also human, which is to say he was limited, and among his limitations was a blindness of a kind that is perhaps not all that unusual among extraordinary men of a certain type. Often right about important things, he was inclined to think himself always right about everything. He found it difficult—could find it impossible—to imagine that those who disagreed with him might some-times be right. Might be acting in good faith, at least. Among his talents was the ability to deceive himself, about his own actions and motives above all, and then to deceive others while remaining certain of his own integrity. These were dangerous traits in the most important man on the planet, at a time when humanity stood on the brink of momentous decisions. Those who do not see what is real are generally doomed to collide with it.

President Wilson, his new wife Edith, and Colonel Edward House
A vision of harmony, but with bitter troubles to come.

In Paris five weeks after the end of the Great War, some things were being concealed from Wilson not only by his own blindness but by other people as well. He had no way of knowing how much, despite the extravagance of the welcome they had prepared for him, Clemenceau and Poincaré did not want him in France, or that England's prime minister, the "Welsh Wizard" David Lloyd George, likewise wished he had stayed home and hoped he would soon return there.

These men led nations that had barely survived fifty months of the most ruinous war in European history, had buried hundreds of thousands of their sons, and had impoverished themselves in carrying on the fight. America's troops, by contrast, had been in combat for barely six months, had operated as an independent army for a mere two months, and in the end had lost only half as many men as Romania or Serbia (never mind France or Britain, or Russia or Germany or Italy).

Against this background, it is understandable if Clemenceau and Lloyd George were inclined to find it not only ridiculous but offensive that an American should now come across the Atlantic for the purpose of showing them how to make peace. Both men had spent their lives in political combat, fighting their way from modest beginnings to the top of the greasy pole. Woodrow Wilson, by comparison, was little more than an amateur, a newcomer, a professional academic who had entered politics at an elevated level a mere eight years before and appeared to regard himself as teacher to the world. The Europeans were accustomed by now to his lofty preachments, and not particularly grateful for them.

Yes, victory would have been long delayed if not impossible without the contribution of the United States. America's vast wealth had come to the rescue just in time to save Britain and France from collapse. By pouring in food and war matériel and an endless flood of fresh troops, America had driven Germany to the desperate measures that hastened her collapse.

But still . . .

It was difficult for America's "associates" (Wilson refused to call them allies, wanting to make clear that his country was operating on its own distinctly higher plane) not to see the president as presumptuous, absurd, perhaps even contemptible. Some of his ideas seemed not only foolish but intolerable. He wanted to guarantee freedom of the seas to all nations even in times of war; this made the British, whose great navy had saved them from starvation while starving their enemies, wonder what the point of that navy was supposed to be if another war came. Wilson also wanted a peace without reparations or retribution; for the French, who saw themselves as innocent victims of aggression and had been left with a wide swath of devastation that cut through their heartland like a bleeding wound from the Belgian border to the Swiss, this was outrageous. As for the League of Nations that Wilson envisaged as the centerpiece of his beautiful postwar world, the Italians may have been especially artful in feigning more enthusiasm for it than they felt, but they were far from alone in their skepticism.

But still . . .

America *had* been indispensable, and all the unsubtle hints from the French and the British had not sufficed to keep Wilson on his own side of the ocean. Now that he was in Paris, there was nothing to do but to make the best of it. If that meant pretending to be sympathetic to his seemingly numberless propos-als, displaying the patience that one would extend to an ignorant and stub-born child, so be it. If it required trying inch by inch to expose him to the realities of postwar Europe, stalling for time while doing so, that was hardly the greatest challenge that his fellow victors had faced in recent months.

Where Wilson's blindness was most willful as 1918 ended was in the realm of domestic politics. Many of the Americans best qualified to judge—Secretary of State Robert Lansing, leading members of Congress from both parties, even Colonel House—had tried to dissuade him from going to Europe. After all, the transatlantic telegraph was now an established fact, so he could direct America's part in the peace conference from the White House. People with his best interests at heart argued that there was no need for him to become so di-rectly involved in what could only be extremely difficult negotiations, thereby putting so much of his own political capital at stake. Some who were not so friendly complained that it was irresponsible for a president to put a wide ocean between himself and Washington. What if there were a national emer-gency?

But no, Wilson said, he had to go. It was a courageous and arguably a self-less decision, proof of his willingness to take risks for the sake of the just and lasting peace that he had promised. But it was something else as well: an ex-pression of his egotism, his vision of himself as *the* indispensable man, *the* one voice able to speak for the freedom-loving people not only of the United States but of the world.

The dangers of such a self-image are apparent in the president's explana-tion of why he could not stay at home. The people expected him to go, he said. They looked to him as the man who could make certain that the high and pure objectives for which America had plunged into history's greatest bloodbath were going to be achieved. He could accomplish this only by personally taking a seat at the bargaining table, face-to-face with his fellow victors. It was his duty to go—a sacred duty.

In this there was nobility and folly. The folly was rooted in the illusions that had always been part of Wilson's understanding of himself.

Had the American public *ever* been strongly behind him in his decision to go to war? That was an arguable if not a downright dubious proposition.

And was he, in December 1918, in a position from which to speak for the people even of his own country? Theodore Roosevelt did not think so. From a hospital bed in New York, as the *George Washington* carried Wilson to France, the former president had issued a statement. "Our allies and our enemies and Mr. Wilson himself," it declared, "should understand that Mr. Wilson has no authority to speak for the American people at this time."

TR was far from impartial. He had long disliked Wilson, and by now he hated him. He had lost the 1912 election to Wilson, fuming in exasperation as the Democrats won the White House for the first time in twenty years despite getting only 42 percent of the vote. Later, Wilson's slowness in going to war convinced Roosevelt that he was weak and cowardly, a deplorable example of how America was becoming effete. Despite his age and infirmities, TR resented Wilson's refusal to allow him to lead a division to the Western Front. And he blamed what he saw as the incompetence of Wilson's War Department—specifically its failure to produce satisfactory aircraft—for the death in France of his adored youngest son, a pilot shot out of the sky.

But about the Wilson who was steaming to France, Roosevelt was not entirely wrong. A month before he issued his statement, 1918's election had become a referendum on the Democratic Party under Wilson's leadership, on the administration's policies and practices at home and abroad, and inevitably on the president himself. It was Wilson who made it so. He injected himself into one congressional contest after another, calling upon voters to rally under his banner and purge those who had failed to support him even if they had strongly supported the war. Midterm elections are usually unhappy experiences for the party of a sitting president, especially a president in his second term. But for the Democrats, the election of November 1918—held, as it happened, in the very week when Germany conceded defeat and the president could claim total vindication of his war policies—was no ordinary setback. When the polls opened on Tuesday, November 5, the Democrats controlled both houses of Congress: the House of Representatives narrowly, the Senate by a commanding margin. A day later the Republicans had majorities of forty-four seats in the House and two in the Senate. There is no way of knowing if the Democrats might have suffered even worse losses if Wilson had not injected himself into the campaign. But perceptions matter in politics as much as in any human enterprise, and the dominant perception as Wilson took ship for France was that he had gambled on the support of the public and lost badly.

In Washington therefore he was suddenly the lamest of lame ducks, a seemingly repudiated leader. The Republicans, jubilant, had no reason to fear or follow him. Conservatives of both parties had always been leery of Wilson the progressive, and across the country millions of liberals were now alienated from him because of the harshness with which his administration had sought to suppress opinions that it found unacceptable. The president urgently needed to repair relations not only with the resurgent Republicans but with important elements of his own party, including those progressive Democrats who had once been his most ardent supporters. But he gave little sign of understanding this, or of caring.

Instead, he proceeded as if nothing had happened. This was nowhere more obvious than in his choice of delegates to the peace conference. There were four of these aside from Wilson himself, and among them were no members of Congress from either party. One was a nominal Republican, the wealthy and semiretired diplomat Henry White, who had supported Wilson both before and after the U.S. entry into the war, had never held elective office, and at nearly seventy years of age was not even on the margins of his party's centers of power. The others were Colonel House, Secretary of State Lansing, and General Tasker H. Bliss, already in Europe as Wilson's military representative on the Allies' Supreme War Council.

It was said, in mocking tones, that in assembling this delegation, Wilson had simply chosen copies of himself four times. If this would keep things simple in Paris, ensuring that none of the delegates would oppose him to any troublesome extent, politically it was shortsighted. The Republican Party, given no voice in whatever was going to happen at the conference, would have little political stake in its success. The same would be true even of many Democrats in Congress, aware as they were of how recently the nation's voters had seemingly washed their hands of the president.

Thus the Woodrow Wilson who arrived in Paris was in a far weaker position than the cheers of the multitudes suggested. At home he was widely seen as a spent force. Here in Europe, his supposedly grateful fellow victors regarded him as trouble, an obstacle standing between them and their own objectives. In spite of the immense sums they owed the United States, in spite of their continued dependence on American largesse, they were going to prove far less tractable than Wilson expected them to be.

So that if December 1918 was for the president a grand apotheosis, the fulfillment of a proud man's most flamboyant dreams, it was also the beginning of the end.

Wilson had reached his zenith. What awaited was nemesis.

Background

How It Happened

It is a rare American who can explain, except in the vaguest terms, how the killing of a man who was not the leader or ruler of any country could possibly have caused a war in which some twenty million human beings perished.

This is as it should be, actually, because the assassination of Archduke Franz Ferdinand, heir to Austria-Hungary's imperial throne, did not *cause* the war at all. It is more usefully understood as having lit a fuse that blew up a keg of gunpowder. The keg was the Europe of 1914. The gunpowder was the system of balance-of-power politics that had separated Europe's most powerful nations into two camps, each fearful that the other was bent on its destruction and therefore desperate not to fall behind in an arms race that in retrospect can seem barely sane.

The fuse was a long one: five weeks of excruciating diplomatic contortions separated Franz Ferdinand's assassination from the unleashing of the armies. It had many twists and loops, barely smoldering at first but later burning hot and fast. There were points at which it might have been snuffed out. These opportunities were missed not because the nations involved wanted to make war but because they feared what might befall them if they appeared to be unwilling to do so. Fear, not aggression, is the theme that runs through the whole story.

Everyone had reason to be afraid. France certainly did; though she had a peacetime standing army of 700,000 men (instantly expandable to 3 million upon mobilization), she shared a long and disputed border with Germany, whose forces totaled 782,000 men in peacetime, 3.8 million upon mobilization. But Germany, too, had reason for fear. Though she had Austria-Hungary on her side (400,000 troops peacetime, 2.25 million mobilized), this could seem almost trivial in light of France's alliance with Russia. Russia's standing army included 1.3 million troops, with 3 million reserves subject to mobilization. The tsar had 25 million male subjects of military service age—for all practical purposes, an infinite resource.

But Russia, too, had much to fear. For all its size, her army was ill trained, ill equipped, run by a corrupt and incompetent bureaucracy, and supported by a deplorably inadequate physical infrastructure. And like her ally France and her potential enemies, Russia was trapped in an unending, apparently unbreakable cycle of escalation. In 1912, for the first time, her military spending exceeded Germany's. But then the First and Second Balkan Wars of 1912 and 1913 both ended with the little kingdom of Serbia profiting at Austria-Hungary's expense, so alarming the Germans that they increased their military budget sharply. This frightened Russia into launching her so-called Great Program. Undertaken at France's insistence and made possible by French loans, this program was approved in June 1914, just days before Franz Ferdinand's assassination. It was, over the next three years, to add four hundred thousand men and modern weaponry and equipment to Russia's standing army and extensively upgrade the railways and other infrastructure needed for fast mobilization. Its short-term effect was not to strengthen Russia but to cause the Germans and Austro-Hungarians to fear that in a few more years their situation would be hopeless. Some of them said that if war was inevitable sooner or later, it had better come soon.

The killing of Franz Ferdinand mattered not only because he was the heir to the throne of Austria-Hungary, one of the three empires that dominated central and eastern Europe, but because he was shot by a Serb, a hapless and tubercular teenager named Gavrilo Princip. This sparked rage in the Austrian capital of Vienna, for which Serbia had long been a headache, taking every opportunity to stir up the kind of trouble that might enable it to grab another piece of territory, always looking to Russia for support. The Austrians assumed from the start, and with reason, that the assassination had been planned in Serbia's capital, Belgrade, and that government officials were involved. They took it as certain that if they did not meet this latest and most outrageous provocation with a punishing response, the subject peoples of Vienna's sprawling multiethnic empire would be encouraged to make trouble as well. The empire was a disjointed hodgepodge, with Germans and Magyar Hungarians making up less than 45 percent of its population. Many of its other subjects—the 12 percent who were Czech, the Polish 10 percent, et cetera—tended to regard themselves as captives with little reason to fight, or even wish, for the empire's survival. Austria-Hungary was also financially hard-pressed, her treasury drained by the Balkan Wars. She was capable of dealing with only a limited amount of trouble. Problems had to be snuffed out as soon as they appeared, because her ability to cope with them was questionable if they grew to be too big.

Serbia was a protégé state, a kind of Slavic little brother, of the great Russian empire. The Russians had long supported the Serbs to strengthen their own position in the Balkans, increasing Austria's difficulties. The Austrians knew that if they threatened Serbia, she would, as in the past, look to Russia for help. They knew also that they were no match for Russia. So they, too, appealed to a stronger ally and patron—to Germany.

When Germany's Kaiser Wilhelm II lunched with a delegation from Vienna and promised to support them in a move against Serbia, giving them what would become notorious as his "blank check," he committed the first of the mistakes with which the road to Armageddon would be paved. He did so almost offhandedly, without deliberation or consultation, not imagining that a major crisis might ensue. His aim was to encourage Germany's junior partner to assert her authority in the Balkans, thereby drawing a line under the relentless erosion of that authority and of Vienna's credibility. He was of course aware of the Russian-Serb connection, but he believed that Russia was not prepared for a showdown. He was confident that her tsar, Nicholas II (who in childhood had seen his grandfather blown to bits by terrorists), would understand the need to

Kaiser Wilhelm II of Germany
Seen by Americans as the devil's disciple, he complained that in wartime Germany no one cared what he thought.

hold regicides to account. They were, after all, family. Nicholas was married to Wilhelm's first cousin, and both the tsarina and the kaiser were first cousins of George V of England.

There was an element of fear in the kaiser's writing of his blank check. He and his ministers and generals were painfully aware that Austria-Hungary, though feeble, was their sole reliable support in a Europe that was growing more militarized every year. They saw that if her decline continued, she could be of little use if war came, that if they did not prove themselves willing to support her, she might be inclined to look elsewhere for protection. Officials in Berlin joked, sourly, that being allied to Vienna was like being shackled to a corpse. But they saw no alternative to propping the corpse up and applying makeup.

If the Austrians had done as the kaiser expected, delivering a fast, chastening blow to the Serbs while making it clear that their objectives were modest and their campaign was going to be short, they would have had the sympathy of a European public still shocked by the murder of Franz Ferdinand and his wife. Undoubtedly there would have been hard words from Russia, and mediation might have been required, but the danger of a crisis escalating out of control would have been considerably reduced.

But Vienna was unable to move swiftly. The mobilization of its army, once started, was going to take sixteen days if everything went smoothly, and would be made especially difficult by the fact that this was high summer and many of the troops had been sent home to help with the harvest. Under the constitution of Austria-Hungary's dual monarchy, mobilization could not begin without the approval of Hungary's government, which was far from eager to proceed. Even the Austrians were unwilling to begin immediately because, as it happened, President Poincaré and Prime Minister René Viviani of France were at that moment in the midst of an official visit to their Russian allies. The Austrians saw the unwisdom of revealing their intentions while the Russian and French leaders were together—something that rarely happened—and able to coordinate an immediate response.

And so the days passed quietly, with nothing apparently happening. The assassination turned into old news. But the Austrians were keeping a dangerous secret: they had no intention of simply giving the Serbs a quick thrashing and withdrawing within their own borders. If free to choose, they would have opted to eliminate Serbia, breaking her up and distributing the pieces among neighbors friendly to Vienna. They had to accept, however, that Russia would never permit such a thing. And so they settled for the lesser goal of reducing Serbia in size—assuming, mistakenly, that Russia would acquiesce in that. They told Berlin nothing, wanting no conditions placed on the blank check. Nor was Russia given even an oblique warning; the plan was to present her with a fait accompli.

The Austro-Hungarian foreign minister, Count Leopold von Berchtold, was a fabulously wealthy bon vivant who thought himself devilishly clever but in fact was only reckless and shortsighted. Not satisfied with merely keeping Russia in the dark, he instructed his ambassador to assure the tsar's foreign minister that Vienna intended to do nothing that St. Petersburg could possibly find objectionable. This ensured that the Russians, when they learned the truth, would become unwilling to believe Vienna about anything.

Meanwhile Berchtold began drafting a list of demands to be presented to Serbia as soon as Poincaré and Viviani departed for home. Vienna's Council of Ministers, its blood up and its confidence inflated by the blank check, agreed that these demands must be so severe as to make acceptance impossible, thereby providing justification for an invasion.

On Thursday, July 23, just hours after the French leaders steamed away from St. Petersburg, Vienna's ten demands were presented to the Serbian authorities in Belgrade. The deadline for an answer was set at forty-eight hours. The Serb response, delivered to the Austrian ambassador late on Saturday afternoon, fully accepted half the demands and requested clarification of most of the others. Its tone was conciliatory, in places almost abject. Nevertheless the ambassador did as instructed and declared that, being unsatisfied, Vienna was severing diplomatic relations. He took the next train out of town, and both countries announced that they were mobilizing their armies. Austria began moving three hundred thousand troops to the border, within easy artillery range of Belgrade.

Russia's foreign minister, Sergei Sazonov, had been so infuriated upon learning of the Austrian demands that he told the chief of the Russian general staff to be ready for mobilization. At his urging and that of the military, Tsar Nicholas declared a Period Preparatory to War. Russian military districts, both those nearest the Austro-Hungarian frontier and others more directly threatening to Germany, were ordered to muster their troops and weaponry. This was supposed to take place in secret, but concealment was impossible. When the Germans made inquiries, they were met with denials that were obviously untrue. The Germans began to wonder what Russia was actually planning. The tension ratcheted upward.

Theobald von Bethmann-Hollweg, chancellor of the German Empire
He struggled to avert a showdown with the United States but was defeated by his own nation's generals.

Sazonov had become convinced, without evidence but with the encouragement of the French and Serbian ambassadors, that the Austrians were being used as German puppets, and that what the Germans intended was to force Russia out of the Balkans. There was no truth in this—Berlin would have been delighted to see Russia exit the Balkans, but had no intention of going to war in hope of making it happen— but that hardly mattered. President Poincaré, before departing, had demanded that the Russians not allow themselves to be bullied by Vienna or Berlin. And now the Serbian ambassador was telling Sazonov, on his own, that Serbia, too, expected him to take a hard line. This was yet another tragic untruth; in fact, the Belgrade government was terrified by the prospect of an Austrian invasion.

The fuse was now short and burning fast. On Tuesday, July 28, Austria-Hungary declared war on Serbia. She did so in spite of being far from ready to attack, and for no better reason than Berchtold's determination to take an irreversible step before Berlin awoke to the seriousness of the situation and stopped payment on its blank check. Vienna's declaration came a day after Kaiser Wilhelm, ignorant of the latest developments, arrived home from his annual yachting holiday in the North Sea. Though the German ambassador in Vienna had provided advance notice of Vienna's intentions, Chancellor Theobald von Bethmann-Hollweg had told Wilhelm nothing. Probably this was because he knew how unstable his master was, how psychologically fragile and how capable of making rash decisions and erratically changing direction. As Otto von Bismarck had declared more than two decades earlier, "The emperor is like a balloon. If one did not hold him fast on a string, he would go no one knows whither." Keeping him ignorant was one way of keeping him from flying off into the unknown.

Shortly after Austria's declaration of war, Russia's ambassador paid a call on Berchtold. The result was disastrous. The ambassador departed believing that Berchtold had told him that he was unwilling to negotiate not just with Serbia but even with Russia. This meant that there could be no communication between the two powers that were best positioned to resolve the crisis peaceably. It is unlikely that even Berchtold was irresponsible enough to have said any such thing—or to have done so intentionally, anyway. But when Sazonov was informed, his fear that war was inevitable turned into certainty. The chief of the Russian general staff agreed; he was receiving reports, false but frightening, that Germany was mustering troops on a massive scale. Later that same day, Thursday, July 30, Sazonov persuaded a deeply unwilling tsar to sign a mobilization order. He accomplished this by claiming to know (as he unquestionably believed) that the Germans were already doing the same thing. The tsar's reluctance did him credit. "Think of the thousands and thousands of men who would be sent to their deaths!" he pleaded. But Sazonov insisted that the survival of the Romanov dynasty—of Mother Russia herself—was now at stake.

This was *the* turning point. Just two days later a dumbfounded Europe would find itself at war. The heart of the tragedy is that there was no need for Russia's mobilization. Nothing had happened to threaten Russia directly or even to put her position in the Balkans in clear jeopardy. The irony is that Germany, the cause of Russia's fears, was now alone in having made no move toward mobilization. The French general staff was moving masses of troops to places within a few miles of their eastern frontier from which they could launch an invasion of Germany. In London, First Lord of the Admiralty Winston Churchill had deployed Britain's Grand Fleet, positioning it to meet any moves by the German navy in the North Sea or the Channel. Nicholas II's signature meant that almost one and a half million troops—some 150 divisions—would begin assembling at points chosen as best for starting attacks on Germany as well as Austria and Hungary. Additionally, Russia's millions of reservists were being called to duty. Viewed from Berlin, these developments were terrifying.

Sazonov gave much weight, in demanding the tsar's signature, to the fact that for Russia mobilization was going to be a slow and cumbersome process. The country was both enormous—the largest on earth—and backward by the standards of western Europe, her railways inadequate and her armies impressive in size only. Even when mobilized, her troops would be merely positioned for action, not launched upon an attack. Viewed from St. Petersburg, Russia's mobilization did not appear nearly as dangerous as it did from Berlin. Sazonov was walking a tightrope, hoping that mobilization would make the Germans see the gravity of the situation while not stampeding them into a panicky response. To accomplish this, unfortunately, he continued to claim that his country's preparations were less extensive than they actually were. The only result was to increase German fears that Russia was readying a preemptive attack.

Britain meanwhile stood on the sidelines. In keeping with her traditional policy of keeping clear of continental alliances, she was not a member of the French-Russian Entente or the German-Austrian partnership. So far as the world knew—so far as most members of the cabinet in London knew—she had no obligations to either side. In keeping with her equally venerable policy of opposing any continental power that threatened to dominate Europe, however, she had unofficially regarded Germany as her prime potential enemy almost from 1871, the year the Franco-Prussian War made possible the unification of the German states in a new empire. Prussia, a German kingdom so warlike that Napoleon I called it an army with a country attached, had led the confederation that defeated France. It was more or less inevitable that her king, Wilhelm I, became emperor of Germany.

France meanwhile had found herself in the unfamiliar role of underdog, without allies. That, however, was sure to change, and in due course it did. Russia had so many border disputes with Austria-Hungary that early in the 1890s she quit the Three Emperors League in which she had been allied with Berlin and Vienna. Unwilling to stand alone, she formed an Entente with France. France, for her part, reached out to Britain and met with a friendly response. In the first decade of the new century, Britain's general staff began working with France's, in deepest secrecy, on preparations for war with Germany. Belgium, like Britain officially neutral, became a third partner in this arrangement; more on that later.

Most of the nations on both sides were thinking defensively, hoping not for conquest but to save themselves from destruction and with luck to become permanently more secure. If there was an exception among the major powers, it was France. In 1871 the victorious Germans had stripped France of the provinces of Alsace and Lorraine, considerable parts of which were in fact historically and culturally German. Bismarck had cautioned that if Germany took the two provinces, she would have to fight to keep them in another fifty years. He was off by less than a decade. Time did not heal France's wound. For many of the republic's citizens, a war to take back what had been stolen would be a holy war. Conquest was entirely justified.

From the start of the 1914 crisis, British foreign secretary Sir Edward Grey found himself obliged to play a devious game, feigning a neutrality that was, because of the secret arrangements with France and Belgium, a good deal less than real. On July 26 and again on July 27, he suggested

Sir Edward Grey,
British foreign secretary
*He managed Colonel House
as skillfully as House
managed Wilson.*

to Prince Karl Lichnowsky, the German ambassador in London, that the dispute between Austria-Hungary and Russia should be mediated by a conference made up of Britain, France, Germany, and Italy. Lichnowsky liked the idea and urged his government in Berlin to take it up. It went no further, however. It was all too obvious that France would favor Russia and Italy would be hostile to Vienna, whose alpine territories she coveted. It seemed unlikely that Britain would want to do anything to antagonize France or Russia. What mattered more, Vienna was emphatically not interested, in this case with some justification. Similar conferences had settled the Balkan Wars of 1912 and 1913, but in a way so unfavorable to the Austrians that they were unwilling to try any such thing again.

It was not until July 30, the day of Russia's mobilization, that Grey peeked out from his shell of impartiality. Speaking without the knowledge of the other members of Britain's divided cabinet, most of whom were only now learning to their shock of the secret military arrangement with France, he told Lichnowsky that in his personal opinion (he made no claim to be speaking for the government), if Vienna refused to negotiate, the result was likely to be a general war. A war that Britain would probably enter on the side of France and Russia.

Lichnowsky, a cordial and capable aristocrat with a passionate commitment to British-German friendship, had been in torment even before hearing this. Four days before this latest talk with Grey, he had wired Berlin that war seemed definitely possible to the authorities in London. He had warned that in his opinion, if war came, "for us there would be everything to lose and nothing to gain." Now thoroughly frightened, he relayed Grey's warning to Chancellor Bethmann, who understood its importance. Bethmann sent a fresh appeal to Berchtold in Vienna, the latest of several, asking him again to make clear to the Russians his willingness to talk. But Berchtold had effectively closed up shop. He gave no answer to Bethmann and sent no assurances to Sazonov. He was determined to allow nothing to interrupt preparations for the attack on Serbia.

The situation was sliding beyond anyone's control. As Bethmann begged Berchtold to change course, the chief of the German general staff, Helmuth von Moltke, sent a telegram to his Austrian counterpart, the bellicose little field marshal Franz Conrad, who had long been urging the destruction of Serbia. Moltke had been distressed to learn of the large number of divisions the Austrians were assigning to the attack on Serbia.

He asked Conrad to shift some of those divisions farther north, to places where the Germans might soon be looking for help in fending off an attack from Russia. More remarkably, and with far less justification, he cautioned Conrad that Austria should not be drawn into any peace proposals that they might see coming from Berlin—from Chancellor Bethmann or even the kaiser.

"What a joke!" Berchtold exclaimed when he saw how completely Bethmann and Moltke were at cross-purposes. "Who's in charge in Berlin?"

The answer was that, not only in Berlin but in St. Petersburg and Vienna and Paris, power was flowing away from the politicians and into the hands of the generals. With Austria-Hungary and Serbia and even Russia mobilized, with France readying her forces and Britain's Royal Navy on station, war seemed ever more certain. Top generals in all the capitals, fearful of what faced them, were demanding to be freed from the restraints of peacetime. The German high command, still not allowed to take any action, was at the edge of hysteria. Hence Moltke's almost treasonous warning to Conrad.

What is most astonishing is that even now, with the crisis this far advanced, Berlin had still done nothing to position her armed forces for action. This was true of Germany alone.

The peace proposal of which Moltke warned Conrad was an idea of Kaiser Wilhelm's, and it was arguably the best to be offered by anyone throughout the entire crisis; even Sir Edward Grey thought it had promise. It called for the Austrians, whenever they attacked Serbia, to advance only far enough to occupy Belgrade—a matter of a few miles. By taking possession of the capital city, they would inflict a significant humiliation on Serbia, and by going no farther, they would signal to Russia that they intended no radical upending of the status quo. They could remain in place while negotiations got under way and the crisis was brought down from a boil. There could be no thought of keeping Belgrade, of course, but an eventual withdrawal on terms acceptable to Vienna was in no way impossible.

The time was ripe for a solution of this kind. Among the generals in all the capitals of Europe, only Conrad was eager for a fight, and he wanted a fight only with Serbia. All the emperors and heads of government, and all the foreign ministers except perhaps Berchtold, understood that if fighting broke out anywhere, it was certain to spread. They understood also that the consequences would be terrible. Never in the history of Europe had so many huge armies gone to war against one another, and never had armies been so monstrously well armed. Expectations of a quick, clean victory were the fantasies of amateur strategists and ignorant superpatriots on street corners. In the army command centers and halls of government, there was widespread appreciation that a terrible ordeal lay ahead.

It was beginning to dawn on Grey that encircling Germany with huge and hostile armies might not have been the wisest way to keep the peace. On July 31, feeling the jaws of a trap closing on Britain almost as surely as on the continental powers, he instructed his ambassador in Berlin to deliver a pledge to the kaiser and to Bethmann: "If the peace of Europe can be preserved and this crisis be safely passed, my own effort would be to promote some arrangement to which Germany could be a party, by which she could be assured that no hostile or aggressive policy would be pursued against her or her allies by France, Russia, and ourselves, jointly or separately."

His epiphany had come too late. Berchtold in Vienna sent no response to Kaiser Wilhelm's Stop-in-Belgrade plan. Wilhelm, desperate, appealed over Berchtold's head to Hapsburg emperor Franz Josef, who had ascended to the throne a dozen years before Abraham Lincoln became president of the United States. Franz Josef informed Wilhelm that what he asked was not possible. Conrad's plan could not be adjusted so as to allow the capture of Belgrade but nothing more. Franz Josef did not want war; he was only repeating what Berchtold and Conrad had told him. All his life he had been presiding over the slow decline of the empire that his forebears had created. His beautiful wife had been assassinated, and his only son had committed suicide (causing his cousin Franz Ferdinand to become heir to the throne). Franz Josef was worn down by his grievous losses and his eighty-seven years. He wanted to die and to do so in peace. But he was not making the decisions.

The Austrian rejection of Stop-in-Belgrade sealed Europe's doom. Moltke and the German war minister, almost beside themselves with anxiety, demanded mobilization. Even now the kaiser refused, but he did approve two less momentous measures. The first was a State of Impending War, which was similar to the Period Preparatory to War that had preceded Russia's mobilization. It recalled soldiers on leave to duty and put the government in control of the infrastructure without which there could be no mobilization: the railways and the telephone, telegraph, and postal systems.

The kaiser also issued what would become notorious as the Double Ultimatum. It informed Russia that if she did not suspend "every measure against Austria-Hungary and ourselves," Germany would have no choice except to mobilize. France was asked for things no sensible person could have expected her to give: not only a pledge of neutrality in case of war between Germany and Russia but the temporary surrender of the great fortresses with which she defended her frontier. To the extent that all this was more than a desperate final effort to avoid mobilization, it was probably intended to make Germany appear the victim of hostile neighbors. What it looked like to much of the world was bullying and bluster. No country on earth was as inept as Germany at the art of public relations.

And now at the eleventh hour, when there was no room for error, something went wrong in a conversation between Grey and Lichnowsky. On the basis of what he understood Grey to have said, Lichnowsky wired Berlin with news that appeared to change everything. Britain, he reported, was offering to remain neutral if Germany would refrain from attacking France. This sent Kaiser Wilhelm into ecstasies; it meant that his armies would have to fight Russia only. (His generals, as we shall see, were less than overjoyed.) It proved to be a transient thrill. Grey quickly made it clear that he had intended no such offer, and the kaiser's hopes were dashed.

Berlin sent an offer of its own to London. If Britain would stay out of war if it came, Germany upon the conclusion of hostilities would restore the borders not only of France but of Belgium as well. (She would also, however, regard herself as entitled to take from her defeated foes whatever colonial possessions she might desire.) This served only to insult Grey. He replied coldly, saying that acceptance of such an offer "would be a disgrace from which the good name of this country [Britain] would never recover."

Grey and his minions in the Foreign Office were taken aback by the Germans' mention of Belgium. London regarded Belgium, because of the proximity of her coast to southeastern England, as an essential element of British security. Britain had insisted on the creation of the Kingdom of Belgium in 1831 in order to ensure that such ports as Antwerp would never fall into the hands of France, then still the continent's leading power and therefore considered a threat. It was likewise at Britain's insistence that the new kingdom committed to "perpetual neutrality . . . towards all other states." All the European powers, the Kingdom of Prussia included, signed a treaty guaranteeing this neutrality.

Why, then, this reference to Belgium in the German communiqué? What could possibly require the restoration of her borders unless those borders were going to be violated? Grey wired Paris and Berlin, asking both governments to affirm their recognition of Belgium's neutrality and by implication her safety from attack. France, for reasons that we will examine later, was able to respond as quickly and affirmatively as London expected. Germany did not respond at all. Her silence was heavy with menace.

The deadline for responses to the Double Ultimatum came and went. Neither France nor Russia responded. On the afternoon of Saturday, August 1, Germany and France both declared general mobilization. Germany declared simultaneously that a state of war existed between her and Russia. Two Russian armies were ordered to advance into Germany.

At this crucial point something was revealed that not even the kaiser or Bethmann knew, never mind London, Paris, or St. Petersburg. It went back to the assumption, first embedded in Germany's war plans by Army Chief of Staff Alfred von Schlieffen in 1905 and retained in all subsequent revisions of those plans, that if war came, Germany would have to fight on two fronts, against France and Russia simultaneously. So far, so necessary: the Franco-Russian Entente made such an assumption inescapable. The planners assumed further that all nations would mobilize upon declaring war, that Germany could not expect to win a protracted war against two such powerful foes, that Russia was too vast geographically to be defeated quickly, and that Germany's survival therefore depended upon a lightning-fast victory in the west. Such a victory would be impossible unless Paris was captured quickly, and this was deemed to be feasible only if Germany's armies began advancing on France from the moment war was declared. The final assumption was that advancing with the necessary speed required avoiding France's border defenses— impregnable strongholds such as Verdun. The only way to do this was to attack through Belgium.

The most fatefully wrong of the German planners' assumptions was also the most understandable: the seemingly self-evident expectation that all the powers would mobilize when they declared war. Declarations of mobilization would, under such circumstances and viewed from a diplomatic perspective, be little more than formalities issued as the various armies set forth to engage one another. Neither Schlieffen nor Moltke nor anyone else had imagined a scenario in which Russia and France would mobilize without first declaring war. That was the sting in the tail of the crisis: Germany had a mobilization plan that did not simply prepare for but began an immediate full-scale attack on France through Belgium. Because of this, just hours after Berlin's mobilization, its troops were advancing on a small country whose neutrality it was pledged to respect.

Here again the motivating force was not a desire for conquest but pure raw fear, in this instance Germany's entirely justified fear of being crushed between the enemies to her west and the vast enemy to her east.

In any case it was done; the July crisis was over, the Great War had begun. On one side were Britain, France, and Russia, calling themselves the Triple Entente.

On the other side were the Central Powers: Germany and Austria-Hungary. The question of who started the war has tortured historians for a hundred years. In the United States it was a crucial question from the start. It assumed a central place in debates about how to respond to the conflict, whether to become involved, and how to deal with the losers after it was won. The men making the decisions, sadly, either never knew or chose to ignore several important facts:

That no one involved in the July crisis wanted a general war, and few wanted even a regional war.

That Germany was the last to put her armed forces in motion and did so to save herself from destruction, not in pursuit of any territorial ambitions.

And that for all of them, except perhaps Britain in the beginning, the war seemed a fight for survival. And therefore a fight to the death.

It is impossible to judge American policy and actions in the five years that followed without keeping these things in mind.

Chapter 2

Neutrality the Wilson Way

LITERALLY FROM THE FIRST DAY OF THE WAR—EVEN BEFORE THE fighting began—the United States loomed large in the thinking of all the belligerent nations. As the world's new economic superpower, vastly surpassing in output both a fading Britain and a fast-growing Germany, America had enormous potential value as an ally and was greatly to be feared as an enemy. That the British understood this is clear in what they did even before declaring war. On August 4, 1914, they sent a little ship called the *Teconia*, a cable layer, into the North Sea to sever Germany's five underwater communications cables, including the two that connected Berlin to New York. From that day no European news could be cabled to the United States except from London and Paris, where censorship offices were put in place to stop the transmission of any reporting not acceptable to the Triple Entente. "The cutting of that cable may do us great injury," an Austrian diplomat stationed in America lamented. "If only one side of the case is given, as may happen if only the English cable is left, prejudice against us will be created here."

He was understating the case. As early as August 6, *The New York Herald* was running a story—improbable on its face and never substantiated—about German soldiers firing at Belgian soldiers being carried on Red Cross stretchers. This set the pattern for what was to follow.

The warring nations' concerns about the United States grew more intense as weeks of fighting passed, casualties mounted, and the belligerents found themselves in a conflict of a kind never before experienced: total war, industrial war, with the potential to go on for years and consume all the resources of the belligerents. By the end of August, it was clear that Count Alfred von Schlieffen had been right to worry, as he did even on his deathbed, about his great plan for a lightning descent upon Paris. As modified by Moltke, the plan failed. It was immensely complex, the obstacles were formidable, and in the end it demanded more than even seven German armies could deliver.

The right wing of the attack force raced across Belgium and into France more or less on schedule, pushed the French and British back and back again until they were almost within sight of the spires of Paris, but finally ran out of momentum. The troops had been on the march for a month, each man carrying some seventy or eighty pounds of weaponry and gear in withering summer heat. Many had had no rations for days, and water was sometimes scarce. Keeping the artillery and ammunition and other essentials moving forward had become an ordeal for men and animals alike. Only token resistance stood between the forward units and the French capital, but large Entente forces were not far away. The more prudent of the German commanders saw no alternative but pulling back to a secure line of defense. The more aggressive generals, their flanks exposed by these withdrawals, had no choice but to follow. They retreated to the Ourq, the first east-west-running river north of the Marne. By the time the French were able to mount a counterattack, they found themselves up against freshly dug but impregnable German fortifications.

The two sides then tried to outflank each other to the north. This turned, willy-nilly, into an unintended "race to the sea." Once the sea was reached, in Belgium's flat and featureless Flanders region, the two sides faced each other along a front that snaked hundreds of miles southward and eastward to the French-Swiss border. That line proved maddeningly static, and along it both sides would mount increasingly massive offensives and repeatedly fail to break through. Meanwhile two Russian armies had invaded Germany from the east and, in spite of immense numerical superiority, were so thoroughly and humiliatingly thrashed that the general in charge committed suicide. To the south and east, in Galicia and the Carpathian Mountains, other Russian armies were savaging their Austro-Hungarian adversaries but also failing to achieve decisive results. By November the Turks had been drawn into the war on the side of the Central Powers. The armies of their Ottoman Empire were fighting the Russians in the Caucasus and the British in the Middle East.

By year-end, five months of combat had driven the casualty figures to nightmarish levels but accomplished little else. A hundred thousand German soldiers were dead, an estimated 700,000 wounded. France and Austria-Hungary had suffered about a million casualties each—the number of French troops dead or missing was in the hundreds of thousands—and the total for

Russia was approximately twice that. Of the 160,000 men who had crossed to the continent with the British Expeditionary Force, more than half were dead or wounded. On both sides there were generals and politicians who believed, and would continue to believe, that with a few more powerful if costly strokes, they could bring the bloodbath to a glorious conclusion.

These optimists were a minority, if an influential one. Wiser men knew better. Field Marshal Earl Kitchener of Khartoum, a national hero newly installed as Britain's war minister, stunned his fellow cabinet members by declaring that to deal with what lay ahead, they were going to have to raise an army of at least two million men. That estimate would prove far too conservative. By early September a call-up of reserves had increased the armed forces of the Central Powers to more than three million. Awesome as this total was, it seemed frighteningly inadequate when measured against the forces being mustered by the Entente: 3.5 million Russians, 1.8 million French, 750,000 British. All the belligerents were enlisting fresh recruits at a rate that would dwarf these numbers.

The war came as a surprise to the American public, of course. It was a surprise to most Europeans, for that matter, in spite of the staggering amounts of money their governments had been spending on arms and the persistence with which they warned that the countries next door were both powerful and wicked. The continent had been mostly at peace for an extraordinarily long time, so that people naturally tended to assume that this was a permanent state of affairs. With the exception of the three quick victories over Denmark, Austria, and France that between 1864 and 1871 led to the unification of Germany, there had been no major wars in the heart of Europe since the fall of Napoleon in 1815.

Few Americans had any knowledge of, or saw much reason to interest themselves in, Europe's power games. Viewed from Main Street, the diplomatic failures of July 1914 and the tragedy that ensued were just the Old World doing its old and decadent thing. Americans liked to think of themselves as above such nonsense, entitled to look down with disdain on kings and emperors, the struggle for global empire, and huge armies butchering each other over nobody exactly knew what.

This was true even in Washington, half empty when the war began, drowsing under the weight of its brutal summer heat. It was true even of President Wilson, less because of any lack of interest in international relations (he had that same summer been pushing the United States to the verge of what would have been an utterly pointless war with Mexico) than because of a searing loss: his devoted wife Ellen died of kidney disease just one day after Britain's entry into the war, leaving him in a state of grief that bordered on despair. It was certainly true of Secretary of State William Jennings Bryan, who would show himself willing, over the next ten months, to destroy himself politically rather than accept the slow slide into a war that was, in his opinion, not worth fighting. It was true of most of America's public men at a time when the State Department had a grand total of 157 employees in Washington. The country was near the end of an era during which, as former secretary of state Elihu Root sardonically observed, "international law was regarded as a rather antiquated branch of useless learning, diplomacy as a foolish mystery and the foreign service as a superfluous expense." In 1893 Champ Clark, then a freshman congressman from Missouri but destined to serve as Speaker of the House of Representatives during the Great War, expressed the spirit of the time by proposing the elimination of the diplomatic service.

Colonel Edward House
*He avoided the limelight,
understanding that
"men often destroy
themselves by being too
much in evidence."*

Within the president's tiny inner circle, however, there was one striking exception. This was Colonel Edward House, who, since first meeting New Jersey governor Woodrow Wilson, had forged a bond with him that could seem almost unnatural in its intensity. Small and frail, faintly mouselike in appearance thanks to protuberant ears and a receding chin, House was a wealthy

Texan with a consuming interest in politics and public affairs. Having decided early in life that he had neither the physical presence nor the robust constitution needed for the pursuit of elective office (he was a bit of a hypochondriac, refusing to leave his New England summer retreat for the heat of Washington even in times of crisis), he set out to become a political professional of a kind more common today than a hundred years ago: a promoter of and adviser to more conspicuously ambitious men, content to work behind the scenes.

At that he was extraordinarily successful, playing a key role in the election of four Texas governors and advising them in office. Early in the new century, in his midforties, he left Texas for New York, his goal now to become influential in the national Democratic Party. He was again successful, building such an impressive reputation that in 1911 Governor Wilson journeyed across the river from New Jersey to discuss his prospects in the following year's presidential election. It is astonishing to read of the speed with which the two men became not only collaborators but best friends. The colonel became the first really close friend Wilson had had since breaking with a supposedly disloyal protégé in Princeton two years earlier. Wilson—especially after he won the White House in 1912—became the figure through whom the colonel could fulfill his dreams of becoming a player in national politics and even on the world stage.

The new president offered the colonel any cabinet post except secretary of state, which had been promised to William Jennings Bryan. House, while managing to place several Texas friends in the cabinet, shrewdly said that he wanted nothing except to be of service in unofficial and unpaid ways. In doing so he kept himself free of administrative burdens and the sometimes petty quarrels of Wilson's official family. And he satisfied the president that his devotion was utterly selfless.

Long after his relationship with Wilson came to a frosty end, House told the man to whom he was entrusting his papers some of the secrets of his success. It was necessary never to disagree with Wilson on any subject about which he appeared to have made up his mind, House said; the president would reject not only the contrary opinion but the person who offered it, and the rejection could very well prove permanent. He recalled that Wilson had a bottomless hunger, an insatiable need, for unqualified praise; House learned to begin discussions of anything Wilson had drafted on a laudatory note "in order to strengthen the president's confidence in himself which, strangely enough, [was] often lacking." But the key to the innermost chambers of Wilson's heart and mind, House said, was his craving for greatness. The way to get him to do something was to tell him that it would contribute to making him a towering historical figure. House's messages to Wilson are studded with innumerable examples of his doing exactly this, often in terms that a less needy spirit would have found laughable.

The examples are almost beyond numbering. On July 1, 1914, the colonel sent a letter telling Wilson that "you have more than fulfilled expectations at home, great as they were, and I have a keen desire for you to become the world figure of your time. Never again can the old order of statesman hold sway, and you are and will continue to be the prophet of a new day." Five weeks later, the war having begun, House consoled the president on the loss of his wife in terms perfectly attuned to what Wilson desperately needed to believe: "It has fallen to your lot to bring a great nation through an epoch making time, and the noble, gentle soul that has gone would be the first to bid you bring to bear that splendid courage, which is yours and yours alone." More followed a week after that: "In my opinion you have already written your name as high as any man America has yet produced, and I am convinced that when the story is told in the future, it will be the first." House could go on endlessly in this vein. No matter how extravagant the flattery, Wilson was always ready for more.

The colonel understood that Wilson was emotionally drained by face-to-face interaction with almost anyone outside his family, and needed frequent and extended doses of solitude. Even the most skilled flatterers were welcome on a limited basis only, and there were few surer ways of alienating him than by demanding too much attention. As his relationship with the president grew increasingly intense, House continued to live in New York and to visit the White House only when summoned—and even then, only when he found the temperature in Washington bearable. "Men often destroy themselves," he observed, "by being too much in evidence." By keeping his distance, he made the president crave his company as he craved that of no one else, even his own three daughters. "Beg you will come here," Wilson said in a telegram to House sent three days after Christmas in 1914. "Lots of room and lots of welcome."

The colonel's keen understanding of the president's psyche had more than a little to do with his early acceptance of American neutrality. Though he was the son of an immigrant from England and himself a fervent Anglophile, having been sent to school in England as a boy, the colonel saw that to urge American intervention in the first months of the war would have been worse than pointless. No one could have persuaded the American public to enter the war at that stage. To urge such a thing would have put him at odds with the president, who from the start insisted both on neutrality and on his own right to determine what the term meant. House would not have remained an always-welcome visitor to the White House, where a bedroom was kept ready for his use, if he had not understood the price of getting out of step with the president.

The evolution of Wilson's neutrality has always been one of the puzzles of his presidency, one that historians continue to explain in contradictory ways. Though few administrations are as thoroughly and accessibly documented as his—all sixty-nine weighty volumes of *The Papers of Woodrow Wilson* are in libraries in every city—its archives do not put the biggest questions to rest. Wilson himself contributed significantly to making himself a mystery. His discomfort in dealing directly with people caused him to become, throughout his presidency, an ever more solitary figure. Writing, however, came naturally to him. Faced with a problem, his instinct was not to reach out for advice and an exchange of views but to put a piece of paper into his little portable typewriter and tap out his thoughts on what the nation or Congress or some foreign country should do. Until his last year and a half in office, he composed his own speeches, diplomatic notes, and other official documents, at the same time maintaining a copious correspondence.

The result is a mountain of source material, almost all of it assembled and published after his death, so vast and varied that extracts from it can be and have been used to depict Wilson in a bewildering variety of ways. To one observer he is a seer and a saint, to another underhanded and repulsively self-righteous. Here he is the twentieth century's Machiavelli, there a credulous and self-deceiving fool. The truth lies between the extremes, as usual, but not all of it is uncertain. Immersion in the sources makes it impossible not to conclude that the president's idea of neutrality was idiosyncratic from the start, that it grew sporadically more dubious in the two years preceding America's intervention in the war, and that the contradictions and ultimately the falsity of his policy were invisible to Wilson himself. He was—necessarily without having any awareness of the fact—a master of self-deceit.

It is equally clear that House, however hard he may have struggled in the beginning to accept neutrality, was much quicker than Wilson to abandon it and much more forthright—with himself—about doing so. His challenge was to deceive not himself but the president. By the time the war was half a year old, he was committed to the Entente, to Britain above all. He concealed this from the president only to the extent necessary to avoid alienating him, finally pushing intervention so persistently as to put their relationship at risk.

The record of House's migration from presumed neutrality to feigned neutrality and finally to flagrant nonneutrality begins more than half a year before the start of the war. In December 1913, as the first year of the Wilson presidency was coming to an end, the United States received a visit from Sir William Tyrrell, a representative of the British Foreign Office whose mission was to ease some points of friction between Washington and London over their interests in Latin America. Colonel House was known, by this time, to be the president's one great friend and principal adviser, and so Tyrrell was interested in getting close to him. House, for his part, saw in Tyrrell an opportunity to involve himself in global affairs, as he had yearned to do since before leaving Texas. Soon the two were having long talks. An eager House laid out various schemes for bringing together major powers from around the world—even faraway and mysterious Japan—and getting them to agree on ways to develop and uplift what he called the "waste places" of the earth. When Tyrrell suggested that a reduction of "militarism" might provide the resources for such good works, House became convinced that the two of them were in full accord.

Tyrrell, accustomed to the dark subtleties of European great-power diplomacy, must have been charmed by the colonel's simple earnestness. He was eager to demonstrate the United Kingdom's receptiveness to his new friend's ideas and a desire for closer ties between Washington and London. He encouraged House to go to Germany and share his ideas with Kaiser Wilhelm. Why Germany? Perhaps he thought that such a journey would give the American a quick lesson in how much less agreeable than the British the Germans were. Perhaps he hoped to spare his associates at the Foreign Office having to listen to the colonel's fantasies. At this point, it should be remembered, no one was thinking about war. Neither Tyrrell nor House had any way of foreseeing that war would soon give a desperate urgency to Anglo-American relations.

Tyrrell's most specific suggestion was that the colonel should urge the kaiser and his henchmen to "evidence their good intentions by agreeing to stop building an extravagant navy, and to curtail militarism generally." This is House's paraphrase of Tyrrell's words, approvingly dictated to a secretary for inclusion in what the colonel called his diary. It suggests the extent to which the English visitor was shaping his American friend's thinking. The German navy was now seen as the "extravagant" one—yet even after 1900, when the

Germans embarked on an ambitious program of warship construction, their naval expenditures were only 42 percent of Britain's, only 8 percent more than France's, and less than 60 percent of France's and Russia's combined. As for "curtailing militarism," that apparently was Germany's responsibility alone.

Five months later House set out for Berlin on exactly the kind of mission Tyrrell had proposed. He carried papers introducing him as the representative of the president of the United States, but he had no official position and was traveling at his own expense.

During his voyage House made the acquaintance of a fellow passenger bearing the famous name Moltke. He was a count, a cousin of the Helmuth von Moltke who headed the German general staff and nephew of the earlier, greater Moltke whose military genius had made possible the unification of Germany in 1871. House was impressed, and in putting his impressions into a letter to Wilson, he revealed something significant about himself. The count, he wrote, "is perhaps the only noble in Germany who has a detached point of view and sees the situation as we do." These words expose a lack of rigor in the colonel's thinking, coming as they do from a man who did not read or speak German, had only scant knowledge of Germany, and could never in his life have exchanged views on any subject with more than a handful of "German nobles." Implicit in this one fraught sentence is the assumption that in order to be credited with a "detached point of view," one had to think what House and Wilson thought. It was an early example of House's tendency to mistake his own prejudices for facts.

In Berlin, House was granted the honor of a one-on-one talk with Kaiser Wilhelm II, evidence of the importance that official Germany attached to its relations with the United States. The colonel was more favorably impressed than he had expected to be. As with Tyrrell, he sketched out his plans for disarmament and international cooperation, and again he got an encouraging response. Now that he had expressions of interest from Britain and Germany alike, he thought it might be possible to take the next step and arrange the negotiation of specific issues. But *what* issues? Disarmament? House's "waste places of the earth"? The colonel needed to get somebody to propose some action. He told the kaiser that he would now move on to Paris and London for that purpose. Wilhelm, no less fluent in English than in German, asked to be kept informed. Whatever the extent of the kaiser's interest in House's ideas—in all likelihood it was minimal—he like Tyrrell wanted to demonstrate goodwill to the personal representative of the president of the United States.

House, whom the Germans believed to be a military man because of the honorific *colonel*, was taken to some of the army parades and ceremonies that marked the arrival of summertime in all the European capitals. It was assumed that he would find this enjoyable. Instead it stirred him to report to his chief that he had encountered "jingoism run stark mad."

Behind the colonel's report was the implication, destined to be embraced as a self-evident truth first by the Entente powers and not long thereafter in Washington, that Germany was the most militaristic (and yes, most jingoistic) of nations and therefore the most mad. The facts, however, make this proposition questionable. From 1900 to 1913 France, Britain, and Russia spent the equivalent of almost £1.5 billion on their armies, exclusive of Britain's expenditures on the Boer War. Germany and Austria-Hungary, in the same period, spent £834 million. France's army was only marginally smaller than Germany's at the start of 1914 and was growing more rapidly. If Russia had had no allies, her army alone would have outnumbered those of Germany and Austria-Hungary together by hundreds of thousands of troops.

House's visit to Berlin was the occasion on which, with almost ridiculously transparent coyness, he sent Wilson a warning that "unless some one acting for you can bring about a different understanding, there is some day to be an awful cataclysm. No one in Europe can do it. There is too much hatred, too many jealousies." That statement, written less than three months before Europe went to war, has been cited as evidence that House was so insightful as to be almost clairvoyant. Which is fair enough, though his purpose in writing it was almost certainly less to predict the future than to put before Wilson a vision of himself as the president who could save Europe from itself. Assuming of course that he had "some one"—guess who—to act on his behalf.

Upon leaving Germany, House spent an uneventful week in Paris. He received little attention there, the French president and prime minister being occupied with their impending visit to Russia. The city's obsession with a sex-and-murder scandal involving the wife of a leading politician satisfied him that jingoism was not as advanced in France as in Germany. In June he crossed to London, where Tyrrell had arranged for him to be much fussed over. He was launched into a whirl of social engagements and invited to meet with Prime Minister H. H. Asquith, Foreign Secretary Grey, Chancellor of the Exchequer David Lloyd George, and other notables. All showed themselves eager to hear about his plans and what he had learned in Berlin. It is no denigration of the colonel to suppose that he must have been thrilled to find himself discussing momentous undertakings with so many of Europe's leading men. Nor was it villainous of his hosts if they saw this improbable little Texan as naïve and presumptuous but nevertheless did everything possible to show that they took him seriously. They, like the Germans, wanted President Wilson to understand that they shared his aspirations. They wanted to convince him of this while committing their nations to nothing.

House remained in London for three weeks after the assassination of Franz Ferdinand. Finally he had to abandon the hope that, in the midst of an increasingly grave crisis, Grey or someone else was going to give him a concrete proposal that he could take back to Berlin. He took ship for America on July 21, two days before Austria-Hungary delivered its ultimatum to Serbia, one week before Vienna's declaration of war. Thus he missed being present for the climax of the crisis, which took place as he approached New York, and had no idea that the "awful cataclysm" of which he had written was now only days in the future. He had accomplished nothing of substance, but his journey solidified the attitudes and assumptions that had first become apparent in his talks with Tyrrell in 1913. Germany was uniquely dangerous. "German nobles," with perhaps one rather obscure exception, lacked a "detached view." The British, by contrast, shared House's yearning not just for peace but for the end of militarism. France was not of the first importance and could be dealt with indirectly, through London.

These assumptions would have consequences. This is clear in what House wrote the president from his summer home on August 22, by which date the war in Europe had already escalated to shocking heights of destruction. "Germany's success," he wrote, "will ultimately mean trouble for us. We will have to abandon the path which you are blazing as a standard for future generations, with permanent peace as its goal and a new international ethical code as its guiding star, and build up a military machine of vast proportions." In short, the whole legacy of the Wilson presidency, Wilson's own bid for immortality, was going to be lost if Germany won the war. Once again the colonel was demonstrating that he knew which buttons to push.

America's first serious entanglement in the war had almost nothing to do with the clash of vast armies across the European continent. What drew the United States in, snaring her in the arcane and rancorous diplomacy of the conflict's first year, was the sea war between Britain and Germany. Paradoxically, this was a small war and a peculiar one, in the early going less a matter of battles between ships than a kind of scholarly dispute over what was and was not lawful in a new age of submarines and steam-powered surface ships made of steel. It gave rise to new and difficult questions about the rights and obligations of the ships of belligerent and neutral nations. The positions that Woodrow Wilson took on such matters raised the first doubts about the nature, the authenticity, of American neutrality. They made his administration complicit—on highly moralistic grounds, of course, this being the Wilson White House—in flagrant violations of international law. Ultimately, the interpretation that the president put on the laws of the sea would become the chute down which the United States slid into war with Germany.

The laws governing the conduct of ships in wartime, thorny and contentious, had been the subject of numerous international conferences, most recently in London in 1908 and 1909. That gathering's mission was to produce a single treaty, approved by the seafaring nations, in which the rules and understandings that had accumulated over the generations could be combined, clarified, and given the force of law. It succeeded, but the resulting draft treaty was never consummated because Britain's House of Lords failed to approve it. This was a setback, Britain being the world's dominant sea power by an overwhelming margin, but the conference's labors did not go to waste. The draft treaty was published as the Declaration of London and was universally accepted as the most authoritative statement of the law of the sea ever produced. Even the British Admiralty adopted it for the guidance of warship commanders.

These matters became suddenly urgent when, on August 6, 1914, the U.S. State Department received from London a list of materials that His Majesty's government was declaring to be contraband and therefore subject to seizure on the high seas. The Declaration of London had upheld a time-honored distinction, relevant only in wartime, between "absolute" and "conditional" contraband. The former consisted of cargo that could have military use only, such as weapons and ammunition; it was always subject to confiscation when ships transporting it were intercepted. Conditional contraband included food, clothing, fuel, and other things with both civilian and military uses.

Among the questions raised by the British list was whether such distinctions were going to be observed in the war that was now beginning. The State Department, sensitive to the implications for the nation's transatlantic trade, sent out a diplomatic note asking all the belligerent countries if they intended to adhere to the Declaration of London. The Germans replied that they intended to do so if their enemies did likewise. The British reply, not delivered until August 22, stated a willingness to adhere to the declaration with certain "additions" and "modifications." These turned out to be significant: Britain was saying in effect that she would follow the rules to the extent that she found it to her own advantage to do so but no further. As if to underscore their determination to take an aggressive approach to this whole subject, the British also now sent what would prove to be the first of many additions to their list of things that would be dealt with as absolute contraband even when found on the ships of neutral nations. Food was conspicuous among the additions. This was a radical departure from precedent, a flouting of the law as then understood by all seafaring nations.

Robert Lansing,
U.S. secretary of state,
1915–1920
*He rose to high office by
having "not too many
ideas of his own."*

Upon taking office in 1913, Woodrow Wilson had appointed to the position of State Department counselor (or legal adviser) a specialist in international law named Robert Lansing. Fifty years old when the war began, married to the daughter of a former secretary of state, Lansing welcomed the opportunity to leave his law practice in upstate New York and join Washington's social elite with its dinner parties and afternoon teas. Possessed of strong convictions if not a powerful personality, a picture of rectitude with his white hair and mustache and high white starched collars, from the start of the war he was candid about favoring Britain and her allies. But he was also punctilious in insisting that all nations, Britain no less than others, must observe the law. He found London's August 6 note offensive and prepared a response. It was addressed to the American ambassador in London, with instructions to deliver it to the Foreign Office, and it rebuked Britain for departing from the Declaration of London and intruding upon America's rights. It asserted that no belligerent had the right to seize neutral ships' cargoes of food and dismissed Britain's claims as "wholly unacceptable."

This message was a legitimate assertion of American rights, solidly based on the law. If it had been sent as Lansing drafted it, it might have changed the course of history. But when Lansing gave it to the president for comment, Wilson passed it on to Colonel House. That was the end of it. House interpreted it in light of his recent experiences in Europe and saw immediately how distressing it would be to his new friends in London. He took it for discussion not to Lansing, not to Secretary of State Bryan, but to the British ambassador, Sir Cecil Spring-Rice. As House must have expected, Spring-Rice expressed horror. He declared that if such a note were sent, it would precipitate a crisis. Wilson, told of this, instructed Lansing to withdraw his draft.

What happened next was heavy with portents. House set out to draft a substitute note to the British government, and in doing so he recruited as collaborator none other than Ambassador Spring-Rice. The result included no assertion of the rights of the United States or neutral nations generally, and no objection to the classification of food and other nonmilitary materials as absolute contraband. The American ambassador was instructed to assure Sir Edward Grey "informally and confidentially" that the United States had no intention of challenging Britain's claims. The point could not have been clearer: the United States was surrendering its freedom to do business with whomever it chose, its rights as a neutral nation. The White House did not even wish to communicate officially with the British government except in terms approved in advance by that government's representative in Washington. This set the pattern for everything that would follow.

There was no need for the United States to submit in this way. It was bestowing a great favor on the Entente, not yielding to necessity. Alone among the world's neutral nations, America had sufficient naval and economic power to force the British to observe the law. That they would have done so is beyond question: Grey himself, years later, would acknowledge that his aim was to push these issues as far as possible without risking a breach in Anglo-American relations, maintaining only as tight a blockade as the United States would tolerate. This underscores the absurdity of Wilson's claim, when he killed the Lansing draft, that sending it would risk war with Britain. The United States would not have needed to fire a shot to bring Britain into line. Simply disallowing shipments of goods to the United Kingdom would have done the trick. The British understood that better than anyone.

Cabled to London, the emasculated note had a powerful effect. Grey and his fellow cabinet members saw that they were free to stop cargoes of any kind from reaching the Central Powers. They no longer had to worry about the fact that the long-range guns of the warships bottled up in German ports, together with the ability of Germany's submarines to stand guard outside those same ports, had rendered obsolete the kind of coastal "close blockade" permitted by law. Or about the fact that the broader blockade of the high seas that they intended to impose instead was of dubious legality at best. The Wilson administration was inviting them to do whatever they wished. Further unprecedented initiatives followed. March 1915 brought the blanket mining of great expanses of the North Sea, all of which London declared to be a war zone. Ships attempting to traverse the North Sea were declared subject to interception, even to being forced into English ports for the unloading and examination of their cargoes. These measures, too, were outside the law. In the ensuing months, Britain's minefields would sink more neutral merchantmen than Germany's *Unterseeboote,* soon known as U-boats.

Eventually a confident Britain would simplify matters by giving notice that she no longer recognized the Declaration of London, with or without modifications. London expected to hear no complaint from the United States about this, and received none.

And so it came to pass that the Royal Navy, with its blockade and with American acquiescence, set out to win a deadlocked war by imposing famine on the populations of central Europe. It defended the strategy in exactly those terms: First Lord of the Admiralty Winston Churchill declared with satisfaction that the aim was to "starve the whole population—men, women and children, old and young, wounded and sound—into submission." When Austria's ambassador in Washington complained of the blockade's illegality, Colonel House made a diary entry that seems almost to cast doubt on his intelligence. "England is not exercising her power in an objectionable way," he wrote, "for it is controlled by a democracy." In fact, the extent to which the Britain of 1915 can be considered a democracy is arguable. Her hereditary aristocracy still had great power, and only 18 percent of adult males were eligible to vote. This compared, rather awkwardly, with 22 percent of Germans and 21 percent of Austrians. Even the *republic* of France allowed only 29 percent of males to vote. Britain's treatment of subject peoples was arguably better than most—Belgium's was incomparably the worst—but the millions living under her rule in Ireland, Egypt, and India could have attested that it had nothing to do with democracy.

It was now up to Germany, her trade links to most of the outside world severed, to decide how to respond. Her surface fleet dared not venture out of its home ports; despite the huge amounts invested in the years before the war, numerically it was so inferior to the Royal Navy that to put to sea would be to invite destruction. (The one great sea battle of the war, 1916's inconclusive Battle of Jutland, proved the point.) The best answer was to get the help of neutral nations—meaning the United States, basically—in stopping the embargo on food. Or to work out a compromise with Britain, somehow. If those options proved infeasible, Germany had nowhere to turn but to the U-boats. But they were small, slow, and fragile and had never been tested in war. And exactly sixteen of them were ready for service at the start of 1915, fewer than Britain's submarines, with the capacity to have perhaps half that many at sea at any one time. They hardly seemed likely to matter.

As far as the German home front was concerned, there was at this early point no urgent need to do anything. People knew of the blockade and were indignant about it, but it was far too new to cause serious inconvenience, never mind hardship. There was no way of being certain that it ever would cause real hardship. International trade and the economies of neutral nations including the United States, however, were affected almost immediately. In the first half of 1914, Germany's gross national product and exports had exceeded Britain's for the first time ever, the culmination of decades of strong economic growth for Germany and near-stagnation for Britain. Thirteen percent of U.S. exports had gone to the Central Powers, and now those markets were closed. The American economy was hit so hard that the New York Stock Exchange was shut down and remained so for four months. American producers and shippers complained loudly.

This might have worked to Germany's advantage, making American acquiescence in the blockade politically unsustainable, had not Britain, France, and Russia put things right. Their hunger for the output of America's factories and farms proved to be literally insatiable. Massive orders from the Entente eased resentment of Britain's interference and then dissolved it: munitions and metals and the numberless other things needed to equip growing armies were demanded urgently and in virtually unlimited quantity. American producers soon had no reason to complain.

There was irony in this. Just a year earlier, responding to American manufacturers wanting to supply forces engaged in Mexico's civil war, Wilson had said, "I shall follow the best practice of nations in the matter of neutrality by forbidding the exportation of arms or munitions of any kind from the United States to any part of the Republic of Mexico." His reasons for departing from "best practice" in dealing with the Entente remain open to speculation.

Almost before the war's first shots were fired, France asked America's mightiest bank, J. P. Morgan and Company, for a loan of $100 million. Secretary Bryan, after conferring with the president, intervened. A statement that the two of them prepared jointly declared that "loans by American bankers to any foreign nation which is at war are inconsistent with the true spirit of neutrality." Morgan and Company retreated.

"We are the one great nation which is not involved and refusal to loan to any belligerent would naturally tend to hasten a conclusion of the war," Bryan said. He was right about that, as the months ahead would show, and right again when he said that if American banks lent to one side in the war, pressure would build in the United States to support that side further because "the value of the securities would be directly affected by the result of the war."

"Money is the worst of all contrabands because it commands everything else," Bryan also said. "I know of nothing that would do more to prevent war than an international agreement that . . . neutral nations would not loan to belligerents."

Wall Street was disappointed but unwilling to proceed in the face of such emphatic official resistance. Its disappointment, however, would be short-lived. Morgan and Company was appointed U.S. purchasing agent for Britain and would become France's agent as well. Over the next four years it would broker fully half of all Entente purchases in the United States, reaping commissions of $30 million by doing so. Its inability to make loans would be nearly as short-lived. Buyers need money, the Entente powers were consuming their financial reserves at an alarming rate, and by the spring of 1915 their purchases were generating an American economic boom. Soon the Entente governments would be joining U.S. banks and manufacturers in insisting that lending on a massive scale had become absolutely necessary.

Background

Coming of Age

The United States of 1914 was an ungainly young giant of a nation, an economic colossus beset with growing pains. In the half century since the Civil War, the simple republic of yeoman farmers and tradesmen idealized by Thomas Jefferson had been utterly transformed. It had become an industrial powerhouse, dotted with bustling cities and dominated by a new class of business barons.

Numbers tell the story:

In 1870 the United States produced less than two million tons of pig iron and barely a third of a million tons of steel. By 1913 it was producing 31.5 million tons of pig iron and 31.8 million tons of steel. That was nearly double the output of its nearest competitor, Germany.

In 1869 there were thirty thousand miles of railway in the United States. By 1920 the total would be a quarter of a million. American refineries processed 26 million barrels of oil in 1880, 442 million forty years later. In 1866 the nation's wheatfields were producing an average of 9.9 bushels per acre. By 1898 this had increased to 15.5, and the total acreage devoted to wheat had tripled. (Among the results of this advance, an example of the way growth could breed trouble, were low grain prices, financial distress for millions of farmers, and agrarian unrest.)

In the 1870s, when skilled workers considered themselves lucky to earn two or three dollars a day, America had approximately one hundred millionaires. This figure rose to approximately four thousand by 1892, and it would quadruple by 1916, when Britain and her allies needed almost everything America could produce, making the accumulation of a fortune almost easy for the bold and well placed. The number of U.S. cities with populations of more than one hundred thousand, nine in 1860, was fifty in 1910.

Such data become even more impressive when compared with the rest of the industrial and industrializing world. The contrast with Britain is especially striking. In 1870 Britain produced more than three times as much pig iron as the United States. By 1914 the situation had reversed, with British output barely a third of America's and half of Germany's. It was the same with steel. In 1875 Britain was producing 40 percent of the world's steel. By 1913 its output was not only less than a fourth of America's but also less than half of Germany's.

Between 1870 and 1913, when the U.S. economy grew at 7 percent per year and Germany's maintained a 6 percent pace, Britain's limped along at a sorry 1 percent. In 1880 Britain's factories accounted for 22.9 percent of worldwide manufacturing, and Germany's for only 8.5 percent; by 1913 German's share had risen to 14.8 percent while Britain's was down to 13.6 percent. Some commentators have maintained that resentment and fear of Germany's industrial success was a significant reason for Britain's entry into the Great War. By this line of argument, the war was an opportunity to wreck an upstart rival and reassert a global supremacy that the British saw as theirs by right. It is certainly true that, in the years leading up to 1914, British newspapers went to extraordinary lengths to depict Germany as a sinister force and inflame public opinion against her.

Thomas Woodrow Wilson grew up with the United States in the years following the Civil War. Born in Virginia in 1856, early enough for him to have indelible memories of that conflict, he spent most of his boyhood in the Deep South state of Georgia, where his father enjoyed a position of local eminence and earned a comfortable living as pastor of a substantial Presbyterian church. In 1870 the family moved to Columbia, South Carolina, where Joseph Ruggles Wilson became professor at a seminary and a senior officer of the Southern Presbyterian Church.

The elder Wilson was a strong, upright, self-confident man and the dominant figure in his son's formative years. Though by no means a domestic tyrant—he could be both playful and affectionate—he set high standards for young Tommy and sometimes shocked visiting relatives by ridiculing the boy when his expectations were not met. Tommy was nevertheless an obedient, submissive, even worshipful son. Biographers of a psychoanalytic bent, Sigmund Freud among them, have hypothesized that his father's demands irreparably damaged the younger Wilson's self-confidence, that the boy must, at some unconscious level, have seethed with an anger that he was unable to express or even admit to himself. They have suggested that the Reverend Dr. Wilson implanted in his son the extreme neediness, the insatiable craving for approval, that Colonel House and others would later turn to their advantage, and that it was repressed anger at his own inability to assert himself against his father that compelled Wilson to be dominant in all his adult relationships, cut off close friends when they displayed independence of thought or action, denounce anyone who declined to do as he demanded, and respond to the acquisition of power by seeking still more power.

Some who have studied Wilson's character say that his father implanted in him an obsession with righteousness, and that this made it impossible for him to accept that he was subject to such commonplace emotions as anger or resentment. He could admit to becoming emotional only for lofty reasons, in the service of high ideals, and could feel justified in acting on such feelings only by deciding that those who opposed him were not merely wrong but morally wrong. To relieve the resulting inner tension, he had to turn differences of opinion into crusades that he alone could lead because he more than anyone else was the champion of justice and truth. He could permit himself to fight only by persuading himself that some great principle was at stake. A dispute over his plans for new buildings at Princeton would thus become, in his eyes, a battle for democracy. Later, in insisting that American citizens were entitled to safety even when traveling on ships of belligerent nations carrying the equipage of war, he would declare himself to be upholding the sacred rights of all humanity.

The one astonishing fact about his childhood, his failure to learn to read until he was nine years old, once was explained as an oblique rebellion against his father's demands. More recently it has been diagnosed as developmental dyslexia. As this form of dyslexia can be caused by emotional problems, especially in youngsters of at least normal intelligence, such a diagnosis does not altogether invalidate the earlier, more Freudian hypothesis.

Presbyterianism, too, was a shaping influence on the future president. In his case, in boyhood at least, it was an undiluted hard-core Scottish Presbyterianism; both sides of the family were Scots and Scots-Irish, and not only all four of young Tommy's grandparents but his mother as well had been born in the old country. His mother's people, the Woodrows, had been Presbyterian clergy of distinction for generations. The Calvinism in which their faith was rooted had at its core the concept of predestination, the belief that even before we are born, the Creator, being omniscient, knows whether we will be saved or damned, and we can do nothing to change our fate. This theology has often been credited with inspiring believers to live disciplined, upright lives, presumably because it reassures them to do so. Doing good and doing well could not win salvation—that question was settled before the world began—but could be evidence that one was among the elect. This does not seem irrelevant to the president's character and career.

Thomas Woodrow Wilson
*He hungered from boyhood
to do "immortal work"
and serve humanity
"in a large way."*

Be all that as it may, Tommy Wilson was better positioned than most young Americans to partake in the surging prosperity of his native land. Though he grew up in a defeated and devastated South, he was a member by birth of a genteel and not-unprosperous postwar southern elite. At a time when only a tiny minority of youngsters went on even to secondary education, it was taken for granted that he would attend university and enter a learned profession. In a nation where most people lived in or on the verge of poverty and child labor was commonplace, he remained financially dependent on his father into his late twenties, free to explore a succession of possible careers.

Not many were so fortunate. The phenomenal economic growth and galloping westward expansion that brought fabulous wealth to a minuscule minority and robust prosperity to middle-class families like the Wilsons also drew floods of immigrants to the United States. Many of the new arrivals found the land and the opportunities that they had left their homelands for. Millions, however, found themselves struggling to wring a living out of soil that never should have been plowed or toiling long hours under miserable conditions for wages barely sufficient to sustain life.

They were not welcome, these newcomers, except as grist for the factories and hardscrabble farmers on the marginal western lands made accessible by the new railroads. They were alien and suspect. Many were Irish—destitute, illiterate, despised. Even more were German, and if somehow they seemed less offensive than the Irish, nonetheless they were guilty of not speaking English and capable of behaving shamefully—of drinking beer in public on the Sabbath, even. There were eastern Europeans with preposterous names, swarthy creatures from Italy, all of them incomprehensible and not only in the languages they spoke. There were Jews, too, piling up in their filthy tenements, performing their weird rites. Not enough of these people seemed properly grateful for having been allowed in, or willing to do as they were told.

Most horrifying of all was the avalanche of Catholic newcomers. It seemed to have no end. Protestant America had from the start viewed Catholics as a threat to the republic and its values: in the presidential election of 1852, a party created for the sole purpose of stopping Catholic immigration received a quarter of all the votes cast. But as their numbers grew, so did the Catholics' political heft and the difficulty of keeping them in their place. As for black Americans, most whites preferred to ignore their existence, especially in connection with politics. Freed from slavery, briefly invited into full citizenship by Reconstruction, they, too, came to seem a threat to true Americanism. But then the Democrats, driven by hatred of Abraham Lincoln and all his works, took control of the former Confederacy and imposed the rule of Jim Crow.

Looming above all this turmoil and tension were the gigantic new corporations that industrialization had brought forth, seemingly out of nothing. Standard Oil, U.S. Steel—they and their counterparts in other industries had not existed when Woodrow Wilson was born. Now they seemed to dominate everything, their vast wealth translating into vast political power, the nation unsure of what to do about them—or of whether anything should be done.

It was the Gilded Age (Mark Twain's name for it), the age of the robber barons: Rockefellers and Vanderbilts, Morgans and Mellons. They were a curious breed. When Andrew Carnegie sold his steel company to the Morgan-led syndicate that was creating U.S. Steel, he used his $800 million in proceeds to become one of the most extravagantly bountiful philanthropists in history. And yet in building his empire—he had come from Scotland as a boy, virtually penniless—he had been ruthless not only as a competitor but as an employer, treating workers as raw material to be consumed and discarded, crushing all resistance. Did he undergo a change of heart upon cashing in? Not at all. His savagery in business and the generosity that caused him to build public libraries across America were two sides of a single coin: social Darwinism, one of the leading intellectual fashions of his time. Applied to industry, it meant that only the most efficient should survive, and not to achieve maximum efficiency was to fail in one's duty. But once he had triumphed, especially if his religious roots were strong, a Carnegie or a Rockefeller might well feel impelled to share.

None of which was of much comfort to farmers who could barely pay the interest on their debts, or to industrial workers in their fetid slums. But neither political party displayed much unhappiness with the status quo. The Republicans, as the 1890s began, were more inclined than the Democrats to support government activism—so long as its purpose was to promote economic growth. They used the government to impose the high tariffs that protected domestic producers from foreign competition. By contrast, the Democrats, heavily influenced by their party's potent southern element, favored states' rights and a small, inert government. For a quarter of a century after the Civil War, government regulation of the economy was scarcely an issue. Few in either party were able to imagine such a thing.

There is nothing surprising about the young Wilson's satisfaction with the state of the nation. He was a Democrat because he was a southerner, and growing up in Georgia, he had little exposure to industrial development, urban slums, the more suspect kinds of immigrants, or non-Protestants. He had much exposure to blacks, of course, but in an environment that, even more than the north, viewed them as inferior and dangerous. All his life he would express nostalgia for the social order that the Civil War had destroyed, and his acceptance of Jim Crow was merely typical of his time and place. He was conservative both by instinct and in conformity with the standards of his class. He saw no contradiction between his Christian faith and the law of the jungle in the economic sphere, and he was no more scornful than other young gentlemen of the idea that government might intrude upon the workings of the market. As an undergraduate, he withdrew from an important debating competition rather than violate his conscience by speaking as assigned in favor of universal male suffrage—allowing even white men who did not own property to vote. His admirers prefer to point to a different college oration, one in which he declared Catholics not to be a threat to American democracy. His position was actually not that Catholicism and American values were compatible but that the institutions established by the Constitution were sturdy enough to withstand papist immigration.

Though some of his attitudes and opinions can be shocking today, in fairness they have to be measured against the standards of his time and place. During the most frustrating period of his young manhood—in 1882, when he was unhappily and unsuccessfully attempting to establish himself as a lawyer in Atlanta—he came for a brief period to seem almost consumed with indignation at the respectful attention given to a Catholic bishop by the Wilmington, North Carolina, *Morning Star*. On January 25 the *North Carolina Presbyterian* carried a letter, written by Wilson under the nom de plume "Anti-Sham," complaining that "in giving unqualified endorsement to the views of Romish prelates, [the editor of the Wilmington paper] is helping on the aggressive advances of an organization whose cardinal tenets are openly antagonistic to the principles of free government."

That this was not just a momentary outburst of bile became evident on February 5, when a second letter from Anti-Sham appeared. It repeated much of the earlier rant, adding that parochial schools demonstrated how "education seems to be the chosen gate of Romish invasion in this country." More of the same appeared in a third letter on March 22, after which Anti-Sham fell silent. It should be remembered that such opinions were commonplace in the polite society of nineteenth-century America, perhaps especially among Scots Presbyterians, perhaps most strongly among *southern* Scots Presbyterians.

What was striking about young Wilson was not his inherited prejudices but his desire, which gripped him with almost painful intensity, to do good and do well, and to do both on the grandest scale imaginable. When he was sixteen, a cousin asked about the picture displayed above his desk. He explained that it was of William Gladstone, three-time prime minister of England. "That is the greatest statesman who ever lived," he said, "and when I grow up to be a man I mean to be a great statesman, too." In his twenties he told his fiancée that he longed to do "immortal work" and not merely serve humanity but serve it "in a large way." When the fiancée became his wife, he told her that "I have the uncomfortable feeling that I am carrying a volcano about with me." Whatever was fueling that volcano—Oedipal rage, fear of damnation, frustration as the fulfillment of his dreams began to seem impossible—in his early years he kept it concealed behind an amiably tranquil facade.

He fed his dream of becoming a Gladstone by honing his gifts, which proved to be exceptional once he began to read, as a speaker and writer. He did so first under the watchful tutelage of his father, then as a college and graduate student, and ultimately on his own. During his months as a clientless young Atlanta attorney, he used his empty hours to practice composition. He was driven by his hunger to be a "statesman" and his conviction that, as he wrote a friend, "statesmanship consists not in the cultivation and practice of the arts of intrigue, nor in the pursuit of all the crooked intricacies of the paths of party management, but in the life-long endeavor to lead first the attention and then the will of the people to the acceptance of the truth in its applications to the problems of government." To do this, of course, a person has to *know* the truth. This posed no problem for Wilson. He was never much inclined to doubt that he had better access to the truth than most men.

He was also untroubled by questions of what exactly leadership was *for.* Of how he would *use* power, if ever it came to him. He preferred to deal in grand abstractions and entered adulthood satisfied that he had the "absorbing love for justice and truth" and the "consuming, passionate devotion to principle" that he saw as making one man worthy to lead the many. But there appears to have been no particular cause or movement of which he wished to take charge or even to join. This vagueness would prove an asset when he embarked at last upon a career in politics. It allowed him to reshape himself into whatever voters appeared to be looking for at the time.

He decided, at an early age, that the career in statecraft that he craved was not open to him. He complained that to succeed in American politics one needed independent financial means—a proposition contradicted by any number of the most significant political figures of his time—and said that he would have had more opportunities under a parliamentary system like Britain's, which he revered. Upon graduating from Princeton, he enrolled in the University of Virginia's law school. He did so not because the study of law interested him—quite the opposite was true—but because he saw it as a portal to politics. What he then saw of local and state politics while attempting to practice law in Atlanta disgusted him and led him to change course.

He decided to settle for academia. He resigned himself to a life of writing and speaking about politics, perhaps advising statesmen rather than being one himself, but he was never entirely comfortable with the decision. He did well all the same, earning a doctorate from the Johns Hopkins University, attracting much attention with the book *Congressional Government,* and moving upward through the educational hierarchy from Bryn Mawr to Wesleyan University and finally to a professorship at his alma mater, Princeton. Along the way he entered upon a thoroughly happy marriage. Ellen Axson, herself the child of a Presbyterian clergyman, regarded Wilson as a great man and abandoned a promising career as a painter in order to become his bride. In four years they became the parents of three daughters. Wilson was a success, a popular lecturer both on and off campus, earning enough as a speaker and writer to provide his family with a more than comfortable lifestyle. He was also deeply, deeply dissatisfied.

He had been at Princeton only a couple of years when, early in the 1890s, the United States was hit by the worst of the financial crises that the Gilded Age called panics. The speculative excesses of the time regularly produced booms and bubbles that were inevitably followed by busts, but this one was uniquely severe, a precursor of the Great Depression. Whole regions suffered as commodity prices plummeted, and great cities found themselves insolvent. By 1894 unemployment was three or four times what it had been a few years earlier. It reached 43 percent in Michigan, 35 in New York. Workers who kept their jobs found their wages savagely cut. Strikes broke out, and much violence. The government had no instruments with which to help the afflicted—not many in authority thought the government should do any such thing—and had only troops as an answer to unrest.

The pain, fear, and despair of the time are expressed in the letter that a farm wife sent to the governor of Kansas in 1893. "I take my pen in hand to let you know that we are starving to death," she wrote. "It is pretty hard to do without anything to eat in this God forsaken country. . . . My husband went away to find work and came home last night and told me that we would have to starve. He has been to 10 counties and did not get no work."

This was happening on a continental scale, and it gave rise to what would be called the populist revolt and a profound change in the politics of the nation. Trouble erupted first among white farmers growing cotton on smallholdings in the South, spread to the wheatfields of the Great Plains, and fed on widespread hatred of the railroads, the banks, and big corporations generally. The idea that government might regulate these concentrations of power entered the nation's political discourse for the first time. A People's Party was formed, with demands ranging from a tax on incomes and direct election of U.S. senators to an eight-hour workday and strict regulation of the railroads and their rates.

It need hardly be said that such notions were widely regarded as incompatible with the nation's core values. The People's Party seemed insanely radical even to many Americans troubled by the power of the corporations. In 1896 a young newspaper editor named Joseph Bristow, who fourteen years later would become a progressive member of the U.S. Senate, wrote that though "we have a horror for the wild excesses of populist doctrines," the situation against which the populists were rebelling was little less intolerable. The corporate elite "represents the cool calculating selfishness of wealth and the desire for power," he complained, while the populists stood for "the wild fury of ignorance, envy and prejudice."

Millions felt similarly torn, and new lines of political affiliation began to appear. The populists attracted discontented Democrats in a number of southern states and discontented Republicans in the Midwest. The results were alarming to the political establishments in both regions. Alone or in fusion with one or another of the major parties, the populists won eleven gubernatorial contests and elected six U.S. senators and thirty-nine House members before their revolt petered out.

Professor Wilson of Princeton was not impressed: the populists and their program had no appeal for Democrats of his conservative stripe. Nor was he better pleased when, in 1896, insurgents seized control of the Democratic Party's national convention and nominated a presidential candidate of strongly populist leanings, William Jennings Bryan. This left the People's Party with little choice but to nominate Bryan as well, thereby rendering itself irrelevant and doomed. Wilson was far from alone in finding the whole situation deplorable. His party was now in the hands of people he scorned, championing a cause he despised.

The 1896 election pitted Bryan against the Republican William McKinley, with Democratic President Grover Cleveland occupying the White House and widely blamed for the economic mess. The most inflammatory issue of the campaign turned out to be one of the populists' favorites: the question of gold versus silver. The United States was on the gold standard, issuing only gold coins, and the populists blamed this for the shortage of credit that had contributed to making the financial panic as destructive as it was. Money had become exceedingly scarce, and fifteen thousand companies, including the Northern Pacific and Union Pacific railroads, went bankrupt. Five hundred banks folded, their depositors not insured. It became dogma with the People's Party, and with the Bryan wing of the Democratic Party, that silver currency would not only increase access to capital but generate enough inflation to ease the debt burden of those farmers who had not yet been ruined. Bryan electrified the convention that nominated him with a speech vowing that the United States would not be crucified on a cross of gold.

Inevitably, Bryan and his following were roundly condemned as socialist. But "if they were," as one historian has observed, "they were advocates of a peculiar brand of socialism." To the extent that many of them advocated public ownership of certain commanding heights of the economy, such as the railroads, the objective, "to their way of thinking, was to serve the interests of millions of small-scale, land-owning farmers, businessmen, and wage-earning laborers." The Georgia firebrand Tom Watson, the People's Party's vice-presidential candidate in 1896, said the purpose of the populist movement was "to destroy class rule and restore to the people the government." It was not, most populists would have agreed, to replace all-powerful corporations with an all-powerful government.

But the Republicans damned the free silver campaign, and the call for reduced tariffs, as irresponsible and worse. Enough voters of the industrial Northeast agreed to give the Republicans a victory that, although narrow, cleared the way for them to regain the dominance that they had enjoyed in Washington in the decades following the Civil War.

Not only the People's Party but the whole populist phenomenon lost impetus after 1896. One reason was the demoralization of many populists by the co-optation, as they saw it, of their movement and the party they had founded by the Democrats. More fundamentally, passions cooled as the economy began to recover. There were also cultural and class reasons for the decline. Even middle-class Americans who saw a need for reform commonly found it impossible to identify with agitators depicted in the newspapers as raving anarchists and ignorant yokels in bib overalls.

William Jennings Bryan
The Great Commoner—and a
three-time presidential loser.

But as the economy resumed the generation of great wealth, once again only a minority felt that they had any share in the benefits. Politically and socially as well as economically, the country remained a tangle of conflicts and problems that few politicians of real influence could see any reason to touch. Where business and government intersected, corruption flourished. The economy became a breeding ground not only for new fortunes but for a new kind of journalist, the muckrakers. Their exposés disturbed the complacency of the middle classes by revealing that the political bosses were not the only ones enriching themselves in dubious ways. Businessmen, some of them pillars of their communities, were in on it, too, often quite as ready to offer bribes as the party chieftains were to accept them.

In both parties, large numbers of educated and active people, though they had spurned the populists, found the state of the nation unacceptable. As a new century approached, they formed the core of a new progressive movement, which cut across party lines and quickly replaced populism as the means by which those who wanted reform strove to achieve it. Much less rural than populism, it had stronger roots in the urban middle classes. Once again, however, Woodrow Wilson stood apart, even from the progressives of his own party. He viewed many of the proposed reforms as unnecessary or worse.

Chapter 3

Quickly to the Brink

AS THE AUTUMN OF 1914 DRIFTED TOWARD WINTER AND EUROPE settled more deeply into its vast, bloody, and stalemated war, public life in the United States was focused on November's midterm election. A third of the seats in the Senate and the entire House of Representatives would go before the voters. The Wilson administration's control of national policy was at stake.

The Republican opposition, already looking ahead to the 1916 presidential election, adopted a strategy that turned out to be a great favor for President Wilson. It called him, sometimes in so many words, a coward and a pacifist, too timid and morally corrupt to join the Entente in its defense of democracy and heroic resistance to Teutonic aggression. The favor lay in the fact that most voters wanted nothing to do with a European bloodbath that appeared to have started over nothing and threatened to go on more or less forever and accomplish nothing. Foes eager to replace Wilson accused him of being exactly what the public wanted him to be: determined to stay out. Theodore Roosevelt, the least temperate of those foes, called the president "the demagogue, adroit, tricky, false, without one spark of loftiness in him, without a touch of the heroic." Wilson was blessed to have such enemies. Their bellicosity repelled even the progressive, reformist Republicans, men who disliked and distrusted their party's dominant Eastern Brahmin wing and were despised by it in return.

When the election results came in, the Republicans made substantial gains in the House. They had accomplished this partly by emphasizing their friendliness to business and their determination to address the deep slump in exports that the outbreak of war had brought on. A more important factor, probably, was that Roosevelt had returned to the fold and was no longer divid-

Theodore Roosevelt
*"There is a sweetness about him
that is very compelling,"* said Wilson.
"You can't resist the man."

ing the Republicans as he had done with his third-party run two years before. Even so, the Democrats retained a thirty-three-seat majority in the House and strengthened their hold on the Senate. This was the first election in which, thanks to the newly passed Thirteenth Amendment, all senators were chosen by popular vote, none by state legislatures. The Democrats lost no Senate seats and took three from the Republicans, giving them a commanding majority: fifty-six to forty.

For Wilson, maintaining a firm hold on both houses against a reunited Republican Party, when registered Republicans still outnumbered Democrats and the economy was staggering under the shock of war, was a thoroughly satisfactory result. He remained free to carry forward the program of progressive reforms that had made his first two years in office so remarkable. (To the chagrin of the progressives in both parties, however, he would display no interest in doing so.) The Republican attacks had positioned him so firmly as the champion of neutrality that in the next two years the public would have difficulty seeing him in any other way. This would help him to favor the Entente in crisis after crisis and draw surprisingly little criticism in doing so.

A month after the election, when Congress reconvened, members introduced a number of bills aimed at prohibiting the export of arms to the warring nations. Trade with the Central Powers having been shut down by the blockade, such a prohibition if enacted would affect the Entente exclusively—

and would have been a hard blow to American manufacturers. The bills received no encouragement from the White House, but some of them had sufficient support to begin moving forward through the slow-grinding legislative mill. Secretary Bryan took a friendly view of them and was increasingly troubled by President Wilson's understanding of what neutrality should entail. Bryan was particularly unhappy about the British policy of impounding ships and cargoes suspected of being bound for the Central Powers. This escalation of the blockade strategy bordered on being a direct affront to American sovereignty. The American ambassador to Britain, Walter Hines Page, exhausted Bryan's patience by failing to follow instructions to take a firm line with the Foreign Office.

And so Bryan bypassed Page, sending Sir Edward Grey a message bearing a title that left no room for doubt about his attitude: "Note to Great Britain Protesting Against Seizures and Detentions Regarded as Unwarrantable." Britain's behavior, the note said, "exceeds the manifest necessity of a belligerent and constitutes restrictions upon the rights of American citizens upon the high seas which are not justified by the rules of international law or required under the principle of self-preservation." These words produced no result. It was understood in London, thanks largely to what the devoutly Anglophile Page was saying unofficially, that Bryan and the president took very different views of the situation—and that Bryan's opinion didn't much matter. Colonel House would not have disagreed.

Bryan himself might not have disagreed by this point. He met with frustration and disappointment everywhere he turned. When he sent the president a memorandum suggesting that the United States should offer to mediate between the warring nations, Wilson's response was once again to turn to Colonel House. House, according to his diary, told the president that he was "certain it would be entirely footless to do this, for the Allies would consider it an unfriendly act, and further it was not good for the United States to have peace brought about until Germany was sufficiently beaten to cause her to consent to a fundamental change in her military policy." Wilson was not, at this early point, nearly ready to embrace such a candid statement of desire for an Entente victory. But he declined Bryan's suggestion all the same.

His doing so should not be interpreted as indicating—as it sometimes has been—that at this point he had any wish to take the United States to war. It would have been surprising, considering his family background and place in the upper middle class of the American East, if he had not favored Britain. In addition to having family roots in the British Isles, he was fond enough of the place to have spent time there summer after summer, thought Britain's political system the world's most perfect, and was among the innumerable educated Americans with far stronger cultural links to Britain than to any continental nation. None of this meant, however, that he was insincere when he said in December 1914 that the chances of achieving "a just and equitable peace, and of the only possible peace that will be lasting, will be happiest if no nation gets the decision by arms." Or when he said that the worst outcome would be one in which "some one nation or group of nations succeeds in enforcing its will upon the others."

Colonel House's chosen role was to keep the president mindful of the opportunity that the war offered the United States to guide the Old World, the Central Powers no less than Britain and her continental allies, to a safer, saner future. And there is no reason to doubt his sincerity, either. If he used his understanding of Wilson to keep him sympathetic to the Entente, exploiting his marrow-deep wish to make himself an immortal by doing great good, the goal of lasting world peace surely justified such devices. And if in devoting himself to that goal, Edward House of Houston put himself at the center of momentous world events, surely there was nothing ignoble about that. He was an idealist as well as an opportunist—not a unique combination—whose robust ego did not negate a genuine desire to serve. And he did admire Wilson. Though his diaries were obviously dictated with posterity in mind, he is entitled to be believed when he writes, as he did in 1915, that "Woodrow Wilson is today the greatest asset the world has. If he should die or become incapacitated, it is doubtful whether a right solution of the problems in this terrible conflict and its aftermath would be possible." If Wilson were lost to the world, of course, House, too, would lose his chance at greatness. The colonel's appreciation of this fact in no way makes him a sinister figure.

It is no mere coincidence that House was speculating about Wilson's possible death or incapacity at just this time. In December 1915 the president's physician, Rear Admiral Cary Grayson (elevated to that high rank from mere lieutenant by presidential order), would tell House that his patient's kidneys were not functioning properly. Wilson was also complaining of headaches, fatigue, and weakness in his right arm. These were symptoms of high blood pressure and the cerebral arterial disease that had been causing him to have recurrent strokes, of varying degrees of seriousness, since the 1890s. They pointed to future trouble.

The war, by contrast, was trouble in the here and now. For Berlin, American passivity in the face of Britain's increasingly aggressive blockade was trouble of a very high order. The question of how to respond was creating angry divisions among the men advising Kaiser Wilhelm. The naval minister, crusty old Grand Admiral Alfred von Tirpitz, bald as an egg but with a forked beard as long as his head, had taken the lead in demanding deployment of the U-boats. He was the father of the modern German navy, the man who had persuaded the young kaiser to spend immense sums on the fleet of battleships and cruisers that he thought appropriate to a world power. The result was an arms race that Germany was doomed to lose because Britain resolutely built two dreadnaught-class battleships for every one of hers. When the war came, Tirpitz was driven half mad with frustration at seeing the fleet that was his life's work bottled up in port, absolutely useless. He saw the U-boats as the way to put things right. But he could not get the kaiser or the chancellor to agree. Even the army's top general disagreed. All of them feared Washington's reaction.

The German public was by now fully aware of the blockade and beginning to experience shortages of various kinds. This naturally received heavy and indignant press attention. People were aware also that the creator of the blockade, Britain, was enjoying unimpeded trade with North America. They were angry and not to be ignored. Imperial Germany was indeed the autocracy that the British never tired of calling it (Britain was one, too, to a quite considerable extent), but she had a cantankerous national assembly, the Reichstag, that was largely socialist in membership and rarely unwilling to make trouble for the government. She also had a press that was markedly less compliant than Britain's.

Finally, the pressure to *do something* about the blockade became more than the kaiser could withstand. At the end of the winter of 1914–15, his government declared that the waters around Great Britain and Ireland were now a war zone, and that the U-boats had orders to sink, on sight if necessary, any Entente merchantmen encountered in it. Neutrals choosing to traverse those waters, Berlin warned, must do so at their own risk. Submarine warfare thus began in earnest.

There was more bravado than substance to this announcement, the Germans having so few submarines to send into the war zone. But in London the government and the press responded with outrage. They ignored the fact that in announcing their war zone, the Germans were merely echoing what Britain had already done in the North Sea. They also ignored the fact that British submarines—more numerous than Germany's—were preying on the Baltic Sea shipping lanes connecting neutral Scandinavia to German ports.

The start of the U-boat campaign was a mistake on Germany's part, and a costly one. Until it was announced, American indignation had been directed mainly at Britain's interference with shipping and her bending of the law to suit her own purposes. But now U.S. newspapers, few of them troubled by or even aware of their dependence on London's censors, followed London's example in treating Berlin's announcement as fresh confirmation of German "frightfulness." Public attention was diverted from Britain's transgressions, and enthusiasm for banning exports of guns and ammunition drained away.

American opinion was also affected, as the spring of 1915 arrived, by a strong resurgence of transatlantic trade. Orders for weapons, ammunition, equipment, foodstuffs, and raw materials of every description were pouring into the United States from Britain, France, and their allies. The nation's economic heart beat more strongly than it had in years. Spoilsports might question how supplying one side only could possibly accord with Secretary of State Bryan's "true spirit of neutrality," but the sales did not break any law. Nor would refusing to supply either side have been in any way unlawful, but any such refusal would have been financially damaging to manufacturers, industrial workers, and farmers. The White House, not surprisingly, showed no interest in discouraging the rising tide of orders, orders for armaments included. Bryan, who loved his job and wanted to be a good party man, kept his concerns to himself.

What the newspapers condemned as particularly barbaric was the Germans' declared intention to sink the Entente's commercial vessels on sight— without warning—when they regarded doing so as necessary. This violated traditional "cruiser rules," which forbade the sinking of any vessels except warships and those merchantmen that attempted to flee or fight when intercepted. Passenger ships were not to be sunk under any circumstances, and compliant cargo ships only after their crews had been placed "in safety" (a vague term understood to impose an obligation to do more than simply allow the crews to launch lifeboats on the open sea).

Cruiser rules originated in the days of sail. They were also known as prize rules, because in those days it had been the practice of warships, upon capturing an enemy vessel, to put a skeleton crew aboard and sail it home. During the Napoleonic Wars, many British commanders got rich from the sale of "prizes" taken in this way. Captured crews were to be taken prisoner or, unless they were already close enough to shore to be left in lifeboats, delivered to some safe place. This was a civilized way of waging war, and when the rules were observed, they minimized loss of life. But in the twentieth century they became a recipe for suicide when applied to small, slow, extremely fragile submarines engaged in the interception of massive surface ships, sheathed in plate steel and plowing through the waves at speeds impossible before the introduction of steam engines. Submarines, when on the surface, were easily destroyed by gunfire or run down and rammed. With their tiny crews, they had no spare men to put aboard captured vessels, and they were too cramped to take even a handful of prisoners on board. In short, they had little chance of observing cruiser rules and surviving. The British and their allies condemned them as criminal enterprises. For the Germans, by contrast, the U-boats were the only possible way of fighting back against a blockade intended to starve them.

This became a crucial issue because Woodrow Wilson personally—not his secretary of state, not even his staunchly pro-Entente State Department counselor, Robert Lansing—chose to make it so. He insisted that American citizens had the right to travel in safety wherever they wished, even on the ships of nations at war, even when those ships were transporting war matériel, even in declared war zones. The simplest and most obvious solution to the whole problem would have been to require citizens to traverse the war zone in neutral ships only, but the president brushed it aside as unworthy. Such a remedy, he said, was dishonorable, craven, an abandonment of American rights and therefore out of the question. (In 1935, by contrast, Congress would authorize the Franklin Roosevelt administration to admonish citizens not to travel on ships of nations at war, and in 1939 the Neutrality Act, drawing on the lessons of the Great War, introduced exactly the measures that Wilson had rejected a generation earlier.)

On January 30, 1915, Colonel House left New York on another mission to London. "The president's eyes were moist when he said his last farewells," the colonel later recalled. "He said 'your unselfish and intelligent friendship has meant much to me,' as he expressed his gratitude again and again, calling me his most trusted friend. He declared that I was the only one in all the world to whom he could open his entire mind." While at sea, House sent Wilson a mes-

sage expressing the hope that "God will sustain you in all your noble undertakings. . . . You are the bravest, wisest leader, the gentlest and most gallant
gentleman and the truest friend in all the world."

He crossed on the crown jewel of Britain's Cunard Line, the mighty *Lusita-*
nia. As the ship approached the Irish coast, the captain had the Union Jack
lowered and the Stars and Stripes hoisted in its place, thereby signaling to any
U-boats within visible range that what they saw through their periscopes was
an American—a neutral—liner. This was sailing under a false flag, another
violation of the law. It compromised the safety of all genuinely neutral ships,
but the British were doing it with increasing regularity. House merely made
note of it, asking no questions then or later.

In London he spent hours every day with Foreign Secretary Sir Edward
Grey and other senior members of the government. Soon all of them learned
that President Wilson had sent the Germans a diplomatic note rejecting the
legitimacy of their submarine campaign. He warned that if it resulted in the
loss of American lives, Germany would be held to "strict accountability." As
usual, he wrote the note himself—his typical workday was short, but there was
always time for the typewriter kept beside his desk—and its words were heavy
with threat. No such language had been used in his complaints about Britain's
departures from the law. It now committed the president to taking forceful
action in the event of submarine attacks involving American travelers. It
thereby reduced his flexibility and the number of options available to him in
case of a crisis. His words would be remembered, and tauntingly invoked, by
Theodore Roosevelt and others, as soon as a crisis arose and Wilson seemed
slow to react.

The overarching question of how to bring the continental bloodbath to an
end was now subsumed in the much smaller matter of U-boats and the blockade. And again it was happening at Wilson's insistence. The situation was rich
in ironies and in historical overtones. President George Washington, in 1793,
had declared that American merchant ships delivering "contraband of war" to
nations at war "will not receive the protection of the United States." But now
the United States was insisting on the safety not of her own merchant fleet
when engaged in such traffic, but of the ships of belligerent nations if they
happened to be carrying American passengers.

A further complication was that the British were now known to be arming
some of their merchantmen, the biggest and most modern of which had been
designed with the ability to serve as auxiliary cruisers in wartime. In 1815

Chief Justice John Marshall, in his decision in the *Nereide* case, had declared that an armed merchant ship "is an open and declared belligerent, claiming all the rights, and subject to all the dangers of the belligerent character." If this ruling was brought to the president's attention, it had no effect. Now and to the end of the war, Wilson would maintain that cruiser rules must be observed and the supposed rights of Americans respected, regardless of whether the ships on which they traveled were armed or were carrying anything besides passengers.

The complications multiplied endlessly and with them the ironies. On the very day that Wilson sent his warning note to the Germans, First Lord of the Admiralty Winston Churchill ordered British merchant ships to try to escape when they sighted U-boats, and to ram the boats when escape was impossible. He warned that any captains who failed to comply would be prosecuted. In addition to being of dubious practicality, this order compounded the legal questions created by the introduction of the submarine as a weapon of war. As Churchill understood clearly—he wanted not compromise but confrontation, and Washington at odds with Berlin—it made German observance of cruiser rules not just dangerous but impossible.

What was not subject to debate, or should not have been, was Wilson's claim that Americans had the right to travel in safety on the ships of a nation at war. From the standpoint of law, there was nothing to debate: no such right existed or ever had. House brought with him to London, on the president's behalf, one overriding question: on what terms might the two sides be willing, if not to make peace, at least to enter into negotiations? This question would loom ever larger as months turned into years, the human costs of the conflict rose to unimagined heights, and neither side came close to victory. The colonel's pursuit of answers drew him ever closer to Sir Edward Grey. This was inevitable: the foreign secretary made himself always available to House, and was as eager to show approval of his ideas as House was to praise Grey's. The two had long talks, often in the study of the widower Grey's London home. They discussed not only the war but their shared love of Wordsworth, the English countryside, and solitude. The colonel gave Grey a book by Woodrow Wilson, and Grey apologized for having nothing better to offer in return than the little treatise he had published on the art of fly-fishing.

It is impossible to tell how much of this rapport was genuine on Grey's part, and how much a calculated application of charm and hospitality to the task of pleasing the American president's alter ego. That it was both seems clear enough; in memoirs written long after the war's end, Grey had only good things to say about the colonel. In any case, his effect on House was all that he or the government he represented could have hoped. In a diary entry of February 13, House writes of how he and Grey "sat by the fire in his library, facing one another, discussing every phase of the situation with a single mind and purpose." How thrilling it must have been for the colonel to find himself the friend and confidant of this eminent and aristocratic statesman, this offshoot of ancient nobility, the archdiplomat of the greatest empire on earth. If confidant is what he was. One would love to know what Grey was thinking in these cozy moments. It is doubtful that he would have confided his "mind and purpose" to even the most amiable and important of foreign visitors when so many questions remained unsettled and so much was at stake. Grey's tenure as foreign secretary was the longest in British history. No one lasts so long in such a post by doing much sharing of innermost thoughts.

This was the point, as Patrick Devlin observes in his incomparable study of America's neutrality, when "peacemaking became for House a collaboration between himself and Grey in which he saw the pair of them as a team working as much against the rapacity of the Allies [France and Russia] as against Germany." Devlin does not mention, however, the use Grey made of that rapacity, which was real enough, in freeing himself from having to do as House and Wilson wished. He would agree that what the Americans wanted was right, profess that he wanted exactly the same things, then explain regretfully that France and Russia were certain to disagree. House made it easy for him to get away with this, relegating France to the status of an unenlightened and remote junior partner that could be dealt with through London rather than directly.

House and Grey do not appear to have given a great deal of attention, in their talks, to the U-boats or the blockade. House's attention was focused, per President Wilson's instructions, on identifying the terms on which the Entente and the Central Powers might consent to enter into negotiations under American mediation. There was much to debate. House, the representative of a president who believed that only an end to the war in which neither side emerged triumphant could lead to a stable peace, was in no position to deviate openly from his master's line. Grey, by contrast, believed, as did the whole Asquith cabinet, that any cessation of the fighting would be transitory unless Germany were severely punished first. In the context of the war as a whole and the challenge of finding a way out of it, the U-boats must have seemed a sideshow to House and Grey alike. Which, in a very real sense, they were. Or should have been.

The priorities looked very different to James W. Gerard, the American ambassador to Berlin. He saw what the blockade meant to the Germans and the bitter divisions at the highest level of the kaiser's government over how to respond to it. From where he stood, in daily contact with leading German officials, the implications for the United States were clearer than they were in Washington, and what he observed alarmed him. A former New York judge with connections to Tammany Hall, Gerard had been without diplomatic or international experience when offered the ambassadorship, and his qualifications for a post as sensitive as envoy to a Germany at war were less than obvious. He soon stood out, however, for his determination to take the initiative to search for ways to defuse the submarines-versus-blockade issue, instead of waiting for directions from Washington. That he did so in spite of a strong dislike for the Berlin regime makes his efforts all the more admirable. Unlike Walter Page in London, he genuinely wanted peace for the United States.

Secretary of State Bryan took his warnings more seriously than did the president or House. On February 16 the State Department, prompted by an appeal from Gerard, instructed Page to explore possible ways of getting Britain to lift the embargo on food. Page, who made no secret of his wish for American intervention in the war, replied with ponderous glumness that "I do not see a ray of hope for any agreement between Germany and England whereby England will permit food to enter Germany under any conditions." Unwilling to settle for this, and once again bypassing Page, Bryan sent a proposal based partly on Gerard's input directly to Grey at the Foreign Office. He suggested that Britain permit the export of food from the United States to Germany, and that this food be distributed to the civilian population by an American agency similar to the Belgian relief organization that was already in operation and proving highly effective. Germany, in return, would be required to adhere to cruiser rules in all interceptions of merchant ships. Both sides would pledge not to allow their ships to display false flags and to stop the indiscriminate mining of merchant shipping lanes.

Berlin replied that it would agree if trade in raw materials were permitted as well as food. This was problematic, but it opened a door to negotiations. It became irrelevant, however, when Britain and France rejected the proposal with almost insulting curtness. As if to punish Washington for making such a suggestion, the Entente powers announced that henceforth German exports as well as imports would be forbidden, and that trade even between neutral ports now required Entente approval. They also formally announced what they had long been doing unofficially: maintaining a general (and unlawful) blockade not of particular ports or coasts but of the open seas. The Admiralty instructed armed British merchantmen to fire on any submarines they sighted. This latest escalation gave Germany further justification, under the law, to treat Entente cargo vessels as warships.

The United States protested Britain's new measures but took no action and said nothing to suggest that the Entente might be held to anything like the "strict accountability" of which Germany had been warned. Paris and London understood that the protest meant nothing. In London, House and Page were offering oral assurances that the Wilson administration would do whatever might prove necessary to save the Entente from defeat. The Entente powers, therefore, could proceed with confidence—with impunity—to do whatever they thought necessary for victory.

Grey's influence was by now evident in almost everything the colonel said and did. In mid-February, having not been in Germany since the war began or talked with any German official except Ambassador Johann Heinrich von Bernstorff in Washington, House wrote to Wilson that Berlin is "now almost wholly controlled by the militarists." What basis could he have had for such an opinion, failing as it did to reflect the divisions within the German government at this time and Chancellor Bethmann-Hollweg's still-firm grip on policy? What except the things that Grey and other British dignitaries were telling him, or that he had read in newspapers that functioned as instruments of British propaganda?

To his diary, he confided his satisfaction with the Entente's unwillingness even to consider peace talks. He himself "did not want [negotiations] to begin one moment before the time was ripe for a peace that would justify the sacrifices of the brave who had already given their lives, for it was even better for others to die if the right settlement could be brought about in no other way." He can have been referring to the sacrifices on one side only—those of the Entente. He was content to let the war go on until the Entente was in a strong enough position to make demands of Germany and get those demands met. His views were at this point more divergent than ever from President Wilson's. His words suggest little discomfort with the idea that it is "better for others to die" than to make a peace that brings no gains.

House's moral imagination, much like Wilson's, appears to have functioned best on the abstract level. He wanted to serve his nation and humanity, and does not appear to have been greatly troubled by the possibility that millions of deaths might be the price of his doing so. In reporting to Wilson that he was urging Grey to "get the machinery in order" in case a need for negotiations somehow emerged, he observed that if such a thing happened and the circumstances were favorable, it would be "foolish" to lose the opportunity. Because "useful" lives might be lost.

British and French generals were promising, as they always would, that the offensives they were preparing for the summer ahead were going to put them on the road to victory. And as would happen again in 1916 and 1917, nothing that they promised came to pass. Germany's strategy for 1915 was to stand on the defensive on the Western Front and take the offensive in the east, where there was an urgent need to shore up the Austrians and the Turks and to keep the whole Balkan Peninsula from falling to the Entente. The results were, from Berlin's perspective, exactly as hoped. The French and British commanders squandered men and resources on attacks that consistently came to naught. Germany meanwhile conquered Russian Poland, killing, wounding, or capturing 750,000 enemy troops in the process. She reduced Serbia to submission, recruited Bulgaria as an ally, and firmed up the Austrian and Turkish lines. In mid-February, as House and Grey exchanged thoughts on the grand things that would become possible once Berlin had been properly chastened, a German force literally obliterated the Russian Tenth Army in a terrible winter battle.

Grey gave Colonel House to understand that in his personal opinion (not necessarily the prime minister's or the cabinet's, and certainly not France's or Russia's) two things might be sufficient to end the war. The first was Belgium: Germany must agree not only to restore Belgian autonomy but to indemnify her for the damage caused by the invasion and the trench warfare that followed. The other was some arrangement to ensure a permanent peace by cleansing Europe of "militarism"—a word now fraught with meanings heaped on it by Entente diplomacy and propaganda. As used in London, it was a thinly veiled synonym for Germany. "Ending militarism" had become code for removing Germany from the ranks of the leading powers of Europe. House was taught the code during his time in London. Not until late in the year did he have occasion to share the secret with the president. He observed in his diary entry for October 8 that in a talk with Wilson, he had "let it be understood that the word 'militarism' referred to the Central Powers."

Grey had no need to fear that in communicating with House in this way he was risking the start of negotiations. There was no possibility that Berlin would discuss an end to militarism if ending militarism meant the end of the Hohenzollern regime. No government in history would have agreed to such a thing, except in extremis. It was only barely more plausible that the Germans would discuss paying reparations or an indemnity to the Belgians; from their perspective, such payments were out of the question. That the German public had not forgotten the lurid news stories about Belgian irregulars waging a guerrilla war on the troops advancing toward Paris, or the lives these *francs-tireurs* had taken, was only part of the problem.

House's request for an explanation of what the Entente wanted out of the war put the Asquith government in an awkward position. The conflict had come upon Britain, France, and Russia so suddenly that, like the Central Powers, they had taken up arms without any objectives except to engage the enemy and fend off disaster. Since then they had had time to think about the longer term, start making plans, and use those plans as a basis for making deals. That France was determined to reclaim her lost provinces of Alsace and Lorraine was understood by all, but not many of the Entente's aspirations were so transparent. Some of the deals being struck were of such a dubious nature that the people making them feared their becoming public. Britain and France had promised Russia the Ottoman capital of Constantinople, thereby casting away generations of opposition to Russian expansion southward to the Mediterranean. They had also committed themselves, in effect, to the liquidation of the same Ottoman Empire that they had long been propping up as an obstacle to Russian expansion.

Italy, having backed out of her prewar alliance with Germany and Austria-Hungary as the shooting began, was being lured into the Entente with promises that she could fatten herself on Austrian possessions in the Alps and the Mediterranean. Romania and Greece were offered gains in the Balkans, South Africa was to get African territory, and Australia and New Zealand, islands in the Pacific. Even Japan was to benefit, in China and the Pacific. There was going to be a global land rush when the war ended, but only if the Entente won. Meanwhile these arrangements had to be kept secret. If made known, they would not fit at all comfortably with the Entente's depiction of itself as a confederation of free peoples fighting for civilization, justice, and the rights of small nations everywhere. Above all, it would not do for Woodrow Wilson to be made aware of how much the Allies were hoping to gain.

Colonel House told Grey that he had just been invited to Berlin. The invitation came from Arthur Zimmermann, Germany's deputy foreign minister. Grey arranged for House to meet with Prime Minister Asquith, who urged him not to accept—at least not yet. House did as his friends advised.

The invitation reflected the Germans' wish not to lose contact with Washington despite the U-boat problem and their concern about their long-term prospects. They were very much ahead on points at this stage of the war, having taken possession of a large part of France and almost all of Belgium and having humiliated the Russians on the Eastern Front. Nonetheless, it was not easy to see how they were going to turn these advantages into an outright victory. Their situation was going to be particularly grim if the Entente continued to be so generously supplied by the United States while Germany remained cut off from imports needed not only to continue the war but to keep her population alive. That would make the conflict a war of attrition plain and simple—one that Germany could not possibly win. Chancellor Bethmann favored a negotiated settlement and wanted it as soon as possible. General Erich von Falkenhayn, who had succeeded Moltke as chief of the general staff after the failure of the Schlieffen Plan, was convinced that Germany could no longer hope for better than a moderately advantageous draw. Others, more optimistic, insisted that there was no need to negotiate anything.

Zimmermann's invitation to House came in the course of an exchange of communications in which the two men touched on the always-sensitive subject of Belgium. Zimmermann said at one point, with a finality and candor that House must have found surprising, that "what you suggest concerning the paying of an indemnity to Belgium seems hardly feasible to me. Our campaign in that country has cost the German nation such infinite sacrifices of human lives that anything in the form of such a decided yielding to the wishes of our opponents would cause the most bitter feeling among our people."

What the people of Germany now knew, and the censors on the Entente side were keeping under tight wraps, was the fact that the whole story of Belgian neutrality was dubious down to its roots. Upon occupying the Belgian capital of Brussels, the invading Germans had discovered government files showing that from 1906 at the latest, Britain had been providing Belgium with funds for the reorganization of her military. This had culminated, in May 1914, in the introduction of universal military training to Belgium and the expansion of the kingdom's standing army to half a million men.

That was by no means the most startling thing that the files revealed. By

1911, Belgium's military was a junior partner in Britain's and France's secret planning for war with Germany. At the start of such a war, British troops were to land in Belgium regardless of whether she was under threat from Germany. The combined British-Belgian forces were then to join France's armies in an invasion of northern Germany via the Rhineland.

Involvement in such planning nullified Belgium's claim to neutral status. Preparations to join nonneutral nations in case of war were a violation of the laws of neutrality, even if done for defensive purposes. The Belgian government's reasons for compromising itself to such a grave extent are unclear; it has been alleged that both Britain and France threatened Belgium's young king with the loss of his crown if he failed to cooperate and to enter the war on their side when it began. In any case, all this remained generally unknown in the Entente nations and altogether unknown in the United States during the years of American neutrality; the story of Belgium's innocence remained unassailable. Years would pass before a postwar British prime minister, Ramsay MacDonald, could describe the story as "a pretty little game of hypocrisy."

President Wilson, upon learning of Zimmermann's invitation, cabled House to express his displeasure that it had not yet been accepted. There was a danger, he warned, if the Germans learned that he was delaying at the advice of the British, that whenever he did go to Berlin he would be regarded as a representative of London, not of the United States. By this time, Prime Minister Asquith was feeling so pleased with America's position on German and British naval policies that he had no lingering objections to the colonel's moving on. The French, Italian, and Russian ambassadors in London disliked the thought of President Wilson's man meeting with the enemy, but House wrote in his diary, "I brought them around to the view that at least it would be well worth while to find how utterly unreliable and treacherous the Germans were, by exposing their false pretenses of peace to the world. That suited them better, and it was not a great while before we were all making merry and they were offering every facility to meet the heads of their governments." No one thought, evidently, that visiting Germany could be more than an empty formality.

House was in no hurry to get to Berlin. He treated himself to a stop in Paris, where he met with various officials but connected with none as he had with Edward Grey. After arriving in Berlin, he did not even go through the motions of asking the Germans about their war aims; that no longer mattered, as he had given Grey his assurance that Britain's enemies were not going to be allowed to achieve anything. Zimmermann, whom House found likable, tried to reinforce what he had written earlier about the anger of the German public and the limit it put on the government's freedom to act. "If peace parlays were begun now upon any terms that would have any chance of acceptance [in London or Paris]," House quoted Zimmermann as saying, "it would mean the overthrow of this government and the kaiser." Zimmermann's candor satisfied the colonel that, as he reported to Wilson, there was at this time simply no possibility of a mediated peace.

House now acquired an appreciation of not just the Germans' anger about the blockade, but their disgust with the peculiarities of American neutrality—Wilson's consistent acceptance of Britain's actions and equally consistent condemnation of Germany's. "The bitterness of their resentment toward us is almost beyond belief," he noted in a letter to Wilson. "It seems that every German that is being killed or wounded is being killed or wounded by an American rifle, bullet or shell." But because of his conviction that an Entente victory was not only desirable but necessary, he began to see German public opinion less as a problem than as an opportunity, one that might in due course be put to very good use. If inflamed sufficiently, public opinion could drive the German government to do exactly the things needed to get the United States into the war. "When the pinch of the blockade becomes greater than even now," House observed, "a revulsion of feeling will probably take place and a sentiment will develop for any measure that promises relief." This is from a letter whose tenor suggests eager expectation, not dread.

One of Wilson's purposes in sending House back to Europe had been to maintain a channel of communications with Berlin in which the bothersome Ambassador Gerard, with his repeated and sometimes urgent appeals for resolution of the blockade issue, would not be involved. With this in mind, the colonel ruminated on what Grey had said about two things being necessary for peace: justice for Belgium, and an end to militarism (however defined). Gerard meanwhile emphasized the dangers for America of the blockade, and his conviction that Germany was open to a resolution of the problem. Putting the two things together, House conceived of a new scheme, a way of possibly getting the two sides to talk to each other—a development that he knew the president would welcome, so long as he could serve as mediator.

When he met with Chancellor Bethmann, whom he found to be "one of the best types of German I have met," the colonel took the opportunity to share what he was thinking. It involved as usual a compromise, a trade-off. The British would accept freedom of the seas—free movement of the merchant ships of neutral nations—and the Germans in return would withdraw their forces from Belgium. Such an arrangement would enable the German authorities to depict their withdrawal as an act of reciprocity, a case of quid pro quo, and therefore less offensive to their own citizens. Berlin could declare that, freedom of the seas having been restored, the German navy no longer needed Belgium's Channel ports and therefore also no longer needed the Belgian territory of which those ports were part. Freedom of the seas having been restored, the Germans would also be able to observe cruiser rules. At a stroke, such an agreement would reduce the question of Belgium's future to manageable proportions. It is not clear, rather oddly, whether House thought his proposal could be implemented during the war or would have to be part of a postwar settlement. Either way, if pursued, it could have gotten the belligerents thinking and perhaps even talking about what kind of settlement they were prepared to accept. It could have put a first crack in the deadlock.

House "shivered" (as he later wrote) to lay out the plan for Bethmann's consideration, so obvious did it seem to him that it favored the Entente. Bethmann delighted him by being interested, even enthusiastic; this was a measure of how desperate the chancellor was to maintain good relations with the United States and move toward negotiations. With surprising speed, however, things spun out of control. The Berlin government's publicists surprised the Americans and the Entente alike by making much of the proposal, and by claiming that the Germans had originated it. The British, seeing the Germans crow about what had not been agreed or even discussed, decided that they wanted nothing to do with it. They felt that they were being asked to give up their command of the seas, a hard-earned and crucial asset, while Germany in return would give up only what she had no right to in the first place. Whether Germany would have proceeded if Britain had been willing is open to question. Even if Bethmann really was willing to give up Belgium—a dubious proposition—it is unlikely that he could have gotten the kaiser and his uniformed chiefs to agree.

House's proposal did have one important result. President Wilson, before the British turned it down, had judged it to be "very promising." Freedom of the seas appealed to him strongly. From this point forward, it would be one of the cornerstones of his program for the postwar world.

In Washington, Congress adjourned without having passed any of the bills prohibiting the export of arms. None had even been released from committee and brought to a vote. Berlin, always sensitive to developments in the American capital, took this as further confirmation that U.S. neutrality was a hopelessly one-sided affair, and that to allow Washington to mediate a settlement of the war would be foolhardy in the extreme.

On March 28 the U-boat campaign claimed its first American victim: Leon C. Thrasher, a young Massachusetts engineer bound for an assignment in Africa. He was a passenger on the *Falaba*, a British steamer carrying thirteen tons of ammunition (even Africa was now at war) and 147 passengers. The case was a murky one where the law of the sea was concerned. The *Falaba*'s captain, upon sighting a U-boat, first attempted to escape, making his ship subject to immediate attack. He changed his mind and hove to, however, and was given ten minutes to get crew and passengers into lifeboats. But then a British warship was seen coming over the horizon—all this was happening just south of England's Scilly Isles. The captain of the U-boat hurriedly fired a torpedo into the *Falaba*'s hull and submerged. The death of an American citizen was sensational news in the States, and the pro-war factions cried out for Wilson to make good on his threat of strict accountability. There were demands for a severing of diplomatic relations with Germany, a likely prelude to war.

Secretary Bryan found himself on the sidelines as these things transpired, given only a pro forma role in discussions, unable to understand the president's thinking and increasingly unhappy with his approach. He had been disappointed when Wilson sent House rather than himself to Europe, but had acquiesced when told the mission had to be unofficial. Now he began peppering Wilson with expressions of concern. Before the *Falaba* sinking, as Britain was tightening her stranglehold on the North Sea, Bryan had called the president's attention to the link between the blockade and Germany's widening use of submarines. He wanted to insist on the right of all neutral nations to trade with whomever they wished. The president said in reply that Britain would refuse to comply with any such demand and that pressing the matter could only damage Anglo-American relations. This was a reprise of what he had done at the start of the war, tacitly accepting Britain's classification of food as absolute contraband. It is difficult to believe that he still failed to see the weakness of Britain's bargaining position. It is at least as likely that he saw it and chose not to make use of it.

Bryan was not satisfied with this response. Five days after the *Falaba* sinking, he sent a message to the president questioning whether it was necessary to risk going to war in order to hold Germany accountable for a single death that had happened under ambiguous circumstances. "Can an American by embarking on a ship of the allies at such a time and under such conditions impose upon his Government an obligation to secure indemnity in case he suffers with others on the ship?" he asked. This seemed absurd, the secretary suggested. The United States, he said, was making demands that had no footing in the law. He did not say outright that these demands made no sense, but obviously they made no sense to him.

Bryan allowed four days to pass before writing again. "The troublesome question," he said now, was "whether an American citizen can, by putting his business above his regard for the country, assume for his own advantage unnecessary risks and thus involve his country in international complications. Are the rights and obligations of citizens so one-sided that the Government which represents all the people must bring the whole population into difficulty because a citizen instead of regarding his country's interests thinks only of himself?"

The next day he wrote twice. First he informed the president of having received confirmation that Britain was in fact arming her merchantmen. In a second message he said, "I cannot help feeling that it would be a sacrifice of the interests of all the people to allow one man, acting purely for himself and his own interests, and without consulting his government, to involve the entire nation in difficulty when he has ample warning of the risks which he has assumed." He added that not enough was known to warrant further unfriendly notes to Germany.

Days later, clearly in torment, the secretary put it this way: "Why be shocked at the drowning of a few people, if there is to be no objection to starving a nation?" The president's answer was to show him the draft of a note that, Bryan's protestations notwithstanding, he intended to send to Berlin. It asserted exactly what Bryan did not want asserted: that American citizens had a right to go anywhere they wished on any ship at any time and expect to be safe. Taking his last shot, Bryan observed that perhaps more weight should be given to the fact that Mr. Thresher had freely assumed the known risks of taking passage on a ship flying the flag of a nation engaged in a naval war. "I cannot see," he pleaded, "that he is differently situated from those who, by remaining in a belligerent country, assume risk of injury. Our people will, I believe, be [slow] to admit the right of a citizen to involve his country in war when by ordinary care he could have avoided danger."

This last message was particularly telling in light of the administration's own record. It should have reminded Wilson—and must have been intended to remind him—of how, after involving the United States so deeply in Mexico's affairs as to create a real danger of war, the president had disclaimed responsibility for the safety of American citizens south of the border. They were there voluntarily, he had said then. If they chose to remain, they did so at their own risk.

Bryan also passed along a dispatch, received from Berlin, claiming that the *Falaba* had attempted to escape when intercepted and had been pursued for a quarter of an hour while firing off flares in an attempt to bring help. The dispatch said also that the submarine did not fire its torpedo until twenty-three minutes after the *Falaba* had come to a stop and her captain was ordered to abandon ship, and that it did so only because a British destroyer was seen to be approaching. If this was true (it was never disputed), the U-boat captain had gone to impressive lengths to stay within cruiser rules.

Bryan was coming close to defying a president whom he knew to have little tolerance for disagreement. That Wilson took it all calmly probably shows how little he cared about Bryan's view of the situation. (He also showed no interest in Lansing's opinion, forwarded by Bryan to the White House, that "if the sinking of the *Falaba* had been the result of an attempt of the vessel to resist or to escape when summoned to stop or to surrender by a submarine, there would be no ground of complaint for the loss of an American life. . . . In that case the submarine would be exercising a belligerent right recognized by international law.")

Before Bryan's refusal to let the matter rest could lead to a showdown, an event occurred that reduced the fate of Leon C. Thrasher to inconsequence. On May 7 the submarine U-20, returning to base after a period on station in the war zone, crossed paths with the great liner *Lusitania*. The U-boat's skipper had three torpedoes remaining and fired one. It hit its target. A powerful second explosion followed, attempts to lower lifeboats went horribly wrong, and the *Lusitania* sank with shocking speed. Fatalities totaled 1,193. Among them were 128 Americans, a number of them children.

Much has been made, over the years, of questions about whether the *Lusitania* was armed and whether she was carrying munitions to the British. Where culpability is concerned, such questions matter less than the impact of British Admiralty instructions to merchantmen on how to respond to U-boat attacks, and the resulting dangers of observing cruiser rules, especially when intercepting vessels as formidable (and possibly heavily armed) as the *Lusitania*. As for the morality of the U-boat campaign itself, like many questions of what is admissible in warfare, it remains shrouded in uncertainty, with things to be said pro and con. The Germans would argue that if the campaign hastened the end of the war, it would stop the slaughter of millions at comparatively low cost, a worthy objective.

At a dinner party at the U.S. embassy in London hours after the sinking, the assembled guests were both stunned by the news and excited about what it portended. Colonel House offered cheery assurances. The United States, he said, would be at war with Germany within the month.

The Tortoise and the Hare

It can come as a surprise to learn that William Jennings Bryan was three years younger than Woodrow Wilson. The history of the time leads one to assume that Bryan must have been older, possibly by a generation. By the time Wilson entered politics in 1910, Bryan had been nationally prominent for two decades and the Democratic Party's dominant figure for most of that time.

He had gotten his career off to an astonishingly fast start, entering the House of Representatives before he was thirty and from then on living a life that Professor Wilson could only dream of. When he became the Democrats' nominee for president in the midst of the economic upheavals of the mid-1890s, he was barely old enough to meet the constitutional age requirement. In 1908, when he was a candidate for president for the third and last time, he was still not fifty.

Though after 1908 he abandoned his pursuit of the White House, his following remained so large and loyal that no one else was likely to win the Democratic nomination without his approval. And he had changed the character of his party in lasting ways. Before Bryan it was a marriage of convenience of the so-called Bourbons of the South and the big-city bosses of the North, people with no wish to let the federal government interfere in their business or their lives. Because of Bryan, the Bourbons and the bosses had to compete with Democrats of a new kind, people who wanted to use the government to attack corruption, curtail the power of the big money, and defend the obscure and vulnerable.

Bryan and Wilson were similar in many ways. Both came out of a growing and upward-aspiring professional middle class, Bryan's father having been a self-made lawyer, gentleman farmer, Illinois state senator, and judge. Both were Presbyterians who took their faith seriously, though Bryan, while still in school, joined a subsect called the Cumberland Presbyterians that rejected the iron-hard doctrine of predestination. This may have contributed to his becoming more easygoing than the often rigid and self-righteous Wilson. More likely it reflects a difference in temperament that was there from the start.

Christianity played a more conspicuous part in Bryan's public life than in Wilson's (though even as president, Wilson prayed daily on his knees). For Wilson, religion was personal and somewhat fraught, a kind of psychic burden in which the belief that one was among the elect was laced with guilt and fear. Bryan, however, saw it as an engine of progress, summoning believers not to salvation alone but also to ever-widening equality and social justice. Wilson in his speeches referred to religion sparingly and obliquely, in ways that even today do not offend secular good taste. Bryan sounded like a revivalist preacher. He said himself that "when you hear a good democratic speech it is so much like a sermon that you can hardly tell the difference." But both grew into young men of what seems a distinctly late nineteenth-century American type: earnest, chaste, incapable of cynicism, and ambitious to rise but also to be and do good.

It is not surprising that both set out to become orators. When they were boys, long before the advent of radio, political debates and speeches were a leading form of entertainment. Holding the attention of audiences was an indispensable political skill, and college debating societies ranked above sports as an undergraduate diversion. Bryan and Wilson became two of the greatest speechmakers of their time, but in person Bryan was the more masterful of the two. One Republican later gave thanks that radio had not been invented in 1896, saying that if more voters had been able to hear Bryan extemporize, the Democrats would have won. Wilson's gift was different, a function of his introverted nature. At its core was the solitary polishing of draft speeches later delivered with artfulness and conviction.

It is more for reasons of style than of substance that Bryan today seems the more antique figure. In his baggy black coat-tailed suits, floppy bow ties, and slouch hats, he appears in photographs as almost a cartoon caricature of a huckster out of the Gilded Age. The paunch and jowls that came with middle age did not help. It is impossible to imagine him as a professor, still less as president, of an institution like Princeton University. The dapper Wilson was, by contrast, the very picture of an Ivy Leaguer.

But Bryan's appeal was by no means limited to rubes from the backwoods. Even that professional cynic H. L. Mencken, in covering the Democratic convention of 1904, compared Bryan's speech there to Beethoven's *Eroica* and went into raptures over it: "What a speech, my masters! What a speech!" Tellingly, he said it had the *simplicity* of all great art. Bryan could be naïve, wrong about important things, foolish in a variety of ways. But he was never in any way insincere. He spent his life crusading for those on the losing end of the American dream. Even those who thought him ridiculous acknowledged the genuineness of his commitment.

Bryan the orator at work
News that he would be speaking was "good for forty acres of parked Fords, anywhere, at any time."

In 1896 he became the first presidential candidate to mount a campaign of travel and speechmaking. He crossed and recrossed the country by rail, denouncing the high tariffs that his followers blamed for keeping prices high, decrying the government's refusal to issue silver currency. Religious imagery came naturally to his tongue, because it expressed the core of what he saw as his purpose. In the words of biographer Michael Kazin, he believed that "the prime duty of pietists was to side with the common man and woman in their perpetual battle with the defenders of privilege, corruption and big money."

Passionate public interest in the contest moved almost 80 percent of eligible voters to turn out on Election Day. Republican William McKinley carried twenty-three states compared to Bryan's twenty-two. Bryan won every western and southern state and received more votes overall than Cleveland had done in winning in 1892. He was, however, shut out in the industrial North. That made the difference.

After the election a new issue came to the fore, one rising out of the nation's stature as an emerging world power. A rebellion against Spanish rule in Cuba attracted the attention of the American government and public, both because of U.S. investments on the island and because of the inherent appeal of a struggle against Old World tyranny. There was pressure for intervention, ardently supported by such press tycoons as Hearst and Pulitzer. When the American battleship *Maine* blew up in Havana harbor, killing 260 sailors, the cause was assumed to be Spanish villainy. "Remember the *Maine*!" became the cry of the hour, though the explosion was almost certainly an accident. The United States launched a hugely popular and ridiculously one-sided war on a Spanish "empire" so decrepit as to be incapable of defending itself. The invasion and conquest of Cuba, accomplished at little cost and with even less difficulty, made a hero of Theodore Roosevelt, a brash and aristocratic young New York politician-turned-soldier. The easy but much-celebrated conquest of San Juan Hill by Roosevelt's regiment of Rough Riders vaulted him first into the New York governorship, then onto a place on the Republican national ticket as candidate for vice president in 1900.

Bryan had no argument with the war, seeing it as a fight for freedom. In fact he joined the National Guard, became the colonel of a regiment of Nebraska volunteers, and spent the months that the war lasted in a mosquito-infested camp in northern Florida. Trouble began when the McKinley administration bought the Philippine Islands in the western Pacific from Spain for a token $20 million. What happened next did not fit Washington's script. Filipinos who had earlier rebelled against Spain now launched a guerrilla war against American troops, demanding independence. The result was a bloody and dirty jungle war marked by horrifying atrocities and dividing American public opinion almost as sharply as another war on the fringe of the western Pacific would do six decades later.

Bryan, having resigned his commission, erupted in indignation. Suddenly the great new issue was imperialism—the prospect of a global

American empire on the European model. Bryan was far from alone in opposition, but his eloquence and fervor carried him back to center stage. "The fruits of imperialism, be they bitter or sweet, must be left to the subjects of monarchy," he declared. "This is the one tree of which the citizens of a republic may not partake. It is the voice of the serpent, not the voice of God, that bids us eat." The echoes of scripture were characteristic of Bryan, and again his rhetoric rose to the level of poetry. The Harvard philosopher William James, as sophisticated an intellect as was to be found on the North American continent, said, "I have fallen in love with [Bryan] so, for his character, that I am ready to forget his following."

Bryan was again nominated in 1900 and again campaigned furiously. McKinley again stayed home, but in Theodore Roosevelt he had a running mate whose showmanship and appetite for political combat were equal to Bryan's. TR (he hated to be called "Teddy") descended upon the electorate with the force of a thunderbolt. He traveled more miles than Bryan, gave more speeches, and generated more headlines. He delighted Republicans by saying that the Bryanite cult was made up of "all the lunatics, all the idiots, all the knaves, all the cowards, and all the honest people who are slow-witted."

Theodore Roosevelt
Denied a general's stars, he called President Wilson a "demagogue, adroit, tricky, false, without one spark of loftiness."

Turnout was lower than in 1896, undoubtedly because of the improving economy, and Bryan's percentage of votes cast declined also. He remained immensely popular, however, and soon returned to being the brightest star of the Chautauqua circuit, which every summer brought famous speakers and entertainers to hamlets and cities across the country. He got $250 per appearance and half the gross above $500. One promoter said that word of an appearance by Bryan was "good for forty acres of parked Fords, anywhere, at any time, day or night."

Professor Wilson was also in demand as a speaker. He served a more sophisticated market than Bryan's, becoming such a public relations asset for Princeton that the university's trustees created a special fund from which to supplement his salary, thereby keeping him from accepting the offers that he received almost every year to become the president of other universities. He was popular with students and smoothly adept at academic politics. In 1902, when Princeton's longtime president announced his retirement, the trustees hastened to put Wilson in his place.

The trustees expected much of him, and he did not disappoint. In short order he enriched the curriculum, raised standards, introduced a tutorial system modeled on those at England's leading universities, and launched an ambitious construction program. His stature, and the prestige of his new position, are evident in the fact that among those attending his installation ceremony were Mark Twain, William Dean Howells, J. P. Morgan, and Henry Clay Frick. Even now, however, he continued to be plagued by the sense of not being in the career he craved. Always, with Wilson, there was what an associate described as "that undercurrent of restless dissatisfaction that was the man's fundamental mood."

Bryan went abroad—he was much more widely traveled than Wilson—and in December 1903 was in Russia, paying calls on Tsar Nicholas II and Count Leo Tolstoy. He and Tolstoy talked for twelve hours. The great author later described Bryan as "remarkably intelligent and progressive." Bryan, asked to explain his admiration for an anarchist who regarded government as evil, said Tolstoy's "philosophy rests upon the doctrine that man, being a child of God and a brother of all the other children of God, must devote himself to the service of his fellows." That could stand as a summary of Bryan's doctrine, too.

President McKinley, meanwhile, had been shot to death by an anarchist assassin. In his successor, Theodore Roosevelt, the country found itself with a whirlwind of a leader, a colorful character and tireless activist who not only began pushing for such innovations as national parks but took up many progressive issues. The Democratic Party, its reformist elements seemingly discredited by Bryan's two losses, responded with a drastic reversal of course. In 1904 it nominated Alton B. Parker, a New York judge who repudiated the Bryanite free silver movement and declared the gold standard "firmly and irrevocably established." As his running mate, Parker chose an eighty-one-year-old anti-union coal and lumber millionaire named Henry G. Davis. The result was an electoral disaster, the worst in the party's history. Roosevelt won every state except those of the Old South. If Bryanism had not quite been vindicated, a strategy based on rejection of Bryanism had definitely been discredited.

Back at Princeton, Woodrow Wilson's life was turning into a race to complete his program of improvements in the face of increasingly serious medical problems. His health had long been erratic or worse. He was susceptible to periods of lethargy and general malaise that he called "colds" and probably were psychosomatic in origin. He had had a breakdown of some sort in 1895 and a year later suffered a stroke (not necessarily his first) that left him with a permanently weakened right hand. Another breakdown followed in 1899, another stroke in 1904. Yet another, a more serious one, came in 1906 when he awoke one morning to find himself blind in one eye. He recovered partial vision, but a specialist physician urged him to retire. A different specialist told him that this would not be necessary if he paced himself and continued to take long restful vacations. His devoted wife Ellen, his closest confidante and the only person able to reason with him when he was in danger of doing something foolish, now put all her emphasis on keeping him comfortable and protected from irritation. This deprived Wilson of almost the only brake on his less advisable impulses.

It became evident—and there are medical reasons why this would be so—that his personality had shifted in a dark direction. Ellen's brother, who admired Wilson and had no ax to grind, would leave an unpublished memoir in which he described this change. After an initial period of depression—understandable in an active and ambitious man threatened with permanent disability or even death—Wilson became harder, less tolerant, and sometimes angrily impatient even in the bosom of his previously serene home. "Although he would have been perhaps the last person to realize it," a member of the Princeton faculty recalled, "he placed everything upon a personal basis—if it were important to him. If you agreed with him you were perfect; if you disagreed you were guilty of a personal insult. You were either his friend or his foe."

It is probably no coincidence that within a year of the 1906 stroke Wilson set out to change Princeton in ways that showed utter disregard for the opinions of students, alumni, and trustees. Or that he dealt with those who failed to embrace his proposals in wrathful and self-defeating ways, destroying relationships built up over years and diminishing his stature. The first cause of trouble was his attempt to reorganize Princeton into colleges built around quadrangles and modeled on Oxford. Then came a protracted and unnecessary battle over the construction and funding of a graduate school. Wilson saw anyone who failed to support him as not merely wrong but a servant of evil. He ended his friendship with his one close friend on the Princeton faculty, John Grier Hibben, and for the rest of his life would rebuff Hibben's efforts at reconciliation. His own position, as he saw it, was unassailable, his objectives not merely best for the institution but the only morally tolerable options. He elevated the fight over the quadrangle plan into a struggle between democracy and privilege and called his proposal a "scheme for salva-

William Howard Taft, U.S. president, 1909–1913
He called Woodrow Wilson "a ruthless hypocrite who has no convictions that he would not barter at once for votes."

tion." This made compromise impossible; even to consider it would be a moral failure.

In the midst of these controversies, Wilson was exposed as having lied to the trustees, denying that he had ever seen a document that he was known to have edited. The purpose of the lie was to discredit a graduate school dean who had once served him as a kind of father figure but whose plans differed from his. It backfired disastrously. For a man as insistent as Wilson on his own rectitude, as protective of his self-image as of his public image, to be caught out in such a way must have been excruciating.

He was embroiled in these troubles as another presidential election approached. Roosevelt, having earlier and to his own eventual regret promised not to seek another term, remained so popular that he was able to choose the Republican nominee, the able, good-natured, and majestically obese William Howard Taft. The Democrats showed their bafflement and disarray by returning to Bryan for another try. He tried to stay closer to the center this time, abandoning such lost populist causes as public ownership of the railroads, and he became the first presidential candidate to receive the endorsement of the American Federation of Labor, two million members strong. But TR's seven years in office had made it difficult for voters to see a sharp distinction between the parties; sometimes it seemed that the whole country had become progressive.

Bryan continued to be disdained by conservative Democrats, Woodrow Wilson among them. "Personally, he is the most charming and lovable of men," Wilson said of Bryan in March 1908, "but his theories are both foolish and dangerous." He declined to appear with Bryan at a dinner of the National Democratic Club because he did not want to be associated even casually with "all the loose notions which he puts forth as a party program."

Wilson was also deploring publicly "the perfect mania for regulation that has taken hold of us." He said that Bryan had "no mental rudder." That was gentle compared to what Roosevelt was saying. He called Bryan "a professional yodeler, a human trombone."

Taft's popular-vote margin was double what McKinley's had been in 1896. For the Democrats the outlook was dismal. They had gone with Bryan and lost, gone with Bryan again and done less well, tried a conservative and lost disastrously, gone back to Bryan and not come close. They could not win with Bryan, could not win without him. Grover Cleveland remained the only Democrat to have won the White House since 1856, and when the next election rolled around, his last victory would be twenty years in the past. The Republicans looked invincible.

For Wilson, too, the future looked dark. In 1908 he had two attacks of "neuritis"—near-disabling shoulder pain caused by the same problems that had caused his recurrent strokes. For those who understood the seriousness of these symptoms, the state of his health was alarming. And his position at Princeton was becoming untenable. He no less than Bryan appeared to be pretty much finished.

He was not, however. By 1910 his health was so improved as to seem no longer a problem. In what was now his home state of New Jersey, by contrast, the Democratic Party was in almost as hopeless a state as it was nationally. In that fact lay a path to the fulfillment of his dreams.

For thirty years the Democrats' most dependable northeastern stronghold, New Jersey by 1894 had become so corrupt that the Republicans were able to win control. But then they, too, gradually became complacent and sank into corruption. By 1910 they were so subservient to big business that virtually every major holding company in the United States was chartered in New Jersey. The state was called "the mother of trusts."

Nonetheless, the Democrats were caught in a bind. To get back on top, they were going to have to attract the growing number of middle-class progressives, voters fed up with the status quo. But they had to do it without threatening the party's chieftains, the bosses who ran the political machines in every major city and had no interest in reforming anything. The Democrats needed a coalition of opposites. It seemed impossible.

Colonel George Harvey, a journalist and financier and power in the Democratic Party of the mid-Atlantic states, thought he had the answer. New Jersey's Democrats needed a candidate for governor who could appeal to the do-gooders on Election Day but afterward make no trouble. They needed a figurehead, someone who looked good and could be depended upon not to do too much. And the bespectacled, pinch-faced Harvey thought he had found the right man.

Like Edward House a "colonel" who had never served in any army, Harvey had come of age in the rough-and-tumble world of Chicago journalism, moved to New York, and at age twenty-seven become managing editor of Joseph Pulitzer's *New York World,* the biggest daily in the country. Along the way he made a fortune in the notoriously shady streetcar syndication racket (wheeler-dealers across the country were getting rich floating streetcar franchise stocks) and used some of his winnings to buy the influential *North American Review.* He also became a protégé of J. P. Morgan, who helped him to take over *Harper's Weekly* as well. His publications and connections made him a force even in national politics—a force of a distinctly conservative, anti-Bryan type.

He had been acquainted with Woodrow Wilson for years, had observed the skill with which Wilson used the presidency of Princeton as a platform upon which to build a national reputation as a speaker, author, and public intellectual. One of Wilson's attractions was his lack of political or business experience. That made him pure, in the context of 1910 America. Nominally a Democrat, in his two decades in New Jersey he had taken no visible interest in the state's politics. Therefore he knew little about the subject and would need guidance—would be grateful for it, no doubt. Better still, he was deeply conservative. He had shown this in a *New York Times* interview of 1907, proposing the creation of a council of wise men to chart the nation's course. And who did he think might lead this "common council of the people"? No less a titan than J. Pierpont Morgan, the king of Wall Street.

Wilson again demonstrated his soundness in 1908 by refusing to support Bryan. Told that he might be under consideration as the Great Commoner's running mate, he had declared unequivocally that under no circumstances would he accept. He refused all invitations to speak at events at which Bryan was on the program and showed no hesitation in expressing his disdain for the Bryanite cause.

Wilson was likewise solid on the great question of organized labor. What impressed was the depth of his contempt not only for the unions but for their members. In the summer of 1909, speaking at Princeton's commencement, he mockingly declared that everyone present knew what "the employee" wanted: "to give as little as he may for his wages." He agreed with the industrial magnates on the Princeton board that unions were seedbeds of decadence and made laziness mandatory.

Similarly, during the 1908 campaign Wilson went on record as opposing "on principle" government programs for feeding needy children. They served only to foster dependency, he said. He likewise could see no reason to give women the vote. "It may be true that women in various parts of the world have to fight against severe odds," he said, "but in America, at least, they are almost too much protected." He hastened to add that he was fully in favor of protecting the ladies, who nevertheless should be kept out of politics because "as a rule, women prefer goodness as a quality to ability, and are apt to be not a little influenced by charm of manner."

With such a paragon at the top of their ticket, Harvey thought, the Democrats might not only win the governorship but recapture the state assembly as well. But he was a New Yorker and could only advise. The decision would be made by the men who ran the New Jersey party, starting with Harvey's old friend James Smith, Jr., "Sugar Jim," who headed the machine that ran Essex County and its throbbing metropolis of Newark. Like Harvey, he had risen from humble beginnings and done well for himself. He had even served a term in the U.S. Senate, his reward for delivering New Jersey to Grover Cleveland in 1892. Tall and silver-haired and always beautifully turned out, he *looked* senatorial and wanted another turn in Washington. He controlled several substantial companies, including a Newark bank, and was the publisher of two newspapers.

Smith was interested if cautious. He and his fellow bosses in Jersey City and Hoboken and other places were having trouble with the progressives and their incessant complaints. They needed a way to keep such people in line. And though the status quo was in no way burdensome to Smith or his fellow bosses, life would be even better, the boodle richer, if they could get control of the governor's office.

But when Harvey and Smith approached Wilson, he was less enthusiastic than they had expected. A likely explanation is that he regarded battling an assortment of New Jersey hacks for the nomination as beneath his dignity and feared that failure, coming on the heels of his setbacks at Princeton, would be one humiliation too many. When he declared that he was willing to do nothing to win the nomination, Harvey asked a question that most politicians can only dream of hearing: "If I can handle the matter so that the nomination for governor shall be tendered to you on a silver platter, without your turning a hand to obtain it, and without any requirement or suggestion of any pledge whatsoever, what do you think would be your attitude?"

Even then Wilson hesitated. He rose to his feet and began to pace the room. His answer, when he gave it, was not a decision but a prolongation of the suspense. He said that under the circumstances Harvey had described, he would consider it his duty not necessarily to accept the nomination, but to "give the matter very serious consideration." This had to be a delicious experience for a man who had dreamed from boyhood of rising to greatness not by seeking to advance himself but simply on the basis of his innate superiority, and by doing what was right.

Wilson's attitude must have unsettled Sugar Jim and may have made him suspicious. He arranged for a mutual acquaintance, a Princeton alumnus and man of influence in Chicago named John Maynard Harlan, to write to Wilson and ask for assurance that he did not aspire to "set about fighting and breaking down the existing Democratic organization and replacing it with one of your own." Wilson replied that he had no such intention and would regard any such action as inexcusable—unless the good name of New Jersey was at stake. He added, however, that upon taking office he would regard himself as "absolutely free in the matter of measures and men." That was fair warning. Smith would regret not paying closer attention.

Wilson himself now wrote to four Chicago-based Princeton trustees, men he regarded as loyal to him. He informed them that he was being asked to run for office and asked if they thought he would fail in his obligations to the university by doing so. One wonders if he was letting the board of trustees know that he still had career options, and that if they wanted to keep him they would be well advised to do as he wished. Be that as it may, all four told him that he need not feel bound in any way. Possibly they welcomed the prospect of being able to part with Wilson on friendly terms, with no more bitter and embarrassing quarrels. What we know is that when he later asked to be allowed to continue as the university's president while running for governor, the trustees turned him down, requiring his resignation. They then overrode his objections in choosing as his successor John Grier Hibben, the professor who had been Wilson's one close friend until he failed to support the quadrangle plan. (It is sadly typical of Wilson that he never forgave either Hibben or the men who elected him president of Princeton. In 1914, when as president of the United States Wilson was the star of the thirty-fifth reunion of the Princeton class of 1879, he refused to shake the hand of a trustee who had voted for Hibben's appointment.)

Harvey's next move was to secure the blessings of other power bro-kers. He introduced Wilson to his fellow machine bosses, the New Jersey party's chairman (who happened to be Jim Smith's nephew), the state's Democratic national committeeman, and Richard V. Lindaberry, an at-torney for U.S. Steel and Standard Oil. All were satisfied with what they saw. Assured that he had the support of these men and others like them, Wilson sent the newspapers an announcement not that he was *running* for governor but was willing to *accept* the Democratic nomination. Thus he kept himself above the muck and mire through which mere politicians are obliged to wade in pursuit of offices high and low.

There was trouble all the same. Progressive Democrats and labor lead-ers looked at Wilson's past speeches and articles, looked, too, at his con-nections with the big money, and decided that he was a Trojan horse and had to be stopped. Liberal newspapers did the same. Among those who saw Wilson as the tool of enemies of reform was a young assemblyman named Joseph Patrick Tumulty. He and his fellow skeptics were beaten before they got started, however. George Harvey's silver platter was real, Wilson's nomination a certainty.

And so began what a New Jersey newspaper editor would recall as Wilson's "strange ascent." Not the least part of its strangeness was the lucky timing. As a Princeton professor observed, if Harvey and Smith had not rescued him, Wilson "undoubtedly would have been forced to resign from Princeton in the near future." Such a resignation would have blemished his reputation and in all likelihood would have led to a move out of New Jersey. The pursuit of the presidency in 1912 could not have happened.

In September, with Wilson waiting in a nearby hotel room, Jim Smith and his fellow bosses extracted their man's nomination as candidate for governor from a not conspicuously enthusiastic state convention. An hour later, in his first appearance before the delegates, Wilson unleashed as never before the power of which he was capable as an orator. He de-clared his independence, telling his audience that he had not sought the nomination and that "not only have no pledges of any kind been given, but none have been proposed or desired." He ticked off the measures the progressives had long and unsuccessfully fought to put in the party platform—reorganization of government, tax equalization, regulation of business, a corrupt practices act—and pledged that if elected he would do his best to enact every one of them. The delegates began to perk up. Soon they were on their feet cheering, some of them weeping. Wilson walked out of the Trenton Opera House the hero of every progressive Democrat in the state and of no few Republicans. Joe Tumulty, who had started the day regarding Wilson's nomination as a disaster, found himself volunteering to work in his campaign.

Having taken on a new political identity, that of a no-holds-barred progressive, Wilson campaigned tirelessly. He asked voters to help him free them from the machines and the corporations. Jim Smith appears not to have been overly disturbed; after all, noble rhetoric was necessary in this so-called age of reform. Some modest legislative initiatives might have to be arranged after the governorship was bagged—so long as they didn't go too far. Smith was satisfied, presumably, that his man was simply doing what any sensible candidate would do: saying things he didn't mean, and creating expectations he neither could nor wished to satisfy.

But Wilson made the voters believe. His appearances pulled in so many disaffected Republicans that he won in a landslide. His coattails were long enough to give the Democrats control of the state assembly and to turn him into a national sensation. He hired Tumulty as his "secretary" (the savvy and amiable Irishman would function as chief of staff,

Joseph Tumulty
*Wilson's jack-of-all-trades and most faithful associate,
destined to be spurned in the end.*

press secretary, and guide to the intricacies of New Jersey politics) and made himself the driving force behind a breathtakingly ambitious legislative agenda. In 1911 the most cherished dreams of New Jersey's progressives became law. Among them were direct primaries, regulation of utilities, workmen's compensation, and the promised corrupt practices act. Across the country, people took note.

If some of the new laws were blows to Sugar Jim, they were not the worst he had to endure. When he attempted to collect the Senate seat that he regarded as now his by right, he was astonished to find Wilson blocking his way. The new governor used all the clout that had come to him with his victory to force the legislature to elect the nonentity who had won the nonbinding preferential primary for the Senate seat. (That primary had seemed so inconsequential that Smith had not bothered to have his name put on the ballot.) Wilson next set out to unseat Smith's nephew, a rough-edged political battler called Little Bob Nugent (the boss of Jersey City, Robert Davis, was Big Bob), as Democratic state chairman. This was another risky move, again putting Wilson's political capital on the line, but again he prevailed. He emerged supreme in the state party.

Wilson's treatment of Smith is sometimes portrayed as a betrayal. It is easy to understand why Smith *felt* betrayed, but to call Wilson dishonorable is naïve. He had been clear from the start about owing nothing— least of all a Senate seat—to Smith or anyone else. If he unveiled a new Woodrow Wilson on the day of his nomination, his new persona served rather than betrayed the interests of the commonwealth. If his crushing of Smith and Nugent came as a surprise after his promise not to challenge the party organization, it should be remembered that that promise had a condition attached to it. Promise or no promise, it is hardly realistic to condemn Wilson for displaying the instinct for the jugular without which no political leader can achieve ambitious objectives. As the popular sage Mr. Dooley observed long ago, politics ain't beanbag. It is, rather, a blood sport.

Smith and Nugent, for their part, never hesitated to play rough. They took their revenge in the legislative elections of 1911, undercutting not only Wilson but the entire state party. They made sure that all Democratic candidates lost in the parts of the state that they controlled, thereby allowing the Republicans to recapture the assembly. In doing this they not only blocked further reform but sowed doubts about Wilson's plausibility as a presidential candidate.

Nonetheless, by the end of 1911 Wilson's accomplishments had made him a major figure nationally. And he had taken every step with the presidential election of 1912—and William Jennings Bryan—in mind. Bryan was certain to have, as usual, the biggest following at the Democratic convention, controlling enough votes make or break other candidates. The Woodrow Wilson of Princeton, who had refused to appear in public with Bryan, was replaced by a Governor Wilson eager for opportunities not only to appear with but to praise him.

It is at this point that Edward House enters the story. He was living in Manhattan, nursing his ambition and looking for a horse to back in the race for the 1912 Democratic nomination. He was also intrigued by what he was hearing and reading about the governor of New Jersey. He wrote to Wilson, Wilson called on him at his apartment, and one of the most complicated and momentous friendships in American presidential history was quickly cemented.

"The first hour we spent together proved to each of us that there was a sound basis for a fast friendship," House would remember. "We found ourselves in such complete sympathy, in so many ways, that we soon learned to know what each was thinking without either having expressed himself. A few weeks after we met and after we had exchanged confidences which men usually do not exchange except after years of friendship, I asked him if he realized that we had only known one another for so short a time. He replied, 'My dear friend, we have known each other always.' And I think this is true."

Soon the colonel was telling his brother-in-law that his new friend the governor "has the opportunity to become the greatest president we have ever had, and I want him to make good. He can do it if the office-seekers will give him leisure to think, and I am going to try and help him to get it." Three weeks later another letter shows House to be thinking of what a Wilson presidency could mean for him personally: "Never before have I found both the man and the opportunity" combined so perfectly in a single package.

Wilson's nomination as Democratic presidential candidate was little short of a miracle. He faced rivals who had long been potent figures in Washington, and he could not have won if Bryan, after a grueling forty-six ballots, had not finally signaled that Wilson was his choice. Bryan did this in spite of the publication of letters in which, some years earlier, Wilson had poured scorn on him. In 1907 Wilson had expressed the wish that "we could do something at once dignified and effective to knock Mr. Bryan once and for all into a cocked hat!" The letters were made public by people wanting to destroy Wilson's chances, but Bryan was accustomed to far worse and had too generous a spirit to allow his mind to be made up in such a way. House found an opportunity to display usefulness. He had a good relationship with Bryan, one of long standing, and took every opportunity to speak well of "the governor" in terms that Bryan would find appealing. Once Bryan became satisfied that Wilson was more genuinely progressive than the other candidates, the issue was settled.

One more miracle was needed to make Wilson president. It arrived on schedule: in 1912 the Republican Party, so long triumphant, unexpectedly fell apart. Theodore Roosevelt, freshly back from overseas adventures, found himself missing the "bully pulpit" of the presidency. He claimed to be disgusted with President Taft's failure to be more activist. He set out to snatch the nomination from his successor, failed, and hastily created a third party that made him its candidate. This split the Republicans and made it possible for Wilson to be elected with only 42 percent of the vote, and for the Democrats to become the majority in both houses of Congress. Bryan became secretary of state, not to honor any deal and not because the new president's opinion of him had improved all that much, but because Wilson didn't expect the position to be particularly important in his administration. And because, wisely, he didn't want to leave the Bryanites on the outside, where they would be free to snipe.

There followed, as in New Jersey, a period of blazing legislative achievement. Wilson drove Congress hard, keeping it in session for an unprecedented year and a half. Because he had firmer control of both houses than Roosevelt or Taft had ever enjoyed, he accomplished more than both. Tariff reform, currency and banking reform including the creation of the Federal Reserve Bank, new controls on trusts and monopolies, and establishment of the Federal Trade Commission all followed his inauguration. Some things that progressives wanted did not follow. Help for organized labor, credit for farmers, limitations on the use of child labor—these and other issues were not addressed because the president had no interest in them. But he stood supreme all the same. It was through his administration, wrote the young journalist Walter Lippmann, that "the middle class has put the 'Money Power' on the defensive" and "big business is losing its control of the government."

But then the president lost interest in reform. The darker, harder Wilson that had first appeared after his 1906 stroke, and had emerged again in his final few years at Princeton, became ever more conspicuous. This Wilson was unwilling to share power with anyone, worked mainly in isolation, and had little interest in the opinions of others. Even now, despite all the amazing things that had happened to him in the past four years, he gave evidence of being chronically dissatisfied, as hungry as ever for admiration, distrustful of anyone who failed to admire him unreservedly, and desperate to become a great president not only by domestic standards but on the world stage.

It was this darker Wilson who brought the United States to the brink of war on her own southern border. Revolution had broken out in Mexico during the Taft administration and turned into a protracted civil war. Within weeks of his inauguration Wilson was faced with the question of whether to extend official recognition to General Victoriano Huerta, the nasty piece of work who had set himself up as Mexico's president. The general had the backing of American companies with substantial investments in Mexico and big American banks also wanted Washington to recognize him. Wilson declared refusal to be the right thing even if not in the financial interests of the United States. When asked to protect American citizens in Mexico, he replied in a way that contrasts curiously with his later insistence on the rights of Americans to travel in safety on the ships of nations at war. "We should earnestly urge all Americans," he said, "to leave Mexico at once. They should take no unnecessary risks when it is impossible for them to leave."

That his intentions were noble is hardly to be doubted. "We shall yet prove to the Mexican people," he told Congress, "that we know how to serve them without first thinking how we shall serve ourselves." But such sentiments did not keep him from making so much unnecessary trouble that war would for a time seem inevitable. There may have been medical—neurological—reasons for his doing so. On the morning of April 11, 1913, still new in the White House, he awoke in a state subsequently described as "ominous from a clinical standpoint." His left shoulder gave him so much pain—probably as the result of another stroke—that he spent the day in bed. Though he was back on his feet on Monday, he went first through a period of euphoria and then fell into a deep depression. This appears to have affected his personality and behavior in much the same way as the stroke of 1906.

The consequences were simultaneously tragic and absurd. A party of sailors from one of the American warships prowling the Mexican coast went ashore at Tampico without seeking permission of the local authorities. They were only looking for fresh water, but an overzealous Mexican officer had them arrested. As soon as the commander of the Tampico garrison learned what had happened, he released the sailors and apologized. When Huerta was informed, he sent a formal apology to Washington. But the admiral commanding the American ships in the area was not satisfied. He demanded that Mexico make amends by giving the Stars and Stripes a twenty-one-gun salute, and President Wilson supported him. When Huerta refused, fearful of showing weakness to his rebellious countrymen, Wilson ordered the U.S. Atlantic and Pacific fleets to mass themselves off Mexico's east and west coasts. This was a gross overreaction. Huerta offered a compromise in which the two neighbor nations would salute each other's flags.

Wilson took this as an affront. He ordered the navy to seize the customs house at Veracruz. Marines went ashore on August 19 and met unexpected resistance. In the ensuing firefight, nineteen Americans were killed. More troops were sent in, and eventually the whole town of Veracruz was under American occupation. Wilson, horrified that his orders had led to so many deaths, forbade further action. But he had precipitated a calamity by refusing a simple compromise that would have resolved an essentially trivial dispute. This echoed the self-defeating inflexibility with which he had pressed his conflict with the Princeton trustees. It foreshadowed his actions during and after the European war.

Chapter 4

Many Sacred Principles

THE SINKING OF THE *LUSITANIA*, WITH ITS TERRIBLE LOSS OF LIFE, sent American public opinion lurching heavily to the Entente's side. It so deepened the differences that separated the president from his secretary of state that Bryan began to find them unbearable. Wilson, regarding Europe and the war as matters to be managed from the White House, was untroubled by those differences. For such counsel and assistance as he required, he looked not to the State Department but to Colonel House, who held no office, scrupulously avoided the limelight, and so posed no threat to the president's determination to be seen as master and sole maker of the nation's foreign policy.

Though the outrage that the sinking provoked was overwhelming at first, the *Lusitania* crisis soon proved to be shrouded in ambiguities. The German embassy in Washington, headed by an ambassador who was horrified by the dangers of his country's U-boat campaign and desperate to avoid a showdown with the United States, had arranged to run newspaper advertisements warning travelers of the risks of taking passage on liners flying the flags of Entente nations. Within forty-eight hours of the sinking, it was generally known that the *Lusitania* had been carrying munitions—six million rounds of small-arms ammunition and 1,250 cases of shrapnel shells, among other things. And anyone taking the trouble to consult the 1914 edition of *Jane's Fighting Ships,* the authoritative source on its subject matter, would have found the *Lusitania* described as an "armed merchantman." A British technical journal of 1913 described her as outfitted with a dozen six-inch guns. (The inches refer to the diameter of shells fired. Six-inch guns are *heavy* artillery.)

Such revelations took some of the edge off public anger, and questions were asked about whether passengers aboard a vessel carrying such cargo should expect to be untouchable. Bryan had already made clear that he thought the answer was no, and he continued to communicate his concerns to the president. "Germany has a right to prevent contraband going to the Allies," he wrote on May 9, "and a ship carrying contraband should not rely upon passengers to protect her from attack. It would be like putting women and children in front of an army."

He was not alone. Even the vice president, Thomas Marshall, said that "when a person boarded an English vessel he was virtually on English soil and must expect to stand the consequences."

Meanwhile Colonel House, from London, was sending cables expressing a sharply different view. He urged the president to take a hard line with the Germans—to demand a promise that there would be no more such attacks or the price would be war with the United States. Thinking that the *Lusitania* had freed him from the need to conceal from the president his wish for war, he nevertheless took care to argue in terms that Wilson was certain to find appealing. "Our intervention will save rather than increase the loss of life," he wired on May 9. "America has come to the parting of the ways, when she must determine whether she stands for civilized or uncivilized warfare. Think we can no longer remain neutral spectators." Viewed from House's perspective in London, the situation left the president with no choice.

But with the public's anger subsiding at a pace that would have dismayed the colonel had he been at home to witness it, few of even the most jingoistic newspapers were suggesting that the nation should go to war. The president's chief adviser on domestic politics, his secretary Joe Tumulty, cautioned him that the public was far from ready for such a step. Not that Wilson needed such a warning. On May 10 he made a long-scheduled appearance in Philadelphia, delivering the speech in which he famously declared that "there is such a thing as a man being too proud to fight—there is such a thing as a nation being so right that it does not need to convince others by force that it is right." News of these words, not the shrewdest Wilson ever uttered, caused dismay when they reached London. The president was derided in the British and French press and by Republican leaders at home. The speech served a purpose, however, even if it expressed little more than a strangely unfocused self-righteousness. It went down well with an American public far more receptive to Bryan's position than to House's.

Wilson *was*, however, determined to take a firm line with Germany, if not as hard a line as House wanted. At a cabinet meeting the day after his speech, he read House's bellicose cable aloud, and from around the table came muttered approval. Bryan, however, was not pleased. He complained indignantly that there were men in that room who were not neutral at all. For stating this obvious truth, he was rebuked by the president, and apologized. Wilson then sketched out a diplomatic note that he had been preparing for delivery to Berlin. It demanded an end to U-boat attacks on merchantmen and financial reparation for the *Lusitania* sinking. It declared the use of submarines against ships carrying passengers a gross violation of "many sacred principles of justice and humanity." It was characteristic of Wilson to offer such flights of rhetoric without saying just what sacred principles he had in mind.

Staying on the same high and abstract level, he said that his note, when complete, would invoke the "sacred duty" of the United States to maintain her rights and those of her citizens. It is revealing of Wilsonian logic that he was able to say such things so soon after surrendering the right of American merchants—a right enshrined in law but evidently not a sacred one—to trade with Germany and with the many neutral ports put off-limits by Britain.

The truth, as before, was simple enough: there existed in law no such thing as the right to a guarantee of safety if one chose to travel on the ship of a nation at war. To claim such a right when traveling on a ship carrying the materials of war to a nation at war was, in the view of Bryan and many others, ludicrous. Wilson was making use of—yielding to the temptations of—his ability to conceal thinness of substance behind grand verbiage. He was reverting to the same pattern of behavior that had become so conspicuous during his final years at Princeton. There, however, he had been confronted by a board of trustees with the power to thwart him. In 1915, in the Cabinet Room of the White House, he faced no such obstacle. There he encountered only men who were dependent on him for continued employment, many of them chosen not by him but by Colonel House, most of them as comfortable as the colonel with the prospect of going to war.

Bryan, again the sole exception, spoke of the likely consequences of leaving the Germans with only two options: a humiliating capitulation or a break with the United States. The subject was then dropped, and the meeting soon adjourned. That the president returned to his office in a state not just of uncertainty but of inner turmoil is apparent in the note he sent to Bryan later that same day. "Both in mind and in heart I was deeply moved by what you said in Cabinet this morning," it said. "I have gone over it again and again in my thoughts since we separated, and it is with no sort of confidence that I am right, but, on the contrary with unaffected misgivings that I may be wrong, that I send you the enclosed with the request that you and Mr. Lansing will be generous enough to go over it and put it into shape for transmission to the German government."

"The enclosed" was of course a completed draft of the note the president intended to send to Germany. If the president's request caused Bryan to hope that he would find the note softened, he quickly learned otherwise. He returned it to the White House the next day, finished and ready for delivery, with his signature affixed along with the following message:

"I join in this document with a heavy heart. I am as sure of your patriotic purpose as I am of my own, but after long consideration both careful and prayerful, I cannot bring myself to the belief that it is wise to relinquish the hope of playing the part of a friend to both sides in the role of peacemaker, and I fear that this note will result in such a relinquishment . . . the jingo element will not only predict, but demand, war." He added that the note was certain to be "applauded by the allies," and that "the more they applaud the more Germany will be embittered." He urged not a change of the presidential mind—clearly there was no hope of that—but the sending of an additional note. It would go to Britain and would protest her illegal acts, particularly "the announced purpose of the Allied to starve the non-combatants of Germany."

When on May 13 Wilson's note was delivered to the German ambassador, acceptance appeared improbable. It seemed more likely that the president would soon be breaking off relations and, not long after that, asking Congress for a declaration of war.

Bryan, however, could not let the matter drop. On May 17, after a conversation with Vienna's ambassador, he wrote again to the president, repeating that a firm note of protest to the Entente would make it easier for Berlin to agree to Wilson's demands; the Germans would no longer feel singled out for blame. "I believe it will have a splendid effect if our note to Great Britain can go at once. . . . I have no doubt Germany would be willing to so change the rule in regard to submarines as to exempt from danger all passenger ships that did not carry munitions of war."

Bryan's desperation, his bafflement in the face of presidential thinking that he confessed to finding incomprehensible, led him to use arguments that he must have known were likely to give offense. "A person would have to be very much biased in favor of the Allies," he wrote in one appeal, "to insist that ammunition intended for one of the belligerents should be safe-guarded in transit by the lives of American citizens."

Even the pro-Entente Robert Lansing agreed that Britain no less than Germany should be sent an admonitory note. U.S. Ambassador Gerard, in Berlin, remained convinced that keeping munitions off passenger ships and passengers off munitions ships could end the crisis, and he said so in repeated cables to Washington. "Why," he asked, "should we enter a great war because some American wants to cross on a ship where he can have a private bathroom?"

Wilson was impervious, his mind made up. He would have no more talk of compromise, or of linking German actions to Britain's blockade. On May 21 he issued a statement of support for an increase in the size of the U.S. Navy, delighting the barons of the steel industry. Colonel House, still in London, was like his friends there disappointed that the president's note had not been stronger. He continued to press Wilson to require the Germans to submit or accept an American declaration of war. "There is no doubt that the position you have taken with both Germany and Great Britain is correct," he cabled on May 25, "but I fear that our position with the Allies is somewhat different, for we are bound up more or less in their success, and I do not think we should do anything that can possibly be avoided to alienate the good feeling that they now have for us. If we lost their good will we will not be able to figure at all in peace negotiations." House and Bryan were like two spirits perched on Wilson's shoulders, each whispering into an ear. One appealed for neutrality and peace, the other for intervention in the war as a necessary prelude to peacemaking.

It was not until May 28 that the Germans responded to the *Lusitania* note. They did so gingerly, sending what they described as a preliminary note and promising something more conclusive later. Berlin's tardiness, and the tentative nature of its response, is explained by the box in which the German government found itself. Neither the kaiser nor his chancellor nor the foreign minister wanted trouble with the United States. In fact they dreaded it. And the U-boat fleet was still so small that not even Naval Minister Tirpitz was prepared to argue that a continuation of the current policy could produce benefits sufficient to justify the risks.

The great problem continued to be public opinion. Ordinary German citizens, faced with an enemy avowedly committed to starving their children and grandparents, wanted exactly what the people of Britain or France or Tannu-

Tuva would have wanted under similar circumstances: a solution or, if that was not possible, retribution. They would be furious if their government capitulated to demands that appeared, from their perspective, to be little more than gratuitous insults.

Wilson dismissed Germany's reply as an effort to buy time, which of course it was. But that he did not actually want war is evident in the way he began, at just this point, to complain with unprecedented vehemence about British disruption of transatlantic trade. He did so quietly, issuing no formal communications, at the same time resurrecting the idea of a compromise in which Britain would lift or loosen its blockade of food in return for a German pledge not to attack merchant ships without warning.

The Asquith government was taken aback by this change in the president's tone. It seemed to make nonsense of Colonel House's assurances that the United States was within weeks of going to war. House's position was becoming awkward—so much so that he decided that he needed to return to Washington and "stiffen," as he put it, the president. When he booked passage on a homebound ship, Grey, in recognition of the value of Britain's most indispensable American friend, arranged for a special destroyer escort through the U-boat danger zone.

Seeing that he had moved too far ahead of the president, House reverted to talking about peacemaking rather than a break with Germany. He understood, if somewhat belatedly, that the bellicosity of his friends in London had caused him to become unwisely bellicose himself in his messages to the White House. That it was not war that the president wanted but the role of peacemaker, and that if he, House, wanted to maintain his place as Wilson's principal instrument, he needed to demonstrate that the two of them still thought the same. Nothing more would be heard from him, for some time after his return home, about threatening the Germans with war.

How to make peace was less clear than House may have been prepared to admit even to himself. Were negotiations possible? If so, on the basis of what preliminary understandings? How could the Entente nations enter into talks when the war was going so badly? In March the British had launched an offensive at Neuve-Chapelle that produced no result beyond a massive loss of life. May brought the joint British-French offensive that kicked off the Second Battle of Artois; when it ended, the French had suffered 100,000 casualties, Britain almost 30,000, and the breakthrough that was the purpose of the whole enterprise had not been achieved. Meanwhile, in the Second Battle of

Ypres, the Germans captured valuable high ground while taking only half as many casualties as the Entente forces, and the Royal Navy's failure to win control of the Dardanelles had been followed by the injection of ground forces that would turn into the disaster of Gallipoli. On the Eastern Front the Germans were driving the Russians relentlessly back and closing in on Warsaw.

Even if the Entente's situation had been less dismal, hard questions would have remained for both sides. What kind of settlement would justify the terrible costs of the conflict? Was it reasonable—was it even sane, in the conditions of 1915—for the Entente to hold out for a settlement that reduced Germany to a second-rate power? How could such a thing possibly be achieved?

As May ended, Kaiser Wilhelm and his ministers gathered at the imperial castle at Pless, behind the Eastern Front in what is now Poland. They were struggling to arrive at a consensus on what kind of definitive reply to make to President Wilson's demands, which were now more than two weeks old. Admiral Tirpitz was adamant as always that no restrictions must be imposed on the U-boats. General Falkenhayn doubted as before that continuing the submarine campaign could possibly be worth the risks. Chancellor Bethmann and Foreign Minister Gottlieb von Jagow, to no one's surprise, agreed with Falkenhayn. The kaiser, who alone could settle the question, was in an agony of indecision. Consensus proved impossible, nothing was decided, and submarines continued to set out for the English and Irish Channels with orders to sink without warning all ships flying Entente flags.

On the first day of June, President Wilson, impatient and annoyed, shared with his cabinet his draft of a second note to Germany, another stern one. There ensued a heated discussion, with Bryan again alone and again becoming emotional. Agriculture Secretary David Houston left a vivid account of an exchange that marked the end of the line for the secretary of state. It begins with War Secretary Lindley Garrison complaining that the Germans, in replying to the president's *Lusitania* note, had not so much as acknowledged what Garrison called an "elemental principle" of international law: the right to safety of citizens of neutral nations even when traveling on belligerent ships. Bryan's response, as described by Houston, was something of a non sequitur: he said that "he had all along insisted on a note to England; that she was illegally preventing our exports from going where we had a right to send them; and that the Cabinet seemed to be pro-Ally." As at the preceding cabinet meeting, Bryan was "sharply rebuked" by the president, who said his remarks were "unfair and unjust" and that he had "no right to say that any one was pro-Ally or pro-German. Each one was merely trying to be a good American."

Wilson closed the subject by saying that he had not decided whether to send the new note. When the meeting adjourned, an unhappy Bryan stayed behind and told the president that if the new note were sent, he would be unable to sign it.

Meanwhile the German ambassador, Count Johann von Bernstorff, was casting about for ways to lower the tension. He had the most difficult assignment in the diplomatic world of the time, trying to represent Germany in a Washington where official and fashionable society was so pro-Entente that he and his American wife were no longer welcome at many functions. He went

Count Johann Heinrich
von Bernstorff
*As Germany's ambassador
in Washington, he had
the most difficult diplomatic
assignment in the world.*

about it with considerable skill, though not always calmly. Fifty-three years old, the tall and gangly Bernstorff was unusually well qualified for his task. He had not only been born in England but had lived there until he was eleven years old, his father being Prussia's and then the newly created Imperial Germany's ambassador to the Court of St. James's. He wanted to follow his father into politics and diplomacy, but the way forward turned out to be difficult. His father made the mistake of getting at cross-purposes with Chancellor Otto von Bismarck, the supreme European politician of the day. Not only was his career wrecked as a result, but the Bernstorff name became non grata in official Berlin.

Young Johann had to go into the army instead of the foreign service but managed to wangle assignments as military attaché and the like in Constantinople, Belgrade, St. Petersburg, London, and Cairo. Having thus acquired much experience of the world, he left the army and won election to the Reichstag. Once settled in Berlin, he was able to make new connections with influential people. With Bismarck first out of office and then dead, doors long shut began to open. In 1908 he was appointed ambassador to the United States, so that by the time the war came, he had been in Washington six years and was considered the dean of the city's diplomatic corps. Wilson and Lansing claimed to find him devious and untrustworthy, but he had been generally well liked until the war turned him into a pariah. Colonel House enjoyed dealing with him.

For a good many weeks now, Bernstorff had been warning Berlin that although Wilson appeared to be trying to avoid war, he was under heavy pressure to do otherwise. He grew increasingly worried as the diplomatic tension increased but held out the hope that if Germany yielded on the U-boat issue, Washington would reciprocate by pressuring the Entente to relax the blockade. His messages produced an odd result. In the aftermath of the *Lusitania* disaster, Chancellor Bethmann used Bernstorff's warnings to persuade the kaiser to sign an order to the effect that the U-boats were not to attack large passenger liners without warning (which meant, in light of the practicalities, not attacking them at all). Though this change was intended to avoid further conflict with the United States, it was kept secret. The high command feared that, if it became known, the Entente would celebrate it as proof of German weakness and desperation. The result was absurd: the effectiveness of the submarine campaign was reduced, but Germany got no credit for reducing it. Not even Bernstorff in Washington was told of the change in policy. Meanwhile Wilson was being ridiculed by Roosevelt and other Republicans for corresponding with the Germans instead of demanding submission.

The German ambassador was not the only man in Washington experiencing severe difficulty. On June 5 a sleepless and distraught William Jennings Bryan sought out Treasury Secretary William Gibbs McAdoo, a tough former businessman who a year earlier had become President Wilson's son-in-law. Bryan declared that he had been forced to the conclusion that his usefulness as secretary of state was ended and he had to resign. He wanted McAdoo to help him do so in a way that would minimize embarrassment to the administration. The treasury secretary tried to dissuade him, but to no effect. Bryan said he was convinced that the administration's actions were carrying the nation toward war and that remaining in the cabinet under such conditions was, for him, impossible.

In what was under the circumstances an extraordinarily generous letter of resignation, Bryan informed the president that "obedient to your sense of duty, and actuated by the highest motives, you have prepared for transmission to the German Government a note in which I cannot join you without violating what I deem to be an obligation to my country. To remain a member of the Cabinet would be as unfair to you as it would be to the cause which is nearest to my heart, namely, the prevention of war." Wilson, like McAdoo, tried to dissuade him from quitting. Bryan replied that he had never had the president's confidence and had never been able to function as a secretary of state should. He was right about that where the European conflict was concerned, although it is equally true that with regular exposure Wilson had come to respect and to like the conscientious, guileless, and openhearted Bryan, of whom he had once been so scornful. This is apparent in what the president now wrote to Bryan. "I accept your resignation only because you insist on its acceptance; and I accept it with much more than deep regret, with a feeling of personal sorrow. Our two years of close association have been very delightful to me."

Until the difficulties over the U-boats and the blockade, Wilson and Bryan had worked together with an ease that must have surprised the president. They found that they had a shared interest in supporting democracy in the Caribbean and South America and peace around the world, and though the results of their attempts to do so sometimes became rather messy, they did not blame each other. Bryan became the only cabinet member Wilson was willing to meet with daily, and it is perhaps a tribute to the secretary's ingenuousness, his obvious lack of any kind of selfish or hidden motives, that he was very nearly the only person who could disagree with the president on a question of importance without becoming the object of bitter scorn.

The decision to resign was painful for Bryan and for his wife as well. He was proud to be secretary of state, the first office he had held since leaving the House of Representatives two decades before, and had worked zealously (his critics said with naïve zeal) to promote peace around the world. Life in Washington had been a joy for his wife, a welcome change from the years that she had spent raising three children and maintaining a base of operations for her famous husband as he traveled the nation and the world as an orator, campaigner, and political celebrity.

Bryan and his family understood that they were going to pay for his resignation and were accustomed to abuse. Theodore Roosevelt had called Bryan "the most contemptible figure we have ever had as secretary of state" (along with describing the president he served in equally biting terms). Still, the price of departure proved to be higher than the Bryans had foreseen. As soon as the resignation became known, newspapers across the country began attacking the former secretary savagely, calling him a traitor not only to the president but to the nation. That he was a coward could almost go without saying, as far as his critics were concerned. The abuse came mainly from the factions and publications that were most hostile to Germany, but these were numerous and influential enough to inflict grave damage. At the time of his appointment Bryan had been at least as popular and influential among grassroots Democrats as the new president. He left office a diminished figure, still adored by millions but with no possibility of ever again holding national office. After twenty years as one of the most famous and controversial men in America, he was, politically, a spent force. Still only fifty-five years old, he was becoming the semipathetic vestige of an America that was passing out of existence.

None of the opprobrium fell on Wilson. For much of the public, he was the man who, while determined to do everything that honor permitted to keep the country out of Europe's war, also had the backbone to oppose Imperial Germany's contempt for "humanity" and trampling of "sacred" rights and principles. That made him admirable even in the eyes of citizens who did not want war.

With Bryan gone, Wilson was relieved of having close at hand anyone who questioned his decisions. He appointed State Department counselor Lansing, as strong as Colonel House in his friendship for Britain but otherwise pliable, to take charge of the State Department on an acting basis. House supported Lansing's promotion, describing him to the president as "a man with not too many ideas of his own," who therefore "will be entirely guided by you." It would not be surprising if the colonel's enthusiasm was heightened by the perception that Lansing was unlikely ever to become his rival. In due course the appointment was made permanent, to the satisfaction of everyone concerned. Lansing understood that he was to run the State Department but not intrude upon the president's management of major issues and not interfere with House. He found this an acceptable arrangement and would continue to do so for the next two years. His principal interest, which only occasionally complicated his efforts to support the Entente and satisfy the president, was in the proper interpretation and application of international law. In this he displayed considerable integrity—within whatever limits the president chose to set down. He felt no compulsion to be making policy or even to be included when policy was being made. His new title brought with it gratifying prestige and invitations to all the best dinner parties.

Less than a week after Bryan's resignation, Wilson sent the Germans his second post-*Lusitania* note, the one Bryan had said he could not sign. It was his own handiwork, as usual, picked out on his little typewriter, then revised and revised again. In its finished form it was at least as strong as the versions Bryan had seen, but its language remained broad and abstract. It declared in now-familiar Wilsonian terms that what the United States was demanding was not "mere rights of property or privilege of commerce"—heaven forfend that the president should stoop to such commonplace matters—but "nothing less sacred than the rights of humanity." Wilson did like that word *sacred.* The Germans, already uncertain about their own policy and still struggling to come up with a conclusive response to the first *Lusitania* note, must have scratched their heads.

When they finally responded, after weeks of hesitation, the Germans reiterated their defense of the U-boat campaign as a legitimate response to the starvation blockade. They also repeated their complaint that Britain, by arming her merchant ships and instructing them to fire on or ram any U-boats they sighted, had turned them into ships of war. They pronounced themselves "unable to admit that American citizens can protect an enemy ship through the mere fact of their presence on board." As before, these were defensible positions under the law. Berlin offered to work with the United States on an arrangement—such a thing would have been easy enough—to allow American citizens to pass through the war zone in safety.

Wilson would have none of it. He saw the Germans as defiant. A third note informed Berlin that the United States "regrets to state that it has found [the German position] unsatisfactory because of its failure to meet the real difference between the two Governments and to apply to them the principles of law and humanity involved in the present controversy." It stated that British policies and practices had no bearing on the dispute between Germany and the United States, and again accused Germany of trampling on "the accepted principles of law and humanity."

In Washington if not in the United States at large, war fever was soon rising once again. It got a bizarre boost when a German commercial attaché, Heinrich Albert, dozed off while riding the Sixth Avenue elevated train in Manhattan, awoke to find the train at his stop and, in hurrying to get off, left his briefcase behind. When he turned back to retrieve it, he was told that another passenger had grabbed it and fled. Albert gave chase, but the culprit escaped. The thief was—this long remained secret—one of the federal agents assigned to follow members of the German diplomatic staff and tap their phones. (Nothing of the kind was being done to representatives of Britain and France, though the British were intercepting and decoding American transatlantic cables.)

There was disappointment at Treasury when no evidence of sabotage or other criminal activity was found among Albert's papers. By this time it was widely believed, even in senior official circles, that German secret agents were everywhere, that the German-American population had organized a secret reserve army sworn to rise up in service of the kaiser if the United States entered the war, and that plans were in place for the disruption of the American army by violent means. Shadowy German saboteurs were blamed every time an explosion or fire occurred at a munitions factory.

Such stories were by no means without a kernel of truth. Not only were diplomats and other Germans stationed in the United States active in gathering information about what was happening there and why—they would have been derelict in failing to do so, so long as they stayed within the law—but there were proven instances of attempted sabotage. At the center of the plot-hatching, such as it was, were German military attaché Franz von Papen (later notorious as Adolf Hitler's first vice-chancellor) and naval attaché Karl Boy-Ed. In December 1915 the two would be expelled from the United States for sending agents to blow up a bridge and a canal in Canada—which was of course at war with Germany. Both attempts were as unsuccessful as they were amateurish. Ambassador Bernstorff was also suspected of involvement but to his immense relief was not required to go home.

Decades later, having survived another world war and been acquitted of war crimes at Nuremberg, Papen would observe of his time in Washington that "I am supposed to have organized a widespread net of saboteurs, to have instigated strikes in the docks and munitions factories, to have employed squads of dynamiters, and to have been the master spy at the head of a veritable army corps of secret agents." He added that "the reputation I acquired in those days was deliberately fostered by the well-organized Allied propaganda services as part of their campaign to arouse emotions in the United States."

The extent of whatever sabotage program the German authorities were operating in the United States should be the subject of its own book; the fact that it has been so rarely examined in depth is probably a function of the elusiveness of the truth even after a century. Two particularly dramatic examples are the explosions that obliterated a large munitions depot on Black Tom Island in New York Harbor in 1916 and a Canadian-owned shell-manufacturing facility in New Jersey's Meadowlands in March 1917. Investigations of and litigation over both incidents went on for decades. A claims commission ruled in 1939 that the German government had been responsible for the Black Tom disaster, which killed seven people and injured hundreds, but evidence was found to implicate members of Ireland's Sinn Fein and an East Indian separatist movement as well. Not until 1950 did West Germany agree to pay $50 million in damages, which it finally paid two decades later. The Meadowlands incident (known when it happened as the Kingsland explosion), in which flames of unknown origin detonated half a million three-inch artillery shells and produced a four-hour fireworks extravaganza within sight of Manhattan, ended even more ambiguously. In 1931 a commission found that the German government had not been involved, but the case dragged on until finally, in 1950, West Germany agreed to pay $50 million without admitting guilt.

Herr Albert's briefcase did contain evidence of a variety of bizarre and sometimes ridiculous activities: buying up both munitions and the machines needed by American manufacturers of munitions in an attempt to slow the flow to the Entente, operating munitions factories in the United States to consume raw materials, paying wages so high that workers at other factories would threaten to strike if not given raises, and buying a New York newspaper in hope of getting a German view of the news past the Entente's censors. All of this, when it became known, was seized upon as fresh evidence of German skullduggery. When Secretary McAdoo handed the materials over to the *New York World,* he did so on condition that their source not be disclosed. Concealment was crucial because of the awkward fact that the materials had been stolen by an agent of the U.S. government from an agent of a government with which America was not at war.

Two days after Dr. Albert lost his briefcase, the complexity of the legal and ethical questions raised by new kinds of naval warfare was thrown into grotesque relief by an incident that occurred just west of the British mainland. A German submarine, the U-27, intercepted a British freighter. After a boarding party established that the freighter was en route to England with a cargo of munitions and mules, her crew was ordered to take to the lifeboats. The U-27 was beginning to shell the abandoned ship—a common practice, intended to save torpedoes—when another merchantman came over the horizon. She was flying the flag of the United States, and as she approached, she sent up pennants signaling her captain's intention to rescue the men in the lifeboats. The U-27 paused in her shelling but, seeing no cause for alarm, neither submerged nor withdrew. But upon drawing near, the new arrival lowered the Stars and Stripes, hoisted the white St. George flag of the Royal Navy, and uncovered deck guns with which she quickly sank the submarine. She was not a freighter at all but the *Baralong*, one of the Royal Navy's recently introduced Q-ships (the Q stood for their home port of Queenstown, in Ireland), heavily armed vessels outfitted with false superstructures that made them appear to be merchantmen. Twelve members of the U-27's crew did not go down with her but swam to the abandoned freighter. Marines were sent from the *Baralong* to kill them, which they did with brisk efficiency. First Lord of the Admiralty Winston Churchill had given orders that U-boat sailors could be executed on the spot, because they were not prisoners of war but criminals.

When the *Baralong* returned to port, the British authorities asked the men in the lifeboats not to tell what they had witnessed. Instead they were to corroborate a concocted story about how the twelve German seamen had died of wounds inflicted during the sinking of the U-27, not later, in cold blood. Certain Americans among them refused to comply, and the story got out. A German demand that the captain of the *Baralong* be court-martialed was dismissed in London with scorn. Wilson, learning of the incident, described it as "horrible." His view of the overall situation, however, was unaffected.

He did react strongly when, on August 19, the British liner *Arabic* was torpedoed off the coast of Ireland, with two Americans among the forty-odd who perished. The commander of the responsible U-boat would later claim to have mistaken the *Arabic* for a freighter; such excuses were common and impossible to prove and made no difference in London or Washington. Ambassador Gerard delivered President Wilson's protest to German foreign minister Jagow and was surprised to be told that the *Arabic* sinking "was done contrary to instructions if the boat had been torpedoed as reported." What instructions? Gerard asked. He, and through him the White House, then learned of the secret order of June 5, the one forbidding attacks on Entente passenger liners.

The revelation lowered the temperature in Washington but probably had little to do with the president's rejection of Colonel House's renewed suggestion that Germany must accept either the rules set by the United States or a severing of relations. Again the colonel was out of step, pushing for a showdown that Wilson did not want and putting a strain on their relationship by doing so. When he sensed a new coolness in Wilson's communications, he again dialed down his belligerence and reverted to a position that at least resembled neutrality. It would become clear, however, that the president was growing wary. He no longer trusted House as unreservedly as he had in earlier years.

It would hardly be surprising if Berlin found it difficult to understand the American government's fury over the unintended loss of two lives so soon after the *Baralong* massacre passed without complaint. Ambassador Bernstorff, in a conversation with House, had recently observed that "you know well enough that nobody in Germany believes in the impartiality of the American Government." In the end, however, the Germans bowed to Washington's demands. First they issued a public pledge not to sink the passenger liners even of the Entente, whatever their size. Then, again publicly, they acknowledged that the *Arabic* had been sunk in violation of German government policy. This was welcomed in Washington as a step, if too small a step, toward getting Germany to admit that its entire U-boat campaign was as indefensible as Wilson claimed. Such an admission, if one could be extracted, would make it extremely difficult for submarine operations to continue. The sense of crisis subsided, and again both House and the British felt thwarted. London could bask, however, in the knowledge that the U.S. government was consistently acting in its favor. And House continued to press Wilson as hard as he dared. "For the first time in the history of the world," he wrote to the president, "a great nation has run amuck, and it is not certain that it is not part of our duty to put forth a restraining hand." Evidently he thought the double negative a way of being subtle.

Sir Edward Grey's frustration drove him to send House a letter that must have taken the colonel by surprise. In Britain, he wrote, there was "disappointment that the feeling in America is not more combative." But he for one would be "content," he added, if two things could be made to happen. First, the United States must recognize that peace would remain impossible until "the cause of Belgium" has been settled satisfactorily—which meant that there must be no possibility of Germany remaining in possession of Belgium when the war ended. Second, once Belgium was put right, the United States must show "no concern with the territorial changes between the belligerents themselves, who must settle things of that kind by themselves."

The point about Belgium was predictable and entirely legitimate; Britain had long regarded the autonomy of Belgium as essential to her own security. But Grey's second point was so presumptuous as to make one wonder how a man usually so cool and self-contained could have allowed himself to make it. He already had House's private assurance that the United States would never allow the Entente to lose the war, and he had been encouraged to believe further that the United States was prepared to help secure an Entente victory. But even this was not enough to put his mind at rest. Now he was insisting that the United States, even if she ultimately made victory possible, must stand aside and not interfere when a victorious Entente redrew the maps of Europe and the world. This put House in a delicate position. Grey was asking for something that Wilson would never accept—a postwar settlement in which the United States would play no part aside from making certain that the Germans gave up Belgium. He was in effect demanding the one thing that, if the president learned of it, was most likely to cause him to turn his back on Britain and her allies.

House had grounds for taking offense, and perhaps he should have done so. But he had no wish to jeopardize his good relations with Grey and the Foreign Office. Grey's letter left him, however, with a formidable challenge. He was going to have to find a way to induce Grey to drop this particular demand while keeping Wilson ignorant of what the demand was.

Money, meanwhile, was becoming an increasingly challenging issue. The departure of Bryan had cleared the way for a reconsideration of the ban on loans to the Entente, and by the end of the summer of 1915 there were powerful commercial and political reasons for doing so. After a year of total war, Britain and France were in financial straits, their costs rising dizzily with no end in sight. This portended trouble not only for the Entente but for the United States, where transatlantic sales had ignited an economic boom of unprecedented magnitude. The White House, with a presidential election little more than a year in the future, had reason to fear that an abrupt drop in those sales could cause a crash. Such concerns weighed heavily on the cabinet, especially after the Morgan bank, in its capacity as Britain's and France's agent, began sounding the alarm. Soon Treasury Secretary McAdoo was telling his father-in-law the president that "to maintain our prosperity, we must finance it." Lansing warned of the "industrial depression" that would follow if the Entente nations became incapable of placing new orders.

Before becoming secretary of state, Lansing had been asked whether loans by a neutral America to either of the belligerent sides would be lawful. He had replied, regretfully, that probably they would not. But he offered a solution: in place of loans, "credits" could be issued. It was a distinction without a difference, and it cleared the way for Morgan to give France a quick and desperately needed infusion of $50 million. It was the largest loan in the history of Wall Street up to that time, but it would be dwarfed by the billions that would be lent over the next three years. Bryan, still secretary of state at this point but conscious of having already made a nuisance of himself over the blockade, quietly acquiesced.

Late in the summer, with Bryan gone, Morgan and Company invited an Anglo-French joint high commission to Wall Street to discuss more substantial sums. This resulted in a September agreement to issue $500 million of British and French bonds in the United States. The offering did not go well; weeks after going on the market, $162 million of the bonds remained unsold. Sales to the public were particularly disappointing. Morgan and Company managed to get all the bonds placed by the end of 1915, but further offerings of the same kind were obviously out of the question. The main problem had been that the bonds were unsecured—not backed with collateral. To get future loans, the Entente nations were going to have to put hard assets behind them. Thus began the process by which the war would cause a massive transfer of wealth from Europe to the United States.

In the same week that Colonel House received Grey's presumptuous letter, he made a remarkable entry in his diary. In the midst of a discussion of how the United States might mediate an end to the war, he wrote, Wilson had disclosed something stunningly new. He told the colonel that "he had never been sure that we ought not to take part in the conflict." House must have been delighted, though his record of the conversation is restrained. Clearly the president's position was shifting, and in potentially momentous ways. Which side he would want to join was too obvious to require statement.

Not long after this revelation, on October 17, House sent what he would call one of the most important letters he ever wrote. He invited Grey, and through him Britain and the Entente, to inform Washington when the time had become right for the United States to call for peace talks. The unmistakable suggestion was that this should happen when the Entente was winning the war and could negotiate from a position of strength or, alternatively, when it was doing so badly that a halt had to be called. Then would come the tricky part: the Americans would issue a summons to negotiations, announcing that the aim was not only an end to hostilities but "universal disarmament." If the Germans refused to participate, the United States would have a basis for entering the conflict and making it—House used these words—"a war to end war." If the Germans agreed, nobody would be under any obligation to make the negotiations pleasant for them.

Once again House was emerging from his shell of feigned neutrality. He was being both extraordinarily bold and extraordinarily duplicitous. This new scheme of his, which historians have labeled his "positive policy," was intended not just to lead to an acceptable end to the war (acceptable, that is, to London) but to do so by trapping Germany between the Scylla of American intervention in the war and the Charybdis of a peace conference controlled by her enemies and their friends. It rose out of his belief that the United States, as he would tell Wilson, "had lost our opportunity to break with Germany, and it looked as if she had a better chance than ever of winning, and if she did our turn would come next." The whole scheme was fundamentally dishonest— erected on a foundation of intentional deceit. It pointed explicitly to the possibility of taking the United States to war through trickery. The most admiring of Wilson scholars have always been inclined to absolve the president of responsibility for this. They say that he was in effect betrayed by House, who concealed from Wilson the devious things he was doing.

This is all too obviously not true. House's diary states that he laid out the ideas that made up the core of his proposal for the president weeks before writing to Grey, and that when he sent his letter he did so not only with the president's knowledge but with his encouragement.

"My suggestion [to the president]," the relevant diary entry states, "is to ask the Allies, unofficially, to let me know whether or not it would be agreeable to them to have us demand that hostilities cease. We would put it on the high ground that the neutral world was suffering along with the belligerents and that we had rights as well as they, and that parleys should begin upon the broad basis of both military and naval disarmament. . . .

"If the Allies understood our purpose, we could be as severe in our language concerning them as we were with the Central Powers. The Allies, after some hesitation, could accept our offer or demand and, if the Central Powers accepted, we would then have accomplished a master-stroke of diplomacy. If the Central Powers refused to acquiesce, we could then push our insistence to a point where diplomatic relations would first be broken off, and later the whole force of our Government—and perhaps the force of every neutral— might be brought against them."

House describes the president as "startled" by all this, as well he might have been, but adds that "he seemed to acquiesce by silence." The diary notes also that House later explained his scheme to Secretary Lansing and State Department counselor Frank Knox and that both liked it. But as Lord Devlin observes, even if House had told no one before writing to Grey, this would matter less than the fact that later, when House's proposal produced diplomatic ramifications that had to be brought to Wilson's attention, the president instructed the colonel to take further steps in the same direction. At no point is there evidence of presidential disapproval.

"It has occurred to me," House told Grey in the letter of October 17, "that the time may soon come when this Government should intervene between the belligerents and demand that peace parleys began [sic] upon the broad basis of the elimination of militarism and navalism. It is in my mind that after conferring with your Government I should proceed to Berlin and tell them that it was the president's purpose to intervene and stop this destructive war, provided the weight of the United States thrown on the side that accepted our proposal could do it. I would not let Berlin know of course of any understanding had with the Allies, but would rather lead them to think that our proposal would be rejected by the Allies. This might induce Berlin to accept the proposal, but if they did not do so it would nevertheless be the purpose to intervene. If the Central Powers were still obdurate, it would probably be necessary for us to join the Allies and force the issue."

While all this was happening, continuing trouble between the United States and Mexico and difficulties arising from American interventions in the Caribbean were fueling congressional demand for a stronger army and navy. On September 24 there was a second *Baralong*-type incident, with a British Q-ship sinking a U-boat and killing all but two members of her crew. German protests were again ignored, and German questions about how cruiser rules could possibly be observed under such circumstances grew more insistent.

For some months President Wilson had been indifferent when not downright unfriendly to what was called the Preparedness Movement, a broad-based campaign for increased military spending. In November, however, he surprised friends and foes alike by issuing his own proposal for increasing the size of the regular army by roughly one-third and creating a ready reserve to be called the Continental Army and made up of four hundred thousand volunteers. He did so in part, probably, to keep the Republicans from making preparedness an issue in the 1916 election, but also because he had come to see the value of military and naval muscle in giving credibility to his foreign policy. Though generally uninterested in military matters (he showed little interest in the work of most government departments, generally leaving the members of his cabinet free to do as they wished), he had begun paying attention to the War Department's capabilities and possible needs when the U-boats first became a problem. Nor is it a coincidence that his proposal came just a few months after the exchange of notes over the *Lusitania.*

There was much opposition. It came from people who did not want to raise the $200 million in new taxes that the president was proposing, or did not want the nation to pursue more proactive policies overseas, or feared that Wilson's plan would require conscription and lead to intervention in Europe. A potent if surprising source of opposition was the National Guard, which was controlled by the states rather than Washington and would have been replaced as the army's reserve by the proposed Continental Army. All this was disputed in both houses of Congress over the winter of 1915–16, with members from the South and West forming the core of resistance to the administration's plans.

Colonel House, who thought increases much larger than those urged by the president should be a national priority, returned to London in January 1916. Soon after his arrival, at lunch with half a dozen British officials including Grey, he was asked point-blank what the United States wanted from Britain. His companions could hardly have hoped for a more delightful answer. "The United States," the colonel would record having told them, "wanted the British government to do what would enable the United States to do whatever necessary for the Allies to win the war." A week later Grey ventured to resurrect the subject that he had raised so boldly late in 1915: he asked House what he and the president would regard as an acceptable territorial arrangement at the conclusion of the war. House was ready with an answer, and it, too, was music to British ears. Not only must Belgium and Serbia be restored—House could have said no less—but Germany must give up Alsace and Lorraine to France and Constantinople should be surrendered by the Turks to Russia. This meant that the Ottoman Empire, with its vast holdings, must disappear. Which meant that almost the whole of the Middle East was going to be available for the taking.

Even this was not the most dramatic thing said that day. According to the recollection of Irwin B. Laughlin, a member of the American embassy's diplomatic staff, Grey also asked House in plain terms the most momentous question of all: did President Wilson want Britain to end its blockade? He cannot have been disappointed by the answer. According to Laughlin's account, House "replied definitely and without qualification in the negative." In so doing, he killed any possibility of a British-German resolution of the blockade-versus-submarines issue. This raises once again the question of how closely House was adhering to President Wilson's directions or acting with the president's knowledge. Was he, by encouraging the British not to compromise on the blockade, undercutting Wilson's hopes of arranging an end to the war that would not require the United States to take up arms? The president's earlier acceptance of House's "positive policy" makes this seem improbable, but certainty is beyond our reach. The absence of conclusive evidence, coupled with the way both Wilson and House could shift from seeming to want intervention to seeming to want a negotiated settlement and back again, shrouds much of the neutrality story in mystery.

It does not appear that House told Wilson anything about this exchange with his London hosts. A few days later, however, he sent an account of having dined with David Lloyd George, then serving as Britain's minister of munitions, because in this case he had things to report that were certain to please the president. Lloyd George had said, according to the colonel, that the war could "only be ended by your intervention," adding however that intervention should be postponed until September, by which time, it was expected, massive Entente offensives planned for the summer would have greatly strengthened the Allies' bargaining position. He said also that once conditions were right, "you [Wilson] can dictate the terms of peace, and he does not believe that any agreement is possible without such dictation." Finally House has the Welshman saying that "no man had ever lived with such an opportunity, and that if the world went on for untold centuries, history would record this as the greatest individual act of which it had record."

In wondering how many of his own words Lloyd George meant, and how many were calculated to seduce House and Wilson, it is helpful to remember what he would write years later in his memoirs. The colonel, he said, was "not nearly as cunning as he thought he was."

Background

Mystery Voyage

The torpedo that sank the mighty *Lusitania* was twenty feet long and twenty inches in diameter. It weighed a ton and a half, so that an early-model submarine like Kapitänleutnant Walther Schwieger's U-20 could carry only seven at a time. It had cost the German navy about five thousand dollars, a princely sum in 1915, and was both an ingenious mechanism and not very reliable.

When it was shot out of one of the U-20's two bow tubes, compressed air was released at a steady rate from an internal tank. This air turned pistons that caused two rear propellers to spin, one clockwise and the other counterclockwise for stability. The torpedo was kept on course by a gyroscope. Its movement through the water caused a small nose propeller to spin itself loose and fall away. This—when everything went as it should—exposed and activated the firing mechanism.

It sped toward its target at forty-plus miles per hour, faster than any ship, producing a stream of bubbles that rose to the surface and left a discernible trail. The sea was weirdly calm that day—smooth as a pane of glass. On the *Lusitania,* passengers who had just finished what they knew would be their last lunch on board—they were scheduled to dock in Liverpool before breakfast the next morning—lolled about on deck. Some of them gazed idly out to sea. Some heard a lookout suddenly shout through his megaphone, "Torpedo coming!" Some saw the torpedo as it churned toward them on the starboard beam. It was "covered with a silvery phosphorescence, you might term it, which was caused by air escaping from the motors," one survivor would recall. "It was a beautiful sight."

No one aboard the *Lusitania* could see her waterline; overhanging decks blocked the view. They saw the torpedo disappear beneath their feet, just below the bridge, and waited breathlessly for they didn't know what. Time seemed to stop. For what seemed an eternally long moment, it seemed possible that nothing was going to happen.

Actually that was possible—more possible than the passengers could have known. The German navy's experience was that 60 percent of its torpedoes malfunctioned. But not this time. The impact of the torpedo's firing mechanism against the *Lusitania's* hull fired a small charge into the 350 pounds of TNT and hexanite packed in just behind the nose. The explosives were instantly transformed into a gas at a temperature of nine thousand degrees Fahrenheit under pressures that no mere steel could withstand. This sent a geyser of water and debris upward into the sky and opened a horizontal hole of approximately forty by fifteen feet below the ship's waterline. It burst rivets and tore steel plates loose across an area many times larger than the hole. Interior damage was massive as well: watertight bulkheads and hatches were twisted open. A Niagara of seawater came pouring in.

A second explosion followed, perhaps thirty seconds after the first. It had a different sound and feel to it, seeming to rumble up from deep inside the ship. There was, however, nothing like panic in these early minutes. Passengers were dumbfounded, but unable to believe that such a massive vessel could *sink*. Most were in no hurry to get to their life jackets.

Within a few minutes the ship was listing fifteen degrees to starboard. There she held steady. Her captain, the experienced and respected W. T. Turner, hurried to the bridge and ordered the engine order telegraph set at full speed astern. That was to force the ship to a halt, so that lifeboats could be launched safely. But the propellers did not respond. The ship continued forward, still making eighteen knots, her thousands of tons creating overwhelming momentum. Turner told the helmsman to steer for Old Kinsale Head on the coast of Ireland, clearly visible to port. He wanted to get closer to help, even, if necessary, to run aground rather than sink. Again nothing happened; the rudder was not answering the helm. The ship swung heavily to starboard, heading farther out to sea. The bow was low in the water now, awash, the stern rising out of the sea.

The torpedo had hit as the watch was changing. Dozens of crew members, half going off duty and half coming on, were assembled belowdecks in the baggage room, organizing passengers' luggage for unloading at Liverpool. If not killed by the explosions, these men drowned in darkness later, trapped when the electricity went out and the elevator that was their only escape stopped working. Among them were many of the men responsible for, and trained in, the launching of lifeboats.

The elevators reserved for the use of first-class passengers stopped, too. They did so between decks, trapping their riders inside. The only electricity was an emergency system serving the radio room. Distress signals and calls for help were, of course, going out one after another. Every inside passageway and cabin was in total darkness. There were more explosions as cold seawater reached the ship's huge boilers. As the list to starboard began to worsen—by 2:25 it was a terrifying twenty-five degrees—water came pouring into portholes that had been opened for ventilation in the midday heat or broken by the explosions. Seventy portholes are believed to have been open on the starboard side. That number was sufficient to let in 260 tons of water a minute.

One of Captain Turner's first orders had been for the lifeboats to be lowered to the boat deck, where passengers were supposed to board them. But the severity of the list suspended the boats on the starboard side in midair, almost out of reach and sixty feet above the surface of the sea. People had to leap to get in them. The boats on the port side came down onto the up-rearing deck and were impossible to launch. Some of the starboard boats, upon being filled to capacity, came loose at their bow or stern ends while being lowered to the water and pitched their passengers out. A good many passengers—not all of them wearing life jackets—gave up on the lifeboats and jumped overboard. Deck chairs and debris rained down on their heads. Other passengers went to the main deck, worked their way forward toward the half-submerged bow, and waded into the ocean as gingerly as if doing it from a beach.

The ship returned to near-upright, indicating that the port side was now as flooded as the starboard. Captain Turner was still on the bridge when, just eighteen minutes after the torpedo hit, the bow took a final downward lurch, the stern rose so high that the propellers were exposed to the sun, and the *Lusitania* slid out of sight. Turner was sucked down with her, but his life jacket brought him back up. He found himself afloat in the middle of a nightmare. Only six of the ship's twenty-two lifeboats had been successfully launched. (A few portable boats were put to use as well.) People of every age and description, hundreds of them, were in the water. They clung to oars, to pieces of wreckage, to whatever they could find. Some were already dead. Some floated upside down, having put on their life jackets wrong. The children were in gravest jeopardy. The water temperature was fifty-five degrees, cold enough to bring on hypothermia and death. The small were especially vulnerable.

The U-20 had departed by then. "The ship was sinking with unbelievable rapidity," Schwieger would recall of his last look at the *Lusitania* through his periscope. "There was a terrific panic on her deck. Overcrowded lifeboats, fairly torn from their positions, dropped into the water. Desperate people ran helplessly up and down the decks. Men and women jumped into the water and tried to swim to empty, overturned lifeboats. It was the most terrible sight I have ever seen." But there was little he could do to help, and there were reasons not to try. A British cruiser, identifiable by the sound of its engines and propellers, had passed directly over the submerged U-20 earlier in the day; obviously danger was nearby. So, low on fuel, Schwieger resumed the long homeward voyage upon which he had embarked the day before. It would take him northward around Scotland, the English Channel being too dangerous to try. A month past his thirtieth birthday on the day of the *Lusitania* sinking, he would continue to command submarines until meeting the fate that awaited most U-boat sailors. In September 1917, trying to escape a pursuing Q-ship, he entered a British minefield. He and his crew and their submarine were never seen again. Fifty-seven percent of the U-boats that saw action in the Great War perished.

Help for the *Lusitania* had set out from the fishing port and naval base at Queenstown, twenty miles or so distant, as soon as Turner's distress calls came in. Speed was literally a matter of life and death, and the fastest of the ships available to help was the *Juno*, the same cruiser that had passed over the U-20 earlier in the day. She had space for all the survivors and was capable of reaching them in little more than an hour. But she was ordered back to port almost as soon as she set out. The Admiralty, after experiencing some dreadful calamities, had forbidden large warships to go to the assistance of vessels attacked by submarines. This removed the danger of their being sunk upon arrival by U-boats lying in ambush. But with the *Juno* out of the picture, only an odd assortment of fishing boats and other small craft were on their way to the *Lusitania*. It took most of them nearly three hours to reach the scene. By then a thousand people were dead.

The aftermath was both ugly and mysterious. Awkward questions arose.

Why had Turner not been instructed to approach Liverpool via the North Channel, which separated Ireland from Scotland, had recently been opened for use by commercial ships, and was known to be much safer than Ireland's south coast? Even Schwieger had written in his log that the fact that the *Lusitania* "was not sent through the North Channel is inexplicable."

Why had Turner not been sent more detailed information—information that the Admiralty possessed—about the threat that the U-20 posed? Schwieger had sunk three ships the day before the *Lusitania* crossed his path, and had done so in waters through which the liner would soon be passing. Turner might have taken a different course, or increased his speed, if the Admiralty had told him more.

Why had none of the destroyers and torpedo boats in the vicinity been sent to guard the *Lusitania* as she approached serious danger? This was standard practice. Perhaps six hours before the U-20's attack, actually, the chairman of the Cunard Line, owner of the *Lusitania*, was so alarmed upon learning of the previous day's sinkings off the coast of Cork that he hurried from his breakfast table to see the senior naval officer at Liverpool. He implored him to send protection and departed believing that this was going to be done. He knew that four destroyers were within reach, along with high-speed torpedo boats. Any one of them probably would have been sufficient to put a submarine to flight.

Shamefully, First Lord of the Admiralty Churchill and First Sea Lord John Fisher decided to pin the blame on Turner. The director of the Admiralty's trade division joined them, declaring that Turner "appears to have displayed an almost inconceivable negligence, and one is forced to conclude that he is either utterly incompetent, or that he has been got at by the Germans." They were foiled when a formal inquiry, which at their insistence had been conducted in unprecedented secrecy, refused to cooperate and instead ruled that Turner was in no way responsible for the tragedy.

Questions remain to this day. What was the cause of the second explosion? Inevitably, Schwieger was accused of having fired a second, murderously gratuitous, torpedo. Thanks partly to its monitoring of U-boat wireless transmissions, the Admiralty knew by the time of the inquiry that there had been no second torpedo, though it kept its knowledge secret.

Possibly it was coal dust, stirred up by the first explosion in the ship's huge and, at voyage's end, nearly empty storage bunkers.

Possibly it was something in the cargo hold. Attention has focused on fifty barrels and ninety-four cases of aluminum powder and fifty cases of bronze powder, en route to England for use in the production of munitions. One theory is that the detonation of these extremely volatile substances blew a hole in the bottom of the *Lusitania* and so caused her to sink as swiftly as she did. This hypothesis cannot be tested, because the wreck lies bottom-down on the seafloor, leaning to starboard and concealing her secrets beneath her.

Was the *Lusitania,* designed for service as an auxiliary cruiser in wartime, equipped with artillery at the time she was sunk? Apparently not; she had been deemed too expensive for military use, burning a thousand tons of coal a day when under way. But why, then, would it later be learned that the British had dropped large numbers of depth charges to the bottom of the sea in an effort to demolish her remains? Was there evidence to be destroyed?

For weeks after the sinking, bodies washed up across a broad expanse of the Irish coast. Ultimately only 173 bodies were recovered, though presumed fatalities totaled 1,193. A corpse found on a beach on July 11 proved to be not from the *Lusitania* at all. It was the mortal remains of Leon C. Thrasher, the American engineer whose disappearance in the sinking of the *Falaba* had created such a stir in Washington more than three months before.

Almost from the start there were rumors that the British authorities had intentionally sacrificed the *Lusitania* in hopes of bringing an outraged United States into the war. Churchill, for one, is on record as hoping for a crisis of exactly that kind. But conspiracy theories are inevitable in such situations, and deserve to be met with the firmest skepticism.

Still . . . questions linger.

Among the doubters was Patrick Beesly. He was a British naval intelligence officer who after leaving active service became a historian and author specializing in the Royal Navy's espionage operations during the Great War, including the secret monitoring of U-boat radio communications. What he had to say about the *Lusitania* near the end of his life is deserving of at least passing attention.

"On the basis of the considerable volume of information which is now available," he told an interviewer, "I am reluctantly compelled to state that on balance, the most likely explanation is that there was indeed a plot, however imperfect, to endanger the *Lusitania* in order to involve the United States in the war. If that's unacceptable, will someone tell me another explanation to these very curious circumstances."

Chapter 5

Marked Cards and a Stacked Deck

OVER THE HALF YEAR FROM SEPTEMBER 1915 TO FEBRUARY 1916, Secretary of State Lansing, hoping as always that the United States would enter the war but do so on legally unimpeachable grounds, had been trying to clear away the difficulties created by Britain's arming of her merchant ships and orders for them to attack any U-boats they could not escape. In January he took a new approach to the old idea of working out a compromise, proposing that Britain agree to disarm her merchantmen in return for a German return to cruiser rules. The president's enthusiastic response to what became known as Lansing's modus vivendi—he said that it had his "entire approval"—might have stemmed from the same thing that had motivated the secretary to suggest it: the expectation, the hope, that the Germans would refuse and by doing so put themselves irretrievably in the wrong. On the other hand, it is not inconceivable that Wilson agreed in good faith, thinking compromise still possible.

In any case it was the British who rejected the idea, and they did so indignantly. They claimed that the modus vivendi would doom their merchant fleet, adding, preposterously, that it showed the Wilson administration to be not neutral at all but pro-German. "I cannot adequately express the disappointment and dismay with which such an attitude on the part of the United States would be viewed here," Sir Edward Grey said in a wire to the State Department. House in a telegram told the president what he said at all such junctures: that pushing any initiative not acceptable to Britain would destroy all possibility of the United States being accepted as a mediator. Wilson responded as House hoped he would, immediately reversing himself and disavowing Lansing's plan.

Wilson scholar Arthur Link has argued that Lansing "blundered badly" in putting his proposed compromise forward. It is difficult to agree except by first accepting House's view that the United States should never attempt anything that Britain was not certain to approve. Be all that as it may, Lansing, like Bryan before him, was being given reasons to resent both House and the president himself. He would prove to have a less forgiving nature than Bryan.

On February 1, 1916, preparing to depart London for home, the colonel sent Wilson a message making clear that he regarded the complications created by the blockade not as a danger but as an opportunity. "I doubt whether a crisis with Germany can be long avoided," he wrote. "The petty annoyances of the blockade will make the demand imperative [by the German public] that an attempt be made to break it by the transcendent sea warfare. We will then be compelled to break relations." This was less a warning of possible trouble than a prescription for making it happen.

Shortly before departing, House received from Grey a written account of the understanding that the two of them had discussed in their latest conversations. This document, famous as the House-Grey Memorandum, took House up on his offer to call for a peace conference whenever the Allies wished. The colonel had been disappointed by Grey's failure, when the offer was first made, to respond with the expected enthusiasm. He had been slow to grasp just how unwilling the British were to discuss even a possible peace conference without an absolute American commitment to enter the war. And he appears to have been almost blind to the skill with which Grey managed, even when at his most receptive, to avoid committing Britain to do or not do any specific thing.

The understanding, as put in writing by Grey, was that if a conference were convened and "failed to secure peace, the United States would leave the conference as a belligerent on the side of the Allies, if Germany was unreasonable." The memo repeated what House had said about Alsace-Lorraine and Constantinople, and it ended by noting—a crucial addition—that Grey had not consulted with his own government or with France or Russia about these matters. This was a delicate way of stating for the record that the memo was nothing more than a summary of some friendly but unofficial talks between its author and Colonel House, and that the men whose approval would be required for implementation of the agreement were not even necessarily aware of it. House was pleased all the same. He thought that he and Grey had worked out a way of ensuring a satisfactory end to the war, eventually if not soon. Both men were playing an intricate double game. House was pretending to Grey that Wilson was ready to commit to war, and pretending to Wilson that the British were ready for serious negotiations. Eager to share the good news, the colonel took ship for home.

Late in January 1916 President Wilson sent war fever up a few degrees by departing on a nine-day speaking tour in support of the fast-growing Preparedness Movement, with its demands for expansion of the American armed forces. This was the latest of his recurrent efforts to go over Congress's head, in this case to mobilize public support for more military spending. When he returned to Washington and found that his tour had done nothing to soften congressional opposition, he washed his hands of the proposed Continental Army of reservists and left the preparedness issue to Congress. His secretary of war, the lawyer and former New Jersey judge Lindley M. Garrison, resigned in disgust, later calling Wilson a man of high ideals and no principles. The president had little reason to regret Garrison's departure. The secretary had made no secret of his desire not only for a bigger increase in military spending than Wilson was willing to propose, but also for conscription. This had made him a lightning rod for congressional opponents of both things and an excuse to distrust the administration. And he had always been less respectful of the chief executive than Wilson expected his lieutenants to be, even daring to interrupt the president during cabinet meetings. If Wilson might have benefited from having more such bold spirits around him, he himself certainly did not think so.

Next came a struggle over a measure called the Gore-McLemore bill, which called for American citizens to be warned about the dangers of traveling on belligerent ships. At the time of its introduction, the bill had broad support in both houses; Wilson, however, saw it as an affront to himself and a challenge to his right to make foreign policy unimpeded. He brought such hard pressure to bear on wavering Democrats that the bill was doomed to defeat. Its supporters were demoralized by being crushed in this way. The Allies were delighted, the Germans disgusted, to see the energy with which the White House had fought to block this small attempt to remove a source of serious diplomatic friction.

The bill's chief Senate sponsor, Thomas Gore of Oklahoma, was undeterred. A progressive powerhouse in spite of having been blind since childhood, he introduced bills to prohibit the government from issuing passports for travel on the ships of belligerent nations, to prevent such ships from carrying American citizens to or from U.S. ports, and to forbid U.S.-registered ships to carry munitions and passengers at the same time. All were smothered in committee, but the president was offended nonetheless. He was becoming increasingly sharp in his dealings with Congress, even with longtime allies when he judged them to be unsatisfactorily loyal. Senate Foreign Relations Committee chairman William Stone, who had given Wilson crucial support at the 1912 Democratic convention and afterward contributed greatly to the success of his legislative agenda, drew a barbed open letter from the president by making it known that he was skeptical about the administration's supposed neutrality and "more troubled than I have been in many a day."

"The honor and self-respect of the nation is involved," Wilson wrote. "We covet peace, and shall preserve it at any cost but the loss of honor. To forbid our people to exercise their rights for fear we might be called to vindicate them would be a deep humiliation indeed. Once accept a single abatement of right and many other humiliations would certainly follow and the whole fine fabric of international law might crumble under our hands." The letter appeared in newspapers across the country. The threat of war was unmistakable in its warning that when the rights of citizens were violated by acts like those of the German U-boats, "we should, it seems to me, have in honor no choice as to what our own course should be." The president was limiting Germany to the two options that House had always urged. She could accept his demands in full or face war with the United States.

Stone was not won over, and he was not the only senator who was showing uneasiness about the president's repeated invocation of "rights" that had never existed, and his apparent determination to raise a solvable dispute over naval tactics to a level so rarefied, even so spiritual, as to make compromise unthinkable. Most of the nations involved in the European death struggle had gone to war in the genuine belief that their survival depended on it. Others later entered the conflict because of what they thought they could gain from it. None had done so for something as diaphanous as the "honor" that Wilson was invoking.

The kaiser's government and military high command, meanwhile, were still struggling with the need to respond conclusively to Wilson's notes. On February 11, with the blockade now creating serious hardship for Germany's civilian population and Q-ships and the arming of British merchantmen making U-boat operations almost impossibly dangerous, Berlin announced that, as of the end of the month, all armed enemy ships would be dealt with as warships. Passenger liners, even the biggest, would no longer be exempt. Army

Chief of Staff Falkenhayn, who previously had been unwilling to provoke the United States because "our situation is so serious that it would be irresponsible to make it worse," had by this time swung around to support Tirpitz and the other naval chiefs. This simplified the dispute: now it was a contest between the men in uniform on one side and Chancellor Bethmann and a few other members of the civil government on the other, with a distressed Kaiser Wilhelm holding the deciding vote but reluctant to cast it in the absence of consensus.

The new submarine rules compromised, if they did not altogether disavow, Germany's *Arabic* pledge. In Washington there was much uncertainty about how to respond. The Foreign Ministry in Berlin sent Secretary Lansing an attempted explanation, saying that the change in policy was necessary because "a submarine commander cannot possibly warn an enemy liner, if the liner has the right to fire on the submarine." The White House made no comment when the story broke in the newspapers. Editorial coverage was muted, and the public, beginning to have some awareness of the more questionable aspects of British policy, reacted calmly. Even the strongly pro-Entente and pro-Wilson *New York World*, perhaps assuming that silence from the White House indicated acceptance of what Germany was doing, editorialized that "nobody ever held that a merchantman could attack anything without becoming a ship of war or possibly a pirate, thus losing its character and immunity as a merchantman."

But Wilson's silence did not mean assent. He had simply gone off for a cruise on the presidential yacht, and upon returning he hastened to make clear that he accepted nothing. On February 15, on the president's instructions, the State Department issued a statement totally at odds with the positions Secretary Lansing had taken earlier. It declared that in arming her merchant ships Britain was acting in full accord with international law, and that U-boats were obliged to observe cruiser rules even if doing so put them in mortal danger. It repeated the president's long-standing insistence that Americans had an unqualified right to travel on armed belligerent ships and be safe in doing so. The questions of people like Senator Gore, who was echoing William Jennings Bryan by asking whether "a single citizen should be allowed to run the risk of drenching this nation in blood merely in order that he may travel upon a belligerent rather than a neutral vessel," were ignored by the White House and its friends.

In Washington, a distraught Ambassador Bernstorff showed Lansing an article in which a legal authority pronounced that armed merchant ships "according to international law cease to be peaceful trading ships." With escalating urgency, the ambassador was continuing to warn Berlin that another disaster on the scale of the *Lusitania* would bring the United States into the war. This strengthened Bethmann's hand, Kaiser Wilhelm being still deeply fearful of antagonizing the United States, but the military and naval authorities argued that unrestricted submarine operations could win the war while failure to permit such operations would lead inexorably to a slow and agonizing defeat. In March, after days of heated discussion, Bernstorff persuaded the kaiser to refuse the navy's demands to lift the remaining restrictions on submarine operations. Tirpitz's resignation followed.

President Wilson, when House returned from London and presented the House-Grey Memorandum like a trophy, shared his friend's pleasure over what appeared to be a great achievement. He accepted the memorandum, House told his diary, in toto. This was not quite true; the president made one small change, the insertion of a single adverb. Once this was done, the memorandum no longer said that if a peace conference were arranged and the results did not satisfy the Allies, the United States would "leave the conference as a belligerent on the side of the Allies." It said instead that America would *probably* leave et cetera. Much has been made of this by some historians, who claim that it made the memorandum a fatally defective instrument in the eyes of Edward Grey. But in fact it was a simple acknowledgment that only Congress can declare war. Grey was too knowledgeable not to understand that.

What surprises is that Wilson appears to have raised no other questions about what was in its essence a profoundly cynical, fundamentally dishonorable scheme for drawing the German government into a diplomatic game in which the deck would be stacked and the cards marked. House and Grey had even agreed that, whenever the United States issued its summons to a conference, it would attempt to ensure German acceptance by telling Berlin, falsely and in feigned confidence, that the British were going to make themselves guilty in the eyes of the world by refusing to participate.

The new trouble that Bernstorff feared and House evidently hoped for was not long in coming. On March 19 a U-boat fired a torpedo into a French-owned cross-channel ferry called the *Sussex*. Once again the circumstances were ambiguous: the *Sussex* was painted black instead of marked as ferries usually were, and it was not within the lanes usually reserved for passenger ships. The submarine commander would say that the vessel he saw in his periscope appeared to be a minelayer. It was not sunk but badly damaged, and though none of the Americans aboard were killed, several, perhaps four, were injured.

Compared to the *Lusitania*, and especially in terms of American interests, this incident was trivial. The president nevertheless reacted wrathfully. Cynics might say that he had been waiting for an excuse to become furious and was prepared to clutch at a straw if nothing more substantial came along. Admirers say that this was the moment when a strong and principled president proved himself capable, under the most trying circumstances, of standing firm for what he knew to be right.

Wilson waited for confirmation that the *Sussex* had been sunk by a submarine and not a mine. Then, satisfied on that score, on April 6 he had House cable Sir Edward Grey and request immediate implementation of the House-Grey Memorandum. Such an oblique approach was necessary, the colonel told Grey, because "we are not so sure of the support of the American people upon the submarine issue, while we are convinced that they would respond to the higher and nobler issue of stopping the war."

House would have been appalled to witness what Grey did with his request. He put it before Prime Minister Asquith and his War Committee but said he was doing so out of a sense of obligation, not because he recommended approval. The committee members gave it a cold reception. Arthur Balfour, himself a former prime minister and future foreign secretary, declared it "not worth five minutes' thought." Edwin Montagu, a junior member of the government but one who had the ear of Prime Minister Asquith, called House's scheme so dishonest, so bizarrely unfair to Germany, as to raise the question of whether some hidden agenda lay behind it—some inscrutable American plot. Even Ambassador Page, whose driving objective was to help get the United States into the war, described it disapprovingly as a "carefully sprung trap"—something that, by implication, had no place in responsible statecraft. When Asquith said he could see no reason to proceed, the matter was settled. Grey did not go into any of this in replying to House's request. He said only that Britain was not ready to act.

Wilson withdrew into solitude. Instead of seeking counsel, he spent three days pecking at his typewriter, drafting and polishing an ultimatum for the Germans. It demanded that Germany recognize the right of American citizens to travel in safety on the ships of nations at war, and that it abandon its U-boat campaign or face a severing of relations. It invoked, in terms by now familiar to Berlin, "sacred and indisputable rules of international law and the universally recognized dictates of humanity."

For one nation to present another with an ultimatum is a grave insult. The grounds for Wilson's ultimatum being as questionable as they were, it seemed improbable that Germany would submit. That the ultimatum all but committed the United States to enter the war on the side of the Entente without requiring anything of the Entente troubled even House, not so much on moral or ethical grounds as because Wilson was not using his leverage with the Allies, above all the urgency with which they wanted the United States in the war, to extract concessions and assert American authority.

But it was sent. When on May 15 Ambassador Gerard presented it to the German authorities, Foreign Minister Jagow laughed sourly. "Right of free travel on the seas?" he said. "Why not right of free travel on land in war territory?"

"They mocked at us when we gave warning," said a Frankfurt newspaper. "Let them turn to those who committed the crime of allowing passengers on a war vessel."

It was not necessary to be German or pro-German to find the White House's position incomprehensible. The American Alan Seeger, whose poem "I Have a Rendezvous with Death" would become one of the most famous of the war, was one of thousands of Americans serving in the trenches as a volunteer member of the French army. In April 1916 he was only weeks from being killed in combat. "I cannot understand the American state of mind," he wrote, "nor why Americans have the temerity to venture into a declared war-zone, much less let their wives and children go there, when anyone with a grain of sense might have foreseen what has happened. They might just as well come over here and go out Maying in front of our barbed wire."

In New York, in this same month, the preparedness people organized a parade that an approving *New York Times* described as "the greatest civilian marching demonstration in the history of the world." More than a hundred thousand people paraded past a reviewing stand that itself seated nine thousand. Fever was again building.

In the end it was not Woodrow Wilson who kept the United States out of war that spring but Imperial Germany. She did so, to the relief of many Americans and the teeth-grinding exasperation of some, by submitting to demands that her government and public regarded as humiliatingly unfair. Berlin announced, after another painful struggle between the civil and military leaders, that henceforth the U-boats would observe cruiser rules at all times. This meant a sharp curtailment of submarine operations and greatly increased risk for the submariners. It amounted to a surrender of what the Germans had claimed (and the law of the sea recognized) as their rightful response to the Entente's blockade. This was a gigantic concession, as they saw it.

They were making this concession, their note said, out of a willingness "to go [to] the utmost limit" to restore amicable relations with the United States. "The German Government must repeat once more," it said, "that it was not the Germans but the British Government which, ignoring all the accepted principles of international law, has extended this terrible war to the lives and property of noncombatants."

This concession was the work of one man, Chancellor Theobald von Bethmann-Hollweg. It could not have happened if he had not taken seriously Ambassador Bernstorff's warnings from Washington and had not agreed that American entry into the war would have terrible consequences for Germany. It was he who persuaded a frightened and irresolute Kaiser Wilhelm that humiliation was a price that had to be paid, but even at the moment of success he found himself isolated. He had almost no allies in the upper reaches of the imperial government except Foreign Minister Gottlieb von Jagow, a diminutive and rather timorous career diplomat who had never wanted the post he now held and was held in contempt by the military leaders.

Bethmann's stubbornness made him, too, a fool and a weakling in the eyes of the advocates of unrestricted submarine warfare. Obviously he was neither, or he could not have stood almost alone as long as he did. But behind his intelligence, persistence, and common sense, there lay only ordinary political and diplomatic gifts. Under the imperial system put in place by Otto von Bismarck at the time of German unification, the chancellor or chief minister was chosen by the kaiser alone. So were all other government ministers; the legislature was not even consulted. Unlike the heads of government in Britain and France, therefore, the chancellors who came after Bismarck did not win high office on the field of political combat, did not have their own sources of support, but instead were creatures of their emperor. The tall, bearded, rather saturnine-looking Bethmann was no exception. Approaching his sixtieth birthday at the time of the *Arabic* crisis, son of a modestly distinguished Prussian family, he was not a politician at all, really, but a career civil servant. He understood that he was free to make policy only to the extent that the mercurial, neurotically insecure Kaiser Wilhelm allowed. His victory over the men in uniform, he knew well, was by no means a permanent one.

The imposition of cruiser rules was of course a boon for Britain, giving her increasingly well-armed merchant fleet an overwhelming advantage in encounters with submarines. But it was also a disappointment and therefore nothing to be celebrated. It was not cruiser rules that London had wanted but an American declaration of war. That remained the overriding objective of the Foreign Office.

For the Wilson administration, Germany's submission was a resounding diplomatic victory, a triumph, a keeping of the peace on terms that upheld the nation's honor as the president himself defined it. It was all these things in spite of Lansing's complaint about what he thought the "decidedly insolent tone" of the German note. But it was not an unconditional victory: the note contained a qualification. "Neutrals cannot expect," it stated, "that Germany . . . shall for the sake of neutral interest restrict the use of an effective weapon if her enemy is permitted to continue to apply at will methods of war violating the rules of international law." In an attempt to conclude on a positive note, it added that "the German Government is confident" that Washington "will now demand and insist that the British Government shall forthwith observe the rules" embedded in the Declaration of London.

Germany expected, in a word, reciprocity. In return for yielding to what they believed to be unjustified demands, the Germans expected—and could hardly have been more explicit about expecting—that the United States would use its influence to end or at least alter the blockade. Bernstorff from Washington had encouraged Bethmann to believe that this would happen, and Bethmann had encouraged the kaiser to believe it as well. The generals and admirals were skeptical; they made it clear that, if it did not happen, they would be demanding the removal of restrictions. Bethmann took pains to make clear to Washington, through Bernstorff, that if nothing was done about the blockade the consequences were likely to be serious. That for Berlin, this was a matter of the highest importance.

President Wilson did not take it seriously at all. In his next note he informed Berlin that the actions of Great Britain had no relevance to the questions that divided Germany and the United States. He was satisfied that the Germans had signed what he called a "Sussex pledge," that it bound them to observe cruiser rules when intercepting merchantmen and not to attack passenger ships at all, and (what would matter most in the end) that it was irrevocable.

Colonel House was no less disappointed than the British. Two days after Berlin's submission, using almost the same words he had used to express his regret that the *Lusitania* crisis had not ended in intervention, he wrote mournfully to the president that "I cannot see how we can break with Germany on this note." It is impossible not to read this as confirmation that he had been hoping for a severing of relations. It confirms also that, if Wilson had not shared this hope, the colonel certainly *thought* he had.

On May 27, with the spring of 1916 fully in bloom, Wilson traveled to New York and delivered to a recently formed group called the League to Enforce Peace a speech in which he called, for the first time, for the creation of an organization of the world's nations the main purpose of which would be the prevention of future wars. This was in no way a new idea. It was the avowed purpose of the organization whose members Wilson was addressing; thus the group's name. In fact, the idea of a global peacekeeping organization had been suggested by Theodore Roosevelt when he accepted the Nobel Peace Prize in 1910, and TR had proposed it again in a magazine article of September 1914. It had been taken up by Senator Henry Cabot Lodge and other prominent figures, but until Wilson's speech it had never been advocated by a serving president. The speech has been described as marking the end of America's traditional isolationism. If that is an exaggeration, the president's focus on the subject does mark the start of a new stage in his determination to make Europe's tragedy the means to a noble end. He and his audience understood that nothing of the kind was going to be possible until the war was brought to an end.

The War Department now had a new chief, the physically diminutive, brilliantly able Newton D. Baker. A onetime protégé of doctoral candidate Woodrow Wilson's at Johns Hopkins University—the two became friends while living in the same boardinghouse—and former progressive mayor of Cleveland, Baker had a qualification seldom found among cabinet officers: he did not want the job and tried to resist the president's insistence that he had a duty to take it. (His reluctance was a repeat. In 1913 he had refused appointment as secretary of the interior, being committed at the time to completing a reform of Cleveland's municipal government.) He was much less abrasive than his predecessor as secretary of war, Lindley Garrison. Though so unimpressed with the military as to be sometimes mistaken for a pacifist, he raised no objections when, in June 1916 and mainly in response to Pancho Villa's border rampage, the efforts of the Preparedness Movement led to the passage of a National Defense Act.

This measure provided for an increase of the regular army to a total of some 175,000 men over the next five years, and of the National Guard to 450,000 within six years. For the first time, National Guardsmen would take an oath of loyalty to the federal government as well as to their home states, and they could be summoned to active duty by the president in times of war or emergency. Wilson called up a hundred thousand Guardsmen to seal the border with Mexico.

Newton Baker, U.S. secretary of war, 1916–1921
An effective secretary of war who didn't want the job.

In Europe, where a hundred thousand troops were almost a triviality, 1916 was turning into a year of catastrophes for the Entente and the Central Powers alike. In January the Entente nations—now known in the American press by the friendlier term "the Allies," and to be referred to as such hereafter—abandoned their disastrously unsuccessful Gallipoli campaign. This had been an attempt to bypass the deadlocked Eastern and Western Fronts by capturing Constantinople, the capital of the Ottoman Empire, which had more or less blundered into the war on Germany's side late in 1914. The failure cost more than forty thousand Allied lives, not only British and French but Australian and New Zealander and others. Some eighty thousand Turks died stopping them. The architect of the campaign, First Lord of the Admiralty Churchill, lost his job.

In February the Germans launched an offensive against the mighty network of fortifications centered on Verdun in eastern France. This turned into one of the most nightmarish battles in history. The German plan was to capture Verdun in an initial assault of overwhelming force, dig in, and allow France to exhaust herself in futile counteroffensives. As usual in war, the plan did not survive its first contact with reality. The opening attack failed to take Verdun, but the Germans were undeterred and prepared to try again. The ensuing bloodbath would go on almost to the end of the year, claiming somewhere in the neighborhood of three hundred thousand lives and turning a huge expanse of French territory into a moonscape.

March brought the Fifth Battle of the Isonzo, barely four months after the fourth bloody conflict of that name. Like its predecessors, it pitted Austro-Hungarian troops against Italians in the Julian Alps of what is now Slovenia. The Italian government, in one of the most cold-bloodedly cynical acts of the war, had in 1915 joined the Entente in return for secret promises of territorial gains. As a result, an atrociously ill-led Italian army was now in a deadlocked struggle with the demoralized forces of Vienna and paying a grievous price for the politicians' dark bargain. Eventually there would be twelve (some say eleven, some only ten) Isonzo battles. As many as three hundred thousand Italian soldiers would perish in them.

Already in preparation was the Battle of the Somme, which the British general staff intended to be the great hammer blow that would smash open the Western Front and send the Germans reeling back to the Rhine. It would be another debacle. On the first day of the attack, July 1, almost twenty thousand British troops would die advancing on German machine guns. Another thirty thousand would be wounded that day. Those who were not cut down succeeded in pushing the defenders back a single mile along a three-and-a-half-mile stretch of front. This achievement, paltry though it was, exceeded what any other British offensive had accomplished since the opposing forces had first dug their trenches a year and a half earlier. The Somme, like Verdun, would go on into winter, the generals continuing to believe that one more effusion of blood would make the difference. As with all the most terrible battles of the Great War, the exact cost in lives will never be known. It is accepted, however, that more than six hundred thousand British, French, Australian, New Zealander, and South African troops were killed, wounded, or captured on the Somme front in 1916, and that German casualties approached half a million.

Equal in scale to all this was the slaughter on the Eastern Front, where the Germans would soon take Warsaw in their drive to expel the Russians from Poland. The unthinkable scale of the carnage on every front was creating bitter hatred among the civilian populations. Every belligerent nation saw itself as an aggrieved victim, and believed that its enemies were intent not just on its defeat but on its destruction. On the Allied side, particularly among the French, there was a belief that never again would any of them be able to make war on Germany with so many other countries on their side, and that this unique opportunity must not be thrown away with a peace short of victory. There was a universal hunger for retribution, and public hostility to any peace that would not bring vengeance down on the heads of the villains. Out of such feelings would come another, even bigger world cataclysm a short generation later.

Anyone wanting to argue that civilization itself was beginning to buckle under the strain did not have to look far for evidence. Technology far more terrible than ships that traveled underwater was newly available, and sooner or later all of it got used. The Germans introduced poison gas at Ypres in Belgium in April 1915, the British followed suit at Loos in September of the same year, and in short order both sides were making regular use of increasingly deadly concoctions. Before the end of 1914, Britain and France were using their primitive aircraft for bombing raids on Germany, and in January 1915 the Germans began sending Zeppelin airships across the Channel to bomb England. Both sides were after military targets, supposedly, but accuracy was unachievable and the inevitable civilian deaths deterred neither side. Eventually it would dawn on the planners that the intentional bombing of civilians might serve useful purposes. Step by ugly step, nations that had long prided themselves on being the most civilized in the world were sinking into barbarism.

Fighting continued in North America, too, but on a distinctly miniature scale. The Mexican rebels had forced the brutal and corrupt Huerta to flee to Spain; he was succeeded as president by Venustiano Carranza, a democrat and reformer. The civil war continued, however, and in its desperate search for a settlement, the United States invited Argentina, Brazil, and Colombia to send representatives to Niagara Falls to help work out a solution. The resulting ABC Conference called for a national election, the interim recognition of Carranza, and the retirement to the United States of the man who was now the chief troublemaker, the bandit-general Pancho Villa.

Villa and his guerrillas did not find these plans acceptable. To discredit the conference and precipitate a new and bigger Yankee intervention, thereby inflaming Mexican public opinion against the United States, they killed dozens of American citizens in a train robbery and an audacious dawn raid on Columbus, New Mexico. A force of some seven thousand U.S. cavalry was sent across the border with orders not to conquer or occupy anything but to pursue and disperse the *Villistas*. The expedition was led by a one-star general out of West Point named John Pershing. Its failure to accomplish anything was made inevitable, much to Pershing's disgust, by the limitations placed on his operations by a White House that was increasingly focused on Europe and wanted as little trouble with Mexico as possible.

These were good times for the United States all the same, and for President Wilson. The country had never been as prosperous as it was now, with fortunes being made in sales to the Allies. The iron and steel industry was typical. Its exports, which generated revenues of $251 million in 1914, soon began rising at a rate that would pass the $600 million mark in 1916 and hit $1.1 billion in 1917. Profits rose even faster: $203 million representing a margin of 7.4 percent in 1915; $634 million and 21.3 percent in 1916; $1 billion and 28.7 percent in 1917. Farmers were prospering, too, and workers found jobs plentiful.

This was good news for an administration that would be going before the electorate in another six months. What was even better, from a personal perspective, the president was blissfully remarried. In December 1915, less than a year and a half after the death of Ellen Axson Wilson, he had wed a forty-three-year-old Washington widow named Edith White Bolling Galt, whom he had courted with an ardor that few adolescents could have surpassed. While courting her, he wrote to her almost every day, sometimes more than once a day in spite of seeing her almost daily also. "Oh, dear kindred spirit, my sweet incomparable friend," he would write. Followed, almost before the first letter could be delivered, by "Ah, my precious friend and comrade, what happiness it was to be with you last night."

Once he had persuaded the lady to become his wife, the former Mrs. Galt devoted herself to Wilson with a commitment equal to Ellen's and a jealous ferocity of which the gentle Ellen would never have been capable. That the president's three daughters were unreservedly in favor of the match testifies to

Edith and
Woodrow Wilson
*The president's
second marriage was
supremely happy.*

Edith's great charm and their understanding of how urgently their father needed a helpmeet.

The bride, like the president, had been born in Virginia—and was, remarkably enough, a descendant of Pocahontas. Her family, for generations part of the southern planter elite, had been ruined by the Civil War. Edith had been rescued from penury by marriage, cordial enough though evidently somewhat loveless on her side, to a successful Washington jeweler some years her senior. Their only child died in infancy, the father in 1908. In some ways she was a surprising choice for Wilson, having had only a few years of formal schooling and virtually no exposure to the world of ideas and great public issues. But her new husband could not endure life without a confidante who adored him unreservedly, and his connection to Colonel House (who continued to keep away from Washington except when invited by the president) was becoming frayed under the pressures of an uncertain neutrality.

Almost from the start of their relationship (they were introduced by a friend concerned about the president's psychological state in the aftermath of Ellen's death), Wilson confided in Edith about matters large and small. She was taught how to decode secret cables, embraced that as one of her domestic duties, and appears to have taken an almost instant dislike to Colonel House. She saw him as a yes-man, not understanding that his willingness to be exactly that was the foundation of his relationship with the president. She may have regarded him as a rival for her husband's affection and trust. House praised her extravagantly, both to her face and to the president, but to no avail. Considering the intensity of the first years of their relationship, it comes as a surprise to find the president writing to Edith that House's "mind is not of the first class. He is a counselor, not a statesman." Obviously this was also an oblique way for Wilson to let his bride know that he, on the other hand, *was* the real thing.

With Berlin's retreat, relations between Germany and the United States entered a less turbulent period. Bethmann, in spite of having been given no encouragement by the White House or the State Department, waited in nervous hopefulness for some indication that the president was now going to do something about the blockade. He was keenly aware that if nothing of the kind happened, and fairly soon, the kaiser's military and naval chiefs would be resuming their demands for a lifting of U-boat restrictions. The American interventionists, meanwhile, waited expectantly for another *Lusitania* crisis.

Britain's relations with the United States entered a prickly new phase at this point, mainly because of new naval initiatives. Wilson and the public reacted angrily when it became known that the British were opening mail on neutral ships intercepted on the high seas. Indignation became outrage with the coming to light of a British blacklist: hundreds of American companies had been banned from doing business with the Allies because London suspected them of selling to the Central Powers. Washington protested, but not really sharply or to any effect.

Then came the Easter Rising, a revolt against British rule of Ireland. It was a smallish affair, led by poets and teachers who knew that it had no chance of success, and it was not popular with the Irish public. But the savage response of the British authorities—much of central Dublin went up in flames, troops broke in to the homes of innocent civilians and shot them in cold blood, and among the killed were some forty children—transformed public opinion in Ireland and awoke the world to the realities of British rule. The hurried and secretive execution of the ringleaders in spite of appeals from America and elsewhere (the U.S. Senate approved an appeal for clemency while the White House remained silent) brought the tragedy to a close. The bitterness engendered both in Ireland and among Irish-Americans, however, led in short order to a bigger and bloodier rebellion and to the creation of an independent Irish republic. It also encouraged independence movements in other parts of the empire.

In the short term, the rising cast a shadow over Allied claims to be waging a war against tyranny. As an embarrassment, it surpassed the presence of Tsar Nicholas II's Russia among the supposedly freedom-loving Allied powers. Revulsion was so powerful in the United States that the interventionists were for a brief period silenced. Bellicose figures as prominent as Roosevelt found themselves in danger of being discredited. Britain nevertheless continued to do as she wished and to bridle when anyone complained. "How difficult it is," Wilson observed, "to be friends with Great Britain without doing whatever it is she wants us to do." In a letter to House he said, "I am, I must admit, about at the end of my patience with Great Britain and the Allies. This blacklist business is the last straw." He told the colonel that he was "seriously considering a ban on loans to the Entente, and a restriction of exports." That he was serious about this is unlikely. Any such steps would have generated economic shock waves, hazardous things in an election year. And if Wilson really wanted to restrain the British, why did he ignore appeals from neutral nations as substantial as Sweden and Holland to join with them in pressuring London to change?

The election, as it drew near, became a convenient excuse for White House inaction on the blockade. Taking as usual the rhetorical high road, Wilson said he wanted to make no new commitments until it was known whether he or his Republican opponent, Charles Evans Hughes, would be setting policy in 1917. In response to Bethmann's demands for an explanation of why nothing was happening, Bernstorff could reply only that no action could be expected until after the election.

At some point in the autumn of 1916, during this period of pre-election diplomatic passivity, Wilson dictated to a stenographer a lengthy rumination about why the war should not end in a decisive victory for either side. His words are uniquely revealing of where he stood on the day he spoke them, and they are impressively perceptive. At their core was an understanding of how the Europeans—France and Germany in particular—had for generations been locked in a cycle in which every conflict left the losing side aggrieved and determined to take revenge. Wilson thought that the horrors of the current war, by exposing the futility of that cycle, might destroy the appetite for war. This could happen, however, only if neither side achieved a decisive victory.

"The aim of far-sighted statesmen," he mused, "should be to make of this mightiest of conflicts an object lesson for the future by bringing it to a close with the objects of each group of belligerents still unaccomplished and all the magnificent sacrifices on both sides gone for naught. Only then would the Europeans see the futility of using war as a means of attaining national ambitions. The world would be free to build its new peace structure on the solidest foundation it has ever possessed."

These words were not published and never used in a speech. In the run-up to the election they would have been dangerously controversial, angering pro-intervention voters and organizations. Three months after the election the president's thinking would be so radically changed as to make them irrelevant.

Background

Choosing Sides

Alexis de Tocqueville, in his classic *Democracy in America,* made note of what he thought the peculiarly strong tendency of the people of the United States to organize themselves into groups. This was in the 1830s, but the tendency had lost none of its potency eighty years later. The United States in the Great War years was a hodgepodge of fraternal organizations, political clubs, associations of farmers and tradesmen, and societies devoted to everything from quilting to the abolition of saloons. Tocqueville would have found it more of the same.

There were American antiwar organizations even before the war in Europe began. Among them was the Anti-Imperialist League, formed in 1898 to oppose American annexation of the Philippines. It made a national figure of Jane Addams, who over the next decade and a half campaigned for pacifism, woman suffrage, and attention to the plight of the urban poor. Within weeks of the start of the world war, she was at it again, helping to establish a Woman's Peace Party (WPP) and becoming notorious in the process. When she appeared at Carnegie Hall to speak in defense of pacifism, *The New York Times* damned her as unpatriotic.

The Woman's Peace Party was quick to make itself felt. Many of its members came like Addams out of the woman suffrage movement. They had experience in organizing as a result and were connected to a national network of tens of thousands of politically active kindred spirits. Not all suffragettes opposed the war, but most of those who did followed Addams when she led the WPP into a broad-based alliance called the Emergency Peace Federation. This was an umbrella group created to enable a variety of organizations (civic, religious, political, labor) to work together for the one objective they had in common: stopping the United States from intervening in the war. The "emergency" to which the title referred was members' perception that intervention was a very real possibility and would be a calamity.

To every action there is an equal and opposite reaction, and before 1914 ended, the Emergency Peace Federation met its answer in the new National Security League. It had an impeccable pedigree, the guiding spirit in its creation being Congressman Augustus Peabody Gardner, who in addition to being a scion of two of Boston's Brahmin families was the son-in-law of one of the Republican Party's most powerful figures, Senator Henry Cabot Lodge. Its roster was studded with such eminent Americans as former secretary of war and secretary of state Elihu Root and Major General Leonard Wood, a former army chief of staff and still the nation's best-known soldier. Its governing committee included prominent educators and industrial and banking magnates.

It professed to be nonpartisan and struggled to be so in its first years. It became a driving force behind the Preparedness Movement and the campaign for an amorphous, never-quite-defined thing called "One Hundred Percent Americanism." Ultimately, it went to extremes that demonstrated just how completely war fever could consume even the most sophisticated elements of society. It opposed the teaching of foreign languages, mainly but not only German. It questioned the loyalty of labor unions, universities, the churches of German-Americans, and, later, the League of Women Voters. From 1915 to 1917 it received contributions of a quarter of a million dollars (only about fifty thousand dollars less than the army's annual budget at the time), much of it donated by such families as the Morgans, du Ponts, and Guggenheims, many of whom were profiting handsomely from the war.

The pendulum continued to swing, and late in 1915 another anti-intervention group came into existence and quickly achieved high visibility. The American Union Against Militarism (AUAM), based in New York, had the advantage of representing the pacifist and antiwar elements of the country's more respectable classes and interest groups. It, too, drew funding from wealthy families—Philadelphia Quakers, for example—and was able to maintain a full-time staff with satellite operations in twenty-one cities. Its members and sympathizers were largely from the elite strata: lawyers, clergymen, editors, and products of the Ivy League. This had disadvantages. Though the AUAM sought to collaborate with groups representing working people, farmers, socialists, and anyone else opposed to intervention, the roughhewn populists of the South and the prairie states and the embattled workers of urban America viewed them warily from across a yawning class divide. This was a small problem, however, in comparison with the increasingly virulent criticism to which all the antiwar groups found themselves subjected.

The Emergency Peace Federation, being more militant than the AUAM and more closely linked to radical unions and socialist organizations, became an early target. It was harassed so relentlessly by local law enforcement and spontaneously formed patriotic groups that it had difficulty holding meetings. Demonstrations became nearly impossible. The AUAM, with its social connections and less provocative tactics, had fewer difficulties of this kind.

The tensions of the time deepened old divisions in American society and opened new ones that spread in all directions. The difficulties of trying to be nonpartisan finally broke the National Security League apart. Many members and potential members felt that it was not sufficiently critical of the Wilson administration and not sufficiently zealous in preaching intervention. In 1915 these dissidents created their own organization, the American Defense Society (ADS). It was like the league, only vehemently more so. It demanded compulsory military training for every American male between the ages of eighteen and twenty-one, the internment of "enemy" aliens and their sympathizers, the exclusion of socialists from the nation's political life, and intervention to be followed by total victory over Germany without possibility of a negotiated settlement. It was as well connected as the league; Theodore Roosevelt became honorary president.

The ADS went beyond depicting the Berlin regime as evil—it encouraged almost every variety of anti-German hysteria and did so with the implied approval of President Wilson. Actually, if German-Americans were notable for anything by 1915, it was for political invisibility. Few of those who hoped for a German victory in the war, or even regretted the hostility toward Germany that increasingly pervaded the country, were willing to say anything that might attract attention. But Wilson was saying, when the war was barely a year old, "I am sure that the country is honeycombed with German intrigue and infested with German spies." Three months later he used his State of the Union speech as a platform from which to complain that "there are citizens of the United States, I blush to admit, born under other flags but welcomed under our generous naturalization laws to the full freedom and opportunity of America, who have poured the poison of disloyalty into the very arteries of our national life; who have sought to bring the authority and good name of our Government into contempt, to destroy our industries wherever they thought it effective for their vindictive purposes to strike at them, and to debase our politics to the uses of foreign intrigue."

Small wonder if patriotic citizens took alarm at hearing their president utter such words and accepted it as their duty to keep suspicious eyes on neighbors lacking English-sounding names. Or if large numbers of German-Americans quietly gave their support to Republican Charles Evans Hughes in the 1916 presidential election, in the process getting Hughes himself accused by zealous Democrats of being the tool of Germany.

The most respectable of the pro-preparedness organizations, one whose legitimacy was beyond question, came into existence when the army appropriations bill for fiscal year 1916 provided the handsome sum of two hundred thousand dollars for a Council of National Defense. Its chairman was the secretary of war, Newton Baker, and it also included the secretary of the navy and the heads of the Interior, Agriculture, Commerce, and Labor Departments. They were joined by leading figures from industry and finance, along with Samuel Gompers of the American Federation of Labor. The council's mission was unarguably sensible: to develop new means of coordinating government, business, agriculture, labor, and national transportation so that all systems could work together in an effective national defense. Even so there were problems. Some conservatives fretted that systematic mobilization of the nation's resources would lead to socialism—to the subordination of the economy to the government. The progressives, inclined as they were to see an active government as the solution to problems of many kinds, had few such qualms.

Chapter 6

"A Dangerous Thing—To Inflame a People"

ACROSS GERMANY AND THE AUSTRO-HUNGARIAN DOMAINS, THE starvation blockade was earning its name. The population was hungry, much of it desperately so. Food riots were becoming something that the authorities had to expect and prepare for.

In the prewar decades, as Germany industrialized, she like Britain had abandoned the thought of feeding herself. There seemed no point—or no possibility. In each of the two years preceding the start of the war, imports had exceeded exports by $640 million, much of the imbalance reflecting a dependence on foreign food and raw materials. Thus the effectiveness of the blockade. As early as the autumn of 1914, the Central Powers were experiencing their first shortages of flour and bread. By early 1915 milk and potatoes were in short supply. By 1916 it was difficult to obtain things ranging from oil and sugar to eggs and soap. By 1917 fat intake per person was 12 percent of what it had been in 1913, and the death rate for civilians was a third higher. A year after that the people of Germany would be living on an average of one thousand calories per day.

Thus the pressure on the Berlin government to *do* something.

The British chose the end of the summer of 1916 to announce the creation of a new government ministry with one responsibility only: to manage the blockade. They thereby demonstrated that they regarded their starvation policy not as an expedient open to negotiation but as integral to their strategy for winning the war. And deepened the anger of a hungry German public.

All this left Chancellor Bethmann in a bind. Germany's only way of responding to the public's anger was to intensify the U-boat campaign against the shipping that was keeping the British population fed. But to do that was to risk further conflict—ultimately war—with the United States. And Bethmann was more certain than ever that American intervention would bring disaster down on Germany.

The generals of the high command did not disagree with him about how America was likely to respond to a lifting of restrictions on submarine warfare, but they did not share his fears. They expected that even if she intervened, the United States would have limited ability to participate in the fighting and might do so with her navy only. She had no army worth speaking of and, if confronted with a fully effective U-boat force, might never get any troops across the Atlantic. And regardless of how dangerous the United States might be militarily, the submarines seemed the only way to save the Central Powers. Their unrestricted use was coming to seem not an option but a necessity, an inevitability.

General Erich von Falkenhayn, who had once supported Bethmann and would soon be replaced as army chief of staff because of the failure of his Verdun offensive, said now that the Allies understood they could never defeat Germany by force of arms. They had decided instead to let the deadlock continue until the Central Powers, encircled and outnumbered and short of essentials of every kind, collapsed of sheer exhaustion. Falkenhayn thought this a workable strategy and saw little hope of foiling it. What hope was there, except to use the U-boats to starve Britain first? And why worry so much about preserving an American neutrality that had been a sham almost from the start?

Bethmann, as Falkenhayn and others saw the situation, was wasting precious time. He was doing so in the sterile hope of getting American help with the blockade. And with the equally futile thought that Britain and France, their lifeline to North America functioning so beautifully, might somehow agree to negotiate. Bethmann was blocking Germany's only possible escape.

The chancellor, for his part, thought that Germany's best hope still lay in the arrangement of a peace conference. But the obstacles were formidable. They began with the fact that for Berlin to publicly call for such a thing seemed out of the question. The Allies could be counted upon to jeer, saying that Germany wanted to talk peace only because her prospects were so bleak. And much of the German public, having lost hundreds of thousands of sons and fathers and husbands, would be hostile to the idea of ending the fighting before those seeking to destroy Germany had been rendered incapable of threatening her again.

Bethmann's answer—an ironic variation on the misfired House-Grey

Memorandum, about which he knew nothing—was to get the United States to convene a conference and to make it appear to be entirely President Wilson's idea. He instructed Bernstorff in Washington, and urged Ambassador Gerard in Berlin, to let the president know that Germany was prepared to respond positively to an American summons. He emphasized that any such call would have to come soon. Told that this, too, would have to wait because of the approaching U.S. election, the chancellor was downcast. He doubted that he had that much time.

None of this is to say that Bethmann should be seen as some kind of angel of peace, offering to give up everything that Germany had gained in the fighting in order to bring the killing to a halt. Even had he wished to do any such thing, it would have been impossible for him to offer terms that an impartial observer could have regarded as generous or perhaps even realistic. No one in official Berlin, not even the kaiser, could have put Alsace and Lorraine on the bargaining table—or Russian Poland, or even the portion of Belgium that the high command had publicly declared to be essential to German security. To do so would have been political, and in the kaiser's case dynastic, suicide. This does not mean that Bethmann's hopes were entirely misplaced, however. The need, at this juncture, was to get both sides to sit down together and talk. Only then would specific terms have to be brought forward. That finding a middle ground would be immensely difficult did not make it impossible. Bethmann was at least attempting a first step.

Any possibility that the Allies might respond positively, if only at the insistence of the United States, was brought to a rude end on September 28. David Lloyd George, now Britain's war minister, declared in an interview with an American journalist that a negotiated settlement was out of the question. "The fight," he said, "must be to the finish—to a knockout." To this he added that "outside interference"—by which he could only have meant an American attempt at mediation—would not be tolerated. Prime Minister Asquith and Sir Edward Grey had been given no warning that Lloyd George was going to say such things and were nonplussed when they heard. But the Welshman's words were taken by Washington and Berlin to be official British policy, and they were so lavishly praised in the London press that it was impossible for the prime minister or the foreign secretary to gainsay or even qualify them. They contributed to establishing Lloyd George in the minds of his countrymen as the leader most committed to the defeat of Germany. They prepared the way for Asquith's fall two months later and Lloyd George's rise to the top.

At about this same time the German navy, without abandoning cruiser rules, was expanding the intensity and geographic reach of its submarine operations. This was possible because almost sixty U-boats were now in service, compared with the mere sixteen of a year and a half earlier. In short order, more tonnage was being sunk monthly than had been the case at the previous peak, before the *Arabic* crisis. And bigger, improved submarines were being launched at five times the rate of loss. All this provided ammunition for the naval authorities in Berlin as they argued that a lifting of restrictions could turn the tables on Britain and bring victory within reach.

Britain meanwhile was arming more and more of her merchant ships, providing them with trained gun crews, and ordering them to fire on any submarines they sighted. This made cruiser rules more hazardous than ever, while rendering the merchantmen ineligible for the protection of those rules. These complications made fresh trouble inevitable. Late in the year there were two instances of armed British freighters being sunk without warning. In one of these cases, six Americans died. They were not passengers, however, but crew members. This new twist made it difficult for Washington to know how much it should be outraged.

The election was bearing down on Wilson, and with the Republicans once again united, it was not at all clear that he was going to be reelected. To rally

David Lloyd George, prime minister of Great Britain, 1916–1922
The "Welsh Wizard" rose to the top by insisting that "the fight must be to the finish—to a knockout."

Charles Evans Hughes,
1916 U.S. presidential candidate,
and his wife, Antoinette
*Thoughtful and honorable,
ambivalent about the war, he offered
no clear alternative to Wilson.*

the voters who had given him the White House in 1912, he became a progressive activist once again, pushing to pass bills providing farm credits and regulating child labor. (The fate of the law putting limits on child labor shows just how much resistance there still was to government involvement in such matters. In 1918 the Supreme Court would find it unconstitutional, after which Congress would pass it in revised form, only to have the Court throw it out again.) Wilson also supported a tax measure that was remarkably progressive by the standards of the time. His ability to adjust his reformist impulses upward and downward was viewed skeptically in both parties, chiefly but not only in the ranks of the progressives. Former president Taft, not a spiteful man and free of bitterness over his defeat in the election of 1912 (he called the White House "the loneliest place in the world"), came to see Wilson as unburdened by principles. "I regard him as a ruthless hypocrite," he wrote a friend, "who has no convictions that he would not barter at once for votes."

The election drew as much attention to the ongoing Mexican imbroglio as to the European war. Republican candidate Charles Evans Hughes, lacking Roosevelt's fire and bite and being himself ambivalent about intervention, made no effort to turn the election into a referendum on foreign policy. Many voters found it difficult to distinguish between the candidates where the war and foreign policy were concerned.

A more striking aspect of the campaign, not a new subject for Wilson but one with which he appeared to be increasingly obsessed, was his sharp questioning of the loyalty of German-American and Irish-American organizations and citizens and other "hyphenates," as he called them. In doing this he worsened a climate of opinion in which it was now acceptable, even praiseworthy, for some Americans to condemn others as suspect or subversive on no evidence except their ethnic origins. The claim that hyphenates were "pouring poison into the veins of our national life" became a commonplace of his speeches. There was however no place, in the darkening Wilsonian worldview, for parallel complaints about those calling for American entry into the war on the side of Allies. Such people were accepted as natural, American, properly patriotic.

In the end the election was so close that Wilson could not be certain that he had won until, three days after the polls closed, it was established that California had gone for the Democratic ticket by the thinnest of margins. The Democrats' net loss of two seats in the Senate still left them with a twelve-seat majority. But the reunified Republicans, with Roosevelt back in their camp, wiped out the twenty-eight-seat majority that the Democrats had enjoyed in the House. For the first time ever, the two major parties emerged from the election with exactly the same number of seats in the lower chamber: 215 each. The Democrats were able to cobble together a majority, however, thanks to the support of five members belonging to minor parties.

Chancellor Bethmann had made it past the election without being overruled on the submarine question, and with Wilson reelected he was once again hopeful. But Wilson continued to do nothing visible to the Germans about either a peace conference or the blockade. Instead he repaired to his typewriter and began to work on a diplomatic note.

On November 14 he confided to House the details of this note. It was to be addressed to all the belligerents and was almost peremptory in tone, in effect a demand that they come together and find a way to bring the slaughter to an end. The colonel was taken aback. He predicted that the Allies would see the president as putting the two sides on the same moral plane, when they of course saw Germany as in the wrong in every way that mattered. He said, no doubt rightly, that they would accuse Wilson of siding with Germany. He urged delay, a wait until the situation clarified. When Wilson suggested that House should prepare to return to Europe, the colonel was for once reluctant. "I was entirely willing to do this *if* it were thought best," he would recall, "although my feeling was that I would prefer Hades for the moment rather than those countries when such a proposal [the demand for peace talks] was put to them." Obviously he did not want the job of delivering to his friends in London a presidential message that they were certain to hate.

Both ideas, the note and the trip, were held in abeyance. Wilson put his draft aside, giving little thought if any to the effect his doing so might have in Berlin. He began instead to work on a speech. All that Bethmann could see was that Wilson appeared to have no understanding of the pressure the kaiser was under to lift the restrictions on the U-boats. If he did understand, he clearly did not care.

Solitary composition and the delivery of orations and diplomatic notes had become Wilson's principal way of governing. More congenial and potentially more effective ways of exerting influence—inviting members of Congress to the White House, or talking things over with experts and opinion leaders— almost never happened during his tenure.

Descriptions of life in the White House at this time invariably draw attention to the president's self-imposed solitude, which became the rule years before bad health made it unavoidable. On a typical day he spent the morning alone in his study, lunched with a few family members, and went off for a drive or a round of golf or both. He was usually accompanied by his wife and his physician, rarely by anyone else. It was not usual for anyone but family to join him for dinner. Colonel House in his diary observed that he had never known a man as isolated as the president, and he attributed this to his discomfort in meeting people. He also commented on the strength of Wilson's dislikes and prejudices, saying that almost every time they met, the president had someone new to complain of, and he complained bitterly. House, too, had a complaint— about the burden imposed on him by his access to the White House. Because "no one can see [the president] to explain matters or get his advice," House said, frustrated officials and others took their problems to the colonel and asked him to intervene on their behalf.

"It is difficult to explain exactly the way business is conducted here," British ambassador Spring-Rice reported to London. "The president rarely sees anybody. He practically never sees ambassadors and when he does, exchanges no ideas with them. Mr. Lansing is treated as a clerk who receives orders which he has to obey at once and without question."

Walter Hines Page, who had been on friendly terms with Wilson for years before being offered the embassy in London, mused that the president "does his own thinking, untouched by other men's ideas. He receives nothing from the outside." Page's description of the organization of the Wilson White

House, written at the end of a visit to Washington, is not flattering: "The president dominates everything in a most extraordinary way. The men about him (and he sees them only on 'business') are very nearly all very small fry or worse, the narrowest twopenny lot I have ever come across. He has no real companions. Nobody talks to him freely and frankly. I have never known such conditions in American life."

A man who receives "nothing from the outside," who has no curiosity and responds to disagreement with annoyance that is poorly concealed when concealed at all, has little protection from his own limitations. He is restricted in his ability to know what is really happening, and vulnerable to stumbling when he ventures beyond his own door.

The war continued to spread like an epidemic even as it remained deadlocked. Bulgaria had joined the Central Powers, while her neighbor and rival Romania went with the Allies. Each had been promised territorial goodies at the expense of the other, but in the early going Bulgaria came out best. General Falkenhayn, upon being displaced as chief of staff, took command of an attack on Romania that knocked her out of the war almost as soon as she came in.

Falkenhayn's successor at the high command was, fatefully, the elderly General Paul von Hindenburg, who at the start of the war had returned to active duty from retirement and found himself a national hero when the forces under his command routed the invading Russian armies in 1914's epic Battle of Tannenberg. That victory was largely the work of Hindenburg's second in command, Erich Ludendorff, who was young enough to be his son, and since then the pair had been achieving great things on the Eastern Front. Hindenburg's promotion to chief of staff was momentous mainly because it brought Ludendorff to general headquarters and to a position from which he could take charge of the entire war effort. Ludendorff was physically unprepossessing, dumpy and double-chinned with strangely short legs, but he was a brilliant tactician and strategist and a superb executive, with an iron will and a driving impulse to command. He was also impatient, short-tempered, socially awkward, and out of his depth when dealing with anything other than military matters. The stolid, grandfatherly Hindenburg, though not really in charge, was more than a mere figurehead. He was a source of calm and steady good sense, balancing the volatile Ludendorff, providing a kind of shield behind which the younger man was able to make himself master first of Germany's military and naval operations and ultimately of the economy, the government, even Kaiser Wilhelm.

Ludendorff was of course far from unique in understanding that the Great War was something new in history, a conflict in which the whole population was almost as involved as the soldiers. Nor was he alone in seeing that, with everything at stake, every possible resource must be poured into the war effort. There were generals who shared that view in all the belligerent armies, and they were by no means wrong. What was different for Ludendorff, what gave him unique opportunities, was the ramshackle system of government that Bismarck had designed to suit his own purposes after creating the German Empire. By vesting all executive power in the monarchy, with no checks or balances, that system enabled anyone capable of dominating the kaiser to dominate everyone and everything else as well. Ludendorff proved to be the first man since Bismarck strong enough to exploit this to the hilt.

When Hindenburg and Ludendorff showed themselves to be unhappy with submarine policy, Bethmann knew that a new hour of decision had come. He could resist only so long as Wilhelm resisted with him. But the kaiser, who even in happier times had never been strong or stable, was by late 1916 too frightened and demoralized to stand firm for long. As he gave way, ironically, the war turned Germany into the kind of military dictatorship that the Allied

Paul von Hindenburg and Erich Ludendorff
Their successes on the Eastern Front brought them to Berlin and to command of the entire German war effort.

powers claimed to have gone to war to resist and destroy. The dictator was not the much-reviled kaiser, a cartoonist's dream with his flamboyant mustaches and preposterous headgear, but a general of middle-class origins unknown even to most Germans until the war was well advanced. Much of Germany's tragedy would flow from the fact that Ludendorff, incomparable as de facto general-in-chief, had no talent for or understanding of politics or diplomacy. The consequences of his incompetence in those fields should stand forever as proof that war truly is too important to be left to the generals.

By November 1916 Ludendorff was already powerful enough to force Bethmann to dismiss Foreign Minister Jagow, thus removing almost the only senior figure who still backed the chancellor. At about the same time Ludendorff ordered that unemployed men in occupied Belgium should be rounded up, transported to Germany, and put to work there. Bethmann foresaw the indignation that this would spark in America and elsewhere. Ludendorff cared only that unemployment was high in Belgium at a time when Germany badly needed manpower. He cared not at all when a formal protest came from Washington. And he would be angry more than abashed when, within a few months, the whole project proved to be unworkable and the Belgian workers had to be returned home.

As in the days leading up to the start of the war in 1914, the tension seemed to become palpably greater with every new day. The insistence of the German military that restrictions on submarine warfare *must* be ended *now,* the growing desperation of Bethmann and Bernstorff as they tried to stop any such thing from happening, Wilson's gradual awakening to the dangers of the situation and the need for peace talks, the determination of London and Paris to make talks impossible—all these things contributed to tightening the screws. In London, in December, Prime Minister Asquith's Liberal government fell. It was brought down by War Minister David Lloyd George, who entered into a coalition with his party's Conservative rivals and seized the premiership for himself. Not for nothing was Lloyd George known as the Welsh Wizard. He was widely distrusted but had a gift for somehow mastering every situation. He had entered the crisis of 1914 as chancellor of the exchequer and one of the Liberal government's most staunchly antiwar members. When he saw which way the political winds were blowing, however, he moved in one smooth leap to the other end of the spectrum. His maneuvers would destroy the Liberal Party, but his 1916 coup ensured that for the remainder of the war and the crucial few years that followed, Britain would be led by a man as strong-willed and capable as he was unscrupulous. His rise brought Sir Edward Grey's long tenure as foreign secretary to an end, removing from the government's innermost circle Colonel House's best friend there.

On December 9, at a meeting of the German leadership at Pless Castle, the contest between Bethmann and the duo of Hindenburg and Ludendorff ended in a deal. Bethmann, having lost hope that Washington was going to call for a peace conference, got approval of a statement that would inform the world of Germany's willingness to engage in talks. The quid for this quo was that if nothing came of the offer, the U-boats would be set free to do their worst.

Bethmann issued his statement three days later. Handled adroitly, it might have put Europe on a new course and saved millions of lives. Instead it became a display of German diplomacy at its most tragicomically inept. Out of fear that it would be seen as an acknowledgment that the Germans were losing the war, the offer to enter into negotiations was encased in boastful verbiage about Germany's strong military position and expectations of victory. This gave the Allies all the excuse they needed to dismiss it as a display of arrogance, an unwarranted demand for surrender, empty and insulting bluster. What was worse, on the day following the statement's release, the kaiser said in addressing an assembly of troops that talks had become possible because the Germans were in the position of "absolute conquerors." This was *pure* bluster, all too typical of Wilhelm's addiction to bombast and strutting. When it was reported in the press, Britain, France, and Russia all responded with understandable contempt. Bethmann's offer was dead on arrival.

Coming on the heels of Lloyd George's tough talk and rise to the premiership, these developments persuaded President Wilson that no White House call for a peace conference could possibly succeed. Instead, therefore, he issued a note—perhaps naïve but unquestionably well intended—asking the two sides to declare their war aims. It observed that, as both sides claimed to desire a just and lasting peace, specifying the means by which they hoped to achieve this shared goal would be a sensible first step. If this appeal came as a particular disappointment to Bethmann, who urgently needed more from Washington, it was not welcomed by the Allies, either. The promises that the original members of the Triple Entente had made to Italy, Romania, and faraway Japan (not to mention to each other) were secret for a reason. It was impossible to disclose them without revealing that the Allies had grandiose territorial ambitions and that achieving them was going to require nothing less than the annihilation of the Ottoman Empire, the radical reduction if not the outright destruction of the Austro-Hungarian Empire, and the demotion of Germany to second-rank status. Nor would it be possible to respond forthrightly to Wilson's request without revealing how Italy and Romania had been bribed to join the Allies. Britain and France could say nothing about their plans for the Middle East, Africa, and the Pacific without contradicting their own propaganda about what they were fighting for.

Bethmann, too, recoiled. His plan had been to get a peace conference started with U.S. help, then get the Americans to step aside while the Germans used their conquests in France, Belgium, and Poland to force concessions from the Allies. Such hopes were groundless, both because the Allies supported Lloyd George in his opposition to peace talks and because President Wilson would never have accepted exclusion from a settlement process. What Bethmann wanted was, however, exactly what the people of Germany had been led to expect. They had been promised that their sacrifices would be justified by the fruits of victory and that their ultimate reward would be a permanent strengthening of German security. Getting out of the war without delivering on such promises was the great challenge facing the leaders of all the warring powers. "It is a dangerous thing," Colonel House had written early in the war after visiting several European capitals, "to inflame a people and give them an exaggerated idea of success. This is what has happened and is happening in almost every country that is at war." He would live to see the government that he served fall into the same pit.

By the end of 1916, in any case, the actions of the U.S. government had made it impossible for the Central Powers to accept Wilson as the peacemaker he so badly wanted to be. The president had poisoned the well by favoring the Allies too often, too openly, and in too many ways for the Germans to be willing to return for another drink. The slanted character of American neutrality made it impossible even for Chancellor Bethmann, never mind the military and naval chiefs with whom he was now chronically at odds, to entrust the future of their nation to any peace conference in which the United States would play a leading part. One of the tragedies of the Great War is that the Germans lost all interest in such a conference at exactly the moment when Wilson was for the first time displaying a real sense of urgency about peace negotiations, and an awareness that talks, if they were to have any chance of success, were going to have to be reasonably evenhanded.

Assuming good faith on Wilson's part, and it is only fair to do so at this point, he appears to have been motivated by two considerations. First was the sense, which he shared with Bernstorff, Bethmann, and many others, that time really *was* running out—that American entry into the war was becoming more likely week by week, bringing a host of horrendous new problems into view. Second was the president's understanding that it would be impossible to take the United States into the war without making victory over Germany the objective, and his conviction that this objective was inherently dubious because—his one great prophetic insight—the decisive defeat of either side would make a stable postwar Europe impossible. That something radically different from victory was needed.

This was the moment, and surely not by coincidence, when Secretary Lansing committed what the dean of Wilson scholars, Arthur S. Link, has described as "one of the most egregious acts of treachery in American history." He met with the British and French ambassadors and urged them to encourage their governments to be demanding in responding to the president's call for war aims. He said it should be made clear that neither nation would accept anything resembling the status quo ante and that both would negotiate only with a new and democratic German regime, not with agents of the kaiser. Lansing of course knew that this second demand would make even consideration of talks impossible.

House, too, if he had never done so before, was now undercutting the president. He was assuring his friends in London that the Allies could respond to Washington in whatever way they wished, because the call for terms was a sham, as empty an exercise as the House-Grey Memorandum had been intended to be, a formality that would precede American entry into the war.

On December 22 Admiral Henning von Holtzendorff, head of Germany's naval general staff, sent the kaiser a lengthy memorandum stating unequivocally that unrestricted submarine warfare, if undertaken soon, would force Britain to the peace table in no more than six months. There was no need to worry about the reaction of the United States, Holtzendorff said, because (this he promised on his "honor as an officer") not a single American soldier would ever reach the continent. Bethmann, defeated by Washington's failure to act and declaring himself unqualified by training or experience to challenge Holtzendorff's bright scenario, sorrowfully withdrew his opposition. He remained certain that the men in uniform were making a tragic mistake but accepted that he was now powerless to stop them.

December 26 brought the Germans' response to Wilson's note. It declined to lay out the war aims of the Central Powers, saying that this was a matter to be broached after "the speedy assembly, on neutral ground, of delegates of the warring states," a category that excluded the United States. It went on to say that "a direct exchange of views"—as opposed to an arrangement in which the United States served as middleman and referee—"appears to the Imperial Government as the more suitable way of arriving at the desired result." Challenged on this by Colonel House, Ambassador Bernstorff said, ingeniously if not credibly, that the aims of Germany and her allies were so modest that disclosing them in advance would be interpreted as weakness. Behind this evasiveness was not only an unwillingness to reveal that Berlin still hoped to emerge from the war with significant gains, but also a distrust of Wilson that was now insurmountable. On Christmas Day, writing to the German ambassador in Vienna, newly appointed German foreign minister Arthur Zimmermann had said it was Berlin's intention to "prevent at all costs any participation on the part of Wilson in peace negotiations." Such were the fruits of Washington's two and a half years of not-really-neutral neutrality.

The president, unable to imagine that any honorable human being could fail to trust him completely, was painfully disappointed, so much so that he became lastingly resentful of the Berlin regime and at least as distrustful of the Germans as they were of him. Out of such small ironies can great tragedies grow. Unwittingly, the Germans were telling Wilson that if he wished to play a part in ending the war and shaping the peace that would follow, he was going to have to go to war first.

David Lloyd George, meanwhile, was playing the Americans more artfully. On December 29 he met with Ambassador Page, who reported to Washington that although the new prime minister was unwilling to meet with the Germans—Lloyd George said, probably not wrongly, that if he attempted any such thing he would be swept from office—he nevertheless saw an immensely important role for the United States in the restoration of peace. "He said that you [Wilson] are the only man in the world to bring this carnage to an end when the time for it should come," Page wrote. "This was true because not only of your high character and disinterested aims but also because you were the head of the great democracy which is as vitally interested as Great Britain itself." It was almost as if Colonel House had coached the Welshman on how to appeal to Woodrow Wilson. Possibly it was Page who had done the coaching—or some editing of whatever Lloyd George actually said.

On that same day, in a joint statement issued from Paris, the Allies formally rejected the German offer to negotiate. They dismissed it as not genuine, a cynical ploy. Their tone hardened the thinking in Berlin, where this refusal was taken as final confirmation that there was no alternative to fighting the war to a conclusion, and that Germany must use every possible weapon because her survival was at stake. The Allies meanwhile were still debating how to respond to Wilson's request for war aims and evidently feeling no great pressure to do so. The French in particular were reluctant even to try to satisfy the president and took comfort in Lansing's advice to take a firm line.

One result of all these developments was that on January 9, 1917, when the German high command again gathered at Pless, Bethmann was a defeated figure and Hindenburg and Ludendorff were in control. Armed with the Holtzendorff Memorandum, the Entente's refusal of peace talks, and Washington's continuing failure even to complain about the blockade, Hindenburg and his iron-willed deputy needed only minutes to get a shaken kaiser to consent to their demands. Effective immediately, U-boat commanders were to be instructed to torpedo "without warning" all Allied "freight ships indisputably recognized as armed." What was vastly more momentous, effective February 1, the same would be true of unarmed ships—even those of neutral nations. This second decision was one of the great crossings of the Rubicon in European history. Everyone at Pless understood it to mean war with the United States.

What made the new policy so momentous, the fact that it applied even to unarmed and neutral ships, was dictated by the brutal logic of the situation. Holtzendorff was promising to remove the dangers of American intervention by cutting off Britain from her sources of supply so effectively that she would be forced to negotiate. But fully one-third of Britain's imports arrived in neutral ships. This meant that the submarine campaign on which Germany was betting everything would be doomed to failure if neutral shipping were not stopped.

German writer Heinrich Pohl explained his nation's view of the situation: "Germany finds herself in the position of a warrior, hemmed in on all sides, whose enemies are all aiming at his heart. Every time this warrior succeeds in disarming the foe most harmful to him, every time the warrior strikes the sword from the hand of the enemy, a so-called neutral comes running from behind and places a new weapon in the hand of the defeated foe."

Again, the logic of the situation was simple and pointed to a hard conclusion. It was necessary to face facts: the "so-called neutral" was not neutral at all and had to be dealt with accordingly.

The Allies of course saw things differently—or saw them in the same way but with themselves as the parties "hemmed in on all sides." Be all that as it may, after the January 9 decision at Pless, the die was cast. The tragedy this time, at least for the Central Powers, was that if that decision had been delayed just a few months, it probably would never have been made. By then the Germans would have known what they could not know in January: the system of exchange by which the United States was financing Britain's purchases was at the point of collapse. The British were, for all practical purposes, insolvent. Their cupboard had been stripped so bare that they no longer had collateral that the banks were willing to accept. Their credit was no longer good. As early as November 27, at President Wilson's urging, the U.S. Federal Reserve Board had issued a warning about unsecured loans to Britain and France, saying that "it does not regard it in the interests of the country at this time that [member banks] invest in foreign treasury bills of this character." If things had gone on as they were, American exports probably would have had to be drastically reduced because the Allies were unable to pay for them.

Nor did the Germans know, in the opening days of the new year, how close they were to victory on the Eastern Front—how close Russia was to collapse. If that had become apparent a few months earlier, Berlin is unlikely ever to have felt the desperation that led to the new submarine policy.

When on January 10 the Allies finally sent a statement of their aims to Washington, they did not disclose the most secret of their arrangements—the ones that had brought Italy and Romania into the war, for example. They did, however, acknowledge what they knew that House already knew, and what it was reasonable to assume that President Wilson must also be aware of: That Alsace and Lorraine must be restored to France. That the Ottoman Empire must be dismantled (though nothing was said about what the Allies intended to do with its component parts). That Austria-Hungary's empire, too, must be taken apart, and Germany diminished. This was, if nothing else, more forthcoming than Germany's response. The president had hoped for more from both sides, but his disappointment would be irrelevant. This whole exchange had been rendered meaningless by the new German policy on submarines.

On January 15 Bethmann sent a cable informing Ambassador Bernstorff of what had been decided. It cited "urgent necessity"—a veiled reference to the fact that North America's 1916 wheat harvest had been bad, causing supplies to fall to alarmingly low levels. This was central to Holtzendorff's calculations; he assumed that Britain could and must be reduced to a state of famine before the next harvest came to her rescue.

Bernstorff, already heartbroken, was now given an impossible assignment: to advise Berlin on how to announce the new policy without precipitating a break in relations with the United States. If the situation did not quite panic him, it did drive him to extremes. He took a train to New York to see Colonel House, and as their conversation proceeded, Bernstorff began saying things that had no basis in fact. He spoke of German willingness to restore the independence not only of Belgium and Serbia but of Poland and territory conquered in Lithuania as well. He said that Berlin would likely be open to reparations and indemnities if they would apply to both sides. All this was wishful thinking—far more than Bernstorff knew to be true.

House was euphoric: perhaps Wilson was right after all, and the United States could take the lead in ending the war without having to enter it. He hurried to inform the president, calling what Bernstorff had told him "the most important communication we have had since the war began," one that created "a real basis for negotiations and for peace." A day later, on January 16, he wrote further that "if a false step is not taken, the end seems in sight." His sudden enthusiasm for peace talks just as the intervention that he had long wanted suddenly seemed imminent can be puzzling. Perhaps the heightening crisis increased his awareness of the risks he had been taking in nudging the president toward war; discovery of what he had been saying and doing might have been fatal to his relationship with Wilson. Perhaps he was even becoming mindful, at this late date, of what the cost of intervention might prove to be in terms of human—of American—lives.

It is not impossible, on the other hand, that something like the House-Grey Memorandum was at the back of his mind—the old but never-quite-abandoned scheme for convening peace talks as a way of entrapping the Germans. He was certainly capable of seeing that if such a stratagem led to an Allied victory without American intervention, and the Allies were aware of how much they owed Woodrow Wilson, that could be the best of all possible outcomes.

On that same day, January 16, Secretary Lansing received from Bernstorff and forwarded to the president the ambassador's last, best attempt to explain his government's thinking and get American help. "We have modified submarine war, waged in retaliation against illegal English starvation policy, to meet

American wishes," he wrote. "In return we expected the U.S. government would contend with us for freedom of seas and obtain from England reestablishment of legitimate neutral trade with Germany. . . . England has conceded nothing but instead boasts of more and more success in strangling Germany. We therefore may expect and should be grateful if America at last takes energetic steps to establish real freedom of sea."

There would be no such steps. Wilson was skeptical about what Bernstorff was telling House and only a little less skeptical, at this point, of House himself. His doubts were entirely justified, of course, because the colonel and Bernstorff were both dealing in illusions. Not only was the ambassador pulling imaginary rabbits out of a nonexistent hat, but House was seeing rabbits where even Bernstorff didn't. The colonel had somehow leaped to the conclusion—Bernstorff does not appear to have told him any such thing—that Berlin was willing to submit the settlement of the war to arbitration and to impose strict limits on U-boat operations while arbitration was in process. The president, not swept away by this supposed new vista, instructed House to get it confirmed in writing. If this proved possible, the colonel was to prepare to go to England with news of Germany's "very striking change of attitude." Bernstorff, unable to confirm anything, soon was backpedaling frantically, informing Berlin as he did so that this time the Americans seemed genuinely interested in talks and begging for postponement of the new submarine policy.

On January 22, addressing the Senate, Wilson delivered the speech on which he had been working since abandoning his call for a peace conference. It was one of the great orations of his life, an echo of the reflections he had dictated but not used in the autumn, and it is sometimes described as among the greatest in American history. Its words, if not the president's most eloquent, nevertheless expressed a profound truth. "Upon a triumph which overwhelms and humiliates," he said, "cannot be laid the foundations of peace." Backward syntax notwithstanding, these words conveyed a wisdom that would be borne out to a terrible extent when babies then being born grew old enough to go to war.

There must be "peace without victory," the president said. An end of hostilities on any other terms "would be accepted in humiliation, under duress, at an intolerable sacrifice, and would leave a sting, a resentment, a bitter memory upon which terms would rest, not permanently, but only as upon quicksand." This was prophecy in both senses of that overused word: it spoke a hard truth, and it foretold the future. Wilson's story might have been less tragic, and Europe's, too, if he had not lost touch with his own most profound insight a mere handful of months after giving it voice.

The speech was also courageous. The president knew that it would bring down the fury of the likes of Theodore Roosevelt, who in his frustration at not being president at such a historic moment had been saying that Wilson was either "at heart an abject coward" or "a heart so cold and selfish that he is entirely willing to sacrifice the honor and the interest of the country to his own political advancement." And it did. "Peace without victory is the natural ideal of the man who is too proud to fight," TR declared. "It is spurned by all men of lofty soul, by all men fit to call themselves fellow-citizens of Washington and Lincoln or of the warworn fighters who followed Grant and Lee."

Wilson's message would not have been welcomed by the Allies or the Central Powers if delivered earlier, but it would have strengthened Bethmann's position in his struggle with the German military. If the White House had then followed it up by putting pressure on both sides, using the leverage that it possessed because of Berlin's pessimistic view of its strategic outlook and Britain's and France's total dependence on loans and purchases from the United States, anything, even peace, might have ensued. But January 22 was at least two weeks too late. Hindenburg and Ludendorff had no interest in surrendering what they had won at Pless on January 9. Thus the speech changed nothing. Two days after delivering it, the president vented his frustration in a note to House. "If Germany wants peace she can get it, and get it now, if she will but confide in me." Genuine though it was, his frustration could do nothing to soften the Germans' distrust.

On January 26 Bernstorff had another conversation with House. He tried to explain the emptiness of his earlier assurances by saying—not quite accurately in terms of chronology—that they had been overtaken by the military's seizure of control in Berlin. House urged the ambassador not to be deterred by the grandiosity of the Allies' stated war aims, which he described as a bluff. This was little short of amazing, considering its source. Little less amazing was House's promise—another expression of what appears to have become his suddenly urgent wish to make peace talks happen—that the United States would not try to involve itself in negotiations over territory. That, if only Berlin would provide Wilson with a candid and confidential statement of its war aims, the United States would set out to arrange two conferences. The first would have as its purpose to bring the war to an end; the United States would not participate. The second would create an international organization to serve as a mechanism for preventing future catastrophes. The United States would insist on a role in it.

House, like Wilson—and like Sir Edward Grey at the climax of the 1914 crisis—was changing course too late. Bethmann had lost hope, though both Bernstorff and Zimmermann were begging him to get the move to unrestricted submarine warfare suspended. Even if he had not given up, at this stage there was no real chance of overturning Hindenburg's and Ludendorff's victory at Pless. At the next gathering of the high command, held on January 29, Bethmann explained for the last time his fears about what had been decided. Once again he asked for a delay, but his appeal was little more than a formality. The chancellor expected it to change nothing, and indeed nothing changed.

Nothing remained but for Bernstorff to deliver the terrible news. At four P.M. on January 31, he called on Secretary Lansing and gave him an official note from Berlin. It thanked Wilson for his speech of eight days earlier, blamed the Allies' "lust of conquest" for making peace impossible, and revealed that unrestricted submarine warfare would commence at midnight.

When they learned of this, the governments of Britain, France, and Russia all were certain that this time the United States really was coming into the war.

Berlin, too, took it for granted that this was true.

Washington did likewise.

One exception was Woodrow Wilson.

Background

The War of Words—and Pictures

The United States, when the Great War broke out, was part of a new kind of "modern world," one still limited to Europe and North America and outposts scattered elsewhere. This civilization was industrial and urban as no other had ever been. Much of it was even, to a varying but unprecedented extent, democratic.

"The public" not only mattered more than it ever had, it *existed* in a way never previously seen. Cities had always been mass markets in some crude sense, but now factories were flooding them with the fruits of mass production and changing their character profoundly. Factory wages, meager though they may have been, generated the cash that made the wheels turn.

Subjects were becoming citizens. Citizens were turning into consumers.

Driving it all was another new phenomenon: daily newspapers of massive circulation and reach. More people were literate than ever before, because that was what the economy required. The newspapers informed and entertained them, created appetites and advertised the means of satisfying them, told people what was happening, and tried, at least, to tell them what to think.

What was right and what was wrong.

What to *do*. How to *vote*.

Newspapers had done such things in the past, but always on a small scale. Now they were industrial machines for mobilizing the public, shaping it, turning it into a force. The governments that were furthest along the road to democracy—the United States and Canada, France and Britain, even Italy and Germany—recognized the importance of public opinion and strove to use it for their own purposes.

Thus the rise of government propaganda, from August 1914 onward, to a significance far beyond anything seen in previous conflicts. Total war was going to require terrible sacrifice for an unforeseeable number of years. It was going to require this of people who were better informed than earlier generations, expected to be kept informed, and felt entitled to have opinions on every subject and to have their opinions heard. It was essential that they believe the cause to be noble, the enemy evil, the sacrifice necessary, and the fruits of victory worthwhile.

Populations not at war had to believe those same things. It was crucial that the people of the United States believe them. Their country was so big, so rich by every measure, that it was capable of destroying any enemy and saving any friend.

The British were uniquely well prepared to meet the challenge. Long experience in the management of the world's greatest empire and the fighting of one colonial war after another had obliged them to become expert in the management of information. They were experienced, too, at finding disagreeable things to say about Germany. The stunningly rapid rise of the new German empire, accompanied as it was by economic near-stagnation in Britain, had aroused incredulity, fear, and a vengeful determination by some in London to restore what they saw as the natural order of things. If that was going to require war, so be it. By the 1890s Britain's press lords knew that they could build circulation by serving up scary stories about German plots to conquer the United Kingdom, and to do so by treachery.

Seventeen years before the start of the war, London's *Daily Mail* ran a series of articles about Germany with the lurid title "Under the Iron Heel." It described the young Kaiser Wilhelm II, by no means a bad-looking fellow even with his waxed mustache, as having "a face at once repulsive and pathetic, so harsh and stony, so grimly solemn . . . like a man without joy, without love, without pity, without hope. He looked like a man who had never laughed, like a man who could never sleep. A man might wear such a face who felt himself turning slowly to ice." Eventually even *The Times*, the most influential newspaper in the world, was crying in alarm that the Hun was coming. American correspondents, who tended to use London as their European base and to read *The Times* with awe, were affected in their own reporting. In the United States, Germany's traditional image as a land of dreamers and poets, philosophers and musicians, began to give way to something harder and darker.

As early as 1900, a French government report paid tribute to Britain's skill in using new communications technology for strategic purposes. "England owes her influence in the world perhaps more to her cable communications than to her navy," the report said. "She controls the news, and makes it serve her policy and commerce in a marvelous manner." In August 1914 she was ready to reassert her supremacy. Her severing of the transatlantic cables connecting Germany to New York was only the start. Further action followed quickly, and most of it was done in secret.

The war was barely a month old when Charles F. G. Masterman, a journalist and member of Parliament, was assigned to set up a bureau for the sole purpose of feeding information to neutral nations around the world. Masterman took several floors of an office building near Buckingham Palace, filled them with staff, and set out to do everything that a big budget and patriotic zeal could make possible. He told his staff that no one would ever know of their contributions to the war effort, because to let the public at home or abroad know that its news was coming from government sources would raise awkward questions.

The most popular authors in the kingdom—Kipling, Wells, and James Barrie among many others—were recruited to write for the cause. Mailing lists made it possible to send a steady stream of information about why the war was being fought and how gloriously well it was going to thousands of influential people—literally *hundreds* of thousands of people—around the globe. Weekly news summaries were prepared for the editors of newspapers large and small, and celebrities were sent out on speaking tours of North America and elsewhere. Soon a special department was created to serve the United States exclusively. It was put under another member of Parliament, Sir Gilbert Parker. He was well suited to the job, having been knighted in recognition of the immense popularity of his novels. They were adventure yarns set in the wilds of Canada's Northwest, a corner of the world Parker had never seen. His imagination and carelessness with the truth made him invaluable. Soon he had a staff of dozens.

Parliament meanwhile had passed the Defense of the Realm Act (DORA), which cleared a legal path for the censorship of all news originating in or passing through Britain. Censors labored with scissors and glue pots to protect the people of the United States from anything that might reflect unfavorably on the Entente or favorably on the Central Powers, and to help them see the Germans as "the Hun"—a collective murderous savage, not really part of European civilization.

Parker was quick to see what most interested North American editors:

reports of German atrocities. Soon the cables were abuzz with reports of the enormities being committed by the Hun as he raped and murdered his way across Belgium. German soldiers cut off the hands of every Belgian boy they could catch, the reports said, to make them incapable of fighting the Fatherland when they grew up. The same soldiers took particular pleasure in cutting off the breasts of the maidens they had gang-raped in public, and in crucifying nuns and prisoners of war. Buckets overflowed with the eyeballs of blinded Belgians. Such stories were picked up wherever they were sent. Readers were horrified and thrilled. Editors wanted more.

Also popular were stories about the heroic resistance of the country now known as Brave Little Belgium. These had to be handled with care, however. *The New York Times* caused an unwelcome stir when it ran a story about what supposedly happened when German troops entered one Belgian town. "The inhabitants of Bernot received them with a heavy fire from the roof and windows," New Yorkers read. "Even the women fought, and a girl of eighteen shot an officer dead with a pistol. She was captured and executed." The problem was that the story—assuming that it was true—confirmed German claims that Belgian civilians were waging a guerrilla war as so-called *francs-tireurs*.

Accounts of unspeakable German atrocities, sent across the Atlantic almost as soon as the war began, had an indelible impact on American public opinion. The question of their veracity remains vexed even today, and conclusive answers, if they exist, lie beyond the scope of this book. The subject is entangled in the ambiguous morality of war, conflicting testimony, and the confusions to be found at the confluence of journalism, propaganda, and the search for historical truth. That some German troops behaved criminally can be taken as settled. That in some cases they did so on the orders of their commanders is probable if not quite certain. That *francs-tireurs* attacked German troops, and that they displayed extraordinary courage in doing so, is beyond question. But in firing on soldiers—green troops with no experience of war, troops unaccustomed to being shot at and frightened by stories of the carnage caused by French *francs-tireurs* in their grandfathers' time—they relinquished the right to be treated as civilians in exactly the same way that merchant ships and liners, in arming themselves and attempting to ram submarines, were no longer entitled to the protection of cruiser rules.

On one hand are such horrors as the story of Leuven, where a never-explained burst of gunfire as German troops entered the town triggered a nightmare of destruction in which 248 Belgians were killed, two thousand buildings were destroyed, and a magnificent medieval library was reduced to ashes. It cannot be considered anything other than an atrocity on a terrible scale, and it was not unique. Other outrages, mercifully smaller ones, were reported in other places.

On the other hand, there is the message received by the New York office of the Associated Press on September 6, 1914, and signed by five American correspondents. All were aware of the impact the atrocity stories were having, and they wanted their countrymen to know what they, at least, had witnessed.

"In spirit fairness we unite in declaring German atrocities groundless as far as we are able to observe, after spending two weeks with German army accompanying troops upward hundred miles we unable report single incident unprovoked reprisal," the message stated in crippled telegraphese. "Also unable confirm rumors mistreatment prisoners or noncombatants. . . . Numerous investigated rumors proved groundless. . . . Discipline German soldiers excellent as observed. No drunkenness. To truth these statements we pledge professional word."

The five were not alone in failing to corroborate the worst of the stories. In 1915 the lawyer Clarence Darrow, skeptical about what he was reading, offered to pay a thousand dollars for one verifiable example of a Belgian boy having a hand cut off. The gesture cost him nothing, as no examples came forward. But that was not what Americans wanted to read, or editors wanted to print, and so it made no difference. The Masterman organization, for its part, had long since seen to it that no more accounts of ambushes by civilians got into print. Belgian civilians could be portrayed as heroic victims but not as heroic fighters.

The message of the Yank reporters may have been one reason the British and French made it their policy to deny access to the Western Front to journalists from neutral nations. There was no need for reporters to generate their own copy when Masterman and Parker were on the job, supplying stories free of charge. When the London *Chronicle* observed that "the debt that England owes the newspaper world of America cannot be overestimated. . . . We have no better allies in America than the editors of the great papers," it does not appear to have been referring to the accuracy of what was appearing in print. What mattered, where the United States was concerned, was less the truth of what happened in and to Belgium than what Americans accepted as the truth. Belgium was the first of three stories—the others being the sinking of the *Lusitania* and a German telegram published in 1917—that cumulatively brought much of the American population to believe that Germany really was a monster among nations and had to be put down.

London's news monopoly paid handsome dividends even in religious circles. Before the war was a month old, *The New York Times* published a letter from the Rev. Dr. Charles Henry Parkhurst of Manhattan's Madison Square Church: "When a mad dog runs amuck, the policeman shoots him on the spot—not by way of revenge, but as a humanitarian contribution to the security of the public. Now has a more rabid creature than Emperor William ever run amuck through the peaceful and prosperous domain of Europe?" Et cetera through two fat paragraphs. In those same first weeks the Rev. Dr. Newell Dwight Hillis of the Plymouth Congregational Church in Brooklyn Heights gave worshippers the good news that "already the hemp is grown to twist into the noose for the royal neck" of the kaiser. For the Huns he had only bad news: "You shall not skewer babes upon your bayonets; you shall not crucify officers upon the trees; you shall not nail young nuns to the doors of the schoolhouse; you shall not violate the sanctities of infancy and old age; you shall not mutilate the bodies of little girls and noble women." These strictures must have come as a terrible blow to the kaiser's troops as they advanced on Paris.

The vividness of the imagery employed by these men of the cloth shows what rich material the atrocity stories provided for the visual arts. Masterman and Parker and their teams quickly exploited the opportunity: posters showing the Hun to be not only inhuman but subhuman were soon everywhere. The chilling pictures of a Dutch artist named Louis Raemaekers were especially valued; he became a hero in London and an international celebrity and ultimately would be credited with helping the Allies win the war. One of his posters shows a gaunt, gore-spattered figure drinking a toast to *Kultur* from a large goblet brimming with red blood. In others, the helmeted figure of Germany cowers in fear and shame under the stern gaze of Jesus, and a satanic figure in a German helmet leers gleefully atop a mountain of skulls. One hundred and forty-eight of Raemaekers's drawings were published in book form in the United States in 1916, with an afterword by the prime minister of Britain. The editor noted in a preface that what ensured Raemaekers's artistic immortality was his lack of "racial and national prejudice." The following year would bring the artist himself to the States, with a traveling exhibition of his greatest hits.

Louis Raemaekers
The Dutch artist's depictions of a monstrously bloodthirsty Germany made him famous in Britain and the United States.

American artists soon outdid Raemaekers in luridness. An example from 1916 shows a fanged, deranged-looking ape arriving on the shore of America, a ruined Europe visible on the horizon behind him. "Destroy This Mad Brute," the poster says, not wasting space by explaining unnecessarily that the brute is Germany. In his right hand the ape holds a bloody club bearing that word *Kultur,* in his left arm a fair-haired damsel whose face is concealed, her bare breasts fully on view. Anticipating intervention by some months, the poster calls upon America's youth to join the army, adding in small print, not far below the bare breasts, that "if this war is not fought to a finish in Europe, it will be on the soil of the United States." Bare breasts feature prominently in American Great War posters, presumably to attract the attention of men of military age, presumably also to indicate that the young ladies to whom they belong have been ravished.

The pattern of the propaganda campaign was set in place in the first sixty days of the war, and it would hold for the next four years and longer. London kept the United States flooded with news that was carefully edited when it was not invented, but was rarely identified as coming from official sources. When Ambassador Bernstorff mounted a ridiculously underfinanced and amateurish countercampaign, cries went up from coast to coast about how the Germans were attempting to poison public opinion. Long before America entered the war, representatives of the Central Powers (but not of the Allies) were put under Secret Service surveillance. There was much wringing of hands over the thought that if Germany triumphed in Europe, her next step would be to invade the United States. In the spring of 1915, when the British government's Bryce Report offered corroboration of the Belgian atrocity stories, it was featured in newspapers throughout the United States. Only years later would investigators set out to check the sources on which the report was supposedly based; they would be told that all such materials had unfortunately and unaccountably disappeared. When Bernstorff's spokesman, Bernhard Dernburg, was foolish enough to publicly defend the *Lusitania* sinking, the backlash was so alarming that the ambassador ordered him to return to Germany.

Worse came in October 1915 with the execution, in Belgium, of an English nurse named Edith Cavell, after her conviction on charges of helping more than two hundred British, French, and Belgian prisoners of war escape from the Brussels hospital where she was employed. Cavell's actions were, in addition to being heroic, a capital offense under international law. And she had confessed her guilt. Evidence has recently come to light that her organization, and possibly Cavell herself, were engaged not only in arranging escapes but in spying for British Intelligence. Her execution was an inherently repugnant act and a gift to the Allied propagandists. It is understandable that few among the Allies or in the United States cared that it was lawful. Nor is it likely that Allied or American editors were informed when the French executed three German nurses under similar circumstances. If any did, they demonstrated no interest and would have been roundly condemned if they had.

As a morale-builder and motivator, propaganda that dehumanizes the

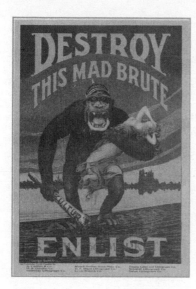

Manufacturing hate
*American poster art showed the Germans as not only inhuman but subhuman,
and contributed to making lasting peace impossible.*

enemy can seem an excellent idea while a war is in process. Obviously it seemed a very good idea throughout the Great War. But there is always a price to be paid. Irrational hatred is more easily turned on than off, especially after it has gone unanswered through four terrible years. The Germans were monsters, the people of the nations fighting them were told repeatedly and with all possible emphasis. But how did you make peace with monsters? What did you do with monsters once they had been subdued? Such questions would prove to be among the greatest obstacles to the achievement of a lasting peace.

Chapter 7

Onward, Christian Soldiers

THE TWO MONTHS THAT FOLLOWED BERLIN'S ANNOUNCEMENT OF unrestricted submarine warfare were electric with suspense. The great question was how the president was going to respond. The world waited for the answer, thinking that it knew but unable to be certain. It watched for clues and thought it found some, but they were never conclusive.

Which is not surprising. The evidence suggests that the president himself was not sure of what he was going to do until at least three weeks had passed, probably more. Members of his cabinet tried every trick to get him to reveal his plans but could learn nothing. It was only after eight weeks that he shared his thoughts even with Colonel House.

The momentum, in any case, was carrying the nation toward war. And Wilson, uncertain though he appears to have been, was contributing to it. On February 3, he went before Congress and announced to loud applause that he was breaking off diplomatic relations with Germany. He reminded his audience of the note with which, after the sinking of the *Sussex* ten months earlier, he had accused the German authorities of using their submarines in ways that violated "the universally recognized dictates of humanity." And of the German response: a promise that no merchant ships would be sunk "without warning and without saving lives, unless those ships attempt to escape or offer resistance."

He acknowledged that, in yielding to his demands, Berlin had warned that it could not be expected to accept restrictions indefinitely if the Allies "continue to apply at will methods of warfare violating the rules of international law"—a reference, obviously, to the starvation blockade and the arming of merchant ships. He did so, however, only to reject the warning as curtly as he had done at the end of the *Sussex* crisis. He repeated his 1916 assertion that German observance of the "sacred rights" of American citizens could not "in any way or in the slightest degree be made contingent upon the conduct of any other government."

Wilson read at length from the German announcement of January 31, saying that it left Washington with only one choice "consistent with the dignity and honor of the United States": to withdraw the American embassy in Berlin and give Ambassador Bernstorff and his staff their passports with instructions to depart. He made no reference to Berlin's complaint about the Allies' "brutal methods of war," perhaps regarding it as a case of the pot calling the kettle black (which it was) and undeserving of comment. He was perhaps less justified in not mentioning Berlin's claim that its "freedom of action"—its right to unleash the U-boats—had been restored by the "openly disclosed intentions" of the Allies to "destroy the Central Powers." When the fight is for survival, the Germans meant, extreme measures come into play. This was, at a minimum, worthy of a response.

Tough though Wilson's words were, and tough though his action was in breaking off relations, at the end of his speech he appealed to Berlin to reverse itself and professed faith that it would do so. "I refuse to believe," he said, "that it is the intention of the German authorities to do in fact what they have warned us they will feel at liberty to do." Nothing would make him believe it, he said, except "actual overt acts on their part," meaning attacks without warning on American ships or on Allied ships with Americans on board. This can hardly be dismissed as trickery—concealing a determination to go to war behind conciliatory verbiage—because trickery was so clearly not needed. If the president had asked for a declaration of war on the day he made this speech, majorities in both houses of Congress would have cheered him for doing so.

On February 7 he received a message in which a newly appointed Austro-Hungarian foreign minister, Count Ottokar Czernin, declared Vienna's support for the peace without victory that the president had called for on January 22. Czernin expressed a willingness to negotiate, adding however that it would be impossible to enter into talks with enemies avowedly committed to the destruction of the empire he served. He asked for assistance in moderating the Allies' intentions.

To say that this was an unimpressive communication is an understatement. It had been overtaken by events more than a week before it was received, and it came from an empire that had entered the war in a parlous state and after two and a half years of fighting was not only destitute but in the early stages of disintegration. The young emperor who had succeeded Franz Josef at the end of 1916, Karl I, knew that a near-miracle would be required for Austria-Hungary to emerge from the war even partly intact. Peace without victory meant peace without defeat, and in 1917 that would be, for Austria-Hungary, a monumental achievement. Wilson had never broken off relations with Vienna, in part because it could no longer pretend to be a major power and seemed scarcely worthy of attention, in part because he thought its empire might be worth saving, albeit in truncated form, as a source of stability in postwar eastern Europe. He therefore responded to Czernin's message by sending off one of his own, not back to Vienna but to London. He instructed Ambassador Page to ask Prime Minister Lloyd George if it might be possible to use the Czernin message as a starting point from which to attempt a general peace conference.

One thing would be necessary, the president said: the Allies would have to agree that Vienna could keep at least the core of her empire. Though it is unlikely that anyone on earth was less interested in peace without victory than Walter Hines Page—from the start of the war, he had displayed far more loyalty to his friends in the British government than to the administration in Washington—on this occasion he appears to have followed orders, keeping his opinions to himself. He could have been neither surprised nor displeased when Lloyd George airily dismissed Wilson's suggestion.

Nothing could have come of any of it in any case. France's and Britain's long-standing reluctance even to discuss the possibility of a peace conference had hardened into an open flat refusal now that Germany and the United States were almost at sword's point. Both allies had long since pledged—whether Wilson in early 1917 had any knowledge of this is unclear—to let Italy and Romania annex substantial portions of Vienna's domains. The president's willingness to make use even of Czernin's transparently pathetic appeal does indicate rather clearly, however, that he was prepared to try almost any door that might lead away from intervention. One wonders if he regretted not having tried harder in 1916, when Kaiser Wilhelm and Chancellor Bethmann were still the decision-makers in Berlin and still hoped that the United States might serve as an honest broker.

The severing of U.S.-German diplomatic relations had caused jubilation among those, in Congress and elsewhere, who were determined to have a war. Those same people were again delighted when, on February 13, the House of

Representatives passed the biggest naval appropriations bill in the country's history. This bill, which originated in the War Department, was ambitious in scope. It aimed at launching new warships at a rate that would in due course make the U.S. Navy equal or superior to the Royal Navy. The British were not pleased, but for once few in Washington cared what they thought. The bill passed by a margin of fifteen pro votes for every one opposed.

Meanwhile the War Department was at work on bills to expand the regular army, introduce universal military service, and conscript young men in numbers that would have been unimaginable just months earlier.

The Treasury Department, for its part, was preparing bills for which there could be little need unless the United States went to war. One would generate the tax revenues with which to pay for a major war. Another would become the basis for future war bond drives, and a third proposed to levy an excess-profits tax both to increase revenues and to clamp down on the profiteering that was already generating much resentment across the country.

The Justice Department, not to be outdone, was drafting legislation to empower itself to ferret out enemy agents and discourage (to put it mildly) criticism of government policy. In March the Council of National Defense, the recently created body that had the secretary of war as its chairman, established a Munitions Standards Board to impose order on the rapidly growing and largely unregulated armaments industry. Before the month ended, this body would be absorbed into a new General Munitions Board with responsibility for coordinating and facilitating the production of ammunition on an ever more massive scale. Many such organizations were being called into existence and expanded and expanded again. All were intended to put the whole national economy at the service of the war.

The sense of crisis was spreading beyond Washington. East Coast ports were clogged with ships, the owners of which were unwilling to order them to sea because of the heightened U-boat threat. Warehouses and docks overflowed with material that was intended for Europe but could not be moved. The railways, in their turn, became jammed with cars that could not be unloaded. One of the concomitants of warfare, inflation, was already a dangerous problem, especially in the East. February 20 brought a riot by working-class housewives in New York City. Enraged by the rocketing price of ordinary foodstuffs, female mobs pillaged and burned grocery stores, overturned the carts of street-side vendors, marched on City Hall, and fought the police sent to restrain them.

The government of Britain, freshly emboldened by the assurances of Colonel House and Ambassador Page that this time intervention really *was* imminent, on February 21 announced a further tightening of the blockade. The Lloyd George government decreed that henceforth all ships traveling to or from a neutral port with connections to the Central Powers must stop at an Allied port en route or be assumed to be doing business with the enemy. This was the equivalent of saying, Lord Justice Devlin would later observe, "that anyone who failed to call at a police station should be presumed guilty."

That the British felt free to make this fresh intrusion upon the rights of neutral nations shows that they now saw almost no possibility of their losing the support of Washington. And indeed, Washington did not object or even comment. London's confidence is all the more striking when one considers that Britain was now spending five million pounds per day on the war, 40 percent of that staggering sum borrowed in the United States.

On the continent the Germans were bringing to completion a project that would change the shape of the deadlocked Western Front to an extent not seen since the two sides first dug their trenches at the end of 1914. All through the winter of 1916–17 they had been constructing a new, massive, and radically innovative system of defenses that they called the Siegfriedstellung and that the British and Americans would call the Hindenburg Line. Intended to be virtually impregnable, this staggeringly ambitious undertaking (which began with the digging of a trench ten feet deep, twelve feet across, and almost a hundred miles long) would when put into operation shorten by twenty-five miles the sector of the front from Arras on the north to Soissons on the south. This promised a huge reduction in the Germans' manpower needs at a time when the Allies had almost a million and a half more men than they on the Western Front.

The Siegfriedstellung was the work of Erich Ludendorff. It expressed what he believed as the war approached the end of its third year: that victory in the west was no longer possible for the Germans, outmanned as they were. At first he intended the new system to be a contingency, something to fall back to if the British and French finally mounted an offensive gigantic enough to achieve breakthrough. Such an option had first been made necessary by the removal of worryingly large numbers of troops from the west in the summer of 1916, when a Russian offensive showed the Austro-Hungarian forces to be unable to hold their ground unassisted. Later Romania's entry into the war on the Allied side required the transfer eastward of still more German troops. Finally, when an intercepted message revealed that the French and British were planning yet another massive offensive for April 1917, one even bigger than 1916's Somme campaign, Ludendorff decided that withdrawal should not be delayed.

American opponents of intervention remained plentiful after the break with Germany and were determined to make themselves heard despite the contempt with which they were treated by nearly every newspaper in the country. William Jennings Bryan brought fresh abuse down on himself by urging the public to pressure the White House to stay out of the war. Across the nation, the pro-war and antiwar factions together were almost certainly outnumbered by the skeptical, the undecided, and the indifferent. The president remained unreadable. In a conversation with French philosopher Henri Bergson, dispatched to Washington to do his part in selling the Allied cause, Wilson drily observed that in his opinion Britain was fighting not to save Belgium or for any similarly grand purpose but to preserve her world leadership in commerce. On February 23, during a cabinet discussion of whether the United States should arm her merchant ships (all the secretaries present were in favor), he declared impatiently that "the country is not willing that we should take any risks of war." He displayed so much uncertainty on so many occasions that it is impossible to agree with those who claim that he had long since made up his mind and was simply waiting for events to bring public opinion into alignment with his thinking. Colonel House, watching for signs that Wilson had accepted the need for war, could detect none.

The president was not wrong about the public's unwillingness. Outside Washington and beyond the East Coast, even at this point most Americans appear to have found the arguments for war less than compelling. Many rejected them outright. But the day after the aforementioned cabinet meeting, on a quiet Saturday evening in Washington, there arrived at the State Department the most sensational message to reach American shores in the entire course of the war, one that would reshape public opinion and free the president from the weightiest of his doubts.

It came from London, from Ambassador Page, and it forwarded to the president the text of a secret message—infamous ever since as the Zimmermann Telegram—that had been sent from Berlin to the German ambassador in Mexico City five weeks earlier. In it, German foreign minister Arthur Zimmermann reported that Berlin was hoping to keep the United States neutral despite the start of unrestricted submarine warfare but, if this proved impossible, wished to offer an alliance to the government of Mexico. The ambassador was instructed, "as soon as the outbreak of war with the United States is certain," to inform the president of Mexico that in return for making war on the United States his nation would receive "generous financial support" as well as Germany's assistance in recovering its lost territories of Texas, New Mexico, and Arizona. As if all this were not fanciful enough, the ambassador was to encourage the Mexican president to—"on his own initiative"—invite Japan to become a third partner in the proposed alliance.

Arthur Zimmermann,
German foreign minister, 1916–1917
*His infamous telegram outraged America—
but was it really outrageous?*

The interception and decoding of this telegram was the supreme triumph of Britain's wartime intelligence service. The authorities in London were left, nevertheless, with the challenge of making its contents known to the United States and the world without alerting the Germans to the fact that their supposedly most secret diplomatic communications were not secret at all. That problem remained unsolved when, chafing to detonate their bombshell in Washington, the British let Ambassador Page in on the secret. He, of course, was thrilled. Lately he had been losing hope that anything, even the submarine campaign, was going to induce President Wilson to intervene. But this was something new, something to stir even hearts worn down by repeated disappointment. Everyone who learned of the Zimmermann Telegram saw how explosive it was. Sir Edward Grey's replacement in the Lloyd George coalition, Arthur Balfour, was no newcomer to the international stage and no stranger to high political drama. His experience included three years as Conservative prime minister. Even he would recall, however, that giving a copy of the telegram to Page was "the most dramatic moment of my life."

The next morning Page sent a cable to Frank Polk, who had succeeded Lansing as State Department counselor and that weekend was filling in as secretary of state while Lansing was away on holiday. It advised him to stand by for a message of the highest importance. The length of the message and the laboriousness of the encryption process delayed transmission until late in the day. Then, in Washington, it had to be decoded. As soon as that was done, Polk hurried it to the White House.

Wilson was stunned, infuriated, offended. He took the telegram as proof that Berlin had been toying with him, pretending to be open to peace talks while scheming to spread the war to North America. (Actually, to the extent that the president had been misled, this was the fault of the German ambassador in Washington rather than his superiors in Berlin. Bernstorff's dread of the consequences of unrestricted U-boat operations had driven him to depict the new Ludendorff regime as more flexible, more open to American mediation, than it was or indeed cared to appear to be.)

Wilson's first impulse was to make the telegram public immediately. There was no longer any concern about revealing Britain's message-interception capabilities, Page and the Foreign Office having concocted a story about obtaining a copy of the telegram in Mexico through bribery. Polk, however, persuaded the president to wait until Lansing could be summoned back to Washington. Lansing, when he arrived, urged deferring release until the telegram could be used to achieve some specific and substantial objective. The telegram therefore produced its first significant effect before its existence was known outside the White House. It prompted President Wilson to go before Congress on Monday, February 26, and request approval of an action for which many members had been clamoring: "armed neutrality." This was the president's term for the equipping of American merchant ships with artillery. He asked for authority not only to put guns and navy gun crews on merchantmen but "to employ any other instrumentalities or methods that may be necessary and adequate to protect our ships and our people in their legitimate and peaceful pursuits on the seas." The vagueness of this language raised eyebrows, but Wilson assured his listeners that there was no cause for concern. "I am not now proposing or contemplating," he said, "war or any steps that need lead to it."

The publicity given the U-boat campaign and the intensity of feeling that it aroused created the impression, which endures to the present day, that Germany's submarines were committing wholesale slaughter on the high seas, sending innocent Americans to watery deaths in droves. The truth, though certainly tragic enough, is not so dire. From the start of the war through 1915 and 1916 and on into the middle of March 1917, exactly two Americans, both merchant seamen, died as a result of a U-boat attack on a U.S.-registered ship. This happened in the Irish Sea on May 1, 1915, and was a mistake: a submarine commander mistook the American tanker *Gulflight* for British. The ship was not sunk but later towed to safety. The German government accepted responsibility, expressed regrets, and paid compensation. Even as attacks and sinkings increased in frequency from February 1, 1917, onward, for a month and a half not one of them resulted in loss of life.

It is likewise astonishing that, in the two and a half years between the start of hostilities in 1914 and American intervention, only six Americans, aside from the 128 who died in the *Lusitania* tragedy, lost their lives as a result of U-boat attacks on British ships. The first four were Leon C. Thrasher, whose story was told earlier, the two American victims of the sinking of the White Star liner *Arabic* in August 1915, and a crewman lost when the freighter *Eaveston* was torpedoed in February 1917. The last two were a Chicago mother and daughter who died in their lifeboat—the cause has never been satisfactorily explained—after the liner *Laconia* was torpedoed off the coast of Ireland. This happened on February 25, and news of it made headlines when it reached Washington the day before the president's call for armed neutrality. The *Laconia* was another of Britain's "armed merchant cruisers," equipped with heavy guns, but this was not immediately clear in Washington. The president's response was to strengthen his armed-ship bill before sending it to Congress.

Press and congressional indignation at the *Laconia* sinking made passage of the bill seem certain. Still, muffled by the howls about German treachery but unmistakable all the same, there were rumblings of dissent. In the House of Representatives, an amendment to prohibit armed merchant ships from carrying munitions as cargo received 125 votes in the process of going down to defeat. At the other end of the combativeness spectrum, old guard Republicans mocked the very idea of armed neutrality and mocked Wilson for not acting more forcefully. The Senate Republican leader, Henry Cabot Lodge, described the president's position as "deplorable."

Lansing thought the time had come to unleash the Zimmermann Telegram. Its release would make passage of the armed-ship bill a certainty, at the same time silencing all but the most intransigent of the president's critics. Late on February 28, the contents of the telegram were handed over to the Associated Press, ensuring that the next morning they would appear at the top of page one in every daily paper in the country. The result was a firestorm of outrage and an explosive boost to anti-German and pro-war sentiment. Members of Congress struggled to outdo one another in expressing their horror at the Hun's perfidy. Before the day was over, the House passed the armed-ship bill by a vote of 403 to 13.

The Senate posed a greater challenge. The margin of support for the president's bill was almost as impressive among the senators as in the House, but the upper chamber's arcane rules meant that even an overwhelming majority was not necessarily enough. Eleven senators—five rebellious Democrats and half a dozen die-hard Republican progressives—joined forces to form an opposition. They made use of one of the hoariest of their chamber's traditions, the filibuster, to keep the armed-ship bill from coming to a vote before the congressional session expired on Sunday, March 4.

A filibuster uses unchecked oratory to paralyze the Senate. As the hour when the Senate would have to adjourn approached and speeches for and against the armed-ship bill went on and on, emotions ran high. A threat of physical violence hung over the proceedings. At one point a group of senators who favored passage rose menacingly from their seats when the leader of the opposition, Robert La Follette of Wisconsin, demanded the floor. As they advanced on La Follette, one of them, Ollie James of Wisconsin, was seen to be carrying a revolver. Another member of the opposition, Harry Lane of Oregon, then brandished a rattail file that he had brought into the chamber after hearing that La Follette might be in danger. Lane said later that he was prepared to drive the sharp point that gave the file its name into Ollie James's heart if necessary. It did not come to that, but in the final moments before adjournment, when La Follette saw that he was to be given no opportunity to deliver the speech with which he hoped to explain his position, he took up a brass spittoon from the floor. He said he was going to brain the presiding senator with it. He was restrained by an ally who imploringly pointed out that the filibuster had achieved its aim. The hour of adjournment had come. There would be no vote.

It hardly need be said that the Zimmermann Telegram was an act of horrendous stupidity. And it was absolutely pointless: what it proposed could never have been accomplished. Mexico, even if she had not been ravage revolution and civil war, was far too feeble to pose a threat to the United States. Germany's financial situation was far too bad to make possible "generous financial support." And the suggestion that Mexico should invite Japan to join her in alliance with Germany was absurd. Japan was by this time a member of the Allies, having been promised the Chinese province of Shantung and islands in the Pacific as her reward for joining. The only result of the telegram's mention of Japan was to inflame American fears of Japanese territorial ambitions. President Wilson himself was much concerned about this "yellow peril," so much so that he sometimes mused that intervention in Europe might leave the western United States vulnerable to invasion from across the Pacific. Obsession with Japan was epidemic on the West Coast, and the telegram caused previously indifferent Californians to become hostile toward Germany.

But was the telegram as villainous as Congress and the newspapers proclaimed it to be? Did it make the case for war unanswerable? No answer is satisfactory that does not make note of the fact that an alliance of Germany and Mexico was not to be proposed until after an American declaration of war. To condemn this as an outrage is to deny nations the right to respond to direct and deadly threat by seeking allies.

It is likewise worth remembering that, in holding out to Mexico the hope of recovering territories seized by force just a single lifetime earlier, Germany was taking a position not easily distinguished from the demand that Alsace and Lorraine be returned to France. Nor is the German offer obviously different in kind from what Britain and France had done in using deeply secret promises of territorial gain to bring Italy, Romania, and Japan into their alliance.

In his undelivered speech, which he soon afterward had printed and distributed nationally, La Follette had wanted to call attention to the passage in the bill authorizing the president to "employ any other instrumentalities or methods" to counter the German threat. This, he argued, would have conferred on the executive branch undefined and therefore unlimited powers— even the power to make war without the approval of Congress. Such power, in his view, was not only unwise but blatantly unconstitutional. He pointed out, too, that the bill would have appropriated $100 million for the president to use, without oversight, in implementing the new law. La Follette was not wrong about the substance of the bill, or the use the president was undoubtedly prepared to make of it. Though it was not passed, it serves as an early indication of how far the president was willing to go in demanding powers that would allow him to fight the war in whatever way he chose.

The Senate if not the nation would have been unmoved by La Follette's speech if he had been permitted to deliver it. Many of his fellow senators were furious with him, and many who were not furious wanted to appear so. Before adjournment, seventy-five of them signed a declaration that they would have voted for the armed-ship bill if given the opportunity. La Follette found himself reviled in the press as little better than a traitor—if better at all. Theodore Roosevelt said he "ought to be hung." A cartoon in the *New York World* showed him receiving an iron cross from a huge hand, apparently sheathed in iron and belonging to the kaiser.

War fever rose to new heights. Two and a half years of unrelenting anti-German propaganda and self-censorship by the American press were bearing the fruit for which Britain had always hoped. If it is possible to point to a single reason for its coming to ripeness at just this time, that reason has to be Herr Zimmermann's telegram. From the morning when it became the talk of the nation, large segments of the American public—the so-called opinion leaders especially—plunged into a frenzy of patriotism that at times resembled a kind of collective madness. That it happened so quickly shows the power of the long-suppressed passions that the Zimmermann headlines released.

The savagery of the attacks on Senator La Follette was one early symptom. Another, even more dramatic and bizarre, was what happened in New York City on March 11, one week exactly after Congress was obliged to adjourn without having passed the armed-ship bill. The New York Federation of Churches held—it would not be an exaggeration to say that it jubilantly celebrated—what was publicized as War Sunday. The stated aim was to "mobilize Christian strength behind President Wilson." Implicit in this, and obviously so, was the expectation that the United States would soon be at war. As part of the proceedings, 158 congregations voted their support of intervention and conscription. They cheered pastors who told them that intervention was morally imperative, opposition a moral failing, Germany the breeding ground of monsters. Clergy who declined to take part were apologized for by their congregants. All this was echoed in other cities.

By the end of March, the Germans had completed the risky process of evacuating the great bulge in the front known as the Noyon salient and withdrawing to the Hindenburg Line. In withdrawing, they destroyed every building, road, and rail line in the salient, leaving their enemies with no infrastructure from which to launch their planned offensive. The move cost the Germans little of strategic value and put them in a position vastly more defensible than the one they had abandoned. But it was, as Ludendorff had foreseen, acclaimed by the Allies as a glorious advance of their forces. It gave fresh encouragement to the pro-war Americans, seeming to establish the truth of what the British propagandists had been claiming from the start of hostilities: that the Germans were beaten, that victory lay just on the other side of the next great offensive, and that the United States, if it intervened, would be enlisting not only in the cause of justice and civilization but on the winning side as well.

A divide had been crossed. The road to war was now downhill all the way.

Background

Troublemaker

To grasp just how strong the impulse to reform was in the United States in the years leading up to the Great War, it is necessary to look no further than to the life story of Robert Marion La Follette of Wisconsin.

That his achievements were in large part La Follette's own doing, the product of his ambition and energy and rare political gifts, cannot be doubted. The proof is in the record: his rise from rural obscurity to become in 1884 the youngest member of the U.S. House of Representatives; three consecutive and eventful terms as governor, won in the face of powerful opposition; and the Senate seat he held to the day of his death and from which he made himself one of the most important public figures in the country.

Robert La Follette, U.S. senator from Wisconsin, 1906–1925
He accused the president of using a double standard in dealing with Britain and Germany.

Nor can it be denied that he was as tireless and effective a champion of the rights of ordinary citizens as the American political system has ever produced. For more than a quarter of a century, first in the Upper Midwest and then on the national stage, he was a leader—more often than not *the* leader—in what at first seemed a hopeless fight to take power from Big Money and put it in the hands of voters. The list of reforms that bear his mark is as long as it is impressive. It includes antitrust legislation, initiative and referendum, open primaries instead of smoke-filled rooms, election of senators by voters instead of by state legislatures, regulation of utilities and banks, better wages and working conditions, restrictions on child labor, and the progressive taxation of incomes.

And that is not all—not nearly. Thanks in no small measure to the influence of his remarkable wife, Belle, the first woman to graduate from the University of Wisconsin Law School and saluted by *The New York Times* when she died as "perhaps the least known, yet the most influential of all American women who have had to do with public affairs in this country," La Follette was from the start of his career far ahead of his time where almost every question of social justice was concerned.

In a society that took it for granted that blacks were inherently inferior and Jews irreparably alien, La Follette positioned himself front and center in opposition to racial discrimination and anti-Semitism. He championed voting rights for women when to do so was to be ridiculed as a crank, and he protected the woodlands of Wisconsin's Native Americans from the predations of timber companies. He was ridiculed for opposing discrimination against immigrants from Asia.

He was widely regarded, especially but not only by those whose privileged position in American society he challenged, as a bizarre figure, a threatening if sometimes pathetically amusing nuisance. Even worse, in the eyes of those he targeted for attack, were his demands—his shocking and preposterous demands, as they saw it—for controls on the wielders of economic power and changes in the ways the nation taxed itself and chose its political leaders. His ideas drew enemies like iron filings to a magnet. To many traditionalists, his progressivism seemed a rejection of core American values, a repudiation of individualism in favor of an interfering government.

Word of what he had done as governor of Wisconsin preceded him to Washington, causing him to be shunned even by his new Republican colleagues when he first took his seat in the Senate in 1906. That he was a wild rebel seemed confirmed when, ignoring the tradition that new senators should keep their mouths shut, he took the floor in support of a bill (regarded as outrageous and soon defeated) to protect railroad workers from having to work more than sixteen consecutive hours.

In due course it became clear even in Congress, however, that he was a force that had to be reckoned with, a man with too large a following to be safely ignored. As other Republican progressives won seats in the Senate, they looked to him as their leader. Even Democratic progressives regarded him as an ally. He was so unimpressed with the reform agendas of two successive presidents from his own party, the "trustbuster" Theodore Roosevelt no less than William Howard Taft, that his relations with both became rancorous. Frustrated at failing to win the presidential nomination in 1912, La Follette lent his support to the progressive agenda of the Democrat Wilson. For much of the national elite, the masters of industry and finance especially, he remained a threat to tranquillity and prosperity—so serious a threat that his removal from office came to seem a patriotic objective.

Powerful enemies were not La Follette's only problem. He had flaws, and they were often on display. He could be self-righteous, disdainful even of well-intended opponents, and unable to conceive that anyone who opposed him could possibly not be stupid or corrupt. His zeal was tinged with paranoia: someone was always spying on him, he thought, or plotting against him. He was not immune to hypocrisy, denouncing his foes as machine politicians while using patronage to build a formidable machine of his own.

Such a man could never have had the career that La Follette had, could never have accomplished as much as he did, if he had not been in some deep way the right man for his times. Or *one* of the right men, at any rate, expressing in his person something that voters in great numbers approved, offering with his legislative agenda things that they, too, wanted. In that sense he was like William Jennings Bryan. And also—though not in the same way—like Woodrow Wilson.

La Follette's similarities to Wilson are striking. Both were morally serious, earnest, courageous, and invincibly certain of their own virtue and wisdom. Both were ferociously ambitious, and in remarkably similar ways: driven to prove themselves worthy of idolized fathers. La Follette's father was in a strange but very real sense a more daunting figure than Wilson's, because he was literally as insubstantial as a ghost. He died when Robert was still a small child, so that the boy grew up without memories of him or even a photograph. He was left with nothing except his mother's tales of what a great and good man he had been, and her insistence that the son must prove himself worthy.

Of course La Follette and Wilson were both crowd-pleasing orators—
"of course" because otherwise they could never have risen as they did.
Like Bryan, La Follette and Wilson became known early in their careers
as speakers who, if you took the trouble to go and hear them, were not
going to disappoint. They, too, were men whom audiences would *pay*
to hear.

But their differences were striking, too, and nowhere more conspicuous than in their speaking styles. The lean, cool Wilson's oratorical gifts
were of a quasi-poetic character. The journalist who wrote his 1912 campaign biography said Wilson's appeal was to the emotions and that he
achieved his effects through "vagueness and reiteration, symbolism and
incantation." He summoned his listeners to contemplate grand and abstract ideals, and offered them stirring if vague visions (of "peace without
victory" and "making the world safe for democracy"). He would have
been brilliant at the advertising game.

The five-foot-five La Follette, as chesty and pugnacious as a bantam
rooster, approached speechmaking from an entirely different angle, one
rooted in his experience as a courtroom lawyer. His orations could go on
for hours, and one can search through pages of them without finding a
memorably ringing phrase. They were by no means just blather, however.
He laid out facts and constructed arguments, painstakingly building a
case for whatever he wanted listeners to believe or do. He was never bor-
ing, because the passion with which he spoke had an electrifying effect
and because the things he talked about—the greed of the railroads, the
unfairness of the tax system, and the exploitation of workers—mattered
to the people who came to hear.

Wilson's penchant for grand generalities, when contrasted with La
Follette's dogged focus on logic and facts, points to the most profound
difference between the two. The young Wilson had honed his rhetorical
skills because of what he wanted to *be:* a leader, a great man, a "statesman." That was also true of the young La Follette, but his ambition had
an additional dimension. He grew up among the pioneering people of
what was called the Middle Border, people who believed that the fruits
of their hard toil were being stolen by the banks and railroads, the packing companies and mill owners, the trusts. He wanted power because
he genuinely wanted to *do* something for these people. From early on
he had a mission, a program, one so specific and clear that he was able

to distill it into a dozen and a half words. "The supreme issue," he said, "is the encroachment of the powerful few upon the rights of the many." That was the basis of his entire legislative program. To stop that encroachment, to reverse it, was the purpose of his life.

This made him—ironically, in light of Wilson's reputation for idealism—the less pragmatic of the two. Though Wilson was nearly incapable of changing his mind once he made it up, before taking a position he was quite capable of considering a wide range of options and choosing the one that would serve his purposes best. He could become a strong progressive when doing so led to the governor's office in New Jersey, do it again when the goal was the White House, do it a third time when his reelection was at issue. But when there was no particular advantage in being progressive, no need to do so, he could revert quite comfortably to the genteel conservatism in which he had been raised. It was enough—so long as he was recognized as a great man—for him to *be* the governor, and then to *be* the president. Nothing in particular absolutely demanded to be *done*—until the war brought him the opportunity to become the savior of the world.

La Follette was incapable of that kind of flexibility. Only one option was open to him: militant, combative, unrelenting reform. With it came things that *demanded* to be done. Americans of the twenty-first century might be puzzled that he saw no contradiction between his lifelong campaign for government intervention in the economy and his adherence to the Republican Party, which from the 1860s had been the party of business. In his eyes, there was no contradiction. If the party happened to be dominated, nationally, by men who spoke for the Big Money and opposed democratizing reforms, nevertheless it was the party of Lincoln, the party that had freed the slaves, the party that had been faithful to the Union in its hour of crisis and now stood for the values of small-town and rural America as well as a growing middle class. To people like La Follette, it seemed the natural home, the only rightful home, of true democracy. It would function as such as soon as it was led back to the right path. The Democrats, by contrast, seemed to men of his stamp to offer no real alternative. They were the party of the disloyal South, of its planter plutocracy, and of the worst big-city political machines.

This orientation helps to explain the force and bitterness of La Follette's opposition to those steps, such as the arming of American merchant ships, by which the United States drew closer to intervention in the European war. He thought the Wilson administration wrong in its stern treatment of the Central Powers and in its indulgence of the Allies. He was convinced that joining the Allies would lead to vastly greater wrongs. But his horror at the drift toward intervention had deeper causes as well. He was early to see what many progressives of both parties would understand only later: that the war and progressivism were fundamentally incompatible, and that the military crusade that Wilson came to adopt as *his* mission in life was going to send more power flowing to those Americans who already had most of it.

Chapter 8

Why

WHAT FOR MANY YEARS WAS PROBABLY THE BEST-KNOWN STORY about Woodrow Wilson, a story treasured by his admirers, is set in the White House in the predawn hours of Monday, April 2, 1917. That was the day on which he was to go before Congress and ask it to affirm that, as the result of the crimes of the German Imperial Government, the United States was at war. The speech with which he would do this, pecked out on his portable typewriter over the preceding days and nights, was ready to be sent to the printers.

As the story goes, the president was in deep agony, tortured by thoughts of what the day ahead, and intervention in the Great War, were going to mean for himself, for the Congress, and for the nation. Sleep being out of the question, he had telephoned one of his most loyal supporters in the realm of journalism, Frank Cobb of the *New York World,* and asked him to get a late train to Washington.

It was one A.M. when Cobb reached the White House. He was ushered into the president's study, becoming there a receptacle into which Wilson poured a dark vision of what lay ahead, his fears about what intervention was going to do to America, and the desperation with which he wished for some way out.

"He said when a war got going it was just war and there weren't two kinds of it," Cobb was reported as having recalled later. "It required illiberalism at home to reinforce the men at the front. We couldn't fight Germany and maintain the ideals of government that all thinking men shared. He said we would try but it would be too much for us."

As the night wore on, Wilson's ruminations became more and more apocalyptic. "Once lead this people into war," he said, "and they'll forget there ever was such a thing as tolerance. To fight you must be ruthless and brutal, and the spirit of ruthless brutality will enter the very fiber of our national life, infecting Congress, the courts, the policeman on the beat, the man in the street."

Cobb recalled afterward that the president "thought the Constitution would not survive it. That free speech and the right to assembly would go. He said a nation couldn't put its strength into a war and keep its head level; it had never been done."

He had done everything possible to avoid war, Wilson said mournfully, but had been thwarted at every turn by Germany. He asked if he could have done anything different, if there was any way to escape having to deliver the speech he had so painfully composed.

"If there is any alternative," he exclaimed, "for God's sake let's take it!"

Cobb assured him that there was none.

So the story goes. Today it does not carry quite the weight that it did in 1924, when it first appeared. Half a century has passed since historians began to ask if the original telling, in a biography of Frank Cobb by John S. Heaton, ought to be believed. Today it is impossible to know if anything like it ever happened at all.

The story's problems are manifold. Cobb himself left no written or corroborative oral account of any such visit to the White House or conversation with Wilson, and he and the president were both dead when Heaton's book appeared. He supposedly told the story to two of his subordinates at the *World,* Maxwell Anderson and Lawrence Stallings, who later passed it on to Heaton. But records were of course kept of comings and goings at the White House, and they contain no evidence of a visit by Cobb on or around the night in question. Nor is it easy to understand why Wilson, who had spent hours laboring in solitude over his speech and was little inclined to trust even friendly journalists, would abruptly summon from New York a man who was not a close friend for a dark-night-of-the-soul venting of his fears. Not one member of his cabinet knew what he intended to say to Congress that day. Would he have unburdened himself to a newsman?

For that matter, is it likely that he remained so racked with doubt at this late point? It was now ten days since Congress had been advised to convene in special session on April 2—and to be prepared for a presidential address of the highest importance. This had led everyone to expect a call to war. Neither Wilson himself nor anyone in his administration had done anything to dampen those expectations. For him to go before Congress and not call for war would, under the circumstances, have brought an avalanche of abuse down on his head.

Conceivably the problem is a simple mix-up about dates. The White House visitors' log shows that Cobb had been there some two weeks earlier, at a point where the intensified U-boat campaign and the release of the Zimmermann Telegram were sparking ever-louder calls for war. Earlier on that same day, just hours before Cobb's arrival was noted in the log, there had been a cabinet meeting at which every one of the assembled secretaries had declared himself to be in favor of war. It is more than merely possible that Wilson and Cobb might have discussed the intervention question at that time; the president would certainly have had it on his mind, and Cobb as a journalist would have felt obligated to ask about it. It is likewise plausible that, feeling extraordinary pressure, Wilson might have become less reticent than usual in the company of the editor of one of the most consistently supportive Democratic newspapers in the country. Nor would it have been remarkable if he put the discussion off the record before unburdening himself. Many of his meetings with reporters were off the record.

Perhaps Cobb, in later gossiping with Anderson and Stallings, changed the date for dramatic effect. Perhaps Anderson and Stallings, or Heaton in his turn, did the changing and for the same reason. It is humanly possible, certainly, that the chronology just became garbled as the story was passed along. Assuming of course that it did in fact start with Cobb. It is perhaps not irrelevant that Maxwell Anderson was a crusading progressive and had been such an outspoken opponent of American intervention that his fervor had cost him at least one job. Or that Stallings, by the time he and Anderson could have been interviewed by Heaton, was a one-legged combat veteran, embittered by his experience of war.

Thomas Fleming, in *The Illusion of Victory,* puts forward the hypothesis that, in talking with Heaton, Anderson and Stallings intentionally embellished whatever Cobb told them. The two were among the many Americans disillusioned by the war and its aftermath, but this need not have kept them from wanting to absolve Woodrow Wilson, that great progressive icon, of blame. What better way than to depict him, on the very eve of intervention, as foreseeing the horrors that lay ahead (even the Constitution would "not survive"!) but powerless to avoid them. This is speculation, but not obviously less credible than the story Heaton told in his book.

Even if Anderson and Stallings (or they in cahoots with Heaton) made up the story out of whole cloth, it remains of interest. If an invention, it nevertheless expresses its inventors' bleak view of the Great War—a view that was already widely held just a handful of years after the conflict's end. If, on the other hand, Wilson said something like the words attributed to him, the story becomes intriguing in a different, more important way. It gives rise to the thought that, in foreseeing the war's effects on American life, the subordination of civil liberties to a "spirit of ruthless brutality," the president might have been lamenting his own fate no less than the nation's. Or perhaps he was foreseeing it without lament. For his words anticipated not only what was going to happen—the creation of something previously unknown in the United States, something very like a police state—but what he himself was going to make happen. The darkest of the plausible theories is that he was cynically paving the way—justifying in advance, not only to the press but to himself—his own wartime transgressions by declaring them unavoidable.

After the fact—meaning after the war—the president would show no regret about what he had done and allowed to be done, and only one big regret about how it had all turned out. That can be taken as evidence that he never foresaw the horrors that the Heaton book said he foresaw. Alternatively, it can be interpreted as an indication of how profoundly the war had changed Wilson, hardening him to such an extent that what he dreaded in 1917 seemed acceptable in later years.

In fact we know, and know with certainty, that the president had already decided on war with Germany at least several days before April 2. He revealed himself to Colonel House when the latter, consumed with curiosity, traveled to Washington on his own initiative on March 27. House's account of their talk on that date gives no suggestion that Wilson was still expressing the uncertainty or reluctance that had earlier caused him so much anxiety and the colonel so much chagrin. What the president talked about was not what he should do but how he should do it: whether to ask Congress for a declaration of war, or simply for a formal acknowledgment that because of Germany's actions a state of war already existed. House advised the second course as the easier one.

When had Wilson made up his mind? We don't know, exactly, but the wind had been thick with straws for weeks. They were visible as early as March 5, the day of the president's second inauguration, the day after Congress had been obliged to adjourn without having passed the armed-ship bill. It was a cold spring Monday in Washington, wet and windy, and the formalities were kept to an austere minimum. Wilson delivered a brief address, making no effort to rise to the rhetorical heights that the nation had learned to expect of him. He limited himself to two clear and simple points. The first was essential to his whole position, the article of faith without which he could never have allowed himself to go to war. It was the conviction, the insistence, that the United States was entirely innocent, with no responsibility for the conflict with Germany. The crisis was a matter "over which we have no control," he said, because it was entirely of Germany's making. "We have been deeply wronged upon the seas, but we have no wish to wrong or injure in return." America was not only blameless but selfless: "We wished nothing for ourselves that we were not ready to demand for all mankind. . . . We desire neither conquest nor advantage."

These can be read as the words of a man who has already decided for war, whose purpose is to assure the people that when called to arms, they will be able to respond with clean hands and hearts as pure as Galahad's. The United States would not be *going to* war, if it came to that. The war—Germany—was forcing itself on the United States. The use of the past tense where one might expect the present—we *wished* nothing for ourselves—strikes a note of finality, of a mind made up.

Wilson's second point was the need for national unity in this time of crisis. "The thing I shall count upon," he said, "the thing without which neither counsel nor action will avail, is the unity of America—an America united in feeling, in purpose, and in its vision of duty, of opportunity and of service." He cautioned his fellow citizens to "beware that no faction or disloyal intrigue break the harmony or embarrass the spirit of our people." On its face this was unobjectionable—either inspiring or familiar political boilerplate, according to one's taste. Only in hindsight does it take on a more troubling hue, becoming a portent of the lengths to which this president would show himself willing to go in suppressing "faction" and enforcing at least the appearance of unity. Few of the progressives who had made him president in 1912 could have imagined, in April 1917, that Woodrow Wilson of all people would soon be making it a crime to dispute his version of the truth.

The inauguration was followed by no festivities. The president and his little party returned to the White House, and he withdrew to his study. There he vented his fury at the previous day's filibuster by typing out a statement that was released to the press later the same day and made headlines across the country. It was an attack on—a condemnation of—Robert La Follette and the senators who had joined him in the filibuster. Wilson called them "a little group of willful men, representing no opinion but their own," and said that by blocking passage of the armed-ship bill they had "rendered the great Government of the United States helpless and contemptible." It takes no great leap of imagination to surmise that Wilson lashed out in this way because he felt that he himself had been made to appear helpless and contemptible. Whether the "willful men" really represented no opinion but their own remained to be seen. The immediate effect of the president's statement was to make them fair game—subject to being depicted as traitors.

Having thus spent himself, the president retreated to his bed, where he spent much of the following ten days. The press was told that he had a cold. Edwin Weinstein, M.D., in his "medical and psychological biography," calls this an improbable diagnosis and notes the frequency with which Wilson's "colds" appear to have been a psychosomatic reaction to extreme stress. It was characteristic of him to cut off contact with others in times of difficulty, complaining of headache and going into deep seclusion where other politicians would have sought discussion and advice. One cabinet meeting was canceled during this period and another severely curtailed, making it easier to keep the whole of the administration in the dark about what lay ahead.

This period was eventful all the same, and even from his sickroom Wilson contributed to making it so. Measures as important as an appropriations bill to fund expansion of the army remained unpassed because of the filibuster, and so the calling of a special session of Congress could not be long postponed. On March 9 the president set April 16 as the date on which Congress would reconvene. The fact that he did not choose an earlier date—there was no practical or procedural obstacle to doing so—suggests that he was in no great hurry.

Shortly thereafter the White House announced that he was ordering the placement of guns and navy gun crews on American merchant ships on his own authority, without the approval of Congress. He invoked a 1797 antipiracy law as his basis for doing so. March 15 brought news that Tsar Nicholas II of Russia had abdicated. He was replaced by a revolutionary government that declared its commitment to democratic reform and to staying in the war. Though the tsar had exhausted his empire and destroyed his dynasty in sticking loyally with Britain and France as his armies were humiliated again and again and Russian society began to unravel, his fall caused jubilation in London, Paris, and Washington. The Allies, now that Russia was throwing off autocracy, would find it less awkward to claim to be a confederation of democracies at war with tyrants. Wilson, for his part, would soon be speaking in public of "the wonderful and heartening things" that were happening in Russia. In fact Russia was sliding into chaos, her government impotent, her population destitute, her armed forces disintegrating.

It remained true that since Germany's introduction of unrestricted submarine warfare, the only American deaths resulting from U-boat attacks had been the mother and daughter who died in their lifeboat after the sinking of the *Laconia* on February 25 and a lone seaman lost in the destruction of a British freighter earlier that same month. Five U.S. merchantmen had been sunk in that same period, but without loss of life. March 18, however, brought news of the destruction of three American ships. The *City of Memphis* and the *Illinois,* both returning to the United States after delivering cargoes to Europe, had been torpedoed on March 17 and 18 respectively, but all aboard had survived. It was a tragically different story with the *Vigilancia,* a merchantman eastbound out of New York carrying iron, fruit, asbestos, and straw. Fifteen members of her crew perished, among them at least two and possibly as many as seven U.S. citizens. (Contemporary reports are inconclusive about the number.) This was the first time in a remarkable twenty-two months that Americans had died in a U-boat attack on a U.S.-registered ship. That when she left New York the *Vigilancia* was the first commercial ship to be armed by presidential order, or that the deaths resulted from the capsizing of a lifeboat as it was being launched, was of no interest to newspapers hungry for fresh examples of Germany's homicidal rampage. If the sinking of the *Laconia* had not been the "actual overt act" that Wilson had said he required, the *Vigilancia* evidently qualified.

Indignation increased when, on March 21, word came of the sinking of the tanker *Healdon* off the coast of Holland. Among the twenty-one men lost were six Americans. It is now accepted that the cause was not a U-boat attack but one of the thousand mines laid in the area a day earlier by British warships. This was not known at the time, and German denials of responsibility, though correct, were dismissed with scorn.

It has to have been at this point, if it had not happened earlier, that Wilson made his decision. On the day of the *Healdon* tragedy, he moved the starting date for the special session of Congress forward to what was now the earliest feasible date: Monday, April 2. He sent word to both houses that on that day he would go before them to deliver a communication "concerning grave matters of national policy," matters requiring to be taken "immediately under consideration." Though he appears to have told no one except possibly his wife what matters he had in mind, most people thought it obvious.

But *why*? Why *now*? For the old guard Republicans, led by the likes of Senator Henry Cabot Lodge and former secretary of state Elihu Root, the answer was too obvious to require statement. The United States had to go to war— under a better man than Wilson it would already be at war—to put right the Rape of Little Belgium, save Britain and France from being enslaved by a cruel tyranny, and liberate all the populations that had for centuries been captives of the German, Austro-Hungarian, and Ottoman Empires. Men of Theodore Roosevelt's stamp, devotees of "the strenuous life," would have added a quasi-spiritual argument: Americans needed a good war to lift them out of the dull and soulless materialism into which they were sinking under the weight of their fabulous new wealth. TR had been saying such things since 1914.

Overall there was tremendous pressure for war—more pressure, probably, than many presidents would have been able, or would even have wished, to resist. It was evident in such events as a huge pro-war rally held at New York's Madison Square Garden on March 22. Elihu Root told cheering thousands that "every true American heart should respond with joy, amid its sorrow," to the opportunity to go to war in fellowship with democracies that now included, "God be praised, the great democracy of Russia." He made no secret of sharing Roosevelt's and Taft's disdain for the president. "We have had weak presidents and wrong-headed presidents," he told a friend, "but never until Wilson have we had an unscrupulous and dishonest president."

To accuse President Wilson of allowing himself to be pressured into going to war by such criticism is, however, to misread him badly. He was not the sort of man to be bullied in any such way. Yielding would have been virtually impossible for such a stiff-necked, self-righteous puritan, and he undoubtedly would have chosen political martyrdom before doing so. In another two and a half years, in fact, we will find him embracing a martyr's role with a kind of bitter satisfaction. Allowing himself to be pushed into war would have made it impossible for him to believe one of the things he most needed to believe about himself: that it was his destiny to do the right thing, regardless of the consequences for himself.

It must not be forgotten that throughout the country, in the Midwest and West and South especially but also among the Irish, Germans, and Jews of the East, there remained much opposition to intervention. This did not translate readily into political pressure on Washington because the newspapers treated it with contempt when they could not ignore it and the administration discouraged it in ways large and small. Wilson certainly could have mobilized and legitimated it, however, had he sought support for nonintervention.

Nothing could have been more obvious, in March 1917, than the importance of the U-boats in the president's thinking. It was so obvious, in fact, that perhaps it is given more weight than it should. The shock of the *Lusitania* was now two years in the past, and nothing remotely comparable had happened since. The force of Wilson's reaction to tiny numbers of deaths at sea at a time when hundreds were being killed even on "quiet" days on the Western Front and when central Europe was being brought to the edge of starvation may seem curious, but that it is true there can be no doubt. Weinstein has traced it to stories that Wilson's mother had told him of nearly perishing in a storm at sea when she emigrated from Scotland to the United States; this seems a stretch. Be all that as it may, deaths by twos and by threes were not exactly a compelling reason to take a largely reluctant nation into a war that measured its casualties in the millions. Wilson himself understood this. Thus the persistence with which he talked not about numbers of lives lost but about abstractions: sacred rights of all humanity et cetera.

The most cynical explanation of the president's motives has always been that he opted for war because by 1917 the Entente, Britain especially, was so deeply in debt to the United States that its defeat would have plunged the nation into depression. Wilson was accused from the start of being in thrall to Wall Street; George Norris of Nebraska infuriated many of his fellow Republicans by claiming on the floor of the Senate that "we are going into this war at the command of gold" and that doing so was "putting the dollar sign on the American flag."

Such words were not indefensible. Between August 1914 and March 1917, the Allied nations spent almost $1.7 billion buying a huge variety of materials from the United States. This total included $700 million for explosives, $92 million for firearms, $322 million for other iron and steel products, and almost half a billion dollars for copper. These sums rose at a faster rate every year. The wealth of rural America exploded little less spectacularly: farm profits from sales of wheat, $56 million in 1913, totaled $319 million just a year later and $642 million in 1917.

By April 1917 Britain owed more than $1 billion to the United States. Canada owed $425 million, France more than $300 million, Russia $121 million, and so on down to Italy and China. Even Germany, early in the war, had somehow succeeded in borrowing $45 million in the United States. A German victory would have put much of this debt in default. Intervention, on the other hand, would not only continue the boom but shift it into a higher gear.

But here again, to accuse Woodrow Wilson of going to war for financial reasons is to do him an injustice. Any such act would have made his whole career a mockery in the way that mattered to him most, which is to say in his own eyes. It must have been a comfort to consider that the course he chose would have good near-term economic consequences and avoid bad ones, but that is not the same as saying that he was driven by such calculations.

It can be argued that Wilson was drawn into the war less by political pressure, or the U-boat campaign, or the greed and fear of American business, than by his own rhetoric. By depicting the submarine attacks as crimes against humanity, by threatening to hold Germany and Germany alone to "strict accountability" for violations of international law, and by insisting that in submitting to his demands at the time of the *Sussex* crisis Berlin had made an absolute and irreversible pledge, he had severely narrowed his own options. He had made changes of course more difficult than they otherwise would have been—more difficult but still not impossible, certainly for a man of the president's powers of persuasion. Ultimately he *chose* not to change course; he was never without options. He took the position that if anyone was going to change course, it would have to be Germany—or possibly, to a much smaller extent, the Allies. There is no evidence that he ever felt trapped by things he himself had said.

And so we are brought back to the question of *why*. The most satisfactory answer is that, his efforts to end the war through mediation having been rejected by both sides, he feared that the United States, and he as president, would be left with no major part to play in the postwar settlement. The only way to change that was to earn a seat at the negotiating table, and by March 1917 the only way to do that was to enter the war. If the United States not only went to war but became the nation that broke the stalemate, that made victory possible, Wilson might well find himself at the *head* of the table. It was not an ideal solution, but from his perspective it was infinitely preferable to being excluded. It would impose on him the responsibility—in no way unwelcome—to stop the Allies from imposing a kind of peace that could never be more than unstable and short-lived. This was a quintessentially Wilsonian aspiration, at once noble and egotistical. It accorded perfectly with his sense of his own great destiny.

By 1917 many knew what Colonel House had learned early about the effectiveness of appealing to the prideful-saintly side of Wilson's nature. It was becoming known even on the far side of the Atlantic. That shrewdest of politicians, David Lloyd George, appears to have discovered the secret by the time he became Britain's prime minister. Certainly he had known what buttons to push by the time Ambassador Page called on him in February and, on the president's behalf, asked for his help in dropping the dismantling of the Austro-Hungarian Empire from the unwritten list of Allied objectives. Lloyd George offered no such help, as we have seen. But in denying the president's request, he displayed a remarkable understanding of how to keep him friendly.

"We want him to come into the war not so much for help with the war as for help with the peace," Page would quote Lloyd George as saying. "My reason is not mainly the military nor naval nor economic nor financial pressure that the American government might exert in their own way against Germany; grateful as this would be [sic] I have a far larger reason. . . . The president's presence at the peace conference is necessary for the proper organization of the world which must follow peace. I mean that he himself must be there in person. . . . The United States wanted nothing but justice and an ordered freedom and guarantees of these for the future. Nobody therefore can have so commanding a voice as the president. . . . American participation in the war would enable him to be there and the mere mortal effects of this participation would shorten the war, might even end it very quickly."

This was balderdash. No one knew better than Lloyd George that by early 1917 Britain and her allies were in desperate need of America's military and financial help. And before two more years had passed, Lloyd George would be showing just how little interest he actually had in allowing the United States to shape the postwar world. But his words were perfectly calibrated to get the president to do what the Entente wanted him to do. And though the president was not deceived about Britain's objectives (he must have laughed inwardly upon reading that Lloyd George had assured Page that Britain "wants nothing for herself"), this would have done little to dilute the prime minister's core message. He was acknowledging that the United States was uniquely free of selfish motives and that only she could bestow upon the world a peace worth having. All this spoke directly to Wilson's deepest core. If, as is possible, Page embellished the prime minister's words before passing them along to Washington, this only shows that he, too, had a good understanding of the president and how to win him over.

Even Secretary of State Lansing ultimately learned the secret and how to use it. In March 1917, having like Page shown himself willing to do what he quietly could to undermine presidential peace initiatives, he was more fearful than ever that not even the U-boats were going to prod Wilson to act. So fearful, in fact, that he was moved to confront the president directly. Late on the night of March 19, arriving home from a social engagement, he went to his desk and composed a letter in which he laid out, for the president's eyes, arguments for intervention without further delay. What he wrote shows a solid knowledge of how to engage Wilson. Perhaps years of watching Colonel House at work had taught him what to say. Perhaps witnessing Wilson's reaction to Lloyd George's words had brought on an epiphany.

"I believe," he wrote, "that our future influence in world affairs, in which we can no longer refuse to play our part, will be materially increased by prompt, vigorous and definite action in favor of Democracy and against Absolutism. This would be first shown in the peace negotiations and in the general readjustment of international relations. It is my belief that the longer we delay in declaring against the military absolutism which menaces the rule of liberty and justice in the world, so much the less will be our influence in the days when Germany will need a merciful and unselfish foe."

The subtlety is impressive. If limited as a statesman, neither a strong nor a remarkably wise man, Lansing was a lawyer of no small ability. Here he shows himself to be a good salesman as well. The cause he supports is just, Germany is evil, America is magnanimous and will be indispensable when the time comes to establish a new world order. Wilson desires to wield not a sword but an olive branch.

If these appeals had no effect, it can only be because they were not needed. Wilson showed repeatedly that his thinking ran exactly in the channels prescribed for him by House, Lloyd George, and Lansing. He never did so more revealingly than when talking with a group of visitors that included the reformer and pacifist Jane Addams in February 1917. "As head of a nation participating in the war," he said in response to Addams's appeal for nonintervention, "the President of the United States would have a seat at the peace table. But if he remained the representative of a neutral country, he could at best only call through a crack in the door."

For Wilson, the thought of being on the outside while other men decided the fate of the world would have been unbearable. He would have seen it as a denial of his destiny and a tragedy for the world. Only he was absolutely disinterested, and only the nation he led was capable of meeting the challenges facing a world teeming with needy and oppressed people. If going to war was the price of admission, it was a terrible price indeed, but not *too* terrible.

Assuming of course that everything worked out according to his plan.

Background

Over There—The War as of April 1917

It is so easy to speak of a million combat deaths, so hard to get one's mind around the reality behind the number. A *million*. A million *violent deaths*. Of young and youngish men, the fittest their nations could muster. Men—many of them boys—with parents and sweethearts, wives and children. With lives to live, and futures.

By the start of 1917 the Great War had claimed a million lives three or four times over. In just the first five months of fighting, August through December 1914, Austria-Hungary and France had both seen at least 200,000 of their soldiers killed. Russian fatalities had been at least twice that total, Germany's perhaps half. Many, many more had been wounded, uncounted thousands of them horribly, and hundreds of thousands were prisoners of war. Of the 120,000 men who had crossed the Channel with the British Expeditionary Force (BEF), more than half had been killed or wounded. As a fighting force, the BEF had been all but wiped out.

And that was just the beginning. Throughout 1915 and 1916 the slaughter went on and on, rising at times to peaks like the first day of the Battle of the Somme, when more than 19,000 British soldiers met their deaths advancing against German machine guns. Season by season, the campaigns became more terrible.

Every major offensive ended in failure and colossal loss. Of the 130,000 men in the Russian Second Army when it invaded Germany in August 1914, some ten thousand escaped being killed or captured. The fighting at Gallipoli in Turkey went on for almost all of 1915, accomplished precisely nothing, and took the lives of 46,000 Allied troops and nearly twice that many Turks. Current estimates are that the death count for the Western Front in 1916 was 143,000 German, 150,000 British, and 268,000 French soldiers. These numbers were almost dwarfed by what was happening on the Eastern Front, where outnumbered Germans repeatedly mauled ill-trained, ill-equipped, and badly led Russian armies. In the south the Austrians and Italians were butchering each other to no effect along the Isonzo River.

To this must be added the toll on civilian populations. Villages and

What awaited the Yanks
Soldiers on the Western Front lived in holes in the ground,
in company with rats and lice.

towns beyond numbering ceased to exist. Cities were devastated. Shell-fire, disease, exposure, starvation, and a general breakdown of order were claiming approximately as many noncombatant as military deaths.

And yet after all this sacrifice, after two and a third years of nightmare, there was no end in sight, no prospect of victory on either side. From a distance of a hundred years, seeing, as few then living could, that none of the belligerents had wanted the war or intended to start it, one inevitably wonders why so little effort was made to bring it to a stop. The magnitude of the tragedy was obvious to all. Europe, which fancied itself the most civilized place on earth, was devouring itself.

Why, then, were the leaders on both sides so hostile to the idea of peace talks? Why did the common soldiers continue to throw themselves into the maelstrom?

There are many explanations. The body count had been so high from the start, and each side's denunciations of the other so extreme, that in short order the belligerent governments found it impossible to talk of compromise. Having sacrificed hundreds of thousands of lives in a struggle with enemies they described as satanically evil, they could not show a willingness to come to terms with those same enemies without risking a terrible backlash.

Though England and France had been enemies from medieval times into the nineteenth century, the rivalry at the heart of the Great War was that between France and Germany. That the two, though neighbors, were not only separate nations but distinct and often mutually contemptuous cultures went back to the time when imperial Rome conquered and absorbed Europe west of the Rhine (Gaul, the future France) but not the territories to the east. The separation was reinforced in the so-called Dark Ages, when Charlemagne's grandsons divided his huge empire. One took what is now France, the other what is now Germany, and a third found himself holding a middle strip that—foreshadowing the troubles that lay ahead—would be fought over inconclusively for a thousand years and more.

In the Middle Ages, France was pulled together by her ruling dynasty to become a united, powerful kingdom. Germany meanwhile, for complicated reasons still being unraveled by historians, became a hodgepodge of independent states. The humiliations that France was able to inflict on her neighbors east of the Rhine continued through the Napoleonic Wars but came to an abrupt end in 1871. In that year, a coalition of German states led by Prussia (but from which Austria was firmly excluded) inflicted a shockingly decisive defeat on the French. A ceremony in the Hall of Mirrors at the Palace of Versailles, occupied by the victors, declared a unified Germany and installed Prussia's king as her kaiser—her caesar, or emperor. Austria, allowed no part in this, had to turn her attention elsewhere—to a partnership with Hungary and a jumbled-together empire of many nationalities in the south and east.

There followed the transformation of Germany into an industrial powerhouse that paralleled, on a smaller scale, what was happening in the United States. The French elite seethed with resentment at no longer dominating western Europe. They fed their hatred on the Germans' seizure of the provinces of Alsace and Lorraine (which France had seized from German rule in the seventeenth century). The British were thunderstruck to see Germany soon surpassing them in manufacturing and other spheres. In a search for security, Germany, Austria-Hungary, and Russia united in a Three Emperors League, but Vienna and St. Petersburg found themselves in conflict in too many places for their alliance to survive. In the 1890s, fatefully, Russia allied herself with France instead, and there came into existence an unstable balance of power that was still in place in the summer of 1914: the Central Powers (Germany and Austria-Hungary) against the Entente (France and Russia). Britain was on the sidelines, officially neutral but not only friendlier to France but secretly planning to join her if the two blocs went to war. Italy was officially one of the Central Powers but not really committed.

When the war came and showed no sign of ending, the Entente grew to include not only Britain and her empire (India plus the dominions of Canada, Australia, and New Zealand) and France and her colonies in Indo-China, Africa, and elsewhere, but Italy, Romania, Greece, and even Japan. Britain, France, and Russia all saw the conflict as an opportunity that might never come again—thought it unlikely that any of them would ever again have so much support in a showdown with Germany. This contributed to making them unwilling to settle for anything less than victory.

But knowledge of how little progress was being made on the road to victory, and the price being paid to maintain the stalemate, had to be kept from the public. Morale had to be maintained at home, and Britain had the added burden of making the United States want to help and ultimately even join the Allies. Victory had to be depicted as the permanent solution to all the world's worst problems. Spreading that story was the job of London's formidable propaganda machine.

The Germans for their part, believing themselves to have been forced to take up arms against an encircling ring of powerful enemies, were likewise inclined to think that only by winning decisively could they break through to a less perilous future. They, too, thought that anything less than victory could be only a postponement of the ultimate reckoning. The two sides were like men with their hands around each other's necks, feeling grievously wronged, crazed with fear, not daring to loosen their grip.

For the rulers and commanders of every belligerent nation, this meant life under horrendous pressure, gambling with stakes that could not have been higher. To be in such a position was to face the possibility of achieving eternal glory or becoming eternally reviled. Year after year, in country after country, men rose to the pinnacle of power only to be cast aside like burned-out ball bearings.

The cost, for ordinary families from the Pyrenees to Siberia, was and remains beyond imagining.

March 1917 brought the most epochal casting-aside of the war: the deposition of Tsar Nicholas II by Russia's revolutionary Duma and the end of the three-hundred-year-old Romanov dynasty. The same month brought to an end the five-month tenure of Aristide Briand as premier of France; his successor would last only one month longer than he, and the next premier after that would stay in office a bare two months. It was also in March that Karl I, the young Hapsburg who had become emperor in Vienna after the 1916 death of Franz Josef I, finally dismissed Franz Conrad von Hötzendorf as chief of staff of the ravaged Austro-Hungarian army.

Conrad (his family name) had been in his post since long before the outbreak of war, and he personally directed military operations after the fighting began. Therefore he bore heavy responsibility for the unpreparedness of his army and its disastrous failures in the field. That he remained in charge for more than two years shows the rigidity of the regime he served so badly. Other countries were not so inflexible. Helmuth von Moltke's failure to defeat France in 1914 led almost immediately to his replacement, and the man who replaced him was replaced almost as quickly after making his own unsuccessful lunge for victory.

The mediocrity of the original commander of the British Expeditionary Force, Field Marshal John French, caused him to be removed in December 1915. He was replaced by Sir Douglas Haig, who would prove to be equally mediocre but in his own distinctive way. This change was less important than the displacing of Prime Minister H. H. Asquith by David Lloyd George, and incomparably less important than the upheaval that brought Erich Ludendorff to Berlin and positioned him to impose a military dictatorship more far-reaching than anything seen under Kaiser Wilhelm.

In France, the rocklike General Joseph Joffre, who had become a father figure for his nation by commanding the armies that stopped the German advance on Paris in 1914, held on to his post until December 1916. Then he was obliged to give way to Robert Nivelle, a dashing, supremely self-assured, and politically adept figure who at the start of the war had been a mere colonel approaching retirement. Nivelle told everyone that he had an infallible plan for shattering the German line.

Erich Ludendorff
*A brilliant military commander
whose political and diplomatic blunders
showed why war is too important to
be left to the generals.*

British General
Sir Douglas Haig,
French General
Joseph Joffre, and
future prime minister
David Lloyd George
*"Our allies,"
an American officer
discovered, "seem to
hate one another."*

Though France's most experienced soldiers and politicians thought his plan had no chance of success, he was allowed to proceed.

The skeptics were right. Almost from the day it began, in April 1917, the Nivelle Offensive was a disaster. It gained nothing of significance and ended with 270,000 Frenchmen dead or wounded. On April 17 French soldiers no longer willing to have their lives thrown away in reckless offensives began what would develop into a widespread mutiny.

Something similar was happening on the Eastern Front at this same time. Discipline was crumbling in the Russian armies, too. The troops were refusing to attack when ordered.

It began to seem possible that the war would be ended not by the politicians or the generals but by ordinary foot soldiers who had decided to say no.

Chapter 9

"A Message of Death"

MONDAY, APRIL 2, WAS A WET GRAY DAY IN WASHINGTON AND A long one for President Wilson. He rose at sunrise, in spite of having slept briefly and badly, and looked over the speech that he had finished writing late the previous night. Joe Tumulty arrived for work early, too, and at nine A.M. sent the speech off to be printed.

This was the first day of the special session of Congress that the president had summoned two weeks earlier. It was the day on which, he had advised members, he would be delivering a message "concerning grave matters of national policy."

Despite the threatening weather, he and his wife set off after breakfast for their daily round of doctor-prescribed golf (terrible golf in the case of the president, who was known to have taken more than twenty strokes on a single hole). He hoped to go to the Capitol at midday to deliver his speech, but upon returning to the White House he learned that that was not going to be possible. A new House of Representatives, the one elected in November, was trying to elect a speaker and not finding it easy.

After lunch the president read part of his speech to Colonel House. As was his practice, the colonel declared it the best thing Wilson had ever written. They waited, but Congress was still not ready. The president, restless, walked to the War Department and called on Secretary Newton Baker. Then he went to the Navy Department and sat in on one of Secretary Josephus Daniels's staff meetings. After a talk with Secretary of State Lansing, he learned that the House of Representatives was in the process of reelecting Democrat Champ Clark of Missouri as speaker because the Republicans, though the majority, were irreparably divided.

Those dining with the president—his wife Edith, his daughter Margaret, and Colonel House—were careful to limit themselves to small talk. Finally word arrived that the representatives had finished their business, were taking an hour's break, and would be ready to receive the president at 8:30. Edith, Margaret, and House departed for the Capitol at 8:10, taking seats in the gallery. Ten minutes later Wilson stepped into his Pierce-Arrow limousine and, in company with Tumulty and his physician, rode to Capitol Hill.

There, in the chamber of the House of Representatives, the members of the Supreme Court, the cabinet, the Washington diplomatic corps, and the Congress awaited him. When he entered the chamber at 8:35, the assembly stood and cheered. No one had any doubt about what was about to happen.

The president, appearing nervous at first, asked not for a declaration of war but for Congress to "formally accept the status of belligerent" that had been "thrust upon" an unoffending nation by Germany. Most of the things he said in explaining this request were familiar to the assembled dignitaries, a repetition of things he had said, sometimes several times, before.

Germany was of course the villain, responsible for everything. It had "put aside all restraints of law and humanity" and was waging "a war against mankind." Its government was a "national foe to liberty," impelling the United States to do its part in "the vindication of right, of human right, of which we are only a single champion."

And the United States had "no selfish ends to serve," the president said. "We desire no conquest, no dominion . . . seeking nothing for ourselves but what we shall share with all free peoples."

The nation would enter the conflict in such "a high spirit of right and fairness," in fact, that "we have no quarrel with the German people . . . no feeling towards them but one of sympathy and friendship."

He condemned the U-boat campaign, as before, in lurid terms. It was "a war against all nations," the dark work of an outlaw regime. But the United States was going to war not only to make the seas safe but to "make the world safe for democracy." With these words, among the most famous ever spoken by any American, the president raised the task ahead to almost the loftiest level imaginable. He staked out a claim that, if justified, would put intervention beyond the reach of criticism. (It should be noted that Wilson never said the United States was entering "a war to end all wars." The honor of uttering those foolish words belongs to David Lloyd George.)

Less familiar today but also loudly applauded was a warning that the president inserted near the end of his speech. If disloyalty showed its ugly head, he assured the Congress, it was going to be met with "a firm hand of stern repression." Two sentences earlier he had praised the patriotism of German-Americans, diluting the effect by adding that this was true of "most of them." Time would have to pass before it became clear just how ominous this part of the speech was. First Wilson would have to reveal just how serious he was about "stern repression."

What was strikingly new—so new that many of his listeners did not take it seriously—was the president's determination to go to war not in some limited or tentative way but on a scale commensurate with what was happening in Europe. When he prescribed "the organization and mobilization of all the material resources of the country," not many could have grasped what a vast enterprise the nation was about to undertake. Nor could his listeners have understood the significance of Wilson's promise of "the most liberal financial credits" for the other nations at war with Germany, because almost nobody in Washington knew how close the Allies were to financial collapse. These words, too, were applauded lustily, as was the president's call for another expansion of the navy and the mustering into the armed forces of half a million men. That was a number almost inconceivable to Americans not old enough to remember the Civil War and therefore easy enough to cheer.

The president reminded Congress that all this was going to have to be paid for. He said it was his hope that this would be done, to the fullest feasible extent, by "well-conceived taxation" rather than by borrowing, which would pass the burden to future generations. This, too, met with approval. It was applauded—for the time being, and in the spirit of the occasion—even by those who in due course would be trying to block almost every tax measure the president proposed.

Everything Wilson said was answered with shouts of jubilation. So loud were the shouts, and so often did the shouters leap to their feet, that those who sat in silence went unnoticed. The sole conspicuous exception was Senator La Follette. He was on his feet, off to the side by himself, arms crossed on his chest and something like a sneer on his face. When Wilson finished and prepared to depart, even his old foe Henry Cabot Lodge was among those pushing forward to offer congratulations. The president had "expressed in the loftiest manner the sentiments of the American people," Lodge told him. Wilson made his way to his limousine and returned to the White House.

Colonel House had watched it all from above. What he later dictated for his diary is amusing and just a bit pathetic. It shows his expectation that one day many would read his words, as well as his hunger for the credit he was sure he deserved.

"It is needless to say that no address he [Wilson] has yet made pleases me more than this one, for it contains all that I have been urging upon him since the war began," House wrote. "It would be interesting to know how much of his address the president thinks I suggested. He does not indicate, in any way, that he is conscious that I had any part of it, I think it is quite possible that he forgets from what source he receives ideas as suggestions."

Almost as soon as Wilson was gone from the Capitol, and in spite of the lateness of the hour, an energized and exuberant Congress got to work on a number of suddenly urgent war-related bills. First among them was the declaration of war itself. It was a mere formality in the sense that there could be no doubt of its passage, but it had to be put through the mill all the same. Also into the hopper went a bill, largely drafted by the Justice Department, to give the president far-reaching powers to censor the press, prevent the use of the mails for subversive purposes (meaning any purpose of which the administration did not approve), and punish anyone interfering with the armed forces. And of course there were the first appropriations and revenue bills, the start of what would become a stream of increasingly huge outlays and increasingly controversial attempts to fund the war effort.

Meanwhile back at the White House, Wilson withdrew to the quiet of an empty Cabinet Room. There—according to Joe Tumulty, the only other person present—he played out a scene no less dramatic than the one in which, in the early hours of that same day, he is supposed to have poured out his forebodings to the newsman Frank Cobb.

A shaken president, Tumulty would write in his postwar memoir, invited his secretary to "think about what it was they were applauding" at the Capitol. "My message today was a message of death for our young men. How strange it seems to applaud that." He spoke of the torture the past two and a half years had been for him. Of how he had long seen the "utter futility" of neutrality. Of having had to endure constant and cruel criticism while waiting for the public to see it, too.

He read aloud an admiring letter sent five days earlier by a newspaper editor in Springfield, Massachusetts. "That man understood me and sympathized," Tumulty quotes Wilson as saying. Then, "the president drew his handkerchief from his pocket, wiped away great tears that stood in his eyes, and then laying his head on the Cabinet table, sobbed as if he had been a child."

Not all commentators on this story believe it happened. To the extent that it shows a side of Wilson not evident elsewhere—such blatant self-pity is not characteristic, the weeping without precedent—it merits a measure of skepticism. But Wilson's description of himself as heroically stoic, as seeing from the start things to which the rest of the country would long remain blind but suffering in silence, is entirely in character. There is no way of confirming Tumulty's story or of disproving it. One must make of it what one will.

When Congress reassembled on the morning of Tuesday, April 3, ready to get down to work, its top priority was a resolution that had been prepared by the House Foreign Affairs Committee, in effect a declaration of war. As soon as it was passed by both chambers and signed by the president, the constitutional niceties would have been served and a state of war would officially exist. Difficulties arose, but at first they were mere annoyances. William Stone of Missouri, the progressive chairman of the Senate Foreign Relations Committee and a strong Wilson ally back in the days when the administration was focused on domestic reforms, startled his fellow committee members by voting against the resolution. Then, after it received majority approval, he startled them again by declaring that he would not present it to the full Senate, as chairmen customarily did. That task fell to Gilbert Hitchcock of Nebraska, who agreed to perform it in spite of having earlier been opposed to intervention. To continue to oppose it as things now stood, Hitchcock said, would be a "vain and foolish thing." In making the presentation, he asked his fellow senators for unanimous approval. If no one objected, the way would be cleared for passage that day—miraculously fast action by U.S. Senate standards.

The danger of a filibuster—assuming that anyone would have dared such a thing in the face of the pressure for swift approval—no longer existed. Almost a month earlier, in indignant response to the filibuster of the armed-ship bill, the Senate had added something new to its bag of parliamentary tricks. This was cloture, a complicated procedure by which three-fifths of the Senate could cut off debate on any measure. No one could have doubted that, if a filibuster of the war resolution were attempted, cloture would immediately be invoked.

But now came another shock, the biggest yet. Robert La Follette, already the most hated man in Congress and probably the country for leading the armed-ship filibuster, loudly refused Hitchcock's appeal for unanimous consent. This meant that another arcane rule came into effect, and no further action could be taken that day. As the senators dispersed, some asked if La Follette had gone insane. He was, they were certain, committing political suicide.

When they assembled again on Wednesday morning, La Follette was more than ever America's number-one villain. His name was on the front and editorial pages of every morning paper, almost always as the target of vicious and often personal abuse. Even in Madison, Wisconsin, where he had spent six years as a crusading and popular governor, a headline suggested that he had lost his mind. He arrived at the Capitol short of sleep, having spent most of the night preparing a speech, but ready for business and seemingly untroubled. He knew there was no way to stop the war resolution from being passed, but he was determined that first there would be a debate.

Lodge of Massachusetts was among the first to speak. Amid a buzz of murmured approval, he urged passage. He did so in terms that his friend Theodore Roosevelt would have applauded, saying that this was a war against barbarism, against Germany's "mad desire to conquer mankind and trample them under foot." To turn away from the challenge would be to embrace "national degeneracy."

Vardaman of Mississippi, on the other hand, said, "I shall vote against this mistake—to prevent which, God helping me, I would gladly lay down my life." If the country's ordinary citizens were allowed to decide, he said, there would be no war.

Stone of Missouri, having been warned by friends that the position he had taken on the previous day was likely to end his career, nevertheless told his colleagues that intervention was going to prove "the greatest national blunder in history."

Kenyon of Iowa, one of the "willful men" who had filibustered the armed-ship bill, now reversed course and decried any criticism of the president, his cabinet, or the Congress. He demanded "one hundred percent Americanism" and with it unqualified support of the war.

Norris of Nebraska, younger than La Follette but already one of the pillars of progressive Republicanism, raised the tension in the chamber with the accusation that his colleagues supported the war because that was what Big Money wanted.

Reed of Missouri said that if Norris's words did not give aid and comfort to the enemy, "I do not know what would bring comfort to the heart of a Hapsburg or a Hohenzollern."

Williams of Mississippi was the first to use the word *treason*. He aimed it at Norris.

And so it went, for nearly six hours, until the clock was almost at four P.M. At last it was La Follette's turn to take the floor. The gallery was jammed with government officials—even members of the cabinet—along with ladies from the highest levels of Washington society and ordinary anonymous folk. The senator would speak for four hours, moving almost ploddingly from point to careful point, repeating one by one the president's reasons for going to war and answering each at length. This was La Follette's approach to oratory, appealing less to emotion than to evidence and to reason. It risked becoming tedious but rarely failed to be powerful in its effects.

His basic point was that one had to look at America's rather than Germany's actions to understand why the country found itself on the threshold of war: "The failure to treat the belligerent nations of Europe alike, the failure to reject the unlawful 'war zones' of both Germany and Great Britain, is wholly accountable for our present dilemma."

And "we have helped to drive Germany into a corner, her back to the wall to fight with what weapons she can lay her hands on to prevent the starving of her women and children, her old men and babes."

And this was the consequence of the administration's double standard, one that had caused every German offense to be "eagerly seized upon" by the United States while the misdeeds of an equally guilty Britain were "met with extraordinary forbearance."

La Follette dealt scornfully with the demand, heard repeatedly in the Senate that day, that it was the duty of every American to stand with the president in this hour of crisis. A citizen's duty, he said, is to support the president when he is right and to stand with the truth when he is wrong.

And Woodrow Wilson was not infallible, La Follette said. He himself had admitted, in calling for war, that he had been wrong about armed neutrality. He had demanded it as the answer to the submarine threat, and it had turned out to be no answer at all. And yet the president was now attacking those who had been right from the start—that "little band of willful men."

Wilson was also wrong in accusing Germany of breaking a solemn pledge by resuming unrestricted submarine warfare, the senator said. Germany's acceptance of restrictions on its U-boats after the *Sussex* sinking had been explicitly conditioned on the United States doing something about the starvation blockade. When the United States did nothing, the acceptance became null.

The blockade was—here La Follette's language appears to have been congested by emotion—"the most ruthless and sweeping in its violation of neutral rights that up to that time had ever emanated from a civilized government engaged in prosecuting a war."

The president was wrong to call the submarine campaign a war against all humanity. Many neutral maritime nations had found no reason to protest it. Many of those same nations tried without success to get the United States to join them in objecting to the blockade.

The president was also wrong to call the war a conflict of democracy against autocracy. Was Great Britain a champion of democracy in Ireland? In Egypt? In India? To what extent could Britain herself, with her king and House of Lords and severely limited franchise, claim to be a democracy?

As for the claim that the United States had no quarrel with the German people, it was absurd to say such a thing while accepting a blockade that was "starving to death the old men, the women and children, the sick and the maimed of Germany."

No less absurd was Wilson's complaint that the people of Germany had not been consulted about going to war. Were the people of the United States being consulted, really? Had the people of Britain, France, or Russia been consulted? The tenacity with which the Germans continued to fight off an enormous enemy alliance, La Follette said, made it likely that they supported their government more strongly than the American people were prepared to support theirs. He said that his office was being flooded with letters and telegrams from people across the country, and that they supported his position by more than ten to one.

Two honorable courses of action were open to the United States, he said. One was to demand that both sides in the Great War stop interfering with America's rights, including the right to trade where she wished. The other was to stop trading with both sides altogether.

At the end there were tears on his cheeks. He attempted no grand final peroration, but simply stopped and sat down. In the two hours of speeches that followed, he was denounced again and again, but the denunciations were almost all on the ad hominem level. "Anti-American president, anti-American Congress and anti-American people" was typical of the things he was called, but there was little response to the points he had raised. Seated together in the gallery were progressive leader Amos Pinchot and journalist Gilson Gardner. When La Follette sat down, Gardner had turned to Pinchot and said, "That is the greatest speech either of us will ever hear. It will not be answered because it is unanswerable."

The last speech was finished shortly before eleven P.M., and the voting began. The resolution was approved eighty-two to six. Of the eight absent senators, seven were quick to make it known that they, too, would have voted yes if able to be present. In happier days Woodrow Wilson had said, "I take my cap off to Bob La Follette. . . . Taunted, laughed at, called back, going steadfastly on . . . I love these lonely figures." But now La Follette was an enemy, a threat to unity, never to be trusted, never to be forgiven.

The House took up the resolution on Thursday, April 5, its members eager to go on record about the war. Most wanted to display their patriotism, meaning their support for the president. With more than four hundred representatives to deal with, Speaker Clark was obliged to allow them only ten minutes' speaking time each. Late in the day, with the list of those requesting the floor seeming to grow no shorter, he cut that to five minutes. On and on it went. When his turn came, the conservative Fred Britten of Illinois used his minutes to tell his colleagues what, in his opinion, all of them knew to be going on.

"Ask your friends around you on the floor of the House," he said, "'Are you going to vote for this bill?' 'Yes, I hate like the devil to vote for it, but I am going to.' Why do they hate to vote for it? The truth of the matter is that 90 percent of your people and mine do not want this declaration of war and are directly opposed to our going into that bloody mire on the other side."

Members of the war party took offense and challenged what Britten had said. He replied that "probably seventy-five percent" of the House was secretly opposed and that he could name most of them. But doing so would be an unkindness. Everyone was aware of the torrents of abuse, the threats of expulsion from the Senate, that had come down on La Follette for his speech of the day before. La Follette himself was in the gallery, looking impassively on, when House majority leader Claude Kitchin declared that he was going to vote against the resolution and added that he would so in the knowledge that "the whole yelping pack of defamers and revilers in the nation will at once be set upon my heels."

While this debate was in process, and virtually unnoticed because the attention of the press was focused on Capitol Hill, the White House issued an executive order. It was directed at the U.S. Civil Service, which was responsible for the administration of thousands of federal jobs, and it gives a remarkably vivid indication of how, even at this early stage, the president intended to manage the government and the nation during wartime.

It read as follows:

> The head of a department or independent office may forthwith remove any employee when he has ground for believing that the retention of such employee would be inimical to the public welfare by reason of his conduct, sympathies or utterances or because of any other reasons growing out of the war. Such removal may be made without other formality than the reasons shall be made a matter of confidential record, subject however to inspection by the Civil Service Commission.

The power of this edict lies in the vagueness of its language. Anyone might be fired if someone in authority decided to fire him for almost any reason or no reason at all so long as the firing was said to have something to do with the war. It contained no provision for appeal or even for allowing the discharged employee to know why he had been dismissed. In light of what would soon follow, there need be no doubt that this bore the stamp of Woodrow Wilson personally.

It was almost three hours past midnight on Friday, April 6, when the last speech ended in the House and voting could begin. As in the Senate, the result was a foregone conclusion. What is surprising is that the minority, the members expressing uncertainty and discomfort instead of eagerness for war, had throughout the night received nearly as much applause as the most bellicose patriots. But if Representative Britten had been correct in what he said on the previous day, the vote did not necessarily reflect the thinking of the members. Three hundred and seventy-three of them voted yes, only fifty no.

The president signed the resolution as soon as it was delivered to the White House at midday, interrupting his lunch to do so. It thereby assumed the force of law, and the United States was at war.

PART TWO

The Price

The object of this war is to deliver the free peoples of the world from the menace and the actual power of a vast military establishment, controlled by an irresponsible Government, which, having secretly planned to dominate the world, proceeded to carry out the plan without regard either to sacred obligations of treaty or the long-established practices and long-cherished principles of international action and honor; which chose its own time for the war; delivered its blow fiercely and suddenly; stopped at no barrier, either of law or of mercy; swept a whole continent within the tide of blood—not the blood of soldiers only, but the blood of innocent women and children also and the helpless poor; and now stands balked, but not defeated, the enemy of four-fifths of the world.

—WOODROW WILSON, AUGUST 27, 1917

←

The first of millions
July 1917: a division of U.S. doughboys is rushed to France.

Chapter 10

Taking Charge

FOR WOODROW WILSON TO EXPECT UNITY WHEN HE LED AN UN-
certain nation into war with a faraway country that did not want war and
posed at worst a dubious threat to the United States was, to say the least, expecting a great deal.

To *demand* unity under such circumstances, to equate disagreement with
subversion and set out to extinguish it, was worse than an error of judgment.
It was to subject the institutions of democracy to strains they were ill equipped
to withstand. It damaged those institutions and did injury to untold numbers
of the citizens they were intended to serve. It set loose in American society
dark currents of mutual distrust that would poison the nation's politics far
into the postwar years.

Unity was impossible because *everything* connected with the war effort was
controversial, and every question turned into a fight. The fault lines ran in all
directions. The ones dividing various pro-war groups from one another were
sometimes little less deep than the ones separating proponents and opponents
of intervention.

In the days following the declaration of war, there was confusion even
about what intervention was going to mean. One veteran senator, Thomas S.
Martin of Virginia, declared after voting for the war resolution that "Congress
will not permit American soldiers to be sent to Europe." The White House
soon set him straight, but among his colleagues there remained widely divergent assumptions about what role the United States was going to play in the
Great War and how much it was prepared to commit.

The most fundamental question, once the president had made clear that he
wanted an army of a million men or more, was how to create such a force and

how to do it quickly. Three possible approaches were obvious: conscription, the recruitment of volunteers, or some combination of the two. The debate brought to the surface incompatible beliefs about the United States, what kind of nation it was, and what its citizens wanted it to be. It aroused deep and powerful passions. Many Americans, perhaps especially the most recent arrivals, associated conscription with the Old World and the autocratic regimes that they or their forebears had come to the New World to escape. The United States was supposed to be different. When her citizens fought, they did so freely, not because the government compelled them.

Such views reached back to the birth of the republic. They had contributed to making conscription ineffective when various colonies attempted it during the Revolutionary War, and to sparking draft riots when both sides introduced it during the Civil War. But not all Americans were opposed. Universal military service on a European model had been advocated in the United States in the years preceding the Great War, and the number of advocates increased as the war dragged on. One of the toughest congressional struggles of 1916 centered, as we saw earlier, on a National Defense Act put forward by the Wilson War Department. The president abandoned it, and with it the idea of a reserve force of four hundred thousand volunteers, when opposition from southern and western Democrats threatened to split the party. The episode made clear that at that point Wilson would have preferred to expand the military on a volunteer basis but was not prepared to fight to make it happen. It showed, too, that he had limited interest if any in universal (which is to say compulsory) military training.

As the months of neutrality turned to years, support for a system in which every young male would be obliged to spend at least some months in military training drew both increasing support and increasingly outspoken opposition. Cost figured importantly in the debate. Universal military training would have required an enormous increase in an army budget that, though it totaled only about $200 million, already accounted for a fifth of federal government spending. (It takes some effort to grasp just how small the American government and its military were before the Great War. Fewer than twenty officers served on the Army General Staff in Washington. The planning staff was only half that size. And yet the War Department, together with the Post Office, accounted for well over half of the federal payroll.)

President Wilson caused much surprise when, shortly after signing the declaration of war, he reversed his earlier position and asked Congress for authority to raise the new army entirely through conscription. The bill he sent to Capitol Hill would allow only enough men to volunteer to expand the Marine Corps and fill vacancies in the small regular army and the National Guard. Though the guard was not much respected by the regular army's professionals, the support that its many units enjoyed as a result of functioning as state militias gave it more political clout than the White House could afford to ignore.

The president's request reignited the anger of southern, western, and rural voters, without whom the Democrats could have no chance of winning national elections. From that perspective it was a courageous move. The reasons for it, in any case, were in no way mysterious. They began with the experience of the Allies in putting their enormous armies into the field and attempting to expand them even while having to replace endless heavy casualties. None of them could have continued the fight if they had tried to rely on volunteers. Even Britain, which had begun the war with a tiny army and taken pride in relying on volunteers to build a force of millions, had in 1916 found it necessary to introduce conscription on a massive scale.

What mattered especially to Wilson and to new secretary of war Newton Baker was what London had learned, to its cost, about how reliance on volunteers disrupted industrial production. Too many of the British who signed up for military service—some of them shamed into doing so by a propaganda machine that encouraged women to give white feathers to apparently healthy young men who appeared in public in civilian clothes—had skills that were indispensable in mines and factories. Shortages of skilled workers eventually became so acute that the government found it necessary to order many soldiers back to their peacetime jobs. This experience caused the Wilson administration not only to insist on conscription but to maintain strict limits on the number of volunteers.

At stake, as the administration sent its bills to Congress, was nothing less than the question of who was going to be in charge of the war effort. Would it be the White House or Congress or both, in some kind of improvised collaboration? The administration's position was clear: it intended to take command. It found itself challenged as early as April 9, when Republican Senator John W. Weeks of Massachusetts introduced a resolution calling for the establishment of a Joint Committee on the Conduct of the War. On the face of it the idea was unobjectionable, a vehicle by which members of Congress from both parties would be able to monitor spending and guard against mismanagement. As with the question of conscription, however, the president's and Secretary Baker's knowledge of history came into play. They knew that a committee of the same name had been created during the Civil War and had been blamed ever since for putting unnecessary obstructions in Abraham Lincoln's path. Wilson went personally to Capitol Hill and got key Democrats to promise that they would keep the Weeks resolution from coming to a vote.

The issue was complicated by that most intemperate of Woodrow Wilson's critics, Theodore Roosevelt. Two decades earlier TR had made himself a national hero by raising his volunteer regiment of Rough Riders for service in the Spanish-American War and leading them to glory in Cuba. Since leaving the White House in 1909, he had itched to get back into uniform and into some war somewhere. He insisted on being called not Mr. President but Colonel Roosevelt, and during the Wilson administration's troubles in Mexico he had sought unsuccessfully to get permission to once again raise his own fighting force. He was determined not to miss out on the greatest war in history. He called on friends from across the country to help him get permission to recruit an infantry division that he would command as a major general.

Those who hated the very idea of conscription welcomed Roosevelt's plan for a force of volunteers (a Democratic congressman spoke for millions when he said that "opposition to compulsory military service is characteristic of every government fit to be called a democracy") and were encouraged to give voice to their objections. It thereby put the administration's plans in jeopardy. On April 18 the House Military Affairs Committee approved a bill to ban conscription and require reliance on volunteers exclusively. On the same day, as though to ensure maximum confusion, the Senate's equivalent committee approved the administration's conscription bill. Meanwhile Roosevelt was expanding his original vision. He now wanted to recruit not a mere division but an army corps of as many as a hundred thousand men. This corps would be commanded not by TR himself but by his friend Major General Leonard Wood, a former army chief of staff still on active duty; Roosevelt would be one of Wood's division commanders. The corps would be mustered at Fort Sill, Oklahoma, and though otherwise privately financed would be equipped by the regular army. It was to be a cross section of the American population, with some units made up of German-Americans ("loyal" ones, of course) and a black regiment led (of course) by white officers. Those officers not cherry-picked from the regular army would be sons of the nation's "best" families, with places reserved for descendants of the nation's past military heroes. In recognition of Lafayette's role in the Revolutionary War, there would also be places for representatives of the French aristocracy.

His corps, TR said, would embark for Europe after sixty to ninety days of training and be ready to engage the enemy by September 1. In this and other ways it was a blatantly harebrained scheme, one that if implemented would have thrown the entire war effort into disarray. TR was fifty-eight years old, in uncertain health (he had less than two years to live), and utterly without qualifications to lead thousands of men in the kind of total war being waged in Europe. His claim that he could have an army corps that did not yet exist in action on the Western Front in about four months exposed the depth of his naïveté. It was also a reflection of the peculiar arrogance that made many Americans contemptuous of the European armies and the soldiers serving in them.

Providing the Roosevelt corps with uniforms, weapons, and other essentials would have stripped the regular army bare. And only a fool could have expected TR, once he was in Europe and in charge of a division, to follow orders or restrain himself from the public airing of his inevitable disagreements with his superiors. Even in the Spanish war, as a mere lieutenant colonel, he had sometimes been nearly unmanageable.

It is astonishing that TR thought he could win White House support for his plan, especially after all the abuse he had been directing at Woodrow Wilson since before the 1912 election. But he did. He even arranged to call at the White House and make his appeal in person. He and Wilson had first met twelve years before, when the Army-Navy football game was played at Princeton: then-president Roosevelt attended, and Wilson served as host. But the campaign of 1912 had turned them into bitter rivals, the bitterness being almost entirely on a frustrated TR's side. Wilson, for his part, now that he was himself a two-term president, found his visitor charming. He said afterward that TR was "a great big boy."

"There is a sweetness about him that is very compelling," he said. "You can't resist the man. I can easily understand why his followers are so fond of him."

Roosevelt was less than sweet in what he said to a companion immediately after leaving the White House. "If any other man talked to me as he did, I would feel assured," he remarked. "If I talked to another man as he talked to me it would mean that that man was going to get permission to fight. But I was talking to Mr. Wilson. His words may mean much, they may mean little. He has, however, left the door open." In ending his visit, he had jovially invited

Joe Tumulty to join his division and come with him to France. Later he said that if Tumulty did join up, he would be regarded as a Wilson spy and kept at a "distance from headquarters except when he was sent for."

It is pathetic to see the former president, a man of formidable intellect as well as inexhaustible vitality, spinning fantasies in this way. Wilson, understandably wary, is not likely to have said anything that a cool-headed listener could have taken as genuine encouragement. He had "left the door open" only to the extent of not saying bluntly that what TR wanted was never going to happen. A politician as experienced as Roosevelt should have understood this—his sour comments upon leaving the meeting suggest that at some level he did understand—but his hopes swamped his judgment. Though he continued to despise Wilson, he ceased for the time being to say so in public. He expected his friends to see to it that, if the president refused him his corps, Congress would give it to him.

Many Americans continued to believe that conscription would bring the end of what made their country unique among the world's great nations. Many others continued to regard conscription as not only necessary but potentially beneficial to democracy, mixing the classes together and showing recent immigrants and the poor how to become good citizens. As the issue became entangled in the struggle over Roosevelt's army corps, the stakes rose. Wilson and Baker knew that they could not afford to lose on such an important question at this early stage. The difficulties of the situation and the bad feeling generated by Roosevelt's relentless politicking hardened Wilson's conviction that attempting to build his new army with volunteers could only end badly.

Time passed, and nothing was decided. On April 23, three weeks after Wilson's call for war, the Senate passed an amendment to the stalemated manpower bill that, if it became law, would compel the War Department to authorize Roosevelt to recruit his hundred thousand volunteers. But the House of Representatives, where pressure from the White House kept the Democratic majority in line, rejected the same amendment. Competing bills were sent to a House-Senate conference committee. Its members, dodging the real question, busied themselves with debating the age at which men should be drafted, if any ever were drafted. They deadlocked on that, too.

Congress was more relaxed about appropriating the huge sums of money the administration had begun requesting within hours of the declaration of war. It showed itself eager, in fact, to approve virtually any numbers the admin-

Women's work,
1917
Recruiting,
volunteering for
the Red Cross,
reporting for
duty as drivers.

istration put before it, and to slow down only when presented with proposals for raising the necessary sums through taxation. Both chambers had immediately approved a loan of $200 million to Britain, and on April 24 they authorized Treasury Secretary McAdoo to raise $5 billion—an eye-watering sum in those days—by selling bonds. Three of those five billions were to be lent to the Allies, a reflection of Washington's new awareness that the Allies were on the brink of financial collapse. London and Paris could hardly have hoped for more, at least where their finances were concerned, and at least in the short term.

Few other matters moved forward so smoothly. Amid universal professions of eagerness to cooperate and avowals that partisan bickering must be suppressed for the sake of winning the war, rancor infected everything. The president's rejection of suggestions that he should invite Republicans to join his cabinet and thus become partners in a kind of coalition government was entirely defensible. But some saw it as petty, and at times Wilson *was* petty. An example was his refusal to invite senators from either party to the receptions that welcomed diplomatic missions from Britain and France during the last week of April. Regardless of whether his disdain for the Senate was justified, it would have been wise of him to do a better job of concealing it.

The purpose of the Allies' diplomatic missions was not only to cement their

U.S. secretary of state Robert Lansing and British foreign secretary Arthur Balfour, 1917
Meeting in Washington, openly allied at last.

new partnership with the Americans but to reveal, now that the United States was committed, just how frightening their situation was. Their first priority was to get the United States to start sending what was most urgently needed without delay. The British arrived first, their delegation headed by Arthur Balfour, Edward Grey's successor as foreign secretary. Balfour was intelligent, immensely sophisticated, and a son of the highest levels of the aristocracy. He was, in short, an impressive specimen of his country's ruling class and perfectly suited to spin a web of enchantment around Colonel House.

René Viviani, former premier of France, and Marshal Joseph Joffre visit America, April 1917 *"The French only asked for all the money in the world."*

The French made their appearance three days later, headed by the odd couple of René Viviani and Joseph Joffre. Viviani, born in the French colony of Algeria, was a socialist and a fiery orator who had been premier in the first year of the war. Emotionally unstable (he would end his life in an insane asylum), he was appallingly ill suited to serve as an ambassador of goodwill. His Washington hosts, inevitably, soon showed a decided preference for dealing with Joffre. A portly, grandfatherly figure, unflappably good-humored, "Papa" Joffre had won international fame for his performance as commander of the French army as it fended off the German invasion of 1914. The long stalemate that followed led to his replacement by a younger general promising quick victory, but instead of being cashiered, Joffre was given the exalted rank of marshal of France and an easy schedule of ceremonial duties. Official Washington embraced him as a hero.

The worst of their money worries having been put to rest by the American government's largesse, the visitors began unveiling some of the hard truths concealed behind years of propaganda. They were not winning the war. In fact, they were in danger of losing it. Their casualties had been much higher than even their own citizens knew, Germany's U-boat campaign was proving alarmingly effective, and it appeared increasingly possible that Russia would before long be removing herself from the war. The great spring offensive organized by Joffre's successor Robert Nivelle, which had reached its climax while Joffre and Viviani were still at sea, turned out to be another disaster. If the French envoys knew that it had cost forty thousand of their countrymen's lives, and that in the aftermath of the slaughter tens of thousands of Nivelle's troops were refusing to obey orders, they did not share that information with their hosts. There was a limit to how much bad news the Americans needed to be told.

What Balfour and Joffre did tell their hosts was sufficient to put the lie to what David Lloyd George had told Ambassador Page, four months earlier, about wanting the United States in the war not because of her wealth or manpower but because she could be a force for good. The need for such pretense was over, and now the talk was about little except American money, American supplies, and American troops. "The French only asked for all the money in the world," the writer and disabled veteran Lawrence Stallings would later observe sourly. The British were "more pragmatic." They wanted only to be able to send America's youth "off to death or mutilation in France."

Joffre saw no point in being subtle. "We want men, men, men!" he declared, stressing the importance of sending at least a symbolic contingent of troops without delay. Only such a demonstration could put heart into soldiers and civilians whose morale was sinking under the weight of Allied losses. A member of the British delegation, Major General G. T. M. Bridges, went a big step further. He proposed that the United States avoid the difficulties and delays of creating its own expeditionary force and instead hurry half a million men, untrained recruits if necessary, to England. There they could be trained under experienced British leadership, then moved to the continent and absorbed into the Allied armies.

Some members of the French mission endorsed this idea enthusiastically. They loved the thought of using American infantrymen to replenish their depleted battalions. Bridges was a credible advocate, having commanded a division on the Western Front, and his American listeners had few grounds for disputing his claim that the British had proved their ability to turn civilians into combat-ready soldiers in no more than twelve weeks. No one could disagree when he argued that his approach was the only conceivable way to get hundreds of thousands of American troops into action in 1917, "before what we would call the fighting season is over for the year."

Bridges said his proposal had the endorsement of the chief of the Imperial General Staff and of Douglas Haig, commander of the British Expeditionary Force. It had appeal even for some of the Americans—not least those civilians faced with the task of building an American Expeditionary Force virtually from scratch. But difficulties were obvious as well. How could Americans serve in a French army whose language they did not understand? How would Irish-Americans react when ordered to put on British uniforms?

Such questions were trivial compared to the insult to American military leadership that was implicit in the Bridges proposal. The Allies wanted masses of ordinary soldiers, not officers. They wanted no officers at all, in fact, above the rank of captain. More senior officers took this as a slap in the face. To become involved in the biggest war in history, to win that war and with it promotions that otherwise might not have come in decades—these things had until recently been only the wildest dreams of the West Pointers. Were they now to be cast aside? And who *were* these Allied generals, to be so presumptuous? What had they done with the millions of men under their command except get them slaughtered? Why should they be given hundreds of thousands of young Americans to replace what they had squandered?

From the administration's perspective, from Wilson's, what made the proposal absolutely unacceptable was what it implied about America's visibility in the war. If Washington did as Bridges was urging, there could be no American army in Europe, no American commanders, no distinctly American victories, no way to prove, when the final victory came, how much the United States had contributed to it. Much of the point of intervention—the earning of a prominent role in deciding the fate of the world after the fighting stopped—would be lost. Even if there had been no other difficulties, even if the army had not hated Bridges's proposal, this would have been enough to keep the president from acceding.

He did, however, agree to Joffre's first and most heartfelt request. A division of American regulars would be dispatched to Europe forthwith: not to be inserted at once into the trenches, but to prepare the way for the greater numbers that would come later and show the Allies that help was in fact on its way. Such a demonstration, a grateful Joffre assured the president, would make all the difference. One small complication would have to be overcome, and its existence showed just how unready the United States was for war on the European scale. In order to send a division, the army would first have to *create* a division. A European division included upwards of ten thousand infantrymen, plus artillerists and men with auxiliary functions of many kinds. The regular U.S. Army contained no unit so large and complex.

Which brought the White House and Congress back to the unresolved question of where the army was going to get the manpower it needed. The reversals through which this question went in the first half of May are too complicated, and in some cases make too little sense, to be detailed here. Congress's inability to decide made it an object of scorn across the country. As Roosevelt's demands came to be seen as a cause of delay, he began to lose some of his heroic luster. Even Senator Henry Cabot Lodge, for whom the former president was almost a brother, lost his appetite for fighting this latest of TR's battles. Finally, on May 17, the conference committee settled on a bill that would introduce conscription on the administration's terms. It *authorized* rather than *required* the War Department to allow Roosevelt and Wood to create their corps.

On the following day TR wrote to the president to "respectfully ask permission immediately to raise two divisions for immediate service at the front," adding that he stood ready to raise four divisions "if you so direct." Upon receiving this message, the president issued a public statement that "I shall not avail myself, at any rate at the present stage of the war, of the authorization conferred on me by [Congress's] act to organize voluntary divisions."

That was the end of it. Everyone understood that Colonel Roosevelt was never going to be a general.

The extent to which Congress and the nation remained uncomfortable with conscription is evident in the fact, astonishing in retrospect, that when the conference committee sent the manpower bill back to both chambers for final approval, the House of Representatives approved it by only 199 yes votes to 178 opposed, with fifty-three members abstaining. When the Senate voted, twenty-three members abstained and eight were openly opposed. Opposition remained strong, support far from unanimous.

Conscription thus became the law of the land a contentious month and a half after the president's bill was introduced. Wilson could proceed, but no one knew how he intended to do so. He could draft men by the millions, but no one knew where he would put them. People wondered how, if the government continued to move at this pace, the United States would ever get into the war.

What the administration had won was, however, of real importance. It cleared the way for the White House not only to raise an army but also to manage the war. A pattern was being set. Issue by issue, fight by fight, Wilson was getting his way.

Colonel House, for his part, was less interested in army building than in geopolitical matters. He found it as delightful to discuss the fate of the world with Arthur Balfour as he had earlier with Edward Grey. The colonel appears to have been rendered almost childishly credulous by the elegant and quietly self-assured Balfour, the nephew of a former prime minister in addition to having served as prime minister himself. He gives every evidence of having accepted without question Balfour's assurances that Britain was committed to standing with the United States in bringing peace and justice to a wicked world and to doing so selflessly.

When Balfour arrived in New York en route to Washington, House arranged to meet with him and afterward dispatched a report to the president. "I told Balfour I hoped England would consider that a peace which was best for all nations of the world would be the best for England," he said. "He accepted this with enthusiasm." House suggested a "tacit understanding" by which neither the British nor the Americans would discuss postwar peace terms with the other Allies, because they were too greedy to take a satisfactorily selfless view. Again Balfour agreed: too much discussion of too many issues could generate friction at a time when everyone had to be focused on the defeat of Germany. Talks were also unnecessary, House assured the president, because eventually "this country and Britain will be able to dictate broad and generous terms—terms that will mean permanent peace." So many dubious assumptions are packed into those words as to make the colonel seem fatuous. It is of course possible that he was expressing not what he believed but what he knew would please Wilson.

House again sounds like an innocent in a diary entry about telling Balfour that "Great Britain and America, I thought, were great enough to rise above all petty considerations." And about how it pleased him to see the Englishman "rise up with enthusiasm to the suggestion." Again, the colonel's diary was a testament to his own importance, composed with future readers in mind, at least as much as it was a candid record of what he was thinking and feeling. He could not have remained as important as he was for as long as he did had he been as guileless as he sometimes makes himself sound.

When they reconnected in Washington, House and Balfour had a ninety-

minute talk about redrawing the map of the world. They agreed that an independent Polish state must be established. (Actually, this had been an aspiration
of the Germans before the war, their aim being to insert a buffer between
themselves and the Russians.) The Austro-Hungarian Empire was to be broken into three autonomous countries, with leftover bits given to various
neighbors. "I said to him what I once said to Grey," House told his diary, "that
if we are to justify our being in the war, we should free ourselves entirely from
petty, selfish thoughts and look at the thing broadly and from a world view-
point. Balfour agreed to this with enthusiasm."

There were limits, however. When House suggested that they should not
"look upon Germany as a permanent enemy" but as a fellow member of the
family of nations once she had been chastised and democratized, Balfour
found no further reserves of enthusiasm to draw upon. The colonel's diary
entry regretfully describes him as remaining "more impressed with the German menace" than with whatever new scenarios the postwar world might
present.

How easy Balfour must have found all this. He wrote of liking House "tremendously," and little wonder. Whatever the colonel said, all Balfour had to do
to satisfy him was demonstrate eager agreement. It was all confidential—in
fact, all of it was entirely unofficial. House was pleased, and Britain was committing to nothing.

This was a good time for House, who found himself restored to the president's favor now that the question of intervention was no longer putting a
strain on their relationship. Wilson welcomed the colonel's opinions as unreservedly as in the past, and appreciated the value of his wide circle of contacts.
His letters to House became nearly as effusive as they had been years earlier. "I
am grateful to you all the time," he wrote on June 1. And on August 16: "I devour and profit by all your letters."

Meanwhile the British and French missions remained in Washington, making their case. Their objective, as one member said, was "to get enormous
quantities of supplies from the United States . . . vast loans, tonnage, supplies
and munitions, food, oil, and other raw materials." The administration found
all this perfectly agreeable and opened wide the horn of plenty.

Needs less crucial than saving the Allies from collapse were treated with
similar urgency by the administration. Before April was out, by executive
order, the president had created a Committee on Public Information and
given the job of running it to the man whose idea it was, the longtime Wilson

admirer and muckraking journalist George Creel. The purpose of what would be known as the Creel Committee was, officially, to help the American public understand that intervention had not only been necessary but was going to change the world. Unofficially, it would have many other objectives.

Curiously, the president acknowledged the dangers of creating such a body in the statement with which he announced it. "I can imagine no greater disservice to the country than to establish a system of censorship that would deny the people of a free republic like our own their indisputable right to criticize their own public officials." What is most curious, and an example of what a paradoxical figure Woodrow Wilson could be, is his uttering such words at precisely the point when he was beginning to do the very thing about which he was warning. It brings to mind the dark thoughts about the consequences of going to war that he is supposed to have told to journalist Frank Cobb not long before asking Congress to declare war.

His first step toward undermining the Bill of Rights was to send to Congress his Omnibus Bill, so called because it cobbled together seventeen legislative measures drafted by the Justice Department in anticipation of a declaration of war. One of its articles, if approved, would have conferred on the president specific authority to censor the press. This was obviously unconstitutional and in calmer times would have been summarily dismissed as such. Wilson nonetheless declared it to be "absolutely necessary to the public safety" and threw all the resources at his disposal behind its passage. The ensuing struggle dragged on into June, with virtually the entire American press unsurprisingly opposed. (Ironically, only foreign-language publications supported Wilson. Their editors apparently hoped that they could escape accusations of disloyalty by surrendering their autonomy voluntarily.) Senator Hiram Johnson of California—the man who famously said that when war comes, truth is the first casualty—was not alone in complaining that such a measure would make it an arguably criminal offense to criticize incompetence, inefficiency, or even outright criminality in the management of the war effort.

In the form finally passed by Congress and renamed the Espionage Act of 1917, the bill was stripped of any reference to press censorship. This was the administration's first significant defeat since the declaration of war, but the setback scarcely mattered. Even in its truncated form, the act set the stage for the most far-reaching assault on the rights of citizens in American history, before or since.

Background

Going Dry

Wartime, with its inflamed passions and angry insistence that all citizens commit themselves to the pursuit of the same towering objective, proved to be very good for people with axes to grind or scores to settle.

If you argued fervently enough that your particular cause was patriotic—better, that the satisfaction of your demands would help win the war—you could sometimes accomplish things that had seemed impossible in peacetime.

If you could persuade the right people that those who opposed you were obstacles to victory, that they fell seriously short of being One Hundred Percent American, those right people could sometimes be persuaded not just to side with you but to attack your rivals on your behalf.

Issues that had long divided Americans thus got resolved with surprising speed once the country was at war: sometimes neither fairly nor democratically, sometimes savagely, not always lastingly, but invariably in favor of whichever side made the best case for its "Americanism" and thereby won official and public approval.

An interesting case in point, because it was also a peculiarly divisive and uniquely American one, was Prohibition. The campaign to free the people of the United States from the curse of John Barleycorn was half a century old when the war in Europe began. Though it had gained strength over the two generations following the Civil War, progress came at a glacial pace. But then two and a half years of increasingly nonneutral neutrality, during which the Preparedness Movement arose with its insistence that the nation gird itself for war, gave the enemies of strong drink a powerful boost.

Intervention provided a still more powerful boost. It allowed those Americans who believed alcohol to be intrinsically evil to position their cause as impregnably patriotic and essential to the war effort. They seized the opportunity with such force that the war became the vehicle on which Prohibition rode to enshrinement in the Constitution.

The drive to purge intoxicating beverages from American life was older than populism, progressivism, or any of the reform movements active at the start of the twentieth century save one—woman suffrage. The importation of "ardent spirits" was banned in colonial Georgia as early as 1733, and Maine outlawed the production or sale of strong drink in 1851. A Prohibition Party was founded in Oberlin, Ohio (earlier a hotbed of the antislavery movement), in 1869. It gave former abolitionists a new goal: to cleanse the nation of beer, wine, and distilled spirits. The party grew to marginally respectable size—from 1900 to 1916 its candidates for president never received fewer than two hundred thousand votes— but never became competitive with the People's and Progressive Parties at their peaks, never mind with the Democrats and Republicans.

The same was true of the Woman's Christian Temperance Union (WCTU). It, too, was founded in Ohio, just a few years after the Prohibition Party, and it held its first national convention in 1874. In addition to preaching abstinence from alcohol, it became involved in such worthy causes as protecting working girls from sexual exploitation. It also displayed a busybody streak, crossing the dim line that separated reform from intrusion into citizens' private affairs. It called for the prohibition of golf on Sundays, sounded the alarm about the practices of immigrants, and even demonstrated a potential for violence as the militant Carrie Nation began taking a hatchet to drinking establishments in the Midwest. Even so, like the Prohibition Party, the WCTU benefited from the reform impulse that had the nation in its grip at the turn of the century. In the first two decades of the new century, its membership doubled to 340,000.

The organization that put muscle into the cause and made it a real political force was not founded until 1893, the year a financial panic sparked a depression and the start of the populist revolt. This was the Anti-Saloon League. Like its two predecessors, it started in Ohio, and it quickly outgrew both. It was something new in American politics: a well-organized, well-financed interest group that used only one criterion—a willingness to vote for prohibition—in deciding which politicians to support and which to oppose. By the time Woodrow Wilson became president, the league was feared and courted by politicians in most parts of the country, the South and Midwest especially.

The work of the league, and the whole prohibition movement, was an expression of the old idea of American exceptionalism, the belief that the United States at the time of her creation was untouched by the pollutions of the Old World and must remain so in order to fulfill her destiny.

These were exalted if naïve ideas, but in the rapidly changing America of the time, an industrial power with fast-growing cities and endangered family farms, they acquired an ugly dimension. Prohibition became very intrusive indeed, and was tainted with the nativism that had made the so-called Know-Nothings of the mid-nineteenth century a potent political force. Its adherents showed an inclination to believe that only people of English and Scots-Irish ancestry, and perhaps only those who still lived on farms or in small towns and remained staunchly Protestant, were fully and truly American. Germans might be conditionally acceptable—at least the Protestant ones, and even they only until 1914. The Irish were seen as barely half civilized and were Papist to boot. As for the Jews and Poles and Italians and people from places no one had ever heard of, they, too, were turning the nation's cities into alien places, pits of ignorance and decadence and corruption. Or so it was said. And widely believed.

Prohibition became a unique reform issue, one that was less economic or political than cultural. It also became divisive in a uniquely toxic way. It could be not just rural but smugly anti-urban, not just nativist but aggressively anti-other, not only militantly Protestant (largely Baptist and Methodist) but fiercely anti-Catholic, anti-Semitic, anti–yellow peril. It was stronger among Republicans than Democrats until 1909, when William Jennings Bryan embraced it publicly for the first time. (He probably acted when he did because, having just failed in his third run for the presidency and having lost hope of ever reaching the White House, he was no longer worried about the big-city vote.) But characteristically, in taking up the cause, he focused on its positive side, the hope of eliminating the harm done by alcohol abuse. He never used the issue to denigrate ethnic or religious minorities, and never tried to use war fever—to which he himself remained immune—to challenge the loyalty of those who did not think drinking sinful.

But Bryan was exceptional. As Richard Hofstadter says in his classic *The Age of Reform,* Prohibition became poisonous, "a means by which the reforming energies of the country were transmuted into mere peevishness." It was "a pseudo-reform, a pinched, parochial substitute for reform that had widespread appeal to a certain type of crusading mind. It was linked not merely to an aversion to drunkenness and the evils that accompanied it but to the immigrant drinking masses, to the pleasures and amenities of urban life, and to the well-to-do classes of cultivated men." It might even have been, at least in part, not a reform movement at all in any true sense but an unreasoning expression of resentment and fear, of hatred for the frighteningly unfamiliar new America to which the post–Civil War era had given rise.

None of which kept it from being, thanks in large measure to the tough tactics of the Anti-Saloon League, a force on Capitol Hill in 1917. In its early years, the league had concentrated on the relatively modest goal of getting state legislatures to enact local-option laws, which did not ban alcohol but gave counties and towns the authority to do so. But as its power grew and with it an impressive record of success, it broadened its horizons to embrace national goals. By 1917 dozens of states had passed local-option laws, others had outlawed alcohol altogether, and prohibition was an issue in nearly every state and local election. The league now looked to Congress for its ultimate triumph: adoption of an amendment to the Constitution.

It had reason to be confident. In the Congress elected in 1916, supporters of Prohibition (the "drys") outnumbered "wets" by two to one. The Preparedness Movement reinforced the trend. It gave force to the argument that, in light of the Allies' need for American exports of food, nothing edible by humans should be converted into alcohol. And that a tipsy America could not possibly be prepared to fight.

Once war was declared, all restraints were off. Distillation was banned by Congress as a waste of food crops, and just drinking beer could draw accusations of disloyalty. The nation's beer barons with their Teutonic names were said to be financing a vast conspiracy in the service of the Beast of Berlin. Prohibitionists celebrated as a sign of divine approval the Supreme Court's upholding, in the very month war was declared, of a 1913 law forbidding the transporting of any kind of alcoholic beverage into any dry state.

The Anti-Saloon League exploited the horror with which virtuous citizens reacted to the thought of innocent boys being exposed to the temptations of military life. The president shared these concerns, as did his secretaries of war and the navy. This, and congressional eagerness to please the prohibitionists, led to the insertion into the conscription law of a provision making it a crime to buy or give a soldier or sailor an alcoholic drink. The young Raymond R. Fosdick, once a protégé of Wilson's at Princeton, was assigned to keep vice away from army training camps.

Eventually he would claim to have put 110 red-light districts out of business in the nine months following the declaration of war. He established detention camps where fifteen thousand women convicted of prostitution were locked away, most of them until 1920.

President Wilson had never taken a clear stand on the prohibition question, fearing that it would split the Democratic Party and interfere with the war effort. He did get the Senate to stop the blanket ban on the use of grain for alcohol production, but later he signed a bill forbidding the production of any beverage with an alcohol content of more than 2.75 percent. This was enough to put many producers out of business. When American troops began arriving in France, they were allowed only "light wines" and beer. Establishments serving anything stronger were put off-limits.

The momentum had become unstoppable, passage of a constitutional amendment more and more probable. The Age of Reform would soon be giving way to the Age of Capone.

Chapter 11

"Skin-Deep Dollar Patriotism"

ONCE THE *BIG* QUESTIONS HAD BEEN SETTLED—THE UNITED STATES was going to create a huge army, it was not going to rely on volunteers, and money would be no object—the *hard* questions came to the fore. They had to do not with *what* the government was going to do but *how,* exactly.

How to turn many hundreds of thousands of raw recruits (not all of them impressively able or willing) into a fighting force capable of taking the field against the German "military machine." (It was one of the achievements of Allied propaganda that no one ever spoke of a British military machine, or a Russian, or a French. The troops of the Allies were of course "boys," and heroes. Those of the enemy were malevolent robots, disposable parts—Huns.)

And how to get the new army into action in time to make a difference.

As the costs of intervention began to come into focus, it became clear also that the Allies were going to be even more demanding than they had been before America's declaration of war. Even after receiving tens of millions of dollars in emergency low-cost loans, even after being assured that additional billions more would be forthcoming (billions that the U.S. government would itself have to borrow and then pass along), they wanted more, and quickly. They seemed incapable of imagining that the New World, a fountain of dollars and foodstuffs and manufactured goods, might not be an infinite one.

This was spectacularly true of the French. Alexandre Ribot, who had been France's premier for all of four days shortly before the start of the war and now in 1917 was back for a term that would last less than six months, had particularly grandiose ambitions where aviation was concerned. He informed Washington that his nation required "a flying corps of 4,500 airplanes—personnel and matériel included—to be sent to the French front during the campaign of

1918," which meant in not much more than twelve months. By "personnel" he meant five thousand pilots and fifty thousand mechanics.

And that was barely the beginning. Altogether, Ribot added, it was going to be necessary for the United States to provide France with 16,500 aircraft "of the latest type" and thirty thousand engines to power them. This was preposterous; in 1917 there was almost no such thing as an American aviation industry. The War Department pointed out that its only air arm, which was part of the Army Signal Corps, could muster thirty-five men who had some knowledge of how to pilot an airplane. It had fifty-five aircraft, all but four of them obsolete and those four classed as obsolescent. The department had ambitions of its own where aircraft production was concerned—time would show them to be nearly as unrealistic as Ribot's—but even its inexperienced planners could see that producing *any* aircraft "of the latest type" was going to be a challenge. At the start of the war France, not the United States, had been the world leader in aviation technology. In the following two and a half years, the Entente nations and the Germans all made amazing technological leaps, leaving the United States further behind than ever.

Where technology and industrial capacity were not barriers, the Wilson administration was inclined to promise nearly anything the Allies requested, and Colonel House for one expected the cost of doing so to yield important diplomatic rewards. "When the war is over we can force them to our way of thinking," he wrote the president in July 1917, "because by that time they will, among other things, be financially in our hands." Here as with regard to other matters, his crystal ball would prove to have been cloudy.

Aircraft production was just one of Washington's weaponry problems, and far from the most serious. In fact, in almost no area was the United States prepared to equip a huge army and provide it with the firepower that modern warfare required. A grand total of fifteen hundred machine guns were available to be sent to France with the initial contingent of troops that Marshal Joffre had been promised. This was an impressive number only to the blissfully ignorant; the machine gun had become the indispensable infantry weapon of the Great War, the killing machine that more than any other was responsible for turning the war into a blood-drenched stalemate. Britain in the spring of 1917 had 80,000 such guns. By 1918 it would have 120,000.

The American army's Springfield rifle was considered the best in the world, but not nearly enough had been produced and the only sources were two smallish factories. American manufacturers had sold huge numbers of artillery shells to the Entente over the past thirty months, but the U.S. Army had only enough to last, at Western Front rates of consumption, about nine hours. The tank, which would eventually prove to be the answer to the machine gun and make wars of mobility once again feasible, was under development in Britain, France, and Germany and was slowly, by a painful process of trial and error, becoming an effective weapon. But not one tank, primitive or otherwise, had ever been built in the United States.

One thing aside from money that the United States had the potential to provide in practically unlimited quantities was manpower. To fulfill the promise that one division would be sent to France without delay, the commander of the southwestern military district was instructed to select three infantry regiments and one regiment of artillery—what would become the core of the army's First Division, the Big Red One—for transfer to the East Coast. There were two reasons for drawing these units from the Southwest. That district was exceptionally rich in manpower at the time, having been sent large numbers of regular and National Guard troops to deal with the Mexican troubles. And the service record and political connections of the officer in charge there, Brigadier General John J. Pershing, made him a leading candidate to take charge of the new division. He knew his troops well, having commanded the expeditionary force sent south in pursuit of Pancho Villa. He understood that a great deal of work would have to be done to get them ready for service on the Western Front.

In short order, Pershing received a telegram from the chairman of the Senate Military Affairs Committee—who happened to be his father-in-law—asking if he spoke French. The general undoubtedly stretched the truth in replying that after spending several months in France in 1908 he had spoken the language "quite fluently," that he "could read or write very well," and that he could "easily reacquire satisfactory working knowledge." Such a white lie is understandable considering the obvious implications of the senator's question, which was soon followed by orders for Pershing to travel to Washington without delay. He could have had little difficulty guessing what was afoot.

The First Division's lack of readiness was of little consequence compared with the fact that hundreds of thousands of men were soon to be drafted and the War Department literally had no place to train them—no place, even, for them to sleep or eat. It was decided that facilities were needed for the training of a million recruits at a time, and that these facilities must be open for business by the first of September. The immensity of the task was obvious. The response, simply stated, was a decision to drown the obstacles in money.

What was needed was little less than the creation of dozens of new cities in no more than three or four months. The War Department decided that there would be thirty-two of these "cantonments": sixteen would have wooden barracks for the men being trained for the new National Army, and others would be tent cities for the National Guard. The cantonments became political prizes, and the question of which states and congressional districts would get them set off intense bickering in Washington. The Democrats' Solid South did well. Georgia became the home of four camps, South Carolina of three. When Florida found itself the only state in the Southeast with none, its senior senator raised such a fuss that Secretary Baker was obliged to find one for him.

"The cost in most cases could not be considered," the colonel in charge of the construction program would testify when called before a congressional committee. "The work had to be done, and the only function we could exercise was to do what we could to get it down as low as possible." Everything was done at maximum speed by hastily chosen contractors working on a cost-plus basis, which gave them no incentive to economize and little reason to worry greatly about the quality of the work being done. By the end of June, all but two of the cantonments were under construction, and by the September 1 deadline, all of them were, if not complete, at least in a state that made it possible for draftees to start moving in.

Two hundred thousand men were employed on the construction. They consumed two billion nails, twelve million square feet of window glass—overall, thirty thousand tons of building materials per day. Not surprisingly, the results tended to be barely satisfactory at best, a scandal at worst. Even some of the new hospitals lacked proper sanitation, and many buildings were unheated. Where metal tubing was in short supply, plumbing pipes were sometimes made of wood. Republicans wanting to make trouble for the administration found a wealth of ammunition in what recruits encountered when they reported for duty. That the cantonments cost $199 million is less surprising than the fact that that amount would turn out to be barely a quarter of wartime spending on military construction.

What many in and out of government expected to be the greatest challenge of all, conscripting hundreds of thousands and eventually millions of men, turned out to be almost the easiest. Secretary Baker, as a student of history, knew of the draft riots that had almost destroyed New York City during the Civil War, and he saw in them a warning. The government's main mistake in 1863, he believed, had been to put the military in charge of conscription, causing it to be seen as something imposed on the population by force. (The Lincoln administration got little for its trouble, by the way. Draftees and men paid to serve in place of draftees ultimately made up only 6 percent of the Union army.)

Baker removed the uniformed services from the conscription process almost entirely. A national network of local volunteers—business and professional men, educators and clergy—was created to implement a new Selective Service System, and these men reported not to the War Department or to any other part of the federal government but to the governors of the states. (*Selective* Service was a term of art. It signaled the authority granted to the administration by Congress to decide, on the basis of national need, which groups of men would be inducted and which would not. *Service* was likewise a felicitous choice—so much less abrasive than *conscription*.)

The administration announced that all males between the ages of twenty-one and thirty, the slice of the population declared to be eligible by Congress, would be required to register on June 5 at their local post offices, not at any kind of military facility. Baker hoped that this approach could turn June 5 into a kind of celebratory event, almost a holiday. President Wilson invited the public to regard it as "a great day of patriotic devotion and obligation." Addressing an assembly of Confederate veterans on registration day, he called it "a very happy day, because a day of reunion, a day of noble memories, a day of dedication, a day of renewal of the spirit which has made America great among the peoples of the world." Still, Washington held its breath amid warnings that Americans would never allow themselves to be herded into the military in the European manner, that the streets were going to run red with blood.

More than nine and a half million men registered that day, and it all went as smoothly as anyone could have hoped. Any inclination to complain or fail to cooperate had been discouraged both by a Committee on Public Information publicity barrage and by the approving newspaper coverage given to the arrest and swift punishment of those who, in the weeks before June 5, dared to speak out against the draft. ("Death for Treason Awaits Anti-Draft Plotters," a *Los Angeles Times* headline crowed on May 25. Readers of *The New York Times* were assured that "the Selective Service Draft gives a long and sorely needed means of disciplining a certain rather insolent foreign element in the nation.")

More often than not—this happened dozens, then scores, ultimately hundreds of times—those considered to be troublemakers were charged with violating the newly passed Espionage Act. This enabled prosecutors to ask for ruinous fines and decades-long prison sentences.

Answering the call
Nine and a half million men registered for the draft on June 5, 1917.

On July 20, after every registered man had been assigned a number between 1 and 10,500, a lottery was held to determine which of the men not exempted on occupational, health, or other grounds would be inducted first. Flashbulbs flared as first a blindfolded Secretary Baker, then other officials including the president, drew numbers out of an enormous glass bowl containing 10,500 capsules. The drawing took more than fourteen hours, but again everything went smoothly. After deductions were made for the men who had volunteered to fill vacancies in the regular army and the National Guard, it was announced that 687,000 draftees would be ordered to report for duty on September 1.

Many thousands of men, by some estimates a hundred thousand or more, did not register as ordered. Over the following five months, six thousand would be arrested and charged with evasion. Criticism of the draft continued all the same, and there were significant disturbances both in cities and in remote rural areas. In August, in probably the largest single incident, some 450 hapless and largely illiterate tenant farmers and sharecroppers were arrested and confined in a penitentiary for participating in an Oklahoma protest that came to be known as the Green Corn Rebellion. A number of them were sentenced to prison terms of as long as ten years, a signal to the nation that further such eruptions would carry a heavy price.

Meanwhile the cantonments were being thrown together, and various offices of the War Department were struggling to figure out who was going to train the recruits and how they were going to be clothed and fed and provided with medical care. Just finding enough cooks to serve three million meals daily was a major headache.

The magnitude of the challenge is apparent in the War Department's calculation that the army, which on April 1 had fewer than six thousand officers on active duty, was going to need two hundred thousand within the next year or so. That number did not include another seventy thousand commissioned officers required in the medical service and other specialized functions. The officer corps was going to have to be more than twice as big as the whole army had been on the day Wilson called for war. Sixteen officer training camps were set up in addition to the thirty-two cantonments. They were modeled on the so-called Plattsburg camps, which General Leonard Wood had begun as a privately organized and financed summer program to make middle- and upper-class volunteers ready to take up commissions when the need arose; these camps had begun to receive federal financing during the preparedness fervor of 1916. An initial intake of more than thirty thousand officer candidates was called to active duty in May. Most were recent college graduates and upperclassmen not willing to wait until graduation to get into the war.

The immense size of the training programs would have unwelcome consequences for many of the men who had been on active duty with the regular army when the United States went to war. The scarcity of commissioned and noncommissioned officers with sufficient knowledge and experience to train recruits meant that more than half of the regulars would still be at home when the war ended. This was intensely frustrating for career officers like Dwight D. Eisenhower, who spent the year and a half after America's declaration of war in Kansas, Maryland, and Pennsylvania. He finally got orders for France but was still waiting for embarkation when the fighting ended and his departure was canceled.

Two great questions remained to be settled that summer, two questions that had become urgent as soon as war was declared. Coming on the heels of

"The cost . . . could not be considered"
Throwing together the training camps employed 200,000 men and consumed thirty tons of building materials a day.

the battles over conscription and the Espionage Act (more about that shortly), they would create lasting bitterness and deepen the distrust that now separated the White House from much of Congress.

The first had to do with food. Consecutive bad wheat harvests in 1916 and 1917, ceaseless demand from overseas, and the shenanigans of speculators were causing shortages, wild price inflation, and smoldering public anger. The situation became critical as demand from the Allies rose to three hundred million bushels annually and an increasing number of transport ships fell victim to the U-boats. The president's first response was to create, by executive order, a food administration to improve supply and distribution. As its head he appointed Herbert Clark Hoover, a Quaker engineer and self-made millionaire whose management of a massive Belgian relief program had made him an international symbol of selfless and efficient public service.

The constitutionality of establishing a large and powerful agency by presidential fiat was dubious. This brought Hoover's authority, and the legitimacy of the food administration, into question. It obliged Wilson to send to Congress a bill that would put the new operation on a solidly lawful footing and extend its powers even to the setting of prices. The article having to do with prices provoked storms of opposition. The middlemen in the long chain of transactions by which agricultural produce moved from farmers' fields to kitchen tables were reaping unprecedented profits, and many thought it outrageous that the government should tell them how much of a cut they could take. Republicans and Democrats alike were wary of extensions of presidential power, and many wanted no government intrusion into the marketplace. Meanwhile farmers and speculators were hoarding not only wheat but other crops as well, knowing that scarcity would make continued price increases all but certain.

Appeals to patriotism and fair play had no effect. Not for the first or last time in Great War America, citizens facing a choice between the common good and fast fat profits showed a decided preference for the latter. As the young but already distinguished journalist Walter Lippmann observed, "There are political and commercial groups who see in this whole thing nothing but opportunity to secure concessions, manipulate tariffs and extend the bureaucracies." The result, for Congress and the White House, was another bitter and protracted legislative battle. The public, looking on, grew ever more indignant.

The House of Representatives did not approve the administration's bill until

Herbert Hoover,
relief administrator
*Having fought to prevent starvation,
he warned that the Paris peace treaty
could only end in new trouble.*

June 23. It empowered Hoover's agency to set some prices and regulate distribution, but the prohibitionists succeeded in inserting a clause forbidding the use of crops for alcohol production. Senate approval appeared improbable. Most of the Senate's old guard Republicans and no few Democrats objected as a matter of principle to what they saw as a socialistic measure. Other Democrats were simply fed up with the Wilson administration's presumption in neglecting to consult Congress except when it had no choice. Even senators long friendly to Wilson were losing patience with his remoteness and apparent expectation that Congress should do his bidding without question. One such senator, the progressive Democrat Henry Hollis of New Hampshire, sent a note warning the president that "it is too late to put the [food] bill through by an appeal to the friendliness of the senators." Wilson was running perilously short of friends.

Organizations representing the cotton growers of the South and the wheat farmers of the western plains were immovable in their opposition to controls. The senators from their states, especially the Bourbon Democrats, were potent voting blocs and chaired a disproportionate number of important committees. They had been the first to oppose the food bill, and other interests soon decided that they could only lose out by failing to do the same. The president reverted to a tactic that had worked for him in the past, appealing over the heads of the legislators to an exasperated public. Though this made a number of senators unhappier than ever, Wilson had much of the press on his side. He was able to generate sufficient pressure that a bill he was willing to sign finally made it to his desk on August 10.

This, too, was a limited victory, one preceded by several subsidiary fights. With much difficulty and no small expenditure of political capital, the administration managed to kill a clause that would have taken food control out of Hoover's hands and given it to an independent board. No less difficult was the defeat of a second attempt to create a Joint Committee on the Conduct of the War. In the end wheat prices were capped, but restraints on cotton proved unachievable. Cotton prices, driven by demand, hoarders, and speculators, continued a rise that would eventually quadruple the prewar level. The Republican establishment, western farmers, Democrats from outside the South—these groups and others emerged from the fray feeling cheated. Many were inclined to blame Woodrow Wilson.

Hanging over everything was the issue of money, still unresolved. The question, as always, was not whether sufficient funds would be found to satisfy the demands of the War Department and the Allies. Everyone accepted that they would be, so that few saw much reason to worry about budgets. But *how* were the needed billions to be raised? The president's preference for taxation, first expressed when he called upon Congress to declare war, was having little effect; there was too much opposition. While bills authorizing the sale of bonds reached his desk in lightning time—they troubled no special interests, as few business barons objected to government borrowing if the alternative was reduced profits—his tax bill remained stuck in Congress, a bone of endless contention. Congress was similarly sluggish in handling appropriations bills, further increasing the government's dependence on bonds.

As originally sent to Capitol Hill, the administration's revenue bill entailed an increase in taxes on the highest incomes, with particular emphasis on profits being made out of the war. This was popular in the South and West, the regions where enthusiasm for the war was faintest and resentment of the eastern business establishment strongest. The industrialists and bankers of the North, to no one's surprise, were loud in their expressions of horror. The arguments used by the likes of J. P. Morgan, Jr., remain both widely held and controversial today: high taxes punish enterprise and initiative and retard productive investment. Low taxes ultimately benefit every level of society. Tax increases might demoralize those patriots without whose humming factories nothing would be possible.

A bloc of progressive senators from both parties—the "willful" few who had voted against the war, joined now by some who had supported intervention—called for a war profits tax of 80 percent. Told by indignant conservatives that such a rate would wreck the economy, they replied that Britain had started with a 50 percent tax on war profits, later raised it to 80, and suffered no obvious ill consequences. Treasury Secretary McAdoo, worried that too high a rate would affect his ability to sell bonds, opined that 31 percent would suffice. Eventually he would get his way.

When in May the House Ways and Means Committee approved a tax increase for individuals and companies in the highest brackets, a closing of loopholes, and the doubling of an excess-profits tax enacted back in March, opponents shifted their lobbying into high gear. The Senate Finance Committee held weeks of hearings that provided a high-visibility platform for antitax views. After sitting through these hearings, Hiram Johnson observed wearily that they had "brought into sharp relief the skin-deep dollar patriotism of some of those who have been loudest in declamations on war and in their demands for blood."

On May 24, two weeks after his arrival in the capital, General Pershing was taken to the White House by Secretary Baker and introduced to the president as the newly appointed commander not just of the First Division but of the

Making soldiers and sailors
*Dental hygiene, calisthenics,
learning to handle a rifle—all
part of getting ready for war.*

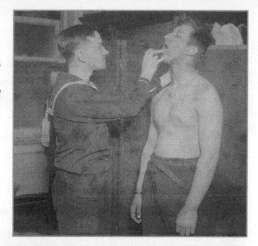

American Expeditionary Force (AEF). Pershing, stunned by how little the general staff had done or was trying to do to prepare for war in Europe, was surprised again by Wilson's failure to ask questions or give him any instructions. He had expected some discussion of what worried the general staff most: British persistence in urging that America's conscripts be handed over to the Allies for training or for integration into the Allied armies after basic training in the States. But the president did not mention the subject. In time Pershing would see the advantages of serving a chief executive who took as little interest in military matters as Wilson did in the work of most government departments. It freed him to make his own decisions and stake out his positions with little fear of interference.

On that same day, the House of Representatives passed a version of the tax bill that provided for only $1.8 billion in new revenue, not nearly enough to meet the need even in the near term. Even so, the Senate soon pared it by 11 percent, after which it hung in the limbo of a conference committee.

Four days after seeing the president, Pershing boarded a ship bound from New York for England. With him went 191 handpicked men, a multiple of the number the general staff had in Washington. This was an early indication of the determination of the expeditionary force's new commander not to operate on the small scale that had long been habitual for the army. He also took with him two sets of written orders, one signed by Secretary Baker, the other by

Doing his bit
*Financier J. P. Morgan, Jr., supports a war bond drive
with a $10,000 check.*

Army Chief of Staff Tasker H. Bliss, although Pershing and his chief of staff had written it themselves. Both instructed Pershing to keep the AEF entirely separate from the armies of the Allies and to refuse all suggestions or requests or demands to the contrary. He, Baker, and Bliss all understood that he was going to need such an order.

When in October the revenue bill reached the president's desk at last, six months after it was first proposed, it was a pathetically puny thing. The revenue stream that it created was scarcely more than a trickle when compared with the Treasury Department's second bond drive, which was then in preparation, would raise another $4.6 billion, and would be followed by a series of later, still larger drives. Meanwhile the head of a steel company noted that he and his counterparts were "all making more money than the average human being ought to." Postwar congressional inquiries would establish that in 1917 the profits of the Savage Arms Corporation amounted to 60 percent of its sales, the Bethlehem Shipbuilding Company increased its profits eightfold between 1914 and 1918, and DuPont's stock dividend was at the war's end sixteen times what it had been at the start.

There could no longer be any doubt that the war was going to be financed mainly through borrowing. This was painless in the short term but worrisome in the long. It transferred immense amounts of wealth to the buyers of the bonds, which were a boon to high-income investors because the interest was tax-free; this increased the initial nominal return of 3.5 percent (later it would be higher) to an actual 9.5 percent. The bonds burdened the future with debt and were powerfully inflationary.

Every answer seemed to bring new questions in its wake, and every solution gave rise to new problems. Troubles rolled in like waves in the ocean. Some were of tsunami proportions.

Secretary McAdoo informed Congress that the government's financial needs just for the current fiscal year were going to be five billion dollars higher than he had estimated in May.

General Pershing, who shortly after arriving in Europe had told Washington that he was going to need a million men by May 1918, now revised his figures, too. In order to do what he had been sent across the water to do, he reported, he was going to need three million.

What had been done and spent so far was obviously no more than a good start. Only a fool would have tried to say where it was all going to end.

Background

Destiny's Child

In February 1917, with American intervention in the Great War seeming not only inevitable but imminent, the identity of the general who would be chosen to command American troops in Europe was pretty much taken for granted in the White House and the War Department.

It was not John Pershing, excellent though his credentials and connections were.

It was not Major General Leonard Wood, whose connections were even better than Pershing's and whose credentials included past service as army chief of staff. He had burned too many bridges with his intrusions into partisan politics and razor-tongued criticism of the Wilson administration's reluctance to go to war. And Secretary of War Baker, who had observed him in the field during summer maneuvers, thought he had grown too fat.

It was assumed, rather, that if an American army did go to war, it would do so under the command of Frederick N. Funston, the most remarkable figure to have risen to the rank of general in the U.S. Army in the half century after the Civil War. Unlike Pershing, he was not a West Pointer; in fact, he failed the West Point admissions test at age eighteen and never graduated from any college. He did not even become a member of the regular army until he was thirty-five years old.

He was a swashbuckler, though a diminutive one at five foot five and 120 pounds, as dashing as a character out of a boys' adventure story. He never put on a uniform until he was thirty, spending his early manhood as a railroad worker, newspaper reporter, and botanical researcher in Alaska. He finally became a soldier by running off to Cuba to join the rebellion against Spain. He rose to lieutenant colonel in the Cuban revolutionary army and saw much action before contracting malaria and finding it advisable, his weight having fallen to ninety-five pounds, to return home to Kansas.

When the United States declared war on Spain, Funston's experience in Cuba (plus, as seems likely, the influence of his father, whose political career had included election to Congress) won him appointment as colonel in the newly formed Kansas Volunteers. Then he was off to the Philippines, and the hard, ugly war to suppress the insurrection there. Funston became a legend. He won the Congressional Medal of Honor and in 1900 was promoted to brigadier general of volunteers. He applied for a commission in the regular army and was turned down. He was slated for discharge and return to the States when, in March 1901, he planned and led an operation that captured the leader of the rebels, Emilio Aguinaldo. For this he was made, at age thirty-five, the youngest general in the regular army.

He was as flamboyant as he was tough, rarely careful with his words. When a reporter asked him about alleged atrocities in the Philippines, he boasted that "I personally have strung up thirty-five Filipinos without trial." He said that Americans calling for withdrawal "should be dragged out of their homes and lynched." President Roosevelt reprimanded him for one such outburst but to little effect. Funston was stationed in San Francisco at the time of the 1906 earthquake and showed firmness bordering on brutality in dealing with looters. Later he applied similarly rough tactics to striking miners in Nevada. Despite criticism, most of the public saw him as both colorful and needed, a pillar of law and order. In 1914 he commanded the troops that occupied Veracruz, Mexico, and later that year was promoted to major general, the army's highest rank at the time. He was not yet fifty, had been a general for fifteen years, and now had overall command in the Southwest, including the Mexican conflict.

John Pershing, though almost five years older than Funston, was junior to him in rank and unknown to the public. When he took his force of cavalry across the border in pursuit of Pancho Villa, it was to Funston that he reported.

But then came the night of Saturday, February 17, 1917. President and Mrs. Wilson were among the guests at a dinner party at the home of Secretary of War Baker. They were at the table when someone knocked at the front door. It was the army major who had duty at the War Department that night. A telegram had arrived, and he thought Wilson and Baker should see it. It reported that Fred Funston had dropped dead of a heart attack in San Antonio.

"What now, Newton?" the president asked. "Who will take the army over?"

Baker turned an inquiring look on the major.

"I cannot of course speak for the army," said Douglas MacArthur, young for his rank, son of a general and Civil War hero, himself a rising star. "But for myself the choice would be General Pershing." That was how MacArthur would remember it. Baker remembered General Tasker H. Bliss as the man MacArthur named.

In any case, no one except the bitterly disappointed Leonard Wood would find much reason to disagree with the choice of Pershing to head the AEF. Not even Wood's good friend Theodore Roosevelt could muster any real indignation, because he was Pershing's friend, too, and in fact had been responsible for his rise to the senior ranks of the army. With Funston out of the picture, there were few alternatives to Pershing, really. The general staff was headed by men whose combat experience had ended with the Indian Wars, some of them too old for the Western Front. Pershing was the only active-duty general with recent experience in leading large numbers of troops against armed enemies. And there was little in his background to which anyone could reasonably object.

Born in small-town Missouri, the son of a family of Alsatian origin and very limited means, Pershing had entered West Point at the unusually advanced age of twenty-one because it offered a college education at government expense. His success as a cadet (he was class president

General John J. Pershing, commander of the American Expeditionary Force, 1918
He "inspired confidence but not affection—personal magnetism seemed lacking."

and held top rank as "first captain") is sometimes attributed to his being older than his classmates, a man among boys, but there was more to it than that. Robert Lee Bullard, who would become one of the highest-ranking generals of the AEF, recalled that First Captain Pershing "inspired confidence but not affection. Personal magnetism seemed lacking." He wrote that Pershing's "exercise of authority was then and always has been since, of a nature peculiarly impersonal, dispassionate, hard and firm." A bit of a cold fish, evidently, if only in the professional part of his life.

There was another part, clearly. Almost paradoxically, Bullard recalled also that Pershing was what the young men of the time called the "spoony" type: fond of the ladies. Like his stern, coldly military bearing, this would be a lifelong trait, one that he would attempt with imperfect success to keep concealed from view.

He graduated in 1886, in time to witness the last of the Indian Wars. This led to the dreary life of a junior officer whiling away the peacetime years in the dusty outposts of a small army whose senior members often stayed on active duty into old age, blocking the paths to promotion. (Douglas MacArthur's father, who as a teenage Civil War hero attained the rank of colonel, later spent twenty-three years as a captain on the western frontier.) Young Pershing, restlessly ambitious, earned a law degree at the University of Nebraska while on active duty. He expected to resign his commission as soon as a sufficiently attractive opportunity came his way, but the Spanish-American War came first. Suddenly the army became interesting.

In Cuba he served with the Tenth Cavalry, one of the army's four black regiments, thereby acquiring a rude nickname that was later domesticated as Black Jack. He had met Roosevelt when TR was New York City's police commissioner, and the two had hit it off. Now he was serving with Lieutenant Colonel Roosevelt. Their units fought side by side in the assault on San Juan Hill. Pershing was commended for gallantry and given the temporary rank of major.

Next came assignment to the Philippines. When Pershing arrived, a captain once again, Fred Funston was already a regular army general in spite of having served no apprenticeship in the lonely weather-beaten forts of the Great Plains. Pershing performed well, as before, but for the rest of his career he would be dogged by rumors that he contracted gonorrhea twice and fathered half-Filipino bastard children. He denied all of it, but to little avail. (A decade later these rumors would still be potent enough to cause him to be denied appointment as superintendent at West Point.)

The most important factor in Pershing's rise happened in 1905. Stationed in Washington, he courted and won Helen Frances Warren, daughter of Francis Warren of Wyoming, Republican chairman of the Senate Military Affairs Committee. From that point, things happened fast. Pershing, accompanied by his bride, was sent to Tokyo as military attaché and from there became an American observer of the war in which Japan astonished the world by inflicting a humiliating defeat on Russia. In 1906 President Roosevelt intervened personally to move his old comrade in arms up four ranks in a single leap, from captain to brigadier general. Pershing thus leapfrogged over 862 more senior officers and was much resented as a result. Between them, however, the president and Senator Warren had more than enough clout to stifle objections.

Nine years later Black Jack Pershing was serving under Fred Funston in the Southwest when a searing tragedy struck. A fire at San Francisco's Presidio, where the general's family awaited his return from the border, killed "Frankie" Pershing and the couple's three small daughters. Only their son, Warren, survived, rescued by a servant; he was sent to live with his grandparents in Washington, and his father went on with what now seemed a blighted life. He was thus on duty, available to answer destiny's call, when Funston keeled over after dinner at a Texas hotel. The timing was crucial: the United States was at the time only seven weeks from going to war.

Pershing knew what was at stake, knew he had a better chance than most of being summoned, and was not prepared to leave things in destiny's fickle hands. On April 10 he sent President Wilson a letter:

"As an officer of the army, may I not extend to you, as commander in chief of the armies, my sincere congratulations upon your soul-stirring address to Congress on April 2d. Your strong stand for the right will be an inspiration to the citizens of this Republic. It arouses in the breast of every soldier feelings of the greatest admiration for their leader."

Colonel House could hardly have done it better. And any questions that Pershing's Republican connections might have raised at the White House were answered by his father-in-law's willingness to cooperate with the administration. First Senator Warren switched from supporting

Theodore Roosevelt's army corps request to opposing it. Then his clout as chairman of the Military Affairs Committee proved crucial in blocking the creation of the proposed Joint Committee on the Conduct of the War. One must assume that he would have acted no differently if the father of the grandson he was now raising had not been in line for the European command. Be all that as it may, less than two months after writing to the president, Pershing was on a ship bound for England.

As he took up his new duties, the two most deeply entrenched aspects of his character made themselves apparent. First, and most conspicuously, there was the strong-jawed man of few words, the consummately professional soldier. Even the British were impressed to see their preconceptions about bigmouthed, excessively friendly Yanks so utterly contradicted. From the start Pershing insisted that, while in France, the American army was going to adhere to the standards of West Point. Officers' tunics, for example, would have no pockets; objects had a way of being deposited in pockets, making the wearer look lumpy. Fraternization between American soldiers and French women was firmly discouraged, and the military police were instructed—to the astonishment of the French—to enforce a ban on prostitution. Men who contracted venereal disease were to be court-martialed and, after medical treatment, would serve three months at hard labor and lose two-thirds of their pay. The wives of officers, even the most senior officers, were forbidden to travel to France.

Behind all this, invisible to nearly everyone, the "spoony" Pershing survived. A wealthy American gave him the use of a fine apartment at 73 rue de Varenne in Paris. With impressive speed Pershing acquired, and installed in the apartment, a twenty-two-year-old mistress, an artist of Romanian extraction named Micheline Resco. The general would keep the apartment, and the girl in it, even after moving his headquarters far from Paris. He would keep them as long as he was in Europe.

Woodrow Wilson would have been shocked.

Chapter 12

Cracking Down

WILSON THE WAR LEADER, NO LESS THAN THE WILSON OF THE NEU-trality years, professed to loathe war and did so sincerely. But the post-intervention version saw *his* war as a unique exception, with a purpose that set it apart from every other war in history. It was going to liberate the whole of mankind. It would lead to just and lasting global peace, and so it was worth any sacrifice of blood and treasure. And because it was such a glorious cause, so incomparably noble, the president found it inconceivable that anyone might not want to join it. Just as Germany, if it was at war with Woodrow Wilson's United States, must be the most monstrous of nations, so, too, there must be something monstrous at work in the hearts of those who refused to follow him at home. If such people couldn't see what he saw, they must be morally tainted if not deranged. They had to be stopped from spoiling everything.

The character of the wartime Wilson, so needful of maintaining an almost superhuman image and self-image and forcing the rest of the world to submit, explains his ferocious support for one of the most remarkable pieces of legislation in American history, the Espionage Act of 1917. Though the act he signed into law on June 15 fell short of what he had originally demanded, it was momentous all the same. What made it so was not a grant of power to censor the press—not even a Congress controlled by his party could bring itself to agree to that, despite the president's insistence—but the right it conferred upon the government to define dissent as treason and punish it accordingly, and to single out for destruction any publications of which it did not approve.

Here is what it made the law of the land:

Whoever, when the United States is at war, shall willfully make or convey false reports or false statements with intent to interfere with the operation or success of the military or naval forces of the United States, or to promote the success of its enemies, or shall willfully make or convey false reports, or false statements . . . or incite insubordination, disloyalty, mutiny, or refusal of duty, in the military or naval forces of the United States, or shall willfully obstruct . . . the recruiting or enlistment service of the United States, or . . . shall willfully utter, print, write or publish any disloyal, profane, scurrilous, or abusive language about the form of government of the United States, or the Constitution of the United States, or the military or naval forces of the United States . . . or shall willfully display the flag of any foreign enemy, or shall willfully . . . urge, incite, or advocate any curtailment of production . . . or advocate, teach, defend, or suggest the doing of any of the acts or things in this section enumerated and whoever shall by word or act support or favor the cause of any country with which the United States is at war or by word or act oppose the cause of the United States therein, shall be punished by a fine of not more than $10,000 or imprisonment for not more than twenty years, or both.

That was far from all. At least as insidious as the act's broad, vague list of ill-defined new crimes, at least as ominous as the draconian punishments it prescribed, was an article that gave tyrannical powers to, of all improbable recipients, the Post Office Department. It authorized the postmaster general to refuse to mail any publication that in his opinion violated any of the provisions quoted above, or that he judged to have advocated treason, insurrection, or "forcible resistance" to any American law.

The man to whom it fell to interpret these provisions and put them to work, Albert Sidney Burleson, had been a seven-term congressman when Woodrow Wilson became president in 1913. Burleson badly wanted a cabinet post and got his wish thanks to his fellow Texan Colonel House. He has been called the worst postmaster general in American history, but that is unfair; he introduced parcel post and airmail and improved rural service. It is fair to say, however, that he may have been the worst *human being* ever to serve as postmaster general. Shortly after taking office, he introduced racial segregation into an organization that had been relatively free of it since the establishment of the U.S. Civil Service in the 1880s. He segregated lunchrooms and toilets, ordered the installation of screens to spare white employees the indignity of having to see or be seen by black co-workers, and had blacks in southern states discharged or demoted. He required photographs to be submitted with job applications, so that supervisors would not have to waste their valuable time interviewing unwanted candidates. The leading African American intellectual of the time, W. E. B. Du Bois, would say that the Wilson administration originated "the greatest flood of bills proposing discriminatory legislation against Negroes that has ever been introduced into the American Congress."

Albert Sidney Burleson, U.S. postmaster general, 1913–1921
The most powerful postmaster general in history, thanks to the Espionage Act.

This side of the Wilson administration, and therefore to some extent of the president himself, has only recently been brought to public attention and become a cause of some embarrassment for Princeton University, where Wilson has long been revered as a kind of secular patron saint. Wilson appears to have viewed Burleson with benign amusement. He called him "the Cardinal" because of his pompous, self-important airs, and although on at least two occasions he suggested that Burleson consider being a bit less aggressive in the exercise of his authority, nothing changed either time. When challenged about his administration's employment and racial policies—Burleson's innovations soon spread to the Treasury Department and elsewhere—the Virginia-born, Georgia-raised Wilson did not deny responsibility for them. He said, rather, that they were intended to protect black employees by keeping them separate as they worked their way toward eventual equality. In the 1910s few white citizens found this explanation unsatisfactory.

The Espionage Act left it to Burleson to decide whether anything in any publication might "cause or attempt to cause insubordination, disloyalty, mutiny or refusal of duty" and to neutralize those he found guilty by denying them access to their subscribers. He was eager to get started, and within twenty-four hours of congressional approval of the Espionage Act was instructing local postmasters to be on the alert for "unsealed matter, newspapers, etc. containing matter which is calculated to [here he repeated at great length the language of the Act] . . . or otherwise embarrass or hamper the Government in conducting the war." All such matter was to be sent to him. There was no need to fear that he would fail to take action.

Many were suspect in Burleson's eyes: Lutheran churches because of their German-American membership, Catholic churches with German- or Irish-American congregations, academic journals, farm journals, labor unions, black organizations, and others. But the juiciest targets, and the ones to which he gave priority, were the country's socialist and left-leaning journals. These were numerous enough, and in some cases successful enough, to keep Burleson busy for quite some time. Socialism had been growing into a substantial force in the years before the war. The American Socialist Party, founded in 1901, still claimed a membership of only 70,000 when the war came, but its presidential candidate received 600,000 votes in 1916 although few voters knew anything about him except that he was a socialist. There were socialist mayors in cities as widely scattered as Minneapolis and Butte, Montana; socialist congressmen had been elected in Milwaukee and New York City; and in the 1914 elections socialists had won more than 160 local and county offices in Oklahoma.

But every indication that socialism might be spreading, every success at the polls, made new enemies for the movement. Every sizable newspaper in the country warned its readers that socialism was an alien and dangerous thing, one of the European pathologies, incompatible with true Americanism. The postmaster general was entirely typical in sharing this view. As a young clergyman and future socialist presidential candidate named Norman Thomas observed, Burleson "didn't know socialism from rheumatism." But he had no doubt that he, and all good Americans, had a duty to exterminate it.

Few socialists tried to conceal their opposition to intervention. The European socialist parties were widely seen as having discredited themselves, at the start of the war, by casting aside their preachments about an international fellowship of the working classes and declaring allegiance to their respective home countries. Many American socialists, seeing this as a betrayal and damaging to the movement, were determined not to repeat it. Days after the president's signing of the declaration of war, delegates to an emergency party convention approved a resolution that condemned intervention as "a crime against the people of the United States." They voted to support resistance to the draft, to censorship, and to the curtailment of workers' right to strike.

Some prominent socialists, among them the muckraking novelist Upton Sinclair, recoiled from such positions and declared their support for the president and the war. A good many did so out of belief in the cause. Others may have been afraid of becoming pariahs or of causing their fellow citizens to equate socialism with subversion. The party as a whole, in any case, held together in opposition. And no small number of the publications associated with it were soon giving the postmaster general exactly what he was looking for. When he moved against them, he did so with the vociferous approval of the most influential people, organizations, and publications in the country. Together, intervention in the war and the Espionage Act had made attacks on the very existence of American socialism seem more legitimate, more patriotic, more necessary than they had ever been. The socialists, for their part, had few friends in high places and enemies beyond numbering.

By one count, Burleson's first move stripped some sixty publications of access to second-class mail delivery. This drew protests from publications that had not yet been targeted, and their turn came next. The June issue of *The Masses,* an irreverently sophisticated monthly that carried the writings of a number of the best-known leftist journalists in the country, published a complaint by editor Max Eastman that "men have already been sent to jail since April sixth on the theory that it is treason to tell an unpleasant truth about one's country." Payback came quickly: the August edition was rejected by the New York post office on orders from Washington.

When Eastman and his associates appealed, the case went before a young federal court judge named Learned Hand, who in a long career would become a judicial legend. He issued a temporary restraining order, which meant that pending a final decision, the post office was supposed to accept and deliver *The Masses* as in the past. Burleson ignored the order, and one can imagine the glee with which he made his next move. He ordered that no future issues of *The Masses* were to be accepted because, having failed to mail an August issue, the magazine was no longer a periodical. A higher court lifted Learned Hand's restraining order, and *The Masses* was beaten. Wilson asked the postmaster general, in passing, if perhaps he was being a bit harsh. Burleson replied that if the president did not wish to support him, he was prepared to resign. That did not prove necessary.

In August one of the oldest and best-known socialist newspapers, *The New York Call*, wrote of Burleson as "the mediocre monarch now mismanaging the post office." It, too, lost its mailing privileges but was able to carry on by delivering copies door-to-door. The socialist *Milwaukee Leader* was less fortunate because more dependent on postal delivery. When Burleson moved against it, it lost the ability to reach all but a small minority of its fifteen thousand subscribers.

Almost anything could get a publication's mailing privileges terminated. It happened to *The Public* for saying what President Wilson had said in asking for a declaration of war: that the costs should be paid more through taxes and less through borrowing. It happened to *The Freeman's Journal and Catholic Register* for printing a statement of Thomas Jefferson's that Ireland should be independent. *The Jeffersonian*, published in Georgia by Tom Watson, once nationally famous as a leader of the populist movement, had to go out of business after writing such things as "men conscripted to go to Europe are virtually condemned to death and everybody knows it."

In October, Congress showed its satisfaction with everything Burleson was doing by passing a new Trading With the Enemy Act to broaden his powers. Now he could require all foreign-language publications to submit to the Post Office, in advance of distribution, English translations of all content that had anything to say about the U.S. government, any other governments engaged in the war, or the war itself. He was authorized to exempt any publications that met with his approval, but of course he was not much interested in exemptions. The new requirements were sufficiently onerous to oblige many small periodicals to cease operations.

Burleson, a canny enough politician, knew better than to interfere with publications of influence in the political mainstream. His biggest target was *Appeal to Reason*, a midwestern weekly that had a circulation of half a million but, being avowedly socialist, few readers capable of making trouble in Washington. William Randolph Hearst's chain of big-city dailies was a different matter. Though it was hostile to the Wilson administration and critical of its conduct of the war, Burleson left it alone.

It is hardly surprising, in such a climate, that local authorities felt called upon to do their part to keep fools and subversives from threatening national unity, giving aid and comfort to the enemy, or complicating the minds and lives of the brave young Americans who soon would be going off to war. In the decades leading up to the Great War, local law enforcement agencies and state militias had usually been more conspicuous than Washington in taking action against socialists, labor organizers, and radicals of every variety. Thus there was nothing particularly novel about the use of such agencies, when the war came, to deal with perceived threats to domestic tranquillity.

It was much the same with private citizens who wanted to play their patriotic part. Even before the Revolutionary War, colonial Americans had sometimes expressed their displeasure with British rule by tarring and feathering agents of the king. And as the young United States expanded westward, mob action often filled the vacuum created by an absence of formal law enforcement, and lynching became its trademark. Lynching also became one of the instruments by which Reconstruction was brought to an end in the post–Civil War South and freed slaves were reduced to quasi-serfdom. In 1917, when men infected with war fever gathered to deal in extrajudicial ways with neighbors whom they deemed insufficiently patriotic, they had reason to see themselves as following in a venerable American tradition. No doubt many of them thought it a *great* tradition.

Everywhere they looked, almost every time they picked up a newspaper, citizens were reminded that they were living through an emergency of the highest order and that extraordinary measures were necessary. "We are at war with the most merciless and inhuman nation in the world," *The Providence Journal* declared. "Hundreds of thousands of its people in this country want to see America humiliated and beaten to her knees, and they are doing, and will do, everything in their power to bring this about. Take nothing for granted. Energy and alertness in this direction may save the life of your son, your husband or your brother." This appeal was reprinted in papers from Connecticut to New Mexico, from North Dakota to Florida. There were warnings, too, that the U.S. Justice Department had neither the manpower nor (some complained) the will to deal with the problem. It is hardly mystifying that readers occasionally felt themselves being called upon to take the law into their own hands.

Attorney General Thomas W. Gregory, though a man of moderately progressive leanings, appears not to have been greatly concerned as reports of mob violence became widespread. Though like Burleson a Texan, he had never been as conservative as the postmaster general, but now that the nation was in crisis, the two became partners in purging it of alleged internal enemies. "May God have mercy on them," Gregory said of those objecting to intervention, "for they need expect none from an outraged people and an avenging Government."

Such words gave state and local officials all the encouragement they needed to demonstrate their own patriotism and the price of nonconformity. As early as mid-April, before the passage of either the Selective Service Act or the Espionage Act, two Seattle men were arrested for distributing a circular titled "No Conscription, No Servitude, No Slavery." Even in the overheated environment of the time, it was impossible to charge them with doing what had not yet been made illegal. They were charged instead with conspiring to block the carrying out of the declaration of war and sentenced to two years in a federal penitentiary.

Thomas Gregory,
U.S. attorney general,
1914–1919
"May God have mercy on them,"
he said of dissenters, "for they need
expect none from an outraged people
and an avenging Government."

When two New Yorkers were sent to prison and fined for passing out notices of an antiwar meeting, the anarchist leaders Emma Goldman and Alexander Berkman denounced the judge who heard the case. They were arrested and taken before the same judge on a charge of conspiring against the government. Each received a two-year sentence and was fined ten thousand dollars.

Objections to the draft became even riskier as the June 5 registration day approached. In West Virginia a man was sentenced to six months in jail for distributing a flyer titled "Are We Facing a Militarized America?" A New Yorker was given ninety days in the city workhouse for, on the Fourth of July, handing out copies of the Declaration of Independence to which he had appended a single question: "Does your government live up to these principles?"

They were lucky. In Philadelphia the editor of a Lithuanian paper wrote an editorial accusing Burleson of intending to destroy any publication daring to say that "American capitalists have drawn this country into war." He got three years. A San Francisco lawyer got five years for being the leader of a group that produced a booklet titled *Legal Opinion and Advice on the Conscription Law to American Patriots.* One of President Wilson's little group of willful men, newly (and voluntarily) retired senator John Works of California, complained upon learning of this sentence that the government was suppressing legitimate dissent. No one who mattered cared.

South Dakota, apparently supposing itself to be a hotbed of spies and subversives, became wonderfully alert. The chairman of the state's socialist party, upon declaring himself a conscientious objector, was sent to prison for twenty years. When twenty-seven German-American farmers sent a petition to the governor objecting to the draft and claiming that the conscription quota for their county was unfairly high, they were rounded up and given sentences of between one and two years each. A man of advanced years got into an argument about the draft, said it was "all foolishness" to send young men to be killed "all for the sake of Wall Street," and found himself sentenced to five years in Leavenworth federal prison. In nearby Iowa, Walter Matthey walked out halfway through a meeting featuring a speaker who vigorously attacked the draft. Someone reported to the authorities that Matthey had been observed not only clapping but making a donation of twenty-five cents. He got a year in jail.

Some sentences were later reduced, and some convictions were even reversed. But this generally happened years later, after the war had ended and passions had subsided, and only in scattered instances as a result of intervention by the president or the Justice Department. In any case, prosecutions were a small part (though the most visible and intimidating part) of the process by which the administration used the Espionage Act to suppress dissent and the appearance of dissent. The Committee on Public Information's appeals for the public to report anyone and anything that seemed suspect produced far more leads than federal agents could investigate, much less take to court. Agents would call on individuals who had been reported, warn them that if they failed to do a better job of demonstrating their patriotism they would find themselves in trouble, and in most cases eliminate the problem if in fact one had ever existed. The Espionage Act served as a kind of universal sword of Damocles, falling on relatively few citizens (some 850 were convicted in the two years following its passage) but frightening untold thousands.

As the crusade for conformity went on, its consequences became ever more gruesome and absurd. Robert Goldstein, the producer of a feature film about the American Revolution titled *The Spirit of '76*, was charged with violating the Espionage Act because of a lurid scene showing British Redcoats bayoneting innocent civilians and dragging women offscreen with obviously evil intent. His crime was fostering hatred for America's ally in the war against tyranny. Conviction was inevitable, Goldstein's company went bankrupt, and he received a sentence of ten years.

As lunacy became epidemic, school districts began to ban the teaching of German. California's state school board declared it to be "a language that disseminates the ideas of autocracy, brutality, and hatred." An Iowa official revealed to the nation that "ninety percent of all the men and women who teach the German language are traitors." Few of the targets of such malignant nonsense were foolhardy enough to try to defend themselves, but resentment simmered. The Wilson administration, by using its own hard tactics and tacitly encouraging local authorities to do worse, was deepening some of the worst divisions in American society—divisions not just of political belief but of race and class and faith. The summer of 1917 brought some of the worst race riots and labor disputes in the nation's history—disasters unlikely to have happened if not for the war. Herbert Croly, co-founder and editor of *The New Republic* magazine and among the most respected progressive thinkers in the country, wrote to Wilson that his intolerance of dissent was "dividing the body of public opinion into two irreconcilable classes" and leaving moderates in an impossible position. Another progressive of national stature, Amos Pinchot, observed with dour amusement that the president was putting "his enemies in office and his friends in jail." And as Senator La Follette's son Philip (himself a future governor of Wisconsin) would observe years later, "the strange thing about World War I, in terms of public reaction, was that by and large the people who seemed to have lost control of their emotions to a greater extent than any other part of our population were the intellectuals."

If perhaps not strictly speaking an intellectual, Elihu Root was in 1917 one of the stoutest pillars of the eastern Republican establishment, a man of monumental attainment and respectability. A former secretary of war and secretary of state, a onetime senator from New York and future recipient of the

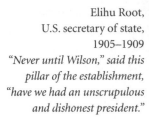

Elihu Root,
U.S. secretary of state,
1905–1909
*"Never until Wilson," said this
pillar of the establishment,
"have we had an unscrupulous
and dishonest president."*

Nobel Peace Prize, he said days after the president signed the declaration of war that "we must have no criticism now." Four months later, his attitude hardened by the failure of so many citizens to take his advice, he was taking a more strident line. "There are men walking about the streets of this city to-night," he told an enthusiastic audience at Manhattan's exclusive Union Club, "who ought to be taken out at sunrise and shot for treason." President Wilson was increasingly inclined to express similar opinions and in doing so to legiti-mate them. "Woe be to the man or group of men that seeks to stand in our way in this day of high resolution when every principle we hold dearest is to be vindicated and made secure for the salvation of the nation," he declared in a Flag Day speech in June. It would appear that he did not regard freedom of speech as among the principles that the nation held most dear.

The courts did nothing to stem the tide. To the contrary, it became clear that the administration could do almost anything it wished without danger of judicial interference. Judges, content to allow prosecutors to interpret the flabby language of the Espionage Act in whatever way they chose, gave them the full benefit of the so-called bad-tendency test. According to this test, first applied early in the nineteenth century in cases involving criticism of public officials, citizens could be punished for speaking or writing in ways deemed likely to cause or encourage illegal acts. Its practical effect was to broaden the ability of the courts to find opinions criminal simply because the person expressing them was believed to be a socialist, or a pacifist, or an anarchist, or otherwise underserving of the protection of the law.

It came to be understood that there was rarely any point in appealing for relief from the government's actions. When federal authorities asked that certain motion pictures not be shown, usually because they were deemed insufficiently patriotic or showed France or Britain in a not entirely flattering light, the unsatisfactory response of producers and distributors led to the movies in question being banned outright. There were no legal challenges, no appeals or repercussions. Occasional court rulings in support of freedom of speech served mainly to spark the anger of self-proclaimed patriots, which served as a warning to other judges not to expose themselves to similar abuse. Appeals of even the most outlandish convictions were moved through the system as slowly as the rules allowed, which was very slowly indeed. The few that reached the Supreme Court typically did not do so until after the war ended. Even then they were not infrequently upheld.

The case of Victor Berger was only one among hundreds, but it is representative enough to be worth recounting. Born into a Jewish family in Austria, Berger had immigrated to the United States in his late teens, apparently to avoid conscription into the Hapsburg emperor's armies. He settled in Milwaukee, where he founded a socialist journal and became a founding member of the American Socialist Party. In 1910, at age fifty, he became the first socialist elected to the U.S. House of Representatives. He attracted the ire of the city fathers of Milwaukee by advocating such shocking innovations as public health programs, old-age insurance, a minimum wage, and woman suffrage. He was not reelected in 1912.

In 1917 Berger ran in a special election to fill a U.S. senate seat vacated by death. He pledged that, if elected, he would work for "an immediate, general, and permanent peace." He again alarmed respectable Wisconsin by getting 26 percent of the vote in a three-way race and carrying eleven counties. In short order he was indicted under the Espionage Act and was convicted in a Chicago trial. The judge presiding, future commissioner of baseball Kenesaw Mountain Landis, complained that "one must have a very judicial mind indeed not to be prejudiced against German-Americans in this country—their hearts are reeking with disloyalty." The sentence was twenty years in federal prison.

The Committee on Public Information was supposed to be, in the words of chairman George Creel, an organ of "expression rather than suppression"— a vehicle through which the truth about the war could be used to "mold the people of the United States into one white hot mass instinct with fraternity, devotion, courage and deathless determination." The chief means by which this was to be accomplished was Creel's most brilliant innovation, a nation-wide network of volunteers who, as Four-Minute Men, made appearances at movie theaters and other places where people assembled in large numbers. In no more than four minutes, the time needed to change the reels of a feature film, they would speak on whatever subject Creel was currently seeking to push. The program was a phenomenal success, certainly in terms of its ability to attract speakers. By the end of the war, no fewer than 75,000 amateur orators had become involved.

The Creel organization joined the Post Office Department in keeping the newspapers of America within bounds acceptable to the White House. Almost immediately upon going into operation, Creel created an organization of academics whose assignment was to monitor the ethnic and foreign-language press, searching for suspect material. The editors of newspapers of every size and kind were asked not to publish anything about peace proposals or any reports of differences among the nations at war with Germany. Few were reluctant to comply. Those few were shown why they should fear the consequences of noncompliance. When in October 1917 the president established by executive order a Censorship Board, it was inevitable that Creel would become a willing and active member.

Intervention made things radically more difficult for the two antiwar groups that had become most visible during the period of neutrality, the Emergency Peace Federation (EPF) and the American Union Against Militarism (AUAM). The relentless hostility of the press persuaded many Americans that the less socially respectable of the two, the EPF, was synonymous with disloyalty, even with treason. The AUAM tried to find a middle path that would offend as few people as possible but succeeded only in alienating its own more militant members.

The result was the creation, a month after U.S. entry into the war, of a new umbrella group called the People's Council of America for Democracy and Peace. Into it moved the federation, the socialists, and others. The AUAM cautiously kept its distance, which caused many of its members to defect and sent it into terminal decline. (Its Civil Liberties Bureau, which had attracted much criticism for offering legal counsel to conscientious objectors, also severed its connections to the parent organization. It began its evolution into today's American Civil Liberties Union.)

In the intensely polarized environment of 1917, with superheated patriotism almost the only acceptable mode of political discourse, the People's Council was soon marginalized and found it impossible to maintain, never mind broaden, its base. Samuel Gompers was approached about bringing his American Federation of Labor into the embattled coalition. "I prefer not to ally myself with the conscious or unconscious agents of the kaiser in America," he replied. He set up a rival organization, the American Alliance for Labor and Democracy, with funding secretly provided by the Creel Committee.

Limited now to a largely radical membership, reviled in all quarters including the White House, the People's Council joined the AUAM on the road to oblivion. Friendless and alienated, its leaders adopted the slogan "Peace by Negotiation Now." As their last suicidal act they embraced the program of the Russian Bolsheviks, which called for a settlement of the war involving no annexation of territory and no payment of indemnities. They were now so remote from mainstream American opinion, so despised, that candidates for public office saw a People's Council endorsement as a curse to be fled. George Creel knew he would draw no rebuke from anyone he need fear when he called the council's members "traitors and fools." Before the end of 1917, the group had become an irrelevancy. Progressivism itself, as a political force, was disintegrating under the pressures generated by Woodrow Wilson's war.

The pro-war forces had no such difficulties. The Council of National Defense, funded by Congress and chaired by the secretary of war, caused much mischief—probably not intentionally—when it encouraged the creation of state defense councils to support and replicate its work at the grassroots level. Governors and legislatures were eager to comply, though their willingness to appropriate funds for the purpose varied as greatly as their views of how their councils should operate. Some state councils became instruments of patronage, dispensing favors in the interests of whoever was in power. Others were left to manage themselves, providing opportunities for local dignitaries to display their patriotic zeal by challenging the loyalty of schools, churches, labor organizations, and individuals. Some were called not councils of defense but committees of public safety, a name redolent of the French Revolution's Reign of Terror. Many became weapons with which "good" Americans, the Hundred Percenters, could strike out at those they deemed not patriotic enough or simply wanted to destroy.

Worse followed. A Chicago advertising executive named Albert Biggs, concerned about all the things he had been reading about ubiquitous enemy subversion and the need for constant watchfulness, went to the Justice Department's Bureau of Investigation with a plan for a nationwide force of volunteer unpaid intelligence agents. The idea was passed along to Attorney General Gregory, who responded enthusiastically. It is understandable that he did so. The Justice Department, now fully absorbed in the policing of public opinion, was overwhelmed by reports of disloyalty, under heavy criticism for not being more aggressive, and eager for whatever help it could get.

Gregory's solution was the American Protective League (APL), officially a private organization, in fact an amateur adjunct of the Justice Department. It recruited thousands of untrained and often overeager would-be counterspies to snoop on their fellow citizens and report whatever they thought suspicious. The appeal of becoming a junior G-man helping to ferret out spies and traitors proved irresistible. By the end of the war, the APL would claim to have a quarter-million volunteers at work in six hundred communities. Its stationery bore the proud words "Organized with the Approval and Operating under the Direction of the U.S. Department of Justice, Bureau of Investigation." Members were given badges identifying them as representing the "American Protective League—Secret Service." The main qualification for membership, evidently, was a willingness to pay dues of seventy-five cents to a dollar.

As a final absurdity, the APL spawned youthful versions of itself: Scout-like organizations with names like the Boy Spies of America, the Sedition Slammers, and the Terrible Threateners. The parent organization was, however, not entirely unhelpful. One historian has found that it did 80 percent of the work of the Bureau of Investigation's Cleveland office, and something similar was undoubtedly true in other cities. But the APL also became an enormous vigilante force, taking part in raids on homes and offices and enjoying implicit immunity when engaged in breaking and entering on its own initiative. Members helped to round up dissidents and break strikes and terrorized people guilty of nothing more (and sometimes less) than not being noticeably enthusiastic about government policy. In Toledo, an APL zealot submitted the names and addresses of library patrons who "read nothing but German books." Others reported people who spoke of the hardships and dangers of frontline service, or predicted that the war would be a long one, or played German music, or played American music but failed to include "The Star-Spangled Banner." People who failed to buy war bonds, or enough war bonds to satisfy snoopy neighbors, drew much attention. (A North Carolina clergyman, challenged on this point, replied that if anyone "could tell him how a man with twelve children drawing $800 a year could clothe, feed them, and buy Liberty Bonds, he would appreciate it.")

With astonishing speed, the APL grew to become the most intrusive and far-reaching (and also most irresponsible) threat to free speech and the right of assembly in the history of the United States.

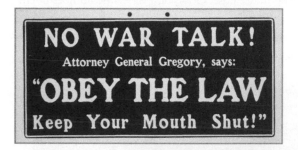

War art was wall art
Posters in infinite variety reminded Americans that the enemy
was evil incarnate—and lurked under every bed.

Writers protective of Woodrow Wilson's reputation rarely fail to point out that, having been told by Treasury Secretary McAdoo that the APL appeared to have "very harmful possibilities," the president asked Attorney General Gregory if it might be "very dangerous to have such an organization operating in the United States" and wondering "if there is any way in which we could stop it." Gregory replied promptly. "The American Protective League is a patriotic organization," he said, "organized with my approval and encouragement."

Gregory wrote to McAdoo as well. "There have been days when as many as one thousand letters came to my Department purporting to give more or less detailed information as to spies, disloyal citizens and plots to destroy ships, factories, railroad bridges, munitions plants, waterworks, arsenals, etc. etc. etc. In perhaps 90 percent of these cases the information furnished was of no value, but in a small number of them it proved to be very valuable indeed, and it has thus become necessary to investigate everything called to our attention. This involved the keeping under observation of a very large number of citizens and situations throughout the United States." He added that the APL was "the largest, best organized and most effective" source of help available to the Justice Department.

In the wrong place at the wrong time
Germans stranded in the United States were held
in prison camps for the duration.

Gregory could have given a simple answer to the president's question: of course the APL could have been stopped. The Justice Department had created and in effect licensed it; it could (and after Gregory left office, it would) shut it down. But the attorney general wanted to expand rather than stop it, and evidently the president was satisfied; he did not intrude again. It has also been argued that Gregory and his lieutenants in the Justice Department saw strict enforcement of the Espionage Act, including the work of the APL, as necessary to keep private citizens from taking the law into their own hands. Actually, this is not as absurd and self-serving as it may seem. The department was scorned editorially for the vast numbers of subversives it was supposedly not sending to prison, and its alleged timidity was not infrequently used to defend mob attacks on suspected traitors.

The ultimate irony is that despite all the things done officially and unofficially to save the nation from enemy subversion—the rampages of vigilante gangs, the reptilian scheming of agents provocateurs, spying by citizens on their fellow citizens, the harassment and the lynchings—not one spy was ever charged. A small number of Germans attached to their country's embassy, men involved in espionage and even sabotage, were sent packing before intervention caused the embassy to be shut down. But the whole apparatus of which the APL was such a prominent part served chiefly to make trouble for people of whom the self-appointed patriots did not approve, and to make the war an excuse to attack the marginal, the vulnerable, and the disreputable even when such persons were connected in no discernible way to national security or what was happening in Europe. That it did not accomplish more raises questions about how much in the way of real spying was actually going on in the United States. Months before the end of the war, *The New York Times,* rarely less than one of the Wilson administration's most dependable supporters, was examining past reports of German espionage and sabotage and reporting that few if any were credible.

Three Faces of Labor

The United States of America and organized labor had always been an awkward coupling. Organizations that we would recognize as unions did not exist at the time of the republic's birth. Generations later, when industrialization gave rise to gigantic railroads, factories, and mines, the idea that their equally gigantic workforces might band together to make demands seemed alien, threatening, and deeply wrong. It seemed to jeopardize not only the rights and profits of employers but what was unique about the American way of life.

These fears were shared by government at all levels, and by the courts. As early as 1805, when a small group of Philadelphia shoemakers attempted to organize, they were indicted for mounting "a combination and conspiracy to raise wages." *The Charleston Mercury* was reflecting the passions of the Civil War when it declared in 1861 that "slavery is the natural and normal condition of the laboring man," but its opinion, if expressed in less abrasive terms, might not have offended the North's industrial elite.

After the Civil War, hostility to workers' attempts to organize was aggravated by the fact that what Karl Marx would have called America's new "industrial proletariat" was made up increasingly of immigrants from the Old World—people penniless and not uncommonly illiterate, prepared to work like beasts for subsistence wages because the alternative was starvation. Many of them came from places where socialism was intellectually respectable and becoming politically important. (In 1912 socialist candidates received more than a third of votes cast in a German national election.) There was no easy way to fit such people into the Jeffersonian vision of America as the land of autonomous farmers and craftsmen, or make them acceptable to Hamiltonian Brahmins. Unionism was alien to both traditions.

Even in 1914, by which time the United States was largely an urban and industrial nation with only about a third of the workforce engaged in agriculture, labor organizations were commonly seen as incompatible with American values. For many of the native-born, they appeared to be a kind of infection. They reeked of the new smokestack cities, the grime of the factories, the dark filth of the mines, the slums in which the newcomers insisted on clustering, and their contemptible religions.

And there hung over them an aura of violence. A magazine of the time reported that during a thirty-three-month period ending in 1904, 198 strikers and strike sympathizers were killed in the United States, 1,166 were injured, and more than six thousand arrested. That this particular magazine cast the strikers as victims rather than perpetrators mattered little; either way, unions were trouble.

The struggle to organize was big, bitter, and bloody enough to amount to domestic warfare: the make-or-break strike at Andrew Carnegie's huge steelworks in Homestead, Pennsylvania; the murderous years-long battle between the coal mine operators of the Northeast and the Molly Maguires, et cetera. The strikers almost always ended up losing, partly because armed force—the U.S. Army as well as state militias and local law enforcement—was repeatedly used against them. Viciously exploited, under relentless pressure and unable to get relief in court or elsewhere, groups of workers were easily pitted against one another. The robber baron Jay Gould was not far off the mark when he boasted that "I can hire one-half of the working class to kill the other half."

Even those among the well-off who acknowledged the plight of the laboring classes often thought them incapable of helping themselves, or even of knowing what kind of help they needed. The president of the Reading Railroad seemed to many to be speaking simple common sense when he declared, in 1902, that "the rights and interests of the laboring man will be protected and cared for—not by the labor agitators, but by the Christian gentlemen to whom God has given control of the property rights of the country." That was comparatively benign, especially when contrasted with Social Darwinism, which still had many adherents among the middle and upper classes. It denied that the workingman had any rights or any interests deserving of representation in the political arena. It held that the common good required that the economy be governed by the law of the jungle, and that to interfere with the strong for the benefit of the weak was against nature and would lead to dire consequences. From both perspectives, that of the gentlemanly Christians and that of the Darwinists, allowing the unions to have anything to say about wages or working conditions seemed a shameful display of weakness, an injury to the social fabric.

Working people had more than one way of responding, of course. Their simplest option was to submit, to accept whatever employers offered and try to make the best of it. Millions did exactly this—understandably, in light of the costs of resistance and the tiny chances of success. Another response was to be cooperative but firm, using whatever leverage workers had in the marketplace to win modest concessions. This was feasible for skilled tradesmen; their skills were their leverage, and they used them as a platform on which to build the nation's only conservative and relatively respectable union, the American Federation of Labor (AFL). A third response, the hard and hated and sometimes heroic one, was to refuse to submit, to fight on in the face of everything employers and government could do.

These different approaches were tried by a variety of labor leaders before and during the Great War. Among them were three men of historic significance: Samuel Gompers, Eugene V. Debs, and William D. Haywood. All three came from far down in the working class, and none had had much in the way of formal education. As they rose to become some of the best-known figures of their time, they became not friends but rivals, even enemies. Two became criminals, at least in the eyes of the U.S. government. The third made himself a buttress if not a pillar of the establishment, if not quite within it then certainly supporting it from the outside.

Gompers, born in 1850 to Jewish parents in London, left school at age ten to become an apprentice in his father's trade of cigar making. In 1863 the family immigrated to New York, where young Sam became active in the cigar makers' union and, at age twenty-five, president of his Lower East Side local. An aggressive organizer and activist, he was elected a vice president of the national union a few years later, and not long afterward he became prominent in the effort to pull a number of trade unions together in a single umbrella group. This led to the creation of the AFL in 1886, and Gompers's emergence as its president. Step by cautious step, shunning all temptations to appear radical, he built the AFL into the most robust labor organization in the country. It received nationwide attention in 1890 by winning the eight-hour day for carpenters in thirty-six cities and the nine-hour day in 234 others. It showed its strength in the panic of 1893, becoming the first American union to survive a major economic downturn.

Gompers himself was a practical man, focused on achieving tangible gains for his members—better wages, better hours, better conditions generally. He tried to avoid confrontations with employers except when victory was certain, and preferred boycotts to strikes. Both personally and strategically he was conservative, supporting the American war with

Samuel Gompers
The head of the "respectable"
wing of the labor movement
was unreservedly pro-war.

Spain and tight restrictions on immigration. Because of the AFL's exclusive focus on the skilled trades and on such noncentralized industries as construction, it represented a kind of blue-collar aristocracy and was capable of looking with disdain on the unskilled toilers of the factories and mines. Tough as he could be—he was once sentenced to a year in jail for refusing to obey a court injunction—Gompers had no aversion to respectability. In fact, he sought it for himself, and he made his organization a platform from which members could lift their families into the middle class. No one could have been surprised when, as the United

States drifted toward intervention, he decided that the objectives of the AFL would be best served by unreserved support for the Wilson administration.

Meanwhile Gene Debs had been following a markedly different path. Born in 1855 to parents who had emigrated from France, he left school early to take a job as a painter and cleaner of railroad cars. Later he became a locomotive fireman, an activist and official in the firemen's union, and the founder, in 1893, of the American Railway Union (ARU), representing the kinds of unskilled and semiskilled workers in which the AFL had no interest. Just a year after coming into existence, the ARU staged a successful strike against the Great Northern Railroad, winning most of its demands. This victory so energized the members that, when not long afterward the Pullman Palace Car Company cut the wages of its workers by 28 percent, an ARU convention responded combatively. Members wanted to boycott Pullman, to refuse to handle cars built by the company and any cars attached to them. Debs urged caution, fearful that his fledgling organization was not ready for such a fight. The boycott was approved in spite of his concerns.

What followed was one of the epic labor battles of the pre–Great Depression decades. The dispute spread from the Pullman factory outside Chicago to involve 150,000 workers in twenty-seven states. The company and its affiliated railroads refused to negotiate, establishing a publicity bureau to keep the newspapers supplied with exaggerated and often utterly false stories about the crimes of the striking rabble. They made use of a new and devastating weapon: the court injunction, by which judges could order unions to immediately do (or stop doing) whatever an employer wanted done or not done. An older, equally effective weapon also was brought into play: the use of army and National Guard troops. Resistance by union members led to increased disorder, to acts of sabotage, finally to the defeat of the boycott and the ruin of the ARU. The conflict had taken twenty-seven lives.

At the crisis, with the outcome still in the balance, Debs asked Gompers to turn the conflict into a general strike by ordering his AFL membership to down tools. Gompers declined. When it was over, Debs was charged with contempt of court and put on trial. Clarence Darrow, until then a railroad lawyer, quit his job to conduct the defense. He was unable to save Debs from being sentenced to six months in federal prison.

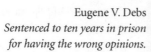

Eugene V. Debs
*Sentenced to ten years in prison
for having the wrong opinions.*

While he was serving his term, admirers sent Debs stacks of socialist and Marxist literature. He read it and was interested. He was visited by the socialist leader Victor Berger of Wisconsin, and that, too, had its effect.

By the time of his release, Debs had become convinced that reform of the economic system was going to require more than unionism. He transformed what remained of his broken union into an organization called the Social Democracy of America. This became the Social Democratic Party, which ran Debs as a candidate for president in 1900. He ran again in 1904, 1908, and 1912, never with the smallest possibility of victory, always on platforms that offended the sensibilities of polite society. By 1917 he was the best-known socialist in the country, and one of the Justice Department's prime targets.

Darrow said, "There may have lived some time, somewhere, a kindlier, gentler, more generous man than Eugene Debs, but I have never known him." Nobody would ever have said anything of the kind about William Dudley Haywood, the hard-drinking, brawling, one-eyed six-footer who would become more notorious than Debs and live to regret it. Born in the Utah Territory in 1869, the son of a pony express rider who died when the future Big Bill was three, he went to work in a remote Nevada mine at age fifteen. Over the next decade he drifted, trying his luck as a prospector, cowboy, and farmer before again taking up employment in a mine in 1896.

He found his destiny upon meeting an official of the Western Federation of Miners (WFM) in Silver City, Idaho. He joined up, soon became president of his local, then was appointed to the WFM's national executive board. Finally he was called to Colorado to become secretary-treasurer. It was in the last capacity that, in Chicago in 1905, he presided at the gathering at which some two hundred socialist and labor leaders including Debs and the legendary Mary "Mother" Jones voted to create the Industrial Workers of the World—the IWW or Wobblies.

Haywood was by this time a hardened veteran of the WFM's violence-ridden struggles to organize workers in the lucrative hard-rock metal mines of the West. He took for granted the kinds of contests in which

Big Bill Haywood
*The driving force behind
the trouble-seeking,
and therefore doomed,
Industrial Workers
of the World.*

employers were offered the services of state and federal troops, had the support of injunction-granting judges, used the spies of detective agencies such as Pinkerton's, and sometimes resorted to what can only be called terrorism. Strikers, too, used violence and intimidation, and disputes about which side was most responsible for which outrage are unlikely ever to be resolved.

Shortly after returning to Colorado from the Chicago gathering, Haywood was arrested (without a warrant) and swiftly and surreptitiously (so that there could be no appeal of extradition) carried off to Idaho. There he was put on trial, accused of responsibility for a bombing that had taken the life of a former governor. Darrow went to Boise to conduct the defense and made it so plain that Haywood was being framed that conviction became impossible. The case made Haywood a hero of the labor movement nationally. He returned to work and by stages became less active in the WFM than in the IWW.

For better and worse, never in American history has there been an organization quite like the IWW. Reviled in its day as a conspiracy of murderers, terrorists, and subversives, it has continued to be depicted in those same dark colors ever since. Certainly it was involved in any number of disputes that descended into violence. The precise truth, however, is elusive, buried beneath the often dubious testimony of the union's numberless and more respectable enemies. What cannot be disputed is that wherever working people were at odds with employers, the IWW was eager—sometimes foolishly eager—to get involved. And that its members, guilty or not (few of the charges against the union can be considered proved), were often not only bullheadedly courageous but good-humored and generous to an improbable degree. If they could be ruthless—and they certainly could—they appear to have been as much sinned against as sinning.

However powerless embattled working people might be, the IWW stood ready to help them organize. In the West in the decade after its founding, alongside its desperate struggles with the mining companies, it engaged in a long series of fights for free speech from which it stood to gain nothing. These fights erupted in places where local authorities had made it unlawful for people with unapproved opinions to give them voice. The IWW's response was to have one person get up on a soapbox or stepladder and speak, send in a replacement as soon as the first speaker was arrested, replace the replacement and then the replacement's replacement until the local jail was full and the officers of the law were unable to cope. The Wobblies became almost as famous for their songs and parades as for their strikes.

Their most celebrated victory came in 1912. In Lawrence, Massachusetts, some 23,000 workers walked out of the town's textile mills to protest a cut in wages. The nature of the workforce made a successful strike improbable: more than half of the strikers were women and children, and many were not only foreign-born but from twenty-seven different ethnic groups. Almost all were unskilled. But under Haywood's direction, the strike turned into a weird mixture of mayhem and festival. Windows got broken and machines were smashed, strikebreakers were sent in and confronted, but through it all there were regular parades through the center of town, the paraders singing selections from the IWW songbook. Every day thousands of picketers and their families and supporters—as many as twenty thousand at a time—would encircle the mills.

Tradesmen of the AFL, meanwhile, were still at work inside those same mills. Haywood asked Gompers to call them out, but like Debs in the Pullman strike he was rebuffed. There were the usual questionable arrests and harassment in a variety of forms, the military was called in, but the strikers stood firm. After nine and a half weeks, the owners gave up. They granted wage increases of up to 21 percent (those making the least got the biggest percentage gains), overtime pay, reinstatement of discharged strikers, and even (especially nice for the children involved) a reduction of the workweek to fifty-four hours. Only two people had been killed— a low body count for a major strike of the time. Mill owners in other New England towns, to avoid being targeted, gave their employees what the Lawrence strikers had won. One unhappy observer said that because of these concessions, a quarter-million workers "look with gratitude from the heart to William D. Haywood." He viewed this as a calamity that "only years of educational effort can overcome."

The IWW's local issued a statement describing the strike as nothing more than a "preliminary skirmish" and saying that the fight would be over "only when the working class has overthrown the capitalist class and has secured undisputed possession of the earth and all that is in it and on it." A dignified silence would have been wiser. It was foolhardy to put out such a clear reminder of just how far out of the mainstream, how unlike the nice people of the AFL, the IWW actually was.

Chapter 13

Welcome to France

IF YOU WERE AN AMERICAN IN THE SECOND HALF OF 1917 AND wanted a safe, simple, and stress-free life, you could do worse than go to France with Major General Pershing's American Expeditionary Force.

You would not want to be in Washington. That was a long-running cockfight. It was where Democrats and Republicans, businessmen and bureaucrats, generals and admirals—all professing to want nothing but to help the nation win the war—were constantly at one another's throats over money, policy, and power.

And you wouldn't want to be in many other parts of the United States, either, unless you were prepared to keep any unorthodox opinions to yourself. America beyond the District of Columbia was where the war could get a

Shipping Out
*By 1918 more doughboys were ready
for transfer to France than ships
could be found to carry.*

person hurt. Right through until the spring of 1918, war-related violence caused more injuries and deaths at home than in the AEF.

Still, you would definitely want to be American, if you wanted to be safe. For every other belligerent nation, the war continued to be a bloodbath. As in 1915 and 1916, almost all of the major battles of 1917 turned out to be disasters for whichever side started them (and usually for the other side as well). April's Nivelle Offensive, which Joseph Joffre's successor as French commander in chief had promised would end the Western Front stalemate, was only the worst of the year's horrific examples. General Henri-Philippe Pétain,

upon replacing the discredited Robert Nivelle, found himself having to deal with the mutinies sparked by the failure of the offensive. Though he had the ringleaders of the mutiny hanged, he also toured the front, promising better treatment for the troops and an end to wasteful campaigns. All this was over before Pershing and his staff set foot in France.

When the next great convulsion came, on July 1, it took place on the faraway Eastern Front. Alexander Kerensky, the young lawyer who headed the provisional government that had taken over in Russia when Tsar Nicholas abdicated, was pledged to keep his country in the war. He ordered a summer

Henri-Philippe Pétain
He saved France twice,
first as commander at Verdun,
then in dealing with troop mutinies.

campaign (it would be named after him and also called the Liberty Offensive) to demonstrate that the new Russia was superior to the old and fully capable of doing its part.

In charge of the offensive was the new Russian commander in chief, the same General Alexei Brusilov who in 1916 had led a fabulously successful attack on the Austro-Hungarian armies in Galicia. He gathered together the last of his nation's military resources, two hundred thousand men and thirteen hundred pieces of artillery, on a thirty-mile stretch of front. With Brusilov commanding, and attacking on familiar ground now held by the Germans, the chances of success seemed excellent. And in the early going, the Russians seemed very successful indeed, overrunning the enemy's forward positions with surprisingly little difficulty. But this was a cruel illusion. It had been made possible by the new German system of defense-in-depth, which intentionally left the front line weak and permeable, designed to be given up after token resistance. The main defensive forces were kept well to the rear, comparatively safe from enemy artillery, poised to counterattack when the opportunity ripened.

Kerensky and Brusilov had failed to grasp one hard fact: that the Russian soldiers, even more than the French, had had enough. As soon as the German counterattack came, they turned and ran, shooting any officers who tried to stop them. They ran not just back to their starting point but as far as their legs would carry them, away from the front, away from the fighting, home. An entire army disappeared that day, as though into thin air.

The debacle left Russia all but defenseless. It discredited Kerensky and his government and gave new credibility to V. I. Lenin's hard-core branch of Russian Communists, the Bolsheviks. They understood that Kerensky's fatal blunder had been to persuade himself, somehow, that a patriotic population had turned on the tsar because it believed him willing to enter into a separate peace with the Germans. The Bolsheviks knew better. They saw that if they could seize power, to keep it they were going to have to get out of the war. The people would have no more of it.

That same July Pershing, accompanied by his aide, Lieutenant George S. Patton, interrupted his work in Paris to accept an invitation to visit Douglas Haig at the headquarters of the BEF. He concealed behind his unflappable soldierly demeanor the shock of learning that the British had lost 125,000 men—killed, wounded, and missing—in their recent Arras offensive. This was triple the number of American troops then in France, more than Pershing expected to have under his command at the end of the year. It had not, however, stopped Haig from preparing still another of the ever-bigger, never-successful offensives that were making his name synonymous with the brainless use of brute force. (He called the machine gun a fad and clung until the end of the war to his conviction that mounted cavalry would ultimately sweep the Germans from the field.)

This new attack, to be launched at the end of July and known as the Third Battle of Ypres, was to be bigger than Nivelle's. It was to be bigger even than

Sir Douglas Haig, commander of the British Expeditionary Force *He approved of Pershing's "quiet gentlemanly bearing—so unusual for an American."*

Haig's own 1916 Battle of the Somme, which had cost the Entente sixty thousand casualties, including almost twenty thousand dead, on its first day. Third Ypres was preceded by an artillery barrage that poured four million rounds, a hundred thousand of them poison gas, down on the German defenses. But when the whistles finally blew and the infantry climbed out of its trenches and advanced, Third Ypres turned into another protracted, heartbreaking failure. It would go on for more than three months, moving the Allied line two miles forward at a cost of three hundred thousand casualties. It would culminate in November in the agony of mud and blood to be remembered forever as Passchendaele.

There were some 65,000 American troops in France by the time of Third Ypres, but not one of them had seen any action. Pershing was sticking firmly to the War Department's plan, to the teeth-grinding exasperation of the British and French. The troops of the AEF, for some obscure reason now called "doughboys" by the war correspondents and headline writers (Pershing had rejected the suggestion that they be called "sammies"), were not to be sent into combat until the two original conditions had been met. They had to be brought up to what Pershing regarded as a professional level of readiness, and there had to be enough of them to take up a position on the front comparable to those of the British and the French. Before the end of September, a report prepared by Pershing's staff informed a surprised Washington that this was not going to be possible until the spring of 1919. New troops were arriving too slowly, and were in need of too much training, for anything better to be possible.

The lead elements of the AEF's First Division, upon arriving in France in late June, had been received with wild enthusiasm everywhere they went. When the French authorities made it known that they wanted Yank troops to march down Paris's Champs-Élysées as the centerpiece of a specially arranged Fourth of July celebration, Pershing at first refused. He knew that even the regiments that had served with him in Mexico now contained large numbers of inexperienced recruits, that they had been given barely enough training to be considered bona fide soldiers, and that their ill-fitting uniforms and soft hats (they had been sent abroad without helmets) were not likely to impress. He finally consented to sending a single battalion. If they looked like beginners, it did not matter. Masses of cheering Parisians poured love on the men come to save them.

Their taciturn general, with his stern demeanor and severely trimmed mustache, made a good impression on his Allied counterparts. Even the snobbish Haig, son of one of Scotland's leading whisky-making dynasties, confessed to his diary that he "was much struck with [Pershing's] quiet gentlemanly bearing—so unusual for an American." The AEF staff was in crowded quarters in Paris, coming to grips with the challenge of bringing into existence and sustaining a fighting force incomparably larger than anything the United States had possessed in the preceding half century. It was a challenge of an entirely new kind. The world had been simpler the last time Washington had a great army. And in Ulysses S. Grant's day there had not been an ocean between his headquarters and Washington.

Training, training, and more training
It was all the troops were allowed to do, until Pershing decided they were ready.

Almost everything had to be built from scratch. Even the organization and command structure of the AEF had to be improvised, the army's directives on such matters having been written by men who could not have foreseen what 1917 would bring. Pershing appointed as his chief of staff a man he had known since his days in the Philippines, James G. Harbord, who had entered the service as a private in 1889 and was now a regular army major. Together they designed a headquarters organization with five divisions (administrative policy, intelligence, operations, coordination, and training) and five assistant chiefs of staff to direct the quartermaster corps, the engineers, and the ordnance, medical, and transportation operations. The quality of the talent pool was high, Pershing having been free to select whichever officers he wished to accompany him to France. In it were future legends, most notably Captain George Marshall and Lieutenant Patton and a man with a visionary's understanding of the potential of military aviation, Lieutenant Colonel William (Billy) Mitchell.

Everything that needed to be done turned out to be an almost overwhelming challenge. Just moving a single division of the size decided on by Pershing (28,000 men, double the total for British, French, and German divisions at full strength) required sixty trains—not railroad cars, but whole trains. All the numbers were astronomical, even the numbers of horses and mules needed for the movement of artillery, ammunition, and food—everything. Early on, at the height of its excitement about the American declaration of war, the French government promised to provide the AEF with 100,000 horses. That was soon reduced to 80,000, and even the lower figure proved impossible. The French armies needed their horses, and when the Americans tried to buy animals on the open market they found few sellers except those hoping to unload sorry nags for high prices. The farmers, too, needed such horses as they still had, as did merchants and tradesmen. It came to be rumored that the French were conspiring to force the Americans to import their own horses, so that when the war ended a superabundance would be available. By hook and by crook, the AEF gradually acquired thousands and then tens of thousands of horses, and their care and feeding became still another headache. Transporting fodder required still more trains on a daily basis.

The AEF needed a supply and transportation system that would be adequate to the need while neither interfering with the Allies nor becoming dependent on them. Before this could be arranged, it was necessary to find a home for the American troops somewhere along the Western Front. It was

Unloading the horn of plenty
*The quantities of equipment and supplies that the United States shipped
to France were measured in astronomical numbers.*

clear from the start that the Americans should operate in closer proximity to
the French than to the British. The attitude that Colonel House and the Anglophile Wilson administration had maintained during the years of neutrality,
regarding France as Britain's distant and distinctly junior partner, was no longer tenable. Now France was the host country, needing to be treated with respect, and her central place in the war had become clear to the newcomers.
Now it was the British who would be left more or less to themselves—to their
part of the deadlocked front, up north in Flanders.

The sectors of front nearest Paris were off-limits; the protection of the capital had to be left to the French. What remained were the areas farther east,
nearer Germany. When he studied his maps, Pershing found something he
liked. It was far to the east, between the Argonne Forest and the Vosges Mountains: the area around the vast Verdun battleground, where France and Germany had nearly bled each other to death in 1916. It was directly opposite, and
therefore perfectly positioned for an attack on, the Germans' St. Mihiel salient,
a protrusion into the French trench line beyond which lay rich iron and coal
mines, crucial rail lines, and the important city of Metz. Better still, the Moselle River ran through the area, down to where it crosses into Germany
proper, becomes the Mosel, and flows into the Rhine at Koblenz. It beckoned

to Pershing as a virtual highway into Germany. The whole situation was ideal in terms of Pershing's ultimate objective: an opportunity, when the AEF was ready, to strike the great blow that would ensure Germany's defeat.

He went to see General Pétain and told him what he wanted. Pétain agreed, and the deal was done. Pershing moved his staff to a château outside the handsome old town of Chaumont, south of Verdun. The First Division followed. The work of making things happen could now begin in earnest.

Their new base can hardly have been what the doughboys had envisioned when given their orders for France. For one thing, there would be no fighting for almost any of them for another half year or more. What hundreds of thousands of them would instead experience through one dreary month after another was endless days and nights of boredom, drill, and discomfort. Because the French lacked decent accommodations even for their own troops, and because building anything like the cantonments back in the States was logistically out of the question, enlisted men as they arrived in Lorraine were billeted in the farm buildings, usually barns and stables and storage spaces, that dotted the countryside. They slept on straw, which soon became damp and dank and provided a breeding ground for the lice ("cooties" to the troops) that were the curse of every army, not only a torment as they feasted on human blood but the cause of trench fever.

Pershing's West Point classmate Robert Lee Bullard would recall one particularly unexpected feature of French rural life: "the *fumier*—the heap of manure piled at the front door of every villager—the sign of his thrift and even of

Home sweet home
Western Front style.

his wealth, but a disagreeable thing, irritating and dangerous in the dark, and a kind of front yard ornamentation to which our soldiers could never become accustomed." This was far from the only source of friction between the soldiers and the people among whom they were living. The Americans, young, looking for fun, and not always respectful of other people's property, sometimes seemed an army of occupation more than of liberation. The French, for their part, could seem to have their hands always out, wanting to be paid for every small thing.

Though the doughboys' diet was generous—more than four thousand calories daily, nearly a third higher than British or French rations—a chronic scarcity of food in the Allied nations meant that the Americans had to be fed almost entirely with imports from the United States. The result was a cumula-

Filling the empty hours
Playing baseball was one way to break the tedium of camp life and rifle drill.

tively disgusting reliance on a variety of beef, imported from Argentina and canned in Chicago, that the troops called "monkey meat." Freshness and variety were rare and became rarer as the transporting of ever-greater numbers of men left less shipboard space for canned fruit and vegetables and the like. Eight hundred million pounds of canned beef were shipped across the Atlantic, along with 150 million pounds of canned pork, a billion pounds of flour, and almost half a billion pounds of potatoes. Lacking mess halls, the men ate in the streets and roadways, out of their mess kits, rain or shine.

They drilled and trained and drilled and trained again, often under French or British combat veterans. Opportunities for diversion were limited almost to the point of nonexistence. A tartly clever eighteen-year-old private named Arthur Yensen, author of an undeservedly unpublished memoir that he titled "War Log of an Underdog," made a list of the people and things he came to regard as his enemies in the empty months before the AEF finally went into action:

Our officers head the list, because they never do us any good; they're cranky, arrogant and unreasonable. They have so much power that they can have us shot for nothing if they want to; and since we have no protection against them, I call them our arch-enemies.

The weather ranks second because in these leaky clothes, the cold rain and must are slowly sapping the life out of us. . . .

The mules come third because they are mostly white-eyed outlaws—so dangerous that the civilians sold them to the army to get rid of 'em. We have to take care of them before ourselves, which is all the way from disagreeable to impossible.

Our leaky clothes come fourth because only our steel helmets turn water—and they sit way up on our heads like pie-pans instead of coming down around our ears where they could do some good. Our wool clothes would be fine if they fit and were of a comfortable design and were protected by rain-coats that were rain-coats. Our feet are wet *all* the time. . . .

The cooties come fifth. . . .

The canned potato-meat hash comes sixth because it gives us heartburn. Our rations are half meat and the other half is made up of potatoes, bread, coffee, rice, dried carrots and too little fruit. We crave sweets, milk and fruit.

Homesickness comes seventh. Most of us have never been away from home before, and we're so hungry for a little womanly affection that it's awful.

The Germans come last, because if it wasn't for them we could go home!

Yensen was hardly exaggerating in saying that the rain, cold, and lack of protection from both were sapping the life of the troops. Pneumonia and other respiratory ailments swept through the ranks, and they and influenza would ultimately account for four-fifths of the AEF's fifty thousand illness-related deaths.

Fantasies about romantic encounters with French damsels had little chance of becoming more than that. Even encounters with members of the oldest profession became difficult and risky when Pershing forbade them and ordered strict enforcement. When Georges Clemenceau became French prime minister, he offered to help the Americans set up licensed houses of prostitution like those provided for his nation's troops, with red lights marking establishments for enlisted men and blue for officers only. Pershing sent this offer to Raymond Fosdick, President Wilson's agent in keeping the stateside army free of vice. Fosdick showed it to Secretary of War Baker. "For God's sake, Raymond," Baker said, "don't show this to the President or he'll stop the war!"

The thoughtful Private Yensen refused to judge the French nation on the basis of what the doughboys found when they went in search of "a little womanly affection." "Ordinarily we get acquainted only with the lowest class here just as we did around Ft. Leavenworth or Kansas City," he wrote. "So it's my contention that we can't judge the women of France by the scum we meet there any more than we can judge the women of America by the chippies that congregate around the army camps back home. If I had a daughter I wouldn't trust her very far with the average man in this outfit, and I suppose the respectable French people feel the same way."

Pershing was almost obsessive about the prevention of venereal disease, demanding daily reports on new cases reported and studying the latest data when visiting his divisions. His vigilance appears to have been effective. Though 57,195 cases were recorded by war's end, they accounted for only about 4 percent of the days lost from duty as a result of disease.

It need hardly be said that VD was not foremost among the problems requiring the general's attention. Among the bigger ones, and incomparably more urgent, was transportation. The men and matériel that were soon arriving in vast quantities from America had to be unloaded somewhere. For this purpose, Pershing requested and was granted the use of three ports on France's Atlantic coast: Pauillac near Bordeaux, La Pallice to the north of it, and St. Nazaire farther north still. None of the three were important to the French or British, and troops and supplies could be transported from them to Lorraine without having to pass through the congested railyards of Paris. A further advantage was that ships crossing the ocean to or from these ports had to go nowhere near Britain or Ireland, where the U-boats most often prowled.

The War Department, having made a close study of the available shipping, replied that it would be able to send only 634,975 men to France by June 15, 1918. This would not begin to meet what Pershing had determined to be the need. In both Washington and Chaumont, this prompted a shift of attention to the one country that had a big enough transport fleet to make a difference— Great Britain. But David Lloyd George claimed to be unable to offer much help. His nation had barely enough merchantmen, he insisted, to feed its people and sustain its own war effort. Thus it remained unclear just when the AEF might become as big and as capable as Pershing said it would have to be in order to join the fighting. Britain and France continued to demand the amalgamation of the American troops into their armies. Pershing, under brutally intense pressure, continued to refuse.

One way to increase shipboard space for troops was to reduce the shipment of other things. One way to do that was to buy as many necessities as possible from European sources. Pershing, endowed with what amounted to an unlimited budget, set out to do exactly that. He had persuaded an old friend, the Chicago banker Charles Dawes, to join his staff and take charge of procurement. It was a wise move, Dawes being a brilliantly effective if personally rather unmilitary manager. His task was made possible by the fact that the war had had little impact on France's production of a good many essentials including raw materials. Eventually the American supply organization, created "to relieve the combatant field force from every consideration except that of defeating the enemy," would employ more than 650,000 men, and Dawes would become a general. His organization ultimately purchased ten million tons of European goods.

The Americans expressed amazement at how little the British and French governments and armed forces cooperated with each other or displayed any interest in doing so. "Our allies seem to hate one another," Pershing's chief of staff, James Harbord, wrote not long after arriving in Europe. This made everything more difficult, including the establishment of a rail system to connect the AEF's ports to its base on the other side of France.

Among the problems was the fact that after three years of war, France's rail network was worn out. It had almost no serviceable locomotives to offer the AEF. Meanwhile between six and seven hundred high-quality locomotives were sitting unused in Belgium, the government of which was hoarding them for use in reconstruction and the revival of commerce whenever the war ended. Dawes managed to pry them loose—the United States had leverage with the Belgians, thanks to years of civilian relief work—and immediately handed them over to the French. That was one problem solved, but more remained unsolved than anyone could count.

Even within the various Allied governments, the failure to communicate and coordinate could be astonishing. By summer's end France was aquiver with rumors that the country's supplies of mined coal were nearly exhausted. It was feared that if winter came and people had no coal, there would be riots, and once riots began in a France thoroughly sick of war, there was no saying what might follow. AEF headquarters naturally took all this seriously; quite apart from the awful prospect of their being a foreign army in a nation on the verge of an uprising, Dawes estimated that by February Pershing's forces were going to need 150,000 tons of coal every month.

He looked to the British and was told that although they had coal in abundance, they had no way of getting it to where it was needed. He proposed importing American miners to increase the output of France's coalfields, drained of skilled workers by the war, and was told that this was likely to cause as much anger as a general coal shortage. Finally an American war correspondent named Hubbard was commissioned an army major and sent out to determine the actual state of France's coal inventory. With surprising speed, he returned to report that there was no cause for concern. How had he learned this so quickly? By calling on the most obvious source of reliable information, the economics section of the French intelligence service. The staff there was delighted to see him. They possessed complete and up-to-date information on the coal situation and could prove that available supplies were sufficient to meet all needs. But they had been unable to get anyone in their own government to pay attention.

As of mid-October the number of AEF combat casualties stood at a virginal zero. Units of the First Division, however, were now being given brief periods of duty in quiet sectors of the front. They were under the supervision of French officers and allowed to take no action without permission. October 23 brought the first wounding of Americans by enemy artillery; the injured were treated at a field hospital and returned to duty. Days later First Division gunners cautiously fired their first round of artillery, and an unlucky German soldier became the Americans' first prisoner of war.

The soldier's second-best friend
After his rifle, his trenching tool.

Then, in the predawn hours of November 3, a force of German trench raiders came across No Man's Land some ten miles east of Nancy. Under cover of an artillery barrage, they rushed an American platoon in a normally quiet part of the line. When they departed, after a short sharp bout of hand-to-hand fighting, they took with them a dozen prisoners and left behind the dead bodies of the first three AEF members to be killed in combat. They were Corporal James B. Grisham, a twenty-seven-year-old former factory worker who had joined the army in 1914; Private Thomas F. Enright, who had enlisted back in 1909 and was thirty at the time of his death; and Private Merle Hay, twenty-one and a green recruit.

It cannot be said that the three did not get their share of glory. They were buried, originally, with full military honors near the place where they died, with a French general giving a speech. A monument was erected over their graves. After the war, in a departure from standard practice, their bodies were returned to the United States and solemnly reinterred in their hometowns with dignitaries presiding and reverent crowds looking on. Hay, the young Iowan, achieved a distinctly American kind of immortality. Not long after his death a highway running northward out of Des Moines was renamed Merle Hay Road. Decades later, when the city's largest shopping mall was constructed along that road, it became Merle Hay Plaza. It is doubtful that one-tenth of 1 percent of the people shopping there know the origin of the name.

The AEF grew by year end to 125,000 men. Many had been in France for half a year, training incessantly, still living in barns, but Pershing continued to insist that they were not ready for combat. To say that this was unacceptable to the Allies, for whom the war was not going at all well, is to understate the case. The doughboys were settling in for a winter that would turn out to be so dark, cold, and wet, so riddled with disease, that they called it "the Valley Forge of the AEF." Back in the States, the human pipeline was full to bursting. The Selective Service System had met its target of getting one and a half million men into uniform by December 31.

Background

Buffalo Soldiers

In the summer of 1917, a nightmare out of the darkest recesses of the American subconscious suddenly seemed to come howlingly to life.

Race riots. Race *war*. Retribution for the primordial sin of slavery, demanding to be atoned for at last.

It began on the first day of July, in East St. Louis, Illinois, a rough-and-tumble riverfront town of railyards and stockyards across the Mississippi from St. Louis. A party of armed white men, probably drunk and out for a jolly time, drove through the streets of the "nigger district" shouting insults and firing their guns. No one was hurt, but many were frightened. When quiet returned, residents peered out cautiously through the windows of their homes. Those who had guns checked that they were loaded and waited for the revelers to return.

Another carload of white men appeared. It stopped, and the men got out; they, too, were armed. Questions were called out, answers were shouted back, and by the alchemy of fear an uncertain exchange of words escalated into a gunfight. Two of the white men were killed. It turned out that they were police detectives.

The next day, after a night of electrifying tension, there came another invasion. It was hundreds of white men this time, armed vigilantes bent on taking revenge and imposing order on their own terms. What followed was a wild melee that had nothing to do with order on any terms. At least thirty-three of the town's black residents were killed, by some accounts more than a hundred. Eight whites died as well. Hundreds of houses were set ablaze as police and National Guardsmen either looked on passively or joined in the rampage.

The story was a national sensation. Theodore Roosevelt condemned the actions of the whites, but his was a solitary voice. Official inquiries were undertaken but were too cursory to accomplish anything. Investigators took less interest in the testimony of survivors than in rumors of how the trouble had been caused by labor agitators, or German agents.

All this was bad enough, especially as it was followed by similar though smaller outbreaks of racial violence in other places. It brought visions of Armageddon to both sides of America's black-white divide. It moved the War Department, in response to southern hysteria, to suspend the induction of black draftees. But in August something even more terrifying happened. This time it was black soldiers of the U.S. Army, men trained in warfare, engaging in a pitched battle with white police and troops.

It took place in the racial tinderbox of Houston, Texas. Deeply southern in their attitudes and culture, the white citizens of Houston had long been uncomfortable with their city's being the home base of the Twenty-Fourth Infantry, which since the Civil War had been one of the regular army's four black regiments (the officers of which were, of course, unanimously white). On the night of August 23, Houston police raided a craps game in which all the players were members of the Twenty-Fourth. In the scuffle that followed, one of the soldier-gamblers (himself a military policeman) was injured and arrested. A black woman was apparently subjected to rough treatment by the white police.

When news of what had happened reached the Twenty-Fourth's barracks, it sparked a furious reaction. Men long fed up with how they were treated by white Houston—and perhaps given an exaggerated account of what had transpired at the craps game—decided that they had had enough. Bizarrely, almost suicidally, they took up their weapons and started for the central city. Whether (as would be alleged) they were intent on a killing spree is unproved. What is known is that they moved on the city's police station, gunfire broke out, and white army troops were dispatched to intervene. By the time the fight ended, fifteen whites and Hispanics including five police officers had been shot dead along with four of the black soldiers. An entire battalion of the Twenty-Fourth Infantry was under arrest.

Enraged black men, armed and intent on mayhem: it was the deepest fear of millions of white Americans, and not of southern whites only. Retribution came swiftly. Sixty-four of the arrested soldiers went before a hastily arranged court-martial, and in short order twenty-nine were sentenced to death. Nineteen were hanged so quickly that appeal was impossible.

The Inquirer, a black newspaper in San Antonio, published a letter in which a Mrs. C. L. Threadgill Dennis expressed regret for the tragedy but told the black soldiers that "we would rather see you shot by the highest tribunal of the United States Army because you dared protect a Negro woman from the insult of a southern brute in the form of a policeman, than have you forced to go to Europe to fight for a liberty you cannot enjoy." The paper's editor, who claimed that he had been away when the letter was published and knew nothing about it, was convicted of encouraging mutiny and sentenced to two years in prison. Clearly, complaints were not going to be tolerated.

White America had for centuries been uneasy about the use of soldiers of African descent in a society most of whose black members were slaves or serfs. Virginia prohibited blacks from serving in its militia as early as 1639, and other colonies, not all of them southern, soon did likewise. Such rules were sometimes relaxed in times of crisis, especially when white volunteers were in short supply, so that freedmen served as soldiers and even officers in the Revolutionary War. They served in the War of 1812 as well, but in 1820 Secretary of War John C. Calhoun, a South Carolinian, imposed a ban on black enlistment that remained in effect until the Civil War. Then the Lincoln administration, under pressure from abolitionists and in need of recruits, began accepting black volunteers and organizing them into segregated units.

Ultimately twenty thousand black soldiers served in the Union army. They performed well and endured high casualty rates. By the end of the war, even the Confederacy, desperately short of manpower, was promising freedom to slaves in return for military service.

In the aftermath of the Civil War, it became a tradition that the regular army would always include four black regiments. Under white officers, these regiments served in the Indian Wars (where they came to be called buffalo soldiers), the Spanish-American War, and the suppression of the Philippine insurrection. The men whom "Black Jack" Pershing led up San Juan Hill on the flank of Roosevelt's Rough Riders were members of one such regiment.

This was accepted even by the South's powerful congressional delegation because of the marginal position of the military in the American society of the time. The enlisted ranks of the regular army were made up largely of immigrants and misfits, ill-paid men many of whom had rejected or been rejected by the civilian world. They were a suspect group, stationed mostly in the distant West, and the black regiments were merely somewhat more marginal than the others. They accepted being led by officers who, this being nineteenth-century America, often regarded them as not quite human.

The Great War impacted the American racial situation long before intervention. First it brought immigration from Europe to a halt. That created a shortage of unskilled labor, a problem that conscription would later make worse. Employers started sending recruiters into the South with promises of a better life elsewhere. Neither the owners of the land on which freed slaves had long toiled nor the white factory workers of the industrial states were happy about this. Companies sometimes used black migrants as strikebreakers, pitting poor whites against poorer blacks, generating the tragedy of East St. Louis and later of cities as large as Chicago. It is estimated that a third of a million southern blacks moved to the North and West between 1910 and 1920.

At the time of the U.S. declaration of war, twenty thousand African Americans were in military service, half with the regular army's four black regiments, half in segregated National Guard units of seven states and the District of Columbia. Many black men were eager to volunteer, if only because an army private's meager pay was more than they could earn at home, but this became difficult when the War Department opted to rely on conscription. Nevertheless, four hundred thousand black men ultimately served, nearly all in the army. (They were excluded from the Marine Corps and were given only the most servile positions—as stewards serving officers, for example—in the navy.) They were a larger percentage of the nation's armed forces than African Americans were of the population, in part because exemptions were granted far more freely to whites.

Military service led less often to liberation than to new forms of humiliation. African Americans found themselves training in the worst facilities. (Those at Newport News, Virginia, spent the winter of 1917–18 in tents without floors, stoves, or blankets.) They had to make do with the least and shoddiest equipment. Many were engaged not in training at all but in brute manual labor. "Our drilling," one conscript would recall, "consisted in marching to and from work with hoes, shovels and picks on our shoulders."

If challenged—which it wasn't, in any serious way—the War Department could have said that there was no need to train most black draftees for combat because there was no possibility of their facing the enemy.

And that was largely correct: 75 percent of all the African Americans who served (and nearly 90 percent of the draftees) were assigned to labor battalions. The same was true of the two hundred thousand sent to France: they made up one-thirtieth of the AEF's combat troops, one-third of its laborers. The laborers wore blue denim instead of khaki, and their contribution was to dig ditches, build roads, load and unload ships and railcars and trucks, and bury the dead. When Pershing complained to Washington that too many of the "colored stevedore troops" assigned to his ports had "tuberculosis, old fractures, extreme flat feet, hernia, venereal diseases all existing prior to induction," he was probably not exaggerating. The reason was the eagerness of many draft boards to be rid of young black males, and the general staff's willingness to put them to work regardless of their physical condition.

Those who later claimed that the army wanted its black troops to fail as fighters could point to the fact that not one of the regular army's all-black regiments was sent to France. If obliged to respond to such accusations, the generals might have replied that most blacks were unfit for the most demanding kinds of duty. And they could have offered evidence: the low scores of most black draftees on what the army called its intelligence test. Never mind that the test judged "intelligence" by asking who wrote "The Raven," why a woman named Rosa Bonheur was famous, and where Overland automobiles were manufactured. Nor were the army's manpower planners likely to have been lying when they said that many black draftees had never heard of Germany and could barely read or write. The average black draftee had had 2.6 years of schooling, versus 4.7 for immigrants and 6.9 for native-born whites. A fourth of all draftees were illiterate, and only 18 percent had ever sat in a high school class. This was a failure of the society, not of the army.

When progressives and organizations such as the NAACP lobbied for the commissioning of black officers, a special training camp was opened for the purpose at Fort Des Moines in Iowa. In the autumn of 1917 it graduated its first class of 639 lieutenants and captains. Almost all were assigned to the newly formed and all-black Ninety-Second Infantry Division, which would later see extensive action. (Uniquely, the Ninety-Second's officer corps was for a time 80 percent black. None of the black officers, however, held a rank above captain. Throughout the war, duty assignments were arranged in such a way as to make it impossible for black officers to qualify for higher promotion.)

By graduation day at Fort Des Moines, the Houston shoot-out had taken place and the presumed culprits had been executed. That may explain why there were no subsequent classes. The army shut the camp down and did not replace it. The number of black officers who served during the war would ultimately reach eleven hundred, or 1 percent of the officers in an army that was 13 percent black. Some were commissioned as doctors, dentists, and the like, though many black professionals found themselves serving as enlisted men in positions that, when held by whites, always brought a commission.

The plain fact is that the army didn't want black soldiers, commissioned or otherwise. Former chief of staff Leonard Wood had refused to admit blacks to the so-called Plattsburg volunteer officer training camps, established before U.S. entry into the war, warning that such a step could lead to interracial marriage and make Americans "a breed of mongrels." No one has ever argued that Wood's views were not typical of the army's senior command, or that they were any less prevalent among the leadership of the AEF in France than in the stateside army.

The white South shared the army's lack of enthusiasm for black troops. Senator James Vardaman of Mississippi spoke for his state's gentlefolk and rednecks alike in warning that soon there would be "arrogant strutting representatives of the black soldiery in every community." The Justice Department, taking such concerns seriously, undertook the systematic surveillance of whatever it was that fell under the heading of "Negro activities." The War Department, when it resumed the induction of blacks, promised that in every cantonment they would be outnumbered by whites by a margin of no less than two to one.

It would be unfair to single out President Wilson for special blame. By the standards of his native South he was a racial moderate, and he was squarely in the mainstream of the United States of his time. His general passivity where racial discrimination was at issue might almost be considered commendable in a southerner who had been almost nine years old when the Civil War ended, and who had heard his adored father deliver sermons about "how completely the Bible brings human slavery underneath the sanction of divine authority." A New Englander who did graduate studies under the young Wilson at Bryn Mawr recalled that he had been something new in her experience, a man "who had no special sympathy for Negroes as human beings." A Princeton acquaintance described him as "the best narrator of darky stories I have ever heard in my life." In his book *Division and Reunion,* Wilson wrote of the white people of the antebellum South that "their relations with their slaves were honorable, their responsibility for the existence of slavery among them remote."

It is in any case certain that he never regarded racial equality as an issue of even minor importance, and that he did nothing to keep the war from becoming another chapter in the unending tragedy of black life in America.

Chapter 14

"A Moblike Madness"

HIRAM JOHNSON, WHO AS GOVERNOR OF CALIFORNIA HAD BEEN among the West's leading progressives and Theodore Roosevelt's running mate in 1912, ran for the Senate in 1916 in the expectation that he could add his voice to those of Robert La Follette and other reformers and help make things happen in Washington. But he found, upon taking his seat in 1917, that the reform impulse had grown feeble there. "Everything here is war," he complained in a letter home. "To suggest a social program or a domestic policy would simply afford an opportunity to those who believe in none to boll [*sic*] you over."

Johnson was among those learning that to be in national politics in 1917, or in almost any position of responsibility in government, was to be entangled in the almost innumerable issues that intervention had either created or brought to the fore. Many of the most sensitive questions—how the war was going to be paid for, whether it was being properly managed, what to do about profiteers—remained, exhaustingly, unresolved. But Johnson was wrong about reform having become impossible. In some ways the opposite was true. After years of conflict and slow progress or no progress at all, advocates of prohibition, woman suffrage, and even racial equality were finding new opportunities to press their demands. In doing so they made the nation's always-contentious capital more turbulent than it had been in decades.

It could almost seem, at times, that everyone hated everyone, most obviously across party lines. That most eminent and powerful of Senate Republicans, Henry Cabot Lodge, reported after a two-hour visit to the White House that he found Wilson "a curious mixture of acuteness, intelligence and extreme underlying timidity, [with] a shifty, furtive, sinister expression." The air was thick with such venomous talk. With the United States now in the war, it could be directed at those who had opposed intervention without fear of repercussions.

Lodge's great friend Theodore Roosevelt, wanting to be either in the White House or at the front, was so consumed with frustration and resentment that he seemed at times to have lost his reason. He condemned pacifism as "the tool and ally of German militarism" and proposed that conscientious objectors be used to clear minefields. Though he continued to speak hatefully of Wilson, the two were no longer all that far apart. The president, once hopeful of ending the war without allowing anyone to win it, now wanted a victory so complete as to leave Europe and the world transformed. He viewed those who did not share his vision as disdainfully as TR viewed him. "What I am opposed to is not the feeling of the pacifists, but their stupidity," he told an AFL gathering. "My heart is with them, but my mind has contempt for them. I want peace, but I know how to get it, and they do not." Contempt: Wilson was a past master. And increasingly it was the lens through which millions of his fellow citizens were learning to view one another.

Congressmen of both parties had questions about the costs and progress of the war effort, and they wanted answers. The unwillingness of Wilson and his cabinet to confer with them, or even to share information, turned their doubts into suspicion. It was self-defeating, the administration's remoteness from Capitol Hill; it kept even friendly senators and representatives from knowing how much was being accomplished by the likes of War Secretary Baker and Navy Secretary Daniels, or understanding the magnitude of the obstacles they faced. Almost as many Democrats as Republicans felt alienated from the cold and distant figure in the White House, and there was much talk of a need for hearings and investigations. The administration was going to be hard-pressed to head such things off when Congress reassembled in December.

December was still four months in the future when, on August 1, 1917, Pope Benedict XV issued a detailed call for peace. It proposed an end to the slaughter on the basis of seven points, among them the evacuation of all occupied territories, no payment of indemnities, global disarmament, freedom of the seas, and the creation of new mechanisms for the arbitration of international disputes. The White House was not pleased—indeed, it was thunderstruck. Wilson, with his Scots-Presbyterian roots, would not likely have found it easy to accept the leadership of the Roman pontiff under almost any circumstances, but in this case the circumstances were particularly unfavorable.

Benedict was trespassing on territory that the president saw as his exclusively. *He* was supposed to be the peacemaker.

And the intrusion came at an awkward time. Wilson, trying to keep the nation focused on the great task of defeating Germany, was discouraging even the mention of peace talks in the American press. Colonel House was somewhat more receptive; he saw that a curt rejection of the pope's message would put the United States and the Allies in a bad light. He got Wilson's attention by reminding him of a danger about which the two of them had long been in agreement: that the crushing of Germany would create a central European power vacuum that Russia might be best positioned to fill. That had always been a worrisome thought. Now, with the Bolsheviks ruling Russia, it was a horrifying one. It pointed to the desirability of halting the war short of Germany's utter destruction.

Nonetheless, Secretary of State Lansing sent a letter warning the president that the pontiff was probably in cahoots with the Central Powers—with Austria in particular, because it was a Catholic country. This was preposterous on the face of it; on the Allied side, Belgium and France were both heavily Catholic, not to mention Benedict's native Italy, and any papal preference for the Hapsburgs of Vienna would have been neutralized by the staunch Lutheranism of the Hohenzollern regime in Berlin. The Austrians knew themselves to be on the verge of collapse, and already saw negotiations as the only way they might possibly escape ruin. But that hardly made the pope their agent, never mind Germany's. Lansing's warning was, in part at least, an expression of the anti-Catholic bias that historian Arthur Schlesinger, Sr., described as the oldest and deepest of American prejudices, reaching back to the Pilgrim Fathers. It was so firmly embedded in establishment Americans of a century ago, so taken for granted, that they were incapable of seeing it as a bias at all.

In 1916 it had nearly broken the heart of President Wilson's devoted private secretary and jack-of-all-trades, the able, amiable, and loyal Joe Tumulty. Through Wilson's first term Tumulty had remained the same invaluable asset that he had been in the New Jersey statehouse, a shrewd guide to the intricacies of Democratic Party politics and a favorite of the Washington press corps. But important people thought it unseemly that such a figure should be part of the president's innermost circle. It was whispered that he must be a secret agent of the Vatican. The second Mrs. Wilson began pushing for Tumulty's dismissal. Edith Galt Wilson, who in girlhood had received exactly two years of formal schooling, decided to her disgust that Tumulty—a university graduate and lawyer who knew Latin and read and spoke Italian and, with his Jesuit education, was at home in the works of Plato and Cicero—was "common." She meant that he was Irish and Catholic and happy to mix with people of all stations in life, even reporters and machine politicians. Colonel House joined her campaign, in spite of having encouraged Wilson to hire Tumulty back in New Jersey in 1910. Possibly he did so in the knowledge that Edith had no liking for him, either, and in the hope (a vain one, if he entertained it) of winning her approval by helping her cleanse the White House of an Irish-Catholic taint. They succeeded—or nearly did.

Wilson and Tumulty
Informed of his dismissal,
the faithful Irishman expressed his
gratitude for the opportunity
to serve "so closely with so
great a man."

Wilson tried to get Tumulty to go by saying he wanted him to run for the Senate in New Jersey. The secretary declined the honor. Wilson then tried to appoint him to a comfortable civil service post away from Washington. Again Tumulty said no thanks, taking the hint this time and adding that if he was not wanted, he preferred to just go home. Wilson agreed that that would be best. Tumulty wrote a letter thanking the president for the privilege of "having been associated so closely with so great a man." His departure was averted in the eleventh hour by a newspaperman named David Lawrence, who had been a Princeton undergraduate when Wilson was the university's president. Lawrence called at the White House one quiet Sunday, saw Wilson alone, and managed to change his mind about dismissing Tumulty. But one of the closest and most positive relationships of Wilson's professional life had been damaged. Throughout his second term, his secretary had to carry on his duties under the unfriendly gaze of the ever-present Edith.

Wilson showed no inclination even to acknowledge the pope's appeal. Weeks went by without his doing anything about it. Colonel House, however, was worried. He urged the president to at least appear to take it seriously, if only for public relations purposes. When Wilson finally did respond, a month after the appeal was issued, he began with language that, if not intentionally condescending, was certainly susceptible to being read that way.

"Every heart that has not been blinded and hardened by this terrible war must be touched by this moving appeal of His Holiness the Pope, must feel the dignity and force of the humane and generous motives which prompted it, and must fervently wish that we might take the path of peace he so persuasively points out," the president wrote. "But it would be folly to take it if it does not in fact lead to the goal he proposes." Which, he went on to explain, it did not come close to doing.

Colonel House, keeping his hand in, told the president that his reply was "the most remarkable document ever written, for surely there was never one approved throughout the world by every shade of political opinion."

If only. Wilson was trying—without success, as he would soon enough find—to walk a thin line of his own drawing. He wanted to show himself to be absolutely committed to the Allies but also well disposed toward the German people, opposed to "punitive damages, the dismemberment of empires, the establishment of selfish and exclusive economic leagues." Knowing that one or more of the Allies wanted each of these things, he attempted to avoid offending them by dismissing negotiations with Germany as impossible because "we cannot take the word of the present rulers of Germany as a guarantee of anything," and because promises, proposals, and offers of agreement, "if made by the German Government, no man, no nation, could now depend on." In short, the Allies need not worry about the possible outcome of negotiations because negotiations were out of the question.

Wilson's response was, in essence, Thank you for the nice thoughts, Mr. Pope, and permit me to explain why you are not being helpful. Those of us who are fighting this war know that there can be no peace worth having until "the free peoples of the world" have been delivered from "the menace and actual power of a vast military establishment, controlled by an irresponsible

Government, which, having secretly planned to dominate the world, proceeded to carry the plan out without regard either to the sacred obligations of treaty or the long-established practices and long-cherished principles of international action and honor."

Wilson and House both hoped the Allies would tell the world that the president's response spoke for them, and the colonel appealed to the British Foreign Office to make this happen. The Allies were united in declining to cooperate. They wanted no part of the president's disavowals of punitive damages, territorial gains, and other fruits of victory.

So none of it mattered in the end, except as a measure of how profoundly the president's thinking had changed since the days when he expressed bafflement at the causes of the war. His actions made it clear that he had no interest in what Berlin or Vienna thought, either about the pope's appeal or about his own response to it. As for the Allies, France's premier had already damned Benedict's message as anti-French. In London, where the papacy was in any case regarded as malignant, ridiculous, and irrelevant, Lloyd George clung to his insistence on winning the war with a knockout blow. Signals of interest in the pope's plan did emerge from the chaos that was now Russia, but no one cared. Benedict's initiative was dead.

The episode served to remind Wilson that, determined though he now was to wage war until the German regime was undone, he also had a pacific flank to protect. He needed to shore up his position as the champion not of war but of a solid lasting peace—of war as the portal to such a peace. He needed to show the world that he remained simultaneously the great visionary and the great realist, a hardheaded warrior but also a beacon of light to the world. To do that, he needed to be able to demonstrate that he knew more than any pope, or any other head of government, about the questions that would have to be answered when the war was finished.

To this end, he invited Colonel House to assemble a collection of experts on Europe, the Middle East, and Asia, on history, geography, warfare, economics, and ethnography. He used secret parts of the White House budget to put these people to work. Their assignment was to identify the key questions that would face the postwar world and develop possible answers. House recruited his brother-in-law, the president of City College in New York, to take charge of the project, and Walter Lippmann of *The New Republic* became its secretary. It was based at the New York offices of the American Geographical

Society and grew rapidly. Called the Inquiry, in short order it was comparable to the faculty of a substantial university.

Soon thereafter the president sent House back to Europe at the head of a special mission including senior representatives of the army and navy and such war-related government functions as food management, finance, shipping, and munitions. The mission's objective was to put these specialists together with their opposite numbers from the Allied governments and work out ways to improve coordination and efficiency. House also had instructions to try to get the leading Allied nations to state their war aims in clearer, more complete terms than they thus far had done. As on previous occasions, this last objective proved impossible, and House's failure to achieve it exposed the limits of American influence even after intervention. The French and especially the British, having seen little need to be submissive to a neutral United States, could see no need at all now that the United States was irreversibly on their side. Where war aims were concerned, House would return home with empty hands.

Unrestricted submarine warfare, meanwhile, was having a devastating effect. In the month of America's declaration of war, the U-boats sank 850,000 tons of shipping, far more than in any previous month and just short of the campaign's monthly goal. What was just as troubling, the number of new submarines going into service was well above the number being destroyed. On the other side of the ledger, however, the blockade that had driven the Germans to declare all commercial ships fair game was also inflicting new levels of pain. Data acquired by the State Department showed that the daily caloric intake of German civilians was now far below—perhaps less than half—the level required to maintain health. Civilian mortality was a third higher than in 1913, and the incidence of tuberculosis had doubled. "The death rate among old people is huge," the department stated, "as it is with small children."

Affecting as it did tens of millions of noncombatants, the blockade was on its way to becoming possibly the most successful and important initiative of the war, though it was not much boasted of at the time and would be largely expunged from the story told by the victors afterward. The whole German nation was on a downward slope to starvation, the old and the small first, with fat intake per person at 12 percent of the prewar level, meat consumption at 18 percent, and calories per day descending toward their 1918 level of one thousand. The situation in Austria-Hungary was if anything worse. After the war, doctors would estimate that between 7 and 11 percent of Vienna's civilian wartime deaths had been caused by starvation, which was a contributing factor in another 20 to 30 percent. More than 90 percent of Vienna's children were mildly to severely malnourished. The overall state of the Hapsburg empire is encapsulated in the fact that its troops were being issued paper underwear.

President Wilson, whether he appreciated it or not, benefited greatly from the fact that while U-boat sinkings were sensational events beautifully suited to the generation of headlines, the starvation of the civilian populations of central Europe happened with excruciating slowness and was a taboo subject for the newspapers of the Allies and the United States. It never had to be thought of by the American public, which in fact knew virtually nothing about it.

Wilson's new approach to the world crisis was producing momentous changes in the government he headed. Never again, even after the war ended and the country's immense new army was disbanded, would the federal budget be less than five times its prewar level. The very tenor of American life was changing, sometimes in disturbing ways. Self-styled patriots were finding in the war an unanswerable justification for attacks on individuals, groups, and movements of which they disapproved or that they viewed as a threat to themselves, their way of life, or (always a favorite phrase) "One Hundred Percent Americanism." Instances of lynching, the ultimate weapon in keeping blacks in their place, would rise from thirty-eight in 1917 to fifty-eight in 1918 and more than seventy in 1919. Overall, with the death count from riots added in, the number of African-Americans killed by mobs during this period probably reached two hundred. On July 26, 1917, at the urging of Joe Tumulty, the president issued a public "Denunciation of Lynching and the Mob Spirit." It was a strong statement, calling lynching a "disgraceful evil." But it put so much emphasis on the damage that lynching did to Americans' stature as "the champions of democracy" that it seems fair to wonder if Wilson would have said anything if he had not been concerned about the effect on America's international reputation and therefore on its propaganda.

Lincoln Steffens, one of journalism's most effective muckrakers, described the state of the nation in December 1917:

> The war is dividing men along the class line. It is becoming a class war. This is the conviction I got on my lecture trip across the country. Business men and the upper class generally are for the war, honestly, but passionately, aggressively. Accused of sordid motives, and conscious of making money, they are developing a moblike madness which is understandable but harmful.

Officials and the press are catching it. Labor and the lower classes are not
exactly against the war, but they are not for it; not yet, and the attitude of the
upper class and the policy (or some acts) of some parts of the government
and press are packing the workers back into a suppressed, sullen opposition.

A particularly ferocious domestic war was waged against those elements of
the American labor movement that did not follow the AFL in giving the government unqualified support. The most notorious remained the Industrial Workers of the World, the Wobblies. They were widely and bitterly despised, often as
a result of their own acts, at least as often because of viciously hostile press

Toil and
trouble
*Labor unrest
contributed
significantly
to domestic
turbulence as
the war came
to an end.*

coverage. The war against Germany became, for the Wobblies' domestic enemies, a chance to get rid of them once and for all. Thus several states, as soon as war was declared, passed "criminal syndicalism" laws intended to make the IWW an outlaw organization, less because of anything the Wobblies were doing than because of what they were—or were perceived as being. Fully 95 percent of IWW members eligible for the draft registered, and few of those called up failed to report for duty. In the six months following the U.S. declaration of war, three Wobbly locals went out on strike, compared with 518 locals of the AFL.

All the same, it was inevitable that the IWW's membership would see the war as a capitalist conspiracy; they saw almost everything as being for the benefit of the rich. The leaders, however, saw the danger of open opposition and were careful not to declare themselves. Their caution made no difference. They found themselves and their organization under attack on a broad front. Just a few months after the declaration of war, the Wilson Justice Department, in cooperation with local and state authorities and the leading industrial associations, took action calculated to put the IWW out of business and its leadership behind bars.

The destruction of the IWW was set in motion on June 8, 1917, in the Anaconda Copper Company's Speculator Mine in Butte, Montana. A fire broke out underground, an estimated 160 miners perished, and the cause was found to be the company's failure to install escape hatches in concrete bulkheads. Some of the dead, rescue teams discovered, had torn away not just their fingernails but the first joints of their fingers in trying to claw open locked doors. Four days after the fire, fifteen thousand members of the United Metal Mine Workers went out on strike. The company refused to meet with their representatives.

Seven days later a veteran IWW organizer named Frank Little, a part-Cherokee whose limp and one blind eye testified to his hard years in the labor wars, arrived on the scene. He gave fiery speeches, rich in the rhetoric of the militants. He condemned the conduct of the mining companies, capitalism generally, the police and state and federal troops, thereby making himself the most conspicuous man in Butte. At three one morning, men identifying themselves as officers of the law showed up at Little's boardinghouse. They pulled him out of bed, tied him to the bumper of a car, and dragged him through the streets until his kneecaps were torn off. They then hanged him by the neck from a railway trestle, disappearing into the darkness after pinning a sign to his dead body. "Others take notice," it said. "First and last warning."

The New York Times, no voice of moderation where labor disturbances were concerned, dutifully described Little's murder as "detestable" but went on to say that "the IWW agitators are in effect, and perhaps in fact, agents of Germany. The Federal Authorities should make short work of these treasonable conspirators against the United States." At no level of government did anyone see reason to investigate Little's murder.

By the time of the killing, the IWW was the target of vigilante and official violence in the copper-mining fields of Arizona, where police and company-paid gunmen were working together to break an organizing campaign. Police did not bother to get a warrant before raiding a dance organized by the Wobblies to raise money for the campaigners and their families. The police chief would later testify that there had been no disturbance at the dance before his men moved in, "but I knew that money would be collected for the IWW, who are known to be enemies of the United States Government."

That belief could justify almost anything. When miners walked out in Arizona, newspapers informed their readers that the whole thing was a plot to cripple the war effort by depriving the nation of urgently needed copper, and that the IWW was financed by Germany. Citizens were assured that action had to be taken, the niceties of the law set aside. Early on the morning of July 2, in the mining town of Bisbee, a vigilante force operating under the auspices of the local Citizens Protective League and supported by three mine-owning corporations went into action. It rounded up 1,146 IWW members, people believed to be friendly to the IWW, and persons unknown to the townsfolk and therefore suspect. They were kept for a while in a baseball park, then loaded into cattle cars and transported to the little desert station of Hermanas, New Mexico, where they were left to fend for themselves. Two days earlier sixty-seven presumed Wobblies and friends of Wobblies had been similarly shipped to California and dumped there.

President Wilson sent a warning to the governor of Arizona about the dangers of allowing citizens to take the law into their own hands. He also appointed a mediation commission to look into the situation; nothing would come of that. The newspapers served as mouthpieces of the companies while denying the strikers any opportunity to explain themselves. The *Los Angeles Times* praised the Arizona vigilantes for providing "a lesson that the whole of America would do well to copy." *The Sacramento Bee* condemned "the idiocy, if not the infamy" of the president in appointing a committee to negotiate with the IWW. A sensible man does not "confer with a mad dog," the paper said, "he shoots the dog."

On September 5, with President Wilson's approval, agents of the Justice

Department assisted by other law enforcement agencies staged simultaneous raids on IWW offices and the homes of Wobblies in thirty-three cities, scooping up every piece of paper they could lay hands on in a search for evidence of German government involvement and violations of the Espionage Act. Further raids followed, not always by men able to show warrants. Eventually five tons of material were collected and shipped to Chicago: personal letters, books, pamphlets, flyers, doodles, all of it scoured for proof of wrongdoing. Traces of German money, unsurprisingly, never turned up. Words that could be interpreted as violations of the Espionage Act's broad language were found in abundance; this, too, was hardly surprising, considering that the source was the IWW. That most of the alleged violations had been committed before the Espionage Act became law was of no concern to the prosecutors.

The penultimate blow came on September 28. The federal district court in Chicago handed down indictments against 166 senior Wobblies: officers and officials of every description in every part of the country, with emphasis in the West, where the union was strongest. One step only remained: to get them convicted and put away. That did not seem likely to be difficult.

In an act as unprecedented as the conscription of millions of men or the attack on the Wobblies, in December 1917 the president by proclamation seized control of the nation's railway system, by far the largest in the world. It was put under a new Federal Railroad Administration, with Treasury Secretary McAdoo as director-general. This was something that railroad-hating populists and progressives had long advocated. Such people immediately applauded Wilson's action, which had been prompted by the threat of a nationwide railway strike. They called for its being made permanent through nationalization of the entire system.

They were in for a surprise. McAdoo in running the railroads took the Wilson administration's approach to most financial problems that had anything to do with the war. He made plain his willingness to spend whatever was required to keep the trains running. He gave the unions almost everything they asked, incurring costs that put a new strain on the federal budget and led to higher charges for passengers and shippers. As all this unfolded, longtime advocates of nationalization found themselves having second thoughts. What was the good of it, if the result was a financial boon for the owners and higher prices for everyone else? Progressivism itself was being thrown into confusion. The movement became increasingly uncertain about what its long-term aims should be and how to achieve them.

Background

"Disgusting Creatures"

The long fight to secure voting rights for women, like the crusade to rid America of strong drink, reached its climax during the war and largely because of it.

And woman suffrage proved to be a tougher issue for the Democratic Party, and for Woodrow Wilson personally, than prohibition ever was. Like prohibition, it pitted core elements of the party against one another, threatening a disastrous split. Unlike prohibition, it did not do the same to the Republicans.

It forced the president to reverse himself first on whether women should have the vote, then on how that objective should be achieved. His changes of direction put him at odds with his adoring wife, who as a demure southern lady found the suffragettes repulsive.

As a political cause, woman suffrage was even older than prohibition. At least as much as prohibition, it was entangled in all the racial, economic, and class issues of America's turn of the century. The question of women's place in public life had been generating heat as early as the 1830s, when women became active in the abolition movement and were denounced for doing so even by some male abolitionists. In those days there was widespread opposition to allowing women to speak in public; few men could imagine them voting, much less running for office. When a series of National Women's Rights conventions was held in the 1850s, the participants, in the midst of being heckled by male onlookers, had heated debates about whether they should seek the franchise. They drew vociferous disapproval from members of the clergy for presuming to raise such questions.

Women's rights, like prohibition, remained in the shadow of abolitionism until the Civil War ended slavery. Peace brought the founding of the American Equal Rights Association, which championed voting rights for freed slaves and women alike. The end of the 1860s saw the introduction into Congress of the Fifteenth Amendment to the Constitution, a Reconstruction measure aimed at prohibiting the denial of voting rights on the basis of race. Two new groups came into existence as the Equal Rights

Association broke apart over the amendment. The National Woman Suffrage Association worked to defeat the amendment, demanding that it be broadened to cover women as well as former slaves. The rival American Woman Suffrage Association supported the amendment as it stood, and as it was ratified in 1870. The two groups would dominate the women's movement over the next twenty years, and remain hostile to each other.

Westward expansion, meanwhile, was bringing into the union new states without the cultural and political traditions of the South or the Northeast. This had dramatically positive consequences for the suffrage movement, divided though it was. Wyoming enfranchised women in 1869, even before becoming a state. Utah did so in 1870, Colorado in 1893, and Idaho in 1896. Washington, California, Oregon, Kansas, and Arizona all followed. Wisconsin remained the only state east of the Mississippi to allow women to vote until 1893, when Illinois approved woman suffrage. But momentum was building everywhere. The Woman's Christian Temperance Union had declared its support as early as the 1870s, the Grange (a fading but still-influential national association of farmers) in 1885, the American Federation of Labor five years after that.

But the South was immovably opposed. Southern mill and factory owners and planters feared that women voters would interfere with the free use of child labor, and their wives and daughters had always been taught that politics was no place for ladies. White southerners saw no advantage in doubling the number of blacks who were constitutionally entitled to vote even if they were rarely allowed to do so, and black males were surprisingly unsupportive of voting rights for their women. Meanwhile the women of the West and Midwest, regions that tended to vote Republican but were not the exclusive property of either party, displayed a readiness to blame not just the Bourbon South but the Democratic Party as a whole for blocking a constitutional amendment. Everywhere but in the South, Democrats had reason to be worried.

Whether to amend the Constitution or convert one state at a time became the key question. In 1872 Susan B. Anthony, a founder of the National Woman Suffrage Association and destined to become the movement's most legendary figure, was arrested for the crime of voting in Rochester, New York. This led to a series of court cases in which female plaintiffs pointed to the Fourteenth Amendment, which granted the prerogatives of citizenship to all *persons* (not *male* persons) born in the

United States, as so clearly giving women the right to vote that nothing further should be required. In 1875 the Supreme Court rejected this argument, ruling that the Constitution "does not confer the right of citizenship on anyone." Many activists became convinced that an amendment was going to be essential after all.

In 1890 the National and American suffrage associations set their differences aside and merged, once again displaying their lack of deftness with nomenclature by declaring themselves the National American Woman Suffrage Association—NAWSA. Official Washington, unimpressed, saw no reason to consider a constitutional amendment. Attention shifted back to the one avenue where progress was possible, the winning of the franchise state by individual state. Many Americans were unsettled on the question, finding it difficult to defend the status quo but wary of what seemed a deeply radical change. *The New York Times,* once a tepid supporter of the suffragists, reversed itself in 1912, warning editorially that if women got the vote, they might go so far as to "serve on juries and elect themselves to executive offices and judgeships." The leaders of Tammany Hall and other political machines had more practical fears: that if women could vote, they might prove less manageable than their fathers, brothers, and sons.

Until the chance to become governor of New Jersey turned him into a crusading progressive, Woodrow Wilson had been a true son of the Old South where voting rights were concerned. As an undergraduate, he had written that "universal suffrage is at the foundation of every evil in this country," suggesting (the year being 1876) that allowing even all white males to vote was a hazardous innovation. He changed little as he matured, declaring in 1911, when he was electrifying the nation with his New Jersey reform program, that he remained opposed to woman suffrage. He said it would make no difference politically and do grave harm to the family.

The pressures that came with the presidency did start a process of change in Wilson, but it was a slow one. By 1913 he was claiming to have no opinion on the suffrage question. In 1915 he announced that he was voting for it in New Jersey (where it was the subject of an initiative that failed) but refused to urge Democrats to support it in Congress. Women should be given the vote, he was now saying, by the states rather than through a constitutional amendment.

In January 1915 the amendment on woman suffrage was again put to a vote in the House of Representatives. It was resoundingly defeated, in a way that intensified pressure on the White House. Democrats voted against it 170 to 85, while the Republicans supported it 81 to 34. (The six representatives from the Progressive Party also voted yes.) Democratic congressmen from the West were shocked by the fury of their female constituents. The Republicans were satisfied to remain on the sidelines and observe the agonies of the party in power.

Only an insensate president could have ignored such developments. At the 1916 Democratic convention, Wilson saw to it that woman suffrage was included in the party platform, but without endorsement of an amendment. Being a half measure, this did not infuriate the South, but it also did not come close to satisfying the voting women of the West or those suffragists of all regions who were tired of waiting for action.

In the aftermath of the convention, a group called the Congressional Union for Woman Suffrage turned itself into the National Woman's Party. It declared itself opposed to the reelection of President Wilson along with all Democratic congressmen who had failed to support the amendment. Its membership was younger and more militant than NAWSA's, and saw no point in being loyal to a Democratic Party that refused to use its control of the White House and both houses of Congress to advance the suffrage amendment.

Winning the vote
*From picketing the White House to tilling the soil,
suffragettes made the war their springboard to victory.*

Division became most painful, where these women were concerned,
when it emerged along class rather than regional or party lines. The most
genteel of the suffragists agreed with the proudly antisuffrage Edith Galt
Wilson that their radical counterparts were "detestable"—"disgusting
creatures." Some of the most prominent of them exploited prejudice
against blacks, white ethnic groups, and recent immigrants in the promotion of their cause. Elizabeth Cady Stanton, long one of the pillars of the
movement, used a snobbish nativism to appeal to the kinds of women
of whom she approved. "American women of wealth, education, virtue,
and refinement," she pronounced, "if you do not wish the lower orders
of Chinese, African, Germans, and Irish, with their low ideas of woman-
hood to make laws for you and your daughters, demand that women,
too, shall be represented in government."

NAWSA president Carrie Chapman Catt took a similar line. "Every
slacker has a vote," she warned. "Every newly made citizen will have a
vote. Every pro-German who can not be trusted with any kind of military or war service will have a vote. Every peace-at-any-price man, every conscientious objector, and even the alien enemy will have a vote."
She pointed to the danger of sending a million American men to Europe

and not replacing them in the voting booth with "the loyal votes of the women they have left at home."

NAWSA supported the Wilson administration unreservedly, even as the president edged ever closer to intervention in the war. It did so largely out of genuine patriotic fervor. But Catt, who had originally opposed intervention, came to believe that continued opposition could only damage the suffragist cause. The administration also had the firm support of the National Women's Trade Union League of America, sponsored by the American Federation of Labor and surreptitiously financed by the government via the Committee on Public Information. At the most conservative extreme was the new National Association Opposed to Woman Suffrage, organized by upper-class and middle-class women and active in a number of states. It warned that giving women the vote would "destroy the family and increase the number of socialist-leaning voters."

The results of the 1916 election amounted to total failure for the National Woman's Party. With Wilson still in the White House and the Democrats still in control of both houses of Congress, the party's leaders decided that the only way to keep their campaign alive was to make a major nuisance of themselves. They began picketing the White House and pledged to go on doing so as long as necessary.

As long as necessary turned out to be a year and a half, and to involve more than a thousand women, many of them university-educated and from well-known, exceptionally respectable families. It achieved both its goals—maximum visibility and maximum annoyance—in large part because it aroused such a strongly negative response. The president observed—more accurately than he understood—that they seemed "bent on making their cause as obnoxious as possible." The picketers were attacked physically by soldiers, sailors, and civilians, and every such incident made headlines. They were arrested for unlawful assembly and blocking the sidewalk, treated with brutish roughness by the police, and sentenced to months in Washington's workhouse. The result was always the same: more headlines.

When the jailed picketers demanded to be treated as political prisoners and went on a hunger strike, they were force-fed through tubes jammed down their throats. Other inmates staged an uprising in their support. The party's young leader, Alice Paul, was given a month in solitary confinement followed by a week in a ward for the insane. The more harshly they were treated, the more sympathy they aroused. Finally Wilson had to concede that this was a more formidable opposition than the socialists or the Wobblies. He pardoned the jailed suffragists, but they foiled him by refusing to be released. When they finally returned to the picket line, they publicly burned copies of speeches in which Wilson had spoken of liberty and burned the president himself in effigy.

The whole thing had become a prolonged and damaging ordeal for the president and the Democrats, and September brought what might have been the deciding blow. A man Wilson regarded as a friend, the reform Democrat Dudley Field Malone, announced that he was quitting as collector of the Port of New York because of the administration's failure to do anything about a constitutional amendment. The president met with him, but Malone was adamant. He explained that he had campaigned for Wilson in the West in 1916, promising women that the president, once reelected, would support their cause in every possible way. In light of the administration's continued inaction, Malone said, honor required him to give up his job. Wilson confessed to feeling hurt.

Most likely it was the plight of the western Democrats, and the resulting danger for the national party, that broke the president's resistance at last. When it was decided that in January 1918 there would be another House vote on the suffrage amendment, Wilson wasted no time in declaring himself to be in favor. He said approval was both just and necessary for the war effort, so that he would be advising the Democrats to vote yes.

Chapter 15

The Law of Selfishness

THE WILSON ADMINISTRATION'S TAKEOVER OF THE ENTIRE NA-
tional railway system, with its three thousand companies and four hundred
thousand miles of track and unnumbered terminals and warehouses and
communication facilities, opened a new chapter in the history of American
business. It gave urgency to the question, already a generation old in 1917, of
whether business was going to dominate government or vice versa, or some
kind of balance could be found. A number of ironies would come to the surface in its wake—deep and portentous ironies such as the eagerness of more
than a few businesses to submit to government control so long as the rewards
were attractive enough.

The consensus in the years following the Civil War, as giant corporations
arose and the nation became an economic colossus, was that government
should promote growth but otherwise not meddle. The young Woodrow Wilson shared this view, but by the 1890s he was beginning to share also, to some
extent, the spreading concern about the extent to which "trusts" were taking
control not only of key markets but of the government as well, and bending it
to their purposes.

Between the outbreak of the war in Europe and America's entry into it,
people worried about how intervention might lead to further entanglement of
government and business. Navy Secretary Josephus Daniels would later quote
President Wilson as saying that "if we enter this war the great interests which
control steel, oil, shipping, munitions factories, mines, will of necessity become dominant factors, and when the war is over the government will be in
their hands. We have been trying, and succeeding to a large extent, to unhorse

government by privilege. If we go into this great war all we have gained will be lost, and neither you nor I will live long enough to see our country wrested from the control of monopoly."

These words bring to mind the forebodings about civil liberties that Wilson was reported to have confided to journalist Frank Cobb before asking Congress to declare war. To whatever extent they were sincerely felt—and assuming, of course, that the president said them—they were soon subsumed under the challenge first of saving the Allies from collapse, then of mustering the resources to defeat Germany. The same Wilson who became the greatest suppressor of free speech in American history moved with almost equal speed to create a wartime regime that was, to a significant extent, of, for, and by the economy's richest and most powerful players.

Of the need for action there could be no doubt. Quite apart from the immense task of creating an army and moving it to Europe, there were the shocking revelations of just how badly the war was going for the Allies in the spring of 1917, and how desperately they needed help. The picture continued to darken as the year went on—so much so that when the Allies' newly formed Supreme War Council met at the end of November, its first major decision was to stand on the defensive in 1918, putting all hopes of winning the war in abeyance until the American Expeditionary Force was ready for action. By then it was no longer possible to count upon Russia for anything; the Kerensky government was tottering, its armies in disorder. France's armies were in a convalescent state after their outbreaks of mutiny and not capable of offensive operations. The Italians had recently taken to their heels in the face of the Germans' Caporetto offensive; three hundred thousand of Rome's soldiers chose surrender over flight. The Third Battle of Ypres (the repetitiveness of Great War battle names shows just how static the Western Front remained) would soon be ending in the nightmare of Passchendaele, having moved a small section of front forward four and a half miles at the cost of a quarter of a million casualties.

The French mutinies gave new force to a question that haunted all the governments engaged in the conflict: how long could they depend upon their fighting men to endure the carnage? The threat of mass refusal was brought home to the British in July 1917, when Second Lieutenant Siegfried Sassoon (not of German ancestry, but given his name by a mother who loved Wagnerian opera) issued a statement that he titled "Finished with the War, A Soldier's Declaration":

I am making this statement as an act of willful defiance of military author-ity, because I believe the war is being deliberately prolonged by those who have the power to end it.

I am a soldier, convinced that I am acting on behalf of soldiers. I believe that this war, upon which I entered as a war of defense and liberation, has now become a war of aggression and conquest. I believe that the purposes for which I and my fellow soldiers entered upon this war should have been so clearly stated as to have made it impossible to change them, and that, had this been done, the objects which actuated us would now be obtain-able by negotiation.

I have seen and endured the suffering of the troops, and I can no longer be a party to prolong these sufferings for ends which I believe to be evil and unjust.

I am not protesting against the conduct of the war, but against the po-litical errors and insincerities for which the fighting men are being sacri-ficed.

On behalf of those who are suffering now I make this protest against the deception which is being practiced on them; also I believe that I may help to destroy the callous complacence with which the majority of those at home regard the continuance of agonies which they do not share, and which they have not sufficient imagination to realize.

This was awkward for the British government on a number of grounds. Sassoon was a Cambridge University man, scion of a wealthy family, and an established, respected poet. Worse, he had not only seen much action on the Western Front but had won the nickname Mad Jack there with his extrava-gantly reckless bravery; a year before issuing his statement, he received the Military Cross for "conspicuous gallantry." He could not be accused of at-tempting to avoid further danger, because at the time he issued his statement he was under orders to take up new duties training military cadets at home. Worst of all, his declaration called attention to the question of what Britain and her allies wanted to accomplish in the war and why none of them were willing to give an answer. Sassoon wanted to be court-martialed, so that such questions might receive a public airing. The War Ministry, to avoid any such thing, declared him a victim of shell shock (*neurasthenia* was the technical term) and sent him to a mental hospital in Scotland, as far from London as possible.

The war was not entirely without bright spots. None was more important than adoption of the convoy system in transatlantic shipping. This involved assembling groups of merchantmen and sending them across the ocean in groups under the protection of warships and, where possible, aircraft. Initially the British Admiralty rejected the idea as self-evidently foolish. It required all the ships in a convoy to move at the speed of the slowest, rather than setting out on their own to outrun the submarines. Even after Lloyd George's war cabinet recommended trying it, the Royal Navy delayed.

The Admiralty changed its mind when the successes of unrestricted submarine warfare became undeniable. By April 1917 the U-boats, operating mainly off the southern coasts of England and Ireland, were sinking merchant ships at a rate that, if sustained, could force Britain to give up the war. Convoys were approved at the end of April, the first set forth from North America days later, and the effect was startling. Sinkings immediately plummeted, falling in May to little more than a third of the April total. Thereafter the monthly tally would never reach even May's level. Sinkings of U-boats, by contrast, began to rise. Eventually they would reach such an unsustainable level that most German submarine operations were transferred to the Mediterranean.

Another positive development, the importance of which would not become clear for some time, was the fourth change of French governments since the beginning of the war. It mattered because it made Georges Clemenceau prime minister. For half a century he had been the wild man of French politics

Georges Clemenceau,
premier of France,
1906–1909 and 1917–1920
*"My foreign policy? I wage war!
My domestic policy? I wage war!"*

and journalism, and at age seventy-six he remained a force, boiling with energy and hatred of the Germans, known to everyone as Le Tigre. He would prove a one-man antidote to the defeatism that staggering casualty numbers had made epidemic in France. He refocused attention on the defeat of Germany to the exclusion of everything else and enabled his weary countrymen to feel a final surge of hope.

The outlook remained bleak all the same. If the collapse of Russia continued, during the coming winter the German high command would be free to move many divisions from the Eastern Front to the west. In these divisions would be scores of thousands of seasoned troops whose successes against the Russians and Romanians had filled them with confidence. Meanwhile General Pershing remained adamant that the AEF would still be neither big enough nor well trained enough to take the field when winter ended. In fact, he said once again, it would not be ready until the spring of 1919. All the United States could do in the meantime, aside from using her navy to protect transport ships and hunt U-boats, was save the Allies from going down to defeat because of shortages of munitions, equipment, raw materials, or food.

There was tremendous pressure on the White House to produce everything the Allies might need and deliver it in astronomical quantities. This was a management challenge above all, and the first of the questions it raised was *who* should do the managing. The administration's answer could hardly have been more sensible: responsibility for getting various industries to supply what the war required should be in the hands of the men who knew those industries best—who had demonstrated their ability to manage production and delivery by actually doing it. The entire structure of the wartime economy would be erected on that decision.

In midsummer 1917 President Wilson announced the creation by executive order of a War Industries Board (WIB) with responsibility for overseeing and coordinating production on a nationwide scale. The WIB stumbled in the early going, in part because it had little statutory authority, but eventually the men chosen to run it learned to use a combination of cajolery and pressure (threatening public denunciation of misfeasance, for example) to induce manufacturers to standardize products, adopt the latest methods of mass production, and cooperate in the allocation of raw materials. Just as important, they learned also to dispense rewards generously. Where producers needed financing, the board could even make government money available.

The WIB became useful in two areas where neither it nor other government agencies had any actual authority: the setting of prices for industrial products, and the settlement of labor disputes. Priority was given to maximizing production, an understandable decision considering the situation in Europe; as with the army's cantonments, cost was a secondary consideration where it was not altogether ignored. Following the example set by Secretary McAdoo in managing the railroads, the board urged companies to accede to union demands that were not downright extortionate, so long as the unions in question were otherwise cooperative and not suspected of disloyalty. The companies were happy to comply, because the WIB rarely objected to their raising prices and thereby passing the increase in labor costs along to their customers, the biggest of which was the government. They were likewise pleased to find that the Justice Department was no longer attempting to enforce the antitrust laws; it turned a blind eye to more than a little profiteering. Most delightfully of all, unprecedented levels of profitability were now virtually guaranteed. Small wonder that the result has been called a "war welfare" economy.

Generous as it was, this approach was not impressively effective in raising productivity. The country's gross national product increased by less than 4 percent from 1916 to 1918. While agricultural output rose marginally, production of copper, pig iron, iron ore, and rolled iron and steel actually declined. This happened largely because of the disruptions inherent in shifting from the manufacture of goods for the civil economy to the materials of war, and because the war ended before converted factories could achieve maximum efficiency. David Lloyd George was being unfair, and probably disingenuous, when he called it "one of the inexplicable paradoxes of history" that "the greatest machine-producing nation on earth failed to turn out the mechanism of war after eighteen months of sweating and toiling and hustling."

The real paradox, but not a mysterious one, is that industry overall prospered so handsomely under the government's wartime regime that more than a few of its leaders hoped they would not have to revert to the prewar system when peace was restored. Not all businessmen were so approving. Some refused government contracts that would have interfered with their use of child labor or imposed the eight-hour day, but they were exceptional.

The way old-fashioned competition came to be supplanted by guaranteed profits is illustrated on a grand scale by the WIB's arrangements with the steel industry. Demand for steel—its importance in armaments, shipbuilding, tank making, and the equipage of modern warfare generally—was causing a dizzying rise in prices that also affected the markets in ore, coke, and pig iron. The WIB, knowing that this price inflation was running far ahead of producers' costs, appealed for restraint and got no response. The Federal Trade Commission (FTC) made noises about a possible federal takeover of the industry. A resolution introduced in the Senate carried a similar threat, but the industry saw all this as bluffing and responded with threats of its own.

In September negotiators for the WIB (themselves recruited out of the steel industry for temporary government service) met with representatives of the producers (their former and presumably future employers) and hammered out an agreement. Thenceforth the government would pay $3.25 per hundredweight of steel plate. This was less than a third of what the producers had been demanding and therefore could be publicized as a huge victory for the WIB. In fact, however, the WIB was inflicting no real pain on the producers but rather was bestowing the government's blessings on a windfall for the whole industry. An FTC report showed that at a price of only $2.90, U.S. Steel Corporation could generate profits amounting to 50 percent of its sales.

The WIB's guiding principle being the production of enormous quantities of steel (and many other things) as quickly as possible, there was little choice except to pay all manufacturers the same price for specific products such as plate. A more sophisticated approach, one taking into account the fixed and operating costs of particular factories or companies, would have been time-consuming, beyond the WIB's resources, and in any case easily manipulated. The simplest answer was to set prices at levels that allowed even the least efficient operators to make an acceptable return. But these same prices, when applied to the biggest, most up-to-date facilities, translated into returns beyond the dreams of avarice. In 1918 the American steel industry would report an overall return on investment of 20.1 percent. Concealed behind this number, munificent enough on its face, were the accounting maneuvers used by companies (often enough with the government's implicit approval) to minimize the impact of the excess-profits tax, and the far higher returns reaped by the industry's leaders. U.S. Steel's earnings, $81 million in 1913, were already at $271 million in 1916 with still better to come; in 1918 the dividend on its common stock would be 14 percent. In that same year, in a foreshadowing of the investment banking industry of a century later, four officers of Bethlehem Steel shared a then-colossal bonus of $2.1 million.

Steel was by no means unique. In 1917 the after-tax profits of lumber companies represented a 17 percent return on investment. Copper producers increased their average return from 12 percent in 1913 to twice that in 1917, all the while refusing pay increases to the IWW. Two of the meatpacking companies most often accused of cheating farmers, Swift and Armour, more than doubled their earnings between 1913 and 1916. (Armour's nearly tripled.) The Cuban-American Sugar Company reported a profit of $365,000 in 1913, $8.2 million three years later. The WIB should perhaps not be blamed for ignoring the conflicts of interest inherent in using recruits from industry to negotiate with companies to which they were likely to be returning after the war. The administration's priorities and approach built conflicts of interest into the system.

Cost-plus contracts, which allowed profits amounting to a set percentage of whatever companies spent to complete some assignment, were not limited to the building of cantonments. And the results could be interesting. One contractor was found to be using high-quality new timber, badly needed for construction, to burn the bodies of dead horses, fattening his bottom line with every dollar thus wasted.

There was much to criticize, but it would have been awkward for the government's representatives to draw too much attention to industry practices. Doing so would have raised questions about the patriotic rhetoric of the Wilson administration, according to which corporations no less than the men in uniform were sacrificing their own interests in order to liberate the world. Those on the inside of the process, however, were sometimes repelled by what they witnessed. The president of the National Lumber Manufacturers Association (a man doing double duty as head of the Council of National Defense's lumber committee) wrote to an associate that in Washington's negotiating rooms "patriotism, in most cases, is nothing much more than a thin veneer." The chairman of the United States Shipping Board, having been drawn into the perpetual negotiations of transportation companies and unions, said that "I find no patriotism on either side when it comes to money." Food czar Herbert Hoover complained late in 1917 that "the law of supply and demand has been replaced by the law of selfishness."

One of the ironies of the situation is that the lengths to which the administration went to increase output, including the burden imposed upon future taxpayers as government borrowing snowballed, might not have been necessary. The industrial capacities of the United States were so immense that the nation was able not only to meet the needs of the Allies and create its own war machine but to do so with surprisingly little disruption of the civilian economy. Industry not only continued to produce automobiles for the commercial market (albeit at a gradually declining rate) but was able to stockpile steel to guard against future shortages. Some fifteen months after the declaration of war, only some 10 percent of the nation's then-numerous automakers had switched to military production.

Price controls that were so lax as to sometimes amount to no control at all, generosity to approved unions, the accumulation of immense amounts of government debt— all this was ferociously inflationary, creating an upward spiral that fed on itself as higher costs of production and a higher cost of living led to fresh demands for higher prices and wages. It also marked the death of President Wilson's hopes of financing the war on a pay-as-you-go basis. That the president's political position was not as solid as it had been early in his presidency, or during the surge of patriotic fervor that accompanied the declaration of war, is evident in the readiness with which Congress approved ever-higher levels of debt while finding it difficult to pass even watered-down tax bills.

The Republicans naturally wished Wilson no good but avoided making themselves seem blindly obstructionist by professing their unqualified support for the war while accusing the administration of mismanaging it. Democrats, for their part, were increasingly disaffected from the president. Those of a progressive bent were particularly uneasy. They were offended by the transformation of Washington into a fountain of cash for contractors of every description, appalled by the whitewashing of dishonesty with buckets of jingoistic rhetoric. Other Democrats resented the president's remoteness and the air of flinty superiority with which he looked down upon Capitol Hill.

It was not until October 3, half a year after a war revenue bill was first introduced, that a badly mauled version finally became law. Through all that time the bill had been kicked from committee to committee in both houses, with progressives demanding an almost confiscatory excess-profits tax while conservatives warned that if America's business leaders were treated unkindly, they might find it difficult to sustain their enthusiasm for the war. Every industrial and agricultural organization in the country was doing its best to make Congress and the administration understand why, although of course it supported fair and responsible financing of the war, the well-being of the nation depended on sparing its members from an increased burden of taxation.

The bill as passed was a setback for the administration. The president either lacked the political muscle to raise taxes on high incomes and high profits to a level commensurate with the need, or decided to follow the path of least resistance. When he proposed a consumption tax of $2.50 per bale on cotton and the Bourbon Democrats rose up in righteous wrath, threatening a comparable tax on wheat, he found it prudent to back down. That was the way the struggle proceeded, with the various interests holding each other hostage in a round robin of legislative blackmail. In the end, farm products escaped being taxed at all—even unregulated cotton producers paid nothing—and the levy on industrial profits was held to little more than a third of what the progressives had proposed.

The wealthy and those becoming wealthy could have found few grounds for complaint. Many ordinary Americans, on the other hand, saw the cost of living rise faster than wages. They were left with an abiding sense that the entire government, the Wilson administration included, was in thrall to special interests. The Republicans, to deflect public attention from industrial profiteering, denounced the Bourbons. They accused the Democrats of being not a national party at all but a southern one.

The consequences of all this should have alarmed more people than they did. By May 1918 federal spending was a billion dollars a month more than income, and the Treasury Department was forecasting total outlays of $24 billion in the 1919 fiscal year. Remember that until the war, the federal budget had been in the neighborhood of $1 billion annually.

If the president was troubled, he kept his concerns to himself. His determination to spend whatever the war required reduced all financial questions to mere administrative details. This was bound to create problems, and it did so soon enough. Trouble emerged first, not surprisingly, in an area where planning and spending had been particularly reckless: the creation of the nation's first combat-ready air force.

Having entered the war with only a rudimentary aircraft industry and a tiny military air service possessing no airplanes comparable to what the Europeans were producing, the United States had a great deal of catching up to do but little understanding of the magnitude of the problem. Intervention brought wildly foolish talk, encouraged by the administration if it did not originate there, of building a hundred thousand planes to "darken the skies over Germany." With lightning speed, Congress appropriated hundreds of millions of dollars to get the program started. The Council of National Defense created an Aircraft Production Board to put those millions to work.

The board sent a delegation of engineers and manufacturing specialists to

Europe to decide which of the Allies' latest aircraft might most usefully be copied. At home, a search began to find companies to manufacture aircraft, engines, and parts. Airframes had to be made of spruce, the supply was limited, and so the government took over the spruce market. Production contracts were awarded wholesale, often with more haste than care. Congress was asked for still more money and granted it without argument. Spending soon passed the half-billion-dollar mark. The program then bumbled along quietly, burning money and managing to produce no aircraft, turning into a political time bomb.

The administration's easiest victories were being won in the courts at this stage. Appeals of Postmaster General Burleson's refusal to allow the mailing of publications of which he did not approve were turned down with numbing consistency. Judges at all levels appear to have taken pleasure not just in finding against plaintiffs but in subjecting them to verbal whippings. The Georgia populist Tom Watson, once a member of Congress and a future U.S. senator, was told by the judge from whom he had requested a restraining order that "had the Postmaster General longer permitted the use of the great postal system which he controls for the dissemination of such poison, it would have been to forgo the opportunity to serve his country afforded by his lofty station." The poison in question was Watson's sour view of the war. It consisted of questions such as "Why is your boy condemned to die in Europe?" and such statements as "Men conscripted to go to Europe are virtually condemned to death and everybody knows it."

Higher courts were no less supportive of the government. The Post Office Department appealed when Judge Learned Hand ordered it to accept *The Masses* for mailing. In nullifying Hand's decision, a circuit court of appeals ruled that "liberty of circulation may be essential to freedom of the press, but liberty of circulation through the mails is not."

To be charged under the Espionage Act was to face near-certain conviction. Of the 180 persons tried for violations of the act in 1917, six were found not guilty. It was even worse for those accused of violating the Selective Service Act: 981 would be charged by war's end, seventeen acquitted. Prosecutors and the advocates of prosecution were not satisfied, however. They demanded more power to deal with the allegedly seditious, the administration agreed, and the Justice Department readied a new and still more draconian measure for presentation to Congress in 1918. Capitol Hill stood ready to approve it sight unseen.

Attacks on dissent reached a level of intensity sufficient to destroy organizations that under other circumstances might have acquired lasting significance. On September 21 Senator La Follette was the featured speaker at the St. Paul convention of a young, fast-growing populist-progressive organization called the Nonpartisan League, which by protesting the exploitation of farmers by grain brokers, packinghouses, railroads, and banks had elected one of its members governor of North Dakota in 1916. Though the league's membership was drawn largely from the plains states west of Chicago, places where enthusiasm for the war was conspicuously limited, its leaders were early to see the dangers of overt opposition. They tried to limit themselves to criticism of profiteering war contractors, controls on wheat prices but not cotton, and the like. Some had misgivings about inviting La Follette to speak, fearing that his appearance would brand the league as antiwar. When they explained their concerns, the senator said he would speak only briefly and say nothing about the war.

When he arrived at the convention hall, however, La Follette found himself being cheered wildly by a capacity crowd of ten thousand, with five thousand others outside in the street, unable to get in. Apparently with the encouragement of the league's leaders, themselves swept up in the excitement of the moment, La Follette decided to talk about the war after all. He had to do so extemporaneously, not having brought a speech with him. He did not attack intervention itself but focused on how it was being financed, the huge profits being made, and the government's suppression of First Amendment rights. His audience was ecstatic, but trouble quickly followed. The worst of it came not from anything the senator said but what an Associated Press reporter *said* he said.

La Follette had told the league members—as most of the journalists present reported accurately—that before the declaration of war, the United States had had "serious grievances" in consequence of German submarine attacks. (He added that those grievances could have been avoided if the country had been truly neutral, and that they were in any case not serious enough to warrant "involving this Government in the loss of millions and millions of lives.") But the story that went out on the AP wire to every paper in the country quoted him as saying "we had no grievances" full stop. The result was a fresh irruption of transcontinental rage. So many demands for La Follette's expulsion from the Senate poured into Washington, with Theodore Roosevelt once again beating his war drum, that a committee was appointed to look into the matter. La Follette's seat hung from such a thin thread that the lawyers he consulted advised him to make no further public comments about anything.

The consequences for the Nonpartisan League were devastating. The industries it had criticized and their political agents condemned it as socialist, anarchist, disloyal, seditious—as everything respectable and patriotic citizens were certain to find alarming. The leader of the Minnesota Public Safety Commission, in arguing that league members and other "traitors" should be tried by military courts-martial, said that "where we made a mistake was in not establishing a firing squad in the first days of the war. We should now get busy and have the firing squad working overtime." The league's founder and driving spirit, Arthur Townley, was convicted on a dubious charge of violating the Espionage Act by urging draft resistance. He would not emerge from prison until the war was long over, Woodrow Wilson was no longer president, and the league was dead. Its legacy, which survives to the present day, is a state-owned terminal grain elevator, a state-owned mill, and a state-owned bank, all in North Dakota.

Clergy deemed to be deficient in Americanism frequently found themselves in search of new employment or worse. In Los Angeles on October 1 police raided a gathering of ministers who called themselves the Christian Pacifists and represented fourteen denominations. Three members of the group were jailed on a curious charge: "discussing, arguing and preaching certain theories in opposition to the orderly conduct of the affairs of the United States of America . . . calculated to cause American citizens then and there present to assault and batter the persons uttering the same." The safest targets were of course clergy in relatively remote places and those belonging to less well-known, therefore less respectable, denominations. In rural Oklahoma, a preacher named William Madison Hicks, who described himself as president of a World Peace League, was first tarred and feathered and then fined ten thousand dollars and sentenced to twenty years for allegedly saying that "the men at the head of this war are nothing but a bunch of grafters" and that he did not believe anyone had an obligation to register for the draft. Presumably he found some comfort in the later reduction of his sentence to five years.

Elementary and secondary school teachers, being by the nature of their calling ill-paid, obscure, unorganized, and subject to the whims of local dignitaries, were most easily crushed under the wheels of One Hundred Percent Americanism. But college professors, even prominent ones at leading universities, were by no means safe. Columbia University president Nicholas Murray

Butler, an antiwar activist and a member of the Carnegie Endowment for International Peace until intervention infected him with war fever, established his patriotic credentials by publicly firing two respected professors whom he accused of a lack of patriotism. When this drew protests, the Columbia trustees defended the firings on grounds that the two men "had done grave injury to the University by their public agitation against the conduct of the war." Famed historian Charles A. Beard resigned from the faculty in protest, his act all the more striking because he had always been and remained a supporter of intervention. Other professors, including the philosopher John Dewey, protested without resigning. *The New York Times*, however, praised Butler and the trustees. Similar things were happening at public and private colleges across the country. The zealots did not always eschew violence in their determination to cleanse the academy of subversion.

Early November was a kind of watershed, elevating the hysteria to a new level both in Washington and in the country at large. One triggering event was the first world-changing result of the war that was supposed to make the world safe for democracy: the establishment of a Communist regime in Russia, putting that nation on the road to Stalinism and further generations of grief. The determination of the Bolsheviks to make peace with Germany provided mainstream America with a new constellation of demons, the country's tiny number of self-styled communists, who found themselves loathed and feared and marked for destruction. The far more numerous socialists did themselves no favor by showing sympathy for the Bolsheviks, though their doing so was usually innocent enough. Neither they nor anyone else knew very much about the Bolsheviks at this point. It was by no means clear what kind of regime Lenin and his cohorts intended to impose, and writers such as John Reed, author of *Ten Days That Shook the World*, were inviting their readers to rejoice at the birth of the workers' paradise. The upshot, in any case, was intensified denunciation of socialists as unfit to participate in the public life of the nation. Woodrow Wilson, with little knowledge of the hardships and losses that the war had brought down on the late tsar's subjects, scornfully dismissed the Russian peacemakers as "fatuous dreamers."

Fresh hysteria led to new attacks on the IWW. In Tulsa, seventeen Wobblies, none of whom had police records, were charged with exploding a bomb at the home of an oil company executive. A judge found them guilty in spite of a total lack of evidence and the incontrovertible fact that the central defendant had not been in Tulsa at the time of the bombing. To further ensure that justice was served, six witnesses for the defense were arrested, charged, convicted, and fined one hundred dollars each. The only thing that any of the accused were clearly guilty of was belonging to the IWW.

The night of their conviction, the seventeen Wobblies were removed from the city jail by vigilantes and driven out of town. There they were stripped, whipped bloody, covered with boiling tar and feathers, and allowed to run for their lives. The authorities made no effort to identify their abductors. When an IWW representative arrived in Tulsa to investigate, he was arrested and transported to Chicago, which had become the headquarters of the anti-Wobbly crusade, to face charges. Another mysterious and ultimately unsolved bombing, this one in Sacramento, California, led to the rounding up of sixty men believed to be connected with the IWW. When the authorities were unable to connect any of them with the crime, they were charged under the Espionage Act instead. Meanwhile 113 of the Wobblies who had been arrested in September were still awaiting trial in Chicago.

In October sixty-nine-year-old Richard Pettigrew, a South Dakota populist lawyer, was indicted after telling a reporter that "there is no excuse for this war" and "we should never have gone into a war to help the Schwabs [Charles Schwab was president of Bethlehem Steel] make $40 million a year." Like all Americans who said such things, he faced a long prison sentence, but the charges were dropped on grounds that his health was bad. The fact that Pettigrew had served two terms in the U.S. Senate, so that a trial would have drawn national attention to his views, was perhaps not irrelevant to the authorities' unwillingness to pursue this particular case.

From the perspective of the White House, the most awkward domestic development of late 1917 must have been New York City's mayoral election. Incumbent John P. Mitchel, the youngest mayor in New York history up to that time and a brilliantly effective reformer, was seeking reelection on a so-called Fusion ticket, representing the most progressive elements of all the leading parties. He faced a trio of challengers: Republican William Bennett, Tammany Hall Democrat John F. Hylan, and Socialist Morris Hillquit, who told voters that electing him would be "a clear mandate for open negotiations for a general peace." The campaign was a complicated affair befitting the nation's biggest and most diverse city, with many factions and interests injecting their own issues, but Mitchel and the newspapers did their best to turn it into a referendum on the war. They smeared not only the socialist Hillquit but also Tammany's Hylan with accusations of disloyalty. "Mayor reveals Hylan as a member of the German propaganda here," the *Times* informed readers. "New York wants no mayor in City Hall to whom enemy spies would have access," said the *Herald*.

The strategy backfired. Hylan, an honest and earnest man of limited talent, won by a big margin. The Socialist Hillquit received only seven thousand fewer votes than Mayor Mitchel; together he and Hylan tallied almost three times as many votes as Mitchel's 150,000. It was another black eye for the Wilson administration, all the more annoying because, unlike the humiliation in Wisconsin, it had come in a fight that the White House had neither sought nor willingly entered. It was also a fresh challenge to one of the president's favorite oratorical themes: that the American people, with the exception of the despised "hyphenates" and small scattered clusters of villains and fools, were unified in their support of him and his war.

Background

The War, Too, Changes

By the autumn of 1917 the war was in its fourth year and, on the Western Front, as solidly deadlocked as ever. The front was not significantly changed from where it had stood at the end of 1914. All the belligerents but one were in a state of exhaustion so far advanced that one of the prime objectives of every government was to conceal the truth from populations teetering on the edge of despair.

The sole exception was, of course, the United States, her banks and factories busily propping up the Allies with money and food and materials of every description, her War Department sending half-trained recruits across the Atlantic as fast as transport could be found for them but still not allowing them to engage the enemy. That would have to come later—later than 1918, General Pershing continued to insist.

But if the war seemed a vampire with its fangs deep in the throat of a slowly dying Europe, it was not actually static. Having changed the world beyond any possibility of a return to what it had been in July 1914, the war itself was inexorably changing.

Even the generals, some of them at least, were learning. The best were working out new tactics. They were adapting to new technologies, new weapons, that would change the nature of warfare forever and make a repetition of the stalemate impossible. Whenever America's doughboys did enter combat, they would find themselves in a different war from that of earlier years. The enemy they confronted would not be the German army of First Marne or the Somme, the army that had fought Britain, France, and Italy to a standstill while bringing Russia to her knees.

The core tragedy of the Great War, what made it so long and costly with no end in sight after years of horror, is the historical accident that it broke out at a time when the military advantage lay decisively on the side of the defense. The machine gun had been perfected, able to fire hundreds of rounds per minute and go on doing so indefinitely, stopping masses of attackers literally dead in their tracks. Artillery was available in quantities and varieties that the gunners of earlier wars could not have imagined; essential to any offensive, it was also devastating in defense.

They also serve . . .
. . . who send sons to the armed services, and cookies to those sons.

Motor-powered heavy machinery had transformed military engineering, too. Many of the "trenches" were actually elongated underground cities, often built of concrete, deep enough, in some places, to be safe from all but the biggest guns.

When the war began, and for a long time afterward, there were no answers to the machine gun. Nor were there airplanes capable of functioning as weapons in any serious way; "bombing" was dropping a hand grenade from an open cockpit. There was no such thing as a tank, a con-veyance that could advance against machine guns without being shot to bits, and only writers of fantasies had ever thought of such a thing. Thus the years of slaughter, of sending men with rifles into torrents of machine gun fire, of losing tens of thousands in a single day while accomplishing nothing. By midyear 1917 Italy's troops were looking for opportunities to surrender en masse, French troops were refusing to attack, and only fear of the political consequences stopped Lloyd George of Britain from sacking Sir Douglas Haig for expending so many men in so many fruit-less offensives.

The status quo was intolerable, unsustainable. And so, gradually but inexorably, tactics began to change. How it happened and who deserves credit is not clear, but a German general named Oskar von Hutier was involved early. A seasoned warrior, married to a cousin of Erich Luden-dorff, Hutier first came to fame in September 1917 when, as commander of the German Eighth Army, he used boldly innovative tactics to bring to a successful conclusion a siege of the Latvian city of Riga that had been dragging on for two years. He was even more spectacularly successful at Caporetto on the Italian front two months later, using the same approach in mounting an offensive that carried his troops down out of the Alps almost as far as Venice. After that he was given a key command on the Western Front, and what was called the Hutier Method was made the centerpiece of plans for a 1918 offensive.

The Hutier Method substituted a brief artillery barrage for the days of saturation shelling that had always begun the offensives of both sides. It thus restored to attackers the lost element of surprise. It replaced masses of men advancing shoulder to shoulder with fast-moving detachments of six or eight "storm troops," trained to penetrate enemy territory as far as possible as quickly as possible, making use of available protective cover, bypassing strongpoints instead of trying to capture them, carrying their rifles slung across their backs and using hand grenades to clear out pockets of resistance. The bypassed strongpoints would be reduced later, by a second wave of larger, slower-moving units equipped with heavier weapons.

That Hutier invented these tactics is questionable. By one account, he found it described in a captured French document that its intended audience had presumably ignored. In all likelihood no one invented the

Hutier Method—it appears to have evolved step by step out of the planning work of the German general staff's tacticians. What matters is that, when tried, it produced stunning results. Ludendorff entered the winter of 1917–18 thinking that it offered a way to clear the way to Paris before the growing American army put victory forever out of Germany's reach.

Earlier we took note of another innovation: Ludendorff's system of defense in depth, which involved maintaining only a thin and intentionally permeable front line, allowing enemy attackers to penetrate far beyond that line, then hitting them hard with a main force positioned far to the rear and driving them back. This, too, proved effective, reducing German casualties sharply. It appeared to Ludendorff that he now had a way to break open the Western Front—and an equally sure way to keep the Allies from doing so.

But then came the next innovation, this one the brainchild of a British general. Sir Herbert Plumer, a dumpy little pear-shaped man with a big white mustache and the mild blank face of a senior clerk, had been in command of the British Second Army since 1915. He and his army were at Ypres when, in the summer of 1917, Haig launched the third of the great offensives that have gone into the history books bearing that devastated city's name. In September, the same month that Hutier captured Riga in the faraway Baltic region, Plumer was ordered to capture the piece of high ground (high by the meager standards of Flanders) known as Messines Ridge. This gave him his chance to demonstrate that he had found the weakness of Ludendorff's defensive system and figured out how to exploit it.

There was never any question about the Second Army's ability to take the ridge, because it was obviously lightly defended. The question was what would happen after it was taken. If Plumer's troops had continued their advance—that was the invariable next step whenever an objective was easily taken and the way forward seemed clear—they would inevitably have run into a counterattack and probably been sent reeling back to their own lines if not farther. He instructed them to do the unexpected—to stop as soon as the ridge was secure, dig in, and wait for heavy machine guns and light artillery to be rushed forward to support them.

The Germans were dumbfounded. What left them flat-footed was the failure of the British to continue advancing until they were thinned out, tired, at the end of their lines of supply and vulnerable. Thanks to his

364 | The World Remade

new tactics, which would be called Bite and Hold, Plumer had captured a valuable piece of ground in a matter of minutes at little cost in lives. A few days later, as soon as he could move his artillery forward, he did the same thing again. And then again. It began to seem possible that the Second Army was going to nibble its way, a mile or two at a time, all the way to the Rhine. Ludendorff could find no answer except to abandon defense in depth, make his front line strong again, and accept the result-

The verdict was unanimous
"Everyone says the same" of the Americans,
the philosopher Pierre Teilhard de Chardin reported. "They're first rate troops."

ing casualties. His reversion to traditional tactics, and atrociously heavy rains heralding the approach of winter, finally brought Plumer to a stop.

But Bite and Hold was no panacea, either. The thing that made it unanswerable against a foe using defense in depth—its acceptance of severely limited gains—made it utterly unsuitable as a way of starting a major offensive. For that the Hutier Method, or something like it, was necessary. The great chess game of infantry and artillery, aircraft and gas, was growing more complicated by the month. The range of options available to armies taking the offensive and those on the defense was growing also, and making it ever more difficult for the generals to out-think one another.

Ludendorff in any case had been shown that defense in depth didn't work as well as he needed it to work, while his new offensive system worked beautifully wherever it was tried. This helped settle the question of whether the Germans should take the offensive when the spring of 1918 arrived.

Pershing was looking on, from his headquarters in Lorraine, and becoming disdainful of his French and British counterparts. He was convinced that the war could be won only by *movement* and that Pétain and Haig and the other Allied commanders had become too accepting of stalemate, too intimidated by the machine gun.

With the doughboys, it was going to be different. Pershing was training them in marksmanship, making them sharpshooters. It was his expectation—in hindsight astoundingly naïve—that when his troops went into action, rifles at the ready, they would force the Germans out of their bunkers, restore the war of movement that had been brought to a bloody halt in 1914, and so bring the conflict to an end.

It does not appear to have occurred to Pershing that the Allied generals wanted movement, too, and always had. Every one of the great and tragic offensives of the preceding three years had been an attempt to restore movement, to force the Germans into the open and get back to the glorious sweeping warfare of Marlborough and Bonaparte and Moltke, the kind that men on horseback could win. And every attempt had failed because men attacking with rifles could never be a match for men firing machine guns through slots in concrete boxes.

Pershing had things to learn, clearly.

Chapter 16

The Last Roll of the Iron Dice

WE DON'T KNOW HOW WELL BLACK JACK PERSHING SLEPT ON THE night of Wednesday, March 27, 1918, but it would not come as a surprise to learn that he slept hardly at all. He had gone to bed after an experience he would not soon forget—a meeting of the Allies' recently created Supreme War Council at which he had found himself in solitary conflict with the president of France, the prime ministers of France and Britain, and both nations' top military commanders. That was formidable opposition for a lone American soldier who had never been in a major or truly modern war and who, until less than a year earlier, had never commanded a unit as big as a division.

When he rose on Thursday morning, he was faced with the fact that none of the previous day's quarrels had been resolved. Clemenceau and Lloyd George, and Generals Foch, Pétain, and Haig, had all refused to agree to his plans for the American Expeditionary Force.

This would have been distressing under any circumstances. But it was happening under the worst of circumstances, in the midst of the most terrifying crisis to have befallen the Allies since the German drive on Paris in the summer of 1914. A week earlier, just before five A.M. on the cold foggy morning of Thursday, March 21, 6,400 pieces of German artillery had erupted in unison along forty miles of front east of the old Somme killing ground, from Arras on the north past St. Quentin to the south. After a four-and-a-half-hour barrage in which torrents of high explosives alternated with shrapnel, poison gas, and long-range machine gun fire, a million German soldiers organized into three armies had begun their advance. Storm troopers trained in the Hutier Method took the lead, routing those British and French troops who had survived the barrage. With astonishing speed they demolished one British army and put two others to flight.

This was the start of Operation Michael (originally called *Saint* Michael, though the prefix was somehow discarded on the way to launch), the first of the series of do-or-die offensives that Erich Ludendorff had been preparing all winter. In the next two weeks it would inflict more than 160,000 casualties on the British and 70,000 on the French. (These totals include 90,000 men taken prisoner, an indication of the extent to which many Allied divisions had simply fallen apart.) Before it was over, the Germans would capture more than a thousand artillery pieces and mountains of desperately needed supplies and take possession of twelve hundred square miles of territory.

They would do so at enormous cost to themselves, hoping in the face of immense odds to force the war to a conclusion before the American horn of plenty made the defeat of the Allies impossible. "If the iron dice roll," Chancellor Bethmann had said when war seemed inescapable in the summer of 1914, "may God help us." Bethmann was gone now, and Ludendorff was throwing the iron dice for what he knew must be the last time. Without the Americans, he might have stood on the defensive and allowed the Allies to grind away until they had nothing left. With the Americans in the picture, that option did not exist.

Pershing's position was excruciating because the AEF now included a quarter of a million men, among them all the foot soldiers and specialists needed to form six of the double-size American divisions. The rate at which still more were arriving would soon reach a quarter of a million a month. Many had been training for half a year or more, yet few had seen any action except what little had come their way as a result of brief postings in quiet sectors of the front. There had been scattered bursts of hard fighting, with scores of doughboys killed and wounded by German raiding parties and hundreds taken prisoner. But even now, at the peak of Operation Michael, the AEF remained an army in waiting. Nine months after a battalion of the American First Division marched to loud cheers through the streets of Paris, U.S. casualties did not yet total one thousand. With the exception of the Big Red One, Pershing still did not consider any of his divisions ready for action.

This was maddeningly frustrating for the Allies. Their impatience had worsened as the AEF grew steadily bigger and better trained and Pershing, with the Wilson administration's support, continued to refuse to put it into action in any significant way or to allow the British or French to have any of its troops. Operation Michael turned frustration into boiling anger. Pershing's stubborn refusals seemed inexplicable and intolerable.

This is what had made the March 27 meeting so difficult. Pershing was outranked by everyone there, he understood how desperate the situation was, and yet he remained convinced that the honor of the U.S. Army, the part that the army and the American nation were going to play in this epic drama, required that the AEF be held together, intact, until it was ready to take the field as a distinct and formidable force. That was what President Wilson wanted, too. Anything less would consign the United States to a supporting role in the war.

The Supreme War Council had been established at Lloyd George's urging in November 1917, after the rout of the Italians at Caporetto. Its purpose was to correct a chronic lack of coordination among the Allied armies on the Western and Italian fronts, but in four months it had accomplished essentially nothing. Its only serious initiative, the attempted creation of a common reserve, came to nothing when both Haig and Pétain refused to contribute meaningful numbers of troops. But the prospect of hanging serves to concentrate the mind, as Dr. Johnson observed, and the shocking success of Operation Michael focused all the minds in the Allied leadership. It demonstrated just how urgently cooperation was needed.

The first day of the council's March meeting brought an apparently modest change that would have far-reaching consequences. It happened when Sir Douglas Haig, whose troops were at that moment battling to keep the Germans out of the crucial communications center of Amiens near the point where the French and British sectors of the front connected, said he needed help. His French counterpart, General Pétain, said he had no help to offer, his troops being fully engaged. When Foch injected himself into the discussion, declaring that help had to be provided because the loss of Amiens would be catastrophic, Haig said he was prepared to do whatever Foch advised.

This was an about-face on Haig's part, testimony to how nearly hopeless he believed his situation to be. His unwillingness to take orders or even accept guidance from the French had long been an impassable obstacle to unified or even coordinated operations. His offer was hungrily taken up by Lloyd George and Clemenceau, who immediately sensed an opportunity. In short order, it led to a resolution making Foch responsible for "the coordination of the action of the Allied Armies on the Western Front." Just what this meant remained

Ferdinand Foch
As supreme Allied commander,
he repeatedly clashed
with Pershing.

to be worked out. Most of those present understood that, considering the plight of the Allied armies and Foch's aggressiveness and powerful will, it was likely to mean a great deal.

Pershing had not been present because he was not a member of the Supreme War Council. President Wilson had welcomed the creation of the council but kept it at arm's length, declining to appoint a political representative on grounds that (as he himself continued to insist) the United States was not one of the Allies but their "associate." As military representative, he had sent Major General Tasker Bliss, currently the American army's chief of staff but close to retirement. This appointment was intended not as a rebuke to Pershing but as a way of keeping him free to focus on the AEF. It had been made clear to Bliss that he was to support Pershing and not compete with him, and he almost always did just that.

Bliss was at the March 26 session. When he learned that on the following day Lloyd George was going to resurrect the old question of how to get America's troops into the fighting, he suggested that Pershing attend. And so Pershing was on hand when, in a conference room in the grandiose Palace of Versailles, Britain's military representative to the council unveiled an unexpected proposal. Obviously speaking with Lloyd George's approval, General Sir Henry Rawlinson suggested that thenceforth only American infantry—riflemen and machine-gunners—should be transported to France, and that all such troops should, upon arrival, be assigned to service with the British army. What made this startling was not the British bid for American recruits—Pershing had been rebuffing such suggestions since before coming to France—but the fact that, if adopted, Rawlinson's proposal would cut off the shipment to France of artillerymen, engineers, transport experts, and the many other kinds of specialists needed for the formation of complete, fully capable divisions.

Pershing did not have to be paranoid to interpret this as a transparent scheme to make the AEF little more than a reservoir of manpower that the British could draw upon to replenish their own fighting units, gradually draining away the very possibility of an independent American army. As he put it later, the British aim was "to put the weight of the Supreme War Council behind the idea of maintaining Allied units by American replacements as a policy." After voicing his objections, Pershing left the meeting, presumably in high dudgeon. The council's members thereupon approved Rawlinson's proposal with modifications that did little to address the AEF commander's objections.

It happened that Secretary of War Baker was on a visit to France at this time, giving himself a firsthand view of problems he had been struggling with back in Washington, and so was able to inject himself into the dispute. After conferring with Pershing, whose concerns he shared, he cabled President Wilson. He proposed that the United States should accept the Allies' demand that only infantry should be transported for the time being, but in doing so it should make clear that all American troops "will be under the direction of the Commander-in-Chief of the American Expeditionary Forces and will be assigned for training and use by him in his discretion." Baker also asked the president to remind the Allies—as he would in fact do—of "the determination of this Government to have its various military forces collected, as speedily as their training and the military situation will permit, into an independent American army."

Did Pershing feel vindicated by this rather one-sided compromise or defeated by it? Perhaps neither, perhaps both. In any case, something about the situation—perhaps his exposure to the Allied commanders at a time when their armies were in peril, perhaps something said by Secretary Baker—clearly affected his thinking. On the same day that Baker sent his message to the White House, the general summoned his car and ordered his driver to take him to Foch's headquarters at Clermont-sur-Oise. There he found not only Foch but Pétain, Clemenceau, and other French leaders.

"I have come to tell you," he said in what must have been barely comprehensible French, "that the American people would consider it a great honor for our troops to be engaged in the present battle. I ask you for this in their name and my own. At this moment there are no other questions but of fighting. Infantry, artillery, aviation, all that we have is yours. Use them as you wish. More will come, in numbers equal to the requirements."

And so the U.S. Army, just days short of the first anniversary of the nation's declaration of war, at last *really* entered the fight against Germany. From that moment, every part of the AEF that could be considered at least conditionally ready for combat was at Foch's disposal. All its units up to and including the division and army corps levels would remain under the command of their American officers, but those officers would, whenever Foch wished, take their orders not from Pershing and his staff but from the commanders of the French armies to which they were assigned. If Pershing's decision was a wise one in terms of his own reputation—he could hardly have escaped condemnation if he had continued to keep his troops out of action at this time of crisis—it was nonetheless generous and courageous. It put in jeopardy his own highest as-

Pétain and Pershing
*The French general
supported the American
in his conflict with
Clemenceau and Foch.*

pirations, and over the next four months it would require him to remain on the sidelines as tens of thousands of his troops, under not his orders but those of the Allied commanders, would help turn the war around. Some of those troops would find themselves in the kind of war of movement that had always been one of Pershing's goals, but not because of anything he, or they, had done.

Operation Michael came to a halt after little more than a week, not so much because the defenders stopped it as because it ran out of momentum, as all such offensives must do. In the speed of their advance the attackers had outrun their logistical support, and in due course they were left as exhausted as the British and French, with no clear sense of what to do next. One difficulty was that, finding themselves in possession of Allied stores of food and liquor, half-starved German troops would stop to gorge themselves and get wildly drunk. Another was the arrival in Europe of what would be called the Spanish Influenza, which put thousands of Ludendorff's best troops more lastingly out of action.

It was not obvious that Operation Michael had been a success in any strategically significant sense. Ludendorff's objective had been to destroy the British armies or, an equally satisfactory result, force them to withdraw across the Channel, leaving the French unsupported and too vulnerable not to agree to talks. Therefore he would have preferred to launch his opening offensive up north in Flanders, where most of Haig's divisions had spent the winter recuperating from the ordeal of Passchendaele. But there was too much danger of Flanders still being a sea of mud in March. In attacking near the Somme instead, Ludendorff expected his right wing to break through more decisively than the center or left, then turn north toward Flanders. This would have forced the British to move troops southward to meet them, thereby weakening them around the Channel ports through which ran their lifeline to England.

But not one major campaign had ever gone according to plan on the Western Front, and Operation Michael failed to break the pattern. It was not Ludendorff's right wing that broke through most decisively but the left, under Hutier, whose expected role had been to protect the offensive's southern flank. Faced with this unexpected development, and with the question of where to insert his reserves, Ludendorff decided to follow one of the oldest maxims of warfare: he would reinforce success, rather than put more muscle into the right wing in the hope that it could then begin to advance more speedily. When the British threw together a new front and it proved stable, the Germans found themselves in a deeply ambiguous position. They had neither driven a wedge between the French and the British nor weakened the British in Flanders.

Ludendorff had considered several possible locations for Operation Michael. A best answer not being obvious, he had ordered the generals commanding several sectors—not only the Somme and Flanders but Champagne and the area around Verdun—to make ready. This created a rumble of activity all up and down the front, so that although it became obvious to the Allies that something big must be coming, they were unable to figure out where. The outlook was little less uncertain in early April, after Operation Michael burned itself out. The Allies could only brace themselves for the next blow, trying to be prepared for it wherever it might fall. Their morale was not high. After the general collapse of March 21, they had limited faith in their ability to deal with whatever was coming.

It would not be accurate to describe Ludendorff's situation as desperate at this point. He and Paul von Hindenburg, the rocklike old Prussian who far more than the kaiser was now a kind of father figure to the German nation, remained confident that sustained offensive action could bring the war to a satisfactory conclusion, and do so soon. After all, Italy was finished, its army able to maintain a line of defense only with British and French support. Romania had been finished since the end of 1916, and now even Russia was def-

Paul von Hindenburg
He, not Kaiser Wilhelm,
became Germany's
father figure and hero.

initely finished, having on March 3 accepted peace terms dictated by Germany. The Russian collapse was beautifully timed. It freed Ludendorff to move scores of divisions to the Western Front.

Britain and France were—like Germany, like Austria-Hungary and Turkey—in a deplorable state. They had sacrificed everything to the war, and their populations went about in a state of perpetual mourning. Ludendorff's hope was that, if those populations could be shown that victory truly was impossible, they would demand a stop. He was not being foolish. Britain and France would likely have had to agree to negotiations as early as mid-1917 if money and materials of every description had not by then been pouring in from America, along with the first doughboys.

At the next meeting of the Supreme War Council, at Beauvais on April 3, Clemenceau took another step toward getting Foch established as the Allies' supreme commander. With his prior encouragement, Foch told the assembled politicians and generals that in order to perform effectively in the role he had been given at Doullens eight days earlier, he was going to need authority not just to coordinate but to initiate, plan, and direct operations. All present agreed, though Pétain and Haig, with the German offensive in a temporary lull, were less enthusiastic than they had been earlier. Haig in fact was trying to revert to his long-standing refusal to subordinate his forces to French command, but Lloyd George was determined not to let him do so. The extent to which he hated Haig, believing him to have squandered the lives of countless British troops, is evident in the urgency with which he set out to put him on a French leash.

Pershing was present at the Beauvais meeting, and he surprised the others by declaring that he wanted it made clear for the record that Foch's authority extended not only to the Allied armies but to the AEF as well. Pétain replied, possibly with a note of condescension, that this was not necessary because there was no such thing as an American army, at least in France. There were just scattered American combat divisions and support functions, and the best of them were now operating under Foch's, not Pershing's, command.

Pétain had immense authority. He had saved France twice, first as commander at Verdun in 1916 and then in containing the mutinies of 1917. Now his strength under pressure was proving crucial in keeping the German breakthrough from turning into a terminal catastrophe. Pershing, however, was not intimidated. "There may not be an American army functioning now but there soon will be," he said, "and I want this resolution to apply to it when it becomes a fact." He wanted an acknowledgment that the day was going to come when all the elements of the AEF could be pulled together to form a single, distinct and significant fighting force, equal in status to the armies of the Allies. His listeners could hardly object, at least in principle. Their assent was a mere formality, however, and might remain one.

Back on January 8, in an address to Congress, President Wilson had expressed his darkening view of the global conflict and its meaning. He laid out the most comprehensive statement yet of what the United States wanted to achieve in fighting the war. The specifics, known to history as Wilson's Fourteen Points (see page 573), were based on the work of the Inquiry, the assortment of experts on global issues that Colonel House had assembled at the president's direction. The points were loftily Wilsonian and would prove in due course to be largely unachievable: self-determination for all peoples (a fine notion indeed to offer the masters of the French and British Empires), open covenants openly arrived at, freedom of the sea, free trade, and the like. The fact that there were fourteen of them trumped Pope Benedict's mere seven.

By stating publicly that Alsace and Lorraine should be returned to France, Wilson gave the German hard-liners, Ludendorff foremost among them, fresh reason to believe that their enemies would never agree to terms that the people of Germany could accept as a sufficient return for their years of suffering. Thereby he contributed, whether inadvertently or intentionally, to ensuring that peace talks would remain impossible. Overall, the president's words reflected his continuing determination to keep the United States on a plane of moral purity, untainted by vengefulness or any ambition except lasting peace for all peoples. Regarded ever since as possibly the president's greatest, the speech was the last the world would hear of the prewar Wilson.

Three months later, speaking in Baltimore at the height of the crisis precipitated by the German offensives, he expressed a still darker view, and the new wartime Wilson came permanently to the fore. The only possible response to German aggression, he said, was "Force, Force to the utmost, Force without stint or limit, the righteous and triumphant Force which shall make Right the law of the world, and cast every selfish dominion down in the dust." He was now in the frame of mind that would enable him to respond positively when, a few weeks later, Clemenceau sent him a message saying that if Washington wanted to ensure victory, it was going to have to send a hundred divisions to France. One hundred American-size divisions meant nearly three million troops. Wilson was willing.

Beyond the frightening success of Operation Michael on the Western Front, the biggest factor in changing the president's tone was the Treaty of Brest-Litovsk, which crowned the Armistice to which Germany and Russia had agreed back in December. It imposed on the Bolshevik regime some of the most brutally humiliating terms in the history of European diplomacy. On the face of it, the treaty was a military and political triumph for Germany. Signed on March 3, it made Germany master of practically the whole world to her east, from Poland to the Pacific Ocean. It stripped Russia of Finland, the Baltic States, Poland, Ukraine, and more. The population of what had been the Romanovs' great empire was cut by a third, as were Russia's rail system, agricultural land, industrial capacity, and most crucial natural resources.

The treaty was also a colossal blunder for Germany, with consequences as ruinous as the move to unrestricted submarine warfare and the Zimmermann Telegram. Strategically it was a recipe for future trouble, destroying any possibility of lasting amity between Germany and Russia. Even in the short term it was folly, burdening Germany with possessions that would prove to be disorderly, rebellious, and in general far more trouble than they were worth. At a time when the outcome of the war was certain to be settled on the Western Front, the Germans had to dispatch a million and a half troops to take control of their new eastern domains. Dreams of feeding the civilians of Germany and Austria-Hungary with the produce of the Ukrainian wheatfields would come to nothing. The only possible justification is that, as useful as a million additional troops could have been in his 1918 offensives, if Ludendorff had moved that many to the west, he probably would have been unable to support them. The four hundred thousand troops sent to Ukraine consumed thirty railcars of food daily. In German-occupied France, those carloads would have been almost impossible to find.

To whatever extent Ludendorff expected the crushing of Russia to impel the remaining Allies to make peace, he was utterly mistaken. Brest-Litovsk strengthened the position of those in London, Paris, and Rome who saw no possibility of ever getting acceptable terms from Germany and insisted that German power must be radically curtailed. It cut the ground out from under those who were willing to settle for less than complete victory, and it satisfied Woodrow Wilson that he had only two options, victory or humiliation.

April confronted the president with a multitude of troubles. On March 25, with Operation Michael at its terrifying peak and the news from Europe spreading alarm through Congress, General Leonard Wood caused an uproar by testifying before the Senate Military Affairs Committee about what he had observed on an inspection tour of AEF facilities in Europe. Still resentful at not having been given the great command that Pershing now held, still disdainful of the president, Wood must have found it satisfying to report that in all of Europe there was still not a single American-made airplane. He knew that the matter would be taken up by Congress and the newspapers, which would demand to know how such a thing was possible almost a year after American entry into the war. It seemed scandalous on the face of it, and only the administration could be responsible.

By the time of Wood's testimony, the War Department had sharply reduced its aircraft-production forecasts. It was now promising to have only twenty thousand airplanes ready for service by the end of 1920, a sharp retreat from previous objectives, and to be training 7,500 pilots a year by that time. Even these numbers were unachievable, although not as wildly out of touch with reality as those given earlier. Congress had appropriated $840 million for the purpose, and still more was being requested. The Committee on Public Information, meanwhile, was continuing to issue boastful and largely baseless press releases about how much was being achieved, and skepticism was growing in Congress. Wood's report forced the issue into the open, and the Republicans went on the attack. Many Democrats saw no reason to rise to the administration's defense, especially as President Wilson was not responding to questions. Secretary Baker became a lightning rod, drawing so much abuse that he considered resigning.

The president's proud silence raised questions about what he was hiding and increased pressure for investigations and hearings. Worse soon followed. The aircraft "scandal" became a factor in Wilson's intervention, with painful consequences for himself and his party, in a special election to fill a vacant Senate seat in Robert La Follette's home state of Wisconsin.

The Senate experienced an extraordinary mortality rate between the elections of 1916 and 1918. Ten senators—fully 10 percent of the membership— died in office. Eight of the ten were Democrats, and three of those eight were replaced by Republicans, causing the Democrats' majority to grow thin. Among the departed was a dependable administration supporter, Democrat Paul Husting of Wisconsin, who had been elected by the thinnest of margins in 1914 when the state's Republicans split into rival factions. His death in a hunting accident was a blow to the White House, and keeping his seat in Democratic hands became a high priority. But White House intervention in the race to replace him was by no means without risk. Congressional Republicans would be angered, and failure was certain to be interpreted as a repudiation of the president.

Postmaster General Burleson urged Wilson to plunge into the fray. Popular revulsion at Robert La Follette's hostility to the war was as strong in Wisconsin as elsewhere, he argued, and the state's Republicans were divided into anti- and pro-La Follette factions. Conditions seemed right for the election of Democratic nominee Joseph E. Davies, a Wilson loyalist since 1912. A Davies victory would demonstrate the president's strength, especially if Wilson helped to make it happen.

The result was the first of a series of blunders that would make 1918 an electoral disaster for the national Democratic Party. And the wound would, like most of those that followed, be almost entirely self-inflicted. Congressman Irvine Lenroot won the Republican nomination for the vacant Wisconsin seat by edging out a rival from the La Follette camp; like most Republicans in the House, he had supported intervention and remained thereafter strongly in favor of a maximum war effort. But in 1917 he had been prominent among the Republicans who led the way in striking a press censorship provision from the Espionage Act, and in 1918 he began charging the president with "exclusiveness, secrecy and intolerance of congressional participation."

Wilson could see such a man only as a nuisance or worse. He wanted him expelled from Congress and decided that the surest way to accomplish this was to impugn his patriotism. Such a thing had to be done with some subtlety, of course. And so the president composed and made public a letter to his man Davies, praising him for selflessly resigning his position with the Federal Trade Commission in order to run for the Senate. The letter said that Davies's position on prewar issues such as the McLemore Resolution (which would have forbidden Americans to travel on the ships of nations at war) and armed neutrality showed that he had passed "the acid test" of "true loyalty and genuine Americanism." Only by implication did the letter accuse Lenroot of failing the president's test and therefore of being not really loyal to the nation. The implication was clear enough to Wisconsin's pro-war Republicans, however, and they were not amused.

Lenroot, too experienced to let himself be thrown on the defensive in the middle of a hard-fought campaign, struck back quickly. And he used the nearest weapon at hand, the administration's allegedly failed management of the aircraft-production program. Other Republicans eagerly joined in, pointing fingers of blame at the White House and raising a chorus of complaints. It was a rather arcane issue for voters a thousand miles from Washington, especially in the absence of evidence of actual wrongdoing, and in all likelihood it would have made little difference to the outcome of the election. But then the White House made its next mistake, and this one would be fatal. It dispatched Vice President Thomas Marshall to campaign on Davies's behalf.

It seemed a harmless idea. Marshall was himself a midwesterner, an amiable and progressive former governor of Indiana who liked to joke about two brothers, one of whom ran away to sea, the other of whom became vice presi-

Irvine Lenroot,
U.S. senator
from Wisconsin,
1918–1927
*He was targeted for
defeat for failing
Wilson's "acid test"
of loyalty.*

dent of the United States, neither of whom was ever heard of again. But by 1918 he was thoroughly infected with the war fever that had most of Washington in its grip. He went forth not to woo the voters of Wisconsin but to scold them, and to do so in keeping with the president's instructions. "Your state of Wisconsin is under suspicion," he told audiences in Milwaukee and elsewhere. "Having purified the stream in the primary"—by rejecting candidates associated with La Follette—"you welcome the sewage vote to help you over the election." The sewage vote, he did not have to explain, was made up of pacifists, traitors, fools, lovers of the kaiser, and enemies of Woodrow Wilson.

The vice president did say that Lenroot was "bidding for the votes of the German sympathizer, the traitor, the seditionist, the pacifist." Such words (for which he would later apologize, telling Lenroot that he had been following orders from "higher up") melded the feuding Wisconsin Republican Party and many of the state's uncommitted voters into a single hot mass of indignation. On Election Day, April 2, Davies received more votes than the late Senator Husting had in winning the 1914 election, but Republicans turned out in even greater numbers and gave Lenroot a comfortable margin of victory. It was a repeat of the New York City mayoral race, only worse because this time Wilson had intentionally made the election a test of his own support. He had tried to save a crucial Senate seat for his party and failed. He had tried to show Congress that the people were with him, and again he failed. The extent to which the Wisconsin electorate was *not* unified is apparent in the hundred thousand votes cast for Victor Berger of Milwaukee, who ran as a socialist on a platform headlined "One Hundred Percent for Peace." His vote total was four times what socialists commonly received, and it happened in spite of Berger's having been indicted, just days before the election, on charges of violating the Espionage Act. This was part of a pattern. Across the country, starting in the summer and autumn of 1917, antiwar socialists were doing increasingly well in local and municipal elections.

There were other, uglier symptoms of discord. One that attracted national attention occurred on April 4 in the coal-mining town of Collinsville, in southern Illinois. A drunken mob seized a thirty-year-old "registered enemy alien," a German-born baker and miner named Robert Paul Prager. The self-appointed patriots stripped him, beat him, and tied him up in an American flag before allowing the police to put him in jail. Those same police stood aside, however, when the mob returned, found Prager cowering in the basement, and carried him away. After allowing him a moment to write to his family in Dresden ("Dear Parents, I must this day, the fourth of April, 1918, die. Please, my dear parents, pray for me."), they strung him up.

Prager had been targeted for voicing socialist beliefs and for going so far as to attend Socialist Party meetings. That he was to any degree hostile to American intervention in the war, however, is simply not credible. He had not only filed an application for citizenship shortly after war was declared, but he had attempted to join the navy. (He was ineligible because he was blind in one eye.) Against the odds and the wishes of the good people of Collinsville, eleven alleged leaders of the lynch mob were charged with murder. Their trial was a farce: the defendants draped in red, white, and blue, a band playing patriotic songs loudly outside the courthouse. Although one of the accused had admitted his guilt to reporters and a coroner's jury, and although the defense focused on establishing their Americanism credentials rather than their noninvolvement in the lynching, jurors needed only minutes to find all of them not guilty. "Well," one of them cried out, "I guess nobody can say we aren't loyal now." His understanding of loyalty, and of what constituted proof of loyalty, was as widespread as it was defective.

Former presidents Roosevelt and Taft were among the prominent Americans who decried the murder and the trial's result. Some newspapers did likewise, though even they seemed reluctant to hold the culprits to account. *The Washington Post*, after acknowledging that the lynching had to be classified among the "excesses" of "true Americanism," added that "it is a healthful and wholesome awakening in the interior of the country." President Wilson remained long silent. Not until late July did he issue a statement about lynching, and even then he may have been prompted mainly by the knowledge that the Prager killing—which he did not mention—was being used by the German government in its domestic propaganda. The war appears to have made lynching a subject of concern for the president in much the same way that it made woman suffrage tolerable to him: as a matter of wartime necessity.

The tone of American public life was becoming as dark as the president's rhetoric. Vice President Marshall, who a year earlier had been unable to muster a shred of enthusiasm for intervention, was now proudly proposing that Americans "not heartily in support of the Government in this crisis" should be deprived of their citizenship and property. John Sharp Williams, a Democrat from Mississippi, spoke for most of his Senate colleagues in declaring that "those who are not with us are against us, and let them take their medicine; and if the law does not give them their medicine, the people will." Such open invitations to mob justice were not unusual and not often criticized. It has been estimated that some thirty-five Americans lost their lives in civil disturbances related to the war in the first half of 1918.

A member of the House of Representatives entered into the *Congressional Record* a list of "crimes committed by German sympathizers against our government." It was a curious hodgepodge, ranging from the sale in Kansas of plaster containing tetanus bacilli to the manufacture in Texas of poison for use by Germans in Mexico and the disabling of mules in Washington State. Also listed were strikes that factory owners and managers blamed on German agents. The dubious character of many such allegations did little to diminish their impact.

They had to compete for headlines, however, with the fact that on April 9, just days after the petering-out of Operation Michael, the Germans attacked again. This time there was no strategic subtlety. Ludendorff was going for his ultimate objective, to clear the British out of Flanders. He was doing so with two armies, and again everything went brilliantly from the start.

Background

The War of the Air—and of the Future

The least bitter irony of the Great War is that its most modern dimension, the war of the air, gave it a dash of old-fashioned military romance and flair that was otherwise almost entirely lacking.

Hard as they tried, until the summer of 1918 the Allied propagandists found it impossible to wring much romance out of the war on the ground. Nor was it easy to find heroes there, except in the unhelpful sense that everyone who endured it might be considered a hero. Courage had nothing to do with whether an enemy shell blew you to bits as you huddled in the mud. It was not likely to save you from being cut in half by machine-gun fire when the whistles blew for an attack.

How different it was when you looked to the sky! Men in flimsy flying machines, up among the clouds, engaged in single combat like knights of old. Bravery mattered up there, and skill could make all the difference. A touch of chivalry was permissible—expected, even. It was all so thrilling, so different from the stink and squalor of the trenches, that even enemy pilots could be admired. (But who in London or Paris could have imagined that Manfred von Richthofen, the fearsome Red Baron, was all of twenty-three years old when he scored his first kill, or that he wrote to his mother daily?)

American pilots, too, became popular heroes when their turn came. Eddie Rickenbacker of Columbus, Ohio, was the most famous, a publicist's dream. A race car driver before the war, he went to France as an enlisted man in 1917, where he managed to talk himself into pilot training in spite of having only a seventh-grade education. By the time the war ended he was a captain and the top American ace with twenty-six kills to his credit. Stories like his served as an antidote to the infantry's appalling casualty lists.

Rickenbacker himself called a much younger American, Frank Luke, "the most daring aviator and greatest fighter pilot of the entire war." Nineteen years old at the time of America's intervention, Luke joined the aviation sector of the Army Signal Corps and after pilot training was sent to France as a member of one of the AEF's newly formed aero squadrons.

He chose as his specialty the dangerous job of attacking German observation balloons, always heavily defended by ground artillery. In the last eight days of his life, in September 1918, he shot down fourteen balloons and four airplanes. Flying low after destroying his last three balloons, he was struck in the chest by a machine gun round fired downward at him from a hilltop. Upon crash-landing, he drew a pistol and prepared to fight rather than be taken prisoner, but died of his wound. A posthumous Congressional Medal of Honor was presented to his parents, German immigrants who had settled in Arizona.

Luke's first distinction had been to live long enough to die in combat. Of the 681 members of the U.S. Air Service killed during the war, almost three-fourths died in training accidents, 263 in the United States and 203 in Europe. Most of the remaining fourth perished in combat.

The glory won by Rickenbacker, Luke, and their fellow American aces helped to obscure the awkward fact that they were flying French-built aircraft. What made it awkward was the prodigious sums spent on the creation of an American-made air fleet and the paucity of the result. The war would end with a billion dollars spent and not a single fighter plane of American manufacture going into action. But the headline-making scandal that this was turned into in Washington, and the howls of outrage emitted by members of Congress, were almost entirely bogus. The problem was less one of mismanagement, never mind of corruption, than of the Wilson administration promising too much as it set out to accomplish the almost-impossible.

Though the world's first heavier-than-air flying machine had been built by the Wright brothers of Dayton, Ohio, by the start of the war the United States was far behind Europe—behind France especially—in aviation technology. A grand total of forty-nine airplanes were built in the United States in 1914. In the years immediately following, even as the contest for air superiority led the Entente and the Central Powers to make astonishing advances and develop aircraft of an ever-growing number of types, American aviation remained barely substantial enough to be considered an industry. The nation's aircraft manufacturers, numbering not much more than a dozen, were in some cases little more than hobby shop operations.

But then, with the country at war and France's Prime Minister Ribot demanding tens of thousands of aircraft, engines, and pilots, Congress and the administration appear to have decided that whatever could be imagined could be achieved. The War Department's Technology Board recommended giving Ribot an affirmative response, and though he was not promised all he asked for, he was promised much. The Committee on Public Information told the press that aircraft were going to be produced by the scores of thousands, and as War Secretary Baker's requests for aircraft program funding approached the billion-dollar mark, he continued to get every penny he requested.

As must always happen, reality finally showed its frowning face. Hard questions could not be indefinitely ignored. What kinds of aircraft were needed, actually? Who in the United States was capable of designing them? Of building them? Of *flying* them? There were no easy answers, not even any hard but satisfactory answers, and backpedaling began on a massive scale. The administration issued a clarification: only 22,000 American-made planes could be in France and ready for action by July 1918. *Only* 22,000. No one in the government, evidently, knew enough about aircraft production to understand that even this number was utterly unachievable.

The new Aircraft Production Board introduced a measure of sanity into the proceedings. Abandoning the idea of designing new aircraft from scratch, it deployed engineers and manufacturing professionals to Europe to select a manageably small number of state-of-the-art Allied planes for production in the United States. In July four choices were announced: two fighters, one British and one French; a British day bomber and observation plane; and an Italian night bomber. Work began immediately on getting them into production. And almost as immediately it broke down, mainly as a result of trying to do too much more quickly than was feasible.

Ultimately there were four investigations, all of them tangled in enmity and intrigue. One was conducted by the Senate, another by the House of Representatives. The third was an inquiry that the administration itself was pressured into launching. For reasons of credibility, and to President Wilson's annoyance, it was put under the direction of the 1916 Republican presidential candidate, Charles Evans Hughes, who had made his reputation exposing utilities corruption in New York State. Still another, functioning at times on the level of comic opera, was headed by the sculptor and amateur aviation buff Gutzon Borglum, who would later become famous by carving the faces of four presidents (Wilson not among them) into the side of Mount Rushmore.

While these investigations were in process, the administration created a Bureau of Military Aeronautics and a Bureau of Aircraft Production and made both independent of the Signal Corps. This eased some of the worst bureaucratic problems, but unified command of all aviation programs was not achieved while the war lasted. Hughes, in reporting his findings in October 1918, said he had found evidence of misconduct by a number of private contractors but only one incident involving a government employee. By that time, with the end of the war at hand, the issue was no longer generating much political heat.

Though the aircraft program never developed into a true scandal, it also never came close to meeting expectations. The only American-built plane to see action was the D-4 day bomber, originally developed by De Havilland of Britain. Its arrival in France was delayed for months by the agreement to ship combat troops only during the Western Front crisis of the summer of 1918. By August, when the first American D-4s were at the front at last, they had been rendered obsolescent by the Allies' ongoing introduction of newer, better designs. Aviation technology was so simple in those days that experienced engineers could often have new ideas in the air in a matter of weeks.

American manufacturers learned just how difficult it was to mass-produce airplanes at a rapid rate while keeping abreast of the latest innovations. More than fourteen hundred French Nieuports and SPADs were in service with the AEF by war's end, and the pilots to fly them had been trained, most of them, at airfields scattered across France. Pershing's original goal had been to build an AEF Air Service of fifty-nine combat squadrons, each including about a dozen and a half planes. This was increased to 260 squadrons when optimism was at its height, then pared back to 202. All these numbers turned out to be fantasies. By November 1918 the AEF had forty-five squadrons available for action. Of their 740 aircraft, exactly one dozen had been built in the States.

The situation would have improved sharply if—as everyone assumed early in 1918—the war had continued into 1919. When the Armistice went into effect, 270 American-built aircraft were being used for pilot training in France, 323 were in supply depots awaiting assignment, 415 were in transit, and more than 2,000 were ready for shipment overseas.

American manufacturers had produced more than 3,500 combat aircraft and more than 6,000 trainers. The pipeline to Europe was full to bursting at last. If it all happened too late, it was an impressive achievement all the same.

By the autumn of 1918 the AEF was engaging in air warfare on a scale, and at a level of sophistication, that would have been unimaginable a few years earlier. Chivalric single combat was giving way to complex operations in which masses of aircraft flew in unison and in careful coordination with the forces on the ground. A total of 1,481 aircraft took part in the first major American offensive, at St. Mihiel. Though half of them were flown by French pilots and 130 by British, strategy and command were in American hands. Only 842 planes were available for the much bigger Meuse-Argonne offensive, but that was sufficient for a numerical advantage over the Germans of nearly two to one and a full array of tactics from bombing behind enemy lines to the strafing of frontline troops.

The United States ended the war an incipient major power in military aviation, vastly ahead of where it had been a year and a half earlier. Starting with almost nothing, it had learned how to mass-produce military aircraft and had turned tens of thousands of foot soldiers and civilians into pilots. In France the commanders of Pershing's Air Service, and of the AEF generally, had seen the potential of aerial warfare in operations large and small. When they returned home, they carried with them the knowledge that when the next war came, aviation was going to be at the heart of it.

Chapter 17

Deadlocked No More

BY THE END, LUDENDORFF HAD THROWN NINETY GERMAN DIVIsions into Operation Michael. Many were so badly mauled in the later stages of the offensive that they were no longer effective fighting units. Many more were simply exhausted, used up, and in urgent need of rest and refitting.

The wise thing, at that point, might have been to put aside all plans for further offensive action. The next step was supposed to have been a pair of massive attacks—St. George One and St. George Two—in which thirty divisions were to hit the British in Flanders and force them to surrender or flee to England. But now, in the aftermath of Operation Michael, Ludendorff had only eleven assault divisions intact and available for use. St. George One had to be abandoned. St. George Two was reduced to such an extent that it was renamed Georgette.

The objective was still the expulsion of the British Expeditionary Force from the Western Front. Just how this was to be accomplished was now less clear than it had been earlier. Asked what was to happen when Georgette achieved a breakthrough, Ludendorff shrugged. "We make a hole, and the rest will take care of itself," he said. "That's how we did it in Russia." But Flanders was not Russia, the BEF was not the Russian army, and Ludendorff was no longer the man he had been earlier in the war. Something more than wishful thinking was required, and Ludendorff was no longer supplying it with his old firmness. He was a chronically lonely man, with no talent for relaxing or for making or keeping friends, and he had been under a crushing burden of responsibility for more than three years. In the prewar years, his austere life had been brightened by marriage to a divorcée with three young sons whom Ludendorff came to love. Two of those boys were dead now, killed in action. He would slip off to visit the grave of one of them, a pilot shot down not far distant from his headquarters, and was seen weeping in his office.

He had lost his resilience. In its place was a fixation—entirely justified—on the relentless growth of the American Expeditionary Force, on what was certain to happen when all those hundreds of thousands of fresh troops entered the fight, and the need to bring the war to a conclusion before that happened. And so on April 9 Georgette was launched. As with Michael, it went exactly according to plan at first, with two armies advancing rapidly on a thirty-mile front. They forced the British back ten miles, then twenty, and appeared to be on the verge of a rout. For the British, the situation became so dire that Douglas Haig, a man with little gift for dramatic utterance, sent out a message that would become one of the most famous of the war. "Every position must be held to the last man," he said. "There must be no retirement. With our backs to the wall and believing in the justice of our cause each one must fight on to the end. The safety of our home and the freedom of mankind alike depend upon the conduct of each one of us at this critical moment."

This was hyperbole. The BEF was in jeopardy, but there was no threat to its homeland. Even if the Germans had driven Haig and his armies back across the Channel—even if the BEF had been annihilated—the Germans would have been little more capable of invading England than of invading Mars. And contrary to Haig's heroic words, a good many positions would be abandoned, a good many withdrawals ordered, before it was all over. But in the end the British line did not break. With every mile the Germans advanced their own losses mounted, their momentum slowed, and they grew more distant from their sources of supply. When they came to a system of canals and found the British dug in on the other side, Georgette, too, was at an end. Strategically it was as empty as Michael.

By this time General Pétain, commander of the French armies, was beginning to make use of the AEF troops that Pershing had put at his disposal. He moved the First Division, Pershing's pride, out of the quiet Ansauville sector at the southern edge of the Germans' big St. Mihiel salient south of Verdun. He shifted it westward to Montdidier, a potential hot spot at the point where Operation Michael had penetrated deepest before running down. There the Big Red One became, in effect, part of the French Fifth Army. Into its former slot at Ansauville went the Twenty-Sixth Division, called the Yankee Division because it was made up of New England National Guardsmen; Pershing had offered it to Pétain in spite of regarding it as not yet adequately trained. As a result of this shift, ironically, the Twenty-Sixth rather than the First became the first American division to fight a bona fide battle nose to nose with first-rate German troops.

A live-and-let-live attitude had long prevailed in the Ansauville sector, part of the hilly and wooded St. Mihiel salient that the Germans had captured in 1914 and fortified heavily. The French, seeing no point in trying to take it, used it as a place where battered units could rest and recuperate. The Germans, for their part, saw no point in trying to expand the salient and were content to stand on the defensive. It was in this spirit that Pétain had inserted the American First Division there, then the even greener Twenty-Sixth. But during its time at Ansauville, the First had refused to follow the French example. It was much more aggressive, and its troops began learning the dangerous game of raiding enemy positions under cover of night. Doing so cost 143 American lives, with another 403 wounded, during the First Division's two months at Ansauville.

The Twenty-Sixth, green or not, continued the pattern set by the First. Deadly clashes in No Man's Land became an almost nightly occurrence. Finally the Germans decided that enough was enough; it was time to show the Americans what real professionals—their *Stosstruppen*, special raiding parties—were capable of doing. At three A.M. on Saturday, April 20, German artillery began raining down shells on a two-mile section of American-held front centered on the village of Seicheprey. Two hours later, a heavy fog having risen out of the ground, a rolling barrage began moving toward Seicheprey. Behind it, advancing unseen, were somewhere between one and three thousand German troops led by a six-hundred-man team of raiders known as Hindenburg's Traveling Circus. They overran the American front line, destroying two companies of infantry as they did so. By breaking through to the east and west of Seicheprey, they encircled and then took the village itself. Every available doughboy—clerks, cooks, and bakers—took up rifles to stem the advance. Their dead lay, a lieutenant said, "in windrows almost, out in front of the fire trenches which by reason of the mud made poor places from which to fight."

The Germans did not attempt to advance beyond the village. In the day that followed, American counterattacks were ordered but for whatever reason never came off. (A major would be court-martialed for failing to attack when ordered.) When the sun rose on Sunday, it revealed that the Germans had withdrawn overnight. The Americans returned to Seicheprey, but 81 of them had been killed and 187 wounded, with another 214 suffering the effects of gas and 187 missing or taken prisoner. The commander of the Twenty-Sixth commended his men for giving as well as they got. The American press celebrated the AEF's first victory. Pershing, however, was not pleased.

Not exactly what the doctor ordered
Healthcare on the front line.

The AEF's star performer in the raiding of enemy trenches was young Colonel Douglas MacArthur. As chief of staff to the commander of the Forty-Second Division, known as the Rainbow Division because it was made up of National Guard troops from across the United States, he was supposed to stay close to headquarters. As soon as the Forty-Second was placed in French sectors of the front early in 1918, however, MacArthur made it almost a game—without the approval of his commanding general—to venture out on raids almost nightly, carrying a swagger stick instead of a weapon, showing almost reckless daring. On one such raid, on February 20, he crept up behind a German colonel and got him to surrender by poking him with the swagger stick and pretending it was a gun. That night's work earned him the French Croix de Guerre and the American Silver Star. Soon thereafter another venture resulted in his being awarded the Distinguished Service Cross, but early in March an encounter with poison gas caused him to be hospitalized for two weeks.

By the end of April, Georgette being finished, an uneasy quiet descended upon the battlefields of the west. The panic of a month earlier was safely in the past, and the sense of imminent peril was subsiding. The Allied side assumed that the Germans would attack again, but the fact that two large-scale attacks had come and gone and been survived made the prospect less fearsome.

The Allied commanders, grateful for this sudden calm, turned their attention once again to the fraught question of American troops: of how many were now in France, how many would be arriving that summer, what kinds of troops they would be, and where they would be assigned.

David Lloyd George would appear to have had good reason to be satisfied on all these points. One hundred and twenty thousand American soldiers were slated for delivery to France in May, which was good news in itself. Still better, in accordance with what had been agreed at Beauvais, all of them were to be infantrymen, armed with rifles or machine guns, and all were to be assigned to the BEF. What better way to ease the slaughter that Britain had been enduring for almost four years than to replace the fallen with Americans? Let Haig throw *their* lives away for a change.

Lloyd George thought the agreement for May a good start, but only that. He wanted more. He wanted the May arrangement repeated in June, and again in July, and so on for as long as possible. The French, however, observed all this with impatience. They wanted their share. To get it, they were prepared to turn the May 1 meeting into what it in fact became: a clenched-teeth, table-pounding clash of words and wills.

At issue was who was going to get how many doughboys and when. Clemenceau and Pétain were on one side, Lloyd George and Haig united for once on the other. Then the supreme Allied commander spoke up. There was no need to quarrel, said Ferdinand Foch, because there would be plenty of Yanks to go around. The transporting of infantrymen only would continue through August at least. And from June 1 they could be parceled out equally to Britain and to France.

Pershing was present, and what he was hearing became more than he could endure. Yes, it had been agreed at the height of the Michael emergency that only infantrymen would be shipped to France *for the time being*. And yes, all those sent in May would go to the BEF. The president of the United States himself had consented to these things. But as he did so, he had reminded the Allies that all American troops in France were ultimately Pershing's to use as he saw fit, and that those serving temporarily under Allied command were to be restored to the AEF as speedily as possible.

But here were Foch and Clemenceau and Pétain, Lloyd George and Haig, all taking it for granted that only infantrymen were going to be sent indefinitely, and all would be given to them. If all this came to pass, there would never be an American army in France. Pershing would never be more than a kind of glorified personnel consultant, advising from the sidelines—if even that—as arriving doughboys moved from their ships into the trenches of the Allies. The U.S. Army would never be more than, in his words, "a recruiting agency for either the British or the French."

He informed all there assembled that they had no authority to decide anything that had not already been agreed. These words were not well received. When Clemenceau protested that Foch must have the power to meet his "great responsibilities," Pershing was unmoved. When Foch said it was "my duty to insist on my point of view," the American was again unmoved. Nor did he care about Lloyd George's disappointment.

Foch, playing his last card, asked Pershing if he was willing to risk a retreat of the Allied armies all the way south to the Loire. The question implied the abandonment of Paris.

"Yes," the American replied, "I am willing to take that risk."

He watched impassively as the others poured out their anger and frustration. "Gentlemen," he said finally, "I have thought this program over very deliberately and will not be coerced." And that ended the dispute for that day. It was clear to all, as Pershing departed, that the heart of the matter was the *kinds* of soldiers to be sent to France. Everyone wanted as many doughboys as possible; when enough of them were on hand, equipped as only the United States could afford to equip them, Germany would be doomed. But if only infantrymen were sent, Pershing would never be able to organize them into divisions. Whatever their numbers, they could never become a fully functional army.

This must have been on everyone's mind as they reconvened the next morning. Tension was high, and another round of fruitless argument seemed inevitable. But then, to the surprise of all, Lloyd George made an announcement that brought the impasse to an end. He had, he said, found the shipping to transport an additional fifty thousand Americans to France every month through the summer. This meant that the full quota of infantrymen could be shipped over as planned, and Pershing could still have the artillerymen, engineers, and supply and transportation specialists he wanted. He could have them now, this summer, not at some uncertain future time.

Pershing and the French were pleased without being exactly grateful. It was impossible not to suspect that Lloyd George had known all along that the additional shipping was available but had kept it a secret in hopes of not curtailing the movement of food and munitions to Britain. The Americans and the French had been given a reminder of why Lloyd George was called the Wizard—too full of tricks for anyone's comfort.

The transatlantic transport problem was thus solved at a stroke. The question of how many of the doughboys would be handed over to the Allies and for how long, however, remained. For the present, everyone was content to leave it that way. They were worn out with fighting each other.

Back in the States, meanwhile, the war in Europe was providing ever-better cover for a war of a different kind, the one that the government was waging on persons and organizations of which it did not approve. The Justice Department, supported by local law enforcement and its nationwide network of quasi-official vigilantes and amateur secret agents, was effectively finishing off the IWW. One hundred and thirteen of the Wobbly officials who had been rounded up in the dragnet of September went on trial in Chicago in April. They did so under monstrously difficult circumstances. In the months preceding, rallies to raise money for their defense had been broken up by federal and local authorities. Sympathizers had been arrested and taken to court themselves for expressing their support. Persons attempting to help prepare the defense found themselves under relentless harassment.

There were numerous charges against the defendants, all of them falling under the general heading of conspiracy to impede the war effort. The prosecution was able to introduce much evidence of Wobbly opposition to intervention, but most of it predated the American declaration of war. The government's lawyers depicted the union's strikes as intended to disrupt the nation's ability to wage war. The defense argued that the strikes had nothing to do with the war, and everything to do with working conditions and wages.

After weeks of testimony by more than three hundred witnesses (eighty-four of the defendants among them), the jury needed only fifty-five minutes to find ninety-six of the accused guilty of all charges and almost all the others guilty of some. Fourteen were sentenced to twenty years in prison, thirty-three got ten years, another thirty-three five, and so on down to the man who got only one year but was fined thirty thousand dollars. The longest sentences and biggest fines usually went together and were imposed on the highest-ranking officials. All this was celebrated in the press. Trials of other Wobblies followed in Sacramento and Kansas City, and the number convicted and given years in prison reached 168. That some of the accused had broken one law or another is undeniable. That most had been proved guilty only of belonging to the IWW is equally certain. The ultimate objective of the raids and trials had been achieved: the evisceration of a hated organization.

Bill Haywood, who had been on the witness stand for three days, was inevitably among those to receive a sentence of twenty years. In 1921, free on bail pending an appeal, he would flee to Russia, there to die seven lonely years later of the effects of alcoholism and diabetes. He had repeatedly expressed his wish to return home. Half his ashes were buried in the Kremlin Wall, half in Chicago near the site of one of the epic events in the history of American organized labor, the Haymarket Riot of 1886.

In France, the British and French were still recovering from Michael and Georgette. For Pershing and thousands of his soldiers of all ranks, it was a frustrating time. They were eager for action, none more so than Robert Lee Bullard, now commander of the First Division. Unhappy at having been moved out of Ansauville too soon to participate in the clash with Hindenburg's Traveling Circus, certain that his men would have done better than their replacements, Bullard wanted an opportunity to show what the Big Red One could do. He went to see General Eugène Debeney, commander of the French corps of which the First Division was now a part. He asked for an offensive assignment. Debeney was happy to give him one. He and Bullard agreed on an attack on the ruined village of Cantigny, at the westernmost tip of a small salient the Germans had punched into the French line as Operation Michael was coming to a close.

The attack on Cantigny was in every way a minor operation, its objective of very little importance. For Pershing and Bullard, however, it was a momentous undertaking. It was their opportunity to demonstrate that the best American divisions were ready to join the war, worthy of being pulled together to form an American army. It would be on such a limited scale, with attackers advancing on a line only fifteen hundred yards wide, that there would be room for only a single regiment. That regiment would be roughly equal in manpower to Cantigny's German defenders.

Success was regarded as certain from the start, with good reason, and everything possible was done to widen the odds. The regiment selected to make

THE WESTERN FRONT: 1917-1918

North
Sea

HOLLAND
(NETHERLANDS)

Rhine

ENGLAND

•Dover

GERMANY

FLANDERS

Calais•

•Ypres

★Brussels

BELGIUM

•Liège

Meuse

•Lille

Arras•

Charleroi•

*Ardennes
Forest*

Somme

Amiens•

Sedan•

LUXEMBOURG

Moselle

•Montdidier

Aisne

Longwy•

Compiègne•

Oise

Soissons•

ARGONNE

Seine

Ourcq

Château-Thierry•

Reims•

Verdun•

Metz•

Argonne   Forest

Meuse

Paris★

Marne

Troyon
•St. Mihiel

CHAMPAGNE

Nancy•

FRANCE

LORRAINE

Seine

•Chaumont

KEY

– – – Western Front 1917

/// U.S. St. Mihiel, Neuse-Argonne Campaigns

- - - German gains spring 1918

—— Front as of November 11, 1918

0 miles   50

0 kilometers   50

© 2017 Jeffrey L. Ward

the attack was taken out of the line and trained, on terrain similar to the approach to Cantigny, in how to follow a rolling artillery barrage as it moved toward enemy positions at the stately pace of four minutes for every hundred yards. Debeney promised to provide 250 artillery pieces, including some heavier than anything the Americans possessed. He would also contribute twelve of France's new Schneider heavy tanks, a flamethrower platoon, and aircraft for observation and bombing. Intelligence reported that one of the defending German battalions was classified as third rate—barely fit for front-line duty. General Bullard was not being unduly optimistic in expecting a walkover.

The attack was scheduled for early on the morning of Tuesday, May 28, and preparations went forward. But one day before, on the Monday, word came that the Germans had launched yet another major offensive, the third of the spring, sending seventeen divisions against fifty miles of the French-held line east of Soissons. The breakthrough was as complete as on the Somme two months earlier, the Germans overrunning one French position after another in a race for the River Vesle and after it the Marne. Every available man and gun was summoned to help plug the holes. The heavy artillery and observation planes that Debeney had promised Bullard immediately went elsewhere.

It is perhaps surprising, in light of this new emergency, that the Cantigny operation was not called off. But it went ahead as scheduled, perhaps because the French understood how much it mattered to the Americans. First came the usual early-morning saturation bombardment. Then Colonel Hanson Ely's Twenty-Eighth Infantry Regiment, heavily laden with equipment, began its long uphill trudge behind the creeping barrage and tanks. The Germans not killed by artillery had positioned themselves in the basements and rubble that were almost all that remained of the village. French flamethrowers made quick work of them. The attackers had possession of Cantigny by about seven A.M., and soon thereafter they reached the ridge, five hundred yards farther on, that was their final objective. They had suffered perhaps fifty casualties, killed no one knew how many Germans, and taken more than a hundred prisoners. It had been a walkover as expected.

The fight had just begun, however. After four hours of silence, time that the Americans used to organize their defenses and dig in, distant German guns opened up with a bombardment that would rain explosives and gas down on the doughboys without pause all through the rest of the day. Evening brought a series of advances by German infantry, but they were poorly coordinated with the artillery, the Americans' light artillery was used to devastating effect, and one by one they failed.

The punishment inflicted on the Americans was extreme. Bullard might have ordered a pullback, and Ely might have started one on his own initiative, if they had not understood that any such step was likely to mean the end of their careers. Pershing saw success as essential to getting the Americans accepted as a credible fighting force. Everyone understood that when he ordered the regiment to hold the village at all costs, he meant exactly what he said. Failure would not be tolerated regardless of the circumstances. Ely's men desperately needed relief, but replacing them with fresh troops under such heavy bombardment would have been high in risk and probably higher in cost than a well-managed retreat. The men could only hunker down, expose themselves to the extent required to bring gunfire to bear on counterattacks, and hope for the Germans to give up. They finally did, but by the time it happened American casualties were in the neighborhood of one thousand. By one count they included two hundred men killed or missing plus 669 wounded, by another 1,069 in all, around 1,300 by a third.

George Marshall, then a lieutenant colonel serving as the First Division's operations officer, would one day acknowledge that "the losses we suffered were not justified by the importance of the position itself." He would maintain, however, that the symbolic value of a first successful American offensive justified the cost in lives. General Bullard, delighted to be able to give Pershing this victory, also took a bright view of what had happened. "To both friend and foe alike," he declared, "it said, 'Americans will both fight and stick.'"

The success at Cantigny got less attention from the Allied high command than Pershing and Bullard thought it deserved, because it was overshadowed by more consequential developments elsewhere. The new German offensive, like Operation Michael, was unfolding in unexpected ways. For Ludendorff, a successful end to the war by year-end, unthinkable a few months earlier, suddenly seemed possible. At the start of their advance, which began on a line between Reims and Soissons, the Germans encountered only three understrength French divisions and two British divisions that had, by a cruel irony, been sent to this supposedly quiet sector to recover from Operation Georgette. None of these units were prepared for what hit them, and all were quickly overrun. So were the reserves sent to reinforce them.

The performance of the troops on both sides was at this point being affected by a new addition to the miseries of frontline life. Across Europe, starting in northern France but spreading rapidly, an infection that the troops called "three-day fever" was making it impossible for thousands and eventually millions of soldiers and civilians to function. Britain's First Army, not an extreme case, reported 36,000 hospital admissions in May as a result; a typical unit of the Second Army reported that only fifteen of its 145 men were able to report for duty. The contagion drastically reduced the effectiveness of Ludendorff's assault troops, but proved fatal only very rarely. Most physicians called it influenza, but some said it could not be that because its effects were so mild and so short-lived.

Influenza or not, the end of the first day of the new offensive found the German vanguard on the banks of the Vesle, a remarkable twelve miles from their starting point. The second day—the day the Americans attacked at Cantigny—brought the capture of the city of Soissons. By the end of the third day, German troops were at the River Marne, thirty miles from where they had begun, little more than a two-day hard march from Paris. They had smashed through every body of Allied reserves sent to stop them, capturing 650 pieces of artillery and taking sixty thousand prisoners. The French government, in one of the numerous echoes of 1914's First Battle of the Marne, was making preparations to leave Paris for Bordeaux on the Atlantic coast. The roads leading southward and westward out of the capital were jammed with civilians— a million of them, according to reports—desperate to escape the Germans.

Ludendorff had not foreseen this. His objective was still to drive the British out of Flanders. This new offensive, like Michael, had been intended to create just enough of a threat to draw Haig's reserves southward out of Flanders, in advance of further attacks to take place there in June or July. But now, as in 1914 but this time unexpectedly, Paris not only beckoned but seemed achievable. The essential next step was to get men, guns, and supplies across the Marne, in position for a direct move on Paris. To do that the Germans needed *bridges.*

Which is what made the town of Château-Thierry, almost directly in the path of the German advance, suddenly loom large. There were two bridges at Château-Thierry, substantial bridges carrying rail and motor traffic, and only one French colonial division was available to keep them out of German hands. General Pétain, seeing the danger and short of troops, asked the Americans if they could help. Pershing had two divisions, the Second and the Third, that were not at the moment committed to any sector but were also not considered entirely ready for active service. He ordered both to proceed to Château-

Thierry and there report to the commander of the French Sixth Army. Both were more than a hundred miles away.

They had to arrange to get to Château-Thierry by a combination of truck and rail travel and marching. The Third Division, however, included a motorized machine gun battalion—"motorized" meaning it had its own transport—that was able to set out immediately. Though some of its trucks broke down en route, seventeen of its machine gun squads reached Château-Thierry on the afternoon of Friday, May 31, at the end of a grueling twenty-four-hour journey. They were just in time. The Germans were at the north edge of the town, trying to enter but being held off by the Tenth French Colonial Division. That night two American squads, led by a young lieutenant not long out of West Point, entered the city, linked up with the colonials, and joined the fight using their Hotchkiss machine guns. Other squads set up their guns south of the river, in positions from which they could spray the Germans with indirect fire (rounds fired into the air to rain down on unseen targets) and guard the approaches to the bridges.

The defenders held their ground through more than two days of heavy gunfire. The French blew up one of the bridges when that became the only way to keep the Germans from taking it. The American machine guns made it impossible for the Germans to approach the remaining bridge. When seventeen thousand of the Third Division's infantry arrived on June 3, a resumed German advance became impossible. Some of the Americans then moved east to Jaulgonne, where they attacked German troops crossing over on a bridge there and forced them back across the river.

Unable to advance, the Germans turned to the west on a route parallel to the Marne. They captured a hill overlooking the surrounding terrain, took possession of the nearby village of Vaux, and drove a body of French troops sent to intercept them into a hunting reserve called the Bois de Belleau—Belleau Wood. By June 6 the Americans had launched an advance that drove the Germans off the high ground. Marine Corps units of the Second Division relieved the French in Belleau Wood and dug in for a showdown. The Germans attacked and were repulsed. When the Americans attacked, they, too, were turned back, with heavy losses. The wood had limited tactical and almost no strategic value, but for both sides it took on symbolic importance. The Germans wanted to give the newcomers a thrashing, to keep them from becoming too confident and the Allies from being encouraged by their performance. The Americans for their part, as at Cantigny, wanted to prove themselves.

In action at last

"It was assuredly the Americans who bore the heaviest brunt of the fighting on the whole battlefront during the last few months of the war," Ludendorff would recall.

For almost the whole month of June, that obscure patch of woodland became a microcosm of the Great War, the Americans' introduction to the war's dark heart. The fighting was savage, profligate of life, and profoundly brutalizing; for a time the Americans were under orders (unofficially of course) to take no prisoners. "Day and night for nearly a month men fought in corpse-choked thickets, killing with bayonet and bomb and machine gun," an American survivor would write years afterward. "It was gassed and shelled and shot into the semblance of nothing earthly. The great trees all went down; the leaves were blasted off, or hung sere and blackened. It was pock-marked with shell craters and shallow dugouts and hasty trenches. It was strewn with all the debris of war, Mauser rifles and Springfields, helmets German and American, unexploded grenades, letters, knapsacks, packs, blankets, boots. A year later, it is said, they were still finding unburied dead in the depths of it."

When the fighting ended on June 26, with the Americans in uncontested control of the wood, eighteen hundred of them were dead and nearly seven thousand wounded, missing, or captured. Those numbers were dwarfed by too many of the war's battles to count, but Belleau Wood had been very much a Great War fight all the same.

American operations around Château-Thierry came to an end on the evening of July 1 with an attack on Vaux by two regiments of the Second Division. The village was defended by a single understrength German regiment, many of its troops sick with flu. The Americans prepared meticulously, even to the point of getting refugees from Vaux to describe the interiors of every building. The six P.M. infantry advance was preceded by twelve hours of bombardment by American field artillery and French big guns. The doughboys, when they made their move, found the Germans gone. The capture of the village and the railway line just beyond it had taken no more than half an hour and exacted zero casualties. That it was a victory was beyond question. Whether it was actually a battle was another matter. In any case, the long stalemate was nearing its end, unsustainable by the depleted and exhausted Germans.

Death from a New Direction

It can be accepted as given that Dean Nilson, Ernest Elliott, and John Bottom meant no harm. It was an accident of history that they happened to live in Haskell County, Kansas, in the winter of 1917–18. And that each of them had a connection to the U.S. Army's Camp Funston, three hundred miles away. And that because of these connections, it was probably one or two or all three of them who set in motion the third worst pandemic in history, one that in less than a year would claim more than twenty million lives around the world and affect the course of the Great War.

It was likewise an accident of history—a freak of epidemiology—that Haskell County appears to have been almost the only place on earth to report an outbreak of influenza in the first two months of 1918. It was a virulent outbreak, leading to more cases of pneumonia and a higher death rate than such things usually did. What caused it will never be known. Probably a virus somehow made the difficult leap from pigs to human beings, but this cannot be proved. Whatever its cause, the disease would run its course and disappear from Haskell County by the end of March. Before that happened, however, it would make a second, more fateful leap.

Dean Nilson came home from Camp Funston on furlough, then returned to duty. Ernest Elliott, not realizing that his young son was at just that time coming down with the flu, went to the camp to visit his brother. And John Bottom, like all draftees from Kansas, reported there for basic training.

These journeys all took place in the last few days of February and the first few days of March. And on March 4 a cook became the first Camp Funston soldier to show symptoms of influenza. This is unlikely to have been a coincidence, the incubation period for flu being one to three days. And at that moment there was no place from which the virus could have come except Haskell County.

Camp Funston, named for the man who would have led the AEF if not for his fatal heart attack, was the second largest of the training cantonments built in 1917, housing some 57,000 men. Like most of the cantonments, it was shoddily built, seriously overcrowded in spite of the warnings of medical authorities, poorly equipped, and inadequately heated. In the three weeks following March 4, more than eleven hundred of the men stationed there were hospitalized with influenza. Of these, 237 developed pneumonia, the complication that can make flu lethal, and thirty-eight died. This was not a remarkably high death rate for an epidemic of this kind, and as the number of new cases began to subside, no one saw reason to be alarmed.

But other leaps were now being made, and in all directions. Troops were constantly moving between Camp Funston, which was part of the huge Fort Riley army reservation in Kansas, and other military installations around the country. From many of these places, men were being ordered to France in a steadily increasing flow. And there was constant contact between soldiers and civilian populations near and far. Once the influenza virus took hold at Camp Funston, its spread was inevitable and followed quickly.

Within a few weeks, twenty-four of the army's thirty-six largest bases were hit, along with thirty of the country's fifty largest cities. In early April influenza showed up in the French port of Brest, the destination of many American transports. From there it spread through the French army and the British Expeditionary Force, to Paris and Rome—basically everywhere. It skipped easily across No Man's Land, soon ravaging the German armies to such an extent that Ludendorff would later blame it for the failure of his spring offensives.

The contagion followed roads and railways into every corner of the Americas and Europe, and it traveled by ship to the Eskimos of the Arctic and the islands of the South Pacific. It affected so many draftees that training became impossible, and it brought commerce to a standstill in cities on every continent.

And yet, despite its disruptiveness, it was not terribly dangerous. Its general mildness and the infrequency of complications caused many physicians to doubt that it could really be influenza at all. Most victims were able to return to their daily routines after a few days of misery.

By high summer, the worst seemed to be over. Between June 1 and August 1, the BEF reported 1.2 million cases, a large majority of them only briefly debilitating, but on August 10 it declared the epidemic to be at an end. It was in decline in the United States as well, and in most places around the world.

But it didn't disappear. It not only persisted in an apparently random assortment of places, but abruptly became much more virulent. The death rate began to soar at Brest, where the French naval hospital was swamped with new cases. U.S. Navy facilities in Boston and Philadelphia were similarly hard hit.

What was happening was a process known to medical science as "passage." Viruses change constantly as they jump from host to host, and by the time this particular virus had passed through fifteen or twenty individuals it was radically different and much more lethal. Doctors now wondered if it could be influenza not because it was so mild but because it was suddenly so dangerous and manifested itself in such varied and unusual ways. Flu epidemics had always occurred between September and March, but now it was August, and this one was growing in reach and potency. Flu usually killed the aged and unwell, but this one was cutting a wide swath through the young and strong. Most vulnerable of all were pregnant women.

If the resulting global pandemic was not made possible by the war— would the virus have escaped from Haskell County if not for Camp Funston?—it was worsened by the conditions and priorities of wartime. This was unquestionably true in the United States, where the mortality rate was markedly higher among soldiers from rural areas than among city boys. The latter, having grown up in close quarters and been regularly exposed to infectious diseases, had robust immune systems. Youngsters from farms and hamlets, even if big and husky, were more vulnerable. Being crowded together in camps, trains, and ships where disease was rampant amounted to a death sentence for many of them.

The belief that nothing was as important as the war, and that nothing must be allowed to interrupt the prosecution of the war, caused people in positions of authority to make decisions that today seem inexcusable. In Philadelphia, where the epidemic was raging in the navy yard but had not yet hit the civilian population, medical experts implored the head of the city's public health department to cancel a big Liberty Loan parade scheduled for September 28. He refused on patriotic grounds, clearing the way for what proved to be the biggest parade in Philadelphia history. Hundreds of thousands watched as a two-mile-long procession of soldiers, sailors, and civic groups marched past. Two days later 117 Philadelphians died of influenza. Soon hundreds were dying daily, two-thirds of them under age forty. The number of sick was so overwhelming that the city's hospitals had to stop admitting patients. Here as elsewhere there was a shortage of doctors and nurses because so many were away doing war service. Many of those still on hand were themselves soon felled by the virus.

On September 26 the U.S. provost marshal, in charge of the Selective Service System, canceled the scheduled induction of 142,000 draftees. He did so not to limit contagion but because the cantonments were in such a state, their hospitals overflowing and corpses piling up faster than they could be buried, that ordinary operations had become impossible. His action saved many lives, but the army made no other changes. The transfer and intermixing of troops continued.

Though the epidemic was rampant at Camp Grant in northern Illinois, 3,100 of the men stationed there were put on a train bound for Camp Hancock in Georgia. Once under way they sickened en masse, turning the journey into a nightmare. Upon arrival at their destination, more than seven hundred had to be taken directly from the train to the hospital. Hundreds ultimately died, and untold numbers of people were infected along their route and in Georgia. The commander at Camp Grant, having approved the journey against medical advice, shot himself.

Still nothing changed. William Gorgas, the army's surgeon general, urged that only men who had been quarantined for at least a week should be allowed to board troopships bound for France. General Peyton March, army chief of staff, refused, agreeing only to the exclusion of men who showed active symptoms at the time of boarding. Nobody knows how many doughboys died of influenza either at sea or shortly after arrival in France, but it is certain that thousands did.

What the men aboard these death ships experienced can scarcely be imagined. Men crammed together in impossibly tight quarters would turn dark blue, a sign of cyanosis, the failure of the lungs to supply oxygen to the blood and more often than not fatal. Men would go wild with delirium, bleed from their noses, their ears, even their eyes. On some ships new deaths were recorded at a rate of almost one a minute, and men were buried at sea in an uninterrupted stream. One survivor, the colonel of the Fifty-Seventh Vermont Infantry Regiment, recalled that aboard the ship that took him to France, "altogether a true inferno reigned supreme."

Few civilians knew what was happening because the United States, like the Allied nations, censored news of outbreaks as potentially bad for morale. The pandemic would become known as the Spanish Flu for no better reason than that Spain, having remained neutral, was nearly alone in not suppressing newspaper coverage of the disaster. Spain was affected, but it had nothing to do with the start of the contagion or its spread to Europe and elsewhere.

Rear Admiral Cary Grayson, President Wilson's physician, learned of the death ships. He agreed with Gorgas that transporting troops without a precautionary quarantine was irresponsible, and persuaded the president to discuss the subject with Army Chief of Staff March. Summoned to the White House, March stood firm. He said that any reduction in troop shipments would cheer the Germans and that every man who died at sea "just as surely played his part as his comrades who died in France." He recalled later that Wilson gazed out the window for a long moment, sighed, and acquiesced. Then, weirdly, the president recited or perhaps sang the words of a ditty that had become popular with schoolchildren.

> *I had a little bird,*
> *Its name was Enza.*
> *I opened the window*
> *And in-flu-enza.*

The president's decision accomplished nothing except a waste of young lives. His meeting with March took place on October 7, by which time the defeat of Germany was a certainty and Berlin and Washington had begun the exchange of diplomatic notes that would culminate in an armistice. Not one of the troopships that left the United States after October 7 arrived in France in time for the doughboys who survived the voyage to get near the fighting. If they had been kept at home, nothing would have been different except that, assuming the taking of minimal precautions, many might not have died.

In eastern France, meanwhile, the AEF was driving northward up the valley of the River Meuse and into the Argonne Forest. They were encountering fierce resistance and taking heavy casualties, but more doughboys were being put out of action by influenza than by the enemy's guns.

The war's end would be followed, with mysterious promptitude, by the end of a pandemic that some doctors had thought might not end until the human race was wiped out. In the century since, researchers have been trying, despite the absence of satisfactory records almost everywhere, to calculate how many died. In the 1920s the agreed-upon answer was somewhat in excess of twenty million. Since then the estimates have continued to rise, and for more than a half century there has been general agreement that the total could be in the neighborhood of fifty million, possibly even a hundred million.

It is likewise agreed that by early 1919 some 675,000 Americans were dead who would have been alive if not for the pandemic. That looks almost negligible compared with the more than twenty million believed to have died in India, but it is thirteen times the number of doughboys who lost their lives fighting.

Chapter 18

The Tide Turns

By late July 1918 it becomes fair to apply the word *desperate* to the German situation on the Western Front and in the war generally. Between late March and the end of May, Erich Ludendorff had launched three of the biggest offensives of the war. All three had begun by shattering the Allied defenses, putting the British and French to flight, and wrecking a good many of their best divisions. But they had yielded nothing but vast expanses of territory of dubious strategic value, and had left the attackers exhausted, many of their best divisions in tatters. German casualties would ultimately total a staggering one million, including almost one hundred thousand dead. The superiority in numbers that they had enjoyed at the start of Operation Michael was gone. And the losses were concentrated among the elite young storm troopers who were all that remained of the cream of the German armies. Such men were no longer replaceable. Meanwhile the Allies were being reinforced with fresh troops from the United States at a rate of more than a quarter of a million monthly—more than three hundred thousand in July alone.

There were signs of a breakdown of discipline in the German ranks. The men, much like their families back home, were subsisting on little more than starvation rations, drinking coffee made from acorns and eating bread containing sawdust and sausages made of horse and rabbit flesh. They made cigarettes from the leaves of beech trees. The demands of the spring offensives made it impossible to rotate troops to allow them to rest and refit by turns, and the high command was angered by reports of men returning from home leave and "spreading high treason and incitement of disobedience." Soldiers were displaying an increasing inclination to surrender, and there were echoes of the French mutinies of the previous year. Bands of deserters roamed the countryside behind the front lines, attacking supply trains and depots. In July, 375,000 troops would be out of action because of influenza.

On the other side, spirits were beginning to rise. Even the English officer Siegfried Sassoon was back on duty, having been discharged from the Craiglockhart mental hospital after changing his mind not about the legitimacy of the war, but about his own refusal to join his comrades. After a period in Palestine he was returned to the Western Front—where, almost immediately and with wild irony, he was shot in the head by a British soldier who mistook him for a German. The wound did no permanent damage, but Sassoon would spend the rest of the war recovering.

The Germans' most pressing Western Front problem was the failure of their third offensive to capture the city of Reims with its crucial railway connections. This meant that they had only a single rail line, one leading southward out of recently captured Soissons, with which to send troops and supplies into the huge new salient that extended all the way to the Marne. Large French forces were near enough to threaten Soissons. If they retook it, the German forces to the south would be cut off and trapped. On June 9 an army commanded by Oskar von Hutier had begun an attack at the River Matz west of Soissons, its purpose being to relieve pressure on the city and widen the mouth of the Marne salient at its western end. It was another impressive early success, as the Germans pushed the French back six miles on the first day and took eight thousand prisoners. On June 11, however, a ferocious counterattack by General Charles Mangin's Tenth French Army caught Hutier's advancing troops in the flank and exposed on open ground. The Germans were thrown back so violently that the offensive had to be brought to an end. The Marne salient remained dangerously vulnerable.

Even as the Germans' problems mounted and their prospects darkened, the Wilson administration's grip on wartime America was growing subtly weaker. Congressmen's questions about the administration's management of aircraft production and other programs, and the White House's disinclination to share information, led to hearings. President Wilson was fortunate to have as spokesman Secretary of War Baker, who when called to testify displayed good humor, calm self-confidence, and an obvious wish to cooperate. A diminutive, unthreatening figure, Baker smoked one cigar after another through days of harsh grilling, disgorging mind-numbing volumes of statistics. Ultimately he persuaded all but the president's most determined enemies that the War Department's management had rarely been less than thorough and conscientious.

The mere fact that Congress regarded hearings as necessary, however, had a corrosive effect on the public's confidence in the administration. And though the Justice Department was by now devoted almost entirely to monitoring the acts and opinions of the citizenry and discouraging dissent, it was increasingly the target of complaints, in the press and elsewhere, that it should have been more aggressive in dealing with the supposedly disloyal.

With Clemenceau of France asking for a hundred American divisions, Theodore Roosevelt demanding an army of ten million men, and President Wilson promising "force without stint or limit," the Selective Service System's manpower needs threatened to outstrip the supply made available by the draft registration of 1917. In June 1918 there was a second registration drive, to bring into the system those who had become twenty-one in the preceding year. A third became necessary when, in August, Congress made all men between the ages of eighteen and forty-five subject to conscription. This added thirteen million names to the Selective Service roster. It was beginning to seem possible that the army would take all of them.

The War Department announced that, with the start of the 1918–19 school year, all qualified male students would be made privates in the army, receiving compulsory military training as a supplement to their other studies and wearing uniforms. This brought thousands of the nation's best-educated young men into the manpower pipeline—and, with a fine irony, into the administration's crusade to rid the world of militarism.

Those young Americans already in France were being drawn deeper into the fighting and were having unexpected experiences along the way. Among the first illusions to be shattered had to do with an idealized France and its delightful females. What the doughboys found along the Western Front was a landscape stripped of vegetation, pocked with shell holes from horizon to horizon, covered with the detritus of war, and literally stinking of death. One new arrival described it this way: "The whole country is littered with rubbish or as we call it salvage—guns and ammunition, trench mortars, equipment and so on—all the litter of war: tanks derelict and desolate by the roadside, and lorries upside down." The only women to be seen, a doughboy wrote, "were haggard and emaciated with hardship," many of them dressed in mourning. The Americans generally got along well with the French troops with whom they served, even though the pay an ordinary doughboy could draw while in France—thirty dollars a month—was ten times that of a French private.

Relations between Americans and the British "tommies" who were often their instructors in training, by contrast, tended to be disagreeable. "Our men seemed to take at once a violent dislike for everything that was British," an American battalion commander wrote. "It is difficult to analyze the reasons for this first impression. It was doubtless due in large part to the fact that the British Tommy had been at the game a long time and he assumed a cocksure attitude toward everything that came his way; perhaps to the fact that most of the Britishers with whom the men came in contact were old soldiers who had seen service and had been wounded in the fighting line and sent back to work in and about the camp, and they looked with some contempt on these striplings who had come in to win the war. Perhaps it was due to the fact that on the surface the average Britisher is not after all a very lovable person, especially on first acquaintance. At any rate our men did not like the British."

The French didn't much like the British, either, perhaps especially at the highest levels of command. No doubt it was fortunate that, as American divisions went into action, they most often did so jointly with French forces and under overall French command. If the worn-down and often cynical French were not very impressed with the battlefield savvy of the newcomers from across the sea, they were often in awe of the eagerness and courage with which the doughboys would throw themselves into danger.

Weeks of relative quiet in most sectors of the front—a quiet resulting from the Germans' need to reposition their troops and guns and shift their lines of supply—ended on July 8 with the launching of Ludendorff's next offensive. The aim this time was to expand the salient that Operation Michael had created at Noyon-Montdidier, merge it with the Marne salient, and so add a threat to Paris from the north to the existing one from the east. Unlike the earlier offensives, this one made little headway even at the start and came to a halt after a few days. Ferdinand Foch deduced that the Germans were at the end of their resources. His suspicions were confirmed when, just a week later, the Germans attacked again, this time on the Marne well to the east of Château-Thierry in the Champagne region, and were again soon stopped.

Short though it was, the Champagne offensive subjected the Americans to their next major trial by fire. The Germans' objective was to capture Reims by enveloping it on its east and west sides, thereby taking possession of the Reims-to-Château-Thierry rail line, without which they could have little hope of holding the Marne salient. As earlier at Château-Thierry, they needed to get across the Marne. The only place where a crossing was feasible, in this case, was at the mouth of a valley through which the River Surmelin flows north-ward to join the Marne. The job of defending this valley, the only gap in a row of hills that dominates the south bank of the Marne and therefore a highway to open country if the Germans could fight their way through, fell to the American Third Division. Its Thirtieth and Thirty-Eighth Infantry Regiments were placed directly in what was expected to be the Germans' line of advance.

The attack came on July 15 and turned into a fight as bitter as anything seen at Verdun or elsewhere. The Thirty-Eighth Regiment was left in an exposed forward position, under attack from three sides, after the Thirtieth on its left and the French troops on its right were forced back. Its commander, a fifty-three-year-old West Point colonel with the splendid name Ulysses Grant McAlexander, had been ordered not to yield an inch of ground and was pre-pared to die rather than do so. When the battle ended after three days of fero-ciously bloody toe-to-toe combat, the Germans were at a standstill and the defending American units were in a wrecked state. One of McAlexander's bat-talions had lost twelve of its thirty-two officers and 461 of its 930 enlisted men. The others were similarly ravaged. The German Sixth Grenadiers, when the shooting stopped, could muster only 150 of the seventeen hundred men with whom they had begun the attack.

"Never have I seen so many dead men, never such frightful battle scenes," a German lieutenant wrote in his journal. The doughboys, he said, had shown not only impressive "nerve" but a "roughness" that, he implied, bordered on the inhuman. "'The Americans kill everybody!' was the cry of terror of July 15, which for a long time stuck in the bones of our men," he wrote. The Third Division's contribution to foiling what would prove to be Germany's last of-fensive had been conspicuous and important. The division won, or perhaps bestowed upon itself, the title "Rock of the Marne." It set a pattern that would become common in future encounters with the enemy, holding its ground in the face of attacks that had forced the French to withdraw, standing firm even while suffering ruinous losses.

The situation on the Western Front was now radically different from what it had been at the start of Operation Michael. Foch decided that the time was ripe to take the fight to the Germans, and for the Americans to play a major part. Ludendorff was at Tournai in the north, conferring with the headquar-ters staff of the German army group in Flanders about yet another offensive, when, on July 18, word reached him of a new crisis. The French Tenth Army, led as before by Charles Mangin and including four American divisions, had again come pouring out of the woodlands and plunged into the west side of the Marne salient. Soissons was threatened, and with it all the German troops to the south. Ludendorff returned to his train and sped south.

Mangin, hated by his troops, called "the Butcher" because of the freedom with which he spent their lives, was possibly the most maniacally aggressive senior officer of the Great War. In 1917 he had been removed from command because of his excessively enthusiastic part in the Nivelle Offensive, the disaster that sparked mutinies. Upon becoming supreme commander, the almost equally bellicose Foch had returned Mangin to the front as an army commander. Mangin saw the advantages, not least as a way of repairing his own reputation, of allowing the Americans assigned to his army to take on a full share of the dying. Thus he had put the AEF's First and Second Divisions, now an army corps under Pershing's former chief of staff James Harbord, at the center of his July 18 attack. It fell to them to take the next step in showing what the AEF could do. They would pass the test, but at as high a price as the Third Division had paid on the River Surmelin.

In preparing Mangin's attack, Foch had been able to pull together twenty-

Signs of weakness, signs of woe
*Their hopes of victory dying, German troops displayed
an increasing readiness to surrender.*

four divisions, twelve hundred guns, eleven hundred aircraft, and five hundred tanks. When these massed forces advanced on twenty-seven miles of front, they quickly overran the first two German lines. The objectives for the first day were taken by 5:35 A.M., and by day's end the attackers had advanced five miles. But an entire German army was now moving to the defense of Soissons, and the French and the Americans had to advance across ground broken by deep and wide ravines that provided excellent cover for the German machine-gunners in their fighting retreat.

Things got almost impossibly difficult after that first day. German field artillery fired point-blank at the French tanks, virtually all of which were soon out of action. The Second Division spent the whole of the second day without food or water, pushing forward under machine gun and artillery fire and bombardment by German aircraft. When relieved on the night of July 19, it had advanced six and a half miles, captured seventy-five artillery pieces, and taken 2,900 prisoners. It had also suffered four thousand casualties, among them Major Theodore Roosevelt, Jr., who had shown extravagant courage until being gassed and taking a nasty bullet wound to the leg. It had failed to

reach its objective for the second day, but the French troops who replaced it would need almost two more weeks to do so, succeeding only when the Germans voluntarily withdrew.

The First Division, which had faced less difficult conditions than the Second at the start of the offensive, remained in action for three days more. It was not relieved until it had taken the heavily fortified village of Berzy-le-Sec, important because on high ground commanding the highway from Soissons to Château-Thierry. By then the First, too, had advanced six and a half miles, capturing seventy-five guns and almost 3,400 enemy soldiers and taking 7,317 casualties. When they were able to re-form their ranks, an officer would recall, the American "battalions looked like companies and companies looked like squads." The Twenty-Sixth Infantry Regiment, having lost all its more senior officers, was commanded by a captain. Some companies were commanded by noncommissioned officers, one by a private.

Pierre Teilhard de Chardin, a Jesuit priest and paleontologist who one day would write *The Phenomenon of Man,* was a corporal and stretcher-bearer (he had declined a captain's commission) with the First Moroccan Division. This was a tough, battle-savvy colonial outfit that had earlier served with the Big Red One in the Ansauville sector, had helped acquaint them with the demands of trench warfare, and then fought beside them in this Second Battle of the Marne. "We had the Americans as neighbors and I had a close-up view of them," Teilhard wrote. "Everyone says the same: they're first rate troops, fighting with intense *individual* [italics in original] passion (concentrated on the enemy) and wonderful courage. The only complaint one would make about them is that they don't take sufficient care; they're too apt to get themselves killed. When they're wounded, they make their way back holding themselves upright, almost stiff, impassive, and uncomplaining. I don't think I've ever seen such pride and dignity in suffering. There's complete comradeship between them and us, born fully fledged under fire."

Another writer observed that "the Americans perished in the same way that all the parties involved in the war had perished during the first years of the war: side by side and wave after wave. . . . At the risk of exaggeration, it can thus be said that the army of the United States set off to battle in 1918 as if the Great War had just begun, and had to discover the hard reality of trench warfare all over again."

Still another noted of the Americans that "after their great fight at Belleau Wood it was remarked how their dead, especially the dead of the Marine

Corps, lay in beautifully ordered lines where the traversing machine guns had caught them."

Such comments point not only to the courage of the American troops but to their newness to industrialized warfare, the deficiencies of their training, and the belief of overconfident senior commanders that they had nothing to learn from veterans of the long Western Front stalemate. They point finally to a waste of life. The AEF staff was not blind to this. Its training section would report that, although valuable lessons were being learned and applied, it remained true up to the end of the war that "assault formations had been too dense and lacked flexibility; scouts were seldom used; supporting arms were improperly employed; and junior officers displayed little initiative."

The early American victories would have come at even greater cost, and might not have been possible, if the doughboys had encountered the German armies of earlier years or even of March 1918. But by the time of Cantigny and Belleau Wood, most of the German divisions were at half their original strength or less, many of their troops were weakened by influenza (which would kill seventeen hundred people just in Berlin on the single day October 5), and their supply system was threadbare. Replacement troops, when replacements could be found, were often boys in their midteens or middle-aged men of dubious fitness. The more wretched the German situation became, the longer the troops had to stay in action—there were no more reserves to relieve them—and the stronger was the impulse to find opportunities to surrender.

The AEF, by contrast, could rotate its troops freely and absorb heavy losses because replacements were pouring into its ports. As July ended, there were 54,224 American officers and 1,114,838 enlisted men in France. One hundred and seventy-five thousand of them were operating the supply system, leaving nearly three-quarters of a million for combat duty. And morale remained high despite the losses, because the doughboys and the Allies were clearly winning. Hindenburg, writing years later of the summer of 1918, paid tribute to the tenacity and self-sacrifice of his beleaguered forces. He added, however, that the situation had become hopeless, that "even heroism such as this could no longer save the situation; it could only prevent an utter catastrophe."

That was the most the Germans could hope for as 1918 entered its eighth month: to escape utter catastrophe. Ludendorff knew it, too. Though Mangin's drive was stopped short of Soissons, the tide of the war had turned. From this point on, the Germans would always be on the defensive and almost constantly under attack. On July 21 the U.S. Third Division advanced into the center of Château-Thierry and found the city undefended, the Germans having withdrawn. The Twenty-Sixth Division, in carrying out orders to take control of positions beyond Belleau Wood, found the Germans gone from there as well. The two divisions set off northward in pursuit and ran into the heavily armed rear guard of an orderly German retreat. Behind them came the Thirty-Second Division. Lieutenant Charles Donnelly described the scene:

> Our recent companions in arms, the Yankee Division, had captured the area we had just entered only a few days before; there had not been time enough in which to clean up the battlefield. Dead men and horses littered the fields and putrefaction, aided by the warm weather, was well along. Of all the odors I have experienced, none is as repulsive as the sweetish, nauseating smell of rotting flesh, especially in hot weather. Up to that time I had never smoked but I needed something to help me cope with the stench. A field agent of the Knights of Columbus [an American Catholic fraternal organization that had sent volunteers to France] came by at about that time, giving away tobacco, writing paper and other things soldiers needed. I told him my problem and he gave me some cigars, Prince Albert, and a corncob pipe; I have been a cigar smoker from that day on.

Just weeks earlier, thrilled by the gains of Ludendorff's early offensives, the ever-more-irrelevant Kaiser Wilhelm had been boasting that he would soon be in Paris. Now he was reeling from exactly the same disappointment he had experienced in 1914: the news that his forces were overextended and had to be pulled back from the Marne. The challenge now was to get those forces, and as much of their equipment as possible, out of the Marne salient before another French offensive took Soissons and cut them off.

On July 24 Foch assembled Haig, Pétain, and Pershing to decide what to do next, now that the front was becoming fluid for the first time in four years. Their spirits were higher than at any time since the first American troops marched down the Champs-Élysées one year and three weeks earlier. The German offensives were obviously at an end and had been survived. The territory lost in those offensives was being recovered. Everyone was eager to stay on the offensive, to prevent the Germans from forming new defensive lines.

Foch wanted coordinated offensives at three distinct points along the front, to put the Germans under more pressure than they could withstand. The British were to strike in the west, in the area of Amiens, and drive eastward. The

French would start at the Marne and push northward. And a newly constituted American army, under Pershing's command at last, would clear the Germans out of the two-hundred-square-mile salient that had been protruding
like a spear point into the French lines at St. Mihiel since it was first captured
by invading Bavarians back in 1914. The ultimate objective in all cases was to
capture the east-west rail lines, without which the Germans would be unable
to maintain their position in France, and with which the Allies and Americans
would be able to shuttle men, guns, and supplies back and forth along the
front as never before.

Foch's plan was the best news that Pershing had received since taking command of the AEF. The supreme commander was not only acknowledging that
there should be an American army distinct from those of the Allies, but approving the creation of that army *now*. He was not only giving it a mission
equivalent to those of the British and French but giving it exactly the mission
that Pershing had always envisioned. In 1917 Pershing had chosen to position
the AEF where, in the fullness of time, it would be able to attack the St. Mihiel
salient. He had done so for exactly that purpose, because once the salient was
taken, strategically vital targets would be within reach. He foresaw a continued
advance to Metz. The capture of that city's junction of rail lines and roads
would sever the communications arteries on which much of the German position in France depended.

Upon returning to his headquarters, a quietly jubilant Pershing issued the
orders necessary for the creation of an American First Army. Young Lieutenant Colonel George C. Marshall, who had been a captain when he crossed over
to France with Pershing in 1917, was given responsibility for planning. He was
told that seven divisions would be available, six American and one French.
That was a challenge. Seven divisions were barely enough for an attack on just
one side of the salient.

Haig and Pétain were not confident that conditions were quite ripe for offensives on the scale that Foch wanted, but they were willing to go along. Their
confidence was bolstered the day after their meeting, when Ludendorff, in a
foredoomed attempt to escape the inevitable, launched a last attempt to encircle Reims. It failed quickly and completely. Haig and Pétain returned to
their respective headquarters and put their staffs to work on ambitious new
plans.

Pershing was impatient to summon his far-flung divisions back to Lorraine
and prepare them for St. Mihiel, but doing so was not possible quite yet. Some

of them were being used by the French to harry the Germans withdrawing from the Marne. From July 18 to 24 the Twenty-Sixth (Yankee) Division was in the forefront of this pursuit, pressing the German rear guard and under constant fire. During this week, which ended with the Forty-Second (Rainbow) Division taking over, the Twenty-Sixth took four thousand casualties.

The Rainbow found itself not pursuing the Germans but attempting to dislodge them from defensive positions in which they had entrenched themselves along the River Ourq (which the members of an Irish-American battalion from New York called the O'Rourke). Five days and nights of hard fighting finally forced the Germans to resume their retreat, but only after units from the American Fourth and Thirty-Second Divisions joined in. The bravery was extraordinary on both sides; the village of Sergy changed hands seven times in a single day. On July 30 the poet Joyce Kilmer was killed. When an American brigade commander suffered a breakdown, he was replaced by Douglas MacArthur, at age thirty-eight the youngest of a number of AEF colonels recently promoted to brigadier general. MacArthur was continuing his feats of frontline derring-do. By virtue of having won his first star, he now became the only American general to literally, physically lead troops in combat in the Great War. In doing so at the Ourq, he received another Silver Star. By the time the Rainbow Division was relieved on August 2, it had taken 5,500 casualties.

The Germans halted their withdrawal for a second time two days later, digging in this time on high ground overlooking the River Vesle. Two American army corps created by Pershing earlier in the year came together here. The First was commanded by one of the most admired (and also most obese) officers in the U.S. Army, Major General Hunter Liggett. The Third's commanding officer was Robert Lee Bullard, who had commanded at Cantigny and was, in keeping with his name, a southerner and a commander of considerable talent and aristocratic demeanor. Some of their divisions would remain in place at the Vesle for most of the following month. The French general in overall command of the sector left them in a riverside position so exposed to enemy fire that the doughboys came to refer to it as Death Valley.

A new pattern was emerging. Sorry as the state of the German army was, even under the most terrible circumstances its commanders could rely on a hard core to go on fighting to devastating effect. It remained capable of inflicting hard punishment on its advancing foes, not least on the Americans, with their fatal combination of fierce bravery and inexperience.

Background

Eggs Loaded with Dynamite

History repeats itself, Karl Marx tells us, first as tragedy and then as farce.

Regardless of whether one sees America's involvement in the Great War as in any way tragic, the smaller military adventure that followed hard on its heels was definitely farcical—grimly so, and with tragic overtones.

This smaller adventure was put in motion by President Wilson's decision, in 1918 after the Bolshevik seizure of power in Russia, to send American troops into the measureless vastness of Siberia. He insisted that in doing so he was not taking sides in Russia's civil war or intruding into the Russian people's business. If he believed what he said—we can accept that he did, having seen his ability to bathe dubious acts in a self-flattering light—he was wrong.

What he accomplished was a poisoning of relations between the United States and the new Soviet Union for years to come, at frightful cost to the American soldiers he had injected into an impossible mess.

The story can begin on August 2, 1918. On that day American General William S. Graves received what he would call, sardonically, "the most remarkable telegram that has ever emanated from the War Department."

Take the first and fastest train out of San Francisco, the telegram said, *and proceed to Kansas City.*

Graves was stationed at Camp Fremont in northern California at this time, overseeing the training of draftees whom he expected to soon be taking to France as the newly formed Eighth Division. Upon arriving in Kansas City at the end of a two-thousand-mile train ride, he found Secretary of War Newton Baker waiting for him.

The two men were friends. Baker, apologetically, informed Graves that he was to turn around immediately and speed back to Camp Fremont. There he was to make ready to depart for, of all improbable places, the remote far north of Russia. He would take command of what was being named the American Expeditionary Force, Russia. Baker said he was sorry that Graves would not be going to France as he had hoped, but neither he nor Chief of Staff Peyton March had been able to dissuade the president from ordering all this.

Baker gave Graves a sealed envelope. "This contains the policy of the United States in Russia which you are to follow," he said. "Watch your step. You will be walking on eggs loaded with dynamite." With that, he boarded a train bound for Washington and was gone. The envelope, when Graves opened it, contained seven pages of text, typed personally by Woodrow Wilson. They were the president's handmade copy of a memorandum to himself, an aide-mémoire dated July 16, 1918, that he had written after the Supreme War Council at Versailles asked him to join the Allies in sending troops into the maelstrom that Russia had become. In it he laid out his reasons for agreeing and his intention to ask all the participating nations to confirm publicly that they intended no "interference of any kind with the political sovereignty of Russia, any intervention in her internal affairs, or any impairment of her territorial integrity now or hereafter."

As guidance for a soldier being given a nightmare assignment in a distant place of which he knew almost nothing, Wilson's typewritten meditation was essentially useless. But Baker and March had shown good judgment in choosing Graves for the job. From September 1, the day of his arrival at the isolated Siberian port of Vladivostok, he found himself knee-deep in a political, diplomatic, and military snake pit. Contingents from Britain, France, Japan, and several smaller Allied nations were already on the scene, all jostling for advantage and entangling themselves in the murderous ramifications of Russia's civil war.

Graves did not have the option of extricating himself, but he resolved not to get drawn in. He made it his policy to keep himself and his men out of the intrigues and maneuvers swirling all around them, and uninvolved in the resulting atrocities. He had the comfort of knowing that all the top men at the War Department, along with General Bliss at the Supreme War Council in France, shared his disgust. His restraint, good sense, and basic decency would save the United States from being more tainted than it eventually was by participation in an absurd, ugly, and painfully protracted affair.

The purpose of the intervention, as stated by Wilson in his memo, was to secure and keep out of German hands the million tons of war matériel that the Allies had sent to tsarist Russia and was now stockpiled in the ports of Archangel, Murmansk, and Sebastopol, thousands of miles from the European war. The Supreme War Council, in agreeing to such a mission and requesting American participation, had stipulated that no nation should send more than ten thousand troops, so that none could dominate. The British and French were eager to proceed, hopeful less of retrieving lost supplies than of overthrowing the Bolsheviks and getting Russia back into the war. Japan was even more eager and paid no attention to the manpower limit. Ultimately the Japanese would pour eighty thousand troops into Siberia, their purpose being to grab a hefty chunk of the collapsed Russian Empire.

Graves found some three thousand American troops waiting for him at Vladivostok. More than half had been sent from the tropical Philippines, without winter clothing. Hundreds more would land at the port of Archangel a few days later. Many were raw recruits who had had absolutely no training; they were equipped with Russian rifles that had bayonets permanently attached and were so inaccurate that the men said they could shoot around corners. Graves himself, as he later wrote, had "no information as to the military, political, social, economic, or financial situation in Russia." He also had little idea of what he or his men were supposed to be doing. He allowed some to guard railway lines under British supervision. Others guarded the ports, where they found mountains of munitions, food, fuel, automobiles, trucks, machine tools, and steel, copper, and brass. All of it had been delivered by Allied shipping while Russia was still in the war, but never moved to places where it might have done some good.

By October a colorful assortment of soldiers was on the scene: a thousand French, sixteen hundred British, four thousand each from Romania, Serbia, and Canada, and twelve thousand Poles. Numerically they were overwhelmed by the Japanese and, most bizarrely of all, by the 120,000 men of what was called the Czech Legion. This last force, sent to Russia in 1917 to shore up the tsar's battered forces, had been left stranded by the Bolshevik takeover. Now, wanting to get to the Western Front but prevented from leaving by the Bolsheviks, it had taken over much of the Trans-Siberian Railway. Its members were living aboard 190 trains on which they shuttled back and forth, making war on the Bolsheviks and any civilians who threatened to get in their way. They were a tough outfit, always ready for a fight.

Eventually there were nine thousand Americans, too. Though all the foreign troops were officially neutral so far as the civil war was concerned, only the Americans, thanks to General Graves, never became engaged in supporting the Bolsheviks' White Russian rivals. Helping the Whites required a strong stomach and deep reserves of cynicism; they were a savage lot, slaughtering so many Siberians that their "campaign" became something akin to genocide and won many friends for the Bolsheviks. Graves, a decade later, would write that "I am well on the side of safety when I say that the anti-Bolsheviks killed one hundred people in Eastern Siberia, to every one killed by the Bolsheviks." He recalled that the Whites, "in roaming the country like wild animals, killing and robbing the people," were under the protection of the Japanese. He believed that the aim of the Japanese was to create a situation so intolerable and hopeless that the Europeans and Americans would withdraw, leaving them permanently in control.

Cossacks were a significant part of the Siberian population. They were on a killing spree of their own, never attacking the Americans but showing contempt for them. In this mad chaos, Graves could only have kept his men safe by confining them to barracks. That would have been as pointless as their being in Siberia in the first place, and so trouble was inescapable. The first U.S. casualties came in Murmansk only sixteen days after Graves's arrival at Vladivostok, when four Americans were killed and four wounded in a clash with Bolsheviks probably seeking to pillage warehouses.

Things went from bad to worse after that. It is always harder to extract troops from an unstable situation than to inject them in the first place, and so it was not until 1920 that President Wilson ordered a withdrawal, and not until 1922 that the last American was out. The official toll was vanishingly tiny by the standards of the Great War but deplorable nonetheless: 137 Americans killed in action, with another forty-three later dying of their wounds. One hundred and twenty-two died of disease, forty-six of accidental causes. Five committed suicide.

And this tally conceals a terrible possibility. The bodies of nearly 90 percent of the men supposedly killed in action were not found or accounted for. There is reason to suspect that many of them were not killed at all but captured and never allowed to return home.

Chapter 19

An Army at Last

IN WASHINGTON, AS THE SUMMER OF 1918 TURNED TO AUTUMN, even the war was coming to matter less—to seem less urgent, certainly—than the approach of November's midterm elections. Election Day was imminent and real, a certainty that had to be faced. The war, by contrast, had about it something of the infinite. It seemed almost to have been there always, as remote as it was terrible, its eventual end a possibility, a vagueness, a mere hypothesis. No one in the White House or the War Department or on Capitol Hill could imagine that a conflict that had been deadlocked for four years now, that the Germans had appeared to be winning only six months earlier, would be ending in victory by the time the voters went to the polls.

What members of Congress did understand was that the fates of many of them were inextricably entangled in the issues to which the war had given rise. Still unresolved, incredibly, and becoming ever more troublesome as the costs of intervention continued to outstrip constantly rising Treasury Department projections, was the old question of how to pay the bills. The administration continued to propose increased taxes, especially on high personal incomes, business profits, and luxury purchases, and continued to be supported by the progressives. But the House of Representatives was not happy. Its members— all of whom would go before the voters in a few weeks—complained that it would be suicidal to raise taxes so shortly before an election. They complained, too, about President Wilson's insistence that they remain in Washington, completing and passing a revenue bill, while back home other politicians were busily campaigning to take their seats. Democrats were complaining more loudly than the Republicans that they wanted to adjourn and go home.

On May 28 President Wilson had addressed Congress and delivered a sermon on the duty of members to stay in the capital and attend to the nation's business. He already had most of the press on his side in this matter—nothing was easier than to ridicule congressmen for not wanting to do their jobs—and newspaper approval of his speech made adjournment unthinkable. The lawmakers stayed in session, if not cheerfully, and began looking for every excuse to slip homeward for a few days of electioneering. Progress toward passage of the administration's $7 billion revenue bill remained so slow as to be nearly imperceptible.

In his speech Wilson had uttered another of the phrases with which he so often snagged the attention of headline writers and the nation. "Politics is adjourned," he declared. "The election will go to those who think least about it." He meant that voters could be depended upon to reward those who devoted themselves wholeheartedly to their duties, to winning, and paying for, the war. At least one historian has argued that the statement was misunderstood from the start, that Wilson meant it to apply to the passage of the revenue bill only, not to the whole of the war effort, much less to all the government's business. Perhaps that is true, though a reading of the speech does not show it to be unquestionably true. Certainly the president would have had to be naïve to a bizarre extent to imagine a national election free of partisan passion, especially with the country and the Congress as sharply divided—along regional, economic, and ideological lines—as they were at that time.

Misunderstood or not, the "politics is adjourned" catchphrase actually worsened partisanship in 1918, turning it more bitter than it otherwise would have been. Coming in the wake of the things Wilson had said earlier about support of his policies being the acid test of loyalty to the nation, it offended Republicans in and out of Congress. They saw Wilson as purposely putting them in a double bind, simultaneously singling them out for blame and warning them not to try to defend themselves. Democrats were not noticeably happier; many felt that they were being bullied into submission, their chances of reelection jeopardized by the administration's actions, particularly its tax proposals and price controls. Though the current ceiling of $2.20 per bushel was a significant increase over the levels of the years preceding, it angered many western growers and others engaged in the grain trade. Such people had looked forward to reaping a bonanza as demand ran further and further ahead of supply. Now they saw their dreams of quick riches evaporating even as their costs—the price of fertilizers and farm machinery and other essentials, all of them uncontrolled—rose crazily and the producers of such things merrily cashed in. There was also long-standing resentment of the government's failure, thanks to the Bourbons, to cap the price of cotton.

Wilson himself made certain that politics could not be adjourned by involving himself in many of the summer's Democratic state conventions and primary elections. The primaries proved to be a mixed bag. A number of congressmen deemed to have been insufficiently supportive of the war or the administration did lose their bids for renomination, much to the president's satisfaction. But in some instances, White House intervention produced only backlash.

Indiana, because its Democratic and Republican organizations could be depended upon to follow the lead of their respective national parties, became a crucible in which the terms of the national campaign were worked out. At Wilson's instruction, his secretary Joe Tumulty and Postmaster General Burleson drafted a platform for Indiana's Democrats. The president carefully edited their work before sending it on to Indianapolis, where it was adopted without difficulty and set the pattern for Democrats everywhere. It emphasized winning the war to the exclusion of all other priorities, and the consequent importance of giving the president a supportive Congress. So as to leave no doubt on this score, the Democratic National Committee declared the election a referendum on the conduct of the war, "drawing special reference to the leadership of Woodrow Wilson."

Implicit in all this was the now-familiar suggestion that the Republican Party, and many Republican officeholders, were deficient in the kind of loyalty on which victory would depend. Colonel House, reverting to his original role as Wilson's political strategist, thought the Democrats could keep the opposition divided by drawing a distinction between bad Republicans, personified by Theodore Roosevelt, and those good Republicans represented by William Howard Taft. This came to naught, however, when TR and Taft met for the first time in years and announced that they had put their differences behind them. Taft, who had often provided the administration with valuable support and refrained from criticizing it sharply in public, was motivated both by his wish to restore a treasured friendship and by dissatisfaction with such things as the administration's high-cost, low-output military aircraft program. What TR wanted was to heal the divisions in the Republican Party well in advance of the 1920 presidential election, which he intended to win.

Colonel House, meanwhile, was confiding to his diary that Wilson appeared to be planning what no American president had ever attempted: a run for a third term. "I sounded him on another term, and I see evidence of his being a candidate," an entry of August 16 says. "I am opposed to a third term in ordinary circumstances, but after looking over the different possibilities, I have come to believe that it may be necessary for the President to undertake another four years. The end of the war is drawing too near the end of his term to make it possible for him to properly solve the many problems arising at the Peace Conference, and the after war problems which are certain to need wise solutions." A change of presidents would of course deprive the world not only of Wilson's "wise solutions" but of House's as well. There is nothing to suggest that the colonel felt ready for retirement.

The Republicans' Indiana convention, coming two weeks after the Democrats', found the party in an exceptionally combative mood. Delegates did exactly what their Democratic counterparts had done, adopting a platform that would serve as the national party's template through the months remaining until Election Day. It damned Wilson first for not doing more to prepare the nation for war, then for bad management after intervention. Later in the summer this would give the party's national convention its theme, with one element added: the fury of the western states over the cap on the price of wheat.

The Republicans out-Wilsoned Wilson in demanding that the war continue until Germany was utterly crushed. This removed any doubt that the 1918 campaign would be about one thing above all, the leadership of Woodrow Wilson, and that it would be an ugly affair. As *The Washington Post* observed, "Politics is not adjourned, and there is no adjournment in sight."

Even with opposition to the war silenced, political discourse continued to be suffused with bitterness. Congressmen resented the president not only because of his policies but even more because of his contempt for Capitol Hill and his inability or unwillingness to conceal it. In May, under White House pressure and trapped by their complaints about inefficiencies in the war effort, both houses had passed the Overman Act, an administration measure that expanded the president's power by authorizing him to reorganize government agencies without involving Congress. Even many who voted for the act disliked it. They were not mollified when the administration used it to good effect.

Congress showed much greater willingness to cooperate with the White House in handling another administration proposal that became law in May. This was a bill to strengthen and broaden 1917's Espionage Act. It was called the Sedition Act to distinguish it from its predecessor, and it carried the suppression of free speech to new extremes. It was both an expression and an intensification of war fever, so far-reaching that even a bellicose Congress inserted a provision that it would become null when the war ended.

Like the Espionage Act, the Sedition Act drew its power from language so elastic and imprecise as to cover nearly any interpretation a zealous prosecutor or judge might choose to impose upon it. It criminalized the use of "disloyal, profane, scurrilous, or abusive language" in connection with the U.S. government, its flag, and its armed services. It outlawed the saying or doing of "anything, except by way of bona fide and not disloyal advice to an investor or investors, with intent to obstruct the sale by the United States of bonds or other securities." Persons convicted of such acts could be, and not uncommonly would be, given fines amounting to several years of the average American's income and sentenced to years, even decades, in prison.

Senate Republicans, conservatives and progressives alike, provided almost the only congressional opposition to this obviously unconstitutional measure. The Senate passed it by a vote of forty-eight to twenty-six all the same, and the House approved it not so much by a landslide as by an avalanche. Of the 294 votes cast, only one, that of New York socialist Meyer London, was against it.

Even a leading historian with unmistakable admiration for Woodrow Wilson, John Milton Cooper, Jr., has called the measure "the most repressive legislation in American history." It was quickly put to use, with socialists and the scattered remnants of the IWW providing the choicest targets as usual. The Justice Department's success in stripping the IWW of its leadership emboldened it to now target prominent socialists. A big step in this direction came on June 16, when the U.S. Attorney for Northern Ohio slipped quietly into a rally organized by the Ohio State Socialist Council in Canton. He was there to observe a speech by Eugene V. Debs, head of the national Socialist Party. The prosecutor had with him a stenographer who took down Debs's words. Federal agents meanwhile moved through the crowd, demanding to see draft registration cards, spreading unease.

In a long speech studded with familiar leftist rhetoric—capitalism was a dirty system, the war was the work of the capitalists, et cetera—Debs never directed any remarks at potential draftees specifically and never advocated resistance to the Selective Service System. His caution didn't matter. On June 29 he was indicted on ten counts of violating the Espionage Act and the new Sedition Act. At his trial, which soon followed, Debs acknowledged that he had said everything he was accused of saying but denounced the criminalization of such statements as a violation of the Bill of Rights. A jury of men whose average age was seventy, and whose average net worth of approximately $50,000 made them unlikely to have much sympathy for socialists, needed little time to reach a decision. Debs became one of more than 850 Americans convicted of violating the Espionage or Sedition Acts between 1917 and 1919. "I ask no mercy," the felon told the court, "and I plead no immunity." By June he was on his way to the federal penitentiary in Atlanta and the start of a ten-year sentence.

One did not have to be well known, or even an activist, to attract the wrath of the government. In Lansing, Michigan, an ill-fated Mr. Powell made the mistake of complaining to a relative about being pressured to buy a war bond, venting as he did so his skepticism about German atrocities and his belief that the wealthy were responsible for American intervention. The relative did what good citizens were being instructed to do: he reported Powell, who was charged with Sedition Act violations. Finding the whole thing absurd, supposing conviction to be impossible, Powell went to court without a lawyer and was shocked to find himself hit with a fine of ten thousand dollars and a twenty-year prison sentence. Lansing's mayor tried to intervene on Powell's behalf and was himself cited for contempt of court. Powell, breadwinner for a wife and five children, was taken off to serve his sentence. A New Hampshire man who said that "this is a Morgan war and not a war of the people" could consider himself blessed by comparison: he got a mere three years.

The Sedition Act, like the Espionage Act, was an administration initiative from start to finish, prepared in the Justice Department, sent to Congress by the president, and pushed to passage by the White House. If intended to spare the president the awkwardness of congressional hearings into his administration's failure to enforce the Espionage Act even more aggressively than it had, it was cowardly as well as a constitutional monstrosity. Senior Justice Department officials would later defend their actions as a way of preventing a rabid Congress from enacting even worse provisions, and as an attempt to reduce instances of mob violence by persuading prospective vigilantes that the government was doing enough. However unsatisfactory this defense might be, it was, unfortunately, not altogether absurd. By the summer of 1918 much of the country was half out of its mind where the war was concerned. It is not inconceivable that Congress, left to itself, might have undertaken something reminiscent of the French Revolution's Reign of Terror. By the end of the war, 1,597 people would be charged under the Sedition Act—enough, one would think, to satisfy even the most demanding patriots.

In Europe the character of the war was changing dramatically. On August 8 a massive assortment of British, French, Australian, Canadian, and American divisions, supported by six hundred tanks and shoals of heavy artillery, attacked the Germans on both sides of the River Somme just west of Amiens. The result was unprecedented and unexpected even by the man in charge, Sir Douglas Haig. For the first time since the war began, Allied forces achieved a true breakthrough on the Western Front. They quickly advanced nearly ten miles, scattering five German divisions, killing, wounding, or capturing at least 27,000 troops, and gathering up four hundred enemy guns. Ludendorff, in despair, called it "the black day of the history of the German army in the war."

But this success was followed by a fresh lesson in how hard it was to sustain an offensive and consolidate its gains even after a stunningly brilliant start. After that first day, the Germans somehow managed not only to close the hole in their line but to mount a counterattack that recovered much of the lost ground. Thus even this Battle of Amiens ended as Allied offensives always had, with the trench line not greatly changed. War-weary and threadbare as the German troops were, happy to surrender as many had shown themselves to be, they were still not behaving like a defeated army.

The German high command had to decide how to respond to the fact that the Allies now had the initiative. In a series of contentious meetings at his headquarters in Spa, Paul von Hindenburg argued for a general pullback to the safety of the Siegfriedstellung, the Hindenburg Line. Ludendorff refused. A new foreign minister, Admiral Paul von Hintze, was present at the gathering. With shaking hands and tears in his eyes, he urged peace negotiations, to begin as soon as possible. Again Ludendorff refused, and Hindenburg agreed with him, saying there must be no peace overtures until the military situation became more stable.

Nothing was decided except that Hintze, distraught over the accelerating disorder he had left behind in Berlin, was authorized to feel out the queen of the Netherlands about her possible service as a mediator. Nothing would come of this, and so nothing at all changed. Kaiser Wilhelm was present as always, and as usual he had no serious part in the discussions. Even at the beginning of the war, he had complained that "the General Staff tells me nothing and never asks my advice. If people in Germany think that I am the Supreme Commander they are grossly mistaken. I drink tea, saw wood, and go for walks." That was truer than ever as the war approached its climax.

There were new difficulties on the Allied side, too. On August 15, when Foch ordered Haig to mount an attack on a particularly well-defended sector of the front, the British commander in chief refused. Years of being accused of throwing away the lives of his men in futile offensives had rubbed him raw, and he wanted no more of the same. Foch cheerfully backed down, the extent of his authority as supreme commander being ambiguous at best, and the two were able to agree on an attack in Picardy, against less formidable defenses, six days thence. This was preceded on August 20 by another attack by Mangin's Tenth Army, which succeeded this time in forcing the Germans out of Soissons. The capture of the city came just a little too late, however, to trap the last of the troops that Ludendorff was pulling out of the Marne salient. In their haste, the Germans were obliged to leave behind quantities of equipment and supplies that they could ill afford to lose.

Mangin's weary veterans continued to hate him for his aggressiveness—his initiatives made a major contribution to the hundred thousand casualties suffered by the French in the last three weeks of August—and had to be bullied into attacking. The men of the American divisions, by contrast, idolized him for that same aggressiveness. He offered the action that many of them were hungry for. One doughboy told him that at war's end he should travel to the United States, where he was sure to be heaped with honors.

On August 21, the day after Mangin's attack, Haig launched his Picardy offensive. The gains it made were small and unimportant, but it contributed to keeping the Germans under pressure and unable to regroup. Mangin's taking of Soissons, meanwhile, had compromised the Germans' defensive line on the River Vesle, forcing a pullback there. The Americans were thus freed to cross the river and leave Death Valley behind.

The Germans still had 197 divisions in the west, organized into five army groups. These formidable numbers concealed the deplorable state of almost every division. Many had seen too much action in the past four months, and taken too many losses, to be capable of more than standing on the defensive in relatively quiet sectors. Strong and weak divisions alike were now being hit by the second wave of influenza, so much deadlier than the first.

American civilians, accustomed by now to making allowances for the propagandistic nature of the war "news" they were allowed to see, had difficulty knowing what to make of the reports from Europe. Accounts of great defeats being inflicted on the Germans did not seem to be followed by corresponding changes in maps of the front. Readers had seen assurances that the Germans were on the brink of collapse before. In Congress and outside it, the two political parties stayed on plan, inviting voters to judge whether Woodrow Wilson should be rewarded for what he had done thus far and whether to believe his promise to bring the war to a conclusion that would justify the nation's sacrifices.

The Republicans gave an added twist to these questions. To their complaints about mismanagement, they added expressions of fear about the terms on which President Wilson might allow the war to end. Ignoring his more recent comments about the need for force without limit and the extirpation of German tyranny, they reminded voters that this was the man who not so long ago had called for peace without victory. Only the Republicans, they declared, could be depended upon to reject anything short of total victory, unconditional surrender, and a Germany facedown in the wreckage it had made of Europe. With Wilson in charge, they said, peace talks might allow the nefarious Hun to win at the negotiating table what he had failed to win on the field of battle.

On August 23, on the floor of the Senate, Henry Cabot Lodge laid out a ten-point program that was in effect a repudiation of Wilson's Fourteen Points. It called, unmistakably though not in so many words, for the restoration of what Europe had been before the war with one momentous exception: Germany would no longer be one of the leading powers. The things that had made her powerful would be parceled out among the victors and their friends. Things that Wilson regarded as essential to his program—free trade, disarmament, a postwar league of nations—were omitted altogether.

Three days later, speaking before an audience of a hundred thousand people observing the centenary of Illinois's admission to the union, Theodore Roosevelt poured his own brand of scorn on what he called Wilson's "internationalism"—a sorry substitute, he said, for old-fashioned American nationalism. "Professional internationalism stands toward patriotism exactly as free love stands toward a clean and honorable and duty-performing family life," TR said. Republicans across the country took up the cry. The chairman of the party's congressional campaign committee said the election of a Republican Congress was the only way to ensure that Germany would never again threaten world peace.

Widespread demands for total victory (voiced by people who rarely attempted to explain what the term meant) did not prevent venomous infighting. Roosevelt appeared at times to have lost his mental balance altogether, publicly demanding military censorship of the press, trial of dissenters in military courts, and the suppression of all German-language publications. Once a voice of sanity where mob violence was concerned, he now praised the acts of vigilantes and urged the ostracism of conscientious objectors. Perhaps he had been driven over some psychic edge by the death in combat of his beloved youngest son, the one he said was most like him. A fledgling fighter pilot, twenty years old and wildly in love with the beautiful heiress who was his fiancée, Lieutenant Quentin Roosevelt had had one kill to his credit when he was shot down over France on July 14.

When Pershing informed Washington that he was going to need eighty divisions by April 1919, the War Department calculated that to accomplish this, the number of soldiers sent overseas each month would somehow have to be trebled. Few questioned the objective even if no one knew how to meet it, but the air turned purple with vituperation all the same. Those who opposed the drafting of teenagers (a step made necessary by the lavishness with which local boards were handing out deferments) were accused of wanting peace without victory, which now ranked as equivalent to treason. A former mayor of Atlanta caught the spirit of the time when, at the end of a public flag-kissing ceremony (such things were held with increasing frequency), he told his audience that "hereafter disloyalists might expect to be branded on the forehead and on either cheek, and the rope would be the end of traitors, in legal process of law or otherwise." The enthusiasm with which such comments were everywhere received heightened TR's confidence that his own preachments were going to carry him back to the White House in 1920.

The Wilson administration, not to be outdone, followed September's Labor Day weekend with the largest of its so-called slacker raids. Some two thousand armed soldiers and sailors and an assortment of federal agents, local police, and volunteers from the American Protective League spent three days scouring New York City and northern New Jersey, accosting any male who appeared to be of conscription age. More than fifty thousand were taken into custody upon being unable to present draft cards. A thousand of them were immediately inducted into the army, and fifteen thousand were reported to their draft boards for irregularities of various kinds. The others were set free—not, however, before being put through a day and night of humiliating and sometimes frightening experiences, and not until a fair amount of public outrage had been provoked.

It was the bad luck of the Justice Department and the Bureau of Investigation to have their dragnet witnessed by people of influence. Joseph Sherman Freylinghuysen, a Republican senator from New Jersey, was one. He reported seeing "soldiers armed with rifles, with bayonets fixed, hold up citizens, compel them to stand waiting while there were crowds around jeering at them, and when they failed to produce their registration cards were put in motor trucks and driven through the streets amid the jeers and scoffs of the crowd." He said they were held in armories with no opportunity to contact relatives and thereby obtain proof of their innocence. A Democratic senator from New York, William M. Calder, said that "in one place I saw a street car stopped and an armed sailor go into the car and take men out of it, in some cases where they were escorting ladies. They were taken out of their places of business and crowded into vans, perhaps fifty or sixty packed in like sardines and sent to the police station houses." There is no way of knowing how many actual draft evaders there may have been. Estimates run as high as three million.

Those Americans who had already been inducted, gone through basic training, and been sent to France remained the objects of an international tug-of-war. On August 30 Ferdinand Foch, recently made a marshal of France, called on Pershing at his headquarters and announced a change of plans. The St. Mihiel attack was to be sharply reduced in scale so that most of Pershing's new army could be diverted elsewhere. American divisions would form the right wing of a French advance northward along the River Meuse and in the Argonne Forest. These things had been proposed to Foch by Sir Douglas Haig, whose view of the Allies' prospects had been greatly brightened by his breakthrough at Amiens earlier in the month.

Having believed at the start of 1918 that there should be no Allied offensives that year, Haig now thought that much might be accomplished before winter. He proposed two massive and nearly simultaneous offensives, one by the British with Mézières as its objective, the other by a Franco-American force aiming for Sedan. The capture of these objectives would sever the communications arteries on which the German forces in France depended, leaving them with no choice except to retreat. Foch liked this plan and agreed with Haig that it made Pershing's proposed advance on Metz through the St. Mihiel salient unnecessary and even pointless. The Americans would be far more useful as part of the French advance.

Foch is unlikely to have been surprised by Pershing's angry rejection of the whole idea.

"I must insist," Foch said.

"Marshal Foch, you may insist all you please," Pershing replied. "But I decline absolutely to agree to your plan. While our army will fight wherever you may decide, it will not fight except as an independent American army." He knew, and showed Foch a letter proving, that he had the support of President Wilson.

The dispute continued for three days, with General Pétain being drawn in and generally supporting Pershing. Finally a compromise was reached. The attack on St. Mihiel would go ahead as planned, its size not reduced, but the sector of front for which the AEF was responsible would be extended northward to the Argonne Forest. Immediately upon securing the salient, the whole American attack force with its six hundred thousand troops was to shift to the west and north and advance up the Meuse River valley. It would be to the east of the French attack force, advancing with it but in no way subordinate to it. This was a victory for Pershing, but in winning it on Foch's terms he committed his staff and his troops to launching two distinct offensives, separated by sixty miles of ruggedly hilly terrain, in two weeks. He was coming perilously close to promising the impossible.

But not quite. Again the planning burden fell on Lieutenant Colonel George Marshall and his small operations staff. Even before Foch's visit, Marshall had been struggling to complete arrangements for the assault on St. Mihiel and encountering difficulties that might have driven a less capable man mad. His original plan had had to be extensively revised when the number of divisions to be involved was increased from seven to ten. Then he was told to plan for fourteen, finally for twenty-two (six of them French, made available by General Pétain). With each increase, the whole approach had to be rethought, the support system reconfigured. Twenty-two divisions made the operation massive, an invasion of the salient from two sides involving nearly half a million U.S. and French troops, 3,000 artillery pieces, and 1,500 aircraft, many of them provided by Pétain. The logistics challenge was correspondingly daunting, requiring first the assembly, then the transporting under combat conditions, of 50,000 tons of ammunition and 200,000 tons of other matériel.

Marshall was aware that his future was on the line. He knew, as everyone on the First Army's staff did, that Pershing had no compunction about ordering promising young officers to do what could not be done in the time provided or with the resources available, then destroying their chances for advancement when they failed. Marshall would write later that the history of the AEF was marred by the "personal tragedies" of the men to whom this happened. His own situation was doubly irksome because this planning assignment had required him to pass up an opportunity to take command of a regiment and be promoted to full colonel.

Fortunately for everyone involved, Marshall was more than merely a promising young officer. He was a miracle of competence, and he handled the burden that Pershing had laid upon him in a way that presaged his rise to chief of staff of the army twenty-one years later, secretary of state eight years after that, then secretary of defense and recipient of the Nobel Peace Prize.

The St. Mihiel offensive, beautifully executed though it was, proved to be the great anticlimax of the war. When it kicked off on September 12, the 448,000 troops of eleven American and French divisions advanced against 75,000 defenders. Not only were the Germans vastly outnumbered, but they were members of fourth-rate, worn-out units that had been sent to St. Mihiel because it was considered safe. And they were caught off balance, midway through a planned withdrawal about which the Americans had known nothing. Their response to the attack was not to try to stop it but to hurry to complete their shift to the sector of the Hindenburg Line that ran along the eastern edge of the salient. To the extent that they resisted, they did so not to hold their ground but to keep their withdrawal from degenerating into a rout.

The Americans were fortunate to be up against such a halfhearted defense. A German noncommissioned officer, writing home at this time, said that his men were "so embittered that they have no interest in anything, and they only want the war to end, no matter how." Among them were survivors of the savage fight with Colonel McAlexander's regiment weeks earlier. Some were so eager to surrender that at times the offensive took on a comic aspect. When Lieutenant Maury Maverick of Texas, alone and on horseback, inadvertently ran into a platoon of German troops, he expected to be shot to pieces. Instead the Germans threw down their weapons and put up their hands. Maverick, who had ridden out in search of a route for bringing ammunition forward, had no time for escorting prisoners. He pointed in the direction of the American rear and told his captives to go there. They begged him not to abandon them, saying that if they were left without an escort, other Americans would shoot them. Maverick was moved to pity—some of the Germans were mere boys, crying—and did as they asked.

Sergeant Harry Adams, when he saw a German soldier run into a dugout, fired the last two rounds in his pistol through the closed door and shouted for the man to come out. The door opened and several Germans emerged, followed by more and then still more, all of them surrendering and addressing Adams as *Kamerad, Kamerad.* In the end, the sergeant and his empty revolver took more than three hundred prisoners.

As soon as the salient was secured, Brigadier General Douglas MacArthur raced off by automobile in the direction of Metz, still a tantalizing possible objective. He went all the way to the city's outskirts, far enough to see that it was undefended. He radioed headquarters, asked Pershing for permission to take possession, and was told to get back where he belonged. "I made a mistake," he said later. "I should have taken Metz and *then* asked his permission."

The Americans took sixteen thousand prisoners that day and captured 450 guns. That they took seven thousand casualties in doing so probably says less about the defense than about the mistakes of inexperienced troops—a failure to make use of available cover, and a tendency to cluster together and advance directly against enemy machine guns rather than working around the flanks.

Though the American and Allied newspapers reported a great victory, what had happened was barely a major engagement in terms of its costs. As the First Army began its ponderous shift to the Meuse-Argonne, struggling against the clock to get its masses of men and masses of artillery and ammunition and supplies properly positioned, it had not yet been really tested.

The test was, however, at hand.

Background

"A Soldier's Soldier"

It used to be said, back when wars could seem glorious and glamorous and had clear beginnings and ends, that a man could have "a good war." This was said of soldiers who saw plenty of action and had escapades that could be turned into dinner party stories, won their share of promotions and medals, wound up on the winning side, and returned home either unscathed or marked just enough to create an air of distinction.

American doughboys had a better chance of having a good war than the soldiers of other nations. By the time they went into combat in great numbers, the long-frozen Western Front was beginning to break up. No Americans had to spend years huddled in rat-infested trenches hoping that death wouldn't crash down on them in the form of a German shell or come creeping in a cloud of poison gas. Not only was theirs a war of movement, but they were moving against exhausted, outnumbered, outgunned, and starving enemy troops.

Some Americans had very good wars indeed. Some even became legends. Probably the most celebrated example was Alvin York, who was drafted out of the Tennessee hill country at age twenty-nine after unsuc-

Sergeant Alvin York, U.S. Army
Denied conscientious objector status, he went on to win the Congressional Medal of Honor.

cessfully filing for conscientious objector status. Among his many decorations was a Congressional Medal of Honor, awarded for an action of October 8, 1918, in which he was credited with killing twenty Germans and putting dozens of enemy machine guns out of action. He also was lauded for single-handedly taking 132 prisoners, but this happened just a month before the end of the war, when many German soldiers were looking for a chance to put up their hands. Be that as it may, exploits like Alvin York's were celebrated back home as proof of just how superior "our boys" were to the despicable Hun—and to Europeans generally. York's ultimate accolade was to be played by movie star Gary Cooper in the Hollywood version of his story.

No one, however, had a better First World War than a man who would be one of the giants of the Second. An adventure story based on Douglas MacArthur's experiences in 1917 and 1918 would be laughed off as too far beyond belief. So would any fictional character based faithfully on MacArthur the man.

Good wars ran in the family. MacArthur's father, Arthur, joined the U.S. Army during the Civil War while still a schoolboy and went on to win the Medal of Honor for leading his men uphill against entrenched Confederate troops at Missionary Ridge. At the war's end in 1865, he was still only nineteen years old and famous as the "boy colonel." He then reverted to being a mere captain in the peacetime army. It was not until 1889 that he received his next promotion: he and his wife and sons spent that long quarter-century at dreary posts in Pennsylvania, New York, Utah, Louisiana, Arkansas, and New Mexico (where the one-time teenage colonel, now a forty-year-old captain, took part in the war with Geronimo's Apaches). Douglas, the youngest member of the family, would one day write, "I learned to ride and shoot even before I could read or write—indeed, almost before I could walk and talk."

By 1903, the year Douglas graduated first in his class from the U.S. Military Academy at West Point, Arthur had had another good war. His performance in the Spanish-American War had vaulted him first to brigadier general and major general of volunteers, then, more important, to brigadier general in the regular army. By 1901 he was a regular army major general and military governor of the Philippines. In the following years he became the army's only lieutenant general, but in 1906 he was passed over for chief of staff because of the opposition of Secretary of

War William Howard Taft, with whom he had clashed when Taft headed the civil government of the Philippines.

Douglas, by virtue of the eminence his father had finally achieved and his own superlative record first at West Point and then in the Philippines, was from the start of his career a member of the army's innermost elite. By the time of America's entry into the Great War, he was a thirty-seven-year-old major on the staff of army headquarters in Washington, incomparably well connected and with a reputation for dash and daring. Early in his career he had gone to the Russo-Japanese War and seen much of Asia as an aide to his father. From 1906 to 1908 he was an assistant to President Roosevelt.

He was never hesitant to make use of his status as a prince among junior officers. His father, then retired, died of a heart attack in 1912, and in 1913 the unmarried Captain MacArthur wangled an assignment in Washington so that his mother, who was in his care, could be near the Walter Reed Army Hospital. (A decade earlier, during her son's years as a West Point cadet, Mrs. MacArthur had lived in a hotel overlooking the academy's grounds.) In 1914 he got himself assigned to the expedition dispatched by President Wilson to Veracruz, Mexico. The commander of that operation, Frederick Funston, had been a protégé of Arthur MacArthur's, and had been nominated by him for the Medal of Honor he received for capturing the leader of the Philippine insurgency.

Captain Douglas MacArthur got his own first nomination for a Medal of Honor in Mexico. Upon deciding that locomotives were needed to support the base established by the Americans at Veracruz, he set out with a small party to steal three of them. He was successful, but the train ride back to Funston's headquarters turned into a running gun battle in which MacArthur shot several attackers with his revolver and got bullet holes in his shirt. The committee that reviewed his nomination decided not to award him the medal because he had undertaken the raid without the knowledge of his superiors. Members feared that rewarding such conduct might encourage other junior officers to embark on ill-judged adventures of their own.

When the United States went to war in 1917, then-Major MacArthur proposed to Secretary of War Baker the creation of a division made up of National Guard units from across the country. This Forty-Second Division, soon famous as the Rainbow Division, was commanded by a major general, but MacArthur became its chief of staff and immediately moved up two ranks to temporary colonel.

The Forty-Second, because it was made up largely of men with some military training, was one of the first four divisions sent to France. When after months of waiting the division was finally sent to the front, MacArthur began doing things that staff officers were expected never to do, starting with his nighttime raids on enemy trenches. He made himself colorful, removing the metal grommets from his hat to give it a slouch, never wearing a helmet except when it rained, going into No Man's Land without a weapon, wearing a seven-foot scarf knitted by his mother and a bulky wool sweater displaying the big letter *A* he had earned playing baseball at West Point. One night he was arrested by soldiers from a different division who thought this odd character must be some bizarre kind of enemy spy.

He won his first Silver Star in February, and his first Distinguished Service Cross not long afterward. By war's end, he would have two of the latter and seven of the former. In June 1918 he was the youngest by far of a number of colonels promoted to brigadier general—presumably the letters his mother had written to General Pershing and Secretary Baker urging his promotion were not a factor—and was commanding a brigade with his usual bravado.

From the time of Ludendorff's spring offensives onward, the Rainbow was in heavy combat, taking many casualties. Though MacArthur was always in the thick of things and usually in the lead, he seemed untouchable. One night a raiding party he was leading was pinned down by artillery fire. When the barrage lifted, he moved among his men, shaking them, telling them to wake up because it was time to move on. No one responded. He was the only one still alive.

During the attack on the St. Mihiel salient, another future legend, George S. Patton, crossed paths with MacArthur on open ground. The two stood talking as explosions from enemy artillery drew closer. Patton wanted to take cover but felt he could not do so with MacArthur standing there, calmly talking. The barrage passed over them safely, and Patton later called MacArthur "the bravest man I ever met."

To the AEF's headquarters staff, MacArthur was a glory-seeking show-off and an interfering, string-pulling nuisance. Pershing himself was annoyed when MacArthur, going over his head, wrote to Secretary Baker and got a reversal of plans to break up the Rainbow Division and distribute its troops among understrength divisions. Nor was he impressed by MacArthur's frontline heroics. He complained that "the days for brigadier generals to rush forward in the firing line waving their hats and yelling 'Come on, boys!' are in actual warfare at least a thing of the past." It was for this reason, apparently, that he refused to endorse the Medal of Honor nomination that would come to MacArthur for his actions during the Meuse-Argonne offensive.

The stern Pershing was also offended by MacArthur's irregular dress and indifference to spit and polish. To the fighting men who served with and under him, however, MacArthur was both a genuine hero and a respected, even loved leader. The fact that he had been twice wounded and twice gassed, in one instance requiring hospitalization for two weeks, carried great weight with his troops. So did MacArthur's treatment of them. "With us he was a soldier's soldier," a Rainbow Division veteran would recall. "He talked beautiful then just like he did later, but there was no ego in him. He was natural and friendly, though he insisted on the attitude of a soldier from all of us. His first thought was always for the soldier, looking out for supplies, trying to check frozen feet and trench foot, getting hot food to them in the line and taking care of everything. I was near him for a year and a half and he never did anything wrong as a soldier."

Even Pershing, who once threw MacArthur out of his office for refusing to stop arguing for something he wanted ("Out! Get out and stay out!"), yielded in the end to the undeniable fact that this was an officer of extraordinary gifts. He approved his appointment as commander of the Rainbow Division and recommended him for promotion to major general. That promotion never went through, because the war ended first. Upon returning home, MacArthur was slated to revert to his regular army rank of major. Before that happened, however, fate and the War Department smiled on him once again. He was appointed superintendent of West Point. That was a brigadier general's post, so he got to keep his star.

Chapter 20

In at the Kill

EASY VICTORIES ARE GOOD FOR GREEN ARMIES, PROVIDING EXPERI-
ence without exacting too painful a price, helping to build confidence. St.
Mihiel, however, may have been too easy to be of much use. It certainly provided no forewarning of what the Americans were going to encounter upon
launching their offensive into the Argonne Forest and up the valley of the
Meuse, where the enemy was determined to hold his ground. What lay ahead
was the last great convulsion of the Great War, a fight in which the tenacity of
the German defenders combined with the mistakes of the Americans to produce horrendous losses and a sadly ambiguous though indisputably decisive
victory.

The Battle of Meuse-Argonne began for the Americans with the same high
hopes that the British and French commanders had felt earlier in the war
when launching their first doomed offensives. And they had reason for optimism. The attacking force would include ten American divisions, more than a
quarter of a million well-equipped combat troops with more than 200,000
more in reserve. It would face at most 125,000 defenders belonging to divisions that were understrength and rated as of middling quality or worse by the
German military authorities. The advance would take place across a twenty-
four-mile section of front, supported by staggering masses of artillery: nearly
150 guns for every mile. Enough aircraft were on hand to guarantee control of
the skies.

With so much force at his disposal, Pershing is perhaps not to be faulted for
making the Germans' main defensive line, the Kriemhildestellung (a name
taken from German legend), his objective for the first day of the attack, September 26. That was ten miles distant, absurdly ambitious by the standards of

the past but not unreasonable if judged by what had happened at St. Mihiel. The ultimate objective, the four-track railway that connected Metz to Lille in the west, was twenty-four miles from the offensive's starting point. It was a great prize, one that if taken could seal the Germans' fate. The First Army could advance much more slowly than it had at St. Mihiel and still cut the rail line in under a week.

Again following the pattern of the Allied armies earlier in the war, Pershing's timetable became irrelevant almost as soon as his troops set out across No Man's Land. They did not start until the enemy's forward position had been saturated with high explosives, shrapnel, and gas, but the Germans were defending ground that they had held since 1915 and that their engineers had turned into a hornet's nest of stoutly built and interconnected trenches, dugouts, and pillboxes. There were four defensive lines, each designed to make maximum use of a hilly landscape studded with woods and cut with deep ravines. Machine gun emplacements were everywhere, positioned so as to lay down overlapping fields of fire. From various high points, artillery spotters were able to direct the fire of batteries concealed by camouflage from the Allies' aircraft.

Advancing against all this was like picking a fight with a buzz saw. In the space of a few days, after never advancing at much more than a crawl, Pershing's lead divisions bogged down in a state not far from disorder. Dirt roads became almost impassable as the rains of autumn turned them to mud. All forms of transport were in short supply, partly because the Allies' insistence on maximum transatlantic shipments of soldiers had limited the import of motor vehicles and animals, partly because horses and mules promised by the French were never delivered. It became impossible to move the artillery or even the ammunition. The whole supply system seized up. The frontline troops had to fight on without food and relied for water on what fell from the sky.

Furious with frustration, desperate for a breakthrough, Pershing issued an order for all officers up and down the line to stay on the offensive "without regard to losses and without regard to the exposed conditions of the flanks." This degree of aggressiveness, of apparent indifference to the rate at which lives were being expended, had rarely been displayed except by the likes of Butcher Mangin or Britain's Haig at the height of his ambition. It was also all too typical of Pershing. Such to-the-last-man tactics, when imposed on troops not facing a high-stakes crisis in which even temporary withdrawal might mean ruin, bordered on irresponsibility. In a campaign like Meuse-Argonne, where the worst Pershing had to fear was not reaching excessively ambitious objectives, his approach deprived officers in direct contact with the enemy of essential flexibility. He appears to have been prepared to pay whatever price in lives was required to show the world that *his* army, the one that *he* had built, was invincible at every moment and in every circumstance. This is one reason why, in spite of his managerial competence, Pershing has never been considered one of history's, or even one of the First World War's, great generals. The severity of his first order, the difficulties that it created, undoubtedly made necessary another that shortly followed—the one authorizing officers to shoot any man who tried to run away.

By October 1 the situation had deteriorated to such a point that orders to fight on could accomplish nothing. The doughboys had advanced perhaps four miles at their farthest points of penetration, and were now stuck in place. In the four days ending on September 29, the First Army had taken 45,000 casualties, putting the start of their campaign among the costliest of the war. The commander of the First Corps, Hunter Liggett, estimated that 100,000 men had become detached from their units and were wandering aimlessly in the rear, adding to the confusion and congestion. More soldiers had to be evacuated because of influenza than because of wounds. More than 70,000 flu victims would be hospitalized by the time the fight ended, and thousands of them would die.

These problems were almost minor in comparison with those of the Germans. Not only were they hard-pressed in all sectors in the west, they were facing disaster in other theaters of the war. Late in September a French army that had long been bottled up in Salonika in Greece began advancing northward against Bulgaria. The Bulgarians asked Berlin for help and were told that none was possible. In short order they were out of the war, as was the Ottoman Empire as a result of British victories in the Middle East. With the remains of Austria-Hungary's armies barely capable even of defending themselves, the Germans found themselves open to attack from the southeast. By September 28 Ludendorff, now little more than a nervous wreck, had finally looked squarely at the facts and seen what they meant. It was over. He went to Kaiser Wilhelm and the kaiser's relative by marriage Prince Max of Baden, the liberal nobleman who had just been installed as chancellor at the insistence of an increasingly rebellious Reichstag. He told them that Germany's only hope was an armistice, a suspension of hostilities. One had to be arranged immediately.

The kaiser was incredulous. Twice in the previous six months, first after Operation Michael and then after the Noyon-Montdidier offensive, he had boasted that he would soon be in Paris. The Treaty of Brest-Litovsk had made him master of Russia and the whole of eastern Europe. And now it was necessary to sue for a cease-fire? How could that be? Prince Max was shocked for a different reason. He had long been an advocate of a negotiated settlement, and had agreed with Bethmann's opposition to unrestricted submarine warfare. But now he was taken aback by Ludendorff's naïveté, his belief that an armistice could be arranged virtually overnight.

But Ludendorff was adamant. Speed was essential; Germany's defenses might collapse at any hour, and at home civil order was disintegrating. And so Prince Max got to work, preparing a note addressed not to the Allies or to the United States but to Woodrow Wilson only. He hoped that the president, the man who had once spoken of peace without victory and later shared with the world his Fourteen Points, would be easier to deal with than the British or the French. Three days later, on October 1, the note was delivered to the government of neutral Switzerland for forwarding to Washington. It informed Wilson that Germany was prepared to accept a cessation of hostilities and discuss a permanent settlement based on his Fourteen Points. Four more days passed before it reached the president's hands.

It was also on October 1 that Pershing, with extreme reluctance but eminent good sense, suspended all combat operations to provide time for restoring order, getting supply lines sorted, and figuring out how to resume the attack. His rage was fed by the knowledge that the French on his left, and beyond them the British, were advancing almost smoothly. That they were more experienced, and had not been obliged to hurry into action immediately after completing anything like the St. Mihiel operation, did nothing to ease his chagrin. Neither did the fact that the Allies were fighting on easier terrain where the Germans were more willing to retreat because they could do so without jeopardizing anything as crucial as the Lille-Metz rail line. What mattered was that the French and British *appeared*—at least to Pershing—to be outperforming the Americans. That he found intolerable.

The revelation that Germany was looking to end the fighting, supposedly on terms that he himself had laid out, complicated President Wilson's situation. For almost a year and a half now, he had focused almost exclusively on the great task of winning the war and on enforcing loyalty to that end. Doing these things had carried him a long way from his prewar advocacy of peace without victory, but the single-mindedness with which he pursued them reduced his differences with the Allies to a manageable level. As an end to the fighting became a real possibility, however, those differences became a challenge and a problem. They were going to give the Republicans new opportunities to accuse him of being soft.

He needed to make a public display of toughness, and did so on the evening of September 27. His witnesses were New York City's social and financial elite, assembled at the Metropolitan Opera House to mark the start of a fourth Liberty Loan drive. It was a festive occasion: the government's reliance on borrowing rather than taxes was good news for the elites of every city, and the president's presence added a gala touch. He told them what many and perhaps most Americans wanted to hear in the autumn of 1918: that "there can be no peace obtained by any kind of bargain or compromise with the governments of the Central Empires" because those governments "have convinced us that they are without honor and do not intend justice." In short, when the war ended, it would do so on terms imposed by the United States and the Allies. And those terms would mean the end of militaristic Germany.

These words were received rapturously by the ladies and gentlemen who filled the opera house that night, and the next morning the press celebrated them. Little attention was paid, however, to other things the president had said, things about the need for a league of nations, things that Colonel House for one had hoped would be seen as the real point of the speech. House, in the audience as Wilson spoke, had noted the audience's hunger for a vengeful peace and its interest in nothing else, and he was disappointed and concerned. It was becoming apparent, now that an end to the war approached, that years of anti-German propaganda and suppression of even mildly neutral opinion had created a monster—one that stood between the president and the kind of postwar world he had always said he wanted. That monster was a climate of public opinion in which no settlement could seem acceptable if it did not only punish the Central Powers but eliminate them where possible and at a minimum cripple them permanently. It was a spirit of unreasoning hatred, and already it was making House uncomfortable.

The president, who was as responsible as anyone for creating that spirit, did not see what House saw. He heard the applause, paid little attention to which of his words were applauded most loudly, and was satisfied that the speech had been a triumph. He was by this point so isolated from almost everyone except his own family and less than a handful of intimates that his knowledge of what was happening even in Congress was dangerously limited. He appears to have been blind to the clamor for unconditional surrender, or unconcerned if he saw it. As he responded to the German offer, and it became known that he was once again exchanging diplomatic notes with Berlin—echoes of the unhappy days after the sinking of the *Lusitania*—the Republicans erupted. It appeared to them, not entirely without reason, that his acts were out of step with his words.

A Republican senator from Washington, Miles Poindexter, proposed making it a crime for the president to communicate with the German government. Even in the autumn of 1918, that idea was too outlandish to go anywhere, but it was very much in the spirit of the time. The man who best expressed that spirit was once again the irrepressible Theodore Roosevelt. He was on a barnstorming tour of the western states, ostensibly to promote war bond sales (which were not going well) but also repeating his demand for an American army of ten million men and laying the foundations of a run for the White House. He lambasted everything from Wilson's League of Nations idea to the alleged pro-Germanism of the Nonpartisan League.

There was reason to wonder if any kind of meaningful league of nations was politically feasible. The Allied governments had never been more than mildly and vaguely tolerant of the idea. Now, with victory certain, they wondered if it remained necessary to humor the Americans. David Lloyd George was saying aloud what he had always believed: that freedom of the seas made no sense for Britain, regardless of how high it ranked among the Fourteen Points. That the starvation blockade was at odds with international law was of no consequence when measured against the fact that it had helped to win the war. To surrender such an advantage, the prime minister said, would be folly. Wilson saw Lloyd George's position as a betrayal, an insult. He had acquiesced in the blockade with the understanding—which existed in his mind only—that once the war was over Britain would agree that no such thing should ever be done again. Now he was being repaid with ingratitude. The French were less forthright in stating their opinion of the Wilsonian vision, but not even Wilson himself could believe that they had much enthusiasm for it.

Clearly the postwar world was going to be loaded with problems. Among the worst of them—but of no interest to those who expected an unconditional German surrender to turn the whole world into a New Jerusalem—was the state of the German homeland. Though Ludendorff's armies continued to stand up under the hammer blows of the Allied and American forces, east of the Rhine society was coming apart. Rebellion was breaking out in city after city, along with a naval mutiny. The shortsighted in London, Paris, and Washington could take delight in this, say it was only what the Hun deserved. Others found it a worrisome replay of what had happened in Russia a year earlier. If the crushing of Germany led to the emergence of another Bolshevik regime, if it made Germany an ally of the Communists to their east, the result could be more years of nightmare.

On October 4, satisfied that the most disabling of his army's problems had been brought under control, Pershing restarted the Meuse-Argonne advance. But the Germans, too, had had three days for recovery, and for adjusting their defenses. As more American divisions arrived on the scene and were fed to the enemy machine guns, ground was gradually and bloodily taken. But with every new day, a little more momentum was lost. On October 12, deciding that the growing size of his army made it unmanageable, Pershing put a new command structure in place. He gave the First Army to Hunter Liggett and created, out of the divisions on the east side of the Meuse, a Second Army under Robert Lee Bullard. He himself became a kind of generalissimo, his position analogous to Haig's with the British Expeditionary Force and Pétain's with the armies of France. With this change, the campaign became more focused if no less bloody. Pershing, Liggett, and Bullard made preparations for yet another new start on October 14.

There were now two major obstacles between Pershing and his objectives: a pair of high, strongly defended ridges, the Côte Dame Marie and the Côte de Châtillon, with commanding views of the surrounding terrain. On October 11 the Forty-Second Division, the Rainbow, was returned to the front line as replacement for the Big Red One, which had suffered severe casualties on the cutting edge of the offensive. The Rainbow was at this time part of V Corps, commanded by General Charles Summerall, and was to take the lead in the attack on the ridges. Its Eighty-Fourth Brigade was commanded by Douglas MacArthur.

Summerall was an almost ruthlessly aggressive general—the *almost* may be unmerited. He was unwilling to accept anything less than success at any price, and therefore he had risen steadily under Pershing's approving eye. On the Eighty-Fourth Brigade's first night on the line, he paid its headquarters an unexpected visit.

"Give me Châtillon, MacArthur," Summerall said, "or a list of five thousand casualties."

MacArthur was just the man to receive such an order. "If this brigade does not capture Châtillon," he said, "you can publish a casualty list of the entire brigade, with the brigade commander's name at the top."

What followed over the next few days was characteristic of MacArthur and of the Meuse-Argonne campaign. He personally conducted a reconnaissance of the approaches to the Côte de Châtillon and found its defenses weak on the flanks. He decided to work around the German left and on October 13 personally led the attempt. Four days of brutal combat followed, with the Americans losing men at a barely sustainable rate but continuing to force their way uphill. By the time they seized the high ground on October 16, they had taken three thousand casualties. One of MacArthur's battalions had begun the fight with 1,475 officers and men and at the end had 306 still in action. A day later the Eighty-Fourth was relieved and returned to the rear, mission accomplished.

That was how it went, day after day and week after week. Pershing accepted no excuses and cast aside those who failed to advance. The pressure to perform penetrated downward through the ranks, falling at last, and with full force, on the backs of the privates. The British and French had operated in much this same way early in the war, or had tried to until forced to see that such an approach was more than mortal men could bear. But the Americans had unprecedented advantages in the autumn of 1918. Their numerical superiority was so great, and growing almost daily, that it was unusual for any unit to have to spend more than several consecutive days in contact with the enemy. This made it possible to maintain relentless pressure on a German army that had little food, no air cover, and few reserves. Even with all their advantages, the doughboys might not have been able to keep attacking while taking so many casualties if they had not been making progress. It always proved possible to force the Germans back just a little farther. That kept feelings of futility at bay.

For most, anyway. On October 10 an AEF officer, Captain D. A. Henkes, sent a letter to the office of the secretary of war asking for release from the army. He had made a similar request before leaving the United States for France, explaining that his father was a native of Germany, they had many relatives and friends in Germany, and being actively engaged in war with them was agony for him. "If my services will not be dispensed with," he had written, "I would suggest duty in another field." That first letter had made no difference: Henkes was sent to France, where he performed his assigned duties but could not shake off the sense of torment. The second letter made a very great difference. He was arrested, court-martialed, and sentenced to twenty-five years' hard labor at Fort Leavenworth.

The surviving officers of MacArthur's Eighty-Fourth Brigade, once in the rear, were instructed to nominate men who they thought had earned the Congressional Medal of Honor. Their commander received more votes than anyone else, so his name headed the list sent to Pershing's headquarters. Most of the nominees were approved, but not MacArthur's. Pershing gave him another Distinguished Service Cross instead and recommended him for a second star.

When the Germans were also driven off the Côte Dame Marie, the way was cleared for a somewhat speedier advance. American casualties had risen to 75,000, but Pershing now had a million men in the fight, an irresistible force pushing day and night against the movable object that the German army had become.

Prince Max of Baden's note of October 1 had by this time proved to be the start of an exchange of messages between the White House and Berlin. President Wilson pressed for proof that the Germans were serious, and for evidence—it is difficult to know what such evidence might be—that he was dealing with parties who spoke not just for the kaiser's regime but for the German nation. Meanwhile the Republicans, with their eyes on an election that was just a few weeks away, were accusing him of waging war by correspondence and undercutting the men on the front. Such criticism kept Wilson mindful of the need to be cautious and to agree to nothing until the Germans yielded to his demands. This was wise not only in terms of domestic politics but because Ludendorff was in fact hoping not for an end to the war but for a pause that would permit him to rest his troops and get them into defensible positions.

On October 12, the day Germany sent off a second note, a U-boat sank a steamer crossing the Irish Sea with the loss of more than four hundred lives. Wilson's next note not only demanded a cessation of submarine warfare—the Germans hastened to agree—but informed Berlin that the terms of any armistice would be set neither by him alone nor by him in consultation with the heads of the Allied governments, but by the commanders of the American, British, and French forces in Europe. This was another clever stroke. It put an end to German hopes of not having to deal with Britain and France at all, and it gave the Republicans in Congress less to criticize. In other respects Wilson was not being clever at all. He was making no effort to consult with the leaders of Congress or even to keep them informed. He was doing the same with the Allies, giving them no information about or part in his dealings with Berlin. This was Wilson at his worst, creating resentment for which he would later pay.

The German leaders met shortly after receiving the president's stern second message. Ludendorff, having decided that he was not going to get an armistice in time to do any good, announced his determination to fight on through the winter and continue the submarine campaign. The kaiser was willing to agree to this, until Prince Max said he would resign unless the president's terms were accepted in full. The prince was supposed to be the symbol of the new, more democratic, less militaristic regime that President Wilson was demanding. To allow him to depart now, so soon after taking office, seemed unthinkable. And so Ludendorff did not get his way. Another watershed had been crossed; the general would never get his way again.

The next American note, dispatched to Switzerland on October 21 and received in Berlin two days later, was in effect an ultimatum. It informed the Germans that they must do as President Wilson directed, taking steps that would render them incapable of renewing the war at some later date, or face a continuation of the fighting. "No arrangement can be accepted by the Government of the United States which does not provide absolutely satisfactory safeguards and guarantees of the maintenance of the present military supremacy of the armies of the United States and of the Allies in the field," the note stated. It declared that "if the Government of the United States must deal with the military masters and monarchical autocrats of Germany . . . it must demand not peace negotiations but surrender." This left the Germans with no room for maneuver.

Three days later, meeting with the kaiser in Berlin, Ludendorff offered his resignation. Perhaps to the general's surprise, possibly to his relief, the kaiser accepted. Hindenburg, too, attempted to resign, but to this the kaiser would not agree. The fourth and final German note, sent just a day later, was little less than a promise of surrender. It assured Washington that the German government "looked forward to proposals for an armistice that would usher in a peace of justice as outlined by the president." In other words, tell us what you want us to do and we will do it. There was no explicit reference to the Fourteen Points this time, but the whole exchange had made it clear that Berlin expected Wilson's points to serve as the foundation for whatever was to come next. This was what the Germans meant in referring to "the president" in their note.

The end of the war was now not only certain but imminent. Wilson, content to leave the Germans in suspense, remained silent for the next nine days. He could afford to wait; the enemy could not. The alliance long centered upon Berlin was falling apart. Hungary seceded from the Hapsburg empire and asked for a separate peace. Austria surrendered, as did the Turks, and all along the Western Front the Allies and Americans continued their attacks. German soldiers were deserting in uncountable numbers.

On October 25 the American and Allied commanders met to consider the terms under which they might agree to a thirty-day cessation of hostilities. Haig's demands were modest: only a German withdrawal from Belgium and Alsace-Lorraine. Pétain said he would be satisfied with a withdrawal to east of the Rhine. Pershing was tougher. He proposed terms so hard as to be barely distinguishable from unconditional surrender, and an invasion of Germany if those terms were refused.

A new division of opinion was emerging. The British and French wanted the war ended now, and not principally because of concern about the lives that continued fighting would cost. By sheer force of numbers and will, the Americans were, at terrible cost to themselves, demolishing the German defenses in the Meuse-Argonne. And hundreds of thousands more of them were still arriving every month. The longer the fighting went on, the more dominant the AEF would be—dominant over not only the Germans but the Allies as well—and the better positioned the United States would be to decide the terms of peace. From the perspective of the Allies, that was an outcome to be shunned. They had paid the highest price by far. To them should go the rewards, and the right to decide who would get what.

Even the implacable Foch, who had lost both his son and his son-in-law in the opening weeks of the war, was unimpressed with Pershing's eagerness to carry the war across the Rhine. Days after the generals' discussion, when Colonel House arrived in France and asked Foch if he would prefer an armistice or more warfare, he got an almost contemptuously dismissive response. "Fighting means struggling for certain results," he said. "If the Germans now sign an armistice under the general conditions we have just determined, those results are in our possession. This being achieved, no man has the right to cause another drop of blood to be shed."

The question of why Pershing was so willing to continue the fighting has no certain answer. One hopes that he aspired to some higher goal than making himself the general who finished off the Germans. That he was not merely frustrated at seeing the war come to an end less than two months after an army commanded by him had gone into action at last.

Also on October 25, against the advice of nearly everyone allowed to offer him advice, without the knowledge of a single member of his cabinet, President Wilson issued a public appeal on behalf of Democrats in the election that was now less than two weeks away. It was a huge gamble, and as Joe Tumulty had warned, it provoked a furious reaction. It also, despite heavy Democratic campaign spending and all the support the White House was capable of providing, led to the humiliation of the president. When the election results were in, the Republicans celebrated having won 237 seats in the House of Representatives, versus 193 for the Democrats and five for minor parties. Even more stunning was what happened in the Senate. In order to win control there, the Republicans had needed to keep every one of the contested seats that they already held and take five from the Democrats. They did better than that, so that when the new Congress convened, both houses would be controlled by the Republicans, and Henry Cabot Lodge would be chairman of the Senate Foreign Affairs Committee. As always in American national elections, the outcome was affected by innumerable factors, many of them local and regional. The extent to which the Republican triumph really was a repudiation of the president, a rejection of his appeal for support, is endlessly debatable. For all anyone really knows, the results would have been even worse for the Democrats if Wilson had not issued his appeal. The fact remains that he himself had made certain that the election would be seen as a referendum on his leadership, and the best that can be said of his decision is that it did not produce the desired result.

The election was still four days in the future when, on November 1, massed American divisions launched a third phase of their offensive and the German lines began to break as never before. That same day Prince Max and the general who had succeeded Ludendorff, Wilhelm Groener, asked Kaiser Wilhelm to abdicate. The kaiser refused and began to fantasize aloud about leading his armies back to Berlin, where together they would restore order. Groener sent a message to his senior Western Front commanders, asking if they thought their men would follow the kaiser to Berlin. One said yes, fifteen maybe, twenty-three no. The kaiser would vacillate for days, finally going into exile in Holland after his abdication was announced without his approval and word reached him at Spa that Bolsheviks were on their way, intent upon taking him prisoner.

The renewed American offensive was now rapidly gaining momentum. The First Army advanced twenty-four miles in a week. Casualties continued at an appalling rate, however, as die-hard German machine gunners maintained a murderously effective rear guard.

One might think, with victory apparently only days away, that the various political and military leaders on the winning side would have been willing to put aside their differences and join in a celebration of their deliverance. It was not to be. Not only did they disagree about the terms of the Armistice, but Premier Clemenceau, in an apparent fit of rage, now undertook to destroy Pershing. Absurdly, he accused the American commander of not really pressing the Meuse-Argonne offensive, saying that the American troops, though splendid, were "merely unused." He suggested that Foch should appeal to President Wilson to replace Pershing. Foch saw how ridiculous this was. He defended Pershing, pointing out the difficult conditions under which the Americans had been fighting, the extent of their losses and gains, and the fact that their offensive had obliged the Germans to use against them many divisions that otherwise would have been fighting the British and the French. Pershing himself would later surmise that Clemenceau's wrath had been feigned for political purposes: to lay a foundation upon which to argue, after the Armistice, that the American contribution to victory had not been all that significant.

German General Max von Gallwitz, commander of the troops defending at Meuse-Argonne, wrote in late October an enemy's-eye view of the doughboys that put the lie to Clemenceau's complaints. "The Americans are particularly fresh and numerically strong," he recorded. "They have also put excellent material into the first combat divisions. Men in their twenties. But these good divisions have suffered absolutely colossal casualties. The Americans are affected by this. Their morale is therefore not elated . . . but they are men of fresh, rude strength and in their prime. . . . They are to be highly rated as enemies, but due to heavy losses their offensive power has now greatly declined. But after reinforcements they will undoubtedly proceed to new attacks."

Ludendorff himself, in memoirs published in 1927, would observe that "the pent-up, untapped nervous energy which America's troops brought into the fray more than balanced the weakness of their allies, who were utterly exhausted. It was assuredly the Americans who bore the heaviest brunt of the fighting on the whole battlefront during the last few months of the war . . . their attacks were undoubtedly brave and often reckless. . . . Their lack of actual field experience accounts for some extraordinarily heavy losses."

Whether the American advance could have been sustained into and beyond late November is a contested question. By that time the AEF would have been so immense, totaling nearly two million men, that its improvised supply and transportation systems would have been strained to the breaking point. Its two armies might well have had no choice but to stop and refit, leading to another winter of stalemate. But then came Wednesday, November 6, and the outbreak of revolution in Hamburg, Hanover, and other German cities. The authorities in Berlin began a desperate search to find someone willing to travel to France at the head of an armistice delegation. This was no easy task; no one holding a position of importance in the government, army, or navy wanted anything to do with what was certain to be remembered as an indelible national disgrace.

Finally a reluctant Matthias Erzberger, leader of the Catholic Center Party, was persuaded to accept the assignment as a matter of duty to the nation. His qualifications were his status as a nonaristocratic civilian—everyone saw the folly of sending anyone from the Prussian aristocracy or the officer class—and a long record of opposition to German war policy. He agreed to serve in spite of the recent death of his young son, a victim of influenza, and his reluctance was fully justified. In 1921 he would be shot to death by nationalist extremists who regarded his role in the Armistice as a betrayal.

In the wee hours of the next day, Hindenburg, from his headquarters in the Hôtel Britannique in the Belgian resort town of Spa, sent a telegram informing the French that Erzberger's delegation was ready and asking how it should proceed. The answer came quickly, with information about where the delegates would be expected. The journey was grueling. Erzberger and three companions traveled all that Thursday by train, then by auto on roads rougher than washboards. Night had fallen by the time they reached the rendezvous point. They then traveled all night, in French custody, not knowing their destination. It was seven A.M. on Friday when they arrived at a rail junction in the Compiègne Forest north of Paris, and nine A.M. when they were taken to a dining car to meet Marshal Foch.

They were given an icy reception. A draft armistice agreement was read aloud. It had thirty-four clauses, each more humiliating than the last. All German forces were to retire in haste to east of the Rhine, and the Allies were to have bridgeheads on the river's eastern bank. The Treaty of Brest-Litovsk was to be nullified, and within fourteen days the Germans were to hand over five thousand locomotives, ten thousand trucks, 150,000 railcars, and impossible numbers of artillery pieces, machine guns, and aircraft. Et cetera. Most distressing to Erzberger and his party, the food blockade was to be continued until the working out of a formal treaty of peace at some future time and, in what appeared to be a sadistic joke, the starving German nation was somehow to turn over 140,000 head of cattle. This was impossible but no discussion was permitted. The Germans were given seventy-two hours—until eleven A.M. on Monday, November 11—to accept. There would be no cease-fire before that deadline, and if it came and went without acceptance, the war would go on.

Erzberger's first concern was time. German communications were in disorder, and the draft armistice was going to have to be reviewed both in Berlin and in Spa, a response decided by the two locations together. He asked for an additional twenty-four hours and was denied.

It was Saturday before a copy of the draft was delivered to the army high command in Spa. Revolution had by then spread to Berlin, where mobs of insurgents roamed the streets. The latest new chancellor, Friedrich Ebert, was finding it difficult to form a government and impossible to restore order. Erich Ludendorff, feeling besieged and threatened in his apartment, prepared to slip out of the city wearing dark glasses and a fake beard.

On Sunday, a Republic of Germany was proclaimed in Berlin. The American First Army's Captain Harry Truman, a Missouri farmer who in thirty years would be president of the United States, wrote to the woman he had been courting without success for years. His new stature as an officer and savior of democracy had caused her to agree to marry when he got home.

"The Hun is yelling for peace like a stuck hog, and I hope old daddy Foch makes him yell louder yet or throttles him one," he told his future first lady. "When you see some of the things those birds did and then hear them put up the talk they do for peace it doesn't impress you at all. A complete and thorough thrashing is all they've got coming and take my word they are getting it and getting it right."

Hindenburg in Spa wired Ebert in Berlin asking for speedy acceptance of the armistice terms. He got his wish. At seven P.M. Ebert addressed a radio message to "the plenipotentiaries at Headquarters of Allied High Command." It stated simply, "The German Government accepts the conditions of the Armistice communicated to it on 8 November."

It was after two A.M. on November 11 when Foch, Erzberger, and their compeers began a final review of the agreement. The French consented to some minor adjustments, conceding that the Germans could not be expected to hand over more than they possessed. Erzberger again raised the subject of the blockade, receiving only a promise that the question would be brought to the attention of the French government. Both sides signed at 5:20 A.M., and shortly thereafter messages were sent out to the military commands on both sides announcing that fighting was to cease at eleven o'clock and that there were to be no communications between troops on the two sides pending further instructions.

Some five and a half hours remained until the cease-fire went into effect. They were hours of relief, suspense, and confusion studded with madness and tragedy. Pershing, unrelenting, issued an order that there was to be "absolutely no let-up in carrying out the original plans until 11 o'clock [and] operations previously ordered will be pressed with vigor." Officers who knew Pershing knew better than to ignore this, whatever their own inclinations. During the morning, officers who were not yet certified as having commanded in combat shamelessly rushed to the front to fill this gap in their service records while there was still time. Some ordered attacks purely for the sake of doing so—for the sake of rounding out their credentials.

Many German soldiers took flight. Surprising numbers remained at their posts, even exchanging fire with Allied troops and driving back attackers. Some of them killed with an abandon that, if it was not simply depraved, was a final outpouring of bitterness and despair. On both sides, sensible men huddled in their trenches and holes and dugouts, eyes on their watches, hoping to be left alone until the historic hour arrived.

A Baltimore man named Henry Gunther, a former bank clerk of German extraction, is believed to have been the last man to die. Once a sergeant, Gunther had been demoted to private when a censor disapproved of the unenthusiastic account of life on the front he had put in a letter to a friend. He wanted his stripes back and evidently thought the best way to get them was to display bravery. On the morning of November 11, he was among those who did not get word of the impending cease-fire. Shortly before eleven o'clock, near the village of Ville-devant-Chaumont in Lorraine, he and a companion came upon a German machine gun emplacement. Thinking that this was his chance, Gunther advanced on the Germans, who had been counting the minutes and wanted no trouble. With less than one minute remaining, they were dumbstruck to see an American soldier charging them, bayonet at the ready. They shouted and waved, trying to make him turn back, but he kept coming. Finally, when he got frighteningly close, they shot him dead.

Perhaps a minute before Gunther's death, at Grandrieu in Belgium, another German machine-gunner opened fire, evidently at random, not taking aim, just filling the air with bullets. He went on firing until his belt of ammunition was spent. By then the clocks had struck eleven. The German stood up, looked across No Man's Land to where South African troops were emerging cautiously from their hiding places, and removed his helmet.

He took a deep slow bow as though acknowledging applause, stood erect, turned his back, and walked away, out of history.

It was over.

PART THREE

✦ ✦ ✦

Sowing Dragons' Teeth

A supreme moment of history has come. The eyes of the people have been opened and they see. The hand of God is laid upon the nations. He will show them favor, I devoutly believe, only if they rise to the clear heights of his justice and mercy.

—WOODROW WILSON, NOVEMBER 11, 1918

←————

The world in their hands
From left: Lloyd George of Britain, Orlando of Italy, Clemenceau of France, and President Woodrow Wilson

Chapter 21

The World the War Made

THE EUROPE UPON WHICH WOODROW WILSON LOOKED OUT FROM his palace in Paris as 1919 began was in a *molten* state. To adapt a phrase from Marx, everything that was solid, if it had not vanished into thin air, had become suddenly, sometimes frighteningly, fluid.

The future had not been so uncertain for centuries, arguably for a thousand years or more. From the valley of the Rhine eastward to the Pacific Ocean, from the Gulf of Finland southward to Arabia, scarcely a border was not in dispute. Three of history's greatest empires—the Russian, the Austro-Hungarian, and the Ottoman—had disintegrated almost simultaneously. A fourth, the younger and more vital German Empire, had been bludgeoned into impotence and was already largely dismantled.

In Winston Churchill's words, it was a "crippled, broken world." All the horsemen of the apocalypse were on the scene. The so-called Spanish Flu had nearly run its course after killing millions (four hundred thousand in Germany alone in 1918), but now typhoid and cholera were rampant in all the places where basic sanitation had become impossible. Herbert Hoover, put in charge of an international food relief program, warned that two hundred million people were starving among the nations that had lost the war, and almost that many among the victors and neutrals.

The capital cities of central and eastern Europe had become madhouses. Their streets ran red with the blood of communists and reactionaries, fighting each other for control. Women emerged from middle-class homes to walk those same streets, trying to sell their bodies to keep their families alive.

Britain and France, opulently wealthy five years before, were sunk in debt. Smaller countries were not only bankrupt but physically devastated; Belgium would never recover her prewar economic vitality. Britain, having stripped herself bare to continue the war, was more than a billion dollars in debt to the United States. Canada owed the United States more than $425 million, France more than $300 million, and so on down through the ranks of the Allies. Even Germany had managed to borrow $45 million from American sources early in the conflict.

Nowhere in Europe was there money to get shattered economies up and running. Altogether, the European combatant nations owed the United States $2.5 billion. That number was dwarfed, however, by the $33 billion that the American government had spent in the year and a half between President Wilson's call for a declaration of war and the start of the Armistice. In the near term, this expenditure had brought roaring prosperity to the American economy. Building a war machine while meeting the demands of the Allies had created a hot market for almost everything America's factories and farms could produce, and the resulting avalanche of profits went largely untaxed. One result was a gross national product that would have been unimaginable a few years earlier. Another was a national debt of unprecedented size, a problem to be dealt with no one knew how, at some uncertain point in the future.

An immense burden of grief, the black shadow of inconceivable loss, lay upon every region of Europe east of the Pyrenees. Two million German soldiers were dead, almost that many Russians, nearly a million and a half French, more than a million from the armies of Vienna, eight hundred thousand Turks, seven hundred thousand British, half a million Italians. Even Romania and Serbia, small as they were, had lost a quarter of a million men each—five times the American total of fifty-three thousand dead as a result of combat.

Almost 3.5 percent of the population of France had died fighting the war. The comparable percentages were 5.7 for Serbia, 3.7 for the Turks, 3.0 for Germany, and 1.6 each for Britain and Italy. But it was only 0.01 percent for the United States, even when the 50,714 who perished of illness or disease are included in the tally.

And then there were the millions who were still alive but maimed in body or spirit or both.

And all the women for whom there were no men.

Such was the world that the Great War had made. Everywhere except in the United States, it could be hard to distinguish the fruits of victory from the price of defeat.

The great question, as the peace conference opened, was what shape a Eu-

Counting the cost
*Much of Europe was in ruins
as 1919 began, and countless
Europeans as well.*

rope ablaze would assume as it cooled and hardened. Who was going to rule where, and by what means? How were the wicked—which of course meant the losers—to be punished? How would the good be rewarded? With revolutions breaking out in so many places, with Austria and Bavaria declaring themselves socialist republics and all Germany in chaos, how real was the danger that half or more of Europe might become socialist or communist? Was it really conceivable, as some claimed, that even western Europe—and then the United States—might fall to the Bolsheviks? What would have to be done to keep this from happening?

Every man, woman, and child in Europe, and millions outside Europe, had a stake in the answer. Many were represented at the peace conference, if only pro forma, by delegates from the more than thirty countries that had been invited. Many more, including the populations of Russia and Germany, of Austria and Hungary and Turkey, were not represented at all. Which did not necessarily put them at as great a disadvantage as one might suppose. Many of the delegates would be present as supplicants only, with almost no voice in deciding the destinies of their nations. They would have little to do beyond waiting in their hotels for an invitation to explain what they wanted and why, and attending plenary sessions almost the sole purpose of which was to rubber-stamp the decisions of the tiny circle of men who had real power. As for Germany and her former allies, it was generally assumed that in due course they would become participants in negotiation of the final peace terms; that was so traditional in postwar European diplomacy as to be almost taken for granted.

That tiny circle of men with real power was called the Supreme Council or, until it became even more exclusive, the Council of Ten. At its core was an even tinier inner circle of three: the triumvirate of President Wilson and Prime Ministers Clemenceau and Lloyd George. Next in importance, but distinctly junior, was the Italian premier, Vittorio Emanuele Orlando. The other six were an essentially powerless majority: the American secretary of state, the foreign ministers of Britain, France, and Italy, and two delegates from Japan. The Japanese were included as a kind of courtesy, partly because they had made useful contributions to the war effort after joining the Allies, mainly because their country was the rising power in the Far East and could not be relegated to the margins. They had limited objectives in Paris and were content to remain silent when other matters were discussed.

The objectives of the council's European members extended around the globe and were by no means always compatible. Italy's were the simplest, though no less troublesome for being simple. The war had been ten months old, with millions already dead, when Italy abandoned her neutrality and joined the Allies. She did so not because she was under threat (to the contrary, both sides were courting her) but in an undisguised bid for territory. In effect, she had put herself up for sale, willing to partner with whoever offered the best deal. The Central Powers found themselves at an impossible disadvantage, because most of what Rome wanted belonged to Vienna, the rest to the Ottoman Turks. The Allies, on the other hand, were prepared to offer prospective new partners almost anything they wanted, so long as the bill would come due only with victory and be paid by the enemy. The result was the secret treaty of London, rich in promises of a generous postwar settlement.

The people of Italy paid a high price. In the following three and a half years, well over half a million of their young men perished, almost all of them fighting Austria-Hungary's armies in the Alpine borderlands. Orlando and Foreign Minister Sidney Sonnino (whose first name came courtesy of his English mother) had one objective in Paris: to make sure that their nation was paid in full for its bloody and cynical bargain. They knew that not only their political survival but their place in Italian history depended on the result. And they were on their guard, aware that their allies were no longer inclined to be so generous now that the danger had passed.

France's priorities were nearly as transparent as Italy's. The collapse of Russia and the defeat of the Central Powers restored France to the position she had enjoyed for centuries and that she regarded as hers by right: once again she was the most powerful nation on the European mainland. Georges Clemenceau's mission—one that he relished, having nursed a hatred for Germany since the Franco-Prussian War—was to make it impossible for the Germans ever again to threaten French supremacy. Achieving this was going to be a matter of old-fashioned power politics. Clemenceau knew from the start that it was likely to put him at odds not only with Woodrow Wilson, with his Fourteen Points and dreams of a new way of managing international relations, but also with David Lloyd George, who like all British prime ministers thought it one of his highest duties to prevent any one country or alliance from dominating the continent.

The British situation, as the conference opened, was in one way simpler than France's, in another way more complicated. Lloyd George was in the unique position of arriving in Paris with most of his country's war aims al-

Squabbling over the spoils, Paris, 1919
*Allies but not friends: from left, Marshal Foch, Premier Clemenceau,
Prime Minister Lloyd George, and Orlando and Sonnino of Italy.*

ready accomplished. Germany was no longer a naval threat, and for the best of all possible reasons: she no longer had a navy. What was in a way even more gratifying, Germany was also no longer a commercial threat: her merchant ships were in the hands of the victors, her economy in collapse, her manufacturers forbidden under the terms of the Armistice to export anything. Germany having been cut off from her overseas possessions, the Ottoman Turks expelled from the Middle East, Britain's overseas empire was not only secure but certain to grow larger as soon as the spoils of war were parceled out.

Just a month before the opening of the conference, Lloyd George's coalition government had won a landslide victory in a general election. In campaigning, the prime minister had given voice to the public's hunger for a vengeful punishment of the defeated foe. He had done so out of expediency rather than conviction, and in spite of his own understanding that the destruction of Germany, even her permanent economic enfeeblement, would not serve Britain's interests. His challenge, at Paris, was going to be to secure the advantages that Britain had already won, keep the wrath of Clemenceau in check, and appear not to betray the voters back home. It was going to require all his legendary shrewdness.

And then there was the United States, in the person of Woodrow Wilson.

He stood apart from, and in his own view above, the Allied chiefs. He was the most important man in Paris because he spoke for what was now unquestionably the mightiest nation on earth, the only one of the great Western powers not reduced to penury by the war. Among the members of the Supreme Council he was the archvictor, the one who had saved the others from more years of bloodshed and possibly from defeat. He never tired of saying that his was the only nation to come to Paris wanting nothing for itself. What he himself wanted had long since been made obvious: an end to the kind of international relations, the kind of world, that had made the Great War possible. He was determined to put in place a new order based on *his* Fourteen Points and kept in place by *his* League of Nations.

The conference over which the council presided was unlike anything the world had ever seen or is likely to see again. For nearly half a year, it functioned as something very like a world government. The council was the place to which the invited nations went to have their futures decided, the place to which the uninvited had to look with hope and dread. If there existed an entity capable of casting the world's temporarily liquid parts into a constructive mold, it could only be the council's inner circle.

What must Wilson have thought? Here he was, *the* central figure in an assembly brought together to restore a desperately disordered world. His most extravagant fantasies, ambitions going back to his boyhood, were being fulfilled to an extent that few men have ever experienced. Was he thrilled? Astonished? Frightened? If he was any such thing, he did a superb job of concealing it. The available evidence, the things that he himself said and wrote and the impressions of those observing him, indicates that he took all of it very much in stride—took his arrival at this global pinnacle for granted. It does not appear to have exceeded his expectations at all.

He would have been astonished, in this his hour of glory, to learn of the impression that King George V of England had formed after playing host to him at Buckingham Palace in December 1918. "I could not bear him," His Majesty confided to a friend. "An entirely cold academical professor—an odious man."

The council met daily, often more than once a day, whenever the principal members were in Paris. It always met without an agenda, which has struck some historians as curious but may be explained by the regularity with which unforeseen crises and disputes erupted and the difficulty of anticipating what problems were going to demand attention on any particular day.

Most of the worst problems emerged from the political rubble that was all that remained of the collapsed empires. The fall of the Romanovs, at first cheered in the West for supposedly turning Russia into an instant democracy, had become the prelude to a sequence of calamities. First was the takeover by the Bolsheviks, despised by the Allies for taking Russia out of the war, feared for wanting to spread revolution everywhere. Then came the ragtag litter of new nations and would-be nations that tsarist Russia had produced in her death throes. For the first time in a century and a quarter, Poland was an independent state. The Baltic countries, too, announced their rebirth: Estonia, Latvia, and Lithuania. To the south, Ukraine, Georgia, Armenia, Azerbaijan, and Dagestan all suddenly found that the Russian boot had been lifted from their necks.

The end of Austria-Hungary followed soon enough, with similar consequences. The Hapsburgs had long been a German dynasty with many millions of non-German subjects: Hungarians, Slavs, and more other ethnic groups than the emperor himself probably could have named. This had caused increasing strain in the nineteenth century, as a kind of nationalism rooted in ethnic identity spread everywhere. Later, when the imperial government began to buckle under the pressures of the Great War, its Polish and Czech and Slovak and Slovenian and Bosnian subjects could see little reason to remain loyal. The end came swiftly: Austrian Poland broke away, then Galicia and Bohemia, finally even Hungary. Austria was reduced to an anomaly, a small, poor country with one of the world's most magnificent capital cities.

None of the empire's fragments were inclined to await anyone's permission to set themselves up as autonomous states. Austrian Poland joined what had been Russian Poland and German Poland to form the resurrected Polish state. The Czechs of Bohemia pressed the neighboring Slovaks to combine with them in creating Czechoslovakia. The South Slavs bullied their neighbors into joining what was called at first the Kingdom of Serbs, Croats, and Slovenes— the future Yugoslavia.

These things happened even before the war ended, and though they were ancient dreams come true, they also had a dark and bloody side. All the collapsed empires had been jumbles of intermixed nationalities and ethnicities and religious denominations, and coming to an objective judgment of whether some particular region was essentially Polish or Lithuanian, Russian or Ukrainian, Serb or Italian, was often difficult and not infrequently impossible. In such a dangerously disordered Europe, with so many borders unsettled, the newborn states cared nothing about objective judgments. They claimed every conceivable patch of ground—for reasons of history or security, if the population data were not in their favor—and denounced the claims of their neighbors.

There were internal conflicts as well. The Russian civil war, though the most terrible by far (ultimately it would kill more Russians than the Great War), was by no means unique. Two rival factions claimed to be the rightful government of Poland. The Czechs pulled the skeptical Slovaks into an iron embrace not because there was any particular affinity between the two peoples—the Czechs were mostly Protestant, the Slovaks Roman Catholic—but for reasons of arithmetic. So many ethnic Germans lived within the borders of what had been the Austrian province of Bohemia that, without the addition of the Slovaks, the Czech claim to be a Slavic country would have been distinctly dubious.

General Tasker H. Bliss, who had served as America's military adviser to the Supreme War Council before becoming a delegate to the peace conference, wrote of Europe's new nations that "as soon as they appear they fly at somebody's throat. They are like mosquitoes—vicious from the moment of their birth." By the time the conference opened for business, the new republic of Ukraine was at war both with its homegrown Communists and with the Bolsheviks of Russia. In the former Austro-Hungarian province of Galicia, the people known as Ruthenians (Roman Catholic Ukrainians) had declared their independence, promptly come under attack by the Orthodox Ukrainians to their east and the Poles to their north, and quickly been eliminated as a possible new member of the family of nations.

In that same month, Lithuanian and Byelorussian Bolsheviks seized control of the Baltic city of Vilna. (In April they would be driven out by the Poles, who a year later would be driven out by the Russians.) Poles and Czechs began fighting over the little duchy of Teschen, which both coveted for its coal mines. German free corps, improvised private armies made up of discharged soldiers who had never done anything but make war and did not know how to stop doing it, invaded the Baltic region to their east, overthrew the government of Latvia, and moved on to Estonia. Meanwhile Poles were at war with Russians over portions of Ukraine and Byelorussia, and Austrians were fighting Yugoslav troops for the Alpine region centered on the city of Klagenfurt. "Central Europe is aflame," Robert Lansing observed in April. "The people see no hope."

In March a Bolshevik revolution in Hungary gave the Czechs an excuse to invade and seize Hungarian territory to which they claimed to be entitled. Their Slovakian compatriots, already unhappy with their subordinate position in the Czechoslovak confederation, attacked the rear of the Czech army as it advanced. By that time the Supreme Council in Paris had dismissed as ridiculous Austria's request for *Anschluss* or absorption into Germany—members saw it as opening the way for Berlin to benefit from the war—and a newly declared Bavarian Soviet Republic was savagely suppressed by what remained of the German army and undisciplined free corps fighters. Communists and free corps were butchering each other in the streets of Berlin.

The nightmare that life in Germany had become was worsened beyond measure by the Allies' refusal to permit the importation of desperately needed food. Herbert Hoover, formerly in charge of Belgian relief and now the head of the international relief organization created at Colonel House's suggestion after the signing of the Armistice, sent investigators into Germany. They reported that the starvation problem was now worse than in the last months of the war, disease and crime out of control.

The problem was solvable in every way except politically. The United States had built up an enormous agricultural surplus by the war's end, and mountains of foodstuffs were stockpiled at East Coast ports. But their delivery to central Europe was blocked by Britain and France, whom Hoover charged with "indescribable malignity." They were motivated, he told President Wilson, not by vengefulness alone but by calculations of political advantage. They feared that if the Americans were seen to have rescued Germany, their status in negotiations of a peace treaty would rise higher than it already was.

The truth about conditions in Germany was both ugly and undeniable, and it made things difficult for Lloyd George, if not for the viciously vengeful Clemenceau. An English journalist wrote of visiting a hospital in Cologne and seeing "rows of babies feverish from want of food, exhausted by privation to the point where their little limbs were like slender wands, their expression hopeless, their faces full of pain." An agent of the British government inspected a Berlin slaughterhouse and submitted a grim report. There being no livestock to slaughter, he wrote, the building was being used to store such potato crops as could be scavenged for the capital.

I can only describe [the potatoes] as being in a rotten and putrid state. . . .
No farmer in Britain would dream of attempting to give this load of pota-

toes to any animal. . . . It is with difficulty that one could believe the potatoes I referred to could be eaten by any human creature; only the pangs of
direct hunger could make their consumption possible. . . . It is easy to understand how public opinion in Germany is so keenly resentful of and de-
plores the demand included in the Peace Terms for the immediate delivery
of 140,000 cows.

Even Winston Churchill was finally driven to relent. From early in the war
he had been unreservedly supportive of the starvation policy. After the Armistice, calling Hoover a "son of a bitch" for objecting to continuation of the
blockade, he had joined Lloyd George in campaigning on a platform of "making the Hun pay." Early in 1919, however, he underwent a change of heart. It
appears to have risen less out of compassion than of fear of the possible consequences of "the entire collapse of the vital structure of German social and
national life under the pressure of hunger and malnutrition."

The great gathering at Paris assumed responsibility for dealing (or in the
case of starvation in pariah states, declining to deal) with all such problems:
for stopping the fighting, assigning contested territories, and deciding who
should be in charge in what places and where borders should be. And even
these things would not be its only work. Among other matters that could not
be long deferred were the future of Germany's colonies in Africa, the Far East,
and the western Pacific, and the vast areas of the Middle East that for centuries
had belonged to the Ottoman Turks. Each of these issues aroused fear or greed
or both among some number of the nations represented in Paris. The British
dominions of South Africa, Australia, and New Zealand were determined to
get permanent possession of what was being taken from Germany in Africa
and the South Pacific. The Japanese expected to be rewarded with islands in
what President Roosevelt had, years before, encouraged them to regard as
their sphere of influence in the Far East. Britain and France already had in
place a secret deal to divide much of the Middle East between themselves: the
Sykes-Picot Agreement of 1916, not made known to the world until the Bolsheviks discovered it in the tsarist government's files. Implementing it, however, was not going to be easy.

Looming over everything was the question of what to do about Germany.
For four years the Allied and U.S. governments had used all the ingenuity of
their propaganda machines to teach their citizens that Germany was the arch-
fiend among the nations of the world, brutal, unprincipled, and contemptu-

ous of civilized standards of behavior. Now, and understandably, great numbers of those citizens thought that nothing would do except to eliminate the fiend, or at least enchain it so severely that it would never again be capable of visiting such horrors upon the innocent and the good.

This was exactly what Clemenceau wanted. And he found that all the force of international public opinion—more important in the new century than it had ever been—was at this moment behind him. For David Lloyd George, the future of Europe was a more complicated question: a problem to be managed, a puzzle to be solved. So long as the voters of Britain remained hungry for vengeance, he would not stand in their way and allow himself to be trampled. But he knew that this was folly, that the new Europe was going to need a healthy Germany, and that Britain would need it, too. He would be ready, when the public mood softened, to nudge it in more constructive directions, even if doing so antagonized the French.

What was for Clemenceau the opportunity of a lifetime and for Lloyd George a waiting game was for Woodrow Wilson a kind of existential show-down, the ultimate test of who he was and what he stood for, what his life was going to mean. Through the years of American neutrality, he had said repeatedly that the United States was not the enemy of "the great German people," whom he numbered among the victims of the Berlin regime (while publicly casting doubt on the loyalty of German-Americans). But from the spring of 1917, needing to justify intervention to himself as much as to the public, he began to shift toward condemning not just the kaiser and his circle but the whole German nation. The newspapers of America were ahead of him in this. By the end of 1918 much of the country was convinced of what continues to be widely believed today: that Germany had started the war bent on world conquest and had fought it in uniquely immoral ways. With the skeptical bullied into silence and dissenters feeling the heavy hand of the law, countervailing opinions were not easy to find. Thus few questions were asked when, on the day the Armistice went into effect, President Wilson went before Congress to declare victory and announce that "the existing blockade conditions set up by the Allies and Associated Powers are to remain unchanged and all German merchant ships found at sea are to remain liable to capture."

In the midst of all the squabbling and logrolling, the president was preaching his Fourteen Points, his League of Nations, his promise of a postwar world so just, so fair to weak and strong alike, and so well designed to deal with aggression that wars would become improbable. The scope of his promises and demands made his situation—the position of the United States—infinitely more complicated than those of Clemenceau or Lloyd George or anyone else at the conference. The complications being largely of Wilson's own making, it was only fair that the burden of dealing with them fell almost entirely on him.

In the conference's first days, Wilson's priority was to put the League of Nations at the center of the Supreme Council's deliberations and keep it there. In attempting to understand what happened in Paris and then in Washington in 1919, it is necessary to keep in mind that ending the war with the Central Powers and creating a League of Nations were entirely distinct objectives. They could have been handled separately—there was no absolute need for the Paris conference to deal with the league proposal at all—and many Europeans and Americans wanted them disconnected. Wilson was determined not to allow this to happen. He insisted that the league had to be inextricably intertwined with the peace treaty and must not be deferred until some vague future time. Implementation of a treaty that created the league was to mark the dawn of the new world order, the lasting peace, for which Wilson had gone to war. This would be impossible if the league were not in place and functioning almost from the day the treaty was ratified.

It was the treaty's creation of the league that caused Wilson, back in the United States later in 1919, to call it "the most remarkable document, I venture to say, in human history." Only the league, he was convinced, could deal with the problems that were certain to arise after the peace conference adjourned and correct deficiencies in the treaty as they became apparent. This last point assumed increasing importance in his thinking as the question of treaty ratification came to dominate American politics. He showed himself willing to accept serious defects in the treaty, even obvious injustices, in the expectation that the league would put things right in due course.

At first, with his prestige still at its peak and the Allied leaders hoping to build up reserves of American goodwill to be drawn upon when they wanted help with their own priorities, the president made fast and substantial progress. As early as January 22, the Supreme Council gave him perhaps his most important victory, agreeing that the league's constitution (which the president, with evangelical flair, was calling its "covenant") should be written into the body of the treaty. Three days later a plenary session of all the nations represented at the conference approved the president's request for creation of a commission to draft this covenant. Wilson insisted on serving as its chairman, and of course no one objected. He had expected to chair the whole peace conference, and had yielded grudgingly when told that that honor had to go to Clemenceau as principal representative of the host country. If he had understood this earlier and foreseen the advantages that Clemenceau would enjoy as chairman, the president likely would have insisted on holding the conference in neutral Geneva, as a number of Americans had urged.

He was not going to make the same mistake with the league, the great achievement of his career and his bid for immortality. It had to stay in his hands. On February 3 he held the first meeting of the league commission, its fifteen members representing ten countries and selected by Wilson himself. Another four members from four smaller countries were soon added. This was far too many cooks for such a broth, especially as from the beginning the commission was under pressure to finish its work by February 14, when Wilson would be departing on a necessary visit to the United States. Most of the commission's members were window dressing, on hand to help create the impression that the covenant was the work of many nations and expressed the will of the world. Their actual function was to look on from the sidelines as Wilson, House, and a few others, including American advisers on international law, got the job done.

The meetings were held in House's expansive suite in the Hôtel de Crillon, almost always at night after the Supreme Council completed its business. The commission did not have to start from scratch; Colonel House had presented a first draft of a covenant, complete with twenty-three articles, to President Wilson back in July 1918. It drew on the still earlier work of league advocates in the United States and Britain, and later in 1918 House and Wilson redrafted it more than once. Calling it a covenant was not House's idea; the president had begun using the word in speeches, then in his reply to Pope Benedict's peace initiative, in 1917.

Between the Supreme Council and the commission and the need to attend to reports and requests from the White House, where Tumulty was managing things, the president was working harder than he had in years. In Washington, even at difficult times, he had kept short office hours, played golf almost daily, and gone on frequent long drives. There was no time for such things now, especially as his refusal to have a secretary burdened him with routine chores that any competent file clerk could have handled. It was a risky workload for a man in advanced middle age with Wilson's medical history.

The Supreme Council's business consisted largely of receiving the delegates of the lesser nations present at the conference and listening to them explain what shards of the old empires they thought their countries were entitled to and why. Even the most vicious of the newly hatched mosquito-states presented a very different face to the council than to their neighbors and rivals. In arguing their cases, they were graciously diplomatic, intent upon seeming ambitious for nothing except what justice and peace required, regretful that the states with which they were in conflict were so deceitful and resistant to the truth. Romania, the member of the Allies that had contributed least to winning the war, was first to be invited to appear before the council, on January 31. The new Kingdom of Serbs, Croats, and Slovenes appeared later on the same day, its delegation dominated by its Serbian element. Three days later it was the turn of Greece, followed in another two days by Czechoslovakia. And so on until the number of issues that the council was being asked to resolve became uncountable. Poland proved to be a particularly troublesome case because of the two factions, mutually hateful, that claimed to be her government. Day after day, week after week, new and impenetrable questions arose about which petitioning country should be awarded some obscure, ethnically mixed place that few members of the Council of Ten had ever heard of.

No one on earth, no ten men as ignorant of the history and geography of eastern Europe as the members of the Supreme Council, could possibly have sorted all this out. The council's response was to set up commissions, each of which was responsible for studying some specific point of contention and reporting back with recommendations. Ultimately there were more than sixty of these commissions, many of them dominated by the teams of American academics and specialists created for the Inquiry and brought to Paris with Wilson. By the end of the conference, they had met more than sixteen hundred times, done immense amounts of work, and presented the council with overwhelming quantities of information and proposals. Human nature being what it is, many questions were decided not on the basis of the experts' findings but according to what various council members found most expedient or most consistent with their personal preferences. Clemenceau, for example, would find it to France's advantage to champion a large, strong Poland incorporating a great deal of German territory and a great many German nationals. Lloyd George would champion Greece's ambitions in the Near East less for strategic than for romantic-sentimental reasons. The result was often resentment, disillusion, and a storing up of trouble for the future.

Wilson's stated objective, where disputed territories were at issue, was to adhere to his Fourteen Points' emphasis on self-determination for all peoples.

He was insistent that, as he had said in a 1918 Fourth of July speech, every territorial question must be resolved with "the free acceptance [of] the people immediately concerned, and not upon the basis of the material interest or advantage of any other nation or people which may desire a different settlement for the sake of its own exterior influence or mastery."

This was nothing less than a call for an end to power politics as traditionally played on the international stage. The nobility of the idea was unmistakable, but even with the purest of intentions it could be almost impossible to put into practice. Europe's turbulent history had intermingled ethnic and religious populations to an extent that in many places was impossible to sort out. The commissions would sometimes find it impossible to obtain conclusive evidence of how many Greeks or Italians or Slavs lived in some contested city or region. As Secretary of State Lansing observed, the notion of self-determination, so central to Wilson's vision for the world, was "simply loaded with dynamite." It raised questions for which there were no answers.

Sometimes with the best of intentions and sometimes not, the Supreme Council gradually turned Europe from the Rhineland to the Black Sea into a mass of festering geopolitical wounds. Populations were consigned to countries that they did not want to be part of and would never have consented to join. In their new countries, people would find themselves treated as aliens and would burn with resentment while waiting for the wheel of history to turn again and give them an opportunity to escape or take revenge. Sometimes this happened inadvertently, out of an unhappy coupling of greed, ignorance, and carelessness. Thus when Vittorio Orlando told Wilson that he wanted Italy's northern frontier to extend to the Brenner Pass, the president offhandedly agreed. He had only the vaguest notion of where the Brenner Pass was, and no idea at all that the consent he had so casually given would turn a quarter of a million ethnic Germans into baffled subjects of the king of Italy.

More often the people making the decisions had some understanding of what they were doing but thought they were justified by having won a terrible war against criminal enemies. The war's losers, naturally, paid the price. The three million Germans of Bohemia's Sudetenland and a million Hungarians were never asked if they wanted to become part of the new nation of Czechoslovakia. They were put there because they were German and Hungarian and therefore had no rights, and because the Czechs had friends on the Supreme Council. Romania, too, fattened at the expense of her neighbors. When someone suggested a plebiscite to find out whether the people of Alsace and Lorraine wanted to be French or German, Clemenceau reacted as though he had been asked to put his mother up for auction. Things got ugly only when the Allies or the favored new nations came into conflict with each other—when Poland and Czechoslovakia, for example, began fighting for possession of Galicia. The result, in the long term, was the creation of grievances that would remain dormant for years, even decades, before erupting in violence.

President Wilson's second success, after getting the league covenant into the treaty, was more ambiguous. It had to do with the disposition of Germany's colonies. The German Empire, not created until 1871, had been a late entry in the European race to acquire overseas possessions. Nevertheless, by 1914 Germany had accumulated four pieces of Africa, three of them substantial in size if not terribly desirable, plus a scattering of islands in the western Pacific, valuable mainly as coaling stations for her navy and merchant fleet. She also shared special status in Morocco with France and had a ninety-nine-year lease on a hundred square miles of China's Shantung Peninsula. When the war came, Germany had no way of maintaining contact with, much less defending, almost any of these possessions.

The victors were agreed that Germany, as an outlaw nation, had no right to colonies. There, however, agreement ended. Wilson was disgusted to discover that the Allies intended to annex not only the African colonies but much of what had been the Ottoman Empire, turning vast tracts of the supposedly liberated Middle East into their property. He declared this to be unacceptable, such a gross violation of the Fourteen Points' assertion of the right of all people to choose their own rulers that it would make a mockery of both his program and the league.

The result was the first great fight of the peace conference. Lloyd George initially showed himself to be sympathetic to Wilson's position, seeing the question as not worth a breach with the United States. His failure to defend what British dominions such as Australia and South Africa saw as their legitimate aspirations, however, drew heavy fire. Jan Christian Smuts, the onetime Boer general so respected by his former British foes that in 1917 he became a member of their war cabinet, insisted that the British Empire must absorb German East Africa (now Burundi, Rwanda, and part of Tanzania), thereby completing a chain of colonies extending without break from north Africa to the Cape of Good Hope. Other South Africans demanded German Southwest Africa (today's Namibia), which would give their country the whole southern end of the continent. Australia wanted New Guinea and German Samoa in the

South Pacific, Japan wanted to take over the German concession in Shantung along with various North Pacific islands, and France wanted (in addition to sharing the Middle East with Britain) the former German colonies of the Cameroons and Togoland and the rights previously enjoyed by Germany in Morocco.

This was old-fashioned smash-and-grab imperialism, impossible to reconcile with the Fourteen Points. The president was prepared to agree, however, that at least some of the territories in question—the "savages" of sub-Saharan Africa and the Pacific islands most certainly—were not ready to govern themselves and might never be. He hoped that all of them could become, temporarily in some cases but if necessary permanently, wards of the League of Nations. He proposed that each, under league auspices, should be governed and developed (economically, politically, and in other ways) as the "mandate" of one or another of the supposedly more civilized powers. They could be assured of the right—when ready—to become autonomous nations.

Benign as this scheme appeared—benign as it was as a theory—it infuriated Britain's dominions and got a cold reception from the French. Feelings ran so strong that it began to appear that the dispute might bring the whole process of working out a peace treaty to a halt. The situation was saved by the resourceful Smuts, who in cooperation with the British diplomat David Cecil came up with a compromise. Everyone was to agree to the introduction of a system of Wilsonian mandates, of which there would be three types. The crucial type, so far as Smuts's plan was concerned, would consist of territories adjacent or near to their "mandatory" powers—the ones responsible for governing and developing them. Mandates in this category could, with minor limitations, be administered as though they were part of the nation or dominion responsible for them. Theoretically they would be prepared for independence, but there would be no monitoring of progress, no consulting with subject populations, and certainly no date by which independence must be granted. In practical terms, this meant that South Africa could absorb German Southwest Africa, Australia could annex New Guinea, et cetera.

In assenting to this, in accepting a fig leaf in place of a program of real progress toward self-government for colonies around the world, Wilson allowed his Fourteen Points to be deeply compromised. He thereby failed the first test of his own seriousness, signaling to those who did not share his aspirations that he might not fight to achieve them. His reasons can only be guessed at, but are not necessarily obscure. He may have seen the Smuts scheme as of relatively minor importance, a mere technicality when balanced against the need to get the entire covenant completed and approved in a matter of days. His acquiescence was an early manifestation of his inclination, which would become increasingly pronounced, to accept measures that were grossly at odds with his own stated principles in the expectation that the league would one day prescribe the necessary remedies. And the mandate's compromise had the advantage of exacting no domestic political costs; few Americans knew anything about Germany's colonies, and most of the politicians who did know were content to let Britain take them.

It is likely that the president, if challenged, would have defended this compromise as being of minor consequence. As irrelevant to what lay ahead.

About that he would have been wrong.

Lost?

As the peace conference got under way, something else was happening in Paris. What is arguably the most romantic myth of the Great War was putting down roots: the notion that the war had left in its wake a Lost Generation.

To be a member in good standing of the Lost Generation, it was necessary to have served in the war or, failing that, to have been in Europe, preferably France, while it was going on. It was also desirable almost to the point of necessity, at least from an American perspective, to *be* an American.

The best candidates were those who could claim to be artists of some kind: writers or painters or sculptors or even all three. If one returned to the United States at war's end, which could be difficult to avoid if one was in uniform, it was advisable to get back to Europe as soon as possible and spend enough time in Paris to become part of the expatriate community there.

But none of this was enough if one did not also look back on the war with bitter contempt, demonstrating that one had been permanently disillusioned by the experience. That one was alienated, torn from one's roots and in that sense *lost*. A fair number of the best young American artists of the time really were these things. They contributed to making the Paris of the 1920s the cultural center not only of Europe but of the world.

There were also, inevitably, lesser souls for whom Paris was an ideal setting in which to strike a romantically antiromantic pose, hangers-on eager to *look* artistic and lost and all the rest.

It is both fitting and ironic that Ernest Hemingway popularized the idea of the Lost Generation and became its supreme symbol. He ticked all the boxes: a midwesterner who entered the war as an eighteen-year-old volunteer ambulance driver, witnessed horrendous carnage before being wounded himself, and after recuperation in the United States moved to Paris in 1921, committed to becoming a literary artist. That he was tall and muscular with movie-star good looks, became a chum of such Paris institutions as James Joyce and Ezra Pound, and happened to be both supremely talented and utterly devoted to his craft—all these things helped. He was perfectly equipped to become an idol to young Americans yearning for liberation from they weren't quite sure what, the ultimate antiromantic romantic hero, the personification of an idea and an ideal.

The ironies of Hemingway's identification with the Lost Generation are manifold. They begin with the fact that the notion of a Lost Generation originated not with him, or with any of its other supposed members, but with a Paris garage owner who was talking about one of his mechanics. They end with Hemingway's rejection of the whole idea as unfair and ridiculous, his denial that he and those like him were part of any such thing.

It happened this way. One day in the early 1920s, Gertrude Stein, the self-anointed queen of avant-garde expatriate Paris, complained about the service she was receiving to the proprietor of the garage that looked after her Model T Ford. The proprietor put the blame on a mechanic who had served in the war, berating him as a typically useless member of a *génération perdue*.

"That's what you are," Stein said later in telling Hemingway of the incident. He was then her starstruck young protégé, an unknown would-be author unpublished except for his work as a newspaper correspondent.

"That's what you all are," Stein continued. "All of you young people who served in the war. You are a lost generation."

"Really?" Hemingway's tone would have been skeptical, impatient, probably a bit indignant.

"You are. You have no respect for anything. You drink yourselves to death. . . ."

"Was the young mechanic drunk?"

"Of course not."

"Have you ever seen me drunk?"

"No, but your friends are drunk."

"I've been drunk. But I don't come here drunk."

"Of course not. I didn't say that."

"The boy's *patron* was probably drunk by eleven o'clock in the morning. That's why he makes such lovely phrases."

"Don't argue with me, Hemingway. It does no good at all. You're all a lost generation, exactly as the garage keeper said."

Despite his protests, the phrase obviously had some sort of interest for Hemingway. Perhaps he meant it when he called it lovely. He made it one of a pair of epigraphs (the less important of the two, he would insist) in his first novel, attributing it to Stein. But it rankled him forever after; he continued to regard it as an insult. Some fifteen years later he would write that thinking of Gertrude Stein and her anecdote put him in mind of "egotism and mental laziness versus discipline." It made him wonder "who is calling who a lost generation."

His last words on the subject were few and blunt: "The hell with her lost-generation talk and all the dirty, easy labels."

Nonetheless, he could never have denied that Paris in the twenties was a magnet for talented young war survivors like himself, that many were there at least in part because they felt genuinely alienated from home, or that their alienation was connected in some way to the war and the changes both in attitudes and objective reality that it had wrought.

Two bona fide members of whatever Hemingway might have permitted his age cohort to be called were E. E. Cummings and John Dos Passos. Both entered the war as Hemingway did, as volunteer ambulance drivers. Both were expelled from the ambulance service when their opinions of what the Allied cause looked like at close range became known to the authorities. Dos Passos returned home, where he wrote *Three Soldiers,* a 1921 novel that depicted the war as irredeemably vicious and army life as dehumanizing. It was hailed by F. Scott Fitzgerald as "the first war book by an American which is worthy of serious notice." Cummings, absurdly, was imprisoned by the French as a suspected spy. He immortalized the degradation to which he and his fellow inmates were subjected in *The L-Shaped Room,* recognized ever since as a minor classic. After he was released and his health recovered, he like Dos Passos returned to Paris.

On the fringes, destined to become a symbol less of the war generation than of the Jazz Age, was Fitzgerald. In 1917 he had dropped out of Princeton (where he was on academic probation) to join the army. He was commissioned a second lieutenant but discharged in November 1918 without having left the United States. Thus he had little to be disillusioned about, at least where personal experience was concerned. He had the good sense not to pretend otherwise. By 1924, when he finally joined the great literary migration to France with his wife and baby daughter in tow, he was one of America's most popular, and extravagantly well-paid, authors. He and Zelda lived and partied in a style commensurate with their princely income. Hemingway became Fitzgerald's friend, but took him to task for compromising his stories to make them acceptable to top-paying magazines like *The Saturday Evening Post*.

France, the Riviera no less than Paris, was by then chockablock with famously creative or soon-to-be-famous Americans: Cole Porter, Thornton Wilder, John O'Hara, Dorothy Parker, Robert Benchley, Malcolm Cowley, and Archibald MacLeish among many others. They were there for as many reasons as any assortment of talented men and women have for going anywhere: the sunshine of Antibes or the somber beauty of Paris, the company of interesting people, the parties, the wish to be somewhere other than the United States. If they were lost, it was not to an extent conspicuously greater than that of most human beings in all times and places. They did have certain things in common, among them a view of the war that Woodrow Wilson could never have recognized. They saw it as a tragedy, a waste, a prolonged act of folly that had accomplished less than nothing at a cost beyond anyone's ability to reckon.

With this came the suspicion that a civilization capable of producing such a catastrophe, and incapable of stopping it once it was under way, might itself not be worth much.

It was Ezra Pound, thirty-three when the war ended and therefore not far from being a member of Hemingway's generation, who expressed this suspicion most memorably. He wrote of the young men who had

> *walked eye-deep in hell*
> *believing old men's lies, then unbelieving,*
> *came home, home to a lie,*
> *home to many deceits,*
> *home to old lies and new infamy;*
> *usury age-old and age-thick*
> *and liars in public places.*

And of how

> *There died a myriad,*
> *And the best, among them,*

For an old bitch gone in the teeth,
For a botched civilization . . .
For two gross of broken statues,
For a few thousand battered books.

But the last word belongs, once again, to Hemingway. He has the protagonist of *A Farewell to Arms* say that, after all the bloodshed and all the bombast of the war years, such words as "glory, honor, courage, or hallow" had become obscenities to his ears.

It was hardly the effect that President Wilson had intended to achieve when he deployed those same words.

Chapter 22

Compromise or Betrayal?

FEBRUARY 14, 1919, HAS BEEN CALLED THE HIGH POINT OF WOODrow Wilson's life. That is a large claim to make about a career that included election and reelection as president of the United States and leading the nation to victory in the most terrible war the world had ever seen. It is not ridiculous, however. Wilson himself might not have disputed it.

On February 14 he was still at the pinnacle of his popularity and prestige— still *the* hero of the Western world. And on that day, at Versailles, he presented to the nations represented at the peace conference his covenant for the League of Nations and received clear signals that their approval was not going to be a problem. It was an achievement, he himself could have had no doubt, that was going to change the world for the better as far into the future as anyone could claim to see.

His destiny had been fulfilled.

There was, however, another, darker sense in which February 14 stands as the zenith of Wilson's career. His appearance before the peace conference's third plenary session, and its embrace of the covenant, was the last unalloyed triumph he would ever know. From that point forward, the arc of his life would bend increasingly downward. Before the month was out, he would be embroiled in the disputes, and faced with the opposition, that by year's end would leave him a defeated and embittered man.

But on February 14 all that lay ahead, not only unforeseen but unimaginable. It is a measure of how he was still perceived in France, two months after his arrival, that at the end of the day's proceedings, as he and his wife left the Versailles palace, they walked to their limousine on red carpet laid down for their exclusive use in spite of rainy weather. Their path was lined with potted palms, and at its end President Poincaré and Premier Clemenceau stood waiting to say bon voyage. The Wilsons were departing immediately for the port of Brest, where the *George Washington* stood ready to carry them home.

Not that his work in Paris was finished. Far from it; work had not even really begun on the treaty needed to bring the war officially to an end. The Council of Ten was far from agreement on what that treaty should entail. Therefore Wilson would be returning to France, and as soon as possible. It was inconceivable, at least to Wilson, that any settlement could be worked out without his direct involvement. He assigned Colonel House to attend the council meetings while he was away, embarrassing Secretary of State Lansing by doing so.

The president was hurrying home because he had to. The last session of the Sixty-Fifth Congress was slated to end on March 3. If he failed to be on hand to sign the appropriations bills that had not yet been passed when he departed for France, much of the government would eventually be brought to a halt. But it would be a flying visit. He would spend twice as many days at sea, coming and going, as on American soil. Then it would be back to work on the treaty that was to draw a line under the Great War and open a new chapter in the history of mankind.

As the *George Washington* steamed out of Brest that night, his success with the league covenant was only one of Wilson's reasons to be satisfied with what had been accomplished thus far. Clemenceau had been persuaded to abandon his demand for the creation of an international army for the purpose of keeping Germany permanently in check. The Supreme Council had agreed, at Wilson's urging, to grant the world's lesser nations two seats, to be filled on a rotating basis, on the league's executive council. Everything appeared to be developing nicely.

There were difficulties, of course. That was to be expected, and even an issue as heated as the colonial mandates had been dealt with in what everyone appeared to regard as a satisfactory fashion. What was in a way the most awkward difficulty had not come up until February 13, just a day before Wilson's departure. Japan's two representatives on the Supreme Council, who usually had little to say, caught the other members off guard with a proposal that could only have shocked European and North American ears in 1919. They wanted the covenant, which in best Wilsonian fashion declared small nations to have the same rights as mighty ones, to acknowledge the equality of races as well. This produced an uproar. The reaction of Australia's prime minister was only a little more extreme than most: if any such statement were adopted, he said, he would take the next ship home. Wilson, who shared the concern about the "yellow peril" that had made the issue politically sensitive on the U.S. West Coast, had nothing to say. The proposal died without serious discussion, leaving the Japanese quietly unhappy. It would be interesting to know what the Japanese thought when, after reading the covenant aloud to a largely uncomprehending plenary session the next day, Wilson told the assembly that "we are all brothers." Colonel House, untroubled and true to form, afterward told the president that "your speech was as great as the occasion."

There seemed every reason to be confident about what lay ahead. The crossing was not as restful as the overtired president and his physician must have hoped—the seas were so heavy that the usual naval escort had to be abandoned—but the Wilsons found pleasure in fellow passengers, including Assistant Secretary of the Navy Franklin Roosevelt and his wife, Eleanor. News of the covenant appeared in American newspapers the day after Wilson left Paris, and the response was favorable. Joe Tumulty, monitoring the coverage from the White House, sent a cable that must have seemed a confirmation of what the president already believed. "Plain people throughout America for you," it said in verb-swallowing telegraphese. "You have but to ask their support and all opposition will melt away."

The president's secretary, if the best of servants, proved in this case to be the worst of prophets. Doubts about the league, the reality of which Tumulty's message obliquely acknowledged, were widespread in the United States and not going to melt away. Some of them had already hardened into outright opposition. Wilson and Tumulty could take a kind of comfort in the unexpected death, on January 9, of the most potent of the league critics and the man most likely to win the 1920 Republican presidential nomination, Theodore Roosevelt. He died in his sleep at his home in Oyster Bay, on Long Island. With him no longer on the scene, the Republicans had no clear standard-bearer. Their opposition to the league seemed fated to be diffuse.

It might have been, for a time at least, if not for the way the president began to conduct himself almost from the moment of his arrival in the United States. His problems began with a bargain worked out before his departure from Paris. He had been planning, upon his return to Washington, to address a joint session of Congress and use his oratorical powers to cement congressional and popular support. Colonel House, knowing how weary Congress was of being lectured like a class of unruly schoolboys, managed to dissuade his master from doing any such thing. How much better, he said, to invite the members of the Senate Foreign Relations Committee and House Foreign Affairs Committee to the White House for dinner and an informal discussion. In return, the prospective guests would be asked to withhold public comment on the covenant until they had met with the president.

It was a reasonable proposal and readily enough accepted. What turned it into a problem, and the first of a sequence of missteps, was what happened when the *George Washington* docked at Boston on the foggy morning of February 24. Ending the voyage at Boston was necessary because of a New York longshoremen's strike. Turning necessity into an opportunity was Tumulty's idea. He said the local Democratic organization could guarantee an enthusiastic welcome. This would provide food for thought for Massachusetts senator Henry Cabot Lodge, who was to become chairman of the Foreign Relations Committee when the Sixty-Sixth Congress was seated in May and the Republicans took control of the Senate. Tumulty was confident that a big turnout in support of the president would have an improving effect on Lodge's thinking, especially if, as seemed certain, the senator intended to run for another term. Wilson agreed, with misgivings, and preparations for a grand occasion were set in motion.

February 24, a Monday, had been declared a public holiday in recognition of the president's visit. The newspapers would report that two hundred thousand people turned out to cheer the president as his ship entered Boston Harbor. His reception was an echo, and a loud one, of the uproarious welcomes he had received when visiting Paris, London, and Rome two months earlier. It is understandable if he took this as confirmation that he, more than anyone else on the planet, was in deep touch with and spoke for the aspirations of common people everywhere, the people of the United States above all. After a simple welcome at the pier, a fifty-car motorcade carried the president through streets lined with well-wishers to a luncheon with dignitaries including the governors of all the New England states. The last of the planned events was a speech—what the president himself had warned would be brief and anodyne remarks—at Mechanics Hall. It was filled to capacity with seven or eight thousand cheerily welcoming people.

Perhaps it was the sheer force of this welcome that encouraged the president to say more than he had intended. His speech was short as promised but anodyne only up to a point. It began with positive rhetoric about how the selflessness of the United States had made her beloved around the world, how

the nations gathered in Paris had been inspired by America's example to be-
have selflessly themselves, and how the conference from which he had just
returned was on course to spread liberation throughout the world. "Now we
will make men free," the president declared. Perhaps it was unnecessary, even
malicious, for influential Republicans and even some Democrats to take offense at what he said next: that the United States could reject the great work
going on in Paris only by limiting herself to "those narrow, selfish, provincial
purposes which seem so dear to some minds that have no sweep beyond the
nearest horizon." The Associated Press certainly found these words provocative. The account that it sent to newspapers around the country said that Wilson had "thrown down the gauntlet."

In any case, it was the speech's combative elements that league skeptics focused on. They pointed to what appeared to be the president's wish not for
consultation and conciliation but for a showdown. "I have fighting blood in
me," he had pridefully if rather obscurely said, "and it is sometimes a delight
to let it have scope, but if it is challenged on this occasion it will be an indulgence." He meant that if getting the league approved came down to a fight, he
would welcome it. This was braggadocio, oratorical strutting. It set the pattern
for what lay ahead: belligerence on Wilson's part, disdain for those members
of Congress who failed to do as he demanded, and anger on both sides.

What mattered more than the president's sharp words was his decision to
begin selling the league and criticizing those hesitant to support it in the most
public way possible literally from the hour of his arrival in the United States.
The congressmen who were to be his dinner guests two days later, and who
had consented to keep their opinions to themselves until then, took this as an
act of bad faith. They regarded themselves as released from any obligation not
to speak out. Some of them, asked by reporters to comment, did so in acid
terms. A few said they would not attend the dinner.

Negative reaction to the president's comments covered a broad spectrum.
At one extreme were the very few senators, progressives all, who were already
saying that they would not vote to ratify the treaty under any circumstances.
They were vastly outnumbered by those who saw the league and the covenant
as potentially positive but in need of being altered. These were Republicans,
mainly; almost all of the Senate's Democrats were prepared to follow their
president, if only to avoid punishment by the White House.

Some of the opposition was partisanship pure and simple. This was intensified in more than a few instances by dislike for Woodrow Wilson the man.

But to characterize the whole of the opposition in this way would be unfair. Among the doubters were people who believed that George Washington had been deeply wise in warning his fellow citizens against "entangling alliances," and who feared that membership in the league would compromise American sovereignty. These were not irresponsible concerns, especially in light of the covenant as approved at the Paris conference. They were shared by such Republicans as William Howard Taft and Elihu Root, who wanted an international organization of some kind but saw reason for caution. Such people understood that the world of George Washington no longer existed and that the United States with her size and power had a role to play in international affairs that went beyond buying and selling abroad. It has always been unjust to call them isolationists.

Henry Cabot Lodge,
U.S. senator from
Massachusetts, 1893–1924
*Haughty, aristocratic, and learned,
he said Wilson had "no intellectual
integrity at all."*

Henry Cabot Lodge would stand out as the most important and interesting of the skeptics, only in part because of his power as chairman of the Committee on Foreign Relations. What is curious is how intense and personal his clash with Wilson became—"I never expected to hate anyone in politics with the hatred I feel for Wilson," he said—in spite of the many values that the two held in common. Both held Ph.D.'s from prestigious institutions and had written numerous books on government and public policy. Both believed that the United States was morally superior to other nations, with an exalted destiny, and that their "race," the Anglo-Saxon, was uniquely gifted in the arts of governance and destined to lead, if not exactly rule, the world.

Both had such strong personal and cultural ties to Great Britain that they were all but fated to be more sympathetic to the Allies than to Germany, though Lodge had from the start been far more passionately convinced than Wilson of the rightness of the Allied cause and incomparably more hostile to Germany. Beyond their shared beliefs, the two had irreconcilably different views of *how* the United States should fulfill its great destiny, and the Great War made the gap unbridgeable. Viewed from one angle, their quarrel can appear to have been played out on a loftier plane than is common in politics, one where foreign policy becomes almost a branch of philosophy. Seen from another angle, it was no more subtle than a bare-knuckle fight over streetcar franchises by two big-city ward bosses who just happened to loathe each other.

At the bottom of their conflict over the peace treaty and League of Nations lay one simple fact: Lodge's thinking about the needs of the postwar world was far more compatible with that of the Allied leaders—Clemenceau in particular—than with Wilson's. Like the feisty old French premier, the senator wanted the league to be a permanent alliance of the war's winners, and he wanted its first purpose to be the permanent subjugation of Germany. Attached though he was to Britain, he parted from Lloyd George in being fully in support of French domination of the European mainland. He actually encouraged Clemenceau and Lloyd George, during the peace conference, to resist the American president.

As early as 1912, Lodge had told a friend that Wilson's abrupt and wholesale shift from Old South conservatism to progressivism showed him to have "no intellectual integrity at all." He added that "I think he would sacrifice any opinion at any moment for his own benefit and go back on it the next moment if he thought returning to it would be profitable."

One might almost expect that Lodge, viewing Germany as by its nature a threat to stability and peace, would have embraced the Wilson who called for war in April 1917 and summoned the nation to save civilization by unseating the kaiser and the villains who served him. Such a rapprochement was, however, never possible. By the time of American intervention, Lodge's natural unhappiness at seeing Wilson become only the second Democrat elected to the presidency since the Civil War had turned into alarm and then contempt. He saw William Jennings Bryan as too ignorant and incompetent to be entrusted with the State Department, and Wilson as so foolishly evenhanded as to be in effect pro-German. The president's call for peace without victory was, in Lodge's eyes, unforgivable. Even the decision to enter the war he took as fresh proof of Wilson's inconstancy; if the things Wilson said in asking Congress to declare war were true, Lodge told Theodore Roosevelt at the time, "everything he has done for [the preceding] two years and a half is fundamentally wrong."

The Armistice was for Lodge a poisoned chalice. He wanted the war to go on until Berlin was in Allied hands, the whole German nation under occupation. And now the United States was represented at the peace conference by a president who was, Lodge fervently believed, as timid as he was inconstant. By the time of the February 26 White House dinner, the senator saw himself as having been made responsible by fate for protecting the United States and the world from what could easily prove to be a blunder of monstrous proportions.

Thirty-three guests showed up at the White House: men who sat on the House Foreign Affairs Committee and Senate Foreign Relations Committee or would become members when the new Congress convened. The gathering was in no way a disaster, but neither did it accomplish anything. At dinner Edith Wilson, seated with Lodge, filled his ear with an effusive account of what a tremendous welcome her husband had been given upon disembarking in Boston. It was hardly the way to put an unsympathetic Massachusetts Republican in a relaxed and receptive frame of mind. In the three hours that followed, Mrs. Wilson having withdrawn, the guests asked questions and the president answered. By all accounts he did so politely, patiently, and forthrightly, but to no discernible effect. Perhaps Wilson was too professorial. Possibly he was at times ever so slightly disdainful—or seen as disdainful, at least, by congressmen grown weary of what they thought his superior airs. It is likewise possible that he did nothing wrong. In any case there was no warmth on either side, no meeting of minds, no minds changed. Upon returning to France, Wilson would waste no time in letting Colonel House know that his dinner idea had been a useless exercise.

The president was in the United States only nine days, doing about as much damage to his cause as was possible in such a short time. On the day after the dinner he met with the Democratic National Committee. It was supposed to be an off-the-record event, but Wilson must have understood that the press was going to be curious about what was said, and that in his audience would be people with other priorities than respecting the president's confidence. As at Boston, he spoke of the league mainly in positive terms, emphasizing its importance to the future of the world. But he went further in heaping scorn on those who hesitated to give him their support—on their "contemptible" character and the "fatuity" of "their poor little minds." These insults appeared in the newspapers in a matter of hours.

If the president was throwing down the gauntlet, the Republicans were not reluctant to pick it up. As March began, with the statutory end of the congressional session only hours away, they filibustered some of the appropriations bills that Wilson had returned to the United States to sign. Sufficient votes to stop the filibuster via cloture were lacking, which meant that the president was going to have to call an extraordinary session of Congress within the next several months. This was a particularly clever stroke on the Republicans' part: by the time of the special session, the men elected in November 1918 would be in office, and those who had lost their seats or were voluntarily retiring would be gone. The Republicans would be in control, and Lodge would be their leader. The Democrats cried foul, but not with great conviction. All but the greenest understood that politics ain't beanbag.

By now the sharper brains in both parties were becoming more specific about what they found troubling in the covenant. Some feared that it would undercut the Monroe Doctrine, by which the United States had for a century told the European powers to keep their grasping hands off the western hemisphere, promising in return to leave Europe to the Europeans. Others feared that the United States, if she joined the league, would not be free to quit if she later wished to do so, would not be able to refuse unwanted mandates, and would lose control of internal matters—tariffs, immigration—that Washington regarded as nobody's business but its own.

Above all there was concern about Article 10—the part of the covenant that Wilson believed to be the most indispensable. It pledged members to defend threatened nations in the following terms:

> The Members of the League undertake to respect and preserve as against external aggression the territorial integrity and existing political independence of all Members of the League. In case of any such aggression or in case of any threat or danger of such aggression the Council [to be made up of the United States, Britain, France, Italy, Japan, and four temporary members elected by the General Assembly] shall advise upon the means by which this obligation shall be fulfilled.

There is no better example of how the covenant was, in historian William C. Widenor's words, "fraught with ambiguities." What did these words mean, really? What, specifically, was the "obligation" to which the article referred? Would the league have its own army? If so, how would that army be raised? If not, what armies would be used? Who would command them and set their objectives? Could the league order the ships and troops of member nations to attack wherever it wished, at times of its choosing? What part would the United States, now the world's most powerful nation, play? Could her armed forces be sent to war at the command of the league, in violation of the Constitution? Would she be obliged to go to war to keep the British Empire intact? To deploy troops whenever any two countries started shooting at each other?

Thoughtful senators and citizens, upon reading the covenant, could hardly avoid asking such questions. Wilson, not wisely but all too characteristically, saw the questioners as enemies. Article 10 was his sole truly original contribution to the covenant, the only part of it not taken from some earlier source. Later in the year, in attempting to sell it to the public, he would say that it "speaks the conscience of the world." Even now, he was ready with a twofold response to questions. He insisted that Article 10 was essential to the league's effectiveness and could not, must not, be altered. He insisted also that there was no need to worry about the details: the league itself, once up and running, would attend to the fine print. Lodge, for one, was not satisfied. "We must have facts," he said. "Glittering and enticing generalities will not serve." He complained that "I read [Wilson's] speeches, and they are all in the clouds and all fine sentiments that lead nowhere." He was not alone.

When supportive Democrats warned that without changes the covenant would have little chance of ratification, Wilson complained in reply that asking the peace conference to debate American amendments would create insuperable difficulties. Again he was particularly adamant about Article 10: it was *the* guarantee of peace and perfect as it stood.

March 4 was his last day in the United States and the most dramatic of his visit. On the floor of the Senate, Lodge presented a declaration—which the press would call the Round Robin—that the league covenant was not acceptable "in the form now proposed." It called for the peace conference to make a treaty with Germany its first priority, setting the league aside for attention later. The drama lay in the fact that this declaration bore the signatures of thirty-nine men who would be Republican members of the Senate when the new Congress convened. This was six more than the number needed to defeat a treaty—and any covenant embedded in a treaty.

That evening, as his final public act before departing for France, the president gave a speech in New York. Big enthusiastic crowds welcomed him, and the Metropolitan Opera House was filled to capacity. The Republicans in the audience were cheered by the appearance onstage of one of their own, former president Taft, who as head of the League to Enforce Peace had become a highly visible advocate of an association of all the world's nations. Now he defended Wilson's league, defended even Article 10, telling his listeners that there was nothing in the essence of the covenant that Americans need fear.

The good-natured Taft did something else, too—something that potentially mattered more than his endorsement of the covenant. He praised Lodge and other senators from his own party for making "suggestions that should prove especially valuable in the work of revising the form of the covenant and in making changes to which the [Paris] conference may readily consent." This was not a grasp at partisan advantage; it pointed the way to a bridge across the divide that had been widening since Wilson's arrival at Boston. By clear implication, it invited the president to make use of the one promising feature of the Round Robin: its assertion that the signers would not accept the covenant *in the form now proposed*. This gaping loophole created ample scope for a working out of differences. In that place and at that moment, Taft's positive tone, generous to both sides in the league debate, was a gift to Woodrow Wilson.

Wilson spurned it. Offended by the Round Robin and by Taft's positive words about Lodge and his followers, his spirits buoyed by the cheering crowds that had lined his route from Pennsylvania Station to the opera house, he used his turn at the lectern to spit venom on all who presumed to question the covenant as he had written it. He professed to be amazed by the "narrowness" of such people, their "comprehensive ignorance of the state of the world," their "doctrine of careful selfishness thought out to the last detail." Again he seemed determined not to negotiate but to fight—even to pick a fight.

He also displayed his growing tendency not just to speak in abstractions—he had always done that—but to use grand generalities to describe a war and a world that never were and never could have been. He said on this night that the armies of Germany—armies invincible when faced with Britain and France and Italy and Russia—had gone into collapse as soon as they made contact with America's doughboys. And they had "continued to break, my fellow citizens, not merely because of the physical force of those lusty youngsters but because of the irresistible spiritual force of the armies of the United States." *Spiritual* force: not so surprising a thing, if God was on America's—on Wilson's—side. One can only wonder what the Yanks mowed down at Belleau Wood and in the valley of the Meuse would have made of it. No doubt they would have regretted not having had a bit more of it, whatever it was.

Having thus made plain his rejection of all doubts and thrown insults in the faces of the doubters, the president steamed off to France. His belligerence fed on the conviction that the voters of America wanted the league pretty much on his terms, and about that he may very well have been right. At this early stage, before the possible implications of league membership came under close public scrutiny, millions accepted Wilson's assurances that an international organization—this particular international organization—was going to be essential to the new world order he had promised. In returning to France, he left behind a nation whose economy was still humming along nicely thanks to the needs of devastated foreign countries, but where millions of people were finding it difficult to get by. Inflation was essentially out of control, at times spiking to an annual rate of 100 percent. Neither government nor industry felt any lingering need to be generous with workers. The war, after all, was over. Even corporations with fat order books and high profits were reducing their workforces, demanding longer hours, and cutting wages. The gains made recently by well-behaved unions such as the AFL were being taken back.

There would be two and a half thousand strikes in the United States in 1919. As in prewar days, the police powers of the national, state, and local governments would be used against the strikers. Irruptions of discontent including a February 1919 general strike in Seattle were becoming almost commonplace, and were blamed on shadowy unnamed Bolsheviks.

For Wilson all this was little more than background noise. Back in December, before his first departure for France, he announced, in what would prove to be his last annual report to Congress, what amounted to the end of the progressive era. "Our people," he had said, "do not want to be coached and led. They know their own business, are quick and resourceful at every readjustment, definite in purpose, and self-reliant in action. Any leading strings we might seek to put them in would speedily become hopelessly entangled because they would pay no attention to them and go their own way. All that we can do as their legislative and executive servants is to mediate the process of change here, there and elsewhere as we may." Domestic reform, in short, not only no longer mattered but was not even achievable. As for himself, he now had more important priorities. The Japanese had been bruised by the Supreme Council's rejection of their racial equality clause and were suspicious of its slowness in granting them the German concessions in China's Shantung peninsula. The Italians seemed to want to erect a kind of new Roman empire on the ruins of the old order. And the Middle East was an impossible tangle: Britain and France were in the process, even as the president spoke, of redrawing its map to suit themselves.

Beyond all this was the still barely addressed challenge of deciding what kinds of peace terms to impose on Germany. A president burdened with such a task could expect to be excused for not giving a great deal of attention to domestic matters, surely, when the world needed him so badly.

Colonel House, who had been dealing with the German question and other matters before the Supreme Council during the month of Wilson's absence, was waiting at Brest when the *George Washington* arrived. His reunion with the president is shrouded in mystery and intimations of intrigue. Edith Wilson, in a memoir written years later, says that House came aboard when the ship docked, talked with the president in private at some length, and sent him into something like a state of shock. "He seemed to have aged ten years," the lady says of her husband as he emerged from the meeting, "and his jaw was set in that way it had when he was making a superhuman effort to control himself. Silently he held out his hand, which I grasped, crying: 'What is the matter? What happened?'"

Wilson "smiled bitterly," according to his wife. She then has him saying that "House has given away everything I had won before we left Paris. He has compromised on every side, and so I have to start all over again and this time it will be harder."

The least of the problems with this little melodrama is that the colonel never went aboard the *George Washington,* but waited for the Wilsons to come ashore. The two men certainly had much to discuss—everything that had happened in Washington and Paris during their separation, all the great and little crises—and not everything House had to report would have been received by the president as good news. But nothing had happened that could possibly have caused Wilson to think House had betrayed him or even let him down in any seriously damaging way.

The colonel had, in keeping with Wilson's instructions, sat in for him at the meetings of the Council of Ten. But he had stayed within the limits that the president prescribed, kept him informed by cable at every step, and committed the United States to nothing. He had not been passive; passivity was not what the president wanted. But his objective had been not to settle the big questions facing the council but to bring as many of them as possible to a point where they would be ready for the president's decision when he returned.

The council, for that matter, had been relatively inactive while Wilson was away. An attempted assassination of Clemenceau on February 19 had left the aged premier with a bullet in his chest, causing him to miss six of the month's eighteen meetings. Lloyd George had a worse attendance record with less excuse, spending much time in England and showing up only six times. Orlando of Italy, typically, attended only twice. Mrs. Wilson's dire story may have been, if not simply the result of a confused memory or excited imagination, an effort to justify a subsequent development in which she would play more than a small part: the end of the House-Wilson friendship in absolute estrangement.

If House did upset the president that morning, he is most likely to have done so simply by giving a candid account of how badly, in his opinion, the peacemaking process had been going during the past month. He was himself in low spirits after prolonged direct exposure to the Supreme Council's arcane divisions, unfocused deliberations, and glacially slow progress. On the day of Wilson's Metropolitan Opera House speech, he had added an almost despondent entry to his diary: "It is now evident that the peace will not be such a peace as I had hoped, or one which this terrible upheaval should have brought about. . . . I dislike to sit and have forced upon us such a peace as we are facing. We will get something out of it in the way of a League of Nations, but even that is an imperfect instrument." The French especially, but the British and Italians, too, were making demands that could only be granted by trampling again on the Fourteen Points. Central and eastern Europe were sinking deeper into disorder. Fear was growing that much of Europe might fall into the hands of revolutionaries.

House shared these fears. Thus he was not insensitive to the appeal of an idea that was winning adherents at the conference as well as in Washington: that for the sake of restoring stability in Europe before it was too late, a treaty of peace should be concluded with all possible speed, if necessary before creation of the League of Nations. "My main drive now is for peace with Germany at the earliest possible moment," says a House diary entry at the time of Wilson's return to France, "and I am determined that it shall come soon if it is within my power to force action." A day later Wilson's physician wrote in his diary of being told by the president that, upon his return to Paris, Clemenceau and Lloyd George had declared their support for "side-tracking of the League of Nations." Worse, the two premiers claimed that the colonel "had practically agreed to the proposition."

Lloyd George and Clemenceau were the real threats to the covenant's place at the heart of the treaty; Colonel House could have done nothing, himself, to separate the two things. It is nonetheless obvious that any sign of willingness on House's part even to consider separating them would have horrified the president. This undoubtedly helps explain the estrangement of the two men that first became apparent at about this point. The fact that the colonel was motivated by nothing more sinister than a recognition of the desperate state of central and eastern Europe and the magnitude of the challenges facing the Supreme Council would not have diminished Wilson's sense of betrayal.

House was learning, if he did not already know, that the Wilson with whom he had worked so intimately in earlier years had passed out of existence by March 1919. The new world-hero Wilson, the Wilson of Paris, deeply hated the thought of having to ask the other members of the council to amend the covenant—hated having to *ask* them for anything. He hated even more the thought of lowering himself (as he saw it) to satisfy senators for whom he had only contempt. He showed his determination to have things his way by issuing an announcement that the peace treaty and the covenant would continue to move forward together.

Postwar Wilson was even more isolated than the earlier versions had been. He trusted no one except his adoring wife—not even House at this stage, certainly none of the other American delegates. He shared his plans with no one except, perhaps, Edith, and allowed no one except her to assist him in his work. He was pushing himself to the limits of his strength. House's fall from grace was hastened by the fact that in Paris he became more visible than he had ever been at home. His role as substitute for Wilson at Supreme Council meetings made anonymity impossible, but beyond that he was making himself more available to the press than he had ever been at home. He granted occasional interviews, and some newspapers suggested that it was he more than Wilson who was making things happen. Mrs. Wilson was aware of this, and it turned her old dislike into open displays of annoyance. For her weary husband, the colonel's growing celebrity was a maddening new source of distress. The role of great peacemaker was his alone.

It has been said of Woodrow Wilson that he could break but not bend. In the days following his return to Paris this was not entirely true. One thing could still induce him to show a modicum of flexibility: fear of losing the league. Thus it took less than a week back in France for him to begin to see the wisdom, even the necessity, of altering the covenant as friends had urged in Washington and House was urging now. Taft was helpful in changing his mind. He cabled Wilson that with just a few changes he could force his opponents to abandon their objections. This was wrong as prediction but exactly the right way to persuade Wilson to take a new approach. It enabled him to stop regarding amendments as a humiliation and see them as a way of bringing the likes of Henry Cabot Lodge to heel.

Working at night, usually alone or with his wife sitting quietly nearby, Wilson drafted four amendments, each one aimed at taking a weapon out of the hands of the opposition back home. They made explicit things that Wilson had been willing to take for granted but others had not. That the league would have no authority to intrude into member countries' domestic affairs. That members were free to quit the league, and also to refuse mandates. That nothing in the covenant should be construed as compromising the Monroe Doctrine.

The care with which the president crafted his amendments would not make them proof against objections in Congress. The first three, however, were accepted without difficulty by his fellow council members. Wilson must have expected that the one dealing with the Monroe Doctrine, a simple confirmation of what had been unchallenged American policy for a century, would be the least objectionable of all. Though no European country had ever formally recognized the Monroe Doctrine, neither had any ever defied it. There was nothing, really, to dispute.

Or would have been nothing, if Clemenceau and Lloyd George had not been on the lookout for leverage in their dealings with Wilson. They understood three things. First, that by asking for their agreement the president was putting them in a position of power. Second, that the American Congress was so hostile to even an implied dilution of the Monroe Doctrine that such a possibility would cause it to reject the league. Third, that of all the issues facing the peace conference, for Wilson the league remained paramount. It seemed possible that he might do or refrain from doing almost anything to keep his covenant essentially intact and in the treaty. This was his Achilles' heel, and it had the potential to outweigh all the advantages he had brought with him to Paris. The Allies set out to exploit it.

Their task was made easier by Wilson's deficiencies as a negotiator and his insistence on not sharing his work with anyone, which made it impossible for House and the other American delegates to help compensate for those deficiencies. Every competent negotiator understands the importance of asking in the beginning for more than he needs or expects to get. There is nothing shameful in this. It is how the game has always been played, making it possible for everyone involved to offer concessions and accept compromises and still get a satisfactory outcome. Wilson regarded such tactics as unworthy of a man as upright as himself. He opened what others expected to be bargaining sessions by exposing his bottom line—the irreducible minimum beyond which he was not prepared to go. This, and his frequently sanctimonious tone, made bargaining difficult if not impossible.

Faced with such an adversary, and presented with the opportunity to deny him something he thought neither he nor the world could do without, Clemenceau and Lloyd George were able to force Wilson to give ground in ways that under other circumstances he would never have considered. He became a sheep among wolves, doomed to be shorn if not devoured.

Clemenceau was first to name his price. Resigned to the impossibility of getting the one thing that might have satisfied him completely, the undoing of the 1871 unification of Germany, he demanded the next best thing. He said he wanted not only Alsace and Lorraine to be stripped from Germany but much of the Rhineland as well. He wanted the Saar valley, which in addition to being heavily industrialized had more coal reserves than all of France. He wanted some German territory to be given to France outright, some to be put under international governance via the League of Nations, and some to be turned into a new Rhine republic that, though formally autonomous and neutral, would function as a French satellite. He also wanted Germany to pay reparations in amounts so vast that the interest alone would keep her financially crippled indefinitely. These exactions, when combined with Polish annexations of territory on Germany's eastern flank, might just suffice, Clemenceau conceded, to meet France's security needs.

Even Lloyd George, pledged though he was to make the Germans pay for their sins, was taken aback by Clemenceau's demands. If for Wilson those demands constituted a gross departure from the letter and spirit of his peace plan, for Lloyd George they meant an end to the European balance of power and the return of France to continental supremacy. They also meant, Lloyd George feared, the creation of new Alsace-Lorraines—annexations certain to create lasting grievances and cause future wars. Nonetheless he, too, had his price and was prepared to bargain if doing so could work to Britain's advantage. He, like Wilson, wanted the league covenant amended, but by no means in the same ways.

Above all, he wanted to expunge the second of Wilson's Fourteen Points, the one guaranteeing freedom of the seas. Wilson could not accept this; it would remove what he saw as one of the essential elements of a lasting peace, the guarantee that, in case of another war, neutral nations would remain free to trade where they wished. For the British, such a guarantee smacked of national suicide. "Germany has been broken almost as much by the blockade as by military methods," Lloyd George said. "If this power is to be handed over to the League of Nations and Great Britain were fighting for her life, no league of nations would prevent her from defending herself. . . . My view is that I should like to see this League of Nations established before I let this power go. If the League of Nations is a reality, I am willing to discuss the matter."

It cannot have escaped notice that he was promising not to accept freedom of the seas but only to discuss the possibility, and not now but later, after certain conditions had been met. He also wanted the United States to scale back its naval shipbuilding program, so that Britain's Royal Navy could remain supreme. Wilson saw these demands as barely disguised insults, a flagrant refusal of what he had been advocating since before the United States entered the war. Clemenceau with his grab at the Rhineland was all but mocking what the president had said the previous Fourth of July: that every question of territory, sovereignty, and political arrangement must be settled "upon the basis of the free acceptance of that settlement by the people immediately concerned." Lloyd George, more excusably if no less annoyingly, was simply making plain that Wilson had been indulging in wishful thinking in expecting the British to agree to a freedom of the seas that would mean no more starvation blockades.

The stage was thus set for a showdown, and it was not long in coming. Partly out of frustration with the peace conference's slow and uncertain progress, possibly in part because he wanted fewer witnesses to what were sure to be tempestuous discussions, in the last week of March Wilson discontinued the Council of Ten and said that henceforth he would meet with Clemenceau,

Lloyd George, and Orlando only. This reduced the Supreme Council to a membership of four and more often than not to a trio; Orlando would continue to be frequently absent, probably because the discussions were in English, and he alone did not speak it. One of the reduced council's first sessions, on March 28, was blown apart by an explosive exchange of recriminations having to do with German reparations. Clemenceau, accused by Wilson of wanting too much, called the president pro-German and stormed out. Once again the peacemaking process seemed in danger of collapse, which would have left the war's winners as well as its losers to shift for themselves amid Europe's spreading chaos.

At this moment of crisis, to calm Clemenceau, Wilson and Lloyd George took an extraordinary step. They told Clemenceau that their countries would join with France in a new triple alliance, committing to come to France's rescue in case of a German invasion. In the short term, this was a meaningless gesture; Germany had demobilized her armies as soon as they returned from the various fronts and was no longer capable of maintaining domestic order, let alone defending herself. With France to her west, Poland's new army of half a million men to her east, and a quarter of a million Czech troops to the south, Germany's ability to attack anyone was nil.

From a longer-term perspective, the proposed alliance was meaningless in a very different way. It was a radical departure for Britain, which had traditionally avoided committing, openly at least, to peacetime alliances with continental powers. Lloyd George did have the power to make it happen, however, and therefore could responsibly make the offer. Wilson had no such power; the alliance he was promising would require Senate ratification and had absolutely no chance of getting it. The president cannot have failed to understand this. It is impossible to believe that the British and French failed to understand it, either. Thus an air of unreality hangs over the entire episode and America's part in it. Wilson had always responded to fears that the League of Nations would drag the United States into "entangling alliances" by saying that, as an alliance of all nations against threats to peace rather than of some countries against others, the league would be liberating rather than entangling. Now he was offering an alliance of three nations, one directed at a single specific adversary. That was entangling by any definition of the term, including Wilson's own.

Clemenceau professed to be pleased by the offer but said that French acceptance required the approval of his cabinet. It must also, he added, be conditional on the assurance that other, more immediate protections would be provided to France. This was a reference to his Rhineland demands, which were not withdrawn. What made the old Tiger happiest, in all likelihood, was this fresh demonstration of how far the American president could be pushed when the future of the league was at stake. Clemenceau had never objected to the league but had always believed that it would be of little use to France unless made to function as an alliance against the Germans. It now appeared that Wilson was willing to think of it in exactly those terms. Small wonder if Clemenceau was delighted. He continued to press for reparations and annexations sufficient to ruin Germany, but now did so with somewhat less heat.

Biographers have long been fascinated by the fact that it was just at this point that the president's health broke down so completely that he had to spend several days in bed. This has been attributed to a small stroke, an attack of the influenza that was still not entirely gone from Europe, or one of the transient nervous breakdowns that Wilson called his "colds." Whatever the cause, he instructed House to once again sit in for him at council meetings. Alexander and Juliette George, in *Woodrow Wilson and Colonel House,* point to this as another instance of the president's lifelong pattern of retreating into illness at times of great stress. They suggest that in this case the necessity of dealing with Clemenceau's and Lloyd George's demands, and the likelihood that concessions were going to prove unavoidable, persuaded him, if only on a subconscious level, that making them would be less painful if done through House.

The weakness in this hypothesis is that the bedridden Wilson showed no inclination to concede anything. The council began meeting in a study adjacent to his bedroom, with Colonel House shuttling between the presidential bedside and the table to which he delivered Wilson's pronouncements. On April 5 the subject of the day was reparations. Clemenceau, who had earlier more than doubled Germany's reparations bill by winning agreement that she must pay the pensions of the Allies' veterans and widows and orphans, now insisted that there must be no limit on the amount owed or the number of years—or decades, or generations—over which payments would continue. Lloyd George, seeing the help that this could be with his government's financial problems, supported Clemenceau. Presumably he was also hoping that by doing so he would have Clemenceau's support when his own demands came up for discussion.

Wilson, with House's encouragement, stood firm: the Allies' reparations demands were out of the question. On Sunday, April 6, he summoned the other American delegates to his sickroom; they must have been surprised, as usually the president paid them no attention. He announced that if within the next few days the French and British did not become more reasonable, either the entire American delegation would be going home or he would tell the world what the Allies were demanding and insist that all future negotiations take place in plenary session, which meant in public view. That same evening he cabled instructions to Treasury Secretary McAdoo to stop extending financial credits to the Allies, and he ordered the *George Washington* to return to Brest from New York and stand by to take him and the others home. If these moves were a bluff—Wilson made certain that the British and French learned of them—they had little discernible effect. Certainly Clemenceau was not intimidated; he moderated none of his demands.

Wilson remained in a combative mood. When he learned that Colonel House, disgusted by the spectacle of Clemenceau, Lloyd George, and Orlando squabbling among themselves, had walked out of a meeting in Lloyd George's apartment, he approved heartily. But in the week that followed, what the president liked to call his "fighting blood" cooled, and by Wednesday he was in retreat. Two cables from Washington exposed the weakness of his position on the home front. In one, Tumulty warned that an exit from the conference would be decried in Washington as an act of petulance, a shirking of responsibility. In the other, McAdoo reported that in the near term it was not possible to cut off credits in any meaningful way; the Allies had already received enough to see them halfway through the summer.

In the end Clemenceau got not everything he had demanded but a very great deal. He could not win Lloyd George's support for the creation of a Rhine republic. That would have been indefensible: five million Germans living on ten thousand square miles of what had always been German soil. Its benefits for France would have been incompatible with Britain's strategic interests. Almost everything else, however, went Clemenceau's way. France was given what amounted to ownership of the Saar mines, which produced seventeen million tons of coal annually, for a period of fifteen years. During those years the entire Saar basin was to be governed by a League of Nations commission, and then the population would vote on whether to become French or rejoin Germany. German military installations were forbidden not only west of the Rhine but for thirty miles to the east, and French troops would control all bridgeheads on both sides of the river for fifteen years. Clemenceau had wanted the bridgeheads for thirty years but was given something better instead: a guarantee that the French would not have to withdraw at all if, when the fifteen years were over, they judged that doing so would leave them insufficiently secure. The way was open to keep Germany under France's heel more or less forever.

Even that was far from all. Wilson's surrender on the issue of reparations was total. No limit was placed on the amount to be paid (it was to be determined at some future time by a commission) or on the number of years Germany would remain liable. France still had the promise of an anti-German alliance with Britain and the United States, fanciful though it was. Lloyd George even got Wilson's assurance that the United States would cut back on shipbuilding.

Why did the president give up so much so quickly? He himself subsequently offered various explanations. He repeated his confidence that, if anything including his compromises proved to be problematic, it would be corrected by the league. He said the peace conference was supposed to usher in a new era of international cooperation, and he had contributed to making that happen by being so cooperative. He said also that it was necessary to get things settled in Europe before Bolshevism spread everywhere. The consensus among recent historians is that the deals struck in the first ten days of April, some of them dubious in the extreme and seen even by Wilson admirers as mistakes, were driven almost solely by the president's determination to keep the creation of the league moving forward. If it died at birth, he had taken America to war for very little. As for the price he was paying to keep the league alive, he put his faith in the ability of the league itself to adjust it downward later.

His reward, when it came on April 11, was meager. The peace conference's covenant commission approved adoption of the president's Monroe Doctrine amendment. The entire revised covenant, with all four amendments, was approved by a plenary session later in the month.

No one was thrilled. Many of the hundreds of Americans employed at the conference believed that the president had sold out. Even some of the delegates—Secretary of State Lansing, General Bliss, and Henry White most notably—were making their dissatisfaction known. Staff members were talking of resigning in protest, and some would do so. Even Clemenceau could not celebrate, for though his cabinet had approved the deal that he had worked out, French leaders as important as President Poincaré and Marshal Foch were, rather incredibly, accusing him of letting Germany off too easily. The premier took no heat for agreeing to Wilson's amendments, however, because no one in France saw them as having the slightest importance. He joked that the Monroe Doctrine was meaningless except as a device for extracting concessions from the United States. He had the same opinion of a League of Nations that had no army of its own; it was never going to matter in any way that France cared about.

Lloyd George found himself under attack in London for allowing France to become too strong. In Washington, congressmen voiced fears that the Monroe Doctrine amendment would encourage Japan to claim a similar sphere of influence in East Asia. Americans were also concerned about the transfer of Shantung to Japan in spite of China's furious objections. That transfer was regarded by the council as necessary to placate Japanese indignation over rejection of the racial equality clause. Again Wilson appeared to many to have betrayed his own principles—and in doing so to have enhanced Japan's growing strength in the western Pacific. Drawing upon ancient myth, General Bliss (an amateur scholar who read the Latin and Greek classics for recreation) wrote to his wife that in yielding to "the Prussianized militarism of Japan," the president was "sowing dragons' teeth"—making trouble inevitable in the long term. Increasing numbers of his fellow Americans were coming to suspect the same thing, and not only about Japan.

This marks the opening of the final and tragic chapter of President Wilson's career. From this point forward, the darkest elements of his character would increasingly dominate his actions and utterances, with unhappy consequences for himself, his legacy, and, not least, the world. He was losing his ability to charm—or perhaps had simply stopped trying. With increasing frequency, other participants in the peace conference wrote of finding him unpleasant to deal with. Lord David Cecil, a key member of the British delegation, was all too typical. "I am coming to the conclusion that I do not personally like him," Cecil wrote of Wilson. "I do not know quite what it is that repels me: a certain hardness, coupled with vanity and an eye for effect."

Background

Strange Bedfellows

The framers of the American Constitution, when they made ratification of treaties subject to approval by two-thirds of the Senate, unknowingly ensured that the ninety-five senators holding office when the Sixty-Sixth Congress convened more than 130 years later would be plunged into one of the most momentous political battles in the nation's history.

Taken as a group, those ninety-five men (one seat was vacant) were almost as mixed, divided, and combative as the vast sprawling country they represented. They responded to the treaty that Woodrow Wilson brought back from Paris, and the league covenant embedded in it, in such wildly divergent ways as to make generalizations nearly impossible.

On one side were forty-six Democrats, in the minority for the first time since 1913 as a result of the 1918 election. They were under heavy pressure to support the president and the treaty without quibble or qualification. Almost all were willing, but there were exceptions, mavericks such as Thomas Gore of Oklahoma, who disliked the treaty and said so loudly. But all of them, as Congress opened, would have fit into a Model T Ford.

The action, the drama, was on the Republican side. Of the party's forty-nine senators (fifty when the vacancy was filled), few were either unalterably opposed to the treaty or ready to vote for it as it stood. William Borah of Idaho, almost as potent a figure as Robert La Follette in the progressive movement, had already declared himself to be "irreconcilable"—committed to rejecting the League of Nations no matter how its covenant might be amended. But in March 1919 the Republican senators prepared to stand with Borah would have fit into that Model T with room to spare. Most were inclined to agree with former president Taft that the league idea had merit, but as proposed by Woodrow Wilson was problematic. Such men hoped that compromise was going to be possible, and many expected that it would.

At the center of the drama, like a conductor charged with turning a random assortment of unruly musicians into an orchestra, was the trimly elegant figure of Henry Cabot Lodge. Delighted that the previous year's election had elevated him to de facto Senate majority leader and chairman of the Foreign Relations Committee at such a critical juncture, he had no illusions about the difficulties that faced him. Though convinced that the covenant as written by the president was unacceptable, he kept clear of Borah and the other irreconcilables. Unlike them, he stood ready to wheel and deal.

His character and personality bring to mind Winston Churchill's quip about Clement Attlee: that he was a humble man with much to be humble about. Lodge was a snob but an impressive one, with much to be snobbish about. Born into the most exclusive reaches of Boston aristocracy and raised on Beacon Hill, he grew up to graduate first from Harvard, then from its law school, and finally to become, in 1876, one of three men on whom Harvard conferred the first Ph.D.'s in history ever awarded by an American university. He was a protégé of Henry Adams, the most revered man of letters in the country, and in young manhood he was painted by John Singer Sargent.

Cold and sometimes arrogant in his dealings with most people, Lodge was not easy to love and not even liked by many of his colleagues. Early in his career, serving as editor of the prestigious *North American Review,* he had accepted for publication an article by the young and unknown Woodrow Wilson. This did not mark the start of a friendship. To the contrary, the two appear to have disliked each other from early on, and on a visceral level. Some have speculated that the problem was an age difference of a decade and a half: it made Lodge a potential father figure, and Wilson always had trouble with those. It is perhaps natural to wonder if the president resented Lodge's superior social, academic, and intellectual credentials.

As 1919 advanced and the new Congress settled in, the fate of the treaty seemed ever more clearly to be in the hands of the undecided Republicans. Everything depended on whether they and the president were going to find common ground. Lodge became less a conductor than a kind of broker, one with a big personal stake in what was being transacted. He was obviously willing to assist in the creation of the league so long as it did not, in his view, make intolerable demands of the United States.

It thus became a matter of old-fashioned political horse-trading, which as Lodge understood is usually best done quietly, in private. Noise, however, was coming from two directions: from the White House, as President Wilson urged the public to demand Senate approval, and from the still-tiny but very slowly growing ranks of the irreconcilables, who had no interest in negotiating with anyone and much interest in damning the treaty. Their minds were made up to an extent that left no room for discussion.

They were a talented and cantankerous lot, the irreconcilables, and some were among the most famous senators of their time. None was more remarkable than Borah. In 1890, an impoverished twenty-five-year-old lawyer, he had left Kansas to seek his fortune in Seattle but was obliged to leave the train in Boise because he was unable to pay the rest of his fare. Seventeen years later the Idaho legislature sent him to the U.S. Senate. By 1919 he was called the Lion of Idaho by his admirers, and the Great Opposer by an exasperated Republican old guard. He was a tireless battler when his passions were aroused. When President Wilson went on the road to sell the league, Borah followed in his wake across thousands of miles, telling the crowds who came to hear him that the president was wrong, the league a mistake.

Borah was a rarity, a bona fide isolationist. He wanted the United States to keep out of the politics of other continents and make sure that the rest of the world stayed out of the western hemisphere. He warned that, the president's amendment notwithstanding, the covenant would undercut the Monroe Doctrine and encourage European and Asian powers to meddle in the Americas as never before. In this respect he differed from most of his fellow irreconcilables, but they were so varied in their views and their motives that not one of them can be considered altogether typical.

For example, George Norris of Nebraska, another leading progressive, joined Borah without sharing his fears that the league would threaten either national sovereignty or the Monroe Doctrine. Before and during the war, he had advocated the establishment of an international court of arbitration for the nonviolent settlement of disputes. The Wilson league, however, he denounced as "offensive to principles of justice" and designed "to maintain the world supremacy of the British Empire." Like many senators, he took particular exception to the granting to Japan of Germany's concessions in China. This part of the treaty was proving deeply objectionable to American voters, many of whom saw it as an injustice to a helpless China and an encouragement of Japanese aggression. It was proving to be an unexpectedly troublesome problem for the president.

Senator Hiram Johnson, two-term governor of California and Theodore Roosevelt's running mate in 1912, joined the irreconcilables because he agreed with Borah that the league threatened American sovereignty and with Norris that the treaty, if implemented, would reinforce tyranny. Robert La Follette dismissed the entire treaty as "a sham and a fraud . . . written in a frenzy of hate." He pointed to President Wilson's dispatch of troops to Siberia as an example of where ratification would lead.

More consequential than any of these men, because he was almost a symbol of the Republican establishment, was Philander K. Knox of Pennsylvania. He had first entered the Senate after serving as attorney general under Presidents McKinley and Roosevelt, then resigned his seat to become Taft's secretary of state, and now in 1919 was a senator again. Early in the Senate's deliberations, he stood among the skeptical but undecided. He showed himself to be especially concerned about whether the treaty was a recipe for lasting peace or for further wars. His final decision, whenever it came and whatever it was, would carry great weight with his fellow Republicans.

With so much uncertainty and so many senators leaning toward opposition, Lodge could simply have stood aside and allowed the treaty to come up for a vote in its original, unamended form. If he had wanted it killed, that might have been his easiest course. That he did no such thing indicates rather conclusively that in fact he did not want it killed—not if it could be made, in his view, both useful to the world and safe for the United States.

He understood that victory in the war had made Wilson's league proposal popular with the public. He knew also that voters had not yet given the matter careful attention, were not yet fully aware of the questions to which the covenant gave rise, and were only beginning to recover from their long bout of war fever. He foresaw that all this would change with time and that, as the public's awareness increased, so would opportunities to change its mind.

He made it his policy to wait, to slow the ratification process, to do what he could to call public attention to the important questions while allowing the issue to ripen. He put his confidence in the informed voter. In doing so, he showed that a Boston Brahmin could be at least as good a small-d democrat as the Democrat in the White House.

Chapter 23

"Hell's Dirtiest Work"

IN PARIS, AS SPRINGTIME CAME TO RIPENESS, THE NUMBER OF PROBlems confronting the Council of Four appeared to be growing rather than shrinking. The reports and recommendations of the dozens of commissions were piling up and not infrequently ignored. It began to seem that the peace conference might go on forever.

In Washington, as the cherry blossoms came and went, the triple alliance offered to Clemenceau by Wilson and Lloyd George quietly met its inevitable obscure death. When presented to the Senate, it was immediately pigeonholed, never to be brought to a vote. The president's amendments to the league covenant, also delivered to the Senate after being approved in Paris, had disappointingly little impact on the undecided. Meanwhile Article 10, the most sensitive issue of all, had not yet been seriously debated. On Capitol Hill as in no other place on earth, because of its possible implications for the richest and most powerful nation on earth, Article 10 cast a shadow over the whole league question.

And now India was erupting in a vast general strike. The turmoil turned into nightmare on April 13, at Amritsar, when British troops opened fire on a huge crowd of demonstrators. The shooting went on for ten minutes, all of it on one side, and the number killed may have exceeded a thousand. Britain's claim to being a bastion of decency and champion of democracy had never sounded more hollow.

Not that less mighty countries were behaving noticeably better. Lloyd George would complain, bitterly and with unintended irony, that "all these small nations are at this moment heading straight toward their own perdition if they conduct themselves as Poland is doing. It will come to pass that we will judge them as did the Prussians and the Russians: we will conclude that they do not have the right to exist. After having been so oppressed, the Poles [who were at this time invading Galicia and Ukraine] think only of oppressing others."

Orlando and Sonnino of Italy were by this time laying out the terms on which they expected the conference to make good on the Treaty of London. Wilson had never accepted the Allies' secret treaties as legitimate, but he had failed to make himself clear on this point at the start of the conference. To raise it now was certain to offend the Italians. They expected to be compensated in full for their country's half-million dead, and did not regard the movement of Italy's border northward to the Brenner Pass as nearly sufficient. When at a council meeting on Easter Sunday they found no support for their claim to the city of Fiume on the Adriatic coast (it is now named Rijeka and is in Croatia), they not only stormed out of the room but boarded a train for Rome. With Japan, too, making noises about withdrawing, a breakdown of the whole peace process threatened. Newspapers declared a collapse to be imminent.

Another problem was that the fighting men who had survived the war wanted to go home. The sailors of a French fleet in the Black Sea, too long stuck in the Allies' futile intervention in the Russian civil war, mutinied. Three thousand British troops rose up in protest at the port of Folkestone when told they were to be sent back abroad, and four thousand went on strike at Calais.

Vittorio Emanuele Orlando, prime minister of Italy, 1917–1919
He stormed out of the peace conference when his demands were not met.

The Allies and Americans between them now had thirty-nine divisions in western Europe, down from 198 the previous November. They were determined to maintain a number sufficient to occupy all of Germany if necessary, but their soldiers and seamen had clearly had enough.

Clemenceau, Lloyd George, and Wilson saw that they had dallied too long. It was time to stop studying and debating and get a treaty nailed down. The German government—meaning the feeble republican administration struggling to restore order in Germany—was instructed to send a delegation to Paris no later than April 25. The conference's various commissions were told to conclude their investigations and submit whatever they wished to contribute to the treaty without delay. A commission on the treaty itself was created to serve as a kind of clearinghouse, winnowing the submissions as they came in and gathering the results into a comprehensive document. It became an affair of scissors and paste—and of unseemly haste.

Astonishingly, there was no draft treaty on which to build. Secretary of State Lansing had offered to prepare one—had in fact begun work on one—but Wilson had refused his help. Nothing of such importance, the president insultingly said, could be left to mere nitpicking lawyers. In contrast to the pains he had taken in drafting and revising the covenant, however, he did nothing to get a treaty written or have someone else do it. Evidently he was not all that interested in anything except the covenant, just as his fellow council members cared about little except what affected their countries directly. Told to start the drafting process, junior staff members found themselves obliged—or free—to make decisions of immense historical significance.

The six German delegates and their support staff, when they arrived, were received like lepers. They were taken to a hotel surrounded with barbed wire and guarded by French troops. Their baggage was dumped at the entrance, and they were told that no one was willing to take it to their rooms. No one met with them. Their only instructions were to wait.

On May 4 the Council of Four sent off a draft treaty to be printed. It filled 413 pages, a French version on the left side and English on the right of every spread. Much of it was a confused and confusing mishmash of half-digested, uncoordinated, ambiguously written bits and pieces. It is unlikely that anyone had read the whole thing. No copies were yet available when on May 6 a plenary session was asked for its approval. A summary of the 440 articles was read aloud in French, which many of the assembled delegates did not understand. Some of them dozed through the reading. They then voted yes.

On that same day, Lloyd George took advantage of the Italians' walkout to get council approval of Greek occupation of the coastal city of Smyrna in Asia Minor. He thereby unwittingly demonstrated that the law of unintended consequences was in full effect, sparking an angry resurgence of Turkish nationalism and setting the Turks, Greeks, and Italians at each other's throats. This put in motion a chain of catastrophes that would lead to the fall not only of the Greek government but ultimately of Lloyd George's as well, and to a monstrously bloody three-year war between Turkey and Greece. That conflict would be won by Turkey, the one nation in the world, ironically, that members of the Supreme Council had thought they could get away with eliminating altogether. Instead Turkey emerged as a regional power, one not to be trifled with.

For Clemenceau and even more for Lloyd George, the day on which mandates were assigned must have been one of the most satisfying of the conference. After weeks of haggling and sometimes childishly acrimonious squabbling, with Belgium and Japan and Romania and the British dominions all adding their demands to those of London, Paris, and Rome, on May 7 more than a million square miles and seventeen million human beings were given new masters. The British Empire got eight million of those people and 862,549 of the square miles. The corresponding numbers for France were five and a half million and 238,168. Belgium was allowed to add territory to her colonial crown jewel the Congo, whose people she had long ruled with cruelty so savage as to defy belief. Even Wilson appears to have been satisfied with this parceling-out of territories equivalent in size to a third of the United States. He had persuaded himself that this was not annexation and not colonialism; rather it was a necessary redistribution of a burden that the white man would put down when men of color became capable of taking it up. Its resemblance to the self-determination of all peoples promised by the Fourteen Points was dubious at best.

The first copies of the treaty, as they came off the press, were delivered to representatives of the leading powers. Herbert Hoover received his in the middle of the night. What he found in it so distressed him that he dressed and went out into the sleeping streets. Wandering, he came upon General Smuts of South Africa and the young English economist John Maynard Keynes. They, too, had received copies and found themselves unable to return to bed. For Keynes, the treaty was "outrageous and impossible and can bring nothing but misfortune." Hoover would later say that "even if Germany signed the present terms, we would not secure stability . . . if she refuses we will have extinguished the possibility of democracy in favor of either Communism or reaction, and . . . wrecked the very foundations of the League of Nations."

The man then serving as German foreign minister, Count Ulrich von

Ulrich von Brockdorff-Rantzau, German foreign minister, 1919
"Those who will sign this treaty will sign the death sentence of many millions of German men, women, and children."

Brockdorff-Rantzau, led the new republic's delegation when it was summoned to Versailles's Trianon Palace to receive the treaty. He was of an ancient aristocratic family related to the Hohenzollerns—one of his forebears was rumored to have been the biological father of Louis XIV of France—but during the war he had urged the generals to offer a compromise peace, and afterward he assisted in the struggle to establish a democratic regime. To the victors waiting at the Trianon, however, his austere figure, complete with monocle, seemed the very essence of haughty Prussianism and therefore a fitting object of their sneers. (The apparent coldness was in fact largely nervousness. Brockdorff-Rantzau, who like the other members of the delegation could only guess at what to expect or why they had been summoned, was struggling to maintain his composure.) Received in icily curt terms by Clemenceau ("You asked us for peace. We are disposed to grant it to you."), he was taken aback to be told that Germany would be given fifteen days in which to submit comments on a fat, sloppily assembled volume that neither he nor any other German had yet seen and was not in their language. Only then did he learn that there were to be no face-to-face negotiations of the traditional kind.

Brockdorff-Rantzau took a seat, which to the onlookers appeared to be an act of calculated rudeness; they were predisposed to regard almost anything the Germans did or said as provocatively offensive. He read aloud a statement that had been all night in preparation. It said that he and his fellow delegates understood that their nation was in a position of utter helplessness, but that they could scarcely believe what the newspapers were reporting about a demand that Germany "shall confess ourselves to be the only ones guilty of the war."

"Such a confession in my mouth would be a lie," he said. "We are far from declining any responsibility that this great war of the world has come to pass. But we deny that Germany and its people were alone guilty." He concluded by calling attention to the continuation of the food blockade half a year after the start of the Armistice, claiming (without exaggeration) that civilians were dying by the thousands as a result. Clemenceau's face grew red. As the Germans withdrew, taking their copies of the treaty with them, he and the other council members vied to outdo one another in expressing their indignation. "The Germans are really a stupid people," Wilson declared. "They always do the wrong thing." Lloyd George, perhaps more stung than contemptuous, said they should never have allowed Brockdorff to speak. Brockdorff-Rantzau himself, upon leaving the palace, made the mistake of pausing to light a cigarette. He was unable to do so without revealing how badly his hands and lips were trembling.

Once back inside their barricaded hotel, the Germans set to work finding out what the treaty said. Their translators were pressed to make haste and announced in shocked tones that their country was to lose 13 percent of its territory and 10 percent of its population. It was to go into financial bondage, be excluded from the League of Nations, and, yes, admit that it alone was responsible for the war. The delegates' response, and that in Weimar and Berlin as the translated text arrived there, was compounded of shock, anger, and a sense of betrayal. These feelings were directed more at Woodrow Wilson than at any other individual. "The unbelievable has happened," said the president of Germany's National Assembly. "The enemy presents us a treaty surpassing the most pessimistic forecasts. It means the annihilation of the German people. It is incomprehensible that a man who had promised the world a peace of justice, upon which a society of nations would be founded, has been able to assist in the framing of this project dictated by hate." Wilson, of course, was mightily offended when such comments found their way into the English-language press.

Brockdorff-Rantzau observed sardonically that "this fat volume is quite unnecessary. They could have expressed the whole thing more simply in one clause—*L'Allemagne renonce à son existence.*" Germany ceases to exist. When his government ordered him to return home, he did not obey. He remained in Versailles, going through the treaty point by point, preparing comments, questions, and counterproposals that were then dispatched to the peace conference. The Supreme Council gave them little attention—understandably enough, as they ran up to fifty thousand words each. They were passed along to the appropriate commissions with instructions not to reply but to rebut.

When on May 10 the Weimar government sent its initial brief response, the core of its message was that "no nation could endure" the worst of the treaty's provisions and that "many of them could not possibly be carried out." Time would prove this to be true, not least where reparations were concerned. Germany would never become capable of paying more than a fraction of what was demanded, and the payments it did make would keep its economy and that of all Europe in a debilitated state up to the start of the Great Depression.

In mid-May a letter of Brockdorff-Rantzau's was published in the *Manchester Guardian*. It focused on the famine in Germany, noting that at the start of the war Germany had, like Britain, been an industrialized nation incapable of feeding her population and therefore importing millions of tons of food annually. Not only had the blockade made most of those imports impossible, but the loss of Germany's colonies now permanently deprived her of what had formerly been essential sources of food. Worse, the annexations prescribed by the peace treaty were now taking away a fifth of the country's domestic supplies of corn and potatoes and a third of her coal. "Those who will sign this treaty will sign the death sentence of many millions of German men, women, and children," the letter declared.

Brockdorff-Rantzau's words struck home with those in London who were beginning to ask how much punishment of the German population made sense and whether the resurrection of French dominance over Europe could possibly be in British interests. Lloyd George, even more attentive to public opinion than the average politician, sensed this shift and anticipated its growing stronger. He arranged for his cabinet to join him for a weekend in Paris to discuss whether the treaty should be revised.

Americans were asking Wilson, too, to reconsider the treaty. When he showed himself to be immovable, some staff members resigned in silent, disgusted protest. The sense of failure, even of betrayal, was becoming widespread. Hoover all but begged the president to relent, but to no avail. Even Ray Stannard Baker, handling the president's press relations, did the same, again to no effect. "We had such high hopes of this adventure," said delegate Henry White. "We believed God called us and now we are doing hell's dirtiest work." Liberal journals for which Wilson had once been a hero—*The Nation, The New Republic*—became bitterly critical of the treaty and the president's actions. He was unimpressed.

May 21 brought an event that gave neither the victors nor the vanquished any cause for rejoicing. A German admiral aboard the flagship of the deposed kaiser's great fleet of warships, interned with their crews at Scapa Flow in the Orkney Islands, ordered the lot of them to be scuttled. The British authorities knew nothing about this until the vessels were seen to be settling lower in the water. By then it was too late: the whole fleet went to the bottom. This was a particular blow to the French, who had planned to augment their navy by taking possession of some of the best German dreadnoughts. The British could be more philosophical. They had already decided that incorporating German warships into the Royal Navy would be difficult, expensive, and ultimately pointless. Nor could they see any point in making France stronger at sea. They had talked of taking the captive ships out into the Atlantic and ceremonially sinking them in a kind of nautical *Götterdämmerung*. If the Germans had made that impossible, they had also made it unnecessary.

On that same day, Clemenceau and Lloyd George began a fresh quarrel over how to divide the Turks' Middle Eastern empire: Iraq and Syria, Lebanon and Palestine, the Arabian desert. This led first to cynical deals and trade-offs and betrayals of the indigenous peoples. Ultimately it set in motion the tragedies that have continued to afflict the region down to the present day.

On May 30 the Germans submitted their formal response. It called attention to the gap between the Fourteen Points, Wilson's other pre-Armistice pronouncements, and the treaty as it currently stood. Some on the Allied side were again sympathetic. Among those supporting a softened approach was British deputy prime minister Andrew Bonar Law, who said he found the German objections unanswerable. General Smuts went further, saying that in light of the importance of the Fourteen Points in the pre-Armistice negotiations, the treaty amounted to a "breach of agreement." Chancellor of the Exchequer Austen Chamberlain, Prime Minister Botha of South Africa, and even the inexhaustibly bellicose Winston Churchill, now serving as war minister, joined in urging a reopening of the treaty while there was still time. Lloyd George was willing.

There could be no doubt that the French would oppose any such move, so the question would be decided by Wilson. Again the president said no. He did so dismissively, saying half-jokingly that Lloyd George was simply "in a funk." He complained that the prime minister now wanted to remove the same punitive provisions that he had earlier insisted on. This was a fair observation as far as it went—Lloyd George was capable of swinging from position to position as easily as a weather vane—but hardly a sufficient one in light of how much was at stake. The treaty went back to the Germans with minor revisions, none of which addressed their deepest concerns. They were invited to take it or leave it, as they wished, and live with the consequences either way.

On the day of the Germans' response, a heartsore Colonel House confided to his diary that "the Treaty is not a good one . . . it is too severe. . . . However, the time to have the Treaty right was when it was being formed and not now. It is a question if one commenced to unravel what has already been done, whether it could be stopped. . . . We desired from the beginning a fair peace, and one well within the Fourteen Points, and one which could stand the scrutiny of the neutral world and of all time. It is not such a peace, but since the Treaty has been written, I question whether it would be well to seriously modify it."

If he shared his feelings with the president, the result can only have been to widen the gulf between them.

Clemenceau, Lloyd George, and Wilson now found themselves in a period of anxious waiting. The great questions were whether Germany would sign and, if she did not, how they should respond. While waiting, they remained as immersed in deliberations as ever, reorganizing the world. Foreign Secretary Arthur Balfour described them as "three all-powerful, all-ignorant men sitting there and partitioning continents."

Wilson had by this point been immersed for so long in global affairs, and was so distant from Washington, that he was no longer attuned to what was happening at home. He was so confident of the peace treaty's eventual ratification by the Senate, so oblivious of the mounting questions about it, that when an extraordinary session of Congress had to be called to secure passage of the appropriations bills filibustered by the Senate back in March, he failed to turn necessity into an opportunity. The special session opened on May 19, but rather than returning home for it, he wrote a speech to be read to Congress on his behalf. Worse, in writing the speech, he limited himself to domestic matters exclusively: labor relations, taxes, tariffs, and the woman suffrage amendment. He promised to speak on "questions which affect the peace of the whole world" upon returning home, presumably thinking that his oratory would work its magic most effectively when delivered personally.

This was a blunder of the first order. A debate on the league was by now far advanced in the United States, and battle lines were firming up. It was time for the president to be arguing his case. In the absence of their leader, the pro-league Democrats tended to keep quiet, remaining passive even in the face of direct challenge. The action was on the Republican side, the side now in the majority in both houses of Congress, the only side where a lively, many-sided, and substantive exchange of views was in full flower.

Leading the nationwide campaign to win public acceptance of the league—not necessarily in quite the form offered by the president—was the League to Enforce Peace (LEP). By 1919 it had three hundred thousand members, thousands of volunteer speakers, a substantial budget, and a printing office capable of producing half a million flyers at a run. Its most visible leader, and much more than a figurehead, was former president Taft. His motivation was expressed in the organization's name: a conviction that the maintenance of peace and the securing of the fruits of victory was going to require an international body with the authority and power to meet trouble with force. This made the group inherently sympathetic to Article 10.

A rival organization, the League for the Preservation of American Independence (LPAI), had recently sprung up. It professed to be opposed not to the league as such but, vaguely, to "unconditional" approval of a peace treaty containing the covenant. It presented a nonpartisan front by recruiting prominent Democrats known to be unfriendly to the president, but never rivaled the LEP in size or impact. The key figure in the debate, Henry Cabot Lodge, declined to openly associate himself with the newer organization but quietly put its organizers in touch with sources of financial support.

The irreconcilables remained a small minority. The debate that mattered, within the Republican Party, continued to take place among those who accepted that the size, power, and economic reach of the United States imposed global responsibilities. The question, for such people, was not how to evade those responsibilities but how to discharge them in ways that were constructive, responsible, and consistent with American interests and values. It was a question that afforded ample space for reasonable people to disagree.

Wilson had in effect denied the legitimacy of questions about Article 10 in refusing to consider amending it, but it was exactly those questions with which the Senate's Republicans found themselves grappling through the summer of 1919. Senator Philander Knox, the former attorney general and secretary of state, generated much publicity with a speech declaring that the league was too difficult a matter, its covenant too fraught with uncertainties, to be undertaken without extensive deliberation. He joined Lodge in demanding that it be separated from the peace treaty and set aside for consideration later. "Beware of the possible consequences of haste," Knox warned. "God forbid that 'the war that was to end all wars' shall conclude with a peace that may end all peace."

Another former secretary of state, Elihu Root, attracted attention with an open letter carried by newspapers across the country. He commented positively on many aspects of the league and did not dispute that it could become a force for good. But he wanted it changed significantly. He said that the Senate must make clear that the United States "refuses its consent" to Article 10 and would insist on its own interpretation of other articles.

The president's response was by now familiar. He said first that the league was so woven into the text of the peace treaty that the one could not be excised without destroying the other. Second, the peace conference had already amended four articles of the covenant at the insistence of the United States, and to ask it to reopen the matter yet again was simply impossible. The first point was true enough; removing the league would require rewriting much of the treaty when no one thought there was time for doing so. Wilson's second point, too, seemed unanswerable at first. But Root, whose intellect kept him among the powers of his party in spite of his holding no office and made him the country's most eminent corporate lawyer, came back with an answer. Instead of demanding new amendments, he said, the Senate in ratifying the treaty should set forth whatever "reservations" it deemed necessary. Unlike amendments, he claimed, reservations would require no action by the peace conference. They would be effective so long as the other signers of the treaty did not explicitly object—something they were not likely to do, for fear of driving the United States out of the league altogether. Though Lodge continued to want amendments, many of his fellow Republicans were delighted with the Root formula and embraced it. It would become the basis upon which they engaged the president when he returned to Washington, and upon which they would come to be known as "reservationists."

In Europe, the final deadline for German acceptance of the treaty was drawing near, and a shaky Weimar government was failing to come to a decision. On June 20 the German cabinet abandoned hope of resolving its deadlock and resigned. Brockdorff-Rantzau, as foreign minister, was among those who quit. He departed Paris, leaving behind a small staff in the vain hope that the Council of Four might show itself willing to discuss Germany's concerns. Suddenly the question was not whether the German government would sign but whether there *was* a German government.

The Supreme Council announced that if Germany did not accept the treaty, she would be invaded. Marshal Foch was ordered to prepare the Allied forces and mustered thirty divisions. The council added a second and rather gross threat: without the treaty, it would not only continue the blockade but tighten it—if such a thing were possible. Learning of this, Herbert Hoover wrote to Wilson that it was his understanding that the blockade was continuing "without any authority from the Council of Four" and that "I should be very glad, if it is in accord with your views, that this order be rescinded." Since the end of March, Hoover had been doing what he could, with extremely limited success, to get some food into Germany. He, along with many of the American soldiers occupying the Rhineland, was sickened by the spectacle of emaciated children, skeletal wraiths with distended stomachs, fighting over the AEF's garbage.

But nothing changed. The blockade had been removed from Austria some weeks before, less out of compassion than because of fears that if the country continued its slide into chaos, the result would be Bolshevism. Hungary did not share in Austria's good fortune because it was already a Bolshevist state, Europe's second after Russia. When ships carrying food managed somehow to reach German ports, they were not permitted to unload. When intercepted at sea, such ships were diverted to Britain.

On June 22 the German National Assembly informed Paris that it was prepared to accept the treaty with a single reservation. This involved the same war guilt clause to which Brockdorff-Rantzau had objected so vehemently. The Assembly declared "with the greatest emphasis" that it "cannot accept Article 231 of the Treaty of Peace which requires Germany to admit herself to be the sole and only author of the war." The vehemence with which the whole German nation—public and press as well as political leaders—persisted in reacting to this article came as a surprise to the victors. As for the treaty as a whole, Weimar told the Council of Four, Germany's decision to sign "is to be understood in the sense that it yields to force, being resolved to spare the German people, whose sufferings are unspeakable, a new war, the shattering of its national unity by further occupation of German territories, terrible famine for women and children, and mercilessly prolonged retention of the prisoners of war.... The conditions imposed exceed the measure of that which Germany can in fact perform."

The council's response was that no reservations, and therefore no such acceptance of the treaty, would be accepted. German politicians conferred with their generals about whether armed resistance might be possible. The soldiers had only to look to Foch's hundreds of thousands of troops, and to the eager and almost equally formidable Polish and Czech forces, to declare the idea ridiculous. In the streets of Berlin and other cities, meanwhile, starving crowds were taking to the streets to beg for peace now, peace at any price.

Admissions of guilt aside, few in Paris were surprised by the Germans' reluctance to sign such a draconian settlement, one so obviously designed to reduce a large and powerful nation, a nation now attempting to function as a democracy, to open-ended servility. Some at the peace conference pointed to the awkwardness of treating a republican government as an outlaw because of the policies and acts of the regime it had overthrown.

Ironically, Article 231 had been inserted into the treaty almost as an afterthought, to provide justification for unlimited reparations. It was drafted by a young American lawyer named John Foster Dulles, a nephew of Secretary of State Lansing's wife, a onetime student of Woodrow Wilson's at Princeton, and himself a future secretary of state. Some historians maintain that it should never have been called the war guilt clause because it was nothing of the kind—that those Germans who insisted on making it an issue were being disingenuous. It is simply not true, they complain, that the clause forced the Germans to accept sole responsibility for starting the war. To test that claim, one must look at what the article says:

The Allied and Associated governments affirm and Germany accepts the responsibility of Germany and her allies for causing all the loss and damage to which the Allied and Associated governments and their nationals have been subjected as a consequence of the war imposed upon them by the aggression of Germany and her allies.

If Dulles—presumably a better lawyer than prose stylist—had stopped after the word "subjected," or even "as a consequence of the war," he would have done no more than state the obvious fact that the German armies had done a great deal of damage. To read the clause's last eleven words and claim that they do not impute exclusive guilt, however, is to strain credibility. What else can be the purpose of "imposed upon" and "the aggression of Germany"? In 1919 surprise at the bitterness of the German reaction required only uncritical assent to the generally accepted Allied account of how the war had begun. Today it requires willful blindness to what has since come to light about the events of July 1914.

The deadline for German acceptance was seven P.M. on June 23. At noon on that day nothing had been heard in Paris. That remained true all afternoon. The wait was almost down to the final hour, and one can imagine the relish with which Foch and the Poles must have been readying their troops for a move into a hated and defenseless enemy's heartland, when the answer came at last. It arrived at 5:40 P.M.: acceptance by a new Weimar government thrown together with a socialist named Gustav Bauer at its head. The message said Germany accepted terms *imposed* by the victorious powers. It said that in doing so it was *yielding to overwhelming force.* Such complaints could have been used by the Council of Four as justification for rejecting this acceptance just as brusquely as it had the one of June 22. Evidently, however, there was not sufficient stomach for a resumption of the war.

If the treaty was an outrage in German eyes, who in Germany would consent to sign it? No one wanted the job, and many were prepared to refuse it. Hermann Müller, a Social Democrat, was now foreign minister and therefore more or less obliged to accept. With him went Johannes Bell, who as minister of colonial affairs held the Bauer cabinet's most laughably empty portfolio. The signing ceremony took place in the glorious Hall of Mirrors at the Palace of Versailles—the very room where the Germans had declared the creation of their new empire after defeating France in 1871. It happened on June 28, the date on which, five years earlier, Franz Ferdinand and his wife had been shot to death.

Clemenceau as chairman presided, and turned the event into a celebration that veered into tawdriness. "They lack only music and ballet girls, dancing in step, to offer the pen to the plenipotentiaries for signing," said France's ambassador to London. "Louis XIV liked ballets, but only as a diversion; he signed treaties in his study." Colonel House would confess to "a feeling of sympathy for the Germans who sat there quite stoically. It was not unlike what was done in olden times, when the conqueror dragged the conquered at his chariot wheels. To my mind, it is out of keeping with the new era which we profess an ardent desire to promote. I wish it could have been more simple and that there might have been an element of chivalry, which was wholly lacking. The affair was elaborately staged and made as humiliating to the enemy as possible."

The two Germans left at the first opportunity. They had maintained a stony reserve throughout, wanting the victors, in Müller's words, "to see nothing of the deep pain of the German people, whose representative I was at this tragic moment."

Wilson departed for Brest and home that night. Almost his last act was to create a diplomatic stink by refusing an invitation to dine with French president Raymond Poincaré, at whom he was suddenly directing all the rage and frustration built up by months of negotiating with the Allies. Colonel House finally persuaded him that refusal was impossible and would create a scandal. But the damage had been done; Poincaré was aware of Wilson's feelings and was furious himself in return.

When the hour of departure came, it brought House and Wilson face-to-face for what neither could have known was the last time. When the colonel himself returned to the United States, he would become the latest but not quite the last of the intimate associates—one hesitates to use the word *friends*—to be banished forever by Woodrow Wilson. A day after bidding the Wilsons farewell, House noted in his diary that "my last conversation with the president yesterday was not reassuring. I urged him to meet the Senate in a conciliatory spirit . . . in reply he said, 'House, I have found one can never get anything in this life that is worth while without fighting for it.'"

He reflected on the question of whether everything might have gone better if Wilson had taken his advice and never gone to Paris at all. "It may be that Wilson might have had the power and influence [to achieve his aims] if he had remained in Washington and kept clear of the conference," the colonel mused. "When he stepped down from his lofty pedestal and wrangled with representatives of other states upon equal terms, he became as common clay. . . . To those who are saying the Treaty is bad and never should have been made and that it will involve Europe in infinite difficulties in its enforcement, I feel like admitting it. . . . I wish we had taken the other road, even if it was less smooth, both now and afterward, than the one we took. We would at least have gone in the right direction and if those who follow us had made it impossible to go the full length of the journey planned, the responsibility would have rested with them and not us."

Lloyd George departed the day after the ceremony, leaving only Clemenceau to keep a wary eye on the battalions of diplomats and functionaries responsible for wrapping up the conference's work. It was not until two weeks later, seven and a half months after the Armistice went into effect, that the blockade of Germany was lifted. It has been called the worst atrocity of the Great War.

Wilson's arrival in the United States on July 8 marked the opening of one of the nation's epic political contests. The struggle to decide whether to join the League of Nations, and if so on what terms, would go on for eight months. It bears comparison with the debates over the drafting of the Constitution and the future of slavery—those rare times when the whole nation focused on a question understood to have profound importance for the future. That big crowds turned out to greet the president when his ship docked in New York, and later when his train arrived at Washington's Union Station, suggests that the public shared in his understanding of the importance of what was being decided and that he had much support. It suggests also that he was not deceiving himself in believing that much of the country still expected that victory in the war was going to change the world for the better, and that it looked to him as the man who could make it happen.

Nevertheless, he should have had no lingering illusions about Senate approval being a sure thing. A newspaper poll indicated that forty senators (almost all of them Democrats) supported ratification of the treaty as it stood, while another forty (almost all Republicans) were ready to support it if certain reservations were attached. The number of irreconcilables had risen to eight, and five senators were classified as too undecided to fit into any more specific slot. This meant that ratification was definitely possible but was going to require winning another two dozen votes. Most if not all would have to come from the reservationists.

The situation called for the kind of political mastery that Wilson had demonstrated in his brief time as governor of New Jersey and at the start of his presidency. The first question was how to proceed: whether to apply his powers of persuasion to the Senate, or to create a groundswell of support by appealing directly to the public. He decided to do both, courting the Senate first and then reaching out more widely. It was a sensible enough decision.

The problem turned out to be not the strategy but the execution. The president misplayed a strong hand, possibly because of the delicate state of his health. Upon returning to the White House, he resumed the habits with which he had husbanded his strength through his first six years there. Once again he stayed away from his office until after lunch, played golf almost every day with his wife and physician, and went for long chauffeur-driven rides. All this helped with his recuperation, but not enough. Paris had taken a heavy toll. In his last weeks in France, the left side of his face had begun to twitch uncontrollably. This did not altogether stop after he got home.

He nevertheless plunged into the fray. On the day after his return, he held a press conference in which, for the first time in a long time, the things he said were not off the record. The questions were almost entirely about the league, Article 10 in particular. He explained his position clearly, firmly, and without belligerence. A day later he appeared before the Senate and formally presented the peace treaty for ratification. Friends and foes alike had awaited with great expectation the speech he gave on that occasion. The irreconcilables had braced themselves for another of the president's stirring orations, a call to action in pursuit of noble goals. Wilson understood this and appears to have been uncharacteristically daunted; the writing gave him more difficulty than any of his previous speeches. On the voyage home, most unusually, he read a draft aloud to five of his fellow passengers, asking for their thoughts. The response was positive, but the men who gave it were ill suited to be of much help: three Wall Street moguls, an economist, and a member of Chicago's wealthy McCormick family. Having limited experience of Congress or politics, they were unable to save the president from wasting a singularly good opportunity.

League supporters were disappointed when the president appeared before the Senate, while opponents had to struggle to keep from gloating. The speech was crafted capably enough, but it was too Wilsonian to suit the occasion. It had too much rhetoric, too little substance. Such an approach had served him well on earlier occasions, when listeners already understood in fairly clear terms what he was asking or promising—a war against tyranny, a progressive legislative agenda—and were eager to demonstrate their support. But in July Senate and nation wanted an explanation of just what this treaty and this league were about, and that they did not get.

They wanted to hear about Article 10, the treaty's implications for the Monroe Doctrine, why Japan was being given a piece of China, et cetera. The president did not even mention these things. His speech was therefore as dull as it was long, a professorial mixture of recent history and worn-out platitudes about America's new and glorious place in world affairs. The treaty itself he seemed almost to damn with faint praise. It was "not exactly what we would have written," he said. "It is probably not what any of the national delegations would have written. But results were worked out which on the whole bear test." These were not words to bring even Democratic senators out of their seats cheering. Nor did he make any effort to explain what the "results" he referred to were or why he found them acceptable.

Here is the reaction of Democratic Senator Henry Ashurst of Arizona, a dependable friend of the administration: "Wilson's speech was as if the head of a great corporation, after committing his company to enormous undertakings, when called upon to render a statement as to the meanings and extent of the obligation he had incurred, should go before the Board of Directors and read Longfellow's Psalm of Life. Wilson was called upon to render an accounting of the most momentous cause ever entrusted to an individual. His audience wanted raw meat, he fed them cold turnips."

The speech instilled no sense of urgency. There followed, instead of a great climactic debate, an intermittent succession of speeches pro and con, with days sometimes passing between one senator's contribution and the next. In a departure from his customary remoteness, in the last two weeks of July the president met individually with twenty-six senators, twenty-two of them Republicans. He made not a single convert. He then fell ill and retreated to his bed. Here again there is speculation that he might have suffered a minor stroke. Senator Ashurst, in describing the president's appearance as he arrived at the Senate to deliver his failure of an address, had noted "a contraction of the back of his neck and a transparency of his ears; infallible indices of a man whose vitality is gone."

Meanwhile the satisfactions of victory were proving to be almost as short-lived in the United States as in Europe. In July, in the nation's capital, rumors that a white woman had been raped by a black man caused angry gangs of whites, many of them servicemen in uniform, to attack blacks wherever they found them. The result, with the police not intervening and blacks fighting back, was not so much a race riot as race war, and it did not end until three thousand army troops had been sent in and fifteen people were dead. This was the first of twenty-five such irruptions across the country that summer. The worst would happen in Chicago, where the downtown Loop was ravaged, thirty-eight people were killed, more than five hundred injured, and the homes of more than a thousand people went up in flames.

Raging inflation, when combined with the determination of employers to reverse the wage gains of wartime, deny recognition to unions, and keep the twelve-hour workday, generated waves of labor disputes. In the course of 1919, one American worker in five would at some point be on strike. By midsummer, workers in industries as massive and essential as steel, coal mining, and the railroads were squaring off for what looked to be an epic showdown with management. The comfortable classes were becoming increasingly inclined to condemn even the AFL as part of the Bolshevik threat to Christian civilization.

All of which must have made approval of the league even more imperative in the president's eyes. With so many things going wrong, at home little less than abroad, the league might prove to be the only positive thing to come out of America's expenditure of so much treasure and so many lives.

Background

The Palmer Raids

Early in 1919, Thomas Gregory having decided that five years as the head of the U.S. Justice Department were enough, President Wilson found himself in need of an attorney general.

There were many qualified and interested candidates. Among them were men who had helped Gregory draft and enforce the Espionage and Sedition Acts and turn the department into an instrument for keeping a close eye on the American population and taking corrective action wherever they saw evidence of unacceptable opinions. None, however, stood out as obviously the right choice.

Among the possibilities was forty-six-year-old Alexander Mitchell Palmer, a loyal Wilsonian Democrat who, in the appointive position of alien property custodian, was responsible for managing hundreds of millions of dollars' worth of assets that belonged to the Central Powers but had been stranded in the United States by the war. The president knew him and had reason to think well of him. At the Democratic Convention of 1912, then-Congressman Palmer had served as floor manager of the Wilson campaign and held his home state of Pennsylvania's delegation firmly in the Wilson camp through long days of deadlocked balloting.

When Wilson became president-elect, he offered Palmer an appointment as secretary of war. Palmer declined, explaining that as a Quaker and a pacifist he would be unable to execute the duties of the office with the vigor it required. He expressed interest in becoming attorney general, but Wilson and House had already filled that position. In 1914, when Palmer gave up his seat in the House to run unsuccessfully for the Senate, he did so at White House urging. He was therefore a man to whom the administration owed a political debt.

He was liked by progressive Democrats because he was one of them, having during his six years in Congress supported such measures as a lowering of tariffs, regulation of child labor, and even woman suffrage. In 1915 Bryanite Democrats and Republicans in the La Follette camp applauded him for publicly questioning whether American citizens should have taken passage on the *Lusitania* in spite of the German government's

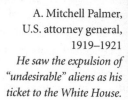

A. Mitchell Palmer,
U.S. attorney general,
1919–1921
*He saw the expulsion of
"undesirable" aliens as his
ticket to the White House.*

warnings. After losing his Senate race, he remained Democratic national committeeman for Pennsylvania and therefore a figure of significance. These connections formed a network of support to which he was able to turn in 1917, when he asked for an opportunity to contribute to the war effort. When the office of alien property custodian was created, he was both available and an unobjectionable choice.

The job involved taking possession, managing, and disposing of German property of almost every description, from ocean liners to industrial patents. Palmer was soon overseeing assets worth more than half a billion dollars and dispensing patronage positions and favors, including the right to buy German property on attractive terms. This added new dimensions to his support network—to the number of people of influence willing to put in a good word for him when he set out to become Gregory's successor at Justice.

It was also an advantage that he had established himself, well before the Armistice, as a solidly pro-war progressive. Years earlier, in declining appointment as war secretary, he had said that if the United States ever found itself at war, he would willingly serve. After intervention, as property custodian, he fulfilled that pledge zealously. In September 1918, called to testify about German holdings in the United States by a Senate committee, he condemned German-American beer barons as fomenters of disloyalty. As the war ended, he professed to believe that Germany, having failed to conquer the world militarily, would next attempt to do so economically and again had to be stopped. This was going to entail making the Germans permanently uncompetitive in the global marketplace. To this end, Palmer got congressional authority to sell off the business assets, including patents and other intellectual property, that had made German companies preeminent in chemicals and other industries before the war. The sales conferred enormous commercial benefits on the American purchasers and gave Palmer yet another cadre of influential friends. (Proceeds from the sales were impounded, not for eventual payment to the former owners but to provide funds for compensating Americans judged to have suffered financial losses as a result of the war.)

As the search for a replacement for Gregory got under way, Palmer was once again an unobjectionable candidate. His greatest asset was the support of fellow progressives with access to the president. From the White House, Joe Tumulty barraged Wilson in Paris with messages praising Palmer as "young, militant, progressive and fearless," and saying that his appointment would "give us all heart and new courage." Navy Secretary Daniels advised Wilson that "in addition to his recognized ability and high character his appointment would be pleasing alike to the bar and to the Old Guard of Democrats." Having no reason to disagree or to prefer other candidates, the president announced his decision at the end of February. There were no notable objections.

At first Palmer seemed determined to end the excesses of the Gregory years and put the Justice Department on a new course. He ordered the release of nearly half of the 239 persons then in prison for violations of the Espionage Act, excluding those (such as Eugene V. Debs) who refused to express contrition. He also freed several thousand citizens, mainly German-Americans, who were in confinement not for breaking any law but because their loyalty had been brought into question. He stopped accepting information offered by the quasi-official vigilantes of Gregory's American Protective League, essentially putting it out of business. He told the president that Debs's sentence was too long and should be commuted—though not quite yet.

In Congress, however, war fever was transmuting into what would come to be called the Red Scare—the fear that Communists, controlled and financed by the Leninists of Russia, were plotting revolution in the United States. Though soon carried to extremes that would give rise to gross misuse of police power and outlandish acts of injustice by government officials, such fears were not totally without foundation. The months following the Armistice were pocked with labor violence across the United States, though it rarely had anything to do with radical ideology, still less with schemes for overthrowing the government. Terrorist bombings were by no means unheard of, though the authorities were rarely able to establish guilt or even identify suspects. Such acts were blamed on phantom Bolsheviks with the same thoughtless ease that strikes and industrial accidents had earlier been blamed on phantom German saboteurs.

Attempts to deal with these matters led to a thicket of confusion in which socialists, communists, and anarchists were all jumbled together. Such people were assumed to be jointly guilty in spite of the scarcity of incriminating evidence, and were seen as a serious threat in spite of being an almost invisibly tiny percentage of the population and in most cases guilty of nothing more than harboring opinions that their more respectable fellow citizens found repellent. The American Socialist Party, which in 1914 had appeared to have the potential to become a national force, was by 1919 so battered as to be incapable of recovery. The Communist Party of America and its rival the Communist Labor Party together had a membership of about twelve thousand nationally.

Further confusing the situation were the anarchists, adherents of a vague and elastic creed embracing everything from libertarian-type individualism to chaotic collectives in which every member was free to make his or her own rules. Almost the only thing anarchists had in common was a rejection of hierarchies, rulers, and authority of every kind. Russian anarchists had participated in and supported the Bolshevik Revolution, but once in power, the Russian Communist Party—hierarchical, authoritarian, and brutal—was quick to expel and suppress them. Around the world, meanwhile, people styling themselves anarchists were making their cause synonymous with terrorism and murder. In the decades before the Great War, they assassinated a tsar of Russia, an empress of Austria-Hungary, kings of Greece, Italy, and Portugal, a president of France, and President William McKinley of the United States.

In the United States the most dangerous anarchists were the so-called Galleanists, followers of an Italian named Luigi Galleani. He had arrived in the United States in 1901, the year McKinley was murdered, and preached "the propaganda of the deed"—the use of violence not for any specifiable political purpose but simply to spread fear and disorder. Apparently random acts of terrorism contributed to an understandable if not really justified fear that revolutionaries lurked everywhere. American nativism was a factor in all this, feeding the belief that newcomers with strange-sounding names did not belong in the United States and should never have been admitted.

Palmer was not yet attorney general when, in February 1919, federal troops were called in to help quell Seattle's general strike. He took office in time, however, to be faced with the strike's consequences, particularly the effects of the mayor of Seattle's claim that the strike was the result not of legitimate worker grievances but of the international Communist conspiracy. At the end of April, thirty-six packages that were labeled "novelties" from the Gimbel Brothers department store but were packed with explosives were mailed to prominent public figures across the country. The press quickly drew a connection to the Seattle troubles and other disturbances elsewhere. Most of the packages were intercepted before delivery because the conspirators had failed to affix sufficient postage. None of the addressees—two senators, Justice Oliver Wendell Holmes, Judge Kenesaw Mountain Landis, John D. Rockefeller, J. P. Morgan, Jr., Postmaster General Burleson, and Palmer among them—were injured. A package that reached the Georgia home of former senator Thomas Hardwick, who before leaving office had sponsored a 1918 law reducing obstacles to the deportation of noncitizens, blew off the hands of the maid who opened it and injured Hardwick's wife.

This was followed by May Day disturbances in several cities, as parading leftists clashed with citizens offended by the public celebration of what they regarded as subversion. Tension continued to rise, climaxing on June 2 when large bombs were detonated late at night in eight cities. One of the terrorists, a Galleanist wanted by the authorities, was himself blown to bits when his bomb went off an instant after he placed it at the door of Palmer's Washington home. The attorney general, who had been up late reading until moments before the explosion, narrowly escaped serious injury or death. His wife and daughter, asleep at the back of the house, were almost blown out of their beds.

The result, not surprisingly, was near-hysteria in Congress and much of the nation. Palmer requested additional funding for his department and undertook a reorganization of its investigative capabilities. An ambitious young law school graduate named John Edgar Hoover took charge of gathering information about radicals and subversives.

In July, with Hoover acting as his field commander, the attorney general went on the offensive. The first of the soon-to-be-notorious "Palmer raids" was launched in Buffalo, New York, and rounded up a number of individuals whose names appeared on Hoover's growing lists of un-American Americans. All were charged with violating the Espionage Act. But a judge spoiled everything, dismissing the charges and rebuking the Justice Department for attempting to criminalize free speech. Foiled, Palmer gave up on the Espionage Act as a tool for cleansing the nation. He urgently needed an alternative, however. In the aftermath of the labor troubles that were sweeping the country that summer, with unexplained bombings continuing sporadically, Congress was under heavy pressure to demonstrate that it was not going to allow the country to slip into chaos. On October 17 the Senate diverted this pressure to Palmer, passing a resolution demanding that he explain what he was doing to contain the radical threat. Hoover eagerly volunteered that his files now contained the names of sixty thousand dangerous persons, and that most of them were aliens. Palmer assured Congress that preparations to deal with these people were well advanced.

Palmer found the weapon he needed in Senator Hardwick's Immigration Act, which simplified the process of deporting noncitizens considered undesirable. On November 7 federal agents under Hoover's direction raided the facilities of a leftist organization that called itself—almost as if it wished to make itself a target—the Union of Russian Workers. Hoover cast a wide net, striking in twelve cities simultaneously. He was hunting not just "dangerous radicals," as in Buffalo, but dangerous and *alien* radicals. The Immigration Act had made them easy pickings.

The raids were little better than police riots. At nine P.M., agents entered the building near New York's Union Square that housed, among other and unrelated things, the Union of Russian Workers' headquarters. They forcibly removed and took custody of everyone found on all the floors, including visitors and persons attending algebra and language classes. People offering no resistance were beaten with blackjacks and metal truncheons and thrown down stairs. Offices were ransacked, typewriters and windows smashed, files strewn across floors. In two nights—

on November 8 local police staged similar raids on the Communist Party and something called the Socialist Left Wing Section—some twelve hundred people were arrested in New York alone. Of that number, seventy-five proved to be members of organizations regarded as suspect by the Justice Department, and only two were found to have violated any law (the violation involving, in both cases, a recently enacted state statute aimed at anarchists). It was much the same across the country. In Detroit, federal agents shut down a play being performed in Russian, detaining and interrogating the entire audience of fifteen hundred, ultimately arresting forty.

The public, on the whole, appeared to be delighted. Most congressmen and most of the press were thrilled. Palmer became a national hero, "the Fighting Quaker." It occurred to him that more such ventures might just propel him into the White House.

Chapter 24

"The Door Is Closed"

As THE SUMMER OF 1919 CAME TO AN END, THOSE WHO HAD DOUBTS about the agreements that President Wilson brought back from Paris held the high ground in the Senate. They had only to stand firm and appear open to being persuaded. Wilson and his Democrats were supplicants, doomed to failure if they could not broaden their support. They had to ask and explain and defend.

At the pinnacle of the high ground, in command, was Henry Cabot Lodge. His first speech as the Republicans' new Senate majority leader had come on August 12, and to no one's surprise he had taken as his subject the League of Nations and its covenant. He gave particular attention to Article 10, the enforcement provision, and did so in a spirit of extreme skepticism. He called the covenant "a deformed experiment upon a noble purpose" and said it was "tainted" because harnessed to a bad peace settlement.

"If Europe desires such an alliance with a power of this kind," the senator said, referring to Article 10's empowering of the league to intervene in disputes around the world, "so be it." But the United States should shun any such arrangement, he continued, and need not fear that doing so would prevent it from "continuing to help in all ways to preserve the world's peace." The claim that his position was in any way isolationist, he said emphatically, was "empty."

Lodge's words did not quite put him in the ranks of the irreconcilables. To go that far, he would have had to declare that the league could never be made acceptable, and he said nothing of the kind. The redoubtable Senator Philander Knox, by contrast, chose this as his moment to do so, thereby lending his considerable prestige to the irreconcilable camp and at the same time showing how the complexities of the treaty made it difficult for even like-minded senators to come into complete accord. He must have pleased Lodge when he said, "I cannot vote for the treaty unless the league covenant is separated from it and unless material modifications are made to the body of the document." But with almost the next breath, he distanced himself from Lodge by saying that the United States should want nothing to do with a coalition of victors, which was more or less exactly what Lodge thought the league should be. While disavowing any sympathy for the Germans, Knox described the peace that the treaty would impose as "hard and cruel" and therefore self-defeating. But again like Lodge, he denied being an isolationist, calling upon the president to summon a new international conference to create a different, better kind of league, one to which "all the world are parties in its formation."

The Senate's slowness in coming to grips with the treaty—members delivered only twelve speeches on the subject in August—was maddening to the president but precisely what Lodge wanted. He devoted half the month to committee hearings, calling as witnesses both members of the Wilson cabinet and spokesmen for groups (such as Irish-Americans and Italian-Americans) that found the treaty objectionable. Every day of testimony served Lodge's purposes, keeping progress at a crawl while building public interest. (There could be no thought of calling the president to testify, by the way. It had always been accepted that, under the Constitution's separation of powers, the chief executive could not be subjected to interrogation.)

Secretary of State Lansing was on the stand for some eight hours over two days. Simmering with long-concealed resentment at how the president had ignored and humiliated him in Paris, he took his revenge with an artful display of passive hostility. He responded in monosyllables to many questions, making no effort to demonstrate support, let alone enthusiasm, for what had been hammered out at the peace conference. While doing nothing to generate headlines, he succeeded in conveying the impression, indistinct but clear enough, that he had no liking for or stake in the treaty and was not the only former delegate who felt that way. He suggested that many of the senators' questions should be directed at the president, because only he could possibly explain everything that had been done and why. He depicted himself as a bystander who had had nothing of consequence to do with the treaty—which was not far from the truth. When asked if in his opinion the transfer of Germany's Shantung concessions to Japan violated the Wilsonian principle of self-determination, he answered with an unadorned yes. This added fuel to a controversy in which the public was showing unexpected interest.

The president needed to seize the initiative, and so on August 14 he took a step that was without precedent. He sent word that he was prepared to meet with the Foreign Relations Committee for a discussion of the treaty and the league. He thereby came closer than any president ever had, or ever would again, to testifying before a committee of Congress. He would do so not on Capitol Hill—that would be going too far—but at the White House, where he could act as host and the press could be excluded. Committee members quickly voted to accept.

And so at ten A.M. on Tuesday, August 19, President Wilson took a corner seat at a table in the East Room of the White House, the executive mansion's largest space, opulent by Washington standards if almost drab when compared with Versailles. Henry Cabot Lodge sat on one side of the president, and pro-league Democratic Senator John Sharp Williams of Mississippi on the other. Their fourteen fellow committee members were arrayed in a square before them. The only other persons in the room were two stenographers and White House head usher Ike Hoover.

The meeting went on for three hours and twenty minutes—it would be Lodge, not Wilson, who finally suggested calling a halt—and by all accounts it was never less than civil. Certainly it was no inquisition; Hiram Johnson of California would complain afterward that Wilson had not been pressed hard enough. His fellow committee members, Johnson suggested, had been overawed by the solemnity of the occasion, too concerned about what history would say of their part in it—"sixteen vain men, sitting around a table, each of whom was certain that the world hung upon his words, and each of whom knew his own ability to outshine his fellows."

That the irreconcilable Johnson was willing to concede that the president had handled himself "generally excellently" shows that the meeting was by no means a setback for the league cause. Neither, however, did it achieve Wilson's purposes. He damaged his credibility and risked offending his visitors by giving obviously and inexplicably false answers to a number of questions. When Borah of Idaho asked when Wilson and Secretary Lansing had first learned of the Allies' secret treaties, the president said they had had no knowledge of such things until the start of the peace conference. Evidence was already available to establish that Wilson knew at least much of the truth more than a year before that, by the end of 1917 at the latest.

He stumbled badly in answering questions about the Shantung concessions, which were becoming notorious both because awarding them to Japan clearly violated the Fourteen Points and because of Americans' concerns about Japanese expansion in the Far East. Wilson first denied having consented to the deal with Japan. Then, pressed, he said he had accepted it in order to keep Japan from exiting the conference. With equal foolishness he denied involvement in redrawing the borders of eastern Europe or in the awarding of the African and Pacific mandates.

Inevitably, many questions had to do with Article 10 and the obligations it would impose on the United States. Here Wilson was prepared and persuasive, pointing out that all league decisions would require unanimous consent of the council, of which the United States would be a permanent member, and that even unanimous decisions would be advisory only, never compulsory. But he allowed himself to be drawn, largely by the persistent if not impressively focused questions of stately and silver-haired freshman Senator Warren Harding of Ohio, into a quasi-philosophical discussion of whether any obligations imposed by Article 10 would be legal or moral. Many citizens would have found it a challenge to follow the president as he declared that Article 10 entailed "a moral, not a legal obligation—binding in conscience only, not in law." Nor did he help himself with the obscure assertion that moral obligations were just as binding as legal ones, "but operative in a different way."

Word of this brought Wilson nothing but scorn. Elihu Root, when he heard of it, accused the president of "curious and childlike casuistry"—of drawing a distinction that was "false, demoralizing and dishonest." Senator Borah expressed the same thought more obliquely. "What will your league amount to," he asked sarcastically, "if it does not contain powers that no one dreams of giving it?"

Wilson appears to have been more annoyed by Harding's questions than by any other part of the meeting. He said later that Harding appeared to have "a disturbingly dull mind" and that "it seemed impossible to get any explanation to lodge in it." The memory of August 19 would add considerably to Wilson's scorn when, fifteen months later, Harding was elected to succeed him in the White House.

President and senators followed their meeting with a cordial lunch and went their various ways. Lodge would opine that the session had exposed Wilson's "ignorance and disingenuousness," but he did so privately. Most public reports of what had transpired were favorable, if only politely so. Hiram Johnson wrote to his sons in California, but did not say publicly, that the president gave the impression of being "hard, cold and cruel, some mysterious, ill-defined monster."

On balance it had been something like a draw. But with his opponents still on the high ground, the president needed more. It was time to try another initiative, one that Tumulty had been planning since before Wilson's return from Europe. Ignoring the warnings of his doctor that such an undertaking could prove beyond his strength, Wilson determined to set forth on a four-week speaking tour that would carry him across ten thousand miles of the American landscape. The schedule called upon him to deliver full-blown orations at a rate of almost two a day on average and to make briefer appearances at frequent whistle-stops along his route. Massive press coverage was ensured: twenty-one reporters from the wire services and leading newspapers would travel on the presidential train, and wherever it stopped, writers from local journals could be depended upon to turn out in force. A private car with a double bed and sitting room was readied for Wilson and his wife. It would be their home for almost the whole of the journey. The train would advance from city to city by night, while the presidential couple rested.

Shortly before departing on the tour, Wilson had the British diplomat Sir William Wiseman to the White House for lunch. Wiseman's account of the visit sheds light on why presidential physician Cary Grayson was opposed to the journey. "The president was cordial as ever," he reported. "I was, however, shocked by his appearance. He was obviously a sick man. His face was drawn and of a grey color, and frequently twitching in a pitiful effort to control nerves which had broken down under the burden of the world's distress."

Nevertheless, the Wilsons set out on September 3, accompanied by Tumulty and Dr. Grayson. They crossed the Alleghenies into western Ohio that first night, and the next day the president gave two speeches, in Columbus and Indianapolis. On September 5 he addressed two audiences in St. Louis, one at midday and the other that night, and on the sixth he spoke first in Kansas City and then in Des Moines. So it went: Omaha and Sioux Falls; two speeches in St. Paul and one in Minneapolis; Bismarck and Billings; Helena and Coeur d'Alene. At every stop he expressed himself in urgent terms. "I can predict with absolute certainty," he said in Omaha on September 8, "that within another generation there will be another world war if the nations of the world—if the League of Nations—does not prevent it by concerted action." He then struck a brighter note—and rather spoiled the speech as a demonstration of prophetic powers—by saying that no such thing was going to happen because the kinds of Americans represented by his audience would never allow it. "The heart of this people is pure," he said. "This great people loves liberty. It loves justice. . . . It is the great idealistic force of history, and the idealism of America is what has made conquest of the spirit of man."

The speeches continued to be substantial and eloquent; Wilson was very nearly in peak form, doing a markedly better job than he had in Washington of explaining the treaty and answering questions. He spoke extemporaneously, without a written script. As soon as he finished each speech, a stenographer's notes were transformed at maximum speed into printed copies that were then handed to the reporters on the scene and mailed to papers across the country. The costs of this improvised publicity operation, about a thousand dollars a day, were paid by the Michigan Democratic Party's narrowly unsuccessful 1918 Senate candidate, league supporter and auto magnate Henry Ford.

Soon almost every speech included a defense of the Shantung settlement, an issue that refused to die. With Tumulty's coaching, Wilson was generally successful at keeping his disdain for congressional skeptics within the boundaries of politeness. He suggested that the skeptics were uninformed, and that some might have parochial and selfish aims, but rarely went further than that.

Trouble pursued him, however, and not just figuratively. At the end of the first week, as his train traversed the blank flatlands of North Dakota, three of the Senate's irreconcilables—Joseph Medill McCormick of Illinois and progressive firebrands Borah and Johnson—began speaking tours of their own, their aim to neutralize the press coverage Wilson's tour was generating. They spoke together at an anti-league rally in Chicago on September 10 and then fanned out, McCormick and Borah across the Midwest, Johnson following the president down the West Coast to Los Angeles. The crowds they attracted were comparable in size to Wilson's.

The question of Ireland, of why promulgation of the Fourteen Points had not brought British rule of Ireland under challenge at Paris, was, like Shantung, a major nuisance. The president was asked about it repeatedly and sometimes heckled. His response was to observe—always without naming particular countries—that the peace conference had not been able to right all the world's wrongs, but that when the league was in operation it would be free to do so. This satisfied few Irish-Americans, who noted that, as a permanent member of the league's ruling council, Britain would have veto power over all proposals. Wilson's position became more awkward when, in the middle of his tour, British authorities in Dublin outlawed a self-proclaimed Irish republican government (winner of a recent election) that was demanding independence. A vicious guerrilla war developed, and Britain would commit two hundred thousand troops to it. It had nothing to do with a September 9 strike by most of Boston's police force—the policemen were motivated by wretched pay and workweeks of up to eighty-three hours—but the fact that most of the strikers were of Irish extraction did not go unnoticed. Nor did the fact that Massachusetts governor Calvin Coolidge used 6,700 troops to crush the walkout, making himself a Republican hero (and a future president) by doing so.

Irish-Americans accused Wilson of hypocrisy. Italian-Americans blamed him for thwarting Italy's aspirations at the peace conference. Many German-Americans, though still fearful of being accused of treason if they spoke out, were deeply unhappy about the consequences of the starvation blockade and the terms of the peace treaty. Though Wilson in his speeches was pointing proudly to the part of the league covenant that he called a Magna Carta of global workers' rights, American unions found nothing to celebrate. They saw no evidence of presidential interest in supporting them in disputes with companies that were unwilling even to acknowledge their existence.

Gradually, the president began to show signs of the strain that the tour was placing on him and the effects of strain on his judgment. As early as Omaha, and later with accelerating frequency, he reverted to his wartime attacks on "the hyphenates," repeating his accusations of disloyalty. "There are a great many hyphens left in America," he said in St. Paul on September 9. "For my part, I think the most un-American thing in the world is a hyphen. . . . It ought not to be there." These words must have undone whatever goodwill he might have generated with German-Americans earlier the same day in Minneapolis, where he said that a democratic Germany would be "as welcome to the league as anybody else."

The news from Washington, meanwhile, was not good. On September 10 Lodge's Foreign Relations Committee sent the treaty to the full Senate with no fewer than forty-five amendments (five of them disavowing and undoing the Shantung settlement) and four reservations. This was so thoroughgoing a repudiation of the president's work in Paris as to amount to a personal insult. Days later the twenty-nine-year-old William Bullitt, a future ambassador to the Soviet Union and coauthor with Sigmund Freud of a contemptuous and controversial "psychological study" of Woodrow Wilson, was called before the

William Bullitt,
junior diplomat at the
Paris Peace Conference
*He testified to the U.S. Senate that
Secretary Lansing and others had
complained of the peace treaty's
"unjust clauses."*

committee to explain why he and a dozen other staff members had quit the peace conference upon seeing the contents of the treaty. Committee members and reporters were less interested in Bullitt's opinions than in what he claimed to have observed of reactions among the American delegates. At least three of them, he averred, had expressed serious dissatisfaction with the treaty. He stunned his listeners—and delighted any number of them—by reading aloud the note in which he had recorded Secretary Lansing's words when the treaty was first printed and distributed. "I consider that the League of Nations is at present entirely useless," the note quoted Lansing as saying. "The great powers have simply gone ahead and arranged the world to suit themselves. England and France in particular have gotten out of the treaty everything they wanted, and the League of Nations can do nothing to alter any of the unjust clauses of the treaty except by unanimous consent of the members of the league, and the great powers will never give their consent to changes in the interests of weaker peoples."

This was particularly stinging because uttered by Wilson's own secretary of state. It was both obviously true and totally at variance with what the president himself was saying in speech after speech about how, for the first time in history, a war had ended in a settlement in which the victors sought nothing and gained nothing for themselves. When the newspapers contacted Lansing, he replied only that "I have no comment to make" and departed on a fishing trip. This, too, was headline news, implying as it did that Lansing had no argument with Bullitt's testimony. Lansing would later tell his undersecretary that he "could not flatly deny" Bullitt's testimony because, if not entirely accurate, it contained enough truth to make a simple denial impossible. He wrote to Wilson, upon becoming aware of what a sensation his failure to answer reporters' questions had been, that "I have made no comment on the Bullitt statement believing that it would only introduce a controversy." Bullitt's testimony he described as "most despicable and outrageous."

Lansing was being disingenuous. Upon returning to Washington, he began composing a letter of resignation in which he intended to blast the president for a "grave breach of faith," as a result of which "a glorious chance to rearrange the world has been lost." Wilson, for his part, told Tumulty that if he were in Washington, he would fire Lansing immediately. The relationship was obviously finished.

The presidential train was on the West Coast by this point, having reached Seattle on September 13. From there it proceeded southward through San Francisco to southern California, then turned eastward back toward Washington. On September 23, at Ogden, Utah, news reached the president that the Senate's "mild reservationists," Republicans whose votes he needed, had come to an understanding of some kind with Henry Cabot Lodge. Details were not provided, but this could not be good news. It was inconceivable that anyone could be both in accord with Lodge on the treaty and prepared to support it on the terms demanded by Wilson. On the bright side, Lodge could not be unalterably opposed to the treaty if he and the reservationists had found common ground.

Such reports gave Wilson no reason to suppose that his tour was changing opinions in Washington. This may have contributed to the increasing sourness of his oratory. In his Ogden address he said things so divisive, so self-defeating that they can easily be taken as early signs of breakdown. "All the elements that tended toward disloyalty [during the war] are against the league, and for a very good reason," he said. "If this league is not adopted, we will serve Germany's purpose, because we will be dissociated from the nations with whom we cooperated in defeating Germany." This was very close to saying that to oppose the league, perhaps even to question the president's approach to the league, was to side with Germany and betray the Allies. Such accusations were hardly likely to be well received by those senators and citizens who, though they had supported the war unreservedly, now thought it their right and duty to examine the treaty and covenant with critical eyes.

How far the president might have gone down this path we can never know, because two days later he came to the end of his strength. He did so in the course of delivering, in Pueblo, Colorado, one of the most rambling and intemperate speeches of the tour. "I find," he said, "that there is an organized propaganda against the League of Nations and against the treaty proceeding from exactly the same sources that the organized propaganda proceeded from which threatened this country here and there with disloyalty. And I want to say—I cannot say it too often—any man who carries a hyphen with him carries a dagger that he is ready to plunge into the vitals of this republic whenever he gets the chance. If I can catch any man with a hyphen in this great contest, I will know that I have caught an enemy of the republic."

The clumsy syntax, almost incoherent at times and utterly untypical of a healthy Wilson even when speaking extemporaneously, suggests that he was no longer himself. In their book, published in Europe in the 1930s but not in the United States until 1967, Freud and Bullitt would claim that the things Wilson was saying at this point in his tour show him to be "very close to psychosis." He was telling his audiences that in restoring peace to Europe, the British and French had been inspired to saintly selflessness; that Germany, though now a republic, remained a "monster" that had to be kept in chains; and that any who disagreed were traitors.

To call such talk psychotic or nearly so is of course extravagant (historian A. J. P. Taylor called the Freud-Bullitt study a disgrace) but hardly without foundation. By the time he reached Pueblo, Wilson had been campaigning without pause for more than three weeks. He had been pummeled by the late-summer heat and humidity of the Midwest. Then, as a result of arteriosclerosis, he had found it difficult to breathe in the thin air of the mountain states. For two weeks he had been afflicted with constant and severe headaches and had driven himself to make appearance after appearance in spite of them.

When he returned to the train after the Pueblo speech, he was in such a state that his doctor, Admiral Grayson, took fright. That night the president had a severe attack of what Grayson wrongly diagnosed as asthma. As the train approached Wichita the next morning Grayson was demanding that the remainder of the tour be canceled. Wilson resisted at first but not for long.

"I don't seem to realize it, but I have gone to pieces," he said to Tumulty.

"The doctor is right, I am in no condition to go on. I have never been in a condition like this, and I just feel as if I am going to pieces." He looked away and, according to Grayson, wept. The train sped off for Washington with the president in bed, nauseated and racked with fits of coughing, unable to sleep. They arrived at Union Station on Sunday, September 28—the day that the last race riot of the year broke out in Omaha—and Wilson was hurriedly delivered to the White House.

Four days later, early on the morning of October 2, while making his way from bed to bathroom, he was felled by a massive stroke. A neurologist summoned from Philadelphia found him entirely paralyzed on his left side. He was conscious, though drowsy, and his life was judged not to be in danger.

There now began one of the darkest, most disturbing episodes in the history of the American presidency. Throughout October, Wilson was not only totally incapacitated by his stroke but brought to the verge of death by a prostate infection that blocked the functioning of his kidneys and could not be surgically corrected because of his fragile state. He lay motionless and silent as Mrs. Wilson took charge, in some sense, of the executive branch of the government. Almost nothing is known of how this was worked out, how she arranged things, or how aware the president was; she allowed no one to see her husband except his daughters, the doctors, the nurses, and those few members of the White House staff who were needed for his care. All took their secrets to the grave. Grayson told reporters that the president was suffering from nervous exhaustion but recovering. For a month and a half not even Tumulty was allowed to see him. Lansing sent appeals for guidance and received no answers. When he called a cabinet meeting, Tumulty told him, falsely but in a convincingly threatening tone, that the president wanted to know by whose authority they were gathering. There were few further attempts to bring the cabinet together.

The life of the nation went on, of course, and in ways that continued to make 1919 an extraordinarily difficult year. A quarter of a million steelworkers had been on strike since September 22, driven to walk out by the refusal of the U.S. Steel Corporation not only to shorten their twelve-hour workdays but to recognize their union. In October they were joined by the coal miners, aggrieved by the government's insistence that they could not have a pay increase commensurate with inflation because, in the absence of a ratified peace treaty, the country was still at war with Germany and wartime wage guidelines continued to apply. Corporations were exacerbating already tense race relations by hiring black strikebreakers, and fears of the Red Menace were inflamed by depictions of virtually the whole labor movement as Communist-led and even Bolshevik-financed. Certainly there were union leaders and organizers whose opinions were far to the left of the mainstream, but they were rarely radical enough and never numerous or influential enough to warrant such intense paranoia. There was real trouble—bombings, and street fights between radical demonstrators and indignant patriots—but hardly on a scale that threatened the future of the republic.

The government continued to function, but on a strange ad hoc basis in which the chief executive played first no part and then a severely limited one. Cabinet members, depending on their temperaments, either feared to act or acted more boldly than they would have dared under presidential supervision. When on October 28 Congress passed the Volstead Act, which created the mechanism for enforcing Prohibition (the Eighteenth Amendment having been ratified almost a year before), it was Joe Tumulty and not the president who wrote the message vetoing it. He did so without being able to see Wilson but was confident that he was doing as the president wished. The veto was in any case an empty gesture; Congress quickly overrode it.

The battle over the peace treaty, too, went on without the president. It is an oversimplification, but not a seriously misleading one, to say that it had come down to a tug-of-war between Senate Democrats prepared to approve the treaty as Wilson wanted it and the far less numerous irreconcilables, unwilling as before to approve it in any form. In the middle, being pulled in both directions, were the reservationists. They were willing to have the country join the league but demanded that the obligations of membership be limited and made absolutely clear. Everything depended, or appeared to, on which way this middle group finally moved. Henry Cabot Lodge kept his colleagues guessing about whether he was going to turn out to be a reservationist or an irreconcilable in reservationist clothing. He was positioned to save the league if he wished but obviously would never do so without exacting a price. In any case, compromise was going to be essential, and most of the senators were willing. The problem for the Democrats was that they didn't want to agree to anything without the approval of their chief, and he was telling them nothing.

It became clear that the Senate was not going to insist on or even accept amendments to the covenant. Therefore the treaty would never be ratified in a form requiring explicit approval of other members of the league; that danger was gone. It was now a question of reservations, which everyone assumed (almost certainly correctly) the rest of the world would accept, without serious complaint, as conditions of American membership. The agreement of which Wilson had learned in Utah, the one worked out between Lodge and the mild reservationists, mainly involved Article 10. Though other parts of the covenant continued to be of concern, this was now the point upon which the debate turned. The White House, whoever was in charge there, did not retreat from the insistence that without Article 10 exactly as the president had written it, the league could never function as it must. Many Americans in and outside the Senate, however, continued to fear that it would oblige the United States to become involved whenever war broke out anywhere in the world, even when the aim of intervention was to maintain a dubious status quo.

This is what Lodge and the reservationists agreed to append to Article 10 and presented to their fellow senators on October 24:

The United States assumes no obligation to preserve the territorial integrity or political independence of any other country or to intervene in controversies between nations—whether members of the league or not—under provisions of article 10, or to employ the military or naval forces of the United States under any article of the treaty for any purpose, unless, in any particular case, the Congress, which, under the Constitution, has the sole power to declare war or authorize the employment of the military or naval forces of the United States, shall by act or joint resolution so provide.

Was this simple prudence or the culmination of a plot by Lodge to eviscerate the league? The available evidence makes it difficult to cast Lodge in the role of villain, impossible to convict him of underhanded behavior. He was, as he insisted, never an isolationist, but he had strong convictions about the importance of integrity in international relations. With Theodore Roosevelt, he had always believed that making commitments that the nation might not be willing to fulfill would damage not only America's credibility and good name but the foundations of international stability. Nor can it be denied that his Article 10 reservation is consistent with, even reinforcing of, the U.S. Constitution. The senator's judgment is as open to question as Wilson's, but that he was in earnest, his intentions good, is hardly to be doubted.

November brought signs that Wilson's physical condition was improving. When the king and queen of Belgium came to Washington and were welcomed as heroes of the recent war, they were invited to visit the president in his bedroom. After a brief and carefully staged greeting, they did as Tumulty requested and spoke to the press of how fit the president appeared to be.

The Senate, aware that its failure even to try to come to a decision on the league compared poorly with Mitchell Palmer's bold pursuit of radicals, picked up the pace at last. In the thirteen days leading up to the climactic final vote, no fewer than sixty-six speeches about the treaty were delivered on the floor of the Senate. One after another, reservations came up for a vote and were variously adopted or, more often, rejected. On November 13 the Lodge-approved reservation on Article 10 passed by a vote of forty-six to thirty-three. There were seventeen votes on November 15 alone, and the daily total would continue to rise.

Senator Gilbert Hitchcock of Nebraska was in a particularly difficult posi-

Gilbert Hitchcock, U.S. senator from Nebraska, 1911–1923
He tried and failed to get Wilson to relent and save the League of Nations.

tion. He had never been one of the Democrats on whom the president could count for support on all questions at all times, but now, as senior Democrat on the Foreign Relations Committee and acting minority leader with aspirations to keep the job permanently, he was doing his best to keep the members of his party in line. But he more than anyone else was required by the president's silence to grope his way half blind through the legislative underbrush. He had been one of the first to be allowed to visit the president after his stroke, later recording his shock at finding him a frail and aged invalid with a scraggly white beard. When he managed to see him again on November 17, with the final vote on the treaty drawing near, he found Wilson stronger and more combative. The president told Hitchcock that the Republican reservations were tantamount to crippling the league, and that he would have nothing to do with them. He said he was going to "get the political scalps" of any who voted for the treaty with the reservations attached, and that "I have no hostility towards these gentlemen, only an utter contempt."

Hitchcock saw the dangers of daring to speak for the president. He therefore drafted a letter from Wilson to himself, a statement of what he understood the president's position to be, and delivered it to Mrs. Wilson. She read it to her husband, made changes per his instructions, used a rubber stamp to affix his signature, and sent it back to Hitchcock in the following form:

> You were good enough to bring me word that the Democratic senators supporting the treaty expected to hold a conference before the final vote on the Lodge resolution of ratification, and that they would be glad to receive a word of counsel from me. I should hesitate to offer it in any detail but I assume that the senators desire my judgment only upon the all-important question of the final vote on the resolution containing the many reservations by Senator Lodge. On that I can not hesitate, for in my opinion the resolution in that form does not provide for ratification, but for the nullification of the treaty. I sincerely hope that the friends and supporters of the treaty will vote against the Lodge resolution of ratification. I understand that the door will probably then be open for a genuine resolution of ratification. I hope therefore that all true friends of the treaty will refuse to support the Lodge resolution.

In giving this letter to Hitchcock, understanding that he would share it with the other Senate Democrats, Wilson killed any possibility of accommodation with the reservationists. He thought the country was with him, that his opponents would be purged in the next election, and that the treaty as he wanted it would be ratified then if not sooner. (Incredibly, despite his stroke, he continued to harbor ambitions of a third term.) Even Lodge was among the prominent figures—Colonel House, recently back from what had turned out to be almost a year in Paris, was another—who sent appeals to the White House, trying to find ways to save a treaty that now faced certain defeat and urging the president to soften his position. None of these messages were answered or even acknowledged. To this day it is not known whether Mrs. Wilson allowed the president to see them. One of the specialists attending her husband had warned that nothing should be allowed to disturb him. Like the first Mrs. Wilson in the final days at Princeton, she saw it as her responsibility to shield her husband from all possible upset. Physicians today say that even from a therapeutic perspective, this was a mistake—that a return to business as usual, if not overdone, could have made a more nearly complete recovery possible.

The Hitchcock letter as revised by Wilson was dated November 18. By then the Senate had approved a dozen reservations, all of them originating in the Foreign Relations Committee. Still more would be proposed and put to a vote in the final hours, and three of those would be approved as well. One—another rebuke for the president—stated that the covenant's labor provisions, the ones that Wilson proudly called his Magna Carta of labor, would not apply to the United States unless approved by a joint resolution of Congress.

Opposition to the labor provisions had been led, curiously, by probably the Senate's foremost champion of organized labor, Robert La Follette. He said they had the potential "to subject American labor to a direct attack upon its existing protective statutes." His success in this matter signaled his reemergence as a political force, and the end of the two and a half years during which even his fellow Republicans had shunned him and threatened him with expulsion from the Senate. His status as an untouchable came to end when, in the aftermath of the 1918 election, the Republicans needed his vote to take control of the almost evenly divided Senate. Now his sins were forgotten, and he was restored to his old place as Capitol Hill's leading progressive. He joined the irreconcilables, mocking the president for demanding "the crushing of the German Republic and the German people" after having said repeatedly that it was the Hohenzollern rulers, not their subjects, who bore responsibility for Germany's sins.

The dynamics of the fight for ratification had by this point changed profoundly. Once the crucial question had been whether the reservationists could be persuaded to accept the president's arguments and join the Democrats in approving the covenant in undiluted form. Gradually, however, the reservationists had strengthened their position, increasing their public support by approving only those reservations that reflected voters' concerns and rejecting those that seemed reckless, ill advised, or simply pointless. With Lodge openly on their side, they felt no pressure to move at all. The question now was whether the Democrats were going to come to them, accepting the reservations.

The unsurprising answer came on the evening of November 19, when a resolution of ratification containing the approved reservations went down to an overwhelming defeat. Thirty-five Republicans voted yes and were joined by four Democrats unwilling to follow the president on this question. The no votes were cast by forty loyal if in many cases regretful Democrats plus the irreconcilables, who now numbered fifteen. (Four senators were absent, not enough to have made a difference.) In a curious move that is worth noting because it suggests how the vote could have gone if Wilson had been less inflexible, forty-five Democrats then voted for a resolution to reconsider—to vote again on—the measure they had just rejected. This was their oblique and rather despairing way of showing what they really thought—of demonstrating support for the treaty without defying the White House. Added to the positive Republican votes, these forty-five senators would have been enough to approve the treaty in a landslide. But when the second vote was taken, the president's strictures were again effective. Only two Democrats switched to the yes side.

And so it was over. Republican Warren Harding spoke for many in both parties when he called the vote "a very grave misfortune, and I am sorry about it." He was speaking for many Democrats when he put the blame on "the towering ambition" of Woodrow Wilson.

One of the unhappy Democrats, Claude Swanson of Virginia, sought out Lodge. "For God's sake," he pleaded, "can't something be done to save the treaty?"

"Senator," Lodge said, "the door is closed. You have done it yourselves."

The hour comes round at last, November 11, 1918
Americans rejoice at news of the Armistice.

Aftermath

"Now It Is All Over"

CARL VON CLAUSEWITZ, FAMOUS FOR DESCRIBING WAR AS THE continuation of politics by other means, defined victory as the achievement of a "better political arrangement." He said also that the improvement must justify the price, and any war in which this proves impossible should be brought to the earliest possible end.

When the first anniversary of the Great War's end came on November 11, 1919, the victors were generally satisfied that the world's new political arrangements were definitely preferable to what the war had swept away. Nor were many inclined to complain, despite the indescribable devastation, that the price had been too high. The British and French Empires, after all, were significantly bigger than they had been in 1914. Italy had spread her borders, while Germany had been rendered incapable of competing with any of them in any way.

The United States once again stood apart. She had made victory possible, had paid the smallest price in blood, and alone had gained in wealth. By virtue of the failure of the Senate and President Wilson to come to terms on the peace treaty and the League of Nations—the Senate's rejection of both came, as we have seen, in this same November—America would be less affected by the new arrangements than any other participant in the war. The doughboys had returned home and, like millions of their fellow citizens, were trying to do the impossible: recover the life that they had lived before the war.

Colonel Edward House had remained in Paris into the autumn of 1919. He did so at President Wilson's request and to his own deepening frustration, the only American delegate to do so. He accomplished nothing—the important work was finished, and the Americans still on hand to help finish the peace conference's business resented his presence—and was unsettled by reports of the president's belligerent attitude toward the Senate and refusal to compromise. His appeals to the White House for a more conciliatory approach went unacknowledged.

There was irony in the colonel's situation. He had never wanted appointment as a delegate and in fact had observed more than two months before the Armistice that unless Wilson decided to remain in Washington "there are many reasons why it would be better for me to be on the outside." Not the least of those reasons was the danger that, as an official participant in the conference, he would not be able to remain behind the scenes. Thus he would run the risk of attracting the attention of the newspapers and arousing the president's jealousy—which of course is exactly what happened. By summer's end it was all too clear that he was not so much needed in Paris as unwanted, by Woodrow Wilson, in Washington.

Late in September 1919, just as the president's western tour was coming to its disastrous end, House informed the White House of his decision to return home. Receiving no response and knowing little of Wilson's condition, he assumed that there were no objections to his leaving Paris. After his arrival in New York, himself so ill that he was taken ashore on a stretcher, his attempts to communicate with the president were answered, when they were answered at all, by the distinctly unfriendly Mrs. Wilson. She made plain her unhappiness that he had departed France without permission and intimated that the president felt the same. House's offers to help in any possible way were brushed aside.

Americans observed their first Armistice Day holiday with picnics and parades and triumphal speeches in every city and town. But like so many things connected with the war, the celebration turned out to be flawed—most notably because of what happened in Centralia, Washington, that day.

The rough laborers in Centralia's lumber industry, some of the last remaining members of the shattered Industrial Workers of the World, had long had an uneasy relationship with the rest of the community. When an Armistice Day parade by two local American Legion posts stopped provocatively in front of an IWW meeting hall crowded with members on the lookout for trouble, the result was mayhem. Four legionnaires were shot dead, including a post commander recently home from army service in Siberia. A number of Wobblies were arrested, and one was lynched. Across the country, the next morning's headlines told readers of what became instantly famous as the Centralia Massacre.

Accounts of how the trouble started are contradictory, as is commonly true of such incidents. Apparently both sides deserve blame, and misunderstanding and panic made their usual contributions. Ultimately, six union members were convicted of second-degree murder and sentenced to long prison terms. Again as usual, the tragedy was said to be the work of traitors and Bolsheviks.

That same month also brought the breaking of strikes by nearly a million steelworkers and coal miners. The courts ruled against the unions—no surprise there—and the trouble was blamed not on hours or wages or working conditions but on subversives. Organized labor went into a defensive crouch from which it would not emerge until the 1930s and the New Deal.

Four days before Christmas, 249 of the aliens rounded up in Attorney General Palmer's November 1919 raids were herded aboard a ship bound for Russia. Many were forced to leave behind dependent wives and children. Palmer and his right hand, J. Edgar Hoover of the Bureau of Investigation, were at the pier before dawn to see them off. They expected to be deporting many, many more.

Palmer, feeling the wind at his back as public and press continued to applaud his anti-Red campaign, was at this time lobbying for a peacetime version of the Sedition Act, one that would give his department new tools for suppressing dissent and punishing dissenters. He would fail in this—though the Senate supported him, the House of Representatives refused to go along—but not until after President Wilson endorsed his proposal. Wilson's intervention in this matter, which if successful would have opened the door to a perpetuation of the government's attacks on the Bill of Rights, generally receives little attention in the books of his more fervent admirers. Is it unfair to wonder if such writers can find no way to make it fit with their hero's image as a champion of liberty?

Twelve days after their first shipload of alleged subversives steamed out of New York harbor, Palmer and Hoover launched a new round of raids. Some five thousand men and women were rounded up in scores of cities and towns. Many were held incommunicado and under appalling conditions—the two sexes crowded together in unventilated rooms without basic sanitation, sleeping on stone floors for days and even weeks. Only aliens with connections to Communist organizations were supposed to be in custody, but the authorities were rarely in a hurry to identify the U.S. citizens and the non-Communist aliens and allow them to go home.

January 1920 brought the peace conference to an end at last. Only the United States was still officially at war with Germany, because only she had not accepted the treaty imposed at Paris. Europe was settling down, if not altogether comfortably. Lenin's Bolsheviks were so solidly established in Russia that Britain and France were inching toward trade relations with them. The Near and Middle East were still in turmoil, with endless bloodshed to come.

President Wilson had by this time recovered to the extent that he was able to take a few steps without assistance. His judgment, however, remained all too obviously impaired. He arranged for a letter bearing his name to be read at Washington's January 8 Jackson Day dinner, an annual gathering of leading Democrats. In it, he announced his intention to make the 1920 presidential election a referendum on the treaty and the League of Nations. He implied, without stating so explicitly, that he himself would again be his party's candidate. Though most of the audience cheered lustily, William Jennings Bryan was present and told all within earshot that the president's plan was ridiculous. The country was too big and diverse, he said, for any national election ever to serve as a referendum on any single issue; he himself had learned this the hard way in 1900, in trying to make that year's campaign a referendum on imperialism. Nationally, the reaction to the letter was disastrously negative. Large numbers of opinion leaders began to see him as "a petulant and sick man and now the principal obstacle to ratification."

Former British foreign secretary Sir Edward Grey, recently ennobled as Viscount Grey of Fallodon and almost totally blind, was in Washington at the time, sent as a special ambassador by the Lloyd George government to encourage ratification of the treaty. Wilson refused to see Grey, supposedly in part because the young diplomat accompanying him and serving as his eyes was accused of having told an off-color joke about Edith Wilson. ("What did Mrs. Galt do when the president proposed to her?" "She fell out of bed!") Annoyed at being rebuffed after making such a long and (for a blind man) challenging journey, Grey returned to England and published a letter in which he said (speaking for himself only, but probably with Lloyd George's approval) that neither Britain nor France had serious objections to the Senate's reservations about the league covenant. He thereby effectively destroyed Wilson's argument that passage of the treaty with reservations would require a reopening of the Paris negotiations.

In February, Edward Lansing resigned as secretary of state. Out of consideration for the president's piteous condition, he did not issue the letter of resignation with which he had intended to air his grievances. His successor, almost inexplicably, was plucked from the obscurity of the shipping board: a figure of small reputation and little diplomatic experience named Bainbridge Colby. His principal qualifications appear to have been his years as a Democratic Party loyalist and his worshipful admiration of Woodrow Wilson, which he had put on display while serving in a minor role at the peace conference. His appointment reflected the president's long-standing conviction that, being in personal charge of international relations, he had no need for a strong secretary of state. It is also explained by his demand for absolute and unwavering loyalty. During a year in office, Colby would cause much mischief by encouraging Wilson's fantasies of winning a third term and taking vengeance on his foes.

The reservationists now mounted a new attempt to get the peace treaty ratified and the United States into the League of Nations. Senators from both parties joined forces in the hope of making it happen. That Majority Leader Lodge allowed his Republican colleagues to proceed makes nonsense once again of the claim, repeated endlessly down the years, that he was unalterably opposed to league membership, an isolationist seeking to wall off the United States from the rest of the world.

Democrats who in November had reluctantly done the president's bidding and rejected a treaty with reservations were eager to vote yes and hopeful that this time the White House would allow them to do so. Most Republicans were equally eager to accommodate them. As in 1919, there were speeches and debates and appeals to the president for compromise, and hopes rose. But Wilson was if anything even more inflexible than at the time of the first vote. Traits that had always been his least attractive—cold hauteur and an ill-concealed sense of personal superiority, contempt for and distrust of others, a readiness to see longtime faithful friends as traitors—had become so dominant as to smother his better qualities. The protective wall thrown up around him by his wife and physician completed his isolation.

On March 8, following in his own footsteps of the previous year, Wilson issued a statement denouncing the Senate's proposed reservations as "in effect a nullification of the terms of the treaty itself." Again he called upon Democrats to reject what remained, for him, the Republicans' utterly unacceptable demands. As before he got his way, but his margin of victory exposed the erosion of his authority. Twenty-three Democrats defied him and voted in favor. This was a solid majority of the Democrats who were not irreconcilables. Overall, fifty-seven senators voted for the treaty, thirty-nine against. It thus fell short of the needed two-thirds by seven votes. This result was entirely the president's doing. Even Democratic newspapers excoriated him.

Did it matter, really? At the end of the next global war, the creation of the United Nations would be hailed as the belated fulfillment of Wilson's grand vision. (Its charter, however, echoed the Senate reservations of 1919 and 1920 and contained not even an echo of Article 10.) Opinions of course differ as to how useful the UN has been, but no one would claim that it has come close to ending war. In the twenty-first century, it cannot claim to affect even the frequency of wars to any measurable extent, or to play much of a part in bringing them to an end. Nor is it possible to do more than speculate about what if anything might have turned out differently if the United States had joined the league in 1919 or 1920, with reservations or without.

Scenting the opportunity of a lifetime, "Fighting Quaker" Mitchell Palmer announced his candidacy for the Democratic presidential nomination. The president he hoped to succeed, meanwhile, remained for the public a mystery, his existence little more than a rumor, never seen in public and rarely receiving visitors. "There never was a moment when he was more than a shadow of his former self," White House chief usher Ike Hoover would recall. "He had changed from a giant to a pygmy." Perhaps the most poignant mark of his decline is the way in which, when presidential messages could not be avoided, Joe Tumulty now had to write them. The master wordsmith could no longer produce his own words, the master orator could not deliver anyone's words. In December 1919, for the first time since taking office in 1913, he had been unable to go to the Capitol to report on the state of the union.

The president had not called the cabinet together in the seven months since his stroke. On April 14, when cabinet members were finally invited to meet with him, they found themselves spectators at a brief and carefully staged affair under the watchful eyes of the first lady and Admiral Grayson. It took place not in the Cabinet Room but in a study adjacent to the president's bedroom on the second floor of the White House. Wilson was propped in a chair at the head of a conference table before the secretaries were admitted. He greeted them by attempting a joke that made little sense but drew forced and scattered chuckles.

Attorney General Palmer, basking in his status as the man of the hour, appears to have dominated the gathering. He gave an expansive, cheerily self-satisfied account of how the wildcat railroad strikes that had begun breaking out across the country after the failure of the big strike were the work of Wobblies and their Bolshevik masters, with the disruption of public order their true aim. When he had talked himself out, the president uttered almost his only words of the meeting: he "told Palmer not to let the country see red," according to an account left by Navy Secretary Daniels. No one present appears to have known what he meant, and no one knows today. Perhaps it was another attempted witticism. Mrs. Wilson and Grayson reminded the cabinet members that the meeting was an experiment and declared it at an end.

The rail strikes petered out, public fear of sedition ebbed, and enthusiasm for Palmer's candidacy subsided with it. He had a powerful rival, Treasury Secretary and presidential son-in-law McAdoo, who had not declared but was known to be planning a run. Wilson's failure to endorse either of them (he was not close to McAdoo, who had married one of the Wilson daughters after his appointment to head the Treasury Department), or take himself out of the running, spread a cloud of uncertainty. As Palmer continued his alarms about terrorists and no fresh violence broke out, people began to complain that he had an inclination to cry wolf. Newspaper stories began to appear about how his raiders often acted without warrants and about his use of agents who were neither government employees nor properly deputized.

Perhaps to rekindle public enthusiasm, perhaps because he was coming to be touched with paranoia, Palmer issued his most sensational warning yet. He said that May 1—May Day, "workers' day" for leftists around the world—was going to bring disturbances of unprecedented violence. Riots were being planned, he said—even assassinations. Police departments and National Guard units were put on alert as the date drew near, often at considerable expense and inconvenience. When May Day came and went without anything happening, Palmer was ridiculed. The Fighting Quaker became the Quaking Quitter. A final blow came on May 28, when twelve lawyers issued a report detailing ways in which Palmer's Justice Department had acted unlawfully in its pursuit and prosecution of aliens. What hurt was the eminence of the accusers: among them were two law school deans including Harvard's Roscoe Pound, seven professors of law including future Supreme Court justice Felix Frankfurter, a former judge, and a former U.S. attorney for Philadelphia. Palmer was not finished as a candidate, but he was a damaged one.

Nothing, meanwhile, shook President Wilson's conviction that the American people wanted what he wanted, and that when this became clear the peace treaty would be accepted on his terms and his enemies routed. He became convinced that the way to bring all this to pass was to consent to serve a third term. He would not seek it but looked forward to receiving it by acclamation at the Democratic National Convention, to be held in San Francisco that summer. He was furious when he learned that a worried Joe Tumulty had asked Mrs. Wilson to persuade the president to announce, for his own good, that he would not be a candidate. Admiral Grayson quotes Wilson as saying at about this time that "the [Democratic] convention may feel that I am the logical one to lead—perhaps the only one to champion this cause. In such circumstance I would feel obliged to accept the nomination even if I thought it would cost me my life." In his own eyes, he was still the indispensable man. In Grayson's, he was risking suicide.

When the convention met in June, Wilson volunteers led by Secretary of State Colby were on the scene, attempting to round up support. The president waited at the White House for news of a stampede in his favor, not knowing that Tumulty, Grayson, Navy Secretary Daniels, and others were explaining to everyone who would listen why his name must not be entered in nomination. They succeeded. When balloting began, McAdoo and Palmer were first and second respectively, but neither had even half the number of votes needed. Forty-four ballots were taken in the next four days. The end did not come until Palmer, his support melting away, released his remaining delegates to do as they wished. The convention was by this time swinging not to McAdoo but to Governor James Cox of Ohio, who won after a few more ballots. He chose the assistant secretary of the navy, the dashing young Franklin Roosevelt of New York, as his running mate.

Upon returning to the East, Cox and Roosevelt paid a visit to the White House—and ended whatever slim chance of being elected they might have had by proclaiming their allegiance to Woodrow Wilson. Repeating the president's proposal of the start of the year, they said they wanted the election to be a referendum on the treaty and the league. The Republicans, with Warren Harding and Calvin Coolidge heading their ticket, declined to take a definitive position on the treaty or the league and paid no price for doing so.

Seven weeks before the election, as if to keep the nation from supposing that domestic tranquillity had been altogether restored, a wagonload of dynamite was set off outside the Wall Street headquarters of J. P. Morgan and Company. The explosion was of Western Front proportions, killing twenty-nine persons (not financial magnates but messengers and clerks and the like), injuring more than two hundred, and breaking windows a quarter of a mile away. If something of the kind had happened a few months earlier, it might have delivered the nomination to Mitchell Palmer. Even coming as late as it did, it probably saved him from being impeached by a Congress that had begun hearings to explore the extent of his excesses. It did not save him from being ridiculed when the Justice Department was unable to come up with a single suspect. It was, to be sure, a difficult case. The wagon and the mule that pulled it had been virtually vaporized in the explosion. The only clues were four iron horseshoes. They were checked against the work of farriers up and down the eastern seaboard, without result.

Harding and Coolidge won the election in an epic landslide: sixteen million votes to Cox's and Roosevelt's nine million.

Eugene Debs, still in prison, received 915,000 votes as the Socialist Party

Eugene V. Debs, 1921
*"A traitor!" Woodrow Wilson
called him, but President Harding
finally set him free.*

candidate.

Mitchell Palmer remained in Washington after leaving office and tried to establish a law practice. But he found himself a nonperson, a lawyer no one wanted to see, much less hire.

Edith and Woodrow Wilson moved in to a stately three-story mansion on S Street in a fashionable section of Washington. There the former president spent the last three years of his life in proud isolation, physically a ruin. He lived to see the start of his enshrinement as one of America's liberal icons, a champion of liberty and peace and lofty ideals. The Woodrow Wilson Foundation was established and handsomely endowed, and Woodrow Wilson clubs were started at colleges around the country. Crowds of admirers would gather outside his door, and sometimes he would show himself. World leaders called on him when in Washington. They were sometimes shocked by the wild bitterness with which he spoke of the many people he regarded as his enemies. Otherwise he saw few people except his family and his wife's.

He must have snorted with contempt when the Senate ratified a separate treaty of peace with Germany, one that departed from the treaty approved at Versailles in no important respects aside from its exclusion of the league and its covenant.

And must have snorted again when he learned that his successor was releasing Debs from prison. Many people had asked him to do the same before leaving office, pointing out that Debs was in his midsixties now, in deteriorating health, showing signs of depression, and no possible danger to anyone or anything. Even Palmer, wanting to end his time in office on a magnanimous note, urged that Debs be set free. Wilson would not hear of it. "This man was a traitor to his country," he said, "and he will never be pardoned during my administration."

One thinks of the closing days of the American Civil War, when the victors were faced with the question of how to deal with citizens who had taken up arms against the United States and killed hundreds of thousands of her soldiers. And of what Abraham Lincoln said about binding up the nation's wounds, "with malice towards none and charity for all." But Lincoln was never what Ray Stannard Baker called Wilson: "*a good hater.*"

From the time of House's return to the United States late in 1919, he and Wilson had no connection, not even an exchange of notes or the briefest of meetings. The colonel survived the president by fifteen years, living quietly except when called upon to voice yet again his support for the League of Nations. "My separation from Woodrow Wilson was and is to me a tragic mystery," he would say, "a mystery that now can never be dispelled, for its explanation lies buried with him. Theories I have, and theories they must remain."

To the end of his days, Wilson remained convinced that the people would see to American entry into the league on his terms. He believed that this could happen with the election of 1924—and really did think that he might be the Democratic nominee that year. But in fact President Harding had put the league question to rest on April 12, 1921, at the end of his first appearance before Congress. Earlier he had promised that the United States would join in "any seemly program to lessen the probability of war." Now he declared that the league could be not such a program, that it was fatally flawed because it had been created to perform the incompatible "dual functions of a political instrument for the conquerors and an agency of peace." He said his position was in accord with the will of the people as expressed in the 1920 election, but that it would also be consistent with public opinion for the United States to "play our fullest part in joining the peoples of the world in pursuits of peace once more."

As Harding's words suggest, it cannot responsibly be argued—though it has been argued with ridiculous frequency—that the Republican electoral victories of the 1920s and the end of "Wilsonism" ushered in a period of American isolation. To the contrary, two exceptionally active and effective secretaries of state, Charles Evans Hughes and Henry L. Stimson, directed the nation's foreign policy during the Republican ascendancy. Their achievements included treaties reducing naval shipbuilding, Japanese withdrawal from the Shantung Peninsula, and extensive though ultimately unsuccessful efforts to reduce German reparations, assist German recovery through trade, and thereby avert Europe's and the world's descent into economic depression.

That notorious isolationist Henry Cabot Lodge was actively engaged in negotiating arms reduction treaties up to the time of his death in November 1924. In that same month his fellow Republican and longtime antagonist Robert La Follette ran for president as a third-party candidate in a last-ditch effort to rally the forces of progressivism. He received a mere 17 percent of the vote, carrying only his home state of Wisconsin, and seven months later he, too, was dead. A month after that, five days after securing a conviction in the Scopes Monkey Trial and getting himself branded a clown by doing so, William Jennings Bryan died in his sleep. The decks were being cleared for a new political era, and a new generation of leaders.

President Wilson, before his death, had repeated an old pattern by banishing almost his last friend from the start of his political career, the devoted Joe Tumulty. When Warren Harding became president, Tumulty had gone home to New Jersey, opening a law practice and again becoming active in the local Democratic Party. In 1922 he wrote to Wilson, asking him for a message that could be read at that year's Jackson Day dinner in New York. Even something quite simple, Tumulty said, would cheer the assembled pols. Wilson refused.

Tumulty asked Mrs. Wilson for help, and she, too, refused. Tumulty managed to get an appointment with Wilson but saw how inflexible and unnaturally aged his longtime chief had become and did not repeat his request. In the end, foolishly, he himself wrote a brief and innocuous (he thought) message and passed it to the dinner's organizers as being from Wilson. Unfortunately, when the message was read aloud, it was interpreted as an endorsement of the evening's main speaker, James Cox, who was known to be planning a second run for the White House in 1924. This was news, and so it appeared in the papers. When Wilson learned of it, he had *The New York Times* informed that the message was a fraud, thereby subjecting Tumulty to public humiliation.

Tumulty left no explanation of why he faked the message. He and his wife had a large family. After a decade in Wilson's service, he needed to reestablish himself professionally. His long association with Governor and then President Wilson made him suspect in the eyes of New Jersey's (and, to a lesser extent, New York's) Democratic Party bosses. Perhaps he hoped to impress such men with a demonstration of his status as an insider, still well connected. Failure to deliver a promised message from Wilson would have been embarrassing. Covering it up with a short counterfeit message must have seemed safe enough. How would the reclusive Wilson ever find out?

Why did Wilson refuse such a trivial favor to a man who had served him so long and so loyally? Why did he then protest in such a hurtful way when he learned what had been done? For the protest there is an explanation, one heavy with pathos. Only a tiny number of people knew (former secretary of state Colby was, inevitably, one) that even in 1922 Wilson dreamed of returning to the White House in triumph. He knew of Cox's hopes of being nominated again. This made Cox a rival. Any suggestion that Wilson might be endorsing him could not be allowed to stand.

The refusal of Tumulty's original request is harder to understand. Wilson might have regarded himself as owing nothing to anyone, and the disdain with which he viewed most people might have extended even to the one man who had served him day and night for a decade. He showed something close to contempt when he told his wife that "Tumulty will sulk for a few days, then come like a spanked child to say that he is sorry and wants to be forgiven."

The prediction was wrong. Tumulty would never again be seen in the house on S Street. Whether he tried, we do not know.

Admiral Grayson, who remained in Wilson's good graces to the end, once raised the subject of the Tumulty rift and was sharply rebuked for doing so. He was neither offended nor surprised. He knew Wilson well. He knew that he "has to hate someone."

One comes at last to the question of legacy, of what was won and what lost, of what it all means or once meant. Where the Great War and the United States are concerned, it comes down to what Clausewitz said about victory, to the question of whether this victory ended in a better arrangement, and if so, whether the betterment justified the cost.

By the time of Woodrow Wilson's death in 1923, there was already much doubt, even among those who had originally supported intervention. The reasons for doubt would multiply as the years rolled on.

The war destroyed the tsarist empire but made possible its replacement by Communist Russia and the reign of Stalin, one of history's great mass murderers.

A better arrangement?

It ended the Hohenzollern regime in Germany. In its place came disorder and a feeble republican government that many Germans saw as the creature of the victors and therefore unworthy of trust. And though it would be outrageous to blame American intervention for Nazism, the peace that intervention produced did put Germany on a path that led to Hitler.

A better arrangement?

The war created a Britain that by the 1930s could see so little justice in the peace imposed on Germany that she was almost fatally slow to stand up to Hitler's aggression—and barely had the resources to do so.

If it did not turn France, which had fought so long and valiantly, into a nation capable first of collapsing when faced with a Nazi invasion and then of collaborating on a shameful scale, it also did not keep such a thing from happening.

It is hardly necessary to mention the Middle East that victory brought into existence. Or Japan's resentment over her experiences at Paris and its effect on her behavior in the following two decades. Or the instability of the settlement that the peace conference imposed upon eastern Europe.

Were these things better?

The United States, for her part, was changed profoundly by the simple fact of being in the war. That years of deadlock culminated in victory barely six months after the doughboys first went into action, that Germany's final collapse followed by only two months the first offensive by an American army under American command—these things had a incalculable effect on the nation's image of itself and of the outside world, and not in entirely positive ways. They aggravated Americans' susceptibility to hubris, to believing that they are inherently superior to all other nations, her warriors inherently superior (and uniquely benign) as well.

But the things that changed the country most profoundly happened at home, and they happened mainly before the war ended:

The government's unprecedented assault on the Bill of Rights, on freedom of speech and assembly, on due process of law, on simple fairness.

The widespread public approval of that assault.

The official telling of lies, and the eager embrace of those lies.

The use of the war as an excuse to attack people guilty of nothing except failing to say only what the government wanted them to say.

These things are central to the legacy of the war—a legacy that lives on. It lives on, for example, in the Espionage Act of 1917. Unlike its equally vile offspring, the Sedition Act of 1918, the Espionage Act did not become inoperative with the end of the war and has never been repealed by Congress. It remains on the books today and is used for the punishment less of spies than of whistleblowers, citizens who reveal things that the government wants to keep secret not from enemies or foreign rivals but from the American public via the American news media. The obvious purpose being to deter other citizens from blowing still more whistles.

It is all part of the price that the United States paid for intervention. That cost is not measurable, and if one wants to argue that it was justified because it produced a better result, fair enough. But that it was a high cost cannot be denied.

If something was gained, even if much was gained, much was also lost. Something that is largely intangible and difficult to put into words. Something that manifested itself as deep and long-lasting disillusionment and that Henry Cabot Lodge attempted to express in a letter to Brooks Adams ten months after the war's end, even before the Senate's struggle over the League of Nations rose to its climax.

"We were all of us in our youth more or less under the spell of the nineteenth-century doctrines that we were in continual evolution," Lodge wrote, "always moving on to something better with perfection as the goal. . . .

"Now it is all over."

Woodrow Wilson's Program for Peace

The following are the Fourteen Points presented in the president's address to a joint session of Congress on January 8, 1918.

1.   Open covenants of peace, openly arrived at, after which there shall be no private international understandings of any kind but diplomacy shall proceed always frankly and in the public view.

2.   Absolute freedom of navigation upon the seas, outside territorial waters, alike in peace and in war, except as the seas may be closed in whole or in part by international action for the enforcement of international covenants.

3.   The removal, so far as possible, of all economic barriers and the establishment of an equality of trade conditions among all the nations consenting to the peace and associating themselves for its maintenance.

4.   Adequate guarantees given and taken that national armaments will be reduced to the lowest points consistent with domestic safety.

5.   A free, open-minded, and absolutely impartial adjustment of all colonial claims, based upon a strict observance of the principle that in determining all such questions of sovereignty the interests of the populations concerned must have equal weight with the equitable claims of the government whose title is to be determined.

6.   The evacuation of all Russian territory and such a settlement of all questions affecting Russia as will secure the best and freest cooperation of the other nations of the world in obtaining for her an unhampered and unembarrassed opportunity for the independent determination of her own political development and national policy and assure her of a sincere welcome into the society of free nations under institutions of her own choosing; and, more than a welcome, assistance also of every kind that she may need and may herself desire. The treatment accorded Russia by her sister nations in the months to come will be the acid test of their good will, of the comprehension of her needs as distinguished from their own interests, and of their intelligent and unselfish sympathy.

7. Belgium, the whole world will agree, must be evacuated and restored, without any attempt to limit the sovereignty which she enjoys in common with all other free nations. No other single act will serve as this will serve to restore confidence among the nations in the laws which they have themselves set and determined for the government of their relations with one another. Without this healing act the whole structure and validity of international law is forever impaired.

8. All French territory should be freed and the invaded portions restored, and the wrong done to France by Prussia in 1871 in the matter of Alsace-Lorraine, which has unsettled the peace of the world for nearly fifty years, should be righted, in order that peace may once more be made secure in the interest of all.

9. A readjustment of the frontiers of Italy should be effected along clearly recognizable lines of nationality.

10. The peoples of Austria-Hungary, whose place among the nations we wish to see safeguarded and assured, should be accorded the freest opportunity of autonomous development.

11. Rumania, Serbia and Montenegro should be evacuated; occupied territories restored; Serbia accorded free and secure access to the sea; and the relations of the several Balkan states to one another determined by friendly counsel along historically established lines of allegiance and nationality; and international guarantees of the political and economic independence and territorial integrity of the several Balkan states should be entered into.

12. The Turkish portions of the present Ottoman Empire should be assured a secure sovereignty, but the other nationalities which are now under Turkish rule should be assured an undoubted security of life and an absolutely unmolested opportunity of autonomous development, and the Dardanelles should be permanently opened as a free passage to the ships and commerce of all nations under international guarantees.

13. An independent Polish state should be erected which should include the territories inhabited by indisputably Polish populations, which should be assured a free and secure access to the sea, and whose political and economic independence and territorial integrity should be guaranteed by international covenant.

14. A general association of nations must be formed under specific covenants for the purpose of affording mutual guarantees of political independence and territorial integrity to great and small states alike.

The president added the following four points in an address
to Congress of February 11, 1918:

1. Each part of the final settlement must be based upon the essential justice of that particular case and upon such adjustments as are most likely to bring a peace that will be permanent.

2. People and provinces are not to be bartered about from sovereignty to sovereignty as if they were mere chattels and pawns in a game, even the great game, now forever discredited, of the balance of power.

3. Every territorial settlement involved in this war must be made in the interest and for the benefit of the populations concerned, and not as a part of any mere adjustment or compromise of claims among rival states.

4. All well-defined national aspirations shall be accorded the utmost satisfaction that can be accorded them without introducing new or perpetuating old elements of discord and antagonism that would be likely in time to break the peace of Europe and consequently of the world.

He next added the following in a 1918 Fourth of July speech:

1. The destruction of every arbitrary power anywhere that can separately, secretly, and of its single choice disturb the peace of the world; or, if it cannot be presently destroyed, at the least its reduction to virtual impotence.

2. The settlement of every question, whether of territory, of sovereignty, of economic arrangement or of political relationship, upon the basis of free acceptance of that settlement by the people immediately concerned, and not upon the basis of the material interest or advantage of any other nation or people which may desire a different settlement for the sake of its own exterior influence or mastery.

3. The consent of all nations to be governed in their conduct towards each other by the same principles of honor and of respect for the common law of civilized society that govern the individual citizens of all modern states in their relations with one another; to the end that all promises and covenants may be sacredly observed, no private plots or conspiracies hatched, no selfish injuries wrought with impunity, and a mutual trust established upon the handsome foundation of a mutual respect for right.

4. The establishment of an organization of peace which shall make it certain that combined power of free nations will check every invasion of

right and serve to make peace and justice the more secure by affording a definite tribunal of opinion to which all must submit and by which every international readjustment that cannot be amicably agreed upon by the peoples directly concerned shall be sanctioned.

Finally, in a speech opening a Liberty Loan campaign on September 27, 1918, the president offered the following "particulars" representing, he said, "this Government's interpretation of its own duty with regard to peace":

1.   The impartial justice meted out must involve no discrimination between those to whom we wish to be just and those to whom we do not wish to be just. It must be a justice that plays no favorites and knows no standard but the equal rights of the several peoples concerned.

2.   No special or separate interest of any single nation or any group of nations can be made the basis of any part of the settlement which is not consistent with the common interest of all.

3.   There can be no leagues or alliances or special covenants and understandings within the general and common family of the League of Nations.

4.   There can be no special, selfish economic combinations within the League and no employment of any form of economic boycott or exclusion except as the power of economic penalty by exclusion from the markets of the world may be vested in the League of Nations itself as a means of discipline and control.

5.   All international agreements and treaties of every kind must be made known in their entirety to the rest of the world.

Sources and Notes

The author of the present work finds himself, not for the first time, faced with the question of how many source notes are appropriate in a historical study aimed at a general readership rather than a community of professional scholars, and with the nonexistence of an incontrovertibly satisfactory answer. To omit such notes would be inexcusable. At the other extreme, to give a documentary source for every fact, opinion, and quotation could require almost as many pages as the book proper—and to no worthwhile purpose.

As with his previous historical works, the author has attempted to find an acceptable middle ground. This means giving no sources for items that are commonly found in earlier books and about which there is no serious disagreement, and providing sources for items that contribute significantly to telling the story and are either controversial or sufficiently obscure that a reader seeking confirmation or further information might have difficulty tracing them. Particular attention is given to direct quotes, which often are exceptionally revealing of what significant figures believed or wanted to be seen as believing.

Abbreviations are used, in the following pages, for the three most used and arguably most authoritative sources:

PWW for the sixty-nine volumes of *The Papers of Woodrow Wilson*, Arthur S. Link, editor.

IPH for the four volumes of *The Intimate Papers of Colonel House*, Charles Seymour, editor.

And *MPWW* for *The Messages and Papers of Woodrow Wilson*, in two volumes.

In all three cases, the first number following the abbreviation indicates the volume in which the relevant information appears, and the second number gives the page.

The Story Overall

Few one-volume works have ever dealt in any depth with all the major aspects of American involvement in the First World War: how the United States came to be involved, the effects of intervention on the nation and the world, the building of a vast army and that army's experiences in Europe, the world-changing peace conference that followed the defeat of Germany, and the American struggle over the peace treaty. An exception is Thomas Fleming's *The Illusion of Victory*, which is rich in interesting detail but unbalanced by the author's contempt for Woodrow Wilson and almost everything he ever did or said.

Unsurpassed on the domestic side of the story—the tale of what intervention in the war did to the United States within her own borders—is David M. Kennedy's 1980 *Over Here: The First World War and American Society*.

Outstanding among studies of the story's central figures are:

Woodrow Wilson: A Medical and Psychological Biography by Edwin A. Weinstein;

Woodrow Wilson and Colonel House: A Personality Study by Alexander L. and Juliette L. George; and

The Warrior and the Priest: Woodrow Wilson and Theodore Roosevelt, by John Milton Cooper, Jr.

Part One: The Crooked Road to War

Christopher Clark's 2012 *The Sleepwalkers: How Europe Went to War in 1914* has no rival among studies of how the Great War began. An older, shorter, but nonetheless meticulously detailed account is *The Lions of July* by William Jannen, Jr. The same story is distilled to eighty-four pages in the first section of *A World Undone: The Story of the Great War, 1914–1918* by the author of the present work. Recent versions are *The War That Ended Peace* by Margaret MacMillan and *Catastrophe 1914* by Max Hastings.

Among studies of the two and a half years of American neutrality, and of the complications arising out of German submarine warfare and the Allies' starvation blockade, Patrick Devlin's seven-hundred-page *Too Proud to Fight: Woodrow Wilson's Neutrality* stands supreme both in thoroughness and in its well-balanced perspective.

Interesting and informative accounts of how the United States moved from neutrality to intervention are *The Politics of War* by Walter Karp and *Road to War: America 1914–1917* by Walter Millis, though both works (Karp's most extremely) are weakened by a hostility to President Wilson that is so relentless as to undermine their credibility.

A thorough and informative study of the manipulation of public opinion during the neutrality period is Stewart Halsey Ross's *Propaganda for War: How the United States Was Conditioned to Fight the Great War of 1914–1918*.

For information about the *Lusitania* and her sinking, the author is particularly indebted to Erik Larson's *Dead Wake*.

Part One

2   "Have you ever heard": PWW, 38:531.

Chapter 1: December 1918: Apotheosis

3   **France had suffered**: MacMillan, *Peacemakers*, 36; Broadberry and Harrison, *Economics*, 27.
5   **"My second personality"**: IPH, 1:118.
6   **"acquire knowledge that we might"**: George and George, *Wilson and House*, 16.
6   **"played a part in the fate"**: Churchill, *World Crisis*, 3:229.
6   **"high-minded things"**: George and George, *Wilson and House*, 22.
7   **He had no way of knowing how much**: Bailey, *Wilson and Lost Peace*, 78.
10   **"Our allies and our enemies"**: Ibid., 72.

Background: How It Happened

12   **France certainly did**: Nicolson, *Longman Companion*, 63.
13   **It was, over the next three**: Herrmann, *Arming of Europe*, 205.
13   **The empire was a disjointed hodgepodge**: Nicolson, *Longman Companion*, 43.
18   **"The emperor is like"**: Ponsonby, *Letters of Empress*, 363.
18   **"Think of the thousands"**: Fay, *After Sarajevo*, 265.
21   **"for us there would be"**: Geiss, *July 1914*, 200.
22   **"What a joke!"**: Fromkin, *Last Summer*, 229.
23   **"If the peace of Europe can be"**: Geiss, *July 1914*, 315.
24   **"every measure against Austria-Hungary"**: Jannen, *Lions of July*, 256.
24   **"would be a disgrace"**: Geiss, *July 1914*, 315.

Chapter 2: Neutrality the Wilson Way

27   **"The cutting of that cable"**: Ross, *Propaganda*, 28.
27   **As early as August 6**: Mead, *Doughboys*, 20.
28   **A hundred thousand German**: Stevenson, *Cataclysm*, 75.
29   **Awesome as this total was**: Nicolson, *Longman Companion*, 63.
30   **It was true of most of America's**: Kazin, *Godly Hero*, 216.
30   **"international law was regarded"**: Devlin, *Too Proud*, 463.
31   **"in order to strengthen"**: George and George, *Wilson and House*, 125.
32   **"you have more than fulfilled"**: PWW, 30:242.
32   **"It has fallen to your lot"**: PWW, 30:359.
32   **"In my opinion you have"**: PWW, 30:385.
32   **"Men often destroy themselves"**: Weinstein, *Medical and Psychological*, 271.

32   "Beg you will come here": PWW, 31:541.
34   "evidence their good intentions": Devlin, *Too Proud*, 221.
34   "extravagant": Ross, *Propaganda*, 17; Herrmann, *Arming of Europe*, 2.
35   "is perhaps the only noble": IPH, 1:254.
36   "jingoism run stark mad": IPH, 1:255.
36   From 1900 to 1913: Herrmann, *Arming of Europe*, 237; Stevenson, *Armaments*, 3.
36   "unless some one acting": PWW, 30:109.
37   "Germany's success": IPH, 1:291.
40   "wholly unacceptable": Devlin, *Too Proud*, 201.
40   "informally and confidentially": Karp, *Politics of War*, 179.
40   That they would have done: Link, *Wilson: Revolution*, 31.
41   "starve the whole population": Karp, *Politics of War*, 176.
41   "England is not exercising": PWW, 31:6.
41   Her hereditary aristocracy still: Ferguson, *Pity of War*, 29.
42   In the first half of 1914, Germany's: Fleming, *Illusion of Victory*, 49.
42   The American economy was hit: Kennedy, *Over Here*, 301.
43   "I shall follow the best practice": PWW, 28:270; Tansill, *America Goes*, 64.
43   "loans by American bankers": PWW, 30:372.
43   "We are the one great nation": PWW, 30:372.
43   Over the next four years it would: Ross, *Propaganda*, 161.

Background: Coming of Age

44   In 1870 the United States produced: Nicolson, *Longman Companion*, 56.
45   In 1875 Britain was producing: Fleming, *Illusion of Victory*, 49.
45   In 1880 Britain's factories accounted: Ferguson, *Pity of War*, 35.
45   Biographers of a psychoanalytic: Freud and Bullitt, *Thomas Woodrow Wilson;* Weinstein, *Medical and Psychological;* George and George, *Wilson and House.*
46   More recently it has been diagnosed: Weinstein, *Medical and Psychological*, 15.
50   As an undergraduate, he withdrew: Ibid., 43.
50   "in giving unqualified endorsement": PWW, 2:98.
50   "education seems to be the chosen": PWW, 2:99.
51   "That is the greatest statesman": Osborn, *Early Years*, 28.
51   "immortal work": PWW, 3:145.
51   "statesmanship consists not": Weinstein, *Medical and Psychological*, 51.
51   "absorbing love for justice": PWW, 1:620.
53   "I take my pen in hand to let": McMath, *American Populism*, 181.
53   "we have a horror for the wild": Clanton, *Populism*, 150.

54   "if they were": Ibid., 130.
54   "to destroy class rule and": Ibid., 86.

Chapter 3: Quickly to the Brink

57   "the demagogue, adroit, tricky": Cooper, *Warrior*, 305.
59   "exceeds the manifest necessity": Millis, *Road to War*, 121.
59   "certain it would be entirely footless": PWW, 31:384.
60   "a just and equitable peace": Cooper, *Warrior*, 275.
60   "Woodrow Wilson is today": Berg, *Wilson*, 371.
60   In December 1915 the president's physician: Weinstein, *Medical and Psychological*, 295.
63   (In 1935, by contrast, Congress would): Bailey, *Wilson and Lost Peace*, 11; Tansill, *America Goes*, 268.
63   "The president's eyes were moist": PWW, 32:121.
64   "God will sustain you in all": PWW, 32:162.
64   As the ship approached the Irish: IPH, 1:365.
64   "contraband of war": Karp, *Politics of War*, 308.
65   "is an open and declared belligerent": Tansill, *America Goes*, 649 note 57.
65   On the very day that Wilson sent: Ibid., 285.
66   "sat by the fire in his library": IPH, 1:378.
66   "peacemaking became for House": Devlin, *Too Proud*, 265.
67   "I do not see a ray of hope": Millis, *Road to War*, 141.
68   "now almost wholly controlled": PWW, 32:237.
68   "did not want": IPH, 1:378.
69   "get the machinery in order": Devlin, *Too Proud*, 266.
69   "let it be understood that": PWW, 35:44.
70   That the German public had not: Fuehr, *Neutrality of Belgium*, 88.
71   "what you suggest concerning": IPH, 1:371.
72   The combined British-Belgian: Fuehr, *Neutrality of Belgium*, 88.
72   "a pretty little game of hypocrisy": Ibid., 108.
72   "I brought them around": IPH, 1:352.
73   "If peace parlays were begun now": IPH, 1:404.
73   "The bitterness of their resentment": IPH, 1:404.
73   "When the pinch of the blockade": PWW, 35:122.
73   "one of the best types of German": Devlin, *Too Proud*, 177.
74   "very promising": Ibid., 278.
76   "Can an American by embarking": PWW, 32:464.
76   "The troublesome question": PWW, 32:487.
76   First he informed the president of having: PWW, 32:487.
76   "I cannot help feeling that": PWW, 32:488.
76   "Why be shocked at the drowning": Devlin, *Too Proud*, 213.

76   **"I cannot see":** PWW, 33:66.
77   **The dispatch said also:** PWW, 32:527.
77   **"if the sinking of the *Falaba*":** PWW, 32:465.
78   **The United States, he said, would:** Millis, *Road to War,* 171.

Background: The Tortoise and the Hare

80   **"when you hear a good":** Kazin, *Godly Hero,* 121.
80   **One Republican later gave thanks:** Ibid., 49.
80   **"What a speech, my masters!":** Ibid., 118.
81   **"the prime duty of pietists":** Ibid., 124.
83   **"The fruits of imperialism":** Ibid., 80.
83   **"I have fallen in love with [Bryan]":** Ibid.
83   **"all the lunatics, all the idiots":** Ibid., 105.
84   **"good for forty acres of parked":** Ibid., 131.
84   **"that undercurrent of restless":** George and George, *Wilson and House,* 24.
84   **"remarkably intelligent":** Kazin, *Godly Hero,* 126.
85   **"colds":** Weinstein, *Medical and Psychological,* 23.
85   **"Although he would have been":** Myers, "President of Princeton," 43.
87   **"Personally, he is the most charming":** PWW, 18:4.
87   **"all the loose notions":** PWW, 18:220.
87   **"the perfect mania":** Weinstein, *Medical and Psychological,* 220.
87   **"no mental rudder":** George and George, *Wilson and House,* 50.
87   **"a professional yodeler":** Cooper, *Warrior,* 272.
89   **"common council of the people":** PWW, 17:520.
89   **"to give as little as he may":** Link, *Wilson,* 1:127.
89   **"It may be true that women":** PWW, 18:4.
90   **"If I can handle the matter":** Link, *Wilson,* 1:142.
91   **"set about fighting and breaking":** PWW, 20:519.
91   **"absolutely free in the matter":** Link, *Wilson,* 1:143.
91   **In 1914, when as president:** Weinstein, *Medical and Psychological,* 257.
92   **"strange ascent":** Kerney, *Political Education,* xv.
92   **"undoubtedly would have":** Myers, "President of Princeton," 49.
92   **"not only have no pledges":** Link, *Wilson,* 1:167.
92   **He ticked off the measures:** PWW, 21:91.
95   **"The first hour we spent":** IPH, 1:45.
95   **"has the opportunity to become":** IPH, 1:85.
95   **"Never before have I found":** IPH, 1:48.
96   **"we could do something":** Kazin, *Godly Hero,* 182.
97   **"the middle class has put":** McGerr, *Fierce Discontent,* 280.
97   **"We should earnestly urge":** PWW, 28:230; Millis, *Road to War,* 12.
97   **"We shall yet prove to the Mexican":** PWW, 28:228.

98   Though he was back on his feet: Weinstein, *Medical and Psychological*, 251.

Chapter 4: Many Sacred Principles

99   A British technical journal of 1913: Tansill, *America Goes*, 284.
100   "Germany has a right to prevent": PWW, 33:134.
100   "when a person boarded an English": Tansill, *America Goes*, 276.
100   "Our intervention will save": PWW, 33:134.
100   "there is such a thing as a man": PWW, 33:149.
101   "many sacred principles of justice": Millis, *Road to War*, 181.
101   "Both in mind and in heart": PWW, 33:155.
102   "I join in this document with": PWW, 33:165.
102   "I believe it will have a splendid": PWW, 33:213.
102   "A person would have to be": Karp, *Politics of War*, 208.
103   "Why," he asked, "should we": Devlin, *Too Proud*, 308.
103   "There is no doubt that the position": PWW, 33:254.
104   "stiffen": Millis, *Road to War*, 186.
105   Agriculture Secretary David Houston: PWW, 33:296.
106   When the meeting adjourned, an unhappy: Baker, *Wilson: Life and Letters*, 5:351.
108   "obedient to your sense of duty": PWW, 33:375.
108   "I accept your resignation": PWW, 33:376.
109   "the most contemptible figure": Cooper, *Warrior*, 305.
109   "a man with not too many ideas": Ibid., 291.
110   "mere rights of property": Millis, *Road to War*, 193.
110   "unable to admit that American citizens": Karp, *Politics of War*, 212.
110   "regrets to state that it has": PWW, 33:527.
111   "I am supposed to have organized": Ross, *Propaganda*, 205.
113   First Lord of the Admiralty: Fleming, *Illusion of Victory*, 67.
113   "horrible": Devlin, *Too Proud*, 414.
113   "was done contrary": PWW, 33:320.
114   "you know well enough": PWW, 33:297.
114   "For the first time in the history": PWW, 33:299.
114   "disappointment that the feeling": Millis, *Road to War*, 227.
116   "to maintain our prosperity": Ross, *Propaganda*, 162.
116   This resulted in a September: Link, *Wilson: Revolution*, 54; Tansill, *America Goes*, 112.
116   "he had never been sure that": Ross, *Propaganda*, 162; Fleming, *Illusion of Victory*, 70.
117   "had lost our opportunity to break": PWW, 35:43.
117   "My suggestion [to the president]": IPH, 2:84.

118 "It has occurred to me": IPH, 2:90.
118 On September 24 there was a second: Tansill, *America Goes,* 380 note 8.
118 In November, however, he: Chambers, *Raise an Army,* 103.
119 "The United States . . . wanted": PWW, 35:474.
120 "replied definitely": PWW, 35:474.
120 "only be ended by your": PWW, 35:484.
120 "not nearly as cunning": Devlin, *Too Proud,* 463.

Background: Mystery Voyage

121 "covered with a silvery": Larson, *Dead Wake,* 242.
124 "The ship was sinking": Ibid., 262.
124 Fifty-seven percent of the U-boats: O'Hara, Dickson, and Worth, *Crown the Waves,* 110.
125 "was not sent through": Larson, *Dead Wake,* 267.
125 "appears to have displayed": Ibid., 318.
126 One theory is that: Preston, *Lusitania,* 157; Simpson, *Lusitania,* 158.
126 "On the basis of the considerable": Larson, *Dead Wake,* 32.

Chapter 5: Marked Cards and a Stacked Deck

128 "entire approval": PWW, 35:498.
128 "I cannot adequately express": PWW, 35:532.
129 "blundered badly": Link, *Wilson: Revolution,* 16.
129 "I doubt whether a crisis": PWW, 36:85.
129 "failed to secure peace": PWW, 36:43.
129 House was pretending to Grey: Cooper, *Warrior,* 293; Ross, *Propaganda,* 154.
131 "more troubled than I have": PWW, 36:209.
131 "The honor and self-respect": PWW, 36:214.
132 "our situation is so serious": Devlin, *Too Proud,* 323.
132 "a submarine commander": PWW, 36:228.
132 "nobody ever held that": Karp, *Politics of War,* 257.
132 "a single citizen should be": Ibid., 250.
133 "according to international": PWW, 36:232.
133 "leave the conference as": PWW, 36:269.
134 "we are not so sure": Karp, *Politics of War,* 278.
134 "not worth five minutes'": Fleming, *Illusion of Victory,* 77.
134 "carefully sprung trap": Devlin, *Too Proud,* 471.
135 "sacred and indisputable": PWW, 36:491.
135 "Right of free travel on the seas?": Mead, *Doughboys,* 34.
135 "They mocked at us when": Ibid., 32.

135   "I cannot understand": Ibid.
135   "the greatest civilian": Ross, *Propaganda*, 187.
136   "to go [to] the utmost limit": PWW, 36:621.
137   "decidedly insolent tone": Devlin, *Too Proud*, 482.
138   "I cannot see how we": PWW, 36:629.
138   In fact, the idea of a global: Cooper, *Warrior*, 279.
138   It had been taken up: Cooper, *Breaking*, 11; Bailey, *Wilson and Lost Peace*, 188.
142   Its exports, which generated: Tansill, *America Goes*, 116.
142   "Oh, dear kindred spirit": PWW, 33:117.
142   "Ah, my precious friend": PWW, 33:124.
144   "mind is not of the first class": Berg, *Wilson*, 373.
145   "How difficult it is": Devlin, *Too Proud*, 502.
145   "I am, I must admit, about": Ibid., PWW, 37:467.
146   "The aim of far-sighted": Link, *Wilson: Revolution*, 26.

Background: Choosing Sides

148   From 1915 to 1917 it received: Chambers, *Raise an Army*, 82.
149   "I am sure that the country": Thomas, *Unsafe for Democracy*, 29.
149   "there are citizens of": Tansill, *America Goes*, 394.

Chapter 6: "A Dangerous Thing—To Inflame a People"

151   In each of the two years: Vincent, *Politics of Hunger*, 36.
151   As early as the autumn of 1914: Healy, *Vienna*, 40.
151   By 1917 fat intake per: Vincent, *Politics of Hunger*, 49.
153   "The fight . . . must be": Devlin, *Too Proud*, 546.
154   And bigger, improved submarines: Ibid., 547.
155   "I regard him as a ruthless": Ibid., 466.
155   Many voters found it: Cooper, *Warrior*, 308.
156   "pouring poison into": Kennedy, *Over Here*, 24; Fleming, *Illusion of Victory*, 65.
156   "I was entirely willing": PWW, 38:646.
157   "no one can see [the president]": George and George, *Wilson and House*, 187.
157   "It is difficult to explain exactly": Devlin, *Too Proud*, 469.
158   "The president dominates everything": Ibid.
161   "absolute conquerors": Ibid., 568.
162   "It is a dangerous thing": IPH, 1:403.
163   "one of the most egregious": Link, *Wilson: Revolution*, 56.
164   "the speedy assembly, on neutral": PWW, 40:331.

164 "prevent at all costs any": Tansill, *America Goes*, 630.
164 "He said that you [Wilson] are": PWW, 40:355.
165 "without warning": Tansill, *America Goes*, 633.
165 But fully one-third of Britain's: Link, *Wilson: Revolution*, 58.
165 "Germany finds herself": Tansill, *America Goes*, 62.
166 "it does not regard it": Ibid., 120.
166 They did, however, acknowledge: PWW, 40:439.
167 He took a train to New York: PWW, 40:477.
167 "the most important communication": Devlin, *Too Proud*, 614.
167 "We have modified submarine war": PWW, 40:464.
168 "Upon a triumph which overwhelms": MPWW, 1:348.
169 "at heart an abject coward": Berg, *Wilson*, 378.
169 "Peace without victory is the natural": Cooper, *Warrior*, 315.
169 "If Germany wants peace she": PWW, 41:3.
169 House urged the ambassador: Devlin, *Too Proud*, 617.

Background: The War of Words—and Pictures

172 "a face at once repulsive": Ross, *Propaganda*, 78.
172 "England owes her influence": Ibid., 28.
174 German soldiers cut off: Ibid., 24.
174 "The inhabitants of Bernot": *New York Times*, August 7, 1914.
175 "In spirit fairness we unite": Ross, *Propaganda*, 48.
175 The gesture cost him nothing: Fleming, *Illusion of Victory*, 54.
175 "the debt that England owes": Ibid., 63.
176 "When a mad dog runs amuck": Ross, *Propaganda*, 191.
176 "already the hemp is grown": Ibid.
176 The chilling pictures of a Dutch: Raemaekers, *Cartoons*, 1.
177 "racial and national prejudice": Ross, *Propaganda*, 43.
178 Evidence has recently come: Souhami, *Edith Cavell*, 106.
178 Nor is it likely that Allied: Ross, *Propaganda*, 70; Fleming, *Illusion of Victory*, 60.

Chapter 7: Onward, Christian Soldiers

182 "consistent with the dignity": PWW, 41:108.
185 "that anyone who failed": Devlin, *Too Proud*, 646.
186 William Jennings Bryan brought: Tansill, *America Goes*, 650.
186 In a conversation with French: Devlin, *Too Proud*, 655.
186 "the country is not willing": PWW, 40:282.
187 "as soon as the outbreak of war": Millis, *Road to War*, 404.
188 "the most dramatic moment": Devlin, *Too Proud*, 651.

188 "to employ any other instrumentalities": PWW, 41:283.
189 From the start of the war through 1915: Carlisle, *Sovereignty*, 35.
189 Even as attacks and sinkings: Ibid., 175.
189 "deplorable": Millis, *Road to War*, 405.
191 "yellow peril": Devlin, *Too Proud*, 636, 638.
192 "ought to be hung": Unger, *Fighting Bob*, 247.
192 "mobilize Christian strength": Millis, *Road to War*, 412.

Background: Troublemaker

195 "perhaps the least known": Unger, *Fighting Bob*, 47.
197 "vagueness and reiteration": George and George, *Wilson and House*, 108.
198 "The supreme issue": Unger, *Fighting Bob*, 103.

Chapter 8: Why

200 "He said when a war got going": Cooper, *Warrior*, 319.
202 Thomas Fleming, in *The Illusion*: Fleming, *Illusion of Victory*, 6.
203 What the president talked about: PWW, 41:482.
204 "over which we have no control": PWW, 41:332.
205 "a little group of willful men": IPH, 2:460.
205 an improbable diagnosis: Weinstein, *Medical and Psychological*, 22, 49.
206 "the wonderful and heartening": PWW, 41:524.
206 "concerning grave matters": Devlin, *Too Proud*, 666.
207 "every true American heart": Millis, *Road to War*, 422.
207 "We have had weak presidents": Devlin, *Too Proud*, 466.
208 Weinstein has traced it to stories: Weinstein, *Medical and Psychological*, 12.
208 "we are going into this war": Zucker, *George Norris*, 129.
208 Between August 1914 and March 1917: Tansill, *America Goes*, 53.
210 "We want him to come into the war": PWW, 40:355.
211 "I believe . . . that our future influence": PWW, 41:425.
211 "As head of a nation participating": PWW, 40:305.

Chapter 9: "A Message of Death"

220 As was his practice, the colonel declared it: IPH, 2:471.
221 "formally accept the status": PWW, 41:519.
222 "expressed in the loftiest": Berg, *Wilson*, 438.
223 "It is needless to say that no": PWW, 40:528.
223 "think about what it was": Fleming, *Illusion of Victory*, 21.
224 "vain and foolish thing": Millis, *Road to War*, 447.
225 "mad desire to conquer": Ibid., 448; Ryley, *Little Group*, 161.

225   "I shall vote against this mistake": Fleming, *Illusion of Victory,* 31.
226   "The failure to treat the belligerent": Ibid., 33.
227   "Anti-American president, anti-American Congress": Millis, *Road to War,* 452.
227   "That is the greatest speech": Fleming, *Illusion of Victory,* 36; Karp, *Politics of War,* 322.
228   "I take my cap off": Millis, *Road to War,* 412.
228   "Ask your friends around you": Ibid., 453.
229   "the whole yelping pack": Ibid., 454.
229   "The head of a department": PWW, 41:547.

Part Two: The Price

The author has found four works to be particularly valuable as sources of information about how the United States began creating an army in 1917 and used it to help win the war in 1918.

To Raise an Army: The Draft Comes to Modern America, by John Whiteclay Chambers II.

The War to End All Wars: The American Military Experience in World War I, by Edward M. Coffman.

Yanks: The Epic Story of the American Army in World War I, by John S. D. Eisenhower.

The Doughboys: America and the First World War, by Gary Mead.

The military climax of the Great War is dealt with in detail in:

The Greatest Day in History, by Nicholas Best.

Hundred Days: The End of the Great War, by Nick Lloyd.

Seward W. Livermore's *Politics Is Adjourned: Woodrow Wilson and the War Congress 1916–1918,* is an excellent account of national political combat during the year and a half when the United States was at war.

Absolutely invaluable, because unrivaled in the thoroughness with which it explores dissent and the suppression of dissent during the war years, is *Opponents of War, 1917–1918,* by H. C. Peterson and Gilbert C. Fite.

Part Two

232   "The object of this war": PWW, 41:591.

Chapter 10: Taking Charge

233   "Congress will not permit": Coffman, *War to End,* 8.
234   They had contributed to making: Chambers, *Raise an Army,* 13.

236 Roosevelt's plan for a force: Livermore, *Politics Is Adjourned*, 18.
237 "a great big boy": Cooper, *Warrior*, 325.
237 "If any other man talked to me": Tumulty, *Woodrow Wilson*, 73.
240 Both chambers had immediately: PWW, 42:25, 42:126.
242 "The French only asked for all": Mead, *Doughboys*, 12.
242 "We want men, men, men!": Coffman, *War to End*, 8.
243 "before what we would call": Mead, *Doughboys*, 16.
244 "respectfully ask permission": PWW, 42:324.
244 The extent to which Congress: Thomas, *Unsafe for Democracy*, 35.
245 "I told Balfour I hoped England": PWW, 42:120.
245 "tacit understanding": PWW, 42:155.
245 "this country and Britain will": IPH, 3:38.
245 "Great Britain and America, I thought": IPH, 3:39.
246 "I said to him what I once said to Grey": IPH, 3:45.
246 "tremendously": Devlin, *Too Proud*, 463.
246 "I am grateful to you all the time": PWW, 42:433.
246 "I devour and profit": IPH, 3:15.
246 "to get enormous quantities": IPH, 3:31.
247 "I can imagine no greater": PWW, 42:304.
247 "absolutely necessary to the public": Fleming, *Illusion of Victory*, 98.
247 Senator Hiram Johnson: Kennedy, *Over Here*, 25.

Background: Going Dry

248 The campaign to free the people: Hofstadter, *Age of Reform*, 289.
250 "a means by which the reforming": Ibid.
251 By 1917 dozens of states had passed: Kennedy, *Over Here*, 185.
251 In the Congress elected in 1916: Fleming, *Illusion of Victory*, 281.
251 This, and congressional eagerness: Ibid., 120.
252 Eventually he would claim to have put: Ibid.

Chapter 11: "Skin-Deep Dollar Patriotism"

253 "a flying corps of 4,500": Mead, *Doughboys*, 93.
254 "When the war is over we can": PWW, 43:238.
254 A grand total of fifteen hundred: Mead, *Doughboys*, 97.
255 "quite fluently": Eisenhower, *Yanks*, 30.
256 Georgia became the home: Livermore, *Politics Is Adjourned*, 46.
256 "The cost in most cases": Coffman, *War to End*, 30.
256 Two hundred thousand men: Ibid.
256 That the cantonments cost $199 million: Ibid., 31.
257 "a great day of patriotic devotion": Fleming, *Illusion of Victory*, 96.

257 "a very happy day, because": PWW, 42:453.
257 "Death for Treason Awaits": Fleming, *Illusion of Victory*, 96.
258 Many thousands of men, by some: Chambers, *Raise an Army*, 211.
258 In August, in probably the largest: Peterson and Fite, *Opponents*, 40.
259 The magnitude of the challenge: Coffman, *War to End*, 55.
261 "There are political and commercial": Kennedy, *Over Here*, 39.
262 "it is too late to put the [food]": Livermore, *Politics Is Adjourned*, 50.
264 A bloc of progressive senators: Ibid., 59.
264 "brought into sharp relief": Kennedy, *Over Here*, 108.
267 "all making more money": Ibid., 135.
267 Postwar congressional inquiries: Ibid., 139.
267 Secretary McAdoo informed: Livermore, *Politics Is Adjourned*, 59
267 General Pershing, who shortly: Coffman, *War to End*, 127.

Background: Destiny's Child

268 It was assumed, rather, that: Eisenhower, *Yanks*, 26.
269 "I personally have strung up": Miller, *Benevolent Assimilation*, 98.
269 "What now, Newton?": Eisenhower, *Yanks*, 27.
270 Born in small-town Missouri: Mead, *Doughboys*, 116.
271 "inspired confidence but not": Ibid., 118.
272 (A decade later, these rumors would): Fleming, *Illusion of Victory*, 102.
272 "As an officer of the army, may I not": Coffman, *War to End*, 46.
272 First Senator Warren switched: Livermore, *Politics Is Adjourned*, 56.
273 With impressive speed Pershing: Fleming, *Illusion of Victory*, 153.

Chapter 12: Cracking Down

275 "Whoever, when the United States is": Peterson and Fite, *Opponents*, 16.
275 Shortly after taking office, he introduced: Berg, *Wilson*, 306.
276 When challenged about his administration's: Ibid., 309.
277 "unsealed matter, newspapers, etc.": Schaffer, *America*, 14.
277 The American Socialist Party, founded: Peterson and Fite, *Opponents*, 26.
277 "didn't know socialism from": Kennedy, *Over Here*, 76.
278 "a crime against the people": Ibid., 26.
278 By one count, Burleson's first: Peterson and Fite, *Opponents*, 47.
278 "men have already been sent to jail": Ibid., 97.
278 Wilson asked the postmaster general: Kennedy, *Over Here*, 77.
279 "the mediocre monarch now": Peterson and Fite, *Opponents*, 96.
279 It happened to *The Public*: Ross, *Propaganda*, 267.
279 The new requirements were: Kennedy, *Over Here*, 74.

279   His biggest target was *Appeal*: Ibid., 27.
280   "We are at war with the most": Thomas, *Unsafe for Democracy*, 52.
281   "May God have mercy": Fleming, *Illusion of Victory*, 189.
281   "No Conscription, No Servitude": Peterson and Fite, *Opponents*, 22.
281   When two New Yorkers were sent: Ibid., 26.
281   "Are We Facing": Ibid., 30.
281   A New Yorker was given ninety days: Ibid., 31.
282   *Legal Opinion and Advice*: Ibid., 33.
282   When twenty-seven German-American: Ibid., 36.
282   "all foolishness": Fleming, *Illusion of Victory*, 191.
283   The Espionage Act served: Thomas, *Unsafe for Democracy*, 49.
283   Robert Goldstein, the producer: Ross, *Propaganda*, 265.
283   "a language that disseminates": Kennedy, *Over Here*, 54.
283   "ninety percent of all the men": Ibid.
283   "dividing the body of public": Ibid., 88.
283   "his enemies in office": Ibid., 89.
283   "the strange thing about World War I": Unger, *Fighting Bob*, 250.
284   "we must have no criticism": Peterson and Fite, *Opponents*, 14.
284   "There are men walking about the streets": Ibid.
284   "Woe be to the man or group of men": PWW, 45:498.
285   "an immediate, general": Peterson and Fite, *Opponents*, 165.
285   "one must have a very judicial": Ibid., 182.
285   "expression rather than": Ross, *Propaganda*, 218.
286   By the end of the war: Ibid., 245.
287   "I prefer not to ally myself": Grubbs, *Struggle for Labor*, 25.
287   American Alliance for Labor: Kennedy, *Over Here*, 29.
287   "traitors and fools": Peterson and Fite, *Opponents*, 76.
287   Some state councils became: Livermore, *Politics Is Adjourned*, 42.
287   Many became weapons with: Ibid., 42, 82; Kennedy, *Over Here*, 68.
288   By the end of the war, the APL: Peterson and Fite, *Opponents*, 19;
      Kennedy, *Over Here*, 82.
288   The main qualification: Peterson and Fite, *Opponents*, 19.
288   Boy Spies of America: Cooper, *Reconsidering*, 197.
288   One historian has found that: Thomas, *Unsafe for Democracy*, 62.
288   "read nothing but German": Ibid., 61.
289   "could tell him how a man": Ibid., 69.
289   "very harmful possibilities": PWW, 45:440.
289   "The American Protective League": PWW, 45:509.
289   "There have been days when": PWW, 45:510.
290   The department was scorned: Ackerman, *Young J. Edgar*, 24.
291   Months before the end: Ross, *Propaganda*, 210.

Background: Three Faces of Labor

292 "a combination and conspiracy": Boyer, *Labor's Untold Story*, 16.
292 "slavery is the natural": Ibid., 13.
292 (In 1912 socialist candidates): Ferguson, *Pity of War*, 29.
292 Even in 1914, by which time: Wright, *Chronology of Labor*, 114.
293 A magazine of the time reported: Lens, *The Labor Wars*, 112.
293 "I can hire one-half": Ibid., 6.
293 "the rights and interests": Ibid., 141.
297 "There may have lived": Ibid., 80.
300 "look with gratitude from": Ibid., 184.
300 "preliminary skirmish": Ibid.

Chapter 13: Welcome to France

306 Before the end of September: Mead, *Doughboys*, 147.
307 "was much struck with [Pershing's]": Coffman, *War to End*, 130.
310 "the *fumier*—the heap": Mead, *Doughboys*, 194.
312 Eight hundred million pounds: Ibid., 197.
312 "Our officers head the list": Ibid., 192.
313 Pneumonia and other respiratory: Fleming, *Illusion of Victory*, 307.
313 "For God's sake, Raymond": Coffman, *War to End*, 133.
313 "Ordinarily we get acquainted only": Mead, *Doughboys*, 203.
313 Though 57,195 cases were recorded: Ibid., 205.
314 The War Department, having made: Kennedy, *Over Here*, 169.
314 "to relieve the combatant field": Coffman, *War to End*, 129.
314 "Our allies seem to hate one another": Ibid., 130.
315 AEF headquarters naturally took all this: Mead, *Doughboys*, 157.
317 Then, in the predawn hours: Eisenhower, *Yanks*, 83.
317 "the Valley Forge of the AEF": Coffman, *War to End*, 141.
317 The Selective Service System had met: Chambers, *Raise an Army*, 78.

Background: Buffalo Soldiers

318 It began on the first day of July: Peterson and Fite, *Opponents*, 87.
319 It took place in the racial tinderbox: Chambers, *Raise an Army*, 222.
319 By the time the fight ended: Schaffer, *America*, 76.
319 Sixty-four of the arrested soldiers: Peterson and Fite, *Opponents*, 89; Chambers, *Raise an Army*, 223.
319 "we would rather see you shot": Schaffer, *America*, 79.
320 White America had for centuries: Chambers, *Raise an Army*, 16.
321 It is estimated that a third: Schaffer, *America*, 75.

321 At the time of the U.S. declaration: Coffman, *War to End*, 69.
321 "Our drilling," one conscript would: Ibid., 71.
322 And that was largely correct: Chambers, *Raise an Army*, 223.
322 And they could have offered evidence: Kennedy, *Over Here*, 188.
322 The average black draftee had: Ibid.
323 "a breed of mongrels": Ibid., 161.
323 "arrogant strutting representatives": Ibid., 159.
323 "Negro activities": Fleming, *Illusion of Victory*, 108.
323 The War Department, when it: Kennedy, *Over Here*, 160.
323 "how completely the Bible": Berg, *Wilson*, 32.
324 "who had no special": Ibid., 104.
324 "the best narrator of darky": Schaffer, *America*, 76.
324 "their relations with their": Berg, *Wilson*, 32.

Chapter 14: "A Moblike Madness"

325 "Everything here is war": Kennedy, *Over Here*, 41.
325 "a curious mixture of acuteness": Fleming, *Illusion of Victory*, 92.
326 "the tool and ally of German": Chambers, *Raise an Army*, 209.
326 "What I am opposed to is": PWW, 45:14.
328 "common": Fleming, *Illusion of Victory*, 22.
328 "having been associated so closely": Ibid.
329 "Every heart that has not been": PWW, 44:57.
329 "the most remarkable document": PWW, 44:149.
329 "punitive damages": PWW, 44:35.
329 "we cannot take the word": IPH, 3:163.
331 In the month of America's declaration: Eisenhower, *Yanks*, 60.
331 "The death rate among old people": Fleming, *Illusion of Victory*, 194.
331 The whole German nation was on: Vincent, *Politics of Hunger*, 49.
331 After the war, doctors would estimate: Healy, *Vienna*, 41.
332 More than 90 percent of Vienna's: Ibid., 31.
332 Instances of lynching, the ultimate: Kennedy, *Over Here*, 283.
332 "Denunciation of Lynching": PWW, 45:381.
332 "The war is dividing men along": PWW, 45:381.
334 "criminal syndicalism": Peterson and Fite, *Opponents*, 51.
334 Fully 95 percent of IWW: Thomas, *Unsafe for Democracy*, 97.
334 In the six months following: Feuerlicht, *Reign of Terror*, 49.
334 "detestable": Peterson and Fite, *Opponents*, 55.
335 "but I knew that money": Ibid., 52.
335 Early on the morning of July 2: Ibid., 53.
335 President Wilson sent a warning: PWW, 43:156.
335 "a lesson that the whole": Peterson and Fite, *Opponents*, 55.

336 That most of the alleged violations: Ibid., 62.
336 In an act as unprecedented: Livermore, *Politics Is Adjourned*, 78.

Background: "Disgusting Creatures"

339 "universal suffrage is at": Levin, *Edith and Woodrow*, 181.
339 He said it would make no difference: Berg, *Wilson*, 488.
341 "disgusting creatures": Levin, *Edith and Woodrow*, 180.
341 "American women of wealth, education": Griffith, *In Her Own Right*, 124.
341 "Every slacker has a vote": Schaffer, *America*, 91.
342 But Catt, who had originally: Ibid., 92.
342 National Women's Trade Union: Kennedy, *Over Here*, 285.
342 "bent on making their cause": Fleming, *Illusion of Victory*, 128; Schaffer, *America*, 93.
343 Dudley Field Malone: Berg, *Wilson*, 490.

Chapter 15: The Law of Selfishness

344 "if we enter this war": Schaffer, *America*, 59.
345 The picture continued: Coffman, *War to End*, 143.
349 "war welfare": Schaffer, *America*, 58.
349 "one of the inexplicable": Ibid., 61.
350 An FTC report showed: Ibid., 56.
350 In 1918 the American steel: Ibid.
350 In that same year, in a foreshadowing: Ibid.
350 In 1917 the after-tax profits: Ibid., 55.
351 One contractor was found: Ibid., 49.
352 Some fifteen months after: Ibid., 52.
353 By May 1918 federal spending: Kennedy, *Over Here*, 110.
353 "darken the skies over Germany": Livermore, *Politics Is Adjourned*, 115.
354 Airframes had to be made: Coffman, *War to End*, 192.
354 "had the Postmaster General": Peterson and Fite, *Opponents*, 99.
354 "liberty of circulation may": Ibid., 97.
354 Of the 180 persons tried: Ibid., 210.
355 Some had misgivings about: Gaston, *Nonpartisan League*, 208.
356 "where we made a mistake": Peterson and Fite, *Opponents*, 190.
356 "discussing, arguing": Ibid., 116.
356 "the men at the head": Ibid., 38.
357 "had done grave injury": Ibid., 103.
357 "fatuous dreamers": PWW, 45:11.

358   The night of their conviction: Peterson and Fite, *Opponents*, 173.
358   "there is no excuse": Ibid., 155.
358   "a clear mandate for open": Thomas, *Unsafe for Democracy*, 162.
359   "Mayor reveals Hylan as": Peterson and Fite, *Opponents*, 160.

Background: The War, Too, Changes

362   That Hutier invented these: Eisenhower, *Yanks*, 104.

Chapter 16: The Last Roll of the Iron Dice

367   "If the iron dice roll": Tuchman, *Guns of August*, 74.
367   Nine months after a battalion: Eisenhower, *Yanks*, 87.
370   "to put the weight": Ibid., 113.
371   "I have come to tell you": Ibid., 114.
374   "There may not be an American": Ibid., 116.
375   "Force, Force to the utmost": PWW, 47:267.
376   It stripped Russia of Finland: Asprey, *German High Command*, 360.
378   But in 1917 he had been: Margulies, *Senator Lenroot*, 245.
378   "the acid test": Fleming, *Illusion of Victory*, 238.
379   "Your state of Wisconsin": Livermore, *Politics Is Adjourned*, 120.
379   "bidding for the votes": Margulies, *Senator Lenroot*, 245.
379   "higher up": Ibid., 247.
380   Across the country, starting: Livermore, *Politics Is Adjourned*, 115.
380   "registered enemy alien": Schaffer, *America*, 23.
381   "Well . . . I guess nobody": Kennedy, *Over Here*, 68.
381   "it is a healthful and wholesome": Ibid.
381   "not heartily in support": Peterson and Fite, *Opponents*, 209.
381   "crimes committed by German": Ibid., 210.

Background: The War of the Air—and of the Future

384   Of the 681 members of the U.S.: Morrow, *Great War*, 340.
384   A grand total of forty-nine: Mead, *Doughboys*, 92.
385   The Committee on Public: Livermore, *Politics Is Adjourned*, 125.
385   The administration issued: Coffman, *War to End*, 190.
385   Gutzon Borglum: Livermore, *Politics Is Adjourned*, 127.
386   Hughes, in reporting his findings: Ibid., 133.
386   Pershing's original goal had been: Coffman, *War to End*, 196.
386   When the Armistice went: Ibid., 210.
387   A total of 1,481 aircraft took: Ibid., 207.

Chapter 17: Deadlocked No More

389 "Every position must be held": Eisenhower, *Yanks*, 117.
390 Doing so cost 143 American: Ibid., 89.
390 "in windrows almost": Coffman, *War to End*, 149.
390 The Americans returned to Seicheprey: Mead, *Doughboys*, 226.
393 "a recruiting agency for": Lloyd, *Hundred Days*, 17.
393 "great responsibilities": Eisenhower, *Yanks*, 119.
394 After weeks of testimony by more: Peterson and Fite, *Opponents*, 237.
398 by the time it happened American: Coffman, *War to End*, 158.
398 "the losses we suffered were": McEntee, *Military History*, 526.
398 "To both friend and foe alike": Mead, *Doughboys*, 236.
399 Britain's First Army: Barry, *Great Influenza*, 170.
402 "Day and night for nearly a month": Mead, *Doughboys*, 248.
402 When the fighting ended on June 26: Coffman, *War to End*, 221.

Background: Death from a New Direction

403 It can be accepted as given: Barry, *Great Influenza*, 91.
404 In the three weeks following March 4: Collier, *Plague*, 9.
405 What was happening was a process: Barry, *Great Influenza*, 177.
405 He refused on patriotic grounds: Ibid., 200.
406 On September 26 the U.S. provost: Collier, *Plague*, 72.
406 William Gorgas, the army's: Barry, *Great Influenza*, 303.
406 On some ships new deaths: Ibid., 306.
407 "altogether a true inferno": Ibid., 305.
407 "just as surely played": Collier, *Plague*, 74.
407 "*I had a little bird*": Ibid., 75.
407 They were encountering fierce: Coffman, *War to End*, 321.
408 In the 1920s the agreed-upon: Barry, *Great Influenza*, 396.
408 It is likewise agreed: Ibid., 397.

Chapter 18: The Tide Turns

409 Meanwhile the Allies were being reinforced: Coffman, *War to End*, 227.
409 "spreading high treason": Lloyd, *Hundred Days*, 90.
410 Ultimately he persuaded: Livermore, *Politics Is Adjourned*, 84.
411 This added thirteen million names: Kennedy, *Over Here*, 167.
411 The War Department announced: Ibid., 57.
411 "The whole country is littered": Lloyd, *Hundred Days*, 134.
411 "were haggard and emaciated": Ibid., 121.
412 "Our men seemed to take": Ibid., 122.

413   One of McAlexander's battalions: Eisenhower, *Yanks*, 159.
413   "Never have I seen so many dead": Ibid., 161.
415   When relieved on the night of July 19: Coffman, *War to End*, 242.
416   "battalions looked like companies": Ibid., 245.
416   "We had the Americans as neighbors": Ibid., 246.
416   "the Americans perished in the": Mead, *Doughboys*, 199.
416   "after their great fight at Belleau": Ibid., 180.
417   "assault formations had been": Ibid., 183.
417   But by the time of Cantigny: Ibid., 190.
417   As July ended, there were 54,224: Ibid., 222.
417   "even heroism such as this could": Coffman, *War to End*, 247.
418   "Our recent companions in arms": Mead, *Doughboys*, 265.
420   By the time the Rainbow Division: Coffman, *War to End*, 253.

Background: Eggs Loaded with Dynamite

421   "the most remarkable telegram": Mead, *Doughboys*, 276.
422   "This contains the policy of the": Ibid., 277.
422   In it he laid out his reasons for sending: PWW, 48:624.
423   "no information as to the military": Mead, *Doughboys*, 281.
424   The official toll was vanishingly tiny: Ibid., 393.

Chapter 19: An Army at Last

426   Progress toward passage: Livermore, *Politics Is Adjourned*, 135.
426   "Politics is adjourned": MPWW, 1:495.
426   At least one historian has argued: Livermore, *Politics Is Adjourned*, 135.
427   "drawing special reference": Ibid., 141.
428   "I sounded him on another term": PWW, 49:275.
428   "Politics is not adjourned": Livermore, *Politics Is Adjourned*, 152.
429   "disloyal, profane, scurrilous": Thomas, *Unsafe for Democracy*, 68.
429   "the most repressive legislation": Cooper, *Reconsidering*, 205.
429   At his trial, which soon followed: Peterson and Fite, *Opponents*, 253.
430   "I ask no mercy": Ibid., 254.
430   In Lansing, Michigan, an ill-fated: Fleming, *Illusion of Victory*, 251.
430   "this is a Morgan war": Kennedy, *Over Here*, 79.
430   Senior Justice Department officials: Thomas, *Unsafe for Democracy*, 283.
430   By the end of the war, 1,597 people: Nelson, *Impact of War*, 36.
431   "the black day of the history": Brown, *Imperial War*, 190.
431   War-weary and threadbare: Coffman, *War to End*, 248; Mead, *Doughboys*, 267.
431   "the General Staff tells me": Lloyd, *Hundred Days*, 72.

433 On August 23, on the floor: Livermore, *Politics Is Adjourned,* 210.
433 "Professional internationalism": Ibid., 212.
434 Roosevelt appeared at times: Cooper, *Warrior,* 329.
434 "hereafter disloyalists might": Peterson and Fite, *Opponents,* 223.
434 More than fifty thousand were taken: Kennedy, *Over Here,* 166.
435 "soldiers armed with rifles": Peterson and Fite, *Opponents,* 231.
435 Estimates run as high as three: Kennedy, *Over Here,* 165.
436 "I must insist": Eisenhower, *Yanks,* 187.
436 The logistics challenge was: Coffman, *War to End,* 268.
437 "personal tragedies": Mcad, *Doughboys,* 289.
437 "so embittered that they": Ibid., 280.
437 Lieutenant Maury Maverick: Eisenhower, *Yanks,* 196.
438 Sergeant Harry Adams, when: Mead, *Doughboys,* 280.
438 "I made a mistake": Perret, *Old Soldiers,* 102.

Background: "A Soldier's Soldier"

442 One night a raiding party: Perret, *Old Soldiers,* 105.
442 "the bravest man I ever met": Ibid., 102.
443 "the days for brigadier generals": Ibid., 89.
443 "With us he was a soldier's soldier": Lee and Henschel, *MacArthur,* 36.
443 ("Out! Get out and stay out!"): Perret, *Old Soldiers,* 102.

Chapter 20: In at the Kill

444 The attacking force would include: Mead, *Doughboys,* 299.
445 "without regard to losses": Fleming, *Illusion of Victory,* 272.
446 The severity of his first order: Ibid., 271.
446 In the four days ending on September 29: Mead, *Doughboys,* 299.
446 The commander of the First Corps: Fleming, *Illusion of Victory,* 271.
446 More than 70,000 flu victims: Mead, *Doughboys,* 317.
448 "there can be no peace obtained": PWW, 51:127.
448 House, in the audience as Wilson: Fleming, *Illusion of Victory,* 285.
449 Miles Poindexter: Ibid., 289.
450 "Give me Châtillon, MacArthur": Eisenhower, *Yanks,* 256.
451 Captain D. A. Henkes: Peterson and Fite, *Opponents,* 83.
452 The surviving officers of MacArthur's: Eisenhower, *Yanks,* 255.
452 American casualties had risen to 75,000: Mead, *Doughboys,* 316.
453 "No arrangement can be accepted": Ibid., 327.
453 "looked forward to proposals": Lloyd, *Hundred Days,* 223.
454 "Fighting means struggling": IPH, 4:9.
456 "merely unused": Coffman, *War to End,* 340.

456 "The Americans are particularly": Mead, *Doughboys,* 189.
456 "the pent-up, untapped nervous energy": Ibid., 180.
457 All German forces were to retire: Eisenhower, *Yanks,* 275.
458 Most distressing to Erzberger: Vincent, *Politics of Hunger,* 168.
458 "The Hun is yelling for peace": Best, *Greatest Day,* 141.
458 "The German Government accepts": Ibid., 157.
459 "absolutely no let-up": Eisenhower, *Yanks,* 263.
459 During the morning, officers: Best, *Greatest Day,* 167.
459 Henry Gunther: Ibid., 199.
460 Perhaps a minute: Ibid., 203.

Part Three: Sowing Dragons' Teeth

Each in its distinct way, the following works shed significantly helpful light on the Paris peace conference of 1919 and the struggle for American ratification of the peace treaty and the League of Nations.

Woodrow Wilson and the Lost Peace, by Thomas A. Bailey.

Breaking the Heart of the World: Woodrow Wilson and the Fight for the League of Nations, by John Milton Cooper, Jr.

Peacemakers: Six Months That Changed the World, by Margaret MacMillan.

Henry Cabot Lodge and the Search for an American Foreign Policy, by William C. Widenor.

Part Three

462 "A supreme moment of history has come": PWW, 53:34.

Chapter 21: The World the War Made

463 "crippled, broken world": Hochschild, *To End All Wars,* 347.
463 Herbert Hoover, put in charge: MacMillan, *Peacemakers,* 68.
464 Britain, having stripped herself bare: Tansill, *America Goes,* 660.
464 Two million German soldiers were dead: Broadberry and Harrison, *Economics,* 27.
469 "I could not bear him": Rose, *King George V,* 232.
471 "as soon as they appear they": MacMillan, *Peacemakers,* 66.
471 "Central Europe is aflame": Sharp, *Versailles,* 130.
472 "indescribable malignity": Walworth, *America's Moment,* 215.
472 "rows of babies feverish": Fleming, *Illusion of Victory,* 353.
472 "I can only describe [the potatoes]": Vincent, *Politics of Hunger,* 168.
474 "making the Hun pay": Fleming, *Illusion of Victory,* 353.

474 "the existing blockade": PWW, 53:40.
475 "the most remarkable document": PWW, 63:468.
476 The commission did not have: PWW, 48:632.
477 Ultimately there were more than sixty: Bailey, *Wilson and Lost Peace*, 135.
478 "the free acceptance [of] the people": MPWW, 1:502.
478 "simply loaded with dynamite": Fleming, *Illusion of Victory*, 319.

Background: Lost?

483 "That's what you all are": Hemingway, *Moveable*, xx.
484 "The hell with her lost-generation": Ibid., 26.
485 "*walked eye-deep in hell*": Matthiessen, *Oxford Book*, 732.
486 "glory, honor, courage": Hemingway, *Farewell*, xxx.

Chapter 22: Compromise or Betrayal?

489 "yellow peril": Devlin, *Too Proud*, 6.
489 "we are all brothers": Berg, *Wilson*.
489 "your speech was as great as": PWW, 43:678.
489 "Plain people throughout America": PWW, 55:198.
491 "Now we will make men free": PWW, 55:238.
491 "thrown down the gauntlet": Fleming, *Illusion of Victory*, 345.
492 "I never expected to hate": Widenor, *Henry Cabot Lodge*, 208.
493 "no intellectual integrity": Ibid.
494 "everything he has done for": Ibid., 264.
495 "contemptible": George and George, *Wilson and House*, 237.
496 "fraught with ambiguities": Widenor, *Henry Cabot Lodge*, 306.
496 Article 10 was his sole truly: Cooper, *Breaking*, 11.
496 "speaks the conscience": Link, *Wilson: Revolution*, 115.
496 "We must have facts": Widenor, *Henry Cabot Lodge*, 294.
496 "I read [Wilson's] speeches": Ibid., 300.
497 "suggestions that should prove": PWW, 55:413.
497 "narrowness": PWW, 55:413.
498 Inflation was essentially out of control: Fleming, *Illusion of Victory*, 415.
498 "Our people . . . do not want": MPWW, 1:564.
499 "He seemed to have aged ten": George and George, *Wilson and House*, 240.
500 "It is now evident that the peace": IPH, 4:362.
500 "My main drive now is for peace": PWW, 55:500.
501 "side-tracking of the League": PWW, 55:497.
501 Mrs. Wilson was aware of this: George and George, *Wilson and House*, 261.

503 He wanted the Saar valley: Bailey, *Wilson and Lost Peace*, 219.
504 "Germany has been broken": IPH, 4:163.
504 "upon the basis of the free": Bailey, *Wilson and Lost Peace*, 229.
506 the president's lifelong pattern: George and George, *Wilson and House*, 256.
507 France was given what: Bailey, *Wilson and Lost Peace*, 219.
509 He had the same opinion: Ibid., 216.
509 "the Prussianized militarism": Berg, *Wilson*, 58.
509 "I am coming to the conclusion": MacMillan, *Peacemakers*, 100.

Background: Strange Bedfellows

512 "offensive to principles": Zucker, *George Norris*, 139.
513 "a sham and a fraud": Unger, *Fighting Bob*, 270.

Chapter 23: "Hell's Dirtiest Work"

515 "all these small nations are": PWW, 59:325.
517 The Allies and Americans between them: MacMillan, *Peacemakers*, 169.
517 Nothing of such importance: Bailey, *Wilson and Lost Peace*, 140.
518 The British Empire got eight million: Fleming, *Illusion of Victory*, 364.
518 Even Wilson appears to have been: Bailey, *Wilson and Lost Peace*, 168.
518 "outrageous and impossible": Cooper, *Breaking*, 96.
518 "even if Germany signed": PWW, 60:137.
519 "You asked us for peace": MacMillan, *Peacemakers*, 474.
520 "shall confess ourselves to be": Bailey, *Wilson and Lost Peace*, 289.
520 "Such a confession in my mouth": IPH, 4:458.
520 "The Germans are really": MacMillan, *Peacemakers*, 475.
520 Their translators were pressed: Ibid.
520 "The unbelievable has happened": IPH, 4:459.
521 "this fat volume is quite": MacMillan, *Peacemakers*, 475.
521 "no nation could endure": Berg, *Wilson*, 587.
521 "Those who will sign this treaty": PWW, 59:305.
522 "We had such high hopes": Fleming, *Illusion of Victory*, 382.
522 Andrew Bonar Law: MacMillan, *Peacemakers*, 478.
522 "breach of agreement": PWW, 59:617.
523 "in a funk": Fleming, *Illusion of Victory*, 382.
523 "the Treaty is not a good one": PWW, 59:623.
523 "three all-powerful, all-ignorant": MacMillan, *Peacemakers*, 446.
524 "questions which affect the peace": MPWW, 2:671.
524 By 1919 it had three hundred thousand members: Cooper, *Breaking*, 91.
525 "Beware of the possible consequences": Ibid., 104.

525 "refuses its consent": PWW, 61:66 note 3.
526 "without any authority from": PWW, 60:606.
527 "is to be understood in the sense": PWW, 61:72.
527 Some historians maintain: MacMillan, *Peacemakers*, 476; Bailey, *Wilson and Lost Peace*, 249.
527 "The Allied and Associated": Bailey, *Wilson and Lost Peace*, 249.
528 *yielding to overwhelming force*: Fleming, *Illusion of Victory*, 386.
528 "They lack only music and ballet girls": MacMillan, *Peacemakers*, 487.
528 "a feeling of sympathy": IPH, 4:487.
529 "to see nothing of the deep pain": MacMillan, *Peacemakers*, 487.
529 "my last conversation": IPH, 4:489.
529 "It may be that Wilson might have": IPH, 4:488.
530 It has been called the worst atrocity: Barnes, *Genesis of War*, 559; Ross, *Propaganda for War*, 47
530 A newspaper poll indicated: Cooper, *Breaking*, 112.
532 "not exactly what we would": MPWW, 2:698.
532 "Wilson's speech was as if": PWW, 61:445.
532 "a contraction of the back": Cooper, *Breaking*, 120.
532 The worst would happen in Chicago: Fleming, *Illusion of Victory*, 399.
533 In the course of 1919, one American: Kennedy, *Over Here*, 272.

Background: The Palmer Raids

534 The president knew him and had: Ackerman, *Young J. Edgar*, 17.
536 To this end, Palmer got congressional: Kennedy, *Over Here*, 311.
536 "young, militant, progressive": Ackerman, *Young J. Edgar*, 20.
536 "in addition to his recognized ability": PWW, 55:264.
536 He ordered the release of nearly half: Ackerman, *Young J. Edgar*, 20.

Chapter 24: "The Door Is Closed"

541 "a deformed experiment": Cooper, *Breaking*, 134.
542 "I cannot vote for the treaty": PWW, 61:565.
542 When asked if in his opinion: Cooper, *Breaking*, 140.
543 His fellow committee members: Ibid., 145.
543 When Borah of Idaho asked: PWW, 62:339.
544 "a moral, not a legal obligation": Widenor, *Henry Cabot Lodge*, 337.
544 "but operative in a different way": Cooper, *Breaking*, 143.
544 "curious and childlike casuistry": Widenor, *Henry Cabot Lodge*, 338.
544 "What will your league amount to": Ibid., 268.
544 "a disturbingly dull mind": Berg, *Wilson*, 618.
544 "ignorance and disingenuousness": Cooper, *Breaking*, 146.

545 "hard, cold and cruel": Ibid.

544 "The president was cordial": IPH, 4:515.

545 "I can predict with absolute": PWW, 63:97.

547 "There are a great many hyphens": PWW, 63:140.

547 "as welcome to the league": PWW, 63:135.

548 "I consider that the League": PWW, 63:337.

549 "I have made no comment": PWW, 63:337.

549 "grave breach of faith": Cooper, *Breaking,* 171.

549 "All the elements that tended toward": PWW, 63:448.

550 "I find . . . that there is": PWW, 63:501.

550 "very close to psychosis": Freud, *Thomas Woodrow Wilson,* 289.

550 "I don't seem to realize it": Cooper, *Breaking,* 188.

551 A quarter of a million steelworkers: Kennedy, *Over Here,* 274.

553 "The United States assumes no obligation": Cooper, *Breaking,* 226.

553 He was, as he insisted, never: Widenor, *Henry Cabot Lodge,* 312.

555 "get the political scalps": PWW, 64:43.

555 "You were good enough to bring me": PWW, 64:58.

556 "to subject American labor": Cooper, *Breaking,* 219.

556 "the crushing of the German": Ibid., 234.

557 "a very grave misfortune": Ibid., 268.

557 "For God's sake . . . can't something": Ibid.

Aftermath: "Now It Is All Over"

560 "there are many reasons why": George and George, *Wilson and House,* 193.

560 House's offers to help in any possible: Ibid., 304.

560 When an Armistice Day parade by two local: Ackerman, *Young J. Edgar,* 124.

561 That same month also brought: Kennedy, *Over Here,* 279.

561 Four days before Christmas: Ackerman, *Young J. Edgar,* 161.

561 He would fail in this: Kennedy, *Over Here,* 87

561 Some five thousand men and women: Fleming, *Illusion of Victory,* 439.

562 President Wilson had by this time: Weinstein, *Medical and Psychological,* 357.

562 The country was too big and diverse: Fleming, *Illusion of Victory,* 440.

562 "a petulant and sick man": Link, *Wilson: Revolution,* 126.

562 ("What did Mrs. Galt do when"): Fleming, *Illusion of Victory,* 441.

563 His principal qualifications appear: Berg, *Wilson,* 681.

563 "in effect a nullification": Widenor, *Henry Cabot Lodge,* 346.

564 "There never was a moment": Berg, *Wilson,* 649.

565 "told Palmer not to let": Ackerman, *Young J. Edgar,* 204.

565 Newspaper stories began: Ibid., 283.
565 He said that May 1—May Day: Fleming, *Illusion of Victory,* 458.
565 A final blow came on May 28: Ackerman, *Young J. Edgar,* 309.
566 "the [Democratic] convention may": Levin, *Edith and Woodrow,* 442.
566 Upon returning to the East, Cox: Fleming, *Illusion of Victory,* 460.
566 Seven weeks before the election: Feuerlicht, *Reign of Terror,* 107.
568 They were sometimes shocked: Levin, *Edith and Woodrow,* 488.
568 "This man was a traitor": Peterson, *Opponents of War,* 277.
568 "*a good hater*": Baker, *Woodrow Wilson,* 552.
568 "My separation from Woodrow": IPH, 4:518.
569 "any seemly program to lessen": Cooper, *Warrior,* 395.
570 "Tumulty will sulk for a few days": Ibid., 720.
571 "has to hate someone": Ibid., 721.
572 "We were all of us in our": Cooper, *Breaking,* 352.

Bibliography

Ackerman, Kenneth D. *Young J. Edgar: Hoover, the Red Scare and the Assault on Civil Liberties.* New York: Carroll & Graf, 2007.

Addams, Jane. *Peace and Bread in Time of War.* New York: Macmillan, 1983.

Allison, J. Murray. *Raemaekers' Cartoon History of the War.* New York: Century, 1919.

Archer, William. *The Peace President.* New York: Henry Holt, 1919.

Asprey, Robert B. *The German High Command at War.* New York: William Morrow, 1991.

Axson, Stockton. *Brother Woodrow: A Memoir of Woodrow Wilson.* Princeton: Princeton University Press, 1993.

Bailey, Thomas A. *Woodrow Wilson and the Lost Peace.* Chicago: Quadrangle, 1963.

Baker, Ray Stannard. *Woodrow Wilson: Life and Letters.* 8 vols. London: Heinemann, 1928.

Baker, Ray Stannard, and W. E. Dodd, eds. *Public Papers of Woodrow Wilson.* 6 vols. New York: Harper, 1927.

Barnes, Harry Elmer. *The Genesis of the World War.* New York: Alfred A. Knopf, 1929.

Barry, John M. *The Great Influenza.* New York: Penguin, 2005.

Beatty, Jack. *Age of Betrayal: The Triumph of Money in America, 1865–1900.* New York: Alfred A. Knopf, 2007.

Bell, William Gardner. *Commanding Generals and Chiefs of Staff, 1775–1987.* Washington, D.C.: Center of Military History, 1987.

Berg, A. Scott. *Wilson.* New York: G. P. Putnam's Sons, 2013.

Best, Nicholas. *The Greatest Day in History.* New York: PublicAffairs, 2008.

Boyer, Richard O., and Herbert M. Morais. *Labor's Untold Story.* Pittsburgh: United Electrical, Radio & Machine Workers of America, 2003.

Bragdon, Henry W. *Woodrow Wilson: The Academic Years.* Cambridge, Mass.: Belknap Press, 1967.

Bridges, Robert. *Woodrow Wilson, a Personal Tribute.* New York: Privately printed, 1924.

Broadberry, Stephen, and Mark Harrison. *The Economics of World War I.* New York: Cambridge University Press, 2005.

Brown, Malcolm. *Imperial War Museum Book of 1918, Year of Victory.* London: Pan Books, 1999.

Carlisle, Rodney. *Sovereignty at Sea.* Gainesville: University Press of Florida, 2009.

Carston, F. L. *War Against War.* Berkeley: University of California Press, 1982.

Chafee, Zecharia, Jr. *Free Speech in the United States.* Cambridge, Mass.: Harvard University Press, 1941.

Chambers, John Whiteclay, II. *To Raise an Army: The Draft Comes to Modern America.* New York: Free Press, 1987.

Churchill, Winston S. *The World Crisis.* Vol. 3. London: Thornton Butterworth, 1923.

Clanton, Gene. *Populism.* Boston: Twayne, 1991.

Clark, Christopher. *The Sleepwalkers: How Europe Went to War in 1914.* London: Penguin, 2013.

Clausewitz, Carl von. *On War.* Princeton: Princeton University Press, 1976.

Coben, Stanley. *A. Mitchell Palmer, Politician.* New York: Columbia University Press, 1963.

Coffman, Edward M. *The War to End All Wars: The American Military Experience in World War I.* Lexington: University of Kentucky Press, 1998.

Collier, Richard. *The Plague of the Spanish Lady.* London: Macmillan, 1974.

Cooper, John Milton, Jr. *Breaking the Heart of the World: Woodrow Wilson and the Fight for the League of Nations.* Cambridge: Cambridge University Press, 2001.

———, ed. *Reconsidering Woodrow Wilson.* Washington, D.C.: Woodrow Wilson Center Press, 2008.

———. *The Warrior and the Priest: Woodrow Wilson and Theodore Roosevelt.* Cambridge, Mass.: Belknap Press, 1983.

———. *Woodrow Wilson, A Biography.* New York: Alfred A. Knopf, 2009.

Devlin, Patrick. *Too Proud to Fight: Woodrow Wilson's Neutrality.* London: Oxford University Press, 1974.

Drake, Richard. *The Education of an Anti-Imperialist: Robert La Follette and U.S. Expansion.* Madison: University of Wisconsin Press, 2013.

DuPuy, R. Ernest. *Five Days to War, April 2–6, 1917.* Harrisburg, Penn.: Giniger, 1967.

Eisenhower, John S. D. *Yanks: The Epic Story of the American Army in World War I.* New York: Touchstone, 2001.

Evans, Martin Marix. *Battles of World War I.* Marlborough, Mass.: Airlife, 2004.

Fay, Sidney Bradshaw. *After Sarajevo: The Origins of the World War.* New York: Free Press, 1966.

Ferguson, Niall. *The Pity of War.* London: Allen Lane, 1998.

Feuerlicht, Roberta Strauss. *America's Reign of Terror.* New York: Random House, 1971.

Fleming, Thomas. *The Illusion of Victory: America in World War I.* New York: Basic Books, 2003.

Ford, Nancy Gentile. *The Great War and America.* Westport, Conn.: Praeger Security International, 2008.

Freud, Sigmund, and William Bullitt. *Thomas Woodrow Wilson.* Boston: Houghton Mifflin, 1967.

Fromkin, David. *Europe's Last Summer.* New York: Alfred A. Knopf, 2004.

Frost, Wesley. *German Submarine Warfare.* New York: D. Appleton, 1918.

Fuehr, Alexander. *The Neutrality of Belgium.* New York: Funk & Wagnalls, 1915.

Gaston, Herbert E. *The Nonpartisan League.* New York: Harcourt, Brace & Howe, 1920.

Geiss, Imanuel, ed. *July 1914: The Outbreak of the First World War: Selected Documents.* New York: Oxford University Press, 1975.

George, Alexander L., and Juliette L. George. *Woodrow Wilson and Colonel House: A Personality Study.* New York: Dover, 1964.

Gibson, R. H., and Maurice Prendergast. *The German Submarine War 1914–1918.* London: Constable, 1931.

Goodwyn, Lawrence. *The Populist Movement.* Oxford: Oxford University Press, 1978.

Gould, Lewis L. *America in the Progressive Era.* Harlow, England: Longman, 2001.

Gregory, Ross. *The Origins of American Intervention in the First World War.* New York: W. W. Norton, 1971.

Griffith, Elisabeth. *In Her Own Right: The Life of Elizabeth Cady Stanton.* Oxford: Oxford University Press, 1985.

Grubbs, Frank L. *The Struggle for Labor Loyalty.* Durham, N.C.: Duke University Press, 1968.

Hale, William Bayard. *The Story of a Style.* New York: B. W. Huebsch, 1920.

Hastings, Max. *Catastrophe 1914.* New York: Alfred A. Knopf, 2013.

Healy, Maureen. *Vienna and the Fall of the Hapsburg Empire.* New York: Cambridge University Press, 2004.

Hemingway, Ernest. *A Moveable Feast.* New York: Scribner, 1964.

———. *A Farewell to Arms.* London: Heinemann, 1971.

Herrmann, David G. *The Arming of Europe and the Making of the First World War.* Princeton: Princeton University Press, 1996.

Herwig, Holger H. *The First World War: Germany and Austria-Hungary 1914–1918.* London: Arnold, 1997.

———, *The War 1914.* New York: Random House, 2011.

Hochschild, Adam. *To End All Wars: A Story of Loyalty and Rebellion 1914–1918.* Boston: Houghton Mifflin Harcourt, 2011.

Hofstadter, Richard. *The Age of Reform.* New York: Vintage, 1955.

Hough, Richard. *The Great War at Sea.* Oxford: Oxford University Press, 1982.

Jannen, William, Jr. *The Lions of July.* Novato, Calif.: Presidio Press, 1997.

Johnson, Claudius O. *Borah of Idaho.* Seattle: University of Washington Press, 1967.

Kaplan, Edward S. *U.S. Imperialism in Latin America: Bryan's Challenges and Contributions, 1900–1920.* Westport, Conn.: Greenwood Press, 1998.

Karp, Walter. *The Politics of War.* New York: Harper & Row, 1979.

Kazin, Michael. *A Godly Hero: The Life of William Jennings Bryan.* New York: Anchor Books, 2007.

Keegan, John. *The First World War.* New York: Vintage, 2000.

Kennedy, David M. *Over Here: The First World War and American Society.* Oxford: Oxford University Press, 2004.

Kennedy, Paul. *The Rise and Fall of the Great Powers.* London: Unwin Hyman, 1988.

Kerney, James. *The Political Education of Woodrow Wilson.* New York: Century, 1926.

Larson, Erik. *Dead Wake: The Last Crossing of the Lusitania.* London: Doubleday, 2015.

Lasch, Christopher. *The New Radicalism in America, 1889–1963.* New York: W. W. Norton, 1965.

Lee, Clark, and Richard Henschel. *Douglas MacArthur.* New York: Henry Holt, 1952.

Lens, Sidney. *The Labor Wars.* Chicago: Haymarket Books, 2008.

Leuchtenburg, William E. *The Perils of Prosperity, 1914–1932.* Chicago: University of Chicago Press, 1958.

Levin, Phyllis Lee. *Edith and Woodrow: The Wilson White House.* New York: Scribner, 2001.

Link, Arthur S. *Wilson.* 5 vols. Princeton: Princeton University Press, 1947–1965.

———. *Woodrow Wilson: Revolution, War and Peace.* Arlington Heights, Ill.: Harlan Davidson, 1979.

———, ed. *The Papers of Woodrow Wilson.* 69 vols. Princeton: Princeton University Press, 1979.

———, ed. *Woodrow Wilson, A Profile.* New York: Hill & Wang, 1968.

Linn, Brian McAllister. *The Philippine War, 1899–1902.* Lawrence: University of Kansas Press, 2000.

Livermore, Seward W. *Politics Is Adjourned: Woodrow Wilson and the War Congress 1916–1918.* Middletown, Conn.: Wesleyan University Press, 1966.

Lloyd, Nick. *Hundred Days: The End of the Great War.* London: Penguin, 2014.

Lord, Walter. *The Good Years: From 1900 to the First World War.* London: Longman, 1960.

MacMillan, Margaret. *Peacemakers: Six Months That Changed the World.* London: John Murray, 2003.

———. *The War That Ended Peace: The Road to 1914.* New York: Random House, 2013.

Manning, Clarence H. *The Siberian Fiasco.* New York: Library Publishers, 1952.

Margulies, Herbert F. *Senator Lenroot of Wisconsin.* Columbia: University of Missouri Press, 1977.

Matthiessen, F. O. *Oxford Book of American Verse.* New York: Oxford University Press, 1960.

McEntee, Girard Lindsley. *Military History of the World War.* New York: Charles Scribner's Sons, 1943.

McGerr, Michael. *A Fierce Discontent: The Rise and Fall of the Progressive Movement.* Oxford: Oxford University Press, 2005.

McMath, Robert C., Jr. *American Populism: A Social History.* New York: Hill & Wang, 1993.

Mead, Gary. *The Doughboys: America and the First World War.* London: Penguin, 2000.

Meyer, G. J. *A World Undone: The Story of the Great War 1914–1918.* New York: Delacorte Press, 2006.

Miller, Kristie. *Ellen and Edith: Woodrow Wilson's First Ladies.* Lawrence: University Press of Kansas, 2010.

Miller, Stuart Creighton. *Benevolent Assimilation: The American Conquest of the Philippines.* New Haven, Conn.: Yale University Press, 1984.

Millis, Walter. *Road to War: America 1914–1917.* Boston: Houghton Mifflin, 1935.

Morrow, John H., Jr. *The Great War in the Air.* Washington, D.C.: Smithsonian Institution Press, 1993.

Mosier, John. *The Myth of the Great War.* New York: HarperCollins, 2001.

Musicant, Ivan. *Empire by Default: The Spanish American War and the Dawn of the American Century.* New York: Henry Holt, 1998.

Myers, William Starr. "President of Princeton." In Link, *Woodrow Wilson, A Profile.*

Nelson, Keith L., ed. *The Impact of War on American Life: The Twentieth Century Experience.* New York: Holt, Rinehart & Winston, 1971.

Nicolson, Colin. *The Longman Companion to the First World War.* London: Longman, 2001.

O'Hara, Vincent P., W. David Dickson, and Richard Worth, eds. *To Crown the Waves: The Great Navies of the First World War.* Annapolis: Naval Institute Press, 2013.

Osborn, George C. *Woodrow Wilson—The Early Years.* Baton Rouge: Louisiana State University Press, 1968.

O'Sullivan, Patrick. *The Sinking of the Lusitania.* Wilton, Cork: Collins Press, 2014.

Peeke, Mitch, Kevin Walsh-Johnson, and Steven Jones. *The Lusitania Story.* Anstey, Leicestershire: F. A. Thorpe, 2015.

Perret, Geoffrey. *A Country Made by War.* New York: Random House, 1989.

————. *Old Soldiers Never Die: The Life of Douglas MacArthur.* London: Andre Deutsch, 1996.

Peterson, H. C., and Gilbert C. Fite. *Opponents of War, 1917–1918.* Seattle: University of Washington Press, 1968.

Ponsonby, Frederick, ed. *The Letters of Empress Frederick.* London: Macmillan, 1929.

Preston, Diana. *Lusitania: An Epic Tragedy.* New York: Walker & Co., 2002.

Raemaekers, Louis. *Raemaekers' Cartoons.* Garden City, N.Y.: Doubleday, Page, 1916.

Rochester, Stuart I. *American Liberal Disillusionment: In the Wake of World War I.* University Park: Pennsylvania State University Press, 1945.

Rose, Kenneth. *King George V.* New York: Alfred A. Knopf, 1984.

Ross, Stewart Halsey. *Propaganda for War: How the United States Was Conditioned to Fight the Great War of 1914–1918.* Joshua Tree, Calif.: Progressive Press, 2009.

Ryley, Thomas W. *A Little Group of Willful Men: A Study of Congressional and Presidential Authority.* Port Washington, N.Y.: Kennikat Press, 1975.

Schaffer, Ronald. *America in the Great War: The Rise of the War Welfare State.* New York: Oxford University Press, 1994.

Seymour, Charles, ed. *The Intimate Papers of Colonel House.* 4 vols. Cambridge, Mass.: Houghton Mifflin, 1926.

Sharp, Alan. *The Versailles Settlement.* New York: St. Martin's, 1991.

Simpson, Colin. *The Lusitania.* London: Longman, 1972.

Smith, Gene. *When the Cheering Stopped: The Last Years of Woodrow Wilson.* New York: William Morrow & Co., 1964.

Souhami, Diana. *Edith Cavell.* London: Quercus, 2013.

Stanford, Karen L. *If We Must Die: African American Voices on War and Peace.* Lanham, Md.: Rowman & Littlefield, 2008.

Stevenson, David. *Armaments and the Coming of War: Europe 1904–1914.* New York: Doubleday, 1996.

————. *Cataclysm: The First World War as Political Tragedy.* New York: Basic Books, 2004.

Stone, Geoffrey R. *Perilous Times: Free Speech in Wartime.* New York: W. W. Norton, 2004.

Tansill, Charles C. *America Goes to War.* Gloucester, Mass.: Peter Smith, 1963.

Thomas, William H., Jr. *Unsafe for Democracy.* Madison: University of Wisconsin Press, 2008.

Tuchman, Barbara W. *The Guns of August.* New York: Macmillan, 1962.

Tumulty, Joseph P. *Woodrow Wilson as I Know Him.* Garden City, N.Y.: Doubleday, Page, 1921.

Unger, Nancy C. *Fighting Bob La Follette: The Righteous Reformer.* Madison: Wisconsin Historical Society Press, 2008.

Vandiver, Frank E. *John J. Pershing and the Anatomy of Leadership.* Colorado: U.S. Air Force Academy, 1963.

Vincent, C. Paul. *The Politics of Hunger: The Allied Blockade of Germany.* Athens: Ohio University Press, 1985.

Walworth, Arthur. *America's Moment: 1918.* New York: W. W. Norton, 1977.

Weinstein, Edward A. *Woodrow Wilson: A Medical and Psychological Biography.* Princeton: Princeton University Press, 1981.

Widenor, William C. *Henry Cabot Lodge and the Search for an American Foreign Policy.* Berkeley: University of California Press, 1983.

Wilson, Woodrow. *The Messages and Papers of Woodrow Wilson.* 2 vols. New York: Review of Reviews Corporation, 1924.

Wright, Russell O. *Chronology of Labor in the United States.* Jefferson, N.C.: McFarland & Co., 2003.

Zucker, Norman L. *George W. Norris, Gentle Knight of American Democracy.* Urbana: University of Illinois Press, 1966.

Zuckerman, Larry. *The Rape of Belgium.* New York: New York University Press, 2004.

Index

Page numbers of photographs appear in italics.

Photo Credits

All of the photographs in this book are from the Prints & Photographs Division of the Library of Congress in Washington, D.C. All can be accessed via the library's online catalog using the call numbers provided below.

Credit for all: Library of Congress, Prints & Photographs Division, [reproduction number, e.g., LC-B2-1234]

310	Troops outside camouflaged shed	LC-B2-4589-12
311	Yanks play baseball in France	LC-B2-4419-5
	Yanks assembled with rifles stacked	LC-B2-4258-4
316	Learning to live in trenches	LC-B2-4405-5
	Digging a zigzag trench	LC-DIG-ds-04284
328	President Wilson and Tumulty	LC-F8-4852
333	Poster: "We Demand the Liberty"	LC-B2-4064-10
	Poster: "Agitation and Defence"	LC-B2-4064-8
340	Suffragettes picketing White House	LC-B2-4112-10
341	Sign: "Woman Suffrage Party Garden Plot"	LC-B2-4268-5
347	Georges Clemenceau, French premier	LC-USZ62-16373
361	Two women with six sons each in uniform	LC-B2-4572-10
	Doughboys with Christmas packages from home	LC-B2-4467-7
364	Pistol training	LC-B2-4596-1
	Marines marching uphill	LC-B2-4402-4
369	Ferdinand Foch, supreme Allied commander	LC-USZ62-103890
371	Pétain and Pershing	LC-B2-4814-14
373	Paul von Hindenburg	LC-B2-4471-8
379	Wisconsin Republican Irvine Lenroot	LC-B2-4174-5
391	Field hospital at trenchline	C-B2-4536-9
401	Marines with field gun	LC-B2-4404-2
	Attacking with hand grenades	LC-DIG-ds-04293
	Attending man with head wound	LC-B2-4519-9
414	German prisoners of war	LC-B2-4268-3
415	Happy German prisoners reclining	LC-B2-4257-10
439	Sergeant Alvin York	LC-B2-4969-8
461	Lloyd George, Orlando, Clemenceau, Wilson	LC-B2-4956-10
465	Ruined street with horse cart	LC-B2-4540-1
	Two men, one heavily bandaged	LC-USZ62-115013
	Wrecked stone buildings	LC-B2-4500-9
468	Foch, Clemenceau, Lloyd George, Orlando, Sonnino	LC-B2-4852-14
492	Senator Henry Cabot Lodge	LC-USZ62-36185
516	Vittorio Orlando of Italy	LC-B2-3322-14
519	Ulrich von Brockdorff-Rantzau of Germany	LC-B2-5858-1
535	Attorney General A. Mitchell Palmer	LC-USZ62-111660
548	William Bullitt	LC-USZ62-133033
554	Senator Gilbert Hitchcock of Nebraska	LC-H261-4200-7
558	Victory celebration, New York	LC-B2-4743-12
567	Eugene Debs on release from prison	LC-USZ62-111659

G. J. MEYER is the author of three popular works of history, *The Borgias,*
The Tudors, and *A World Undone: The Story of the Great War,* as well as
Executive Blues and *The Memphis Murders.* He received an M.A. from
the University of Minnesota, where he was a Woodrow Wilson Fellow,
and later was awarded Harvard University's Nieman Fellowship in Journalism. He has taught at colleges in Des Moines, St. Louis, and New
York, and now lives in Wiltshire, England.